INTERNATIONAL TRADE AND ECONOMIC LAW
AND THE EUROPEAN UNION

D0421660

WITHDRAWN
THE LIBRARY OF
TRINITY COLLEGE DUBLIN

AUTHORISED: MK

DATE: 22/9/23

BR1645

BR1645

International Trade and Economic Law and the European Union

SARA DILLON
PhD (Stanford), J.D. (Columbia),
Associate Professor of Law,
Suffolk University Law School, Boston, Mass

·HART·
PUBLISHING

OXFORD – PORTLAND, OREGON
2002

Hart Publishing
Oxford and Portland, Oregon

Published in North America (US and Canada) by
Hart Publishing c/o
International Specialized Book Services
5804 NE Hassalo Street
Portland, Oregon
97213-3644
USA

Distributed in the Netherlands, Belgium and Luxembourg by
Intersentia, Churchillaan 108
B2900 Schoten
Antwerpen
Belgium

© Sara Dillon 2002

The author has asserted her right under the Copyright,
Designs and Patents Act 1988, to be identified as the author of this work

Hart Publishing is a specialist legal publisher based in Oxford, England.
To order further copies of this book or to request a list of other
publications please write to:

Hart Publishing, Salter's Boatyard, Folly Bridge,
Abingdon Road, Oxford OX1 4LB
Telephone: +44 (0)1865 245533 or Fax: +44 (0)1865 794882
e-mail: mail@hartpub.co.uk
WEBSITE: http//www.hartpub.co.uk

British Library Cataloguing in Publication Data
Data Available
ISBN 1–84113–113–X (paperback)

Typeset by Hope Services (Abingdon) Ltd.
Printed and bound in Great Britain on acid-free paper by
TJ International Ltd, Padstow, Cornwall

Perm
Res.
341.57
P26

TRINITY COLLEGE
3 1 OCT 2002
LIBRARY DUBLIN

Foreword

With the accession of China, and the successful launch at Doha of a new round of international trade negotiations (however fraught with contradictions the opening ministerial declaration), it would seem that the World Trade Organisation (WTO) is here to stay. Whatever doubts there may have been after the Seattle Ministerial debacle of late 1999 with respect to the long-term viability of WTO law have apparently been put to rest after the events of September 11, 2001. At moments of global crisis, economic integration re-emerges as a symbol of stability. The more difficult question, however, is what form this economic integration should take.

With the anti-globalisation movement in a state of some confusion in the wake of September's events, the WTO's Doha conference moved forward, and an uneasy basis for future action agreed upon. It would be folly, however, to imagine that the intellectual difficulties presented by WTO law—with its unsettling relationship to national regulatory goals—have also disappeared.

As trade negotiations proceed under the new round in the months to come, there will be an urgent need for far greater numbers of people than heretofore to involve themselves in shaping global trade law. The outcome of the new round should be, and hopefully will be, the result of more complex intellectual and political inputs than was the case with the Uruguay Round Agreements, the substantive law of which came into force in 1995, generating controversy and street conflict in the years that followed.

The Doha Ministerial Declaration reflects in places the variegated protests that hounded trade meetings in the late 1990s wherever they occurred, prominently mentioning the special difficulties of developing countries, trade and environment concerns, and the matter of an improved "dialogue with the public".[1] There are indications of a general commitment to further liberalisation in the areas of agriculture, investments, and trade in services; also to taking up the issue of a "multilateral framework to enhance the contribution of competition policy to international trade and development". Commentators are already making predictions as to where the concessions and climb-downs will come from; will the EU hold firm on agriculture? Will the developing countries give in on the introduction into WTO law of new subject areas?

There are also signs that the most high-profile of the contentious WTO issues will be addressed in the spirit of preserving the WTO as a whole; notably, the fact that a separate Declaration on the TRIPS Agreement and Public Health calls for an interpretation of the Agreement on Trade-Related Aspects of

---

[1] Ministerial Declaration, WT/MIN(01)/DEC/1, 20 November 2001.

Intellectual Property (TRIPS) to allow for the granting of compulsory licenses for patented drugs in the event of national public health emergencies.[2] There is little question but that many WTO insiders would like to move on from this persistent controversy, which has had the effect of characterising the entire WTO as harsh and unfair in the public mind.

It is unclear at this juncture the degree to which the issues around which anti-globalisation protests have taken place over the last several years will be reflected in the actual WTO negotiating agenda as it takes shape in the near future. To the extent that the interests of developing countries (not to mention disparate groups within those countries), environmental activists, labor advocates, and anti-debt campaigners pursue very different, and sometimes conflicting, agendas, the possibility of fundamental reform of the global trade regime is correspondingly lessened.

This book suggests that the EU model of economic integration offers a far more fruitful and complex human endeavour than what has been seen from the WTO thus far. But as we enter the new negotiating round, it is important to consider that the ultimate shape of WTO law is still to be determined. What GATT/WTO law has undertaken so far—including its purposes, methods and achievements—is the principal subject of this book.

I would like to offer sincere thanks to Richard Hart of Hart Publishing, to friends and colleagues at University College Dublin, Brooklyn Law School, and Suffolk University Law School. Special mention and gratitude go to my research assistant *extraordinaire*, Mr Marc Monte, 2001 graduate of Brooklyn Law School; thanks also to Ms Anne Gates-Gurski of Suffolk University Law School.

---

[2] WT/MIN(01)/DEC/2, 20 November 2001.

Contents

PART III   EXTERNAL TRADE RELATIONS OF THE EUROPEAN UNION

Table of Cases

GATT PANEL REPORTS

WTO PANEL AND APPELLATE BODY REPORTS

EUROPEAN COURT OF JUSTICE

Part I

Global Context

1

Introduction: The Problem of Europe in a Globalised World

THE POSITION OF the European Community in the unfolding narrative of international trade and economic law in the period since the end of World War II is unique, and uniquely problematic. In many ways, the integrationist ambitions of the EC have tracked those of the world trading system, previously embodied in the General Agreement on Tariffs and Trade (GATT), and now the World Trade Organisation (WTO). As the scope and ambition of the global trading regime expanded, so the EU moved closer towards the establishment of a "European economy".

The EU is, along with the United States, one of the two "titans" of the GATT/WTO system. While the WTO is the single most important external entity with which the European economy must come to terms, so too is the EU seen as one of the most formidable players at the WTO. The number of scholars literate in both systems, and able to analyse their relationship, remains strikingly small. As the world trading system extends its reach into new subject areas, as it continues its drive towards genuine judicial procedures, and as WTO disputes proliferate and gain in complexity, there is an increasingly urgent need for the system to be made more intellectually accessible. Unfortunately, the voluminous quality of the panel and Appellate Body decisions, and the forbidding technicality of the underlying agreements, has meant that the "audience" for this subject remains the academically intrepid, despite the ever more profound effects of the WTO on our lives.

It is with this in mind that this book has been undertaken. As the trading system becomes more truly "legal", there is a clear necessity to subject its terms to academic scrutiny. Unfortunately, it often proves exceedingly difficult to find the right guide to such a study. I have approached the book on the theory that there are those who, even if well versed in economics and/or in international law, nevertheless find the "law" of the WTO too impenetrable, and thus tend to turn away from the task of mastering it. The contrast between scenes of protest on the streets of cities where economic summits take place, and the process of reading a WTO panel report, is stark; academic explorations of WTO law tend to be ponderously self-referential, and much of the protest against it mainly visceral.

In fact, despite its numbingly technical appearance, contemporary trade and economic law is an engaging reflection of the major themes of our time. The degree to which we decide to cede national sovereignty to international trade institutions, particularly the WTO, will determine the overriding values of our world for decades to come. It is impossible to form an accurate sense of whether this is a direction we should take, if we do not have ready access to this developing area of the law, and the opportunity to place it in historical context.

In addition to accessibility and intelligibility, there has been a profound failure to generate a conceptual framework for even considering the desirability or otherwise of recent developments in international trade law. It is absolutely natural for there to be a comparison drawn between the EU and the WTO, since these two systems provide contrasting models of economic integration. But as I will attempt to show, there is far more to compare in this regard than the techniques of economic de-nationalisation employed by the two systems. The EU provides the only contemporary evidence that in fact complex, multi-dimensional, supranational regime-building is possible. The principal point is not the relative stringency of the two systems *vis-à-vis* national regulatory freedom; rather, it is the degree to which supranational governance might dare to embrace both the public and the private interest. In this regard, the academic community, and that still small group of scholars with access to the legal techniques employed by both the EU and the WTO must begin to analyse in terms capable of resonating in a larger intellectual world. The WTO is the largest and most important set of trade obligations with which the EU must deal; at the same time, the EU is the most important counter-model with which the WTO must deal. Both models must be re-evaluated in light of their underlying rationales; yet it would appear that most discussion still focuses on the legal symbols tossed up on the shore by each system. Understanding of the WTO system in particular must be re-connected to the world in which it operates. Only in that way can we understand what the EU has to offer an evolving global governance, and only then can we see what the EU stands to lose from too close an encounter with the WTO as it is presently configured.

In key ways, the relationship of the EU to the WTO system is more subtle and complex that that of the US to the WTO. On the one hand, there are two distinct schools of thought in Europe as to whether the developing European entity should be increasingly based on free trade/neo-liberal principles, or instead remain firmly in the tradition of "social Europe". (It is surely the case that the neo-liberal wing, though, stops far short of advocating the sort of "law and economics" vision so popular in American law schools. While many might advocate a leaner and more competitive Europe, socially conscious policy is so entrenched in even the European right wing that its complete demise is unthinkable. This is a factor that is insufficiently understood in the US.) Having struggled for decades with stubborn Member State allegiances to national economies, and the wish of the Member States to protect national social and cultural features against the demands of Community law, the EU as a whole is now faced, and faced dramatically, with the problem of how to configure itself within the WTO order. What effect will the EU's participation in the WTO have on its internal regulatory values? And, even more interestingly, can Europe be—or does it wish to be—a genuine counterweight to the US in the construction of real and effective global legal values?

In terms of the recent past, the question might be posed: Did the creation of the European Single Market take as its main purpose the more effective protection of a Europe already enormously changed by the demands of that market; or, alternatively, was the Single Market programme merely a step along the path towards a truly efficient, "reformed" Europe, whose ideals will come to resemble more closely those of the WTO? In the EU, internal stringency in economic integration has not necessarily translated into greater adherence to free trade principles at global level. To paraphrase the European Court of Justice, the EU is not simply about economics; indeed, it is possible that its central internal economic requirements, necessary for integration, have had as their main purpose the preservation of non-economic values. But there is no easy formula for determining what the EU "wants to be", and what relationship with the larger trading world will assist in the achievement of such a collective goal, assuming it can be identified.

While the United States reacts more vocally to fears of losing "national sovereignty" to the WTO, it is clear that the EU is not in a position to emphasise loss of sovereignty, having invested decades in downgrading the concept of national sovereignty. Unlike the case of the European debate over the WTO, the question of whether the United States is somehow standing in the way of America's transnational businesses by WTO-illegal forms of protectionism is not really a major issue. One reason for this is that the US has for much longer taken market-based values as its mainstream creed; it is not especially traumatised by the thought of the WTO imposing a greater degree of market discipline. Its objections are political, perhaps best understood by analogy to national security concerns. What's more, the American states have hardly considered themselves in the guise of sovereign rivals to the United States—at least not in the modern period. In that sense, the US has little to fear from the discourse of "sovereignty".

This also means that while Europe can protest that its own vision of a socially protective and humane life for its citizens is threatened by the excesses of WTO, there is perhaps less conceptual resistance than in the United States to the notion of the supremacy of external rules, rules based on abstract ideas of the market, rather than more complex inputs, including social policy. In a continuing historical parallel, both the EU and the WTO are still "in evolution", while by contrast the United States is more conceptually static, and will likely be far less affected in its central character by its relationship with the WTO. The United States is not a rival model of integration to the WTO; the EU is. (The North American Free Trade Association (NAFTA) could hardly be said to qualify, as important as it is in raw economic terms.)

So one underlying question posed here will be whether the EU is, through the agency of WTO law, seeking to maintain the notorious "fortress Europe" of social protection and purposive inefficiencies, or whether on the contrary the WTO could or should become Europe's ongoing opportunity to move from internal integration to a super-state characterised by citizens' "rights to free trade". Without attempting to reach a definitive conclusion on this vital topic, this book will propose to introduce the reader to the nature of this massive legal presence called the WTO, and to its precise relationship with the EU, historically and to come.

Popular discussion of the EU and the WTO as systems have often centred around the problems of legitimacy and the democratic deficit. It is hardly surprising that as a supranational entity gains the power to essentially invalidate a national law or regulation, not to mention the tradition bound up in that law or regulation, the general population will question the source of this power and its rationale. Such questions cannot be answered by hermetically sealed analyses of either EU or WTO law; neither can a satisfactory answer come from abstract economics. The EU, for all its deficiencies, has had an actual response: it can claim at least to have delivered peace and stability, a high level of social and environmental protection, as well as economic rights and freedoms. The EU legal system also early on created an alternative route to influence for citizens, bypassing the national state; the EU was able to marshal resentments against individual Member States held by citizens of those states. Concrete requirements emanating from the EC, such as equal pay for equal work, made sense as obvious benefits available from the centre. And for the elites of the Member States, the EC system made available new and previously unimagined avenues for career advancement and influence.

As to justifications for the WTO's new powers (as of 1995), justifications are thinner on the ground, and tend to be without content that can be recognised and understood by persons outside economics, transnational business, or trade law studies. It does not appear that the trade sceptics will be satisfied by reference to incremental changes taking place in the reasoning of the WTO's Appellate Body; a larger, more systemic, more "real" justification alone will suffice.

There *is* no public interest dimension to WTO; at best, the WTO bodies (the panels and Appellate Body) can decide, or not, that a national public interest measure with restrictive trade effects is consistent with WTO law (for reasons to be explored at length throughout this book). The EU, by contrast, is a multi-dimensional political and economic project, with binding law in many areas of concern to the non-economic aspects of life. This multi-dimensional quality acts as a recognition that economic integration in and of itself creates dangers for social and other protections developed over time within the confines of the nation state. It is part of the logic of economic integration that economic and social losers may be created; it is also apparent that the "race to the bottom" in terms of regulatory structures is a natural product of integration across national borders. It is plain that there was an acute awareness among the drafters of the modern European project that economic integration posed dangers to protections that had been developed at national level; hence the requirement that prior to accession, candidate countries would receive funding to bring their economies up to a certain standard (cohesion); and also that they would create a broad range of legislation that would qualify them for membership. This must be contrasted with the willy nilly integration that is taking place at global level, where only economic law is binding, and laws protecting other and more vulnerable aspects of human life are aspirational.

It could be said that the EU offers the only concrete proof that multidimensional integration is in fact possible; to that extent, it offers the best model for a different and enhanced idea of global governance. While the EU had everything to do with devising the current shape of the WTO (which serves the EU's interests *vis-à-vis* developing countries), it will also have everything to do with the WTO's future development. It is possible that the principal EU institutions believe that European standards in consumer, environmental and social protections, as well as human rights, can withstand the pressure exerted by the WTO and the liberalising tendency it represents, and that it is not in the overall interests of European business to advocate for labour, social or environmental protections at global level. It is also the case that if the EU does not shoulder this task, there will likely be no progress towards a complex global governance agenda. What could occur in its stead, though, by default, is a grand disaffection of citizens in many countries, and a consequent rollback of the drive to globalisation begun in 1995.

Legal academia in Europe is very conversant with the concept that liberal economics has been "constitutionalised" in the Treaty of Rome, and solidified in the interpretations by the European Court of Justice of the Treaty's provisions. The result of this constitutionalising is of course that these principles cannot be undone by "short term" majoritarian impulses. There is naturally less confidence as to whether it is safe or desirable to extend this status to include global trade principles as well. Should European citizens be seen to have a "legal guarantee" of economic freedom, even if this conflicts with the notion of a social Europe? Should economic freedom be placed on a par with human rights?

Much depends of course on how tightly Europe's major trading partners (notably the US) decide to embrace WTO law; also on what those partners insist upon in the upcoming round of WTO negotiations. As indicated, however, this comparison between Europe and its partners is not a perfect fit, since the effect in Europe of greater efficiency, along with inevitably less emphasis on social protection and planned markets, will be significantly greater. And it may be that Europe can find a middle ground, neither completely committed to competitive values, nor completely protectionist, but selective in its approach to the global rules. This leads us to the question of whether those rules in fact allow for such selectivity. And that in turn is a question that cannot be answered unless one fully understands the trade rules, and the disputes that they are, at an ever increasing pace and volume, generating. And the disputes are at the heart of the narrative of the domestic versus the global; local or regional legislation as opposed to trade rules.

There are many descriptions of the world trading regime in the abstract. The purpose of this book is to make that trading system more concrete and legally transparent. In particular, the nature of the WTO disputes in the post-Uruguay Round world demonstrate the dramatic conflict between national (or supranational) regulation and trade rules, although, due to the technocratic nature of WTO panel discourse, these profound legal/historical issues are not readily apparent, even to an informed readership.

The watershed date for global trade law was 1 January 1995, in that the Uruguay Round Agreements, including the Agreement Establishing the World Trade Organisation, came into effect. Before that date, the old "GATT" system could have been accurately described as an arm of "international law", in its reliance on diplomacy and willing state compliance. However, with the adoption of the Uruguay Round Agreements, bringing enormous subject areas of national economic regulation under GATT/WTO discipline, as well as subjecting the whole to a new and far more binding dispute resolution system, the regime took on unique properties not easily conceptualised within any one legal category. The WTO is certainly not just "international law" in the conventional sense. Neither is it the multifaceted supranational creature described by the European Court of Justice in *Costa* v. *ENEL* Case 6/64, [1964] ECR 585. If there is a world government, it has only a Department of Commerce.

As will be explored below, the Uruguay Round negotiations, spanning 1986 to 1994, brought such economic sectors as services, investments, agriculture, intellectual property and textiles into the global rule-based trading system. The single most important change was in dispute settlement, in that an adverse ruling against a defending member country by a panel or by the new Appellate Body could not be avoided, as panel rulings had been in the past. From 1995 onwards, in the event of an adverse decision, that ruling has had to be complied with, or substantial amounts of money foregone. The prevailing party can now withdraw concessions in the event of non-compliance, as long as the amount of the "sanction" has been approved by the WTO. This change from diplomacy to a more recognisably judicial system, with binding consequences, has been described over and again. Indeed, WTO studies have been characterised by far more attempts at description than comprehension or contextualisation.

Despite criticisms of the form of remedy available (trade sanctions as the principal and paradoxical remedy in the quintessential free trade regime), the WTO system has nevertheless become a system based on enforceable penalties; it was after 1995 a system with legal teeth.[1] Regardless of the sensitivity of the national legislation being challenged, no matter the political cost at home, the system could now demand compliance. It is unlikely, though still possible, that this newly "binding" aspect of the global trade regime will be reversed, street protests and dissatisfaction notwithstanding. The constituencies most critical of

---

[1] Steve Charnovitz, "Rethinking WTO Trade Sanctions", 95 *American Journal of Int'l Law* 792–832 (Oct 2001). Note to trade sactions underlying free trade.

the WTO—because of its lack of transparency, threats to the global environment, indifference to labour concerns, and harsh effects in developing countries—are disparate and disunified, and hardly capable of undermining the
superior lobbying position of international corporations arguing in favour of
further legal steps in the direction of a global market. On the other hand, legal
rigor demands intellectual justification going beyond market considerations, as
discussed above.

"TRADE RIGHTS AS EUROPEAN RIGHTS"

The most extreme, and certainly the wittiest, version of this doctrine appeared in
a book several years ago by Kees Jan Kuilwijk, who likened the EC's passage
through stages of development to that of Dante's spiritual journey.[2] In Kuilwijk's
vision, "after centuries of seemingly interminable struggle", a "ray of hope"
appeared with the foundation of the EC. The common market was consolidated
during the Single Market programme of the late 1980s, but could not reach its
proper zenith without fully providing for "free trade rights" to European citizens. This could best be effected through decisions of the European Court of
Justice, Kuilwijk argued, giving full direct effect to GATT law.[3]

The opening up of "fortress Europe", according to Kuilwijk, would make a
"true level playing field" for European companies and allow European consumers "true freedom of choice".[4] The third stage, which will involve a full
implementation of GATT/WTO law by the EC, requires the "divine guidance"
of the European Court of Justice. As Kuilwijk put it, "the neglect of GATT law
is an internal problem which can be solved only internally.[5]

Under this view, the EC is a neo-liberal way station, and restrictions on "trading rights" by the Court of Justice are the equivalent of restrictions on human
rights. As will be discussed in chapters 11 and 12 below, the Court of Justice has
long affirmed rights to property, trade and business within the Community, but
always legally circumscribed by the greater general interests of the Community
as a multi-faceted entity. Kuilwijk pointed out that there are a number of similarities between GATT and the EC; inevitably so, in that the General Agreement
provided one of the main models on which the EEC Treaty was based. Both
systems are founded on the "rule of law", and principles of non-discrimination
in trade.[6] Kuilwijk did acknowledge that "the objective of the EC Treaty
transcends that of the GATT", and quotes the Court of Justice in *Van Gend en*

---

[2] Kees Jan Kuilwijk, *The European Court of Justice and the GATT Dilemma: Public Interest versus Individual Rights* (Beuningen Center for Critical European Studies Series, 1996).

[3] See Judson Osterhoudt Berkey's critique of Kuilwijk's book, in "The European Court of Justice
and Direct Effect for the GATT: A Question Worth Revisiting", *Jean Monnet Program Working
Papers* No. 3/98, Harvard Law School (1998).

[4] Kuilwijk, *supra* n. 2, at 26.

[5] *Ibid.* at 28.

[6] *Ibid.* at 45–46.

Loos to the effect that the Community constitutes a "new legal order", distinct from what had come before.[7] But even while making reference to Pierre Pescatore as to the "originality" of the European "task", Kuilwijk did not satisfactorily treat the problem of the interaction of sectoral concerns: how should trade principles and "rights to trade" be reconciled with concerns for the protection of labour, environment and social policy? And how can a court charged with the protection and vindication of all parts of the Treaty be expected to lead the charge in the full and total embrace of a GATT/WTO law that might well threaten many aspects of the full European "project"?

While it is true that rights to property, business and trade are important rights, they are likely to occupy a position of opposition to other kinds of rights; other rights have tended to be protected as a result of controls being placed on property rights. It is insufficient to say that the European Court of Justice should provide for the full integration of GATT/WTO law into the legal system of the Community, without coming to grips with how the Court might balance this innovation against the tradition of protection for non-economic values within the EU. Kuilwijk wrote that

> "There is still a widespread misunderstanding that GATT law requires the Members to give up their own economic or social policy objectives. GATT law only restricts, and in some cases prohibits, the use of trade policy instruments which are generally considered to be harmful to the domestic economy".[8]

He went on to say that GATT law ranks trade policy instruments in line with the "economic theory of optimal intervention".[9] That is to say, when government intervention is needed for the sake of a social policy goal, for instance, interventions as close as possible to "the distortion in question" will be the most efficient; whereas the more trade-distorting solutions call forth limitations in the form of GATT law. "GATT law", Kuilwijk wrote, "offers numerous ways to pursue economic and social policy in a responsible and effective manner".[10] However, this insight is not terribly useful in devising EU-wide solutions to the problem of beef hormones, the banana trade, or GMOs. And going far beyond this, there are the indirect threats posed by globalisation to high standards of labour and social protection; what in GATT/WTO law can possibly provide guarantees for these non-economic values? It does not seem that it is open to the European Court of Justice to consider economic rights in isolation from the complex inter-connectedness of the EC/EU treaties and secondary European legislation, as well as long-term political goals, which inevitably provide subtext and context.

Kuilwijk also wrote, powerfully and compellingly, that the Court of Justice should realise that the Community public interest is an "amorphous concept",

[7] Kuilwijk, *supra* n. 2, at 46.
[8] Kuilwijk, *supra* n. 2.
[9] Kuilwijk, *supra* n. 2.
[10] *Ibid.* at 239–240.

one which "cannot exist independently from the disclosed preferences of private traders in the Community".[11] He rejected the notion that the public interest is a truth which can be discovered "regardless of the equal rights and individual preferences of the citizens".[12] But this, in one sense, begs the question; who shall decide the nature of the public interest, and the nature of the relationship between laws made in the public interest and laws made at the GATT/WTO, is precisely what is being argued over at street level around the world, albeit in an often uninformed fashion. Kuilwijk argued, apparently seriously, that the Community can intervene on behalf of some, but certainly not all, its constituents (for instance, farmers, but not consumers); thus, it should relinquish this doomed task to the invisible hand.[13] This seems to acknowledge that the EU could not fully embrace GATT/WTO law, by granting it direct effect, without at the same time ceasing to be the multi-faceted "intervenor" that it has attempted to be.

An array of European scholars have blended together the processes of European and global economic integration, pointing to a simultaneous rise of "deregulation, market economies, protection of human rights and democracies".[14] But it is crucial to note that the EU was not formed by a process whereby the protection of economic and non-economic values simply emerged from the activity of the market. Perhaps it is understandable that the 1990s fostered a view that democracy and human rights were automatically spawned from market economies, that issues of war and peace would be settled through the operation of the market, and that the only necessary element was the firm establishment in law of free trade principles and rules. But despite its underlying free-trade ethos, the system of European integration clearly did not evolve without significantly restraining market impulses at many stages. Economic integration through shared liberal principles might well be the necessary pre-condition for the creation of a general world peace of the kind posited by Professor Petersmann. However, the ideal citizen who is the subject and object of the constitutionalisation process is surely not named "modern homo economicus".[15] With a general focus on the development of the common market, and in the general belief that politics follows economics, it is easy to overlook the massive expenditure of human resources represented by the non-economic protections offered by the EU as a system.

These protections may not be perfect, but they were planned, and executed with an unparalleled determination. The EU limited the concept of competition to actual economic activities, and worked to prevent competition between Member States based on a race-to-the-bottom. This the global system has not

---

[11] Kuilwijk, *supra* n. 2.

[12] *Ibid*. at 257–258.

[13] *Ibid*. at 349.

[14] See, for example, Ernst-Ulrich Petersmann, "Constitutionalism and International Organizations", (Winter 1997) 17 *Journal of International Law and Business* 398.

[15] *Ibid*. at 401.

come to grips with, and appears to have no organised intention of coming to grips with in the near future. However, reminders will continue to appear in the form of noisy confrontations, now taking place with regularity.

It is not the case that these issues have been lost on recent scholarship; indeed, there have been admirable attempts to link globalisation with fair and balanced development, as well as with environmental and social protections.[16] However, a serious problem with these attempts is that they lack realistic prescriptions regarding how to achieve the link. It would seem that unless the seriousness of purpose that created the EU is present at global level, objections to the one-sidedness of binding economic law will remain aspirational. Certainly the UN has identified the opportunities and pitfalls of globalisation, and suggested ways in which the beast might be tamed in the service of humanity.[17]

Professor de Waart was correct when he noted that the introduction of a social clause in international trade relations "is revealing as it is met with opposition by both poor and rich countries". Poor countries, he said, are concerned about interference in their internal affairs, whereas the wealthier countries do not wish to see any restrictions on the market.[18] Professor Weiss stated much the same thing about opposition by poorer countries to linking labour protections to trade agreements, as they suspect this to be a "protectionist ploy".[19] In many ways, this often cited opposition of developing countries to inclusion of labour or environmental standards is the hardest obstacle to the creation of a complex, fair and sensible global regime. Again, the EU example is instructive. The inclusion of such standards involves wealth transfers, and large-scale investment not based purely on market considerations. It is likely that there is no political will to bring this about at global level, even within the EU. However, not to bring this about, and to hope for the best from the operation of international markets as currently regulated, is to court the failure of globalisation as a process.

METHODOLOGIES OF INTEGRATION: THE EC AND THE WTO

In the wake of the breakdown of the WTO's first Millennium Round talks in Seattle, the WTO has been experiencing a crisis of legitimacy. Political constituencies from around the world, each with important stakes in various kinds of national regulation—environmentalists, labour advocates, rural development groups, and so forth—have called the WTO legal structure into question,

---

[16] See, notably, *International Economic Law With a Human Face*, F Weiss, E Denters and P de Waart (ed.) (The Hague: Kluwer Law International, 1998).

[17] See *ibid.* at 10. Weiss and de Waart claim that "international economic law is beginning to turn its faces to humanity in the best tradition of Roosevelt's freedoms from not only fear but also want".

[18] Paul J I M de Waart, "Quality of Life At the Mercy of WTO Panels: Article XX An Empty Shell?", in Weiss, Denters and deWaart, *supra* n. 13, at 109.

[19] Friedl Weiss, "Internationally Recognised Labour Standards and Trade", in Weiss, Denters and deWaart, *supra* n. 13, at 89.

albeit in a disjointed fashion unlikely to greatly influence its future development. For a system on the defensive, the strikingly technocratic approach taken in so much international trade scholarship is particularly unsuited to answering these challenges, or suggesting meaningful reforms.

By contrast, the framers of the original EC system were acutely aware that economic integration was a means to an end: peace through overcoming the impulse towards economic rivalry. The war and peace dimension, and the grand assumption that politics would not only follow but also inform economics, has allowed for the development of EC law in such diverse areas as labour protection, social equality, consumer and environmental protection, and lately human rights more explicitly. The European system was able to create a direct link between citizens and the Community institutions; in many and complex areas, the benefits on offer from the Community could often surpass those available from the nation (member) state.

Perhaps the most distinctive aspect of European integration is the manner in which Europe has pursued enlargement. Far from an *ad hoc* tacking together of uneven and unequal national economies in the service of a free trade ideal, the European system demands the most painstaking, and expensive, form of pre-accession convergence imaginable. European integration and expansion are not based on the notion of comparative advantage—alone, or perhaps even at all. European integration has not relied on the doctrine of welfare maximisation, although improving standards of living has been one of many key justifications for the development of the EC. Rather, as a matter or policy, the EU has insisted upon a multi-faceted, multi-sectoral legal development that attempts to mimic the complexities of the nation state. The EU has been able to absorb cultural and economic contrasts because of this elaborate process of legal convergence through years of assisting in the adoption of the entire *acquis communautaire* by new entrants to the Community.

It is clear that if the sole justification for the European project were seen as economic in nature, this could hardly be so. (Admittedly, the limits or perhaps the ultimate confirmation of this theory arises at the borders of traditional "European" territory, and its implications for a barrier based mainly on race and religion, under the guise of a "shared cultural tradition".) It can be assumed that generations of European policy-makers have perceived grave dangers to existing Member States *and* new entrants to the Community should this process of pre-accession convergence not occur.

Although the pre-accession process for aspiring EU members could appear as a kind of penance (witness the impatience with which some applicants have awaited a final timetable for entry), it can also be assumed that the process of advance convergence is for their benefit. Without experiencing a big bang, and without inviting massive political resistance, aspiring members can work in an orderly, detailed manner, negotiating on items of particular concern, to make the internal legal changes necessary for smooth entry into the Community system. Tellingly, Europe also makes available significant funding for projects that will assist in allowing these new states to reach European standards in environmental and social protection, and for the modernisation of industry. This represents an investment in long-term stability.

Seen from the point of view of existing Member States, there is a clear intention to avoid a race-to-the-bottom scenario, as discussed above. Haphazard enlargement and integration could potentially endanger standards within the Community by creating unwanted competitive pressure in areas well established as being part of the Community acquis. Indeed, what is most striking about this process (particularly when compared with the creation of NAFTA, not to mention the establishment of the WTO) is its thoroughness and level of detail. This economic and political investment is proof of the danger inherent in thoughtless expansion, and is proof of a European commitment to economic integration that actually works at many levels in the long term. Anything less, one can assume, would not be "good enough" for the EU. To say that it is essentially the task of states to deal with non-economic issues, while undermining the influence of the state through the process of transnational law-making, is disingenuous.

In contrast is the process that led to the establishment of the WTO at the end of 1994. Many commentators have discussed the fact that the WTO and the entire range of the Uruguay Round Agreements had to be accepted by would-be WTO members in their totality; the "all or nothing" quality of the new WTO. This was to be the end of the former "GATT *a la carte*". It also meant that a huge variety of countries with dissimilar interests and needs were required to take on a wide range of new substantive laws, without regard to the domestic impacts of any particular agreement. Thus, if a developing country remained firmly opposed to the Agreement on Trade-Related Aspects of Intellectual Property (the TRIPS Agreement), for example, in order to be a participant at the WTO, that country would nonetheless have to accept TRIPS in its entirety.

It is curious that for the EU, the pre-accession process is an absolute requirement; whereas at global level, there has been almost no discussion of the dangers of imposing broad areas of substantive law on countries of often profoundly conflicting interests. It could be argued that the WTO has no political aspirations comparable to those of the EU; for that matter, neither does NAFTA. This is no wish at WTO level to create a world citizenry; there is no inclination towards global free movement of persons, at least on the part of the major trading nations. Also, representative governments made the decision to proceed despite the apparent dangers, and dissatisfactions can be dealt with during the upcoming round of WTO negotiations. If this is so, is there any basis for saying that the EU and WTO systems are enjoying a gradual convergence?

Professor Weiler posits the "emergence of a nascent Common Law of International Trade",[20] although it would seem that his principal emphasis is on

---

[20] J H H Weiler, "Cain and Abel—Convergence and Divergence in International Trade Law", in *The EU, the WTO and the NAFTA: Towards a Common Law of International Trade?* (Oxford: OUP, 2000).

comparison between the techniques of the EU, GATT/WTO and NAFTA techniques of economic integration. Surely whether or not an individual state is allowed latitude in regulatory autonomy can only be evaluated in light of the overall validity of the transnational/supranational regime. In other words, it is a very different matter to examine the degree of regulatory freedom left to the European Member States, as opposed to that left to WTO members. It is precisely because the EU is more than a "free trade system" that only a part of its methodology bears comparison with the WTO; the early activism of the European Court of Justice can only be seen in the context of an overarching, even sometimes unarticulated, drive towards a very large project encompassing the various sectors and layers of social organisation. An historical examination of the techniques of economic integration will show any system more or less stringent over time—now favouring the transnational regime, now easing up and allowing more freedom to the constituent states. However, that the WTO has taken on such an authoritative role, without the corresponding complexity, is what causes the true crisis of legitimacy—a legitimacy impossible for the WTO itself to salvage or solve from within.

An enormous problem in the academic discourse surrounding WTO studies, and infecting comparisons between the WTO and EU, is that the most important questions do not primarily involve markets as markets—but rather, market forces and their effects on constituencies. A constituency losing out due to a rule of economic integration has no interest in a long-term or abstract justification for that historical movement. The EU has at least given serious thought and taken legal moves to deal with the losing constituencies deriving from economic integration. This the WTO has not done, and this the academic community must confront.

It would seem that more is required to establish legitimacy in "adjudicating competing values" than fair procedures, coherence and integrity in legal interpretation and institutional sensitivity.[21] Long before one reaches that point, there is a problem to do with the regime's very source of power itself. Pre-1995 GATT law was characterised by the fact that when a particular country found the compliance with an adverse decision too politically difficult, the adverse ruling could be ignored. Quite obviously, this meant that the confrontation between political constituencies and the free trade rule was not taken to the bitter end in hard cases. The bitter battles were state-to-state, contracting party to contracting party. This was never true in the Community system, because the system showed an early intention to uphold Community principle over national need, but then to deal with legitimacy issues by offering substitute benefits, even to losers. This was not always a smooth ride; there have been periods of retrenchment in the development of Community law. But the general approach

---

[21] See Robert Howse, "The Early Years of WTO Jurisprudence", in Weiler (ed.) *The EU, the WTO, and the NAFTA: Towards a Common Law of International Trade* (Oxford: OUP, 2000) 35–70; 41–42.

has remained consistent, and this should not be confused in any way with the much narrower concerns of the GATT/WTO system. It has been suggested that the critics of the WTO are perhaps not so much motivated by "a reaction against the legal rules of international trade themselves, but the institutional and interpretative behaviour of the official guardians of those rules",[22] but it seems only common sense that there is a broad, substantive justification that the system's critics find lacking, that has little to do with the quality of the Appellate Body's decisions.

The inertia characteristic of the pre-WTO global trading system was overcome in extraordinary fashion during the Uruguay Round because of the political strength of transnational market players. This new system can only, in turn, be altered by a similarly powerful set of forces, and this may not be possible to achieve. It remains to be seen whether the EU has the will to impose a more complex agenda on global legal relations, by bringing together a disparate set of actors whose common element is fear of the purely market character of the WTO. It is hardly a question of being in favour of or against the global trading system; it is rather a question of recognising the reality and staying power of resistance to the singularly market emphasis of the WTO.

EU IDENTITY IN THE DEVELOPMENT OF GLOBAL GOVERNANCE

It is worth noting that at least at the level of rhetoric and policy development, the EU is attempting to "complexify" the process of global integration, based on its own past and model of inputs. Recently, a working group participating in the creation of the White Paper on Governance generated a report called "Strengthening Europe's Contribution to World Governance".[23] Despite an unavoidable quality of abstraction, the report made a number of important points concerning the EU identity within the construction of a global legal regime. The report stated that within the EU

> "it has been possible over time to persuade Member States to pool sovereignty and thus to incur a direct 'loss' in exchange for the broader benefits to be reaped from integration".[24]

The working paper also stated that the demands of anti-globalisation protestors could be seen as

> "a call to return to a more integrated world-view that Aristotle would have found familiar, so that such a desire for more coherent policy-making should not be controversial in principle".[25]

---

[22] See Howse, *supra* n. 18.
[23] White Paper on Governance, Working Group No 5, "An EU Contribution to Better Governance Beyond Our Borders" (May 2001).
[24] *Ibid.* at 35.
[25] *Ibid.* at 13.

It cautioned, however, that "coherent policy-making is not easy: it faces resistance to new approaches, the lack of analytical tools and the lack of political leadership in changing old ways".[26]

At least one could say that the EU has an instinctual drive towards complex global system-building, and not only at the level of rhetoric. Whether there is an intention to attempt genuine "global governance" is debatable. The posture of the EU in WTO negotiations is far less remarkable than its advance statements would lead one to believe. While a multi-dimensional EU is essential and fundamental, it would seem that a multi-dimensional world order is expendable when EU-wide interests are threatened; nevertheless, such ideas as "sustainability impact assessments" and good global governance are abstract but resilient notions in the discourse of the EU institutions.

In that regard, the structural foundations of the recently agreed "Conotou Agreement", successor to the Lomé Conventions, are instructive. The Agreement has been criticised for containing laudable objectives, but failing to address the distinct needs of the developing world as a bloc, since it will in effect replace the traditional European emphasis on the ACP countries as a group, instead creating numerous individual free trade pacts with individual countries in the developing world. From the EU's point of view, this new emphasis is on "partnership" rather than the traditional paternalism. What is of interest from a global governance point of view is the strong political dimension of the Agreement, and the multi-dimensional approach taken to solving social problems and human rights matters through economic integration. A basic feature of the Agreement is that starting in 2002, the parties will commence negotiations to create individual "economic partnership agreements", to take effect in 2008.[27] Interestingly, a further objective of the EU is to bring its trade-related international development policy in line with the demands of the WTO, and no doubt to avoid disputes of the sort that arose in relation to bananas.

Article 1 of the Cotonou Agreement calls for an "integrated approach" that takes account of "political, economic, social, cultural and environmental aspects of development". It also emphasises involving the private sector, and creating conditions for "an equitable distribution of the fruits of growth". The language of the EU itself—including references to "social cohesion" and an active "civil society", with sustainable management principles informing "every level of the partnership"—is also much in evidence. Article 4 insists that various "non-State actors" will be involved in development strategies and will be provided with financial resources—again, in terms of regime-building strategy, similar to the methodology of the EU itself.

---

[26] *Ibid.* at 13.

[27] For strong criticism of the Cotonou approach, see Tetteh Hormeku and Kingsley Ofei-Nkansah, "Thematic Reports 2001: The Cotonou Agreement", Instituto del Tercer Mundo—Social Watch, *at* http://www.socwatch.org.uy/2001/eng/Thematic_reports/cotonoue_agr_2001.htm.

Article 9.2 of the Agreement states that

"respect for human rights, democratic principles and the rule of law, which underpin the ACP-EU Partnership, shall underpin the domestic and international policies of the Parties and constitute the essential elements of this Agreement".

How strict a condition this language is intended to place on participation remains to be seen; it does, however, provide an interesting paradigm for integrating trade and other non-economic conditions, here termed "essential" and "fundamental". Article 13 tackles such wide-ranging issues as fair treatment of immigrants, poverty reduction, and access to educational facilities for ACP students. It is clear that complex global governance would ultimately require wealth transfers; it is possible that in the future international trade agreements, such as the WTO agreements, will have to "earn" the participation of developing countries through technology transfer, and investment aimed not so much at preventing "distortions" as in equalising the global playing field.

Such an approach may come to be seen as practical and realistic, rather than fanciful. Indeed, on 30 July 2001, the Director-General of the WTO issued a warning to WTO members that continued failure to reach consensus on the agenda for the upcoming trade negotiations, in the light of the "earlier failure in Seattle", may well lead to a questioning of the WTO as a forum for negotiation. He warned that the WTO could enter a "long period of irrelevance".[28] With developing countries threatening to veto the entire process if their concerns are not met, it would seem that the WTO stands at a crossroads; the Uruguay Round was a one-time event, with the unknown leading to ambiguous compliance, even by those whose interests were not apparently being served. Conflicting interests are a fact, not a political position.

It could be said that the Cotonou Agreement is excessively interventionist at the level of rhetoric, and that massive funding would be needed to make such far-flung aspirations real. However, it is at least impressive to read that "[t]he central objective of ACP-EC cooperation is poverty reduction and ultimately its eradication; sustainable development; and progressive integration of the ACP countries into the world economy (Article 19)." The economic sections include provisions on macroeconomic reform as well as microeconomic assistance. Article 25 on "Social sector development" calls for assistance to health care and housing projects, under the guise of "cooperation". There are provisions on environmental co-operation and gender equality, legal reform and institution building. It is striking that the WTO system has not involved any wealth transfers beyond what is ideally supposed to occur in the process of international trade liberalisation. One returns to the issue of whether economic integration is possible or desirable in a situation of entrenched and ongoing dissimilarity of economic and social development; the EU system has answered that in its

[28] Doha WTO Ministerial 2001: Statement by the Director-General, 30 July 2001, at http://www.org/english/thewto_e/mini...n01_dg_statement_gcmeeting30july01_e.htm.

approach to accession; the WTO system is in the throes of dealing with the question, though no answer is yet apparent.

While it is not at all clear whether the Cotonou Agreement can achieve its lofty goals, there is a certain sanity to its structure that the WTO system could learn from. Article 36 makes clear that one of the principal objectives is to conclude new trade agreements that will be compatible with the WTO. The EU is not rejecting the WTO system, and indeed is working to WTO-proof its international trade and aid policies. Non-reciprocal trading arrangements will be denied to countries that have reached higher levels of development; the EU will no longer treat all ACP countries as one bloc. As mentioned above, there will be a "preparatory period" between 2002 and the end of 2007 wherein the parties will be in the process of negotiating country-specific trade agreements. Article 37.3 states that

> "the preparatory period shall also be used for capacity building in the public and private sectors of ACP countries, including measures to enhance competitiveness, for strengthening of regional organisation and for support to regional trade integration initiatives, where appropriate with assistance to budgetary adjustment and fiscal reform, as well as for infrastructure upgrading and development, and for investment promotion".

This is not mere idle speculation on the likely beneficial effects of "more free trade;" rather, at least in outline form, the Agreement offers a blueprint for "capacity building" in the developing world. It may be that what the WTO lacks most sorely is not so much more transparent procedures, as a clear and practical plan for capacity building aimed at the poorer members. This would make possible the introduction of environmental and labour standards, since the developing world will not agree to these changes without a clear indication of targeted wealth transfers. Those who are convinced that trade liberalisation alone will deliver this multiplicity of benefits will be opposed to complicating the global regime in this manner. However, as even the WTO's Director-General seems to indicate, the current configuration of conflicting national interests is leading to stasis and threatening the world trade system itself. For the system to continue and legal development to continue, substantive provisions addressing and altering the clash of interests is probably inevitable.

To this extent, no analysis of international trade law as such, in comparison with the internal trade aspects of the EU, can capture the nature of the current legitimacy crisis gripping the WTO in particular, and offer new modes of understanding the EU's methodology. It is not really open to the WTO to merely "engage with" the world's multiple political, social and cultural constituencies. The crisis, as this work sees it, is in the disproportion between the legal powers of the WTO, as opposed to the far less definite international structures meant to deal with health, labour and human rights. Thus, the WTO's Appellate Body, for instance, almost certainly does not have the power or capacity to provide a "perfect example of the interplay between external and internal legitimacy".[29] Allowing *Amicus* briefs submitted by NGOs is not sufficient recognition of the outside world. Indeed, the future will in all probability reveal that the issue is not whether or not the WTO recognises those constituents making up the outside world, but how the main players in the development of global governance create new legal structures to take into account these constituencies. It has been my contention that the EU is best positioned to guide this work, as it seems most capable of thinking in these regime-building terms, and best able to communicate with players clearly at odds with one another.

A principal motivation for the writing of this book is the conviction that the field of international trade studies is too small and too insular; that there should be a new field of legal studies created round the notion of "legal aspects of global governance". In this way, the structural differences between international trade law and other sectors of law can be examined. That is why it is so crucial for WTO panel reports to be written in human form, made accessible, far shorter, far less reliant on unreadable technical jargon, more analogously to judicial decisions, and for more law students to be brought into the field. For many years, there was an entrenched belief that international trade law, notably GATT law, was based on immutable principles (such as "comparative advantage"), and that this arcane branch of legal knowledge was best left up to insiders and experts. This worked reasonably well, until the 1995 shift, much discussed, from diplomacy to legalism. All the shift really means is that the consequences of adverse panel and Appellate Body decisions are no longer avoidable in the manner of diplomacy. Rather, there are real penalties and genuine financial consequences. This has inevitably brought to bear an intensity of questioning that did not exist before. Nevertheless, the discourse of the academic writing on the subject has remained in large measure locked in a dull technocratic box, with the panel reports in particular nearly a parody of the turgid and unreadable. By contrast, the European Court of Justice, dealing with similarly technical and difficult economic issues, has consistently been almost poetic. But this is not praise reserved only for the ECJ; the same could be said of nearly any good court in any jurisdiction. It must be said, there is no need for the panel reports and Appellate Body reports, the essential decisions of the WTO, to go on presenting such a forbidding face to the world, daring students to enter, deterring the imaginative and the interdisciplinary to stay, to analyse, and to influence.

It is not uncommon for panel reports to spend many pages parsing the meaning of a small phrase; and the entirety of the pleadings by both sides are likely to be intertwined with the core reasoning of the decision. It is not the case that WTO subject matter is uniquely difficult; it is, however, uniquely isolated from other human concerns. Thus has developed a legal discourse that, consciously or unconsciously, cannot be perused by ordinary, even highly educated, mortals.

---

[29] See J H H Weiler, "The Rule of Lawyers and the Ethos of Diplomats: Reflections on the Internal and External Legitimacy of WTO Dispute Settlement" Jean Monnet Program Working Papers, No. 9/00, Harvard Law School (2000).

This has the effect of further limiting the circle of those familiar with WTO law, and intensifying the gap between those who protest and those who explicate the system. It also tends to reinforce a scholarship dominated by description, as opposed to contextualisation.

By virtue of being "closed", the modern nation state managed to deliver certain benefits to its citizenry. In the twentieth century, along with the nationalistic nightmares brought about by inter-state rivalry, relative labour and capital immobility led to demands for redistribution as compared with the early days of the Industrial Revolution. It should go without saying that transnational economic integration can hardly succeed if it is perceived as eliminating many of those hard-won social benefits. In this lies the most impressive achievement of the EU, whatever its negative consequences might be: it has succeeded in economic and political integration, without allowing backsliding from the social attainments of the twentieth century.

The lesson of the history of EU legal developments, as well as the recent breakdown in the forward march of the WTO, may be that economic integration does not exist in isolation from other sectors of law dealing with non-economic values. There can probably be no ongoing WTO, with dispute resolution continuing to threaten national regulatory values, unless non-economic values are somehow factored into a global system in a more "legal", more compelling manner than is currently the case. It may be said that the WTO has no interest in reducing the regulatory autonomy of individual members, but this is not the perception for many of the world's peoples. Public interest theories and practices need not be the sole preserve of the nation; nor of the region, as with the EU. Nor can economic theory genuinely substitute for the public interest at global level.

If one considers a notion such as the "Community interest", a concept that reappears on a regular basis in the reasoning of the European Court of Justice, and in turn transcribes this notion onto a global regime, one gets a sense of what might be needed. It is to be hoped that the debate will soon shift from determining who is a "critic" and who a supporter of the WTO system, to something far more complex, and at the same time far less impenetrable. For the record, it should be stated that this work would like to be part of the drive towards the creation of a global system; it does not advocate localism or unilateralism in trade matters. It does not deny the power of the market. The point, however, is that there is a problem with the fact that true legalism at world level involves only trade concerns. The fact that Article XX of the GATT may be interpreted by the WTO's Appellate Body to allow more national regulations to be declared GATT/WTO-legal than heretofore is not a solution to this essential disproportion.

HOW THIS BOOK SHOULD BE READ

The intention underlying the writing of this work was to present the clash between national regulation and international trade rules in a dramatic, or at least narrative fashion that would be of interest to all those who care about the construction of transnational regimes. In addition, the hope was to demonstrate how the EU offers a separate, though in many ways closely related, model for economic integration; and further to show how, in embracing and rejecting the GATT/WTO, Europe has the power to influence the future development of global trade law as no other existing nation or group of nations can.

It is not easy, especially for law students, to find a more or less comprehensive work on the subject of WTO law as it actually is, that at the same time bears some relationship to other areas of law and society. In fact, it may be that the principal reason Professor Robert Hudec became such a central figure in trade law studies was that he was able to make GATT law come alive through discussions of individual trade disputes in language that appealed to thinking people and non-specialists. It must be said that it is impossible to determine whether or not the WTO system is performing a valid service to global welfare without understanding what it is in fact doing. Whether or not the WTO has something of value to add to the European legal regime is similarly a question that depends on whether one believes the EU has somehow failed to reach the heavenly stage posited by Kuilwijk, discussed above.

Needless to say, each topic taken up in this book could provide the basis for much more discussion than is found here. For instance, "trade and intellectual property" could also encompass an investigation of the European intellectual property regime; the extent of harmonisation, differences from TRIPS and so forth. However, it seems that what is most urgently lacking at this moment in global development is a coherent framework for understanding the globalisation process, for assessing its characteristics and offering alternative intellectual modes for approaching the next trade round.

In this light, I have attempted to present recent legal developments at GATT/WTO level as an overarching strengthening of trade rules as against national discretion. This is not to suggest that national discretion has always been exercised wisely; but rather to examine the specific manner in which the GATT/WTO system is now empowered to invalidate national laws that do not meet the standards developed since the inception of the General Agreement in the 1940s, and also those renewed and expanded after 1995. There are no doubt those who would quibble with the use of the word "invalidation", since, after all, it is impossible to actually coerce a member country into compliance with a WTO ruling. However, the economic costs of non-compliance are undoubtedly high, even if the edifice rests on mutual consent to recognise the WTO system as a valid and functioning one. Should the conflicts in worldviews and essential national interests become too acute, it is certainly still possible that the WTO system will lose that basic component of credibility, relevance and viability. The EU, despite the waxing and waning of the impulse towards greater integration, has managed to avoid a fatal crisis in its years of operation, and seems set to survive into the foreseeable future. As it generates more instruments of integration—such as the single currency—and as it enlarges to the East, this ability of the EU regime to endure will undoubtedly come to be seen, if it has not already, as self-evident.

This is not to say that the EU is beyond reproach; rather, it is to recognise that in light of the need for peace within Europe, and the decision to base this new era on the structure of a common market, the EU was able to offer general compensation in many fields for the loss of national autonomy and discretion. The WTO is not yet able to offer such a justification, except in the minds of certain economic theorists or specialists in international trade law. It is to a new generation of readers, intrigued by the possibilities of integration, but willing to imagine other legal models in the construction of global governance, that this book is primarily aimed.

STRUCTURE AND PURPOSE OF THE BOOK

The main purpose of this work was to set out the story of the manner in which the WTO has scrutinised national and EU law; then to examine the legal relationship of the EU to the external trading world, followed by a discussion of the reaction of the European Court of Justice to granting GATT/WTO law direct effect within the European legal regime. The objective was not to provide an exhaustive list of legislative responses at EU level to GATT/WTO law, since this has been carried out by others. Rather, the not very modest intention has been to map out a new way of understanding the relationship between these two regimes, at a time when reaction to globalisation is at times violent. The spectacle of a European Member State's police force turning against anti-globalisation protesters is, to say the least, a historically interesting and important phenomenon.

The book first examines the nature of early GATT law and takes up several key disputes from the early years of GATT. Once the GATT's central methodology is established, later chapters explore developments in recent GATT/WTO law, beginning with intellectual property and trade. Since the issue of patent protection for pharmaceuticals reaches into the problem of public health in the developing world, this has been one of the flashpoints for resistance to full implementation of WTO law by developing countries.

The next chapter, on free trade in investments, also looks at the general question of freedom for developed countries to invest in developing countries, and the nature of conditions and restrictions traditionally placed on such investments by developing countries. The next topic, trade and environmental protection has, along with the public health debate, been one of the most contentious. The chapter covers some of the most high profile of the recent trade and environment disputes, including the *Beef Hormones* and *Sea Turtles* cases. The chapter on trade in agricultural products examines questions relating to this idiosyncratic area of trade; the separate and different approach traditionally taken towards primary products in the world trading regime, and recent attempts to bring these products within the scope of GATT/ WTO "discipline".

The chapter on safeguards explores the subject of national opt-outs, and examines the nature of the GATT/WTO emergency safeguard provision after 1995. The conclusion is that this is not a very attractive or realistic option for WTO members seeking to protect themselves and their domestic constituencies against low-cost imports. The section on the textile trade suggests that this is one of the areas of genuine benefit to developing countries resulting from the Uruguay Round negotiations; with the caveat that the labour conditions in this industry world-wide are very problematic. The chapter on trade in services looks at why integration of markets in services involves alterations in domestic market organisation at a far deeper level than integration through freer trade in goods. Because of the interesting and important use of the General Agreement on Trade in Services (GATS) in the *US–EC Banana* dispute, a discussion of that case is located in this chapter.

The final chapter on WTO law specifically deals with the matter of national anti-dumping law. It is suggested that with restrictions having been placed on so many avenues to protectionism through the new substantive agreements created during the Uruguay Round, as well as due to the new and more genuinely binding dispute settlement procedures, national and EU anti-dumping law is an area where members retain an unusual degree of discretion in reacting to low-cost imports, even though the use of national anti-dumping instruments is ostensibly restricted by the fairly elaborate WTO rules designed to prevent protectionist reliance on anti-dumping measures.

The latter sections of the book are devoted to the topics of European external trade relations generally; and the role of GATT/WTO law within the European legal regime. The reasoning of the Court of Justice in denying GATT law direct effect within European law is given special attention. It is hoped that it will have become clear what would be at stake were the Court to give the GATT such a privileged role *vis-à-vis* Community regulation from within. Defending EC law before a WTO panel is one matter; striking down Community law because of its inconsistency with GATT/WTO law as an internal matter is quite different.

FOCUS ON THE DISPUTES

In recent times, there has been an enormous amount of discussion concerning the power of an unaccountable, unelected set of persons in Geneva to strike down domestic regulation, on the one hand; and on the other, a great deal of writing describing in enormous detail the slightest changes in the relationship between the WTO bodies and certain key provisions of WTO law—notably Article III on national treatment. This book, by contrast, places its emphasis on the working out of the specific trade disputes that have come before the WTO, comparing them to the earlier GATT disputes and also demonstrating the manner in which the Uruguay Round Agreements have been applied in scrutinising national laws. It would seem that the heart of the debate over the validity, legitimacy and viability of WTO law could be located within the disputes themselves. The WTO has enormous potential power, and it now also has a record.

It is no doubt quite difficult for law students or other non-specialists to appreciate the finer points of an internally referential WTO law debate; whereas the disputes set out a national law to be scrutinised, a provision of GATT/WTO law to be interpreted and applied, and a result that either leaves the national or EU law in tact, or strikes it down as GATT/WTO unlawful. This exercise of power is significant. It has global implications. It leads naturally to the question: Was this exercise of power worth it? Where a national law has been invalidated, the question must be: what has been lost, in terms of the national constituency or transnational constituency for that type of law? Is the fact that the WTO rule prevailed a preferable outcome to the retention of the national or EU regulation?

An equally important question has to do with the basis upon which the WTO has exercised its power. It is clear that huge swathes of humanity have no idea what ratification of WTO law entails, or on what set of criteria this hierarchy of laws has been created. Again, the EU alternative is instructive. While often criticised for leaving ordinary citizens baffled, it is likely that there is not the same degree of general confusion about why the Community was originally created, and what its main objectives are.

At the very least, it can be said that if one is searching for models of international governance, as opposed to diplomacy-based "international law", then the EU has attempted with varying degrees of success to base the development of its legal regime on complex inputs. EU white papers and speeches and legislation overflows with references to stake holders and social partners; with structures of consultation and elaborate processes of assent. Its legislative structures involve representative inputs from the Member States, the Community executive, and the directly elected, as well as specialised bodies representing political constituencies within and across Europe. It should be recognised that this can lead to an artificial, stylised set of procedures, a separate language not really spoken by anyone, formalistic and hypocritical. However, the ambition and successes of the regime cannot be ignored. If the EU system is really to be compared with that of the WTO, the EU version is notable for having avoided the sort of crisis of legitimacy that now faces the world trade body. This could be because, in light of what was said above about the EU's "complex inputs", the WTO has in one sense been about reducing inputs, where national or EU level inputs conflict with trade rules. This may be the case with the Uruguay Round's Sanitary and Phytosanitary (SPS) Agreement, discussed in the context of the *Beef Hormones* case, in chapter 5. Perhaps even in the context of a legal discussion, it is crucial to bear in mind that to the extent that the interests of constituencies are not simple—and cannot be made so through abstract theory—global law cannot long remain simplistic. GATT/WTO law is not just about imposing rationality on domestic regulation, or altering it slightly to fit a superior paradigm. But it is for an ever-broader set of scholars, reading the disputes and considering the substantive WTO Agreements, to help decide whether trade law should be slightly reformed, fundamentally altered, combined with other and equally binding areas of non-economic law, or indeed left alone to operate as it is now.

2

Early GATT

WHATEVER ELSE THE European Community may be, its original identity is that of a customs union, a free trade area, with political union following the often painful and always incremental process of economic integration.[1] While the GATT's foundation preceded the formal creation of the European Communities, that there would in due course be a common market in Europe was, of course, understood at the time of the GATT's inception. The stance of the GATT drafters towards the prospect of the creation of such regional free trade entities, as described below, is instructive.

While the EC demonstrates a collective tendency to consider itself unique, and while the doctrines of supremacy and direct effect of Community law undoubtedly did create an entity that was able to move far beyond the strictures of conventional international law, the EC—and more recently the EU—cannot be fully understood without also taking into account the conceptual roots of the GATT trading system.[2] Both systems grew out of the idealistic spirit of internationalism that succeeded a period of horrifying warfare in Europe and elsewhere. In the late 1940s, it was an article of faith, and understandably so, that "free trade" could offer an antidote to national strife and competition. This idealism took the form of very specific, almost inanely simple, legal building blocks, many of which the GATT was to share with the European Communities.[3]

At the time the basic GATT articles were being drafted, the reputation of nationalism was at a low ebb, and the concept of a "world economy", founded on peace and prosperity, accepted with relative ease. Historically speaking, the GATT system, the International Monetary Fund, the World Bank, the EC, and the United Nations, were built on the same belief in ever-increasing integration that would bring an end to chaos and poverty.[4] While the GATT regime has seen its fortunes rise and fall over the intervening decades, the resiliency of this central concept is remarkable.

While the enormous differences in intention and scope between the regime established by the Treaty of Rome and that of the General Agreement must be

---

[1] See Wolf Sauter, "The Economic Constitution of the European Union", (1998) 4 *Columbia Journal of European Law* 27; J H H Weiler and Joel P Trachtman, "European Constitutionalism and Its Discontents", (1996) 17 *Journal of International Law and Business* 354.

[2] See Kees Jan Kuilwijk, "The WTO and the European Community: The Historical Dimension", in *The European Court of Justice and the GATT Dilemma: Public Interest versus Individual Rights?* (Beuningen: Center for Critical European Studies Series, 1996) 45–76.

[3] *Ibid.* at 335–337.

[4] John H Jackson, *The World Trading System: Law and Policy of International Economic Relations*, 2nd edn. (Cambridge, MA: MIT Press, 1997) 35–43; Kuilwijk, *supra* n. 2, at 47–62.

acknowledged, they do in fact share a basic methodology of open-endedness, and "ongoing progress". Perhaps never before had international agreements been so ambitious for the future. Future developments, while invisible, had an unquestioned presence. Participating countries were to be induced to sign up to Step One; the integration machine was switched on, and the process of never-ending union begun. The legal question for the drafters and planners was how best to devise rules most suited to this process.

The GATT system was born from the idea that the major disasters of the twentieth century could be traced to trade protectionism and economic nationalism; the so-called "beggar thy neighbour" policies pursued by the nations of the Western world during the early part of the century.[5] The Great Depression of the 1930s and World War II in particular were generally thought to be symptoms of national protectionism run amuck.[6] During the latter stages of the war, when it was clear that the allied countries would need to have a plan in place to remould the post-war economic world, the US and UK in particular began negotiations to devise a regime for post-war monetary and trade co-operation.[7]

The famous conference at Bretton Woods, in New Hampshire in the United States in 1944, had as its objective drafting a charter for the International Monetary Fund and an International Bank for Reconstruction and Development.[8] Here, too, one cannot but be struck by the resiliency of the regimes devised for these institutions. The parties at Bretton Woods actually managed to negotiate a stable currency exchange system for the major trading nations that lasted until the early 1970s.

As the Bretton Woods mythology goes, the delegates at the conference, composed in the main of representatives of ministries of finance in the allied countries, realised that there was little point in regulating the flow of international funds in isolation from patterns of trade in goods.[9] A recommendation came from the conference, directed at their respective governments, that work should begin on the task of reducing the sorts of trade barriers that had led to disaster in the recent past.

It is clear that there was nothing inevitable or haphazard about the legal system that resulted from this initial impulse. As with the creation of the European Communities several years later, the drafting of the GATT system was the result of political purpose and careful planning. Given the strong mistrust of economic nationalism—though it would make a comeback of sorts not long afterward—there were calls on all sides for the creation of an actual international trade

---

[5] See Robert L McGeorge, "Revisiting the Role of Liberal Trade Policy in Promoting Idealistic Objectives of the International Legal Order", (1994) 14 *Northern Illinois University Law Review* 305, 309–312. See also John H Jackson, *World Trade and the Law of GATT* (Indianapolis: Bobbs-Merrill, 1969).

[6] See generally Robert E Hudec, *The GATT Legal System and World Trade Diplomacy* 2nd edn. (Salem, NH: Butterworths Legal Publishers, 1990).

[7] John H Jackson, *supra* n. 5; Jackson, *supra* n. 4 at 35–36.

[8] Jackson, *supra* n. 4, at 36.

[9] Jackson, *supra* n. 5.

entity—an organisation capable of overseeing the functioning of the projected world trade system.[10] While this organisation did not come to pass in the 1940s, it is again a tribute to the central insights of the post-war planners that such an organisation—powerful, capable, and based in law—did come into being, albeit nearly fifty years later: the World Trade Organisation.[11]

The early preoccupations of trade planners were, perhaps, primitive by the standards of today's complex trade disputes. The first few decades of the twentieth century had been characterised by very high tariffs in particular, along with strict quotas placed on imported products, the manipulation of exchange rates as a form of protectionism, and a constant, unpredictable changing of import regulations.[12] These techniques were relied upon by all the major trading powers of the time. It was against this historical background that the US, based on the extensive negotiations that had taken place with its wartime allies, published a draft proposal for an International Trade Organisation ("ITO"). This original charter contained a free trade agreement, along with dispute resolution procedures, and proposals for a permanent organisation able to carry out the dispute resolution function. Consideration was given to the possibility of appeal of organisation decisions to the International Court of Justice.[13]

Not every component of this programme came into being at the time, the simplest explanation for which is that such a surrender of sovereignty was politically premature. Indeed, it is generally acknowledged that the fault for failure to adopt the complete liberalisation programme lies with the US, whose executive branch of government by 1950 had decided to abandon attempts to gain legislative approval for entry into an actual international "organisation".[14]

In this regard, it is worth noting that international trade is an area of commerce where competition and conflict between the US President and Congress is particularly intense. In the US, then as now, the Congress was determined that the executive would not gain too much power in the area of foreign trade relations. Thus from the 1930s onward, Congress granted the President limited authority to enter into trade agreements of a reciprocal, bilateral nature. Clearly, the implications of this are very different from the prospect of entering into a multilateral organisation. In light of these limitations on presidential action, there could be no entry into the proposed ITO without specific Congressional authorisation.[15]

---

[10] Jackson, *supra* n. 5. Jackson, *supra* n. 4, at 36–38.

[11] Kevin C Kennedy, "The GATT-WTO System at Fifty", (1998) 16 *Wisconsin International Law Journal* 421.

[12] McGeorge, *supra* n. 5, at 309.

[13] Jackson, *supra* n. 5.

[14] Jackson, *supra* n. 5.

[15] See Gerald A Bunting, "GATT and the Evolution of the Global Trade System: A Historical Perspective", (1996) 11 *St. John's Journal of Legal Commentary* 505, 514–519; see also William Diebold, "Reflections on the International Trade Organization", (1994) 14 *Northern Illinois University Law Review* 335.

The US was not alone in requiring parliamentary approval for entry into a planned ITO. However, given the overwhelming power and prestige of the US—a dominance that was to fade with interesting consequences in the 1970s—it was felt that if the US was not going to enter the ITO, there was little point in expending the political capital necessary for other governments to put the ITO proposal before their parliaments either.[16]

It is in this twilight zone of pre-ITO ambiguity that we must look to understand the manner in which the GATT system functioned for the first 45 years of its existence. The GATT system came into being even though the ITO, which was to be the parent organisation, did not. The question to be put in this preliminary examination of the nature of the early GATT system relates to its underlying legal character: Was the GATT a legal system? To the extent that it proved effective, in what way did it manage to be effective, given what are frequently called its "constitutional defects?"[17]

By relying on available powers, the US executive pushed ahead with initial negotiations designed first and foremost to reduce tariffs. On that narrowly focused basis, between 1946 and 1948, already four separate conferences (these came to be called "rounds") were held. The work of drastically cutting tariffs was begun.[18] Even in these earliest days, the central genius of the GATT system was in evidence.

Major exporting countries and major importing countries involved with a particular product or sector would hammer out agreements involving specific tariff reduction commitments. Each individual nation would then produce its own tariff "schedule", containing the myriad national commitments entered into after any given round of negotiations, based on essentially bilateral talks. But the GATT system required that the bilateralism of the past be transcended, and the commitments entered into were generalised to include all participating nations. In other words, a tariff reduction (for instance) granted to one's major supplier of a product was required to be offered to all suppliers from other participating nations as well.

This concept, called "most favoured nation",[19] is central to GATT law, and represented a new departure in economic history. The requirement of reciprocity was eliminated from national wish-lists, largely as a result of a collective embrace of the theory of comparative advantage. The justification offered for being required to grant one's best level of trade terms to all participating countries (not just the partner with whom one has been negotiating) was that even unreciprocated trade liberalisation, in reducing trade barriers, would be beneficial to the nation granting the general concession.[20]

[16] See Arie Reich, "From Diplomacy to Law: The Juridicization of International Trade Relations", (1996/7) 17 *Journal of International Law and Business* 775, 784–786.

[17] See Ernst-Ulrich Petersmann, *Constitutional Functions and Constitutional problems of International Economic Law* (Boulder, CO: Westview Press, 1991), 221, 221–244.

[18] Jackson, *supra* n. 5.

[19] See Michael J Trebilcock and Robert Howse, *The Regulation of International Trade* 2nd edn. (London: Routledge, 1999) 27–28.

[20] See Jackson, *supra* n. 4, at 14–21.

Soon after the initial negotiations, a problem became apparent. Because the schedules of national tariff reduction were, on their own, comparatively informal, there was a fear that they could be revoked or ignored by the countries that had agreed to them. From this concern came the idea of formalising one part of the overall ITO package—the section comprising a "general agreement" on trade rules and behaviour. The reasoning was that in the absence of the institutional structure represented by the ITO, it would be possible to adopt the rules of the agreement to safeguard tariff commitments being made.[21]

The purpose of the rules found in the general agreement was to prevent the substitution of other kinds of protectionist behaviour after the more obvious and transparent one of tariff barriers had been lowered.[22] The agreement provided a model of trade behaviour—legal rules that could prevent backsliding via such expedients as quantitative restrictions. The concept was identified as "safeguarding the value of concessions", a major topic of concern in the early days of GATT.

All systems have foundational principles, and in the GATT, it was imperative to convince potential participants that they could negotiate to receive concessions that would retain a certain value. If the cost of this "investment" in the new multilateral system was vulnerability for economic sectors exposed to new international competition, the compensation for such potential losses would have to be access to new markets and a guarantee that risks taken were backed up by an assurance of overall wealth enhancement. This concept is reflected in the dispute settlement provisions of the General Agreement itself, as will be shown below.

So, as efforts continued to gain parliamentary willingness to adopt the ITO, the General Agreement on Tariffs and Trade (the "GATT" Agreement) was lifted out of the whole ITO package, and presented as stand-alone substantive obligations for participating countries. The plan was that each country would, without the need for the cumbersome and politically difficult process of parliamentary approval, sign the Agreement as a preliminary step, thus making it more difficult for them to engage in trade-impeding behaviour. The long-term hope was that the ITO would be ratified in due course by the various parliaments.[23]

The role and function of the Agreement to a large extent also determined its terms and its diction. Because of the generally held view that the Agreement should be entered into by executive decision, enormous care was taken to prevent any language suggestive of a formal international organisation or preemption of national legislative powers. This was an especially sensitive matter in the United States, where the President had to avoid the giving the impression that he was, on existing authority, committing the US to membership of an international organisation with separate powers of its own.

---

[21] Thomas J Dillon Jr., "The World Trade Organization: A New Legal Order for World Trade?", (1995) 16 *Michigan Journal of International Law* 349, 353–355.
[22] Jackson, *supra* n. 4, at 37.
[23] Jackson, *supra* n. 4, at 38–43.

Into such an atmosphere came the General Agreement on Tariffs and Trade,[24] signed by 22 countries initially in October of 1947, along with a brilliantly conceived "Protocol of Provisional Application",[25] to be described below. The original Contracting Parties, as they were called, were a relatively diverse group, including of course the UK and the US, along with Belgium, France, Australia as well as Brazil, India, Norway, Pakistan and South Africa.[26] The most important issue to bear in mind in approaching the text of the GATT Agreement is that it was never intended to carry the entire weight of global trade liberalisation in the modern period. It was expected at the time of adoption that it would soon be supplemented by the constitutional coherence of the ITO.

It is also crucial to understand that the bare, technocratic look and feel of the original GATT functioned historically—it served to conceal the ambitious political nature of the Agreement, and gave it the appearance of a specialist agreement dealing with such dry matters as tariffs and quantitative restrictions on imports. In other words, the GATT aspired to, and for many years achieved, invisibility. This in no way meant that it was ineffective. For those who knew and understood the GATT system, its power and effectiveness was clear, long before 1995.

The Protocol of Provision Application ("PPA") was further designed to dampen opposition to adoption of the General Agreement. A separate legal instrument, the protocol set out the precise nature of the commitments being entered into by the signatory parties to the GATT.

Specifically, the PPA stated that Parts I (the most favoured nation provision; and rules for the creation of individual tariff schedules), and III (largely the procedural sections), were to be applied fully; but that Part II, containing the principal substantive commitments of the agreement, was to apply "to the fullest extent not inconsistent with existing legislation". The PPA in this fashion granted all-important "grandfather rights" to participating countries with regard to their then-extant legislation that might be inconsistent with the Part III obligations of the GATT.[27]

Those vitally important Part II provisions cover such areas as customs procedures, quotas on imports, subsidies, anti-dumping duties and national treatment. The PPA sent out the comforting signal that no country would be forced, by virtue of its participation in GATT negotiations, to alter its domestic legal regime to conform to the provisions of the new agreement. It is obvious that the protocol would have had the effect of lessening parliamentary opposition and given the (perhaps misleading) sense that GATT participation would be relatively cost-free from a sovereignty point of view.

---

[24] General Agreement on Tariffs and Trade, opened for signature 30 October 1947, 55 UNTS 194.
[25] Jackson, *supra* n. 4, at 39–41.
[26] Jackson, *supra* n. 5.
[27] It is important to realise that this exemption did not apply to new legislation, even in the same subject area. Once the conflicting legislation lapsed, the right to retain similar conflicting legislation was also lost.

The PPA has of course ceased to have legal effect with the advent of the WTO and the Uruguay Round Agreements. However, it is worth comparing the genesis of the GATT system with that of the EC, in the sense that the GATT was deliberately presented in a constitutionally low-key manner; attempting to assure national representatives that this was hardly a system at all, but rather a set of guidelines. The European system, though also gradualist, announced itself with constitutional flourishes. And while the GATT founders apparently believed that the agreement on its own would act as a temporary expedient leading to a proper organisational structure in time, the agreement, and the PPA (though much of the relevant national legislation had of course expired) limped along as the sole basis—along with the evolving jurisprudence of panel reports—for the world trading system until 1995.

In the years following, a larger body of countries became contracting parties to the GATT. Representatives of these countries would meet approximately every six months and there was maintained the essential fiction that the GATT was not an "organisation"—thus the word "member" was not used until 1995.[28] Negotiations aimed at lowering tariffs continued, and disputes began to arise and to be taken before the GATT, with the dispute settlement bodies first called "working parties", and then "panels". It became clear that the lack of organisational structure was inefficient and unworkable, and by convention, smaller specialised committees began to take over GATT business between formal sessions of the representatives.[29]

The General Agreement itself was last formally amended in the 1960s, largely for the purpose of adding sections on the special role of developing countries.[30] Since that time, in order to avoid the technical difficulties of reaching consensus on changes to the basic text of the agreement, changes to overall GATT law have been negotiated outside the agreement itself, in the form of separate codes or agreements. This tendency was first seen in the Tokyo Round negotiations (1973–1979);[31] and continued in far more elaborate form during the Uruguay Round negotiations. This feature of "GATT/WTO" law can make the overall body of trade law, based on legal accretions, difficult to conceptualise. The panel and Appellate Body law, post-1995, has had to grapple with this complexity.

The General Agreement is an unprepossessing document; 38 articles, with several appendices, its tone is both technical and opaque.[32] Its most effective features could easily be overlooked, since the agreement does not provide within its own provisions any interpretative signposts of the sort one finds, for instance, in the Treaty of Rome. The GATT did not announce its own philosophy; instead, it retained an appearance (for the reasons already outlined above) of self-evident, above all technical rules. However, in the broadest sense, this

---

[28] Jackson, *supra* n. 4, at 59–60.
[29] Jackson, *supra* n. 5.
[30] Jackson, *supra* n. 5.
[31] Jackson, *supra* n. 4, at 75–78.
[32] General Agreement on Tariffs and Trade 1994 incorporates GATT 1947.

apparently modest GATT Agreement purported to make unlawful certain specific legislative acts by national governments, acts not taken in accordance with the philosophy of progressive economic interdependence.

The first and most basic GATT concept, "most favoured nation", is found in Article I.[33] This provision provides that the citizens of the contracting states may enjoy the same level of privileges accorded by any other GATT party to their "most favoured" trading partner.[34] The concept is not about a right to special treatment, but rather a right to equal treatment. While leaving in place some preferences based on historic relationships, the GATT Agreement attempted to eliminate the concept of "preferences" with respect to specific product sectors.[35]

The second essential principle of non-discrimination is found in Article III, "national treatment".[36] "National treatment" requires that a nation party to the Agreement treat an incoming product, after it has passed customs and moved into its "stream of commerce", in the same way it treats its own products. In other words, within its domestic market, a nation is not allowed to demonstrate commercial preference for its own products, as distinct from any action at the border in the form of a customs duty or other barrier.[37] Along with MFN, these two rather innocent sounding principles made up the heart of the transformation of the global economy that developed in the wake of the GATT Agreement.

From the EC's point of view, the most significant exception to the GATT principles of non-discrimination is to be found in Article XXIV, on customs unions and free trade areas.[38] While the GATT system might have been expected to resist and reject the formation of such trade blocs, it instead took quite the opposite approach; Article XXIV makes clear that, under certain conditions, the GATT system will welcome free trade areas, despite the inherent contradiction between them and the principles found in Articles I and III of the Agreement.[39]

The Article XXIV exception was far from open-ended, though. To be GATT-legal, a free trade area or customs union had to involve "substantially all" trade between the constituent parties, thus eliminating the possibility of

[33]   Trebilcock and Howse, *supra* n. 19, at 27–28; Jackson, *supra* n. 4, at 157–173.

[34]   MFN is often mistakenly believed to involve special and privileged treatment for one trading partner or set of trading partners, but in fact it refers to the right held by any GATT participant to seek treatment equal to that which is given to the most favoured or preferred. Thus no GATT party could (in the absence of some other justification) offer differential tariff rates on the same product to different nations acting as suppliers of that product.

[35]   A vitally important exception to this rule is found in Article XXIV on regional trade arrangements.

[36]   Trebilcock and Howse, *supra* n. 19, at 29–30; Jackson, *supra* n. 4, at 213–228.

[37]   Article III, para. 1 says that internal taxes and other internal charges should not be applied in such a way as to afford protection to domestic production.

Article III (4) provides a summing up of the national treatment concept, in that imported products shall be accorded treatment no less favourable than that accorded to like products of national origin in respect of all laws, regulations, and requirements affecting their internal sale. (Note that government procurement was initially excluded from the scope of Article III.)

[38]   A customs union is of course distinguished by the fact that it has a common external tariff.

[39]   Trebilcock and Howse, *supra* n. 19, at 27; Jackson, *supra* n. 4, at 165–167.

selective discrimination. Further, the general level of duties charged on imports after the creation of the bloc was not to be higher than the average level of duties in existence for the constituent countries before the formation of the bloc.

It would have been clear to the drafters of the GATT Agreement that the creation of the EC was on the horizon; thus one could perceive Article XXIV as a mere recognition of necessity. However, an alternative interpretation is that a trading bloc acts as a stepping stone towards a global economy, despite its inherent discriminatory tendencies. Since the common enemy of both a regional and global trading system is the idea of a national economy, it would seem that persons who have been trained in a regional trading bloc, especially one extensive enough to meet the Article XXIV standard, would have foregone their attachment to more traditional, locally-based economic activities in favour of scale and efficiency.[40]

OTHER GATT PROVISIONS OF PARTICULAR IMPORTANCE

Article VI,[41] on anti-dumping and countervailing duties,[42] should be read in conjunction with Article XVI, on the subject of subsidies.[43] It must be noted that the GATT system never attempted to outlaw dumping, since dumping is considered to be private behaviour, and GATT obligations fall, in the formal sense, only on the governments of participating countries. What the GATT did in the dumping context was to allow a proportional response by parties who believed themselves to be the recipients of dumped goods. Article VI allows a duty to be placed on such goods, but only in proportion to the margin of the dumping.[44]

[40] Note the deeply contradictory language of Article XXIV, para 4: "The contracting parties recognise the desirability of increasing freedom of trade by the development, through voluntary agreements, of closer integration between the economies of the countries parties to such agreements". But then, "They also recognize that the purpose of a customs union or of a free trade area should be to facilitate trade between the constituent territories and not to raise barriers to the trade of other Contracting Parties with such territories".

[41] Trebilcock and Howse, *supra* n. 19, at 31–33; Jackson, *supra* n. 4, at 247–303.

[42] Anti-dumping duties are customs duties placed on imports to counteract the effects of dumping; countervailing duties are similar in nature, placed on imports to respond to subsidisation in the home country of origin.

[43] While both these articles have been expanded upon enormously by later agreements, the underlying substance of each is still relevant.

[44] Article VI defined dumping fairly precisely, giving several choices as to how dumping could be ascertained. Generally speaking, dumping occurs when the products of one country are introduced into another country at less than the "normal value" of the products. Normal value may be determined in any one of the following three ways: firstly, if the price is less than the comparable price for the like product when consumed in the exporting country itself. If that information is not available, dumping can be determined to exist if the price is less than that charged for the like product in third countries. Or finally, in the absence of such data, if the price charged is less than the price represented by the cost of production plus a reasonable amount for costs and profit.
GATT rules have always made clear that anti-dumping duties should only be assessed when injury is shown to producers of "like" products; or, as the 1979 Anti-Dumping Code put it, at least "closely resembling in all respects". It has been pointed out that this is an impossibly strict standard

The concern reflected in the GATT rules was that anti-dumping or counter-vailing actions could become protectionist devices in themselves. Neither anti-dumping duties, as mentioned, nor countervailing duties, may exceed the gap between the real cost of the product and the advantage provided to the producer by the dumping or subsidy. Precisely to prevent this remedy from becoming a device of national protection, it is a requirement that before either an anti-dumping or countervailing duty is levied, the importing country must show that material injury is being done to an established industry, or that the development of such an industry is being materially hindered.

Article XVI on subsidies started out with the vague and general Section A, a mere exhortation to parties to "notify" other parties in the event of a subsidy being created which could have the effect of increasing exports from or reducing imports into its national territory. In the event of harm being shown to a contracting party because of the other party's subsidy, all that was required was a discussion between the subsidy-granting party and affected parties, with a view to limiting the subsidy!

This strikingly cautious provision was soon supplemented with Section B, which acknowledged that export subsidies could hinder the objectives of the GATT. Thus in para. 3: "Accordingly, contracting parties should seek to avoid the use of subsidies on the export of primary products". It was in this section that the GATT drew a fateful distinction between primary and non-primary products, with export subsidies on manufactured goods essentially forbidden from 1958, but with far more generous possibilities for continuing to subsidise primary (or agricultural products).[45] One of the most extraordinary features of the Uruguay Round Agreements is, of course, the fact that agricultural products have for the first time been brought, at least to a certain degree, within GATT "discipline", with a commitment to significant lowering of export subsidies for virtually all agricultural products.

Along with tariffs, one of the most common forms of protectionism is the "quantitative restriction", some form of numerical limit on imported products, including those created through national quotas or licensing schemes.[46] Article XI of the GATT Agreement addresses this problem.[47] Article XI's basic dictate was that no such quantitative restrictions were to be instituted or maintained on

---

for anti-dumping administrators to maintain, since it would then be an option for foreign producers to circumvent any dumping law by making superficial changes to the relevant product. In fact, most administrators take commercial reality into account and are flexible in their interpretation of "like" products in the anti-dumping context.

[45] If subsidies do increase the export of primary products, Article XVI states, "[s]uch subsidy shall not be applied in a manner which results in that contracting party having more than an equitable share of world export trade in that product". To arrive at an equitable share, the parties are told that account should be taken of relative shares in a "previous representative period", along with any other factors that might have affected trade levels.

[46] Ironically, although tariffs constituted the earliest preoccupation of the GATT system, tariffs are the favorite trade restriction of that system, since tariffs are considered to be obvious and transparent, and thus the easiest form of protection to eliminate.

[47] Trebilcock and Howse, *supra* n. 19, at 29–30; and Jackson, *supra* n. 4, at 153–154.

imports or exports. Of course, a number of exceptions were offered, notably for agricultural products.[48]

Article XII allowed contracting parties to safeguard their balance of payments under certain circumstances by restricting imports. Article XIII requires that where quantitative restrictions are applied, they must be applied in equal fashion towards all third country exporters of a product. In other words, shares in the restricting country's market must be allocated fairly and equitably among all supplying nations.

Article XVIII, governmental assistance to economic development, was added as a way of softening the effect of GATT policies on developing countries.[49] Following agitation by developing nations that became GATT parties in the 1960s, a more extensive set of differential considerations responsive to the needs of such countries was added to the original GATT provisions. These special conditions, while largely aspirational, are found in Part IV of the Agreement, on trade and development. As will be seen in discussions of the later WTO agreements, developing countries do generally receive separate and, ostensibly, special treatment in the various trade sectors. However, bearing in mind the effect of the debt crisis and other economic disasters on decision-making in the developing world, it is an open question as to whether this differential treatment amounts to a substantial overall benefit.

Every free trade system provides its participant countries with the possibility of emergency protective action. This is because of the fact that free trade rules will have unforeseen and painful effects on participating economies, as free trade creates winners and losers within each constituent economy, and not to provide a safeguard would risk political instability in the bloc. GATT's original Article XIX,[50] which has been substantially altered with the new Uruguay Round Agreement on Safeguards,[51] created a fairly undefined safety valve, allowing countries to take emergency action without setting time limits on the action.

Article XIX allowed a GATT country to react in a protectionist way, including through the imposition of quantitative restrictions, when it felt itself adversely and unexpectedly affected by concessions made under the GATT Agreement. The point is that the obligation incurred as a result of the GATT negotiation could be suspended if products were, as a result of a concession made, flowing into that country in such a way as to injure domestic injury. There was certainly political comfort in the open-endedness of the original Article XIX.

---

[48] Most significantly, Article XI (2)(c) stated that such a restriction could be GATT-legal if necessary to enforce government measures operating to also restrict quantities of the same product produced locally, or to remove a temporary surplus of a like domestic product. Such restrictions were not to reduce the total proportion of imports relative to domestic production, due regard being had to a "representative period".

[49] Jackson, *supra* n. 4, at 319–322.

[50] Trebilcock and Howse, *supra* n. 19, at 30–31; Jackson, *supra* n. 4, at 175–181.

[51] As will be shown, the new emphasis is upon the so-called "opportunity to adjust".

As will be shown below, the desirability of invoking Article XIX, and the willingness of participating countries to rely on it, would depend very much upon the general degree of autonomy allowed individual countries in imposing their safeguard actions. Was Article XIX to be subjected to the non-discrimination provisions of Article XIII, for instance? A continuing theme of GATT/WTO jurisprudence is the relative cost of the various protectionist devices remaining to participating countries. The higher the cost to the invoking party, the less likely it is that a particular device will be used. Inevitably, substitute means of national protection will be sought; in the post-1995 world, the reality is that fewer such devices than ever can be found.

Article XX on "general exceptions" allows for otherwise GATT-illegal behaviour, if necessary for the implementation of some other national law or public policy.[52] (Article XX is often associated with the recent trade and environment controversies, since it is the provision under which countries seek to defend themselves in the event of being accused of "green protectionism".) Article XX allows parties to adopt otherwise unlawful national measures for a variety of reasons, including the protection of public morals, protecting national treasures, protection of human, animal or plant life or health, or the conservation of exhaustible natural resources. Article XX can also be invoked when the measures adopted are necessary for the enforcement of another national law that is not, in itself, GATT-illegal.

The Article XX general exceptions are only valid if the national measures are not applied so as to constitute arbitrary or unjustifiable discrimination between countries where the same conditions prevail; neither, the provision says, can these measures be a disguised restriction on international trade.

Before the new dispute settlement procedures came into force in 1995, Article XXIII of the GATT,[53] a genuine legal oddity in terms of its historical position and drafting, provided the principal mechanism for the resolution of trade disputes between contracting parties. The early GATT, with its diplomatic, rather than adversarial, emphasis, was notably weak in the area of dispute settlement and penalties for non-compliance. To understand the revolution in dispute settlement wrought by the Uruguay Round Dispute Settlement Understanding, it is first necessary to have a full understanding of Article XXIII, the original GATT grievance provision.

Article XXIII relied on the notion of "nullification or impairment of benefit". The "benefit" referred to benefits expected to accrue from participation in the GATT system itself, and from favourable concessions made by other participants. The object of the dispute settlement system was to restore the value of the benefit gained—a favourable tariff or other concession of value. The central concept in early dispute settlement was that the behaviour of a party could be complained of, whether or not it actually violated a substantive provision of the

---

[52]   Trebilcock and Howse, *supra* n. 19, at 35; Jackson, *supra* n. 4, at 232–238.
[53]   Trebilcock and Howse, *supra* n. 19, at 51–58; Jackson, *supra* n. 4, at 114–115.

GATT Agreement, if that behaviour was having the effect of obstructing the realisation of an expected GATT benefit. Behaviour could also be complained of if it had the effect of impairing the objectives of the agreement itself.

Readers may note a similarity between this seminal GATT concept to the idea of legitimate expectations in contract law. The GATT was framed as a sort of collective contract with its participants able to obtain relief for behaviour of trading partners that interfered with these expectations. In a larger sense, the drafting of Article XXIII created a sense of inherent value arising from participation in the GATT, with Article XXIII designed in effect to preserve and protect the value of the investment of political capital for participating countries.

The Article XXIII dispute procedures, as they developed over time, were conducted as follows. When a party believed itself to be losing a benefit, either from GATT-illegal or GATT-legal behaviour of another party, representations were made to the offending party, who was then obliged to consult about the problem.

Should no satisfaction emerge from this stage of the process, the Contracting Parties as a collective were empowered to investigate. This step came, understandably, to be handled by a panel of independent persons, generally from trade ministries of disinterested countries (with regard to the dispute at hand), and familiar with GATT law. These bodies came to be called first working parties and then "panels", and were set up on an ad hoc basis to hear the merits of a particular dispute.[54]

Article XXIII simply stated that the Contracting Parties can give a "ruling" on the matter. The Contracting Parties (CPs) as a group were empowered to recommend a suspension of concessions or other obligations toward the offending party. The last sentence in the article, quite a fanciful scenario, says that the party against whom such action is taken can withdraw from the GATT itself, although in fact no party has ever withdrawn from the GATT on such grounds.

Of the greatest significance is the fact that, while the post-1995 GATT/WTO law also relies upon "withdrawal of concessions" by the complaining party as the principal sanction against the offending party, only in the post-1995 legal situation does this provision have real meaning. Panel reports did not have, and still do not have, legal effect before being adopted by the Contracting Parties (now membership) as a whole, thus preserving the notion of action by consensus. However, prior to 1995, the concept of consensus was very different from what it is in the WTO.

Prior to 1995, any party, including the party against whom an adverse judgment was made, could block the legal effect of the decision. Thus, no party actually had to accept an adverse ruling, and thus sanctions could not become legitimated except through the consent of the defending party. This situation, infused with the ethos of diplomacy, and scarcely an adversarial legal system, meant that the threat of litigation at the GATT was far less worrisome a

---

[54] After 1995, panels are still formed for the purpose of a particular dispute, and thus have no permanency. However, the new Appellate Body is court-like in that it is composed of appointed members serving for a fixed period of years.

prospect than it is today. The effect of these changes on contemporary disputes will be explored in full in later chapters.

Between the time of its legally ambiguous inception in 1947 and the end of the 1950s, the GATT remained a comparatively small body, although it included many of the world's most important trading nations. Even by 1960, it still had only 37 members. Its functioning was characterised by diplomatic consultation, whereas truly complex and sophisticated trade disputes had not yet arisen. Goals during that period were common to all participants: the continued reduction of tariffs, and assurance that these tariffs would not be replaced by other forms of protectionism.[56]

The GATT developed a consultation system that had the effect of preventing conflicts from reaching the stage of formal dispute, rather like informal arbitration. Over the early years, the number of formal complaints brought before GATT panels accelerated, though not as dramatically as in recent times. Between 1948 and 1959, a respectable 53 formal legal complaints were brought before panels.[57]

The normal GATT panel consisted of three to five persons, selected as indicated above from among delegates to the GATT from national trade ministries, as long as these were countries without a direct interest in the dispute at hand. Selection of panel personnel was by the General Secretariat, with the consent of the parties to the conflict.[58] The panels heard arguments, presented in oral and written form, both from the parties directly involved, and from any other party with an interest in the matter. This tradition has continued into the post 1995 legal regime. Because of the fact that defendant parties could block panel decisions,[59] larger trading powers such as the US and the EC often managed to keep adverse rulings at bay for years.

The question must then be asked at this stage, whether prior to 1995, panel decisions had any great effect or meaning. If rulings were essentially adopted on a voluntary basis, in what sense was the GATT a "legal system" in its early days? While characterised by a heavily diplomatic approach, it must be pointed out that even in its early years, the GATT was more coercive than traditional international law. The GATT system created a certain momentum towards liberal inter-penetration of economies. This, in turn, made the possibility of retreat from that direction increasingly costly to contemplate. Adverse rulings in this

---

[55] For an exceptionally complete discussion of the early history of GATT disputes, see Robert E Hudec, *Enforcing International Trade Law: The Evolution of the Modern GATT Legal System* (Salem, NH: Butterworths Legal Publishers, 1993).

[56] *Ibid.* at 11–13.

[57] *Ibid.* at 11–12.

[58] Jackson, *supra* n. 4, at 116.

[59] Jackson, *supra* n. 4, at 117, 125.

context did matter, in that the reputation of a participating country for behaving in a manner contrary to the larger interests of free trade could affect economic prospects on the global front. Indeed, it was often the case that, though a party continued to block a panel ruling, it would over time tend to revise the domestic law that had been challenged and found to violate GATT rules. Therefore, while it would be difficult to quantify the precise long-term effect of adverse panel rulings on parties unwilling to accept them, it would be wrong to dismiss the pre-1995 dispute settlement system as mere diplomatic negotiation. The early GATT panel system was a precursor to the post-1995 legal regime, yet with a few key elements missing, for which the trading world was not yet ready.

THE INTERVENING DECADES

The 1960s saw a rise in the level of internal conflict at the GATT, and significant changes in the balance of power. One reason for this was that the EC took over the negotiating function for the six founding member countries of the Community (Germany had become a GATT participant in 1951).[60] From the point at which it assumed a common position at the GATT for the six, the Community set the stage for the later development of a relentless rivalry with the United States within the context of the GATT dispute system.

A second reason for the change in the existing GATT balance was the large increase in the number of developing countries contracting parties to the GATT. While there had been only 16 CPs so categorised in 1960, there were as many as 52 in 1970. No longer was the GATT a small group of like-minded trading partners; global conflict in the post-colonial period found its way into the GATT as well.[61]

The addition of Part IV to the General Agreement as a result of this change in composition was mentioned above. As a parallel to these events, the United Nations Conference on Trade and Development (UNCTAD) was held in Geneva in 1964, with the intention of establishing a permanent organisation of the same name.[62] The objective of UNCTAD was, through its organisation, to influence trade issues on behalf of the developing world; much in the same manner that its opposite number in the Organisation on Economic Co-operation and Development (OECD) continues to exert influence on behalf of major industrialised countries.

It is generally agreed that by the time of the end of Kennedy Round in 1967, the original GATT goal of drastic tariff reductions had been largely accomplished. Historically speaking, it was only natural that the trading powers should have sought out new areas of liberalisation starting in the Tokyo Round

[60] Hudec, *supra* n. 55, at 12.
[61] *Ibid.*
[62] Jackson, *supra* n. 4, at 7.

in 1973. The post-war systems of liberalisation have been continuously in motion; conceived in the spirit of historical progress, their objectives have never been static.

Regarding dispute settlement activity, the peculiar nature of the 1960s has been well documented.[63] From around 1963 through 1970, the US and the EC colluded in nearly suppressing the operation of the GATT dispute settlement system, this being known as the period of "anti-legalism". Especially given the rapid entry of developing countries into the GATT, it was in the temporary interests of the two trading superpowers to avoid being subjected to legal rules and quasi-judicial procedures by parties with significantly different overall interests. This period was in this sense unique in GATT history. The US and EC actually managed for this period to create a trading climate wherein legal disputes brought before the GATT were seen as "unfriendly" actions in the diplomatic meaning of the word. This, of course, caused a near eclipse of the GATT legal system, such as it was at the time.

The 1970s was the decade of the Tokyo Round, lasting from 1973 through 1979. It was during this time that the economic power of the US saw its first real decline in the post-war period, with an ironic increase in the US appetite for a return to a more "legalistic" approach to the GATT rules. During the 1970s, internal constituencies in developed countries also became more aware of the internal effects of free trade, with many sectors staking out their opposition, notably labour unions. The Nixon Administration relied on the same "big promise" approach to free trade that is invoked by politicians today: when the dangers of free trade become apparent (that is, the real possibility that one's producers are losing out to foreign producers in the export wars), the antidote is said to be not protectionism, but more free trade. If the problem is free trade, then only freer trade can fix it. Reflecting this decision to forge ahead with the free trade agenda begun in the 1940s, the Tokyo Round negotiations proposed stricter rules in a number of key areas.[64] The most ambitious negotiating round prior to the Uruguay Round, Tokyo established clearer standards and a more credible enforcement mechanism, with the benefits of these global achievements being celebrated politically in a manner not seen before.

During the 1970s, the dispute resolution system was accordingly revived to some degree, and 32 new disputes were decided under the panel procedure.[65] Not only were the cases increasing in volume as the years of this decade passed. They were also increasing in legal complexity and in significance for a world economy increasingly obsessed with the issue of competitiveness. Starting in the late 1970s, in response to the growing volume of world trade, along with the growing threat posed to the traditional trading powers by Japan's aggressive,

---

[63] Hudec, *supra* n. 55, at 12–13; Jackson, *supra* n. 4, at 114.

[64] See John H Jackson, Jean-Victor Louis and Mitsuo Matsushita, "Implementing the Tokyo Round: Legal Aspects of Changing International Economic Rules", (1982) 81 *Michigan Law Review* 267.

[65] Hudec, *supra* n. 55, at 13.

export-driven policies, new techniques were developed apart from the GATT system to restrict the entry of goods in certain sensitive trade sectors.

It was the late 1970s that gave rise to a device that would be perfected in the 1980s: the Voluntary Export Restraint, or VER.[66] VERs were bilateral agreements entered into outside the GATT, in which an exporting country would agree "voluntarily" to restrict exports, in the hope of avoiding some kind of threatened trade sanction. The GATT legality of such agreements was questionable, and the danger posed to the functioning of the GATT system obvious, but what was not clear was who had standing to challenge such agreements, and in what forum. There was no GATT cause of action to deal with these situations directly.

Because such agreements were ostensibly "consensual", and their terms relatively secret, the participants would certainly have no interest in exposing them to legal scrutiny.[67] And on what grounds would some other party bring a GATT action? One of the most striking aspects of the changes brought about by the Uruguay Round Agreements is that such agreements are now clearly contrary to WTO law. There is little question but that the proliferation of VERs had posed a threat to GATT theory and practice, and threatened to create an alternative regime that would ultimately undermine the official one.

Despite the dangers posed by VERs, by the end of the 1970s it could be said that the major trading powers were investing more heavily in bringing and defending GATT actions. The disputes had taken on greater political meaning, and there was greater public relations value attached to prevailing before a panel.

The 1980s act as a bridge between the old GATT system, which had become inadequate to the task of managing important disputes, and the WTO, which came into being after the eight year long Uruguay Round negotiations, begun in 1986. During the decade, 115 complaints were argued before GATT panels.[68] Yet parties were no longer satisfied with what the system had to offer, and there was widespread questioning of the efficacy of the dispute resolution procedures. Naturally, the more sensitive and urgent the trade issue, the more likely a ruling would be blocked by an adversely affected party. It became increasingly common for countries, each of which of course retained a veto power in this regard, to simply block the creation of a panel to hear the case in the first place. Indeed, nearly all of the more important panel decisions remained in legal ambiguity as a result of the national veto.

The 1980s are seen as a watershed for economic integration, both at European and global level. Just as the prospect of "Eurosclerosis" jolted European Member States to push for further political unification, so too the tendency

---

[66] Jackson, *supra* n. 4, at 203–204.

[67] For a discussion of the contrast between GATT Safeguard Measures and VERs, see Ernesto M Hizon, "The Safeguard Measure/ VER Dilemma: The Jekyll and Hyde of Trade Protection", (1994) 15 *Journal of International Law and Business* 105.

[68] Hudec, *supra* n. 55, at 14.

towards unilateralism in international trade led directly to the ambitious Uruguay Round negotiations.[69] The US in particular, under siege from Japanese exports, and enduring record trade deficits, began to rely on unilateral pressure as a major component of its trade policy in the 1980s. Trade demands on troublesome competitors, like Japan, could be backed up by the threat of retaliation in the form of quantitative restrictions or other GATT-illegal measures. Had the Uruguay Round not taken place, it is possible that the GATT system would have broken down irretrievably during the 1980s.

THE EARLIEST GATT DISPUTES: NULLIFICATION OR
IMPAIRMENT OF GATT "BENEFIT"

The earliest GATT disputes are generally cited for the key jurisprudential concepts they established. However, from the post-Uruguay Round vantage point, they are of interest for comparative purposes; the disputes demonstrate clearly that the early GATT years were based on a specialised kind of international diplomacy. The GATT regime was new and uncertain in the 1950s. It has been noted that the dispute resolution language of Article XXIII was based on the concept of legitimate expectation, a benefit derived from participation in the GATT. It is not an exaggeration to state that the early panel rulings were motivated by a desire to grant satisfaction to all participants—complainant and defendant. Both parties were, if possible, to be sent away contented; the complainant with a promise of further negotiations towards a satisfactory settlement, and the defendant without being marked out as a "violator" of the GATT.

The "*Ammonium Sulfate*" dispute, based on a complaint brought by Chile against Australia,[70] and resulting in a panel report in 1950, is still cited for its useful interpretation of the Article XXIII phrase "nullification or impairment".[71]

During the early GATT rounds, Australia had offered Chile major tariff concessions with regard to sodium nitrate. Chile was contentedly exporting this material to Australia, when in 1949, the Australian government withdrew its official involvement from trade in sodium nitrate, lifting price controls and subsidies, while retaining these for the rival ammonium sulphate.[72]

---

[69] Regarding eurosclerosis, see Philippe Manin, "The Treaty of Amsterdam", (1998) 4 *Columbia Journal of European Law* 1 1–2; and Paul D Marquandt, "Subsidiarity and Sovereignty in the European Union", (1994) 18 *Fordham International Law Journal* 616, 622–623.

[70] *Australian Subsidy on Ammonium Sulfate*, Working Party Report (1950), BISD vol. II, at 188 [hereinafter *Australian Subsidy* Working Party Report].

[71] The background facts involve a wartime scarcity of fertiliser inputs in Australia, following upon which the Australian government created an agency for dealing in both sodium nitrate and ammonium sulphate, to be sold with government subsidies at uniform prices. While only ammonium sulphate was produced domestically, both types of fertiliser were also purchased from abroad.

[72] *Australian Subsidy* Working Party Report, at 189–191.

The working party first found that the actions of the Australian government were not inconsistent with the General Agreement; in other words, there was no violation of its terms. The working party reasoned that the Australian government had created no actual restrictions on the imports of interest to Chile; thus Article XI and Article III were found not to be relevant.[73]

Similarly, Article I could not be invoked, since it refers to "like" products, and not to directly competitive products.[74] These products were separate, listed and treated differently for purposes of customs classification in various countries. Chile also attempted to challenge the legality of the remaining subsidy itself under Article XVI. However, the working party concluded that Article XVI was meant to deal with subsidies that gave financial aid to domestic producers in order to improve their competitive position on domestic or international markets, and this was not the case here. It also doubted that Chile could demonstrate the necessary level of "injury" to its domestic producers because of the Australian subsidy per se.[75]

So the first part of the working party's analysis found that there was no violation of the General Agreement by the Australian government. However, what is noteworthy in the decision is that Chile was not turned away empty handed from the dispute settlement process. Nullification or impairment of GATT benefit is treated by the working party as severable from the question of violation of the agreement. The working party agreed that

> "such impairment would exist if the action of the Australian government which resulted in upsetting the competitive relationship between sodium nitrate and ammonium sulfate could not reasonably have been anticipated by the Chilean government, taking into consideration all pertinent circumstances and the provisions of the General Agreement at the time it negotiated for the duty free binding on sodium nitrate".[76]

The working party concluded that Chile did have reason to assume during its negotiations that the subsidy would not be removed from one of the two products without also being removed from the other.[77] The working party did not go so far as to say that removal of the subsidy was in itself a cause of nullification or impairment. Rather, the conclusion was that Chile could not have foreseen this sudden inequality of treatment of the two products.

We have seen that a foundational feature of the GATT system was that relief might be available even in the absence of violation. Here, the ultimate focus is on a readjustment of the balance in treatment between the two fertiliser types. The working party presented a draft recommendation for achieving this.[78] It

---

[73] *Australian Subsidy* Working Party Report, at 191.

[74] *Australian Subsidy* Working Party Report, at 191.

[75] *Australian Subsidy* Working Party Report, at 192.

[76] *Australian Subsidy* Working Party Report, at 192.

[77] The working party offers practical and factual reasons as to why it feels that Chile would have expected both subsidies to be treated in the same way: that the system was in place at the time of the negotiations, the similarity of the products, etc. See *Australian Subsidy* Working Party Report, at 193.

[78] *Australian Subsidy* Working Party Report, at 195.

made clear that it was not ordering a cancellation of the remaining subsidy, which it was not in any event authorised to do.[79]

The emphasis in the Australian case was on the assurance offered by the system to participants that their expectations could be gratified and their risk minimised. The early GATT employed its resources to prevent unauthorised and unnegotiated retaliation by parties; in particular by featuring the right of parties to retain legitimately hoped-for benefits, reached through the process of supervised discussions and the granting of concessions.

Another well-known dispute from the same period involved the import by Germany of Norwegian sardines.[80] As with the Australian fertiliser dispute, the facts in this case seem distant and obscure, and extraordinarily simple. However, this group of early cases gains force when seen thematically and in the aggregate.

In this dispute, Norway complained that it had lost the value of an advantageous rate of tariff negotiated through the GATT for its exports of herring and sprat to Germany.[81] Traditionally, these two fish had been treated in the same way as sardines. However, having received this GATT concession, Norway then discovered that sardine imports from Portugal were receiving a still better rate of tariff into Germany, based on a European trade liberalisation programme.[82] In this case, as in the Australian Subsidies case, Norway failed to convince the panel that Germany had acted in a GATT-illegal fashion, and its Article I arguments failed.[83] Just as in the Australian case, having decided that Germany had not failed to live up to GATT obligations, the panel then turned to Norway's expectations. The panel determined that Norway could not have anticipated the imbalance in competitive conditions caused by the unilateral action of the German government; that is, could not have so anticipated at the time it was negotiating tariff reductions on its fish of export interest.[84]

The panel made the interesting observation that it was on the basis of its expectations that Norway "assessed the value of the concessions offered by Germany".[85] So in this context, the meaning of nullification or impairment is that the value of the German concessions to Norway had been reduced.

It can be speculated, based on the discourse of these two cases in particular, that in the early days of GATT, the permanence and ongoing value of GATT participation were largely unknown. The panels had to ensure this value, or insure it, by granting relief to complaining parties who could not establish

---

[79] The working party states that "The ultimate power of contracting parties under Article XXIII is that of authorizing an affected contracting party to suspend the application of appropriate obligations or concessions". Australian Subsidy Working Party Report, at 195.

[80] *Treatment by Germany of Imports of Sardines*, Panel Report (1952), BISD 1st Supp, 53 [hereinafter Sardines Panel Report].

[81] *Sardines* Panel Report, at 54–56.

[82] *Sardines* Panel Report, at 56.

[83] *Sardines* Panel Report, at 57–58.

[84] *Sardines* Panel Report, at 58–59.

[85] *Sardines* Panel Report, at 59.

GATT violations. This can be thought of as a "protective" GATT jurisprudence, which relied more heavily on inducements and restoration of lost value than on the letter of the law or adversarial relationships.[86]

With the growing contentiousness of disputes, even by the late 1950s, and the inevitably more complex legal issues, this type of analysis by GATT panels ceased to be the norm. Yet such reasoning probably acted in the early days of GATT to maintain the momentum of negotiations and prevent disappointments, followed by destructive unilateral trade retaliation. The greatest nightmare of GATT's founders was undoubtedly the possibility of slipping back into the habit of *ad hoc* "self help" solutions to trade conflict and economic rivalry.

A decision from the mid-1950s in an action brought by Italy against Sweden[87] demonstrates the concern of the early GATT system that national measures taken under the banner of anti-dumping could act as a disguise for discrimination against low-cost producers. Here the subtext involves the need for the GATT to allow such low-cost producers their full comparative advantage. Italy came before the GATT to complain that Sweden had devised an anti-dumping mechanism that had the effect of making low cost imports undesirable to Swedish importers.[88]

Sweden was alleged to have established a minimum "basic price", which worked to exempt products from dumping enquiries if their prices were above the basic price. Italy argued that use of an officially set minimum price of this sort was contrary to Article VI of the General Agreement, and that it constituted systematic discrimination.[89] The Swedish system, Italy maintained, deprived efficient and competitive producers like themselves of the advantages to which they were entitled under the "most favoured nation" clause of the General Agreement. Since the Swedish system tended to impose a minimum price, this, in turn, fundamentally altered the conditions of competition that Italy might reasonably have expected under the General Agreement.[90] Again, the central concept is that of the legitimate expectations of GATT-participating countries.

---

[86] Also see a complaint brought by Norway and Denmark against Belgium—*Belgian Family Allowances* (1952), BISD 1st Supp, at 59. This interesting case, which challenged the GATT-legality of a Belgian law which levied a charge on foreign goods purchased by public bodies when these goods originated in a country whose system of family allowances did not meet specific requirements, is notable for the extreme diplomacy of its conclusion. Having heard all the arguments, "The Panel felt that the legal issues involved in the complaint under consideration are such that it would be difficult for the contracting parties to arrive at a very definite ruling. On the other hand, it was of the opinion that the Belgian legislation on family allowances was not only inconsistent with the provisions of Article I (and possibly with those of Article III, paragraph 2), but was based on a concept which was difficult to reconcile with the spirit of the General Agreement and that the contracting parties should note with satisfaction the statement made . . . by the Belgian representatives and should recommend to the Belgian government to expedite consideration and the adoption of the necessary measures, consistent with the General Agreement, including a possible amendment of the Belgian legislation, to remove the discrimination complained of . . .".

[87] *Swedish Anti-Dumping Duties*, Report of the Panel (1955), BISD, 3rd Supp, 81 [hereinafter *Swedish Anti-Dumping Duties* Panel Report].

[88] *Swedish Anti-Dumping Duties* Panel Report, at 82–83.

[89] *Swedish Anti-Dumping Duties* Panel Report, at 81–86.

[90] *Swedish Anti-Dumping Duties* Panel Report, at 82–83.

The panel concluded that the Swedish system was worrying, but not on its face GATT-illegal, if applied fairly.[91] No clear inconsistency with Article VI or with the MFN clause was found. The panel did, however, find that the administration of the system might easily run into conflict with those obligations. As a system, it would require strong supervision, lest it be "turned into a general protection against low-cost producers".[92] The outstanding factual issues in the dispute were acknowledged, and the panel encouraged the two parties to continue negotiations to resolve their differences in the light of the GATT "normal value" standard. The panel recommended possible improvements to the administration of the Swedish system, to minimise impediments to Italian imports.[93]

Another national "system" was examined for its discriminatory potential several years later, with a somewhat different result. In a case that anticipated many of the long-running GATT agricultural battles, Australia took France before the GATT to complain of France's system of subsidising wheat and wheat flour for export, claiming that this violated Article XVI:3.[94] Australia argued that France had displaced Australia's traditional export markets in South and Southeast Asia, and thus that Australia's expected benefits under the GATT had been impaired.[95]

The panel had first to answer the question of whether the French system of "price equalisation" amounted to the grant of actual subsidies for wheat exports.[96] After deciding that France's provision of a "guaranteed price" for its producers to meet the going world price was indeed an export subsidy, the panel had to determine whether France had obtained more than an "equitable share" of world trade in a manner inconsistent with Article XVI:3, and whether the French system had, in fact, impaired benefits accruing to Australia under the GATT system.[97]

France argued that after its post-war recovery period, it had merely regained the strong position it traditionally held in the disputed markets.[98] But the panel, as it reviewed the significant rise in French exports over the course of the 1950s, pondered whether the rise was attributable to the complained of subsidy system. There was, the panel noted, no statistical definition for the term "equitable share" in world markets. But based on the data, the panel said, its conclusion must be that the increase could be largely traced to the subsidy system, and that the French share was, relative to other competing suppliers, more than was equitable.[99]

[91] *Swedish Anti-Dumping Duties* Panel Report, at 86.
[92] *Swedish Anti-Dumping Duties* Panel Report, at 86.
[93] *Swedish Anti-Dumping Duties* Panel Report, 90–91.
[94] *French Assistance to Wheat and Wheat Flour* (1958), BISD 7th Supp, 46 [*French Wheat Flour* Panel Report].
[95] *French Wheat Flour* Panel Report, at 46.
[96] *French Wheat Flour* Panel Report, at 50–52.
[97] *French Wheat Flour* Panel Report, at 52–53.
[98] *French Wheat Flour* Panel Report, at 53.
[99] *French Wheat Flour* Panel Report, at 53.

The case provides an interesting twist on the concept of nullification or impairment of GATT benefit. Australia argued that the expected benefit which was impaired by the French action was the assurance that its export trade would not face subsidies going beyond the limits permissible under Article XVI of the General Agreement.[100] As for the requisite injury, Australia had been displaced from its export markets, and suffered industry-wide damage.

The panel agreed that this displacement had occurred, and made documentable displacement a relevant factor in interpreting the concept of "equitable share" of world markets.[101] Australia had, the panel concluded, suffered both direct and indirect damage. In an interesting contrast to the finding in the Swedish anti-dumping case, the panel concluded that the French system was flexible and open-ended, thus making it possible to reduce or increase the subsidy amount. But rather than finding the system on its face *not* GATT-illegal, but with a caution regarding its manner of administration, the panel declared it defective in that there could be found no guarantee within the system that it would conform to the standards set out in Article XVI:3.[102] So the panel was unable to declare the system GATT-legal. One might think of this as a transitional finding; neither purely diplomatic, nor truly adversarial.

The panel set out recommendations for a mutually satisfactory resolution. The French government was to consider measures to avoid the system of payments to exports "in such a manner as to create adverse effects on normal Australian exports". The panel also offered specific negotiating suggestions.[103] This decision was obviously not even a beginning to a solution for the vexing problem of agricultural export subsidies, which until the Uruguay Round Agreement on Agriculture, would appear and recede on a regular basis within the GATT dispute settlement system. The vagueness of Article XVI contributed to the long-running battle over agricultural subsidies. Without sufficient clarity in the relevant provisions, an occasional flare up of old grievances would send complainants to the GATT, often to challenge the elaborate subsidies granted to agricultural producers under the EC's Common Agricultural Policy.

The possibility of more expansive uses of the GATT system was evident in an action brought by the UK against Italy, decided in 1958.[104] The UK complained that a 1952 Italian law granting credit facilities to farmers' co-operatives for the purchase of machinery was inconsistent with Article III of the General Agreement, in that the terms of the credit were appreciably better if the machinery to be purchased was of Italian origin.[105] Implicit in the dispute is the question of how deeply a GATT panel could delve into national laws, in order to

---

[100] *French Wheat Flour* Panel Report, at 54.

[101] *French Wheat Flour* Panel Report, at 55.

[102] *French Wheat Flour* Panel Report, at 56.

[103] *French Wheat Flour* Panel Report, at 22–23.

[104] *Italian Discrimination Against Imported Agricultural Machinery* (1958), BISD 7th Supp, 60 [hereinafter *Italian Agricultural Machinery* Panel Report].

[105] See *Italian Agricultural Machinery* Panel Report, para. 5.

uncover negative trade effects. The UK made broad use of Article III:4, which contains a general requirement that laws, regulations and requirements affecting internal sale should not be applied to imported products so as to afford protection to domestic producers.

It is hardly surprising that the Italian side argued that the General Agreement is a trade agreement, with its scope necessarily limited to matters affecting trade.[106] Thus, Article III:4 could only be seen, the Italians maintained, as applying to regulations actually concerned with conditions of sale, and "should not be interpreted in an extensive way".[107] A programme concerning the development of the Italian economy and Italian employment could not fall under Article III, the argument went.[108]

However, the panel took the more expansive view of Article III, understandably one of the most heavily litigated provisions in GATT law. The words "affecting internal sale", the panel said, would imply that the drafters of the article

> "intended to cover in paragraph 4 not only the laws and regulations which directly governed the sale or purchase, but also any laws or regulations which might adversely modify the conditions of competition between the domestic and imported products on the internal market".[109]

With predictable emphasis on the "value" of GATT participation, the panel stated that if the Italian interpretation of Article III were to be accepted, the value of tariff bindings and of the general rules of non-discrimination as between imported and domestic products could be easily evaded.[110] Protection for one's industries must be accomplished in a GATT-legal manner; through the action of tariffs, for instance.[111]

The panel then looked at the question of whether there was nullification or impairment of the UK's benefits under GATT. It noted the fall-off in the proportion of foreign-made tractors entering Italy in the preceding years.[112] Calling the bluff of the Italian delegation, the panel stated that "if the considered view of the Italian government was that these credit facilities had not influenced the terms of competition of the Italian market, there would not seem to be a serious problem in amending the operation of the Law so as to avoid any discrimination . . ."[113]

Although the case moves us closer to an adversarial model, with strongly-conceived arguments put forward on both sides, definitions and standards of review considered, and a prevailing party clearly identified, the panel did not go beyond recommending that it be pointed out to the Italian government that

---

[106] *Italian Agricultural Machinery* Panel Report, para. 6.
[107] *Italian Agricultural Machinery* Panel Report, para. 6.
[108] See *Italian Agricultural Machinery* Panel Report, para. 8.
[109] *Italian Agricultural Machinery* Panel Report, para. 12.
[110] See *Italian Agricultural Machinery* Panel Report, para. 15.
[111] See *Italian Agricultural Machinery* Panel Report, para. 16.
[112] See *Italian Agricultural Machinery* Panel Report, para. 19.
[113] *Italian Agricultural Machinery* Panel Report, para. 22.

"it consider the desirability of eliminating within a reasonable time the adverse effects of the Law on the import trade of agricultural machinery by modifying the operation of that Law or by other appropriate means".[114]

ANTI-LEGALISM AND THE TUMULTUOUS 1960S

It has already been noted that during the 1960s, the major trading powers acted in concert to prevent GATT rules from being used against them in the dispute settlement system.[115] As the GATT began to evolve into a more complex entity than the small, like-minded group of countries that had been eager to lower tariffs and eliminate most quantitative restrictions, issues of power and public relations, likewise, became more prominent.

Symbolic of this time of legal ambiguity and political flux is an action brought by Uruguay against a large number of wealthy developed countries.[116] A kind of "structural" case, Uruguay presented far-reaching complaints regarding the treatment of Uruguayan exports. The vague and technocratic nature of the panel's response, consisting mainly of abstract recommendations for future consideration, is oddly out of sync with Uruguay's systemic grievance.

It was clear from this time onwards that the earlier GATT system, based on diplomacy, co-operation and shared interests, could not cope with a more complex international situation and fundamental alterations in the balance of world economic power. This situation could only grow more serious as the 1970s commenced.

THE AGE OF THE TOKYO ROUND: NEW AREAS OF CONCERN REFLECTED IN STAND-ALONE CODES

In the light of the far more dramatic Uruguay Round agreements, the achievements of the Tokyo Round appear rather colourless, and have understandably ceased to attract much attention. However, the codes produced by the Tokyo Round,[117] and the legal questions raised by the Tokyo Round methodology, form an indispensable milestone on the road to the creation of the WTO.

After the amendments to the actual text of the General Agreement in the 1960s, the contracting parties made no further attempts to tamper with the basic provisions. This was in part because of the complexity of the Article XXX procedure for amending the GATT. A far more efficient technique developed, which allowed for the expansion of the GATT system into new areas of trade

---

[114] *Italian Agricultural Machinery* Panel Report, para. 25.
[115] Hudec, *supra* n. 55, at 12–13.
[116] *Uruguayan Recourse to Article XXIII*, Panel Report, (1962) BISD 11th Supp, 95.
[117] For the texts of the codes, see (1980) BISD 26th Supp, 201.

concern hitherto left outside the GATT structure. This was first seen in the adoption of the Tokyo Round codes.[118]

With the major participants eager to bring the GATT out of its rapidly out-dated preoccupations with tariffs, the codes expanded the GATT into such sectors as government procurement and technical barriers to trade. However, as the GATT's first foray into separate side agreements, a major conceptual hurdle lay in the way of this subject matter development. Since not all contracting parties were willing to sign onto the new codes, a GATT "heresy" was for a time promoted by the major trading powers: that only those parties adopting the codes should be able to benefit from the enhanced liberalisation they represented. This would amount in effect to "conditional MFN", a clear departure from the most basic GATT doctrine of the 1940s and 1950s.[119] Although this doctrine was eventually rejected by the parties as a whole, the Tokyo Round Codes continued to project an image of incompleteness and partiality, if not quite a backslide towards the pre-GATT trading basis of "reciprocity".[120]

The new Tokyo Round codes tended to have separate dispute settlement mechanisms, and the more important ones gave an automatic right to the seating of a panel. At least in the limited subject matter of an individual code, there was to some degree an attempt to bypass some of the structural inadequacies of the original GATT system.

The best-known Tokyo Round codes are those on Anti-Dumping and Subsidies.[121] It is important to note that the Tokyo Round codes attempted to raise the evidentiary burden on parties invoking dumping or export subsidies as a reason for engaging in national protective measures. Already, the move towards legal restriction on the ability of nations to decide when and how to protect themselves from these activities was apparent. These two codes, though now largely superseded by the developments of the Uruguay Round, are significant in that they represent the beginning of a long-running trend towards restricting the ability of participating countries to invoke "GATT-legal" protectionist measures.

Other important codes were the following:[122]

The Standards Code (Agreement on Technical Barriers to Trade): This code was the first step towards restricting the use of national product standards as disguised barriers to trade.

---

[118] See John H Jackson, *The World Trading System* 1st edn. (Cambridge, MA: MIT Press, 1989) 51–52.

[119] See *ibid*. at 56–57, 143–145.

[120] As will be demonstrated, all such ambiguity has been definitively swept away with the Uruguay Round agreements, in that all participants in the WTO system must accept virtually all instruments of WTO law. While this is seen by many mainstream GATT/WTO scholars as evidence of the WTO's legal effectiveness, it also has troubling implications for democracy and national choice.

[121] See Jackson, Louis, and Matsushita, *supra* n. 64, at 271–273; see also Hudec, *supra* n. 55, at 24–25, 26–28, 119–126.

[122] Brief descriptions of all the Tokyo Round codes can be found in Jackson, Louis and Matsushita, *supra* n. 64, at 272–277.

The Government Procurement Code: Items to be used for governmental purposes, and not intended for commercial resale, had been specifically exempted from Article III (national treatment) of the GATT Agreement. This code, not surprisingly worked in a modest and incremental manner, allowing countries to set out in positive commitments precisely which products they were willing to subject to national treatment in the government-purchasing sphere.

The Customs Valuation Code (Agreement on the Implementation of Article VII of the GATT): This code confronted the problem of national disparities in the manner of placing a value on imported goods for purposes of setting customs duties. These methods traditionally varied from country to country, and obscure methods of calculation were thought to act as definite impediments to trade. The US system, based on a so-called "American Selling Price", was particularly unpopular, in that it tended to overestimate the price of goods. The code set out a preferred method of calculation known as the "transaction value".

The Licensing Code: This code attempted to simplify and harmonise national laws relating to application procedures for obtaining import licenses. Among other requirements, the code called for transparency through the publication of procedures used.

In addition to these codes, there was a number of lesser agreements in specific sectors of trade, including the Civil Aircraft Agreement, designed to bring some measure of commercial discipline into an industry characterised by intensive government subsidies and a small number of extremely expensive transactions.

From the time of the Tokyo Round codes, there was an awareness that the GATT system could grow to accommodate new areas of trade concern, through the relatively efficient mechanism of creating side agreements, or stand-alone treaties. The exact relationship of these agreements to the original GATT agreement, and the relationship of the Tokyo Round to the concept of MFN, were never fully resolved. Despite the incomplete aspects of the codes, they were nevertheless a methodological breakthrough for the major GATT trading nations anxious to move beyond more traditional, and limited, trade preoccupations.

It was also from this time that there developed a sense of a complex GATT "jurisprudence", linking the underlying General Agreement—a constitution of sorts—to disputes decided under the General Agreement, as well as the new codes, with their own sets of negotiations and disputes. In the background, of course, could be heard a grinding of gears as the system became increasingly unwieldy. Panel reports were routinely blocked; unilateral pressure against trading partners and VER agreements became more common, and the nature of disputes far more complex. By comparison, the era of disputes over fish tariffs is remarkable for its simplicity.

GATT'S ADOLESCENCE: THE DISC CASE

The famous "DISC" dispute,[123] that continued throughout the 1970s, demonstrated clearly that the GATT system had, by this period, either to reform itself or risk becoming irrelevant. Its clumsy diplomatic structures, created for another time, could not react to the complex interests of a world made unquestionably more integrated because of several decades of GATT having done its work.

The DISC case began in 1973, when the EC brought a GATT challenge to US tax laws, which it alleged favoured US exporters in an unfair manner.[124] The US in turn filed a complaint against French, Belgian and Dutch export-promoting tax laws. The parties became embroiled in bitter debates as to the proper composition of the panels, with the US insisting on the presence of tax experts. It took a full three years for the panels to be seated. At US insistence, the two panels had identical personnel. The DISC case is also seen as a watershed in GATT history, since it demonstrated the extent to which contracting parties were beginning to invest substantial resources in pursuing GATT cases. Diplomatic finesse on the part of panellists was no longer sufficient.

The target of the DISC case was a US law dating from 1971, the Domestic International Sales Corporation. The EC charged that this law violated Article XVI:4 of the GATT, prohibiting export subsidies. In fact, all major trading countries maintained laws that favoured export industries by reducing their domestic tax burden; the US DISC law was simply different in method from those of the European trading partners.[125] For this reason, the US argued that its system offered no greater advantages to its exporters than was available to European exporters, who benefited from European governments' policy of not pursuing taxes owed on profits earned outside the national territory, with only small amounts falling due on the repatriation of profits.[126]

The principal US strategy was to insist on the same panel hearing both cases, in the hope that if the US system was found to be GATT-illegal, then the

---

[123] *The Domestic International Sales Corporation*, Panel Report, (1976) BISD 23rd Supp, 98 [hereinafter *DISC* Panel Report].

[124] See Hudec, *supra* n. 55, at 59–100. Hudec provides an exhaustive discussion of this unique case. He writes that ultimately the GATT system had no choice but to accept the European tax system as it affected exporting companies, since a wide range of governments (in and out of Europe) relied on similar principles and could not be induced to alter their approach. Hudec maintains that the case, lengthy and acrimonious as it was, represents the first time the US passed a national law the only purpose of which was to bring US law in compliance with an adverse GATT ruling.

[125] Under the US version of tax relief, US exporters would set up a separate domestic corporation (rather than the handy foreign subsidiary favoured by European corporations), to which they would "sell" their products for export. A certain level of taxation owing to DISC profits would then be "deferred" indefinitely.

[126] The main discussion of the *DISC* case follows the *DISC* panel report. See Hudec, *supra* n. 55, at 59–100.

European systems would as well; thus creating an incentive for the EC to veto the adoption of any such panel report. The cases were heard separately, but by the same panel.

The panel concluded, in quasi-diplomatic language, that "[t]he DISC legislation in some cases had effects which were not in accordance with the US obligations under Article XVI:4" on export subsidies.[127] The panel noted the large increase in exports as a result of the creation of DISCs. But at the same time, the panel found the European territorial tax principle to be an export subsidy under Article XVI, and as with the US DISCs, found that "in some cases [the European tax laws] had effects which were not in accordance with the defendant's obligations under Article XVI:4".[128]

The case is justly famous because of its transitional and hybrid nature. There was general dissatisfaction among contracting parties in the wake of the panel ruling, in that the tax territoriality principle was followed in most countries, and there was a belief that the panel was mistaken in its view of the GATT-illegality of European tax laws. The US, according to plan, stated that it would accept the panel's ruling if the Europeans did. The political standoff continued for years afterward.

Finally, in 1981, a decision of the GATT Council provided a peculiarly GATT "understanding" that altered the original ruling. All the panel's findings were adopted at that time, but with the understanding that the GATT-illegal ruling on European law should be considered repealed. In time, the dispute faded away, although the legal issues raised clearly did not.[129]

ANTICIPATING THE URUGUAY ROUND

The Uruguay Round Agreements,[130] though based on years of GATT tradition and methodology, changed the course of modern trade history. The very legalism that entered the GATT as it became the new WTO is the reason that recent disputes have gained such public prominence. Since panel rulings can no longer be evaded, and because postponing compliance costs large amounts of money in concessions revoked, the revisions that were to regularise the GATT legal system had the ironic effect of raising the political stakes, and thus the international temperature during disputes.

---

[127] *DISC* Panel Report, at 113.
[128] *DISC* Panel Report, at 126; 136; 146.
[129] See Hudec, *supra* n. 55, at 59–100.
  See discussion below, of an action brought by the EC against contemporary US tax law—*EC v. US: Tax Treatment for Foreign Sales Corporations*, Report of the Panel, 8 October 1999 (WT/DS108/R); and Appellate Body Report, 24 February 2000 (WT/DS108/AB/R).
[130] See Jackson *supra* n. 4, at 305–317.

It is unfortunate that the Uruguay Round Agreements tend to be studied in sectoral isolation. In fact, the agreements are held together by certain dominant themes. To understand the Uruguay Round Agreements, it is first necessary to understand the negotiating postures of the key participants and alliance groupings from the old GATT. The wealthier developed countries shared a view that the rising areas of trade were not covered under the old GATT rules. While they were forced to maintain open markets, and to absorb the export drive of the newly industrialised world, sectors of greatest trade interest to themselves were simply not addressed in the existing GATT system. It is not unrealistic to suggest that, had the GATT system not adapted by expanding to include these newer areas of trade, the developed countries would have eventually lost their incentive to remain within a multilateral trade regime.

The range of new agreements that came into force in 1995 is astonishing. The Agreement Establishing the WTO created the necessary institutional basis for administering the newly ambitious legal structure. The new Dispute Settlement Understanding ensured that the new subject matter would prove legally meaningful.

In terms of substantive additions to available causes of action, The Agreement on Trade Related Aspects of Intellectual Property (TRIPS) was of key significance to the developed countries. Their position was that penetration of newly industrialised country markets was severely restricted by the practice of those countries in copying research-intensive products without paying the costs of intellectual property rights. In one sense, the TRIPS Agreement was quid pro quo for the further trade liberalisation represented by the Uruguay Round. Unusually for the GATT/WTO system, TRIPS actually mandates a significant level of legal protection in the substantive sense to be implemented in national law.

The Agreement on Trade-Related Investment Measures (TRIMS) was a deceptively modest foray into the area of national conditions on inward direct investment. The TRIMS Agreement restricted the freedom of WTO member countries to condition inward investment on investor commitments to use domestic product inputs over imported products. The Agreement on Subsidies and Countervailing Measures (SCM) had two effects: first, it unequivocally prohibited certain types of subsidies, while making other types actionable where they have adverse trade effects; it also set a more rigorous standard for the application of countervailing duties against unfairly subsidised imports. The Agreement on Safeguards made it far more difficult to invoke the Article XIX safeguard provision, by imposing significant limitations on its use. Most notably, the Safeguards Agreement created a firm time limit for national safeguard measures; it also outlawed VERs.

The Agreement on Agriculture was the first true step in creating a world "free market" in primary products—a matter that bedevilled the old GATT throughout its history. The Agreement on the Application of Sanitary and Phytosanitary Measures (SPS) and the Agreement on Technical Barriers to

Trade (TBT) created clear, indeed harsh, standards for determining whether or not a member country's environmental or technical standards posed an unlawful impediment to global trade.

Perhaps the most conceptually far-reaching of these is the General Agreement on Trade in Services (GATS), which enjoys a separate legal status from the agreements on trade in goods. GATS has created a wide range of new causes of action, many of which have not yet been explored in the context of disputes. The GATS Agreement involves an area of economic life that can be contrasted very dramatically with trade in goods; an area that challenges the very concept of national borders, and reaches deeply into the structure of national commercial life. Since expanding trade in services had also become of central economic concern to developed countries, the march of globalisation clearly proceeded in part on the basis of hope for greater access to service markets in the rest of the world.

One sector of trade in which developing countries were indisputably granted a major Uruguay Round benefit was in textiles. The Agreement on Textiles and Clothing (ATC) phases out, over a period of ten years, the traditionally "managed" forms of textile trade, thus guaranteeing that this labour-intensive industrial production will shift almost completely in that period to the developing world. In some ways, it could be said that the Uruguay Round Agreements reflect traditional notions of comparative advantage. In another sense, they reflect quite obvious economic and political interests, with trade-offs between the developed and developing worlds tilting heavily in favour of the former.

Seen in the aggregate, the Uruguay Round Agreements represent a fundamentally changed ethos at the level of the global trading regime. In the case of each agreement, previously available modes of unilateral national protection are made far more difficult. Opportunities to protect vulnerable national constituencies, to shield national labour markets against the harsh winds of international competition, to protect the farm sector, to subsidise, to invoke environmental reasons for restricting imports, and finally to decide that emergency action is required—each of these means of traditional protectionism has become far more costly, with an "opportunity to adjust" the best that the nation can now hope for.

The Uruguay Round results are only intelligible in the context of the shifts in global economic life that had occurred as a result of the work of the old GATT, which, despite the effect of national resistance, still managed to transform participating countries from national economies to players in a competitive global web. The political courage to adopt the Uruguay Round agreements was a direct result of "reality on the ground", forged over several decades. The new subject matter in turn was only meaningful because of the stick provided by the new dispute settlement procedures. If it is the case that, post-1995, the entire world is living in the first stages of mutually assured competition, the high profile trade disputes of the past five years are perfectly understandable.

THE DISPUTE SETTLEMENT UNDERSTANDING[131]

The Dispute Settlement Understanding (DSU) transformed the former GATT system into a recognisably legal regime.[132] While it could be said of the old GATT that, because of its special power of economic coercion, its effects had not been confined to those of public international law, neither had it completely separated itself from the methods and limitations of international diplomacy. The Uruguay Round's Dispute Settlement Understanding, despite its deceptively technical appearance, gave the panel (and now Appellate Body) decisions the strength of enforceable rulings.[133] Once this is fully appreciated, the provisions of the DSU seem completely straightforward.

Under the DSU, an entity called the "Dispute Settlement Body" is created.[134] One might be tempted to assume that the DSB is a separate entity within the WTO, but this is not the case. The DSB is, in fact, merely the General Council, or overall membership, acting in a specialised capacity of giving legal effect to decisions of the panels and Appellate Body. The DSB is, in this sense, a kind of fiction, the arm of the WTO capable of authorising "sanctions" in the form of GATT/WTO benefits withheld by prevailing parties from parties against whom an official ruling is handed down.

Indeed, very broad procedural powers were conferred on the "DSB", including the authority to establish panels, to adopt panel reports, to maintain surveillance of the implementation of rulings, and to authorise the suspension of concessions.[135] It must be noted that the power to veto any of these events has been completely removed from the hands of individual WTO members.

As a general matter, the DSU preserves the old GATT notion that action would be by consensus, although the notion of consensus shifts, depending upon the DSB activity at hand. Consensus is generally deemed to exist if there is no formal objection to a particular decision from within the body itself.[136] (Consensus has a separate meaning in the context of the adoption of panel and Appellate Body rulings, as described below.)

As with other of the WTO agreements, to be explored below, the dispute system is to be held to clear time lines. In sharp contrast to its notoriously slow pace prior to 1995, the dispute settlement system is now required to proceed at a rate

---

[131] Understanding on Rules and Procedures Governing the Settlement of Disputes [hereinafter DSU].

[132] See Friedl Weiss, "WTO Dispute Settlement and the Economic Order of WTO Member States", in Pitou van Dijk and Gerrit Faber (eds.), *Challenges to the New World Trade Organization* (The Hague: Kluwer, 1996) 77–91.

[133] For detailed discussions of the DSU, see Robert E Hudec, "The New WTO Dispute Settlement Procedures: An Overview of the First Three Years", (1999) 8 *Minnesota Journal of Global Trade* 1; see also Dillon, Jr., *supra* n. 21 at 349; and Joel P Trachtman, "The Domain of WTO Dispute Resolution", (1999) 40 *Harvard International Law Journal* 333.

[134] DSU, Art. 2.

[135] DSU, Arts. 6, 16, 17, 20, 21, and 22.

[136] DSU, Art. 2.

that is certainly faster than most national litigation. Initial requests by members for consultation with an alleged offender must be responded to within 10 days of the request, and actual talks must begin within 30 days.[137] Should these time constraints not be honoured, the complaining party has the unequivocal right to move forward to the establishment of a panel to hear the complaint.[138] Shorter time frames are possible where the situation is urgent.[139]

As before, all interested parties have a potential right to be included in the proceedings.[140] Where a request for a panel has been lodged, one shall be established, at the latest, at the next meeting of the DSB (which complainants also have a right to have held within 15 days), unless the DSB decides by consensus not to establish a panel.[141] "Consensus" here is a specialised consensus and would literally *require all parties to agree that a panel should not be established*, a quite unthinkable scenario.[142]

Panel proceedings are given a target deadline of six months, and in no case should the time required for submission of a decision exceed nine months.[143] The most significant of the changes contained in the DSU is that within 60 days of the issuance of the report to members, the report will be adopted unless, again, either *the DSB decides unanimously not to adopt it*; or if one or both of the parties notifies its intention to appeal the decision to the Appellate Body.[144] The old GATT had no Appellate Body; the only method of "appeal" under the former system was to prevent the adoption of the panel report through individual veto power.

Appellate decisions are also time bound, to between 60 and 90 days at the maximum. As with panel decisions, the Appellate Body decision will only not be adopted *if there is a unanimous decision by the DSB (i.e., by the members as a whole) not to adopt*.[145]

The final sections of the DSU are of interest, in that they reflect WTO principles with regard to implementation of panel rulings. Article 21(1) states that "prompt compliance with recommendations or rulings of the DSB is essential in order to ensure effective resolution of disputes to the benefit of all members". Members must inform the DSB of intentions as to implementation of rulings;

---

[137] DSU, Art. 4(3).

[138] Similarly, where the consultations are undertaken but fail within 60 days, there is an automatic right to request a panel. See DSU, Art. 4(7).

[139] DSU, Art. 4(9).

[140] While it was thought that the DSB requirement that a "substantial interest" be shown, in reality, almost any party expressing an interest will be allowed to make submissions. DSU, Art. 10(2).

[141] DSU, Art. 6(1).

[142] Parties to the dispute are not to oppose panel nominations except for compelling reasons. DSU, Art. 8(6).

[143] DSU, Arts. 12(8)–12(9).

[144] DSU, Art. 16. Under both the old and new systems, the panels are put together *ad hoc* for the purpose of the dispute at hand. While panellists would be required to be experts in trade law, this *ad hoc* quality is not likely to lead to a coherent body of law. However, the Appellate Body is appointed for terms of four years, and it is already evident that the Appellate Body is establishing a core set of firm WTO law principles.

[145] DSU, Art. 16.

implementation is kept under surveillance by the DSB.[146] Implementation is clearly preferred over compensation and/or suspension of concessions. Where defendant members have not complied, and complainants are then authorised to suspend concessions as a means of imposing a "sanction", there must first be an attempt to suspend concessions in the same sector of trade in which the violation occurred.[147]

It is of the greatest significance that, while the WTO system does not literally have a system of "court ordered" fine or penalty, in an integrated global economy, authorisation of the suspension of concessions acts in a similar manner, and very literally causes economic harm to the non-complying defendant. The situation in which proper levels of suspension have to be determined by arbitration under the DSU[148] will be explored in the section on the banana trade wars.

INSTITUTIONAL BASIS: THE WTO ITSELF

The Agreement Establishing the WTO creates the firm structure so clearly lacking in the pre-1995 GATT system. With this agreement, all participating countries were obliged to accept the WTO itself, all the multilateral trade instruments (the Uruguay Round Agreements) appended to the WTO Agreement, and the GATT Agreement. (The PPA, of course, is now obsolete.)[149]

The activities of the World Trade Organisation, abstract as they are, are fully described in the Agreement Establishing the WTO: to provide a forum for negotiations, to administer the DSU, and to co-operate with the other major institutions of global economic governance—the IMF and World Bank. The Ministerial Conference of all members is to meet at least every two years; the General Council, also composed of representatives of all the members, is to meet "as appropriate" to carry out functions the Ministerial Conference may be unable to carry out.[150]

The General Council must convene as required to discharge its function as the DSB[151]—a change of hat that allows the members to give legal effect to rulings of the panels and Appellate Body. There are more specialised councils created to oversee the functioning of the various sectors of trade—trade in goods, services, intellectual property matters, and so forth.

The agreement formally establishes a WTO Secretariat and an office of Director General.[152] The WTO must continue the GATT practice of "decision-making by consensus". Where decisions cannot be arrived at by consensus, the

---

[146] DSU, Art. 21(3).
[147] DSU, Art. 22.
[148] DSU, Art. 22(7).
[149] WTO Agreement, Art. II.
[150] WTO Agreement, Arts. III, IV, V.
[151] WTO Agreement, Art. IV(3).
[152] WTO Agreement, Art. VI.

matter in question must be decided by majority voting.[153] Waivers may be granted to members for a limited period of time, with the agreement of three fourths of members.[154] Amendments to the MFN provision of the GATT Agreement would require consent of all members; other provisions of the GATT/WTO corpus could be amended by two-thirds or three-quarters of all members, depending on the gravity of the subject matter involved.[155]

NEW AREAS OF GATT/WTO LAW: TRADE POST-1995

Each of the new areas brought within the GATT/WTO net after 1995 represents a point of global contention with a significant conceptual history. It was well known that the old GATT was unable to cope with issues relating to investments, intellectual property, agriculture and services, yet it was not until the remarkable push forward of the Uruguay Round that these elements of global economic activity could be brought within the scope of the regime. For each of these areas, and in virtually each WTO member country, there are important national constituents opposed to subjecting a formerly protected or uninvolved economic sector to the winds of global competition. It is always important to remember that the WTO system works not only according to blocs of nations with common external interests, but also according to transnational alliances of economic forces, with consequences for winner-loser configurations within nations as well. This fact has enormous implications for cultural life and the nature of national economic activity. To the extent that the forces of globalisation and modernisation are in the ascendancy, the general tenor of life itself in otherwise widely disparate regions of the world will tend towards a uniform emphasis on dynamism and heightened productivity, as opposed to other possible values.

In this sense, the WTO should be understood as an ever-increasing web of economic benefits and obligations. It is misleading to approach the subject by attention to the rules of discrete sectors, agreements, or provisions exclusively. There is an incremental methodology common to all parts of the GATT/WTO system, and a coherent and purposeful drive to institutionalise the competitive imperative.

Our examination of the WTO system can only be a snapshot of the GATT/WTO in its current state of development. If its intellectual founders continue to dominate global decision-making, the contours of the system will be certain to continue shifting outward, increasingly ambitious, provision by provision.

---

[153] WTO Agreement, Art. IX. Note that the EC has been granted a number of votes equal to the total number of Member States.
[154] WTO Agreement, Art. IX(3).
[155] WTO Agreement, Art. X.

Part II
The Effects of the Uruguay Round[1]

<hr/>

[1] Note on methodology

It was frequently the case that in the "new" areas of trade rules introduced by the Uruguay Round Agreements, there had previously been disputes that attempted to raise related issues, but were only imperfectly developed because of a lack of specific law within the GATT system on the point.

The following chapters will each concentrate on Uruguay Round subject matter innovations. Where earlier disputes highlight the gap that existed prior to 1995, that history will be examined.

3

Intellectual Property Rights and Trade: Creating the TRIPS Agreement

IN THE YEARS leading up to the Uruguay Round, the developed countries, those capable of making huge investments in industrial innovation, had urged newly industrialised countries to cease their practice of mass copying of products that had cost dearly to develop. But from the point of view of the developing world, paying the full cost of industrial innovation to wealthy corporations was unthinkable, if only because under the existing situation, copied products could be delivered on a mass scale to populations generally unable to pay the price of intellectual property rights. From the developing or newly industrialised point of view, what could be wrong with availing themselves of products that had already provided great profits to their inventors, when the alternative would preclude most people in the developing world from obtaining such products at all? Was it not a win-win situation?

The reluctance of the wealthier countries to continue providing market access to the newly industrialised countries in the event of a continued failure to honour intellectual property rights was understandable. The traditional, uni-focus intellectual property conventions could not possibly persuade the countries of the developing world to alter their domestic regimes, since these conventions had no broader economic leverage over the offending parties.[2] Along with the new dispute settlement system, and the "all or nothing" acceptance requirement for prospective WTO members,[3] for the first time, there was a chance that even the most recalcitrant intellectual property violators could be made to provide legal protection for non-national rights holders. Thus was created the Agreement on Trade-Related Aspects of Intellectual Property (TRIPS), one of the most ambitious of the Uruguay Round Agreements.[4]

---

[2] Administered by the World Intellectual Property Organisation (WIPO) under the auspices of the United Nations, the principal intellectual property conventions are the Berne Convention for the Protection of Literary and Artistic Works (1971); the Paris Convention for the Protection of Industrial Property (1967); and the International Convention for the Protection of Performers, Producers of Phonograms and Broadcasting Organisations (Rome Convention) (1961).

[3] See John Jackson, *The World Trading System,* 2nd edn. (Cambridge, MA: MIT Press, 1997) at p. 47 (". . . foremost is the 'single package' idea, which the negotiators had embraced some years earlier and had resolved to make an important aspect of the negotiation. The idea was that there should be one complete elaborate text to which all those who wanted to become members of the new structure must adhere and accept".).

[4] For an exhaustive discussion of the developing world's perspective on TRIPS, see Carlos M Correa, *Intellectual Property Rights, the WTO and Developing Countries: the TRIPS Agreement and Policy Options* (The Hague: Kluwer Law International, 2000). Correa writes at 3: "Industrialized

Marking it as a unique GATT/WTO instrument, the TRIPS Agreement requires that members bring substantive protection for intellectual property rights into their domestic law.[5] For a GATT/WTO regime that is generally characterised by negative requirements—that national laws shall not restrict trade—TRIPS represents a move towards harmonisation of the required level of intellectual property protection within each national jurisdiction. This intrusive legal move has been politically contentious, not least because it demonstrates a natural gap between the fundamental interests of the developed and developing worlds.[6]

However, not to be overlooked is the fact that, although at a less politically charged level, the TRIPS Agreement has also provided the means for countries at the same level of development to bring complaints against each other before WTO panels.[7] To the extent that TRIPS demands convergence, with only a limited amount of flexibility, it is to be expected that a relatively large number of actions, some with overarching political themes, and many far more modest, will be brought before the WTO. It may be said without exaggeration that the creation of the TRIPS Agreement is the most dramatic attempt at supranational law-making by the GATT/WTO system since its foundation.[8]

INTELLECTUAL PROPERTY AND THE OLD GATT

There were attempts to bring intellectual property issues before the GATT prior to 1995,[9] despite the fact that the former GATT imposed no separate obligations on countries with regard to their treatment of the intellectual property rights of non-nationals. Canada attempted to push the boundaries of GATT to include intellectual property concerns, by bringing an action against the US in 1981 concerning alleged discriminatory treatment of suspected foreign counterfeit goods,

---

countries forced developing countries to initiate negotiation of an agreement on TRIPS with a clear objective of universalizing standards of intellectual property rights protection that the former had incorporated in their legislation, once they had attained a high level of technological and industrial capability".

[5] See Paul Vandoren, "The Implementation of the TRIPS Agreement", (1999) 2:1 *Journal of World Intellectual Property* 25–34.

[6] See, for example, Michael W Smith, "Bringing Developing Countries' Intellectual Property Laws to TRIPS Standards: Hurdles and Pitfalls Facing Vietnam's Efforts to Normalize an Intellectual Property Regime", (1999) 31 *Case Western Reserve Journal of International Law* 211; and David K Tomar, "A Look Into the WTO Pharmaceutical Patent Dispute Between the United States and India", (1999) 17 *Wisconsin International Law Journal* 579.

[7] See, for instance, the action brought by the EC against Canada, *EC* v. *Canada: Patent Protection for Pharmaceutical Products*, Report of the Panel, 17 March 2000 (WT/DS114/R) [hereinafter *Canadian Patent Act* Panel Report].

[8] Adrian Otten, "Implementation of the TRIPS Agreement and Prospects for Its Further Development", (1998) 1:4 *Journal of International Economic Law* 523–536.

[9] See Jackson, *supra* n. 3, at 310.

under the terms of section 337 of the US 1930 Tariff Act.[10] Canada's principal argument was that since these imports received harsher treatment than US products in the same circumstances, section 337 violated GATT Article III (national treatment).[11] Because there were no substantive rules on intellectual property matters at GATT level, Canada was restricted to arguing for an expansion in the panel's understanding of the sorts of discriminatory behaviour that could fall within Article III:1 and III:4. Canada maintained that US products suspected of having been produced in violation of a patent would have the benefit of more complete procedures in a federal court.[12] In particular, the accused party would then have the right to counterclaim—something denied parties dealing in the imported product.[13] Canada also complained of the fact that imported products could be caught up in a sweeping exclusion order at the border, and alleged violation of Article XI:1.

The US built its defence around Article XX (d)—an exception allowing for measures necessary to secure compliance with laws or regulations not inconsistent with the provisions of the GATT agreement, including those relating to "customs enforcement . . . the protection of patents, trade marks and copyrights . . .". Limited to the causes of action available to it under the basic General Agreement, Canada had argued that the US law was prejudicial to foreign suppliers because potential purchasers would be dissuaded by the fact that the entire foreign source could be summarily cut off under section 337. The US countered that procedures applicable to foreign suppliers accused of patent violations had to be distinct, because of inherent difficulties in obtaining relief if the target of the suit is a foreign supplier.[14]

The panel concluded that the standards required for an Article XX defence had been met by the US, in that section 337 did not constitute an arbitrary means of discrimination or disguised restriction on trade; also, that section 337 could be seen as "necessary" as that term is used in Article XX.[15] The panel did say that section 337 could in some circumstances create unnecessary burdens, and go beyond what was necessary to protect the interests of a particular patent holder. But in this instance, involving relatively simple technology, for violations to be left unchecked would soon leave the patent holder without any value in his patent.[16]

The *Spring Assemblies* case demonstrates legal peculiarities characteristic of pre-1995 GATT, similar to those outlined above in the examination of the *DISC* case. When the *Spring Assemblies* panel report came down, many delegations

---

[10] *Imports of Certain Automotive Spring Assemblies*, (1983) BISD 30th Supp, 107 [hereinafter *Spring Assemblies* Panel Report].

[11] *Spring Assemblies* Panel Report, at 119.

[12] *Spring Assemblies* Panel Report, at 113.

[13] Canada would have availed itself of such a right in this case, had it been possible. The Canadian manufacturer of the product in question believed the original patent to be invalid.

[14] *Spring Assemblies* Panel Report, at 121–123.

[15] *Spring Assemblies* Panel Report, at 124–128.

[16] *Spring Assemblies* Panel Report, at 125–126.

disagreed strongly with the idea that section 337 was "necessary" as that term is used in Article XX. The parties adopted the panel ruling, but made it subject to a written understanding that there could be further legal challenges to section 337.[17] Accordingly, in due course, that provision of US law was declared GATT-*illegal*, by a different panel, hearing essentially the same arguments in a case brought by the EC against the US several years later.[18]

This time, the panel ruled quite squarely against the "necessity" of this aspect of section 337, and rejected the US defence.[19] While recognising that section 337 was designed to enforce compliance with US patent laws as provided for under Article XX(d), the panel said that it was first of all an internal law subject to the national treatment requirement of Article III.[20] Article III:4 requires that no internal laws treat imports less favourably than domestic goods, and the panel found that on balance section 337 did give less favourable treatment with regard to patent claims procedures.[21]

With some narrow exceptions, the panel found that the US system of determining allegations of violations of US patent law under section 337 was not justified. The US declared that it would delay full compliance until intellectual property issues were included in an agreement under what were, at the time, the still-ongoing Uruguay Round negotiations.[22]

The resulting TRIPS Agreement is certainly not comprehensive enough to eliminate all disparities in levels of intellectual property rights protection offered across the WTO membership. Nevertheless, it represents an unprecedented effort to harmonise law in this area; it has likewise generated an unparalleled level of controversy.[23] TRIPS is without question more powerful than any intellectual property convention of the past, even though it relies heavily on the standards established in those earlier conventions. By incorporating intellectual property

---

[17] For a critique of the Panel's reasoning, and the peculiar manner of adoption of the Report, see Robert E Hudec, *Enforcing International Trade Law: The Evolution of the Modern GATT Legal System* (New Hampshire: Butterworth Legal Publishing, 1993) 142–143.

[18] *Aramid Fibres: Section 337 of the Tariff Act of 1930* (1989) BISD 36th Supp, 345 [hereinafter *Aramid Fibres* Panel Report]. The dispute arose from a complaint under the "New Commercial Policy Instrument" of 1984. See Hudec, *supra* n. 17, at 219–221.

[19] *Aramid Fibres* Panel Report, at 392–396.

[20] *Aramid Fibres* Panel Report, at 384–386.

[21] The Panel made a significant contribution to the Art. XX-related jurisprudence by determining that Art. XX(d) can permit GATT-inconsistent enforcement measures only when there is no GATT-consistent measure available to achieve the same level of enforcement. Where there is no GATT-consistent measure available, Art. XX(d) only allows the least inconsistent measure available to be used. See *Aramid Fibres* Panel Report at 392–393.

[22] Jackson points out that the US implementing legislation for TRIPS did make a number of changes to the objectionable statute. Respondents were given the immediate opportunity to file counterclaims, which were removed to federal court, and there were clear limits placed on the circumstances in which general exclusion orders on foreign source products could be enacted. See John H Jackson, William J Davey, and Alan O Sykes, Jr., *Legal Problems of International Economic Relations*, 3rd edn. (St. Paul, Minn: West Publishing, 1995) 517–521; 874–876.

[23] See John G Byrne, "Changes on the Frontier of Intellectual Property Law: An Overview of the Changes Required by GATT", (1995) 34 *Duquesne Law Review* 121.

law, at least as it relates to international trade, into the WTO, the complex method of coercion peculiar to the WTO has made all the difference.

THE COMING OF TRIPS

Intellectual property law is prominent in jurisdictions where industrial development depends directly upon major investment in intellectual resources. Without full legal protection of intellectual property rights, these expenditures would become unrecoupable, and thus, the theory goes, would not take place. Intellectual property protection assumes a sufficient level of wealth to allow for such investments in the first place;[24] those newly industrialised countries which, prior to 1995 failed to honour intellectual property rights (either in general or on a selective basis) were acting rationally, in that they had nothing immediate to gain and much to lose from paying such costs.[25] It was completely predictable that the coming of TRIPS, which newly industrialised countries participating in the WTO had no choice but to accept in its entirety, would cause enormous political upheaval and conflict between the developed and developing worlds.[26]

Intellectual property regimes generally seek to strike a balance between the need to protect investments in innovation, and the countervailing need to avoid monopoly possession of ideas. The TRIPS Agreement covers the traditional areas of intellectual property law, as well as some cutting edge matters: thus, along with copyright, trademark and patent, TRIPS also deals with trade secrets and special protection for high technology industrial products.[27]

The potential exists for a wide range of international trade disputes involving intellectual property rights, as reflected in the extensive TRIPS subject matter. Where a foreign producer is making and selling products that infringe intellectual property rights outside the market of the holder of the rights (whether in the home market of the infringer or in a third country market), it is obviously difficult to pursue remedies by taking legal action in the home country of the right holder, or indeed in the home country of the infringer.

---

[24] See Frederick M Abbott, "The Enduring Enigma of TRIPS: A Challenge for the World Economic System", (1998) 1:4 *Journal of International Economic Law* 497–521 (exploring the relationship between level of development and the protection of intellectual property rights).

[25] There is, of course, a school of thought which holds that if these NICs were to commence a solid intellectual property rights regime, then they would also, in due course enter the top ranks of industrial innovators, driven by a natural resulting tendency to investment in innovative industries. See, for example, Martin J Adelman and Sonia Baldia, "Prospects and Limits of the Patent Provision in the TRIPS Agreement: The Case of India", (1996) 29 *Vanderbilt Journal of Transnational Law* 507, 530.

[26] See, n. 6 above. Rosielyn Alviar Pulmano, "In Search of Compliance With TRIPS Against Counterfeiting in the Philippines: When is Enough Enough?", (1999) 12 *The Transnational Lawyer* 241.

[27] For an overview of the contents of TRIPS, see Adrian Otten and Hannu Wager, "Compliance With TRIPS: The Emerging World View", (1996) 29 *Vanderbilt Journal of Transnational Law* 391.

Where offending goods are being imported into the home market of the holder of the right, at least there is a greater possibility of pursuing some domestic law remedies. However, this gives rise to the potential problem of discriminatory procedures, as seen in mild form in the section 337 cases, described above. It is also clear that forcing developing countries to pay the full cost of intellectual property rights would make certain products prohibitively expensive in the developing world. The developing world, in turn, has far less ability to invest large sums in the development of innovative industries of its own. TRIPS, however, has not attempted to deal with this latter issue; in common with all the WTO Agreements, TRIPS is all but silent on the matter of global wealth transfers.

It has already been mentioned that during the 1980s, developed countries had become increasingly unhappy over the fact that many products of greatest export interest to them required strict intellectual property protection, leading to a situation where the GATT had ceased to serve their needs.[28] It is outside the scope of this study to examine individual intellectual property regimes among the major GATT/WTO participants. However, even acknowledging the legal variation present among developed countries, TRIPS has clearly sought to impose, at one swoop, a global level of protection roughly equivalent to a norm or average in a wealthy developed country. TRIPS did not re-invent an appropriate level, taking into account regional needs. While, as will be explored, it allows for variation in strictness of implementation, it does not posit a fundamentally different standard for developing countries, despite a range of special social and economic needs on the ground in those countries.

The limited effectiveness of the single-focus World Intellectual Property Organisation (WIPO), administered by the UN, has been discussed. Without the possibility of economic coercion in a non-intellectual property context, it was more or less impossible for WIPO to compel participants to raise their level of intellectual property protection. Many, if not most, of the developing countries with industrial capacity were not even signatories to the major conventions administered by WIPO. The TRIPS Agreement, while adding some innovative subject matter of its own, has transformed the effectiveness level of the main global intellectual property conventions, by attaching their substantive provisions to the newly powerful dispute resolution system created by the WTO.[29]

Part I of the TRIPS Agreement sets out a national treatment clause for foreign nationals, and an MFN provision.[30] Part II deals with the substantive intellectual property rights members have committed themselves, through TRIPS, to recognising. For copyrights, the 1971 version of the Berne Convention is invoked,

---

[28]   See Michael L Doane, "TRIPS and International Intellectual Property Protection in an Age of Advancing Technology", (1994) 9 *American University Journal of International Law and Policy* 465.

[29]   For a general discussion of the global situation after TRIPS, see Laurinda L Hicks and James R Holbein, "Convergence of National Intellectual Property Norms in International Trading Agreements", (1997) 12 *American University Journal of International Law and Policy* 769.

[30]   TRIPS, Arts. 3–4.

though without the obligation to protect moral rights.[31] Computer programs are to be protected, as well as certain databases.[32] A minimum of 50 years' protection is made standard.[33] Authors of programs, recordings and films can authorise or prohibit commercial rental.[34] Performers are granted specific protection against bootleg recordings of their performances.[35]

As for trademarks, the types of signs to be protected are defined and minimum protection is guaranteed.[36] Any misleading indication of product origin is to be regarded as unfair competition for GATT purposes.[37] Industrial designs must receive ten years of protection.[38]

With patents, there is created a general obligation to live up to the terms of the 1967 Paris Convention; 20 years of patent protection is made available for all inventions in nearly all areas of technology.[39] Inventions may be excluded from patentability if their commercial exploitation is prohibited for reasons of public order or morality. Other permitted exclusions are for diagnostic, therapeutic and surgical methods, as well as plants and animals (other than micro-organisms). However, plant varieties must be protected either by patent or by an effective sui generis system, or both.[40] Rights conferred under patents for processing must extend to products directly obtained by that process. TRIPS is noted for the fact that it also states that trade secrets and know-how must be protected against breach of confidence and other commercially dishonest acts.[41]

In a stunning intrusion into the deep structure of the legal regimes of WTO members, Part III of the TRIPS Agreement sets out the obligations on governments to provide remedies under their own domestic laws to ensure that these rights mentioned above can actually be enforced, both by nationals or non-nationals.[42] Procedures should not be too costly or complex, or involve unwarranted delay.

The Agreement states that procedures and remedies should include judicial orders to destroy offending goods and the ability to take swift provisional action. Action may be taken at the border to prevent the entry of any counterfeit goods. Parties in their domestic systems must also provide for criminal penalties in cases of "wilful trademark counterfeiting or copyright piracy on a commercial scale". Available remedies should also include imprisonment and sufficient fines.[43]

---

[31] TRIPS, Arts. 9–14.
[32] TRIPS, Art. 10.
[33] TRIPS, Art. 12.
[34] TRIPS, Art. 11.
[35] TRIPS, Art. 14.
[36] TRIPS, Arts. 15–21.
[37] TRIPS, Arts. 22–24.
[38] TRIPS, Art. 26.
[39] TRIPS, Arts. 27–33.
[40] TRIPS, Art. 27.
[41] TRIPS, Art. 39.
[42] TRIPS, Arts. 41–61.
[43] TRIPS, Art. 61.

The TRIPS Agreement establishes a Council for Trade-Related Aspects of Intellectual Property Rights to monitor international compliance with the terms of the agreement.[44] Dispute settlement, as indicated above, must take place under the WTO's DSU.[45] The section on the transition period leading to full TRIPS implementation is politically significant, and generated the first litigation under the agreement.[46] Developed countries were given only one year, with no other exceptions, to bring their national regimes into conformity. Developing and former non-market countries were to have a five year period of transition. The so-called least developed countries, mainly located in sub-Saharan Africa, were given an 11 year transition period.[47] However, it should be recalled that the TRIPS Agreement was not primarily aimed at countries without strong industrial copying capacity.

Many countries that maintained in their national legislation a certain level of protection for patent holders generally had nevertheless excluded from patentability certain products of special interest and importance, such as basic medicines. In apparent deference to that reality, the TRIPS Agreement stated that if a developing country was lacking patent protection in a certain area of techno- logy, that country was allowed ten years to introduce such protection.[48] However, as evidence of the strength of the pharmaceutical and chemical lobby, a special provision stated that despite the ten year transition for new patent areas, countries availing themselves of the transition provision must also accept the fil- ing of applications for patents in the pharmaceutical and agricultural chemical fields from 1 January 1995.[49] This is the so-called "mailbox" requirement.

It remained for a high-profile dispute to work out the precise legal require- ment contained within the mailbox provision. Members were obligated to "provide a means" by which patents for new inventions in the areas of pharma- ceuticals and agricultural chemical products could be filed. In addition, the "cri- teria of patentability" would have to be applied from the date of filing as if those criteria were already being applied in the member state.[50] This would seem to constitute a "patent without a patent", or an anticipatory patent. The eventual granting of the patent must be counted from the date of the original application. While the special transition seemed to allow a generously long period of time for developing countries to create patent protection in these areas, it was also designed to ensure that the practice of mass copying of such goods would end, at least with regard to new inventions.

---

[44] TRIPS, Art. 63.
[45] TRIPS, Art. 64.
[46] TRIPS, Part VI, Art. 65. See *US* v. *India: Patent Protection for Pharmaceutical and Agricultural Chemical Products*, Report of the Panel, 5 Sept 1997 (WT/DS50/R) [hereinafter *Indian Pharmaceuticals* Panel Report].
[47] TRIPS, Art. 66.
[48] TRIPS, Art. 65(4).
[49] TRIPS, Art. 70(8).
[50] TRIPS, Art. 70(8)(b).

To further guarantee protection in these key product areas, the Agreement also required that where such a product has, after the coming into effect of the Uruguay Round Agreements, received patent protection and marketing rights in another member state, and where an application has been made in the member state invoking the ten year transition for new patent areas, then the right holders should also receive exclusive marketing rights in that member state.[51] These exclusive marketing rights are to last up to five years or until actual patent protection is granted, whichever is shorter. It is clear that the "transition" opportunity would not allow continued copying of pharmaceutical or agricultural chemical products.

INDIAN PHARMACEUTICALS[52]

The first dispute under the TRIPS Agreement was dramatic and deeply political. There is little doubt that countries such as India, China and Brazil, developing countries with massive markets and huge industrial capability, were the principal targets of the TRIPS agreement. While many less politically charged disputes are sure to follow, the first dispute highlighted the most disturbing elements of the agreement, and left untouched many more issues for the future than it solved in the present.

The US brought this complaint based on the fact that India had not created a sound "mailbox" system for filing patent applications for pharmaceutical and agricultural chemical products; nor had India created any mechanism for granting exclusive marketing rights for such products under the conditions laid down in the section of TRIPS dealing with transition rules for products previously unpatentable under national law.[53] With the coming into force of the Uruguay Round Agreements, the Indian parliament had balked at making the necessary changes to domestic legislation, and the relevant patent application filings had been allowed to take place under the authority of an executive order, the contents of which were not formally notified to the WTO.[54] The Indian intention was to store the relevant applications separately, until such time as Indian's patent law, which made it impossible to seek patents in these areas, was changed to reflect TRIPS provisions.

During this period of legal ambiguity, India continued to receive and store patent applications, although Indian law retained its prohibition against the

---

[51] TRIPS, Art. 70(9).

[52] *Indian Pharmaceuticals* Panel Report, n. 46. *US* v. *India: Patent Protection for Pharmaceutical and Agricultural Chemical Products*, Report of the Appellate Body, 19 December 1997 (WT/DS50/AB/R) [hereinafter Indian Pharmaceuticals Appellate Body Report]. See also *EC* v. *India: Patent Protection for Pharmaceutical and Agricultural Chemical Products*, Report of the Panel, 24 August 1998 (WT/DS79/R) [hereinafter *EC* v. *India* Panel Report].

[53] See TRIPS, Arts. 70(8)–70(9).

[54] *Indian Pharmaceuticals* Panel Report, paras. 2.1–2.9.

patentability of these socially and economically sensitive products.[55] The US argued that India had not created an adequate mechanism for recognising these applications, and thus had failed to preserve their novelty. The US also demanded that recognition of exclusive marketing rights be brought into Indian legislation.[56] India rejoined that its then-existing means for filing applications was capable of attaining the objectives of the transition provisions of TRIPS. Also, since there had been no request to date for exclusive marketing rights, there could be no failure to honour these obligations.[57]

The panel's approach to this dispute is symptomatic of the early tendency displayed by WTO panels to go beyond, in their liberal zeal, the precise terms of the agreements themselves.[58] As will be shown below, it remained for the Appellate Body to attempt to impose legal regularity and predictability on interpretation of the complex new agreements. But as the panel described TRIPS at the outset of its ruling in *Indian Pharmaceuticals*, this agreement is an integral part of the WTO system, "which itself builds upon the experience [of] over nearly half a century under the GATT 1947".[59] The panel asserted[60] that "adopted panel reports create legitimate expectations among WTO members and therefore should be taken into account where they are relevant to any dispute".[61]

The panel set forth its view that "the protection of legitimate expectations of members, regarding the conditions of competition, is a well-established GATT principle, which derives in part from Article XXIII . . .".[62] The panel further asserted that the protection of legitimate expectations "is central to creating security and predictability in the multilateral trading system".[63] While the earlier trade disciplines were aimed at trade in goods, the TRIPS Agreement involved mainly a member's treatment of foreign nationals. Nevertheless, as the panel saw it, there was between these two ideas a shared, underlying principle of legitimate expectations of a competitive relationship based on GATT

---

[55] *Indian Pharmaceuticals* Panel Report, para. 2.10.

[56] *Indian Pharmaceuticals* Panel Report, paras. 4.1–4.5. The EC's submission in this case was highly supportive of the US position. See *Indian Pharmaceuticals* Panel Report, paras. 5.1–5.4. It is noteworthy that the EC took a nearly identical case soon after the completion of this one; no doubt on the theory that India would require extra pressure before complying fully with the panel and Appellate Body rulings. See *EC v. India* Panel Report.

[57] *Indian Pharmaceuticals* Panel Report, paras. 4.6–4.9.

[58] See *Indian Pharmaceuticals* Panel Report, para. 7.1, and following.

[59] The panel also points out that Art. XVI:1 of the WTO Agreement states that "[e]xcept as otherwise provided under this Agreement or the Multilateral Trade Agreements, the WTO shall be guided by the decisions, procedures and customary practices followed by the contracting parties to the GATT 1947 and the bodies established [in that framework]". Indian Pharmaceuticals Panel Report, para. 7.19.

[60] Quoting from the Appellate Body Report in *Canada, EC and US v. Japan: Taxes on Alcoholic Beverages* (WT/DS8/AB/R).

[61] *Indian Pharmaceuticals* Panel Report, para. 7.19.

[62] The Panel gives, as an example of such "expectation" in action, the *Italian Agricultural Machinery* case of 1958, and the *Section 337* case on US intellectual property law, adopted in 1989. *Indian Pharmaceuticals* Panel Report, para. 7.20.

[63] *Indian Pharmaceuticals* Panel Report, para. 7.21.

discipline; it being the task of the WTO legal system to protect the conditions of competition flowing from multilateral trade agreements.[64]

On its face, this might seem a harmless summing-up of GATT legal concepts. However, to the extent that this formulation influenced the panel's interpretation of the actual nature of India's obligations under the TRIPS Agreement, it was problematic. The panel began its substantive analysis by stating that the mechanism required to preserve the novelty of inventions (the subject matter of patent applications) under the transition rules must have a firm legal basis in national law, with legally sound filing dates.[65] The point, the panel said, is that the patent must be available at the moment the transitional period runs out.

What is startling about the panel's approach is that it extends this formulation to include the idea that a WTO-consistent "mailbox" system must also

"take away any reasonable doubts as to whether mailbox applications and eventual patents based on them could be rejected or invalidated because, at the filing or priority date, the matter for which protection was sought was unpatentable in the country in question".[66]

The panel seemed to be demanding that, even where the member country puts in place a "mailbox" application system, that is not a sufficiently "sound" basis—if other provisions of national law indicate that the patent in question is essentially unlawful. The panel insisted that predictability is an essential component of the global intellectual property regime. The question then naturally arises as to whether the Indian regime is capable of protecting these legitimate expectations of other WTO members.[67]

India insisted quite understandably that a special situation obtained during the transition period; however, the panel said that it did not agree

"that the transitional arrangements of the TRIPS Agreement necessarily relieve India of the obligation to make legislative changes in its patent regime during the first five years of the Agreement".[68]

So, does the transitional period have any meaning at all? The panel agreed with India that, under Article 1.1 of the TRIPS Agreement, members are free to determine the appropriate method of implementation within their own legal systems and practice.[69] However, the panel's notion of "legitimate expectations" came into play, as it stated that the relevant question is whether the Indian system provides sufficient "legal certainty and predictability". "There appear to be a few serious problems", the panel said.[70]

We are reminded that the Indian Patents Act of 1970 requires that patent applications in the areas of pharmaceuticals be refused by the relevant authorities. In

---

[64] *Indian Pharmaceuticals* Panel Report, para. 7.21.
[65] *Indian Pharmaceuticals* Panel Report, para. 7.28.
[66] *Indian Pharmaceuticals* Panel Report, para. 7.29.
[67] *Indian Pharmaceuticals* Panel Report, para. 7.31.
[68] *Indian Pharmaceuticals* Panel Report, para. 7.31.
[69] *Indian Pharmaceuticals* Panel Report, para. 7.33.
[70] *Indian Pharmaceuticals* Panel Report, para. 7.34.

the light of these provisions, the panel concluded that the administrative practice governing the Indian "mailbox" system "creates a certain degree of legal insecurity", especially since Indian administrators were obliged, in effect, to ignore mandatory provisions of Indian law. The panel took this further, stating that economic operators (here, applicants for patents) are influenced by this legal uncertainty created by the continued existence of the legislation is question. Literally speaking, India is entitled to maintain the provisions in question until 2005; thus, the existence of the legislation is not the problem. Rather, it is the legal uncertainty created by the continued existence of the legislation that is troublesome.[71]

The panel posited a situation wherein a competitor would seek a judicial order to force a patent official to reject an application made under the "mailbox" system. An Indian court might, the panel imagined, find the filing mechanism to be illegal in light of the mandatory legislative provisions to which it seemed to be logically opposed. There is no guarantee, the panel continued, that an Indian court would uphold an administrative practice that was clearly at odds with such a legislative provision. More applications might have been filed during the transition, the panel said, had the system not been so uncertain—and it would remain uncertain until 2005.[72]

Thus, the panel concluded that the current Indian mailbox system failed to achieve the purposes of the TRIPS transition rules, and failed to "protect the legitimate expectations of inventors of pharmaceutical and agricultural chemical products". Planning trade moves requires predictability, the panel stated, and the Indian system does not provide that.[73]

The second major issue in the case involved the failure of India to create the legal authority for exclusive marketing rights, as required by the TRIPS Agreement.[74] Here, too, the lack of legal authority on the part of the relevant officials to grant such rights was said to "frustrate legitimate expectations".[75] The panel acknowledged that the question of timing—*when* the authority to grant these marketing rights must be in place—should be addressed,[76] and proceeded to reject the Indian idea that the marketing rights can only be meaningful during the five years immediately preceding the end of the transition period, leading up to 2005.[77]

Rather, the panel said that the exclusive marketing rights

"partly compensate for the absence of effective patent protection in countries which avail themselves of the transitional periods under the TRIPS Agreement".[78]

---

[71] *Indian Pharmaceuticals* Panel Report, para. 7.35.
[72] *Indian Pharmaceuticals* Panel Report, paras. 7.36–7.38.
[73] *Indian Pharmaceuticals* Panel Report, paras. 7.39–7.43.
[74] *Indian Pharmaceuticals* Panel Report, para. 7.51, and following.
[75] *Indian Pharmaceuticals* Panel Report, para. 7.53.
[76] India makes the entirely logical argument that the rights need only be available for the five years immediately preceding the year 2005. Otherwise, a situation could arise where rights were granted for five years, after which there would be a gap until the time when the patent could be granted.
[77] *Indian Pharmaceuticals* Panel Report, paras. 7.57–7.62.
[78] *Indian Pharmaceuticals* Panel Report, para. 7.57.

Such rights have to be granted as soon as the conditions are met any time after the entry into force of the WTO Agreement".[79] As for India's contention that this makes no commercial sense, the panel brushed these objections aside. The panel called this "mere speculation" as to how economic actors might react to a specific legal situation. Furthermore, speculation cannot justify delay; and finally, the panel itself speculated that companies could use the five-year period to set up their position in the relevant market.[80] The panel was firm in its conclusion that the power to grant the marketing rights must be available from the coming into force of the TRIPS Agreement.

Re-emphasising its conviction that expectations are at the heart of the Agreement, the panel stated that India must take into account the interests of those who—in addition to those who have, in fact, filed applications—would have filed, but did not feel that the system was secure enough.[81] When it called upon the DSB to request that India bring its domestic regime into line with its TRIPS obligations, the panel seemed to have interpreted TRIPS primarily in the light of the rights of those who had gained "legitimate expectations" from the existence of the agreement.[82] The panel appears to have believed that this conclusion rested on GATT's foundational principles.

On appeal, the Indian government argued that the panel had applied the wrong standard of review in the case, particularly in that the panel failed to seek guidance as to the manner in which Indian authorities interpret Indian domestic law.[83] India insisted that the agreement allowed it to postpone legislative changes for a certain period, and that the panel's view would eliminate the effect of the transition itself. Interestingly, India also argued that the panel had justified an expansive approach by invoking the "need to establish predictable conditions of competition".[84] The panel had in effect, it was argued, turned an obligation to take legislative action in the future into an obligation to take action immediately.[85] The US, not surprisingly, insisted on the centrality of protecting legitimate expectations in the intellectual property area.[86] The US also insisted that the quid pro quo for taking advantage of the extended transition period for these products was the grant of exclusive marketing rights.[87]

This dispute is notable not least for the fact that it established a particular relationship between panel and Appellate Body reasoning. While the Appellate Body clearly disapproved of the more imaginative and expansionary approaches

---

[79] *Indian Pharmaceuticals* Panel Report, para. 7.57.

[80] *Indian Pharmaceuticals* Panel Report, paras. 7.58–7.60. The panel says: "Competitors, knowing that the grant of subsequent patent protection is imminent, are likely to be discouraged from entering into the market during this brief window of opportunity".

[81] *Indian Pharmaceuticals* Panel Report, para. 7.62.

[82] *Indian Pharmaceuticals* Panel Report, para. 7.65–8.2.

[83] *Indian Pharmaceuticals* Appellate Body Report, para. 9.

[84] *Indian Pharmaceuticals* Appellate Body Report, para. 13.

[85] *Indian Pharmaceuticals* Appellate Body Report, para. 12.

[86] *Indian Pharmaceuticals* Appellate Body Report, para. 20.

[87] *Indian Pharmaceuticals* Appellate Body Report, para. 21.

taken by the panel in its interpretation of the obligations created by the TRIPS Agreement, the ultimate effect of the panel ruling were left undisturbed.

Turning to the question of legitimate expectations, the Appellate Body reminded the reader that the panel had relied upon past GATT case law (panel reports) wherein legitimate expectations of contracting parties were discussed. The Appellate Body stated that the panel was wrong in its view that the legitimate expectations of private rights holders from different member countries should also be taken into account under the TRIPS Agreement.[88] The panel's attempt to extend the early GATT notion of the need to protect expectations of countries participating in the GATT to the need to protect the expectations of economic players affected by the WTO rules was repudiated. Yet what was the ultimate effect of the Appellate Body's more restrained approach?

Addressing the question of the Indian "mailbox" system, the Appellate Body stated that the panel was correct in its finding that the purpose of this provision was to prevent the loss of the novelty of an invention, and thus that national implementation must have a sound legal base. Without legally sound filing and priority dates, the mechanism to be established on the basis of Article 70.8 would be inoperational, the Appellate Body said, backing up the panel on this point. Here, the Appellate Body said, the panel's interpretation was consistent with the object and purpose of the TRIPS Agreement.[89]

But this is to be further distinguished from the notion that a country is obliged to eliminate any reasonable doubts regarding whether the patent applications could be rejected, since the subject matter was unpatentable at the time of the application.[90] India is entitled, the Appellate Body maintained, to delay the creation of patents for these products until 2005. However, India is obliged to create a "mailbox" system with a "sound legal basis to preserve both the novelty of the inventions and the priority of the applications as of the relevant filing and priority dates. No more".[91]

India's view, the Appellate Body recounted, was that its administrative instructions on the "mailbox" system provided just such a legal basis.[92] The Appellate Body mentioned that these instructions had not been provided to the panel or the Appellate Body.[93] And as for the question of whether legal certainty was harmed by the fact that a judicial order could be sought by a competitor to

---

[88] The Appellate Body faults the panel for having confused the distinction between protection of legitimate expectations in the context of violation and non-violation disputes under the GATT. In addition, the Appellate Body cites Art. 3.2 of the DSU, which refers only to the rights and obligations of members. *Indian Pharmaceuticals* Appellate Body Report, paras. 33–47. The Appellate Body writes: "For these reasons, we do not agree with the Panel that the legitimate expectations of Members and private rights holders concerning conditions of competition must always be taken into account in interpreting the TRIPS Agreement". *Indian Pharmaceuticals* Appellate Body Report, para. 48.

[89] *Indian Pharmaceuticals* Appellate Body Report, para. 57.

[90] *Indian Pharmaceuticals* Appellate Body Report, para. 58.

[91] *Indian Pharmaceuticals* Appellate Body Report, para. 58.

[92] *Indian Pharmaceuticals* Appellate Body Report, para. 60.

[93] *Indian Pharmaceuticals* Appellate Body Report, para. 61.

prevent acceptance of a "mailbox" application, the Appellate Body said that upon examination, "we are not persuaded that India's administrative instructions would survive a legal challenge under the Patents Act".[94] Consequently, the Appellate Body said that it was not persuaded that the administrative instructions constituted a sound legal basis to preserve the novelty of inventions and priority of applications.[95] Thus, on the ultimate point—that India's administrative instructions alone do not bring India into compliance with TRIPS—the Appellate Body was in agreement with the panel. As for exclusive marketing rights, the Appellate Body, without significant elaboration, upheld the panel's ruling that India was required to implement the relevant provision in legislation as of the beginning of 1995.[96]

Perhaps fearing an interpretative free-for-all on the part of panels, the Appellate Body displayed caution in limiting its own findings to the strict letter of the TRIPS Agreement. Nevertheless, in no major respect, except for the more philosophical conclusions to be drawn from the existence of the TRIPS Agreement, does it differ from what the panel ruled with respect to India's obligations. The Agreement demands that the novelty of inventions be preserved, and that there be legally sound bases for filing and priority dates. It is only common sense that the interests of rights-holders create a common bond between the two decisions. But the Appellate Body indicated that this subtext could not be used as an *interpretative* tool. Obligations of members would be interpreted literally; not through speculative interpretation of the larger purposes of the agreements.

When the EC brought a virtually identical case in 1998, arguing that India had not acted to alter its domestic legal regime in the light of the earlier rulings, India maintained that successive complaints based on the same facts and legal claims were unprecedented in GATT/WTO law.[97] The *Pharmaceuticals II* panel did not take any position on the question of whether the "system" would be put in jeopardy if such a re-hearing could take place, as argued by India. Instead, the panel adhered to Article 11 of the DSU, which merely requires that the panel "make an objective assessment of the facts", in the light of the "relevant covered agreements".[98] While stating that it was not literally bound by the earlier panel decision, this panel concluded, in the light of GATT history, that there is a need for security and predictability in the world trading system which implies a need to avoid inconsistent rulings.[99]

India took the occasion of the second panel to argue that its domestic law would, under Indian rules of statutory interpretation, be interpreted by a court in accordance with Indian international obligations, and thus that the

---

[94] *Indian Pharmaceuticals* Appellate Body Report, para. 70.
[95] *Indian Pharmaceuticals* Appellate Body Report, para. 70.
[96] *Indian Pharmaceuticals* Appellate Body Report, 76–84.
[97] See *EC v. India* Panel Report, n. 52.
[98] *EC v. India* Panel Report, paras. 7.22–7.23.
[99] *EC v. India* Panel Report, para. 7.30.

Pharmaceuticals I panel's conclusions about the unsuitability of its domestic regime were incorrect.[100] However, this panel concluded that the Indian legislation was only capable of one interpretation, and that the earlier panel was correct in seeing a threat of litigation by a competitor in the Indian courts.[101]

Concerning the rather simpler matter of exclusive marketing rights, India continued to insist that it need do nothing until an actual application for such rights should arise. This panel reiterated the view that the Indian obligation dates from the beginning of 1995.[102]

Given the serious social and political consequences for India, it is worth noting that GATT/WTO law grants few, if any, opportunities for arguing the equity of the matter; the parties are limited to arguing in the essentially one dimensional space of the agreements' provisions. However, India made the perfectly cogent argument that the Pharmaceutical I panel's conclusions "entail the absurd consequence that the transitional arrangements would allow developing countries to postpone legislative changes in all fields of technology, except in the most sensitive ones"—that is, pharmaceutical and agricultural chemical products.[103] India's now more elaborately argued view was that this conclusion could not be justified in terms of the objectives of the transitional arrangements in the TRIPS Agreement.[104]

However, the panel was free to ignore the drift of India's argument; there was no obligation on the panel to make complete sense of the demands of the agreements. The requirement of the exclusive marketing rights was, the panel stated, "a special obligation imposed on those members benefiting from the transitional arrangements".[105] Then, India might well ask, what is the actual benefit? The panel continued with what must have been a maddening consistency from the Indian point of view.

> "Exclusive market rights were a quid pro quo for the delay of the availability of product patents for pharmaceutical and agricultural chemical products until January 1, 2005, based on a careful balancing of obligations between interested parties during the Uruguay Round negotiations".[106]

Having lost on the same issues twice, against important trading partners, the cost of non-compliance had obviously risen substantially for the Indian government. Irrespective of the social and political consequences, India subsequently announced that they would be complying with the rulings against them, and would act to bring their legislative scheme into line with the demands of the TRIPS Agreement, as interpreted by two panels and the Appellate Body.

---

[100] *EC v. India* Panel Report, para. 7.46.
[101] *EC v. India* Panel Report, paras. 7.49–7.54.
[102] *EC v. India* Panel Report, paras. 7.60–7.65.
[103] *EC v. India* Panel Report, para. 7.71.
[104] *EC v. India* Panel Report, para. 7.71.
[105] *EC v. India* Panel Report, para. 7.71.
[106] *EC v. India* Panel Report, para. 7.72.

The Indian Pharmaceuticals cases sent a clear message to the NIC countries at which the TRIPS Agreement was principally aimed, that transition cannot be taken to mean non-compliance. The understandable political resistance in countries like India to altering foundational beliefs concerning the relationship between fairness and intellectual property rights was the ultimate target of these actions. The developed world lost no time in ensuring, by forcing the issue in the dispute format, that in the war between certain national parliaments and the TRIPS Agreement, TRIPS would have to prevail. India's silence on the question of public access to life-saving pharmaceutical and indispensable agricultural chemical products stems from the fact that such concerns form no part of WTO law, and have no place in the dispute settlement system.

A principle theme in the study of the Uruguay Round Agreements is the greatly increased cost of participation for member countries in the new multi-lateral trading system. Whereas prior to 1995, a GATT requirement that involved too high a domestic political cost could in effect be resisted, that is no longer the case.[107] At least with regard to patents, TRIPS involves obligations that could well cost some citizens in WTO member countries their lives. Even in the name of the future development of efficient research-based industries, that is a political cost of the highest order. It is to be expected that non-compliance will continue to be a prominent feature of the TRIPS Agreement in particular.[108] Indeed, how to deal with this continued tendency to resist the full rigours of TRIPS has been a major source of contention in the run-up to the Millennium Round of negotiations.

While less politically explosive, there have been significant disputes between developed countries brought under TRIPS. It could be said that these disputes involve public policy issues at the margins, rather than issues of life or death; nevertheless, TRIPS provides an important vehicle for clearing up long-standing grievances with regard to weak or protectionist aspects of national intellectual property laws.

CANADIAN GENERIC DRUGS

An example of a somewhat more "garden variety" dispute under TRIPS is the case brought by the EC against Canada regarding the scope of exclusive patent rights under Canadian legislation.[109] The dispute once again confirms the

---

[107] See Sara Dillon, "Fuji-Kodak, the WTO, and the Death of Domestic Political Constituencies", (1999) 8:2 *Minnesota Journal of Global Trade* 197.

[108] See John E Giust, "Noncompliance with TRIPS by Developed and Developing Countries: Is TRIPS Working?", (1997) 8 *Indiana International and Comparative Law Review* 69; and Keshia B Haskins, "Special 301 in China and Mexico: A Policy Which Fails to Consider How Politics, Economics, and Culture Affect Legal Change Under Civil Law Systems of Developing Countries", (1999) 9 *Fordham Intellectual Property, Media and Entertainment Law Journal* 1125.

[109] *EC v. Canada—Patent Protection of Pharmaceutical Products*, Report of the Panel, 17 March 2000 (WT/DS114/R) [hereinafter *Canadian Patent Act* Panel Report].

extraordinary importance of the interests of the pharmaceutical industry in the creation of the TRIPS Agreement, and in particular, highlights the struggle between primary drug developers and the generic drug industry.

At issue were provisions of Canadian law which allowed companies to complete the process of gaining marketing approval for a patented drug, to be sold after the expiration of the existing patent rights; and also to stockpile manufactured drugs during the last six months of a patent in anticipation of the expiration of the original patent.[110] The EC complaint was that these provisions of Canadian law conflicted with Article 28.1 of TRIPS, which states that owners shall have the right to exclude others from making, using and selling the patented product during the term of the patent. Article 33 of TRIPS states that the term of patent protection available shall not end before the expiration of a period of 20 years, counted from the filing date of the application for the patent.

The dispute centred on the proper interpretation of Article 30 of TRIPS, the so-called "limited exceptions" provision.[111] While this provision states that there may be some exceptions to the principle of exclusivity of rights, it also requires that normal commercial expectations of patent owners should be kept intact. Canada maintained that its exceptions met all three conditions set out in Article 30 of TRIPS.[112] It further argued that in light of other provisions of TRIPS, notably Articles 7 and 8 (which make reference to social values), a balance must be struck in national law between patent rights and other important national policies.[113]

The EC countered with the view that Articles 7 and 8 of TRIPS already represent the balancing of goals that took place in the course of drafting the TRIPS Agreement. The three limiting conditions found in Article 30, Europe argued, are part of this pre-existing balance, and there must not be, in addition, any "double-counting of socio-economic factors".[114] The Panel agreed with Europe that the three limiting conditions indicate that Article 30 was not intended to "bring about what would be equivalent to a re-negotiation of the basic balance

---

[110] Canadian Patent Act, Sections 55.2(1)–55.2(2).

[111] TRIPS, Art. 30 (reading "[m]embers may provide limited exceptions to the exclusive rights conferred by a patent, provided that such exceptions do not unreasonably conflict with the normal exploitation of the patent and do not unreasonably prejudice the legitimate interests of the patent owner, taking account of the legitimate interests of third parties").

[112] *Canadian Patent Act* Panel Report, paras. 7.20–7.24.

[113] *Canadian Patent Act* Panel Report, para. 7.24. Art. 7 of TRIPS reads: "*Objectives* The protection and enforcement of intellectual property rights should contribute to the promotion of technological innovation and to the transfer and dissemination of technology, to the mutual advantage of producers and users of technological knowledge and in a manner conducive to social and economic welfare, and to a balance of rights and obligations". And Art. 8 on *Principles* reads: "1. Members may, in formulating or amending their laws and regulations, adopt measures necessary to protect public health and nutrition, and to promote the public interest in sectors of vital importance to their socio-economic and technological development, provided that such measures are consistent with the provisions of this Agreement.

2. Appropriate measures, provided that they are consistent with the provisions of this Agreement, may be needed to prevent the abuse of intellectual property rights by right holders or the resort to practices which unreasonably restrain or adversely affect the international transfer of technology".

[114] *Canadian Patent Act* Panel Report, para. 7.25.

of the Agreement". The focus then became the precise meaning of the three conditions, and precisely what they in fact permit.[115]

The Panel turned first to the stockpiling exception, which Canada argued is limited in scope because it preserves the right of the patent owner to sell commercially during the entire life of the patent.[116] The EC countered that ultimate sale to the consumer is only one of the rights guaranteed under the patent provision of TRIPS—that the rights to make and use are also significant, and that these were clearly infringed by the Canadian stockpiling exception.[117] As the Panel framed the question, to determine whether a particular exception constitutes a limited exception, the extent to which the patent owner's rights have been curtailed must be measured.[118] In the Panel's view, the exclusive right to sell to an ultimate consumer is only one among several rights required to be preserved, and thus agreed with the EC that the stockpiling exception violated Article 28.1 of TRIPS.[119]

By contrast, the Panel found no violation of Article 28.1 with regard to the Canadian "regulatory review exception".[120] The Panel decided that this exception was "limited" within the meaning of TRIPS Article 30, in that it was confined to conduct "needed to comply with the requirements of the regulatory approval process", such that "the extent of the acts unauthorised by the right holder that are permitted . . . will be small and narrowly bounded".[121]

The Panel dealt straightforwardly with the question of economic effects, acknowledging that

> "if there were no regulatory review exception allowing competitors to apply for regulatory approval during the term of the patent . . . the patent owner would be able to extend its period of market exclusivity, de facto, for some part of that three to six and a half year period" [needed to gain regulatory approval].[122]

But because member countries are in broad disagreement over which interests are to be preferred in this matter, the Panel left the policy choice to political debate, rather than attempting to decide this unresolved matter through adjudication. For WTO purposes, under the current state of TRIPS law, the

---

[115] *Canadian Patent Act* Panel Report, para. 7.26.
[116] *Canadian Patent Act* Panel Report, para. 7.27.
[117] *Canadian Patent Act* Panel Report, para. 7.29.
[118] *Canadian Patent Act* Panel Report, para. 7.32.
[119] *Canadian Patent Act* Panel Report, paras. 7.36–7.38. The Panel writes that "[i]n theory, the rights of the patent owner are generally viewed as a right to prevent competitive commercial activity by others and manufacturing for commercial sale is a quintessential competitive commercial activity, whose character is not altered by a mere delay in the commercial reward". *Canadian Patent Act* Panel Report, para. 7.35.
[120] *Canadian Patent Act*, Section 55.2(1). This provision states that it is no infringement of a patent if the use in question is solely related to the submission of information required under any national law—in other words, for compliance with regulatory controls for safety purposes on products such as pharmaceuticals.
[121] *Canadian Patent Act* Panel Report, para. 7.45.
[122] *Canadian Patent Act* Panel Report, para. 7.48.

panel ruled that the Canadian regulatory review exception was sufficiently narrow to meet the standard of Article 28.1, read in the light of Article 30.[123]

Canada indicated its willingness to implement the terms of the panel decision,
and decided not to appeal.[124]

CANADIAN TERM OF PATENT PROTECTION

Certain TRIPS disputes between developed countries may provide even less in
the way of subtextual debates over public policy. An example of a purely economic case is one taken by the United States against Canada over the fact that
some of Canada's "Old Act" patents (patents applications filed before 1
October 1989) provided fewer years of protection than the 20 year standard
established by Article 33 of TRIPS.[125] The case is significant to the extent that it
clarifies the scope of non-retroactivity in the TRIPS Agreement.

At issue was Section 45 of Canada's Patent Act, which stated that patents
issued on the basis of applications filed before 1 October 1989 would be granted
for seventeen years from the date on which the patent was issued. Because the
Act was not brought into force for several years, Canada maintained that
approximately 60 per cent of Old Act patents would not expire until at least 20
years after their application dates.[126] But, based on the fact that a large number
of such patents would in fact expire before 20 years of filing date, the United
States argued that the Canadian provisions were in violation of Articles 33 and
70 of TRIPS.[127]

Canada defended on the basis that Article 33 should be applied prospectively
to acts of grant occurring on or after 1 January 1996, the date on which TRIPS
would have taken effect in Canada; and not retrospectively to acts or grant
occurring before that date.[128] At issue was the language of Articles 70.1 and 70.2
of TRIPS.[129] Thus, the question, as framed by the panel, was whether "existing
subject matter which is protected", as that phrase is used in Article 70.2 of

---

[123] *Canadian Patent Act* Panel Report, paras. 7.78–7.84.

[124] *Canada—Patent Protection of Pharmaceutical Products*, Arbitration under Art. 21.3 of the
Understanding on Rules and Procedures Governing Settlement of Disputes, 18 August 2000
(WT/DS114/13), para. 1.

[125] *US v. Canada: Term of Patent Protection*, Report of the Panel, 5 May 2000 (WT/DS170/R)
[hereinafter *Canadian Term of Patent Protection* Panel Report]. See Art. 33 of TRIPS (reading, "The
term of protection available shall not end before the expiration of a period of twenty years counted
from the filing date".)

[126] *Canadian Term of Patent Protection* Panel Report, para. 2.6.

[127] *Canadian Term of Patent Protection* Panel Report, para. 3.1.

[128] *Canadian Term of Patent Protection* Panel Report, para. 6.19.

[129] Art. 70—Protection of Existing Subject Matter:

1. This Agreement does not give rise to obligations in respect of acts that occurred before the date
of application of the Agreement for the Member in question.

2. Except as otherwise provided for in this Agreement, this Agreement gives rise to obligations in
respect of all subject matter existing at the date of application of this Agreement for the Member in
question, and which is protected in that Member on the said date, or which meets or comes subsequently to meet the criteria for protection under the terms of this Agreement.

TRIPS, includes inventions protected by Old Act patents that were in force on the date of application of the TRIPS Agreement in Canada. Canada insisted that Article 70.1, not Article 70.2, was relevant to this situation, such that "acts" of the Canadian authorities occurring prior to 1 January 1996 would not be included.[130]

The principal US argument was that the "acts" of the Canadian Patent Office prior to 1 January 1996 were not at issue. Rather, the violation was related to the subject matter—in this case, the protected inventions—that existed in Canada on 1 January 1996. The US position was that the Article 70.1 rule—stating that pre-1996 acts are not subject to TRIPS obligations—does not imply that subject matter existing at that time was similarly not subject to the obligations of the Agreement.

The panel first established that the term "subject matter" as used in Article 70.2 refers to material including literary works, industrial designs and inventions. Thus, the panel concluded, the reference in Article 70.2 also includes inventions that were under patent protection in Canada on 1 January 1996. Therefore, the US had established a prima facie case that Article 70.2 is applicable to inventions protected by Old Act patents. Canada had argued that Article 70.2 is set aside by Article 70.1 in this case, in that the term "acts" in Article 70.1 encompassed the acts of the Canadian authorities.

However, the panel declined to rule on the scope of the term "acts" as used in Article 70.1, since the administrative granting of a patent would in any case be distinct from "subject matter . . . which is protected", as that phrase is used in Article 70.2. As the panel pointed out, this "subject matter" had already been determined to include Canada's Old Act patents. The non-retroactivity rule of Article 70.1 does not govern inventions protected by Old Act patents, the panel said, because the protection granted to this subject matter is ongoing.[131]

In response to the US argument that its law provides no sound legal basis for patent applications filed before 1 October 1989 to obtain a period of protection that did not end before twenty years, Canada attempted to argue that the "effective" term of protection available under Section 45 of the Patent Act met or exceeded the TRIPS requirement. As added insurance of this, Canada maintained, applicants can obtain a period of protection of not less than twenty years by readily available procedural delays. The panel rejected these arguments.[132]

In the panel's view, Section 45 did not meet the minimum standard imposed by TRIPS Article 33 in all cases; it was irrelevant that a large number of the patents in question exceeded the twenty year term.[133] Not surprisingly, the panel also decided that requiring applicants to resort to procedural delays for the purpose of obtaining the required period of protection would constitute

---

[130] *Canadian Term of Patent Protection* Panel Report, para. 6.7.
[131] *Canadian Term of Patent Protection* Panel Report, paras. 6.38–6.41.
[132] *Canadian Term of Patent Protection* Panel Report, paras. 6.82–6.99.
[133] *Canadian Term of Patent Protection* Panel Report, para. 6.88.

unreasonable procedures, inconsistent with Canada's obligations under Article 62.1.[134] The panel's rulings were upheld by the Appellate Body.[135]

THE US "FAIRNESS IN MUSIC LICENSING" ACT

Europe also relied on TRIPS to gain a legal victory over the United States in the matter of an amendment to US copyright law granting a broad exemption to small business owners from paying royalties for the playing of background music.[136] The dispute originated in a complaint made by the Irish Music Rights Organisation that Irish music was being played in small eating and drinking establishments across America, without the payment of appropriate royalties to Irish musicians. The EC brought an action at the WTO, complaining that Section 110(5) of the US Copyright Act, as amended in 1998 by the "Fairness in Music Licensing Act", violated Article 9.1 of the TRIPS Agreement, under which WTO members were required to comply with Articles 1 to 21 of the Berne Convention (1971), the major international convention on copyright.

Under the 1976 US Copyright Act, owners of small establishments such as fast food outlets were entitled to play background radio music, as long as they did not use a commercial sound system. Referred to as the "homestyle" exemption and based on decisions of the United States courts,[137] the theory behind this exemption was that such establishments were unlikely ever to seek a license to play music in any event.[138] In the 1998 amendments to the Act, this exemption was preserved in its original language as subparagraph (A) of Section 110(5) of the Act, although in light of subparagraph (B) as described below, now taken to refer only to broadcasts of "dramatic" musical works.

A new subparagraph (B), inserted in 1998 as part of the "Fairness in Music Licensing" amendments, significantly expanded the scope of the exemption. Called the "business exemption", this section covered broadcasts of "non-dramatic musical works intended to be received by the general public". The beneficiaries of this exemption were divided into two groups, establishments dealing with food and drink, and those that did not. For each of the two categories, establishments under a certain size were exempted, regardless of the equipment they use; if over the size limit for each category, the exemption applied if the establishment did not exceed the limit on number and size of sound outlets.[139]

---

[134] *Canadian Term of Patent Protection* Panel Report, para. 6.115.

Art. 62.1 states that "members may require, as a condition of the acquisition or maintenance of the intellectual property rights provided for under Sections 2 through 6 of Part II, compliance with reasonable procedures and formalities".

[135] *EC v. US: Canadian Term of Patent Protection*, Report of the Appellate Body, WT/DS170/AB/R, 18 September 2000.

[136] See *Section 110(5) of the US Copyright Act*, Report of the Panel, WT/DS 160/R, 15 June 2000 [hereinafter *Copyright Act* Panel Report].

[137] See particularly *Twentieth Century Music Corp.* v. *Aiken*, 422 US 151 (1975).

[138] See *Copyright Act* Panel Report, paras. 2.1–2.17.

[139] *Copyright Act* Panel Report, paras. 2.2–2.10.

It is common practice for copyrights in music to be licensed through "collective management organizations", whose task it is to collect payment for these general licenses, and in turn to distribute revenues collected to individual right holders in the form of royalties.[140] The EC alleged that the exemptions provided under US Section 110(5) were incompatible with Articles 11(1)(ii) and 11*bis*(1)(iii) of the Berne Convention (1971); and that the exemptions could not be justified under any limitation permissible under the Berne Convention or TRIPS.[141] It was noted that Section 110(5) did not apply to the use of recorded music (either CDs of tapes), or to live performances.[142] The principal US defence was that insofar as TRIPS incorporates the major substantive provisions of the Berne Convention, that convention also allows members to place minor limitations on the exclusive rights of copyright owners. The US further argued that Article 13 of TRIPS provided the standard by which to judge the appropriateness of such limitations or exemptions, and that the Section 110(5) exemptions did meet that standard.[143]

The EC position, by contrast, was that Article 13 of TRIPS only applies to exclusive rights newly introduced under the TRIPS Agreement itself, and thus that the rights granted under the Berne Convention could be derogated from only on the basis of pre-existing exceptions that had been available under the Berne Convention itself.[144]

While the text of the Berne Convention itself does not contain explicit reference to exceptions, the reports of conferences revising the convention affirm "implied exceptions" allowing member countries to provide limitations and exceptions to certain rights. This so-called "minor exceptions" doctrine was first mentioned in the General Report of the Brussels Conference in 1948.[145] A choice was made not to insert any provision into the body of the convention that would clearly allow members to retain such exceptions; nonetheless, the report made clear that the conference did not question the right of members to retain minor exceptions in national law.

---

[140] *Copyright Act* Panel Report, para. 2.17.

[141] *Copyright Act* Panel Report, para. 3.1. Art. 11(1) of the Berne Convention provides that "Authors of dramatic, dramatico-musical and musical works shall enjoy the exclusive rights of authorizing: (i) the public performances of their works, including such public performance by any means or process; (ii) any communication to the public of the performance of their works.

Art. 11 *bis* (1) states that "Authors of literary and artistic works shall enjoy the exclusive right of authorizing: (i) the broadcasting of their works or the communication thereof to the public by any other means of wireless diffusion of signs, sounds or images; (ii) any communication to the public by wire or by re-broadcasting of the broadcast of the work, when this communication is made by an organization other than the original one; (iii) the public communication by loudspeaker or any other analogous instrument transmitting, by signs, sounds or images, the broadcast of the work".

[142] *Copyright Act* Panel Report, para. 2.16.

[143] *Copyright Act* Panel Report, paras. 3.1–3.3.

TRIPS Art. 13 states that "Members shall confine limitations or exceptions to certain special cases which do not conflict with a normal exploitation of the work and do not unreasonably prejudice the legitimate interests of the right holder".

[144] *Copyright Act* Panel Report, para. 6.34.

[145] *Copyright Act* Panel report, paras. 6.50–6.52.

As to the nature of these exceptions, the WTO panel stated that the "non-commercial character of the use in question is not determinative provided that the exception contained in national law is indeed minor".[146] In the absence of any indication in the TRIPS Agreement to the contrary, the panel accepted the US argument that Articles 11 and 11 *bis* of the Berne Convention have brought with them into the TRIPS Agreement (via Article 9.1 of TRIPS) the minor exceptions recognised in connection with the Berne Convention itself.[147] With respect to those exceptions, the panel also concluded that

> "the application of Article 13 of the TRIPS Agreement to the rights provided under Article 11(1) and 11*bis*(1) of the Berne Convention (1971) as incorporated into the TRIPS Agreement need not lead to different standards . . .".

In accordance with the US position, the panel proceeded to "examine the scope for permissible minor exceptions to the exclusive rights in question by applying the conditions of Article 13 of the TRIPS Agreement".[148] Thus, if an exception meets the three conditions of Article 13—"certain special cases"; "which do not conflict with a normal exploitation"; and "do not unreasonably prejudice the legitimate interests of the right holder"—a government may then choose among different options for limiting the right in question.[149]

With respect to the first condition, that the exception involves "certain special cases", the panel stated that the exception in national legislation should be clearly defined and narrow in its scope and reach.[150] The panel rejected the notion that Article 13 requires that the exception be justified in terms of a legitimate public policy purpose in order to fulfil the first condition.[151]

The panel agreed with the European position that "it is the scope of potential users that is relevant for determining whether the coverage of the exemption is sufficiently limited to qualify as a 'certain special case' ".[152] In light of the detailed factual evidence indicating that a substantial majority of eating and drinking establishments, as well as close to half of retail establishments, are covered by the "business exemption" of subparagraph B of Section 110(5), the panel concluded that this exemption could not be considered a "special case" in the sense of the first condition of Article 13 of TRIPS.[153]

However, with regard to the exemption provided by subparagraph A of Section 110(5) of the Act (the "homestyle" exemption, as amended only applicable to "dramatic" musical works), the panel found that in view of its narrow limits, as well as the legislative history, this provision was sufficiently well-defined to meet the standard created by the first condition of Article 13 of

---

[146] *Copyright Act* Panel Report, para. 6.58.
[147] *Copyright Act* Panel Report, paras. 6.62–6.63.
[148] *Copyright Act* Panel Report, para. 6.81.
[149] *Copyright Act* Panel Report, para. 6.87.
[150] *Copyright Act* Panel Report, para. 6.112.
[151] *Copyright Act* Panel Report, para. 6.111.
[152] *Copyright Act* Panel Report, para. 6.127.
[153] *Copyright Act* Panel Report, para. 6.133.

TRIPS.[154] The panel then proceeded to analyse the two exemptions, subparagraphs (A) and (B), under the other two conditions imposed by Article 13 of TRIPS.[155]

After a lengthy discussion of the meaning of "normal exploitation", the panel concluded that "exceptions or limitations would be presumed not to conflict with a normal exploitation of works if they are confined to a scope or degree that does not enter into economic competition with non-exempted uses".[156] In the panel's view, not every use of a work involving commercial gain necessarily conflicts with "normal exploitation" of that work. Otherwise, the panel concluded, hardly any exception or limitation could pass the test of Article 13's second condition, leaving Article 13 "devoid of meaning".[157]

Rather, the exempted use would have to enter into economic competition with the *ways* in which right holders normally extract economic value from the copyright, thereby depriving them of tangible commercial gain, in order for "normal exploitation" to have been prevented.[158] Because right holders would expect to be in a position to authorise the use of broadcasts of radio and television music by many of the establishments covered by the subparagraph B exemption, and receive compensation as appropriate, the panel found that subparagraph B did not meet the second condition of TRIPS Article 13.[159]

Treating the subparagraph (A) exemption under the second condition, the panel noted that in the US view, this exemption was limited to establishments that were not large enough to justify a subscription to a commercial background music service in any event.[160] Since there would be no license in any case, there was consequently no conflict with the expectation of right holders concerning the normal exploitation of their works. The panel found that the subparagraph (A) exemption was indeed confined to a situation where one was "listening to the radio or television", as opposed to using equipment that would create a "new public performance" of the music contained in the transmission. Therefore, the panel concluded that the subparagraph (A) exemption did not conflict with a normal exploitation of works, within the meaning of the second condition in Article 13.

---

[154] *Copyright Act* Panel Report, paras. 6.143–6.159.

[155] Although in terms of judicial economy, it would hardly have been necessary for the panel to deal with subparagraph (B) in light of the other two conditions, having found that it failed to meet the first, the panel explained that an earlier ruling of the Appellate Body required it to deal with all the claims necessary to secure a positive resolution of the dispute. See *India* v. *US: Shirts and Blouses* Appellate Body Report, to the effect that it would be a "false judicial economy" not to do so. *Copyright Act* Panel Report, para. 6.162.

[156] *Copyright Act* Panel Report, para. 6.181.

[157] *Copyright Act* Panel Report, para. 6.182.

[158] *Copyright Act* Panel Report, para. 6.183.

[159] *Copyright Act* Panel Report, para. 6.210. The panel further noted that it saw no reason for the distinction drawn in subparagraph (B) between the use of radio and television broadcasts on the one hand (covered by the exemption), and the use of CDs and tapes on the other (not covered).

[160] *Copyright Act* Panel Report, para. 6.212.

As for the final condition, that the exemption "not unreasonably prejudice the legitimate interests of the right holder", the panel decided to confine its view of "legitimate interests" to the "economic value of the exclusive rights conferred by copyright on their holders", even while acknowledging the incomplete and conservative nature of that definition. The panel made clear that there could be other "legitimate interests" than these, but also that it was "possible to estimate in economic terms the value of exercising, e.g., by licensing, such rights".[161]

The US and EC presented widely differing estimates of the losses to copyright holders because of the US exemption in question. With regard to the subparagraph (B) business exemption, the US attempted to emphasise that, were the exemption not available, many businesses would simply not play the music, or otherwise pay any royalty. The panel cautioned against attributing too much relevance to the factors cited by the US in its attempt to reduce the EC's estimated losses, stating that the ultimate burden of proof concerning whether the conditions of Article 13 are met lies with the member invoking the exemption. The panel went on to rule that the US had not demonstrated that the business exemption of subparagraph (B) does not unreasonably prejudice the legitimate interests of the right holders.[162]

Not surprisingly, the panel found that playing music by the small establishments covered by the "homestyle" exemption (subparagraph (A)) "has never been a significant source of revenue collection for CMOs". Especially in light of the 1998 amendments which further limited the scope of the "homestyle" exemption, the panel concluded that the potential effects of this exemption "are not of sufficient practical importance" to give rise to an "unreasonable level of prejudice to the legitimate interests of right holders".[163]

It should be borne in mind that the primary importance of TRIPS in the global trading order is not in disputes "on the socio-economic margin" between developed countries with traditionally similar levels of intellectual property protection. Under international political pressure, the US decided not to pursue a case of symbolic proportions, based on a complaint it filed against Brazil, and which led to the establishment of a WTO panel in February, 2001. At stake was a provision (Article 68) of Brazil's 1996 Industrial Property Law, which obliges the holder of a patent in Brazil to ensure that the subject matter of the patent is worked in Brazil, either by producing the good in Brazil, or by allowing the process to be used in Brazil. Where these terms are not met within three years of the issuing of the patent in question, the Brazilian government can issue compulsory licenses to allow parties in Brazil to use the patent, despite the opposition of the patent holder.[164] A further provision of the

---

[161] *Copyright Act* Panel Report, para. 6.227.
[162] *Copyright Act* Panel Report, paras. 6.237–6.265.
[163] *Copyright Act* Panel Report, para. 6.271.
[164] See *International Trade Reporter*, Vol. 18, No. 8, Bureau of National Affairs, Washington, at 320.

Brazilian law, Article 71, allows for compulsory licensing for production of drugs in Brazil in order to combat health crises.[165]

The language of TRIPS with respect to "exceptions to rights conferred" on patent holders is extremely guarded. Article 30 states that

"Members may provide exceptions to the exclusive rights conferred by a patent, provided that such exceptions do not unreasonably prejudice the legitimate interests of the patent owner, taking account of the legitimate interests of third parties".

Article 31, which discusses "other use without authorization" (including use by governments or third parties authorised by them), would presumably govern the Brazilian situation described above, and is also circumscribed. Where the use is allowed by a Member's law, "such use may only be permitted if, prior to such use, the proposed user has made efforts to obtain authorization from the right holder on reasonable commercial terms and conditions", and those efforts have not been successful. (Article 31(b))

This requirement can be waived in the case of "extreme emergency or in cases of public non-commercial use", Article 31(b) continues. The list of provisions to be "respected" also includes a requirement that "the right holder shall be paid adequate remuneration in the circumstances of each case, taking into account the economic value of the authorization". (Article 31(h)) This would seem to conflict with the concept of emergency use, but has not yet been interpreted in context; nor has the interaction of the provisions been explored.

The US publicly insisted that it was not challenging Brazil's Article 71, allowing for compulsory licensing in a health crisis. Rather, the US complaint focused on Article 68, which allows the Brazilian government to license local companies to manufacture a product not being used in Brazil by a foreign company/patent owner.[166] International health organisations expressed fears that the case could act as a brake on Brazil's impressive AIDS treatment plan, whereby locally produced AIDS-drugs were being provided without cost to poor citizens.[167] It was hoped, on the other hand, that Article 31 of TRIPS would be clarified to allow for local production of life-saving drugs in the face of a public health emergency.[168]

Such an outcome would have reflected awareness on the part of the WTO decision-making bodies of the increasingly organised opposition to this aspect of the TRIPS Agreement. In light of the special protections given to the pharmaceutical companies under Article 70.8, as discussed in connection with the Indian Pharmaceuticals case above, it is scarcely conceivable that the drafters of TRIPS intended a very generous reading to be given to Article 31(b),

---

[165] US Says Its Patent Complaint Does Not Target Brazilian Generic AIDS Drugs, *Agence France Presse* (Financial pages), 2 February 2001.

[166] *Ibid.*

[167] See *International Trade Reporter, supra* n. 164.

[168] For a discussion of the ambiguous nature of the exception provided for in Art. 31, see Sara M Ford, "Compulsory Licensing Provisions Under the TRIPS Agreement: Balancing Pills and Patents", (2000) 15 *American University International Law Review* 941.

although this original intention may come to be seen as irrelevant. Given the many and varied health crises in existence at any one time, it is extraordinary that a requirement of patentablity for "any inventions, whether products or processes, in all fields of technology", would have been inserted into a world-wide intellectual property agreement.[169]

A second major point of contention between developed and developing countries with respect to the TRIPS Agreement involves the matter of biodiversity and genetic engineering. Under Article 27 (Patentable Subject Matter), TRIPS allows members to

> "exclude from patentability: (a) diagnostic, therapeutic and surgical methods for the treatment of humans or animals; (b) plants and animals other than micro-organisms, and essentially biological processes for the production of plants or animals other than non-biological and microbiological processes. *However, Members shall provide for the protection of plant varieties either by patents or by an effective sui generis system or by any combination thereof*".

These provisions, along with the special protection afforded to "agricultural chemical" inputs in Article 70.8 (see discussion of pharmaceutical patents, above), caused enormous resistance to the conclusion of TRIPS among farmers in the developing world. The principal fear is that powerful multinational corporations in the developed world will be able to appropriate and patent valuable elements of bio-diversity from the developing world without providing compensation, while at the same time patenting, and rendering prohibitively expensive, other forms of vital agricultural ingredients, such as seeds and chemicals.

In another indication that the legal logic of the WTO may necessitate the integration of WTO with other sectors of law, India has tabled an elaborate proposal to integrate TRIPS with the 1992 Convention on Biological Diversity.[170] The core of India's proposal is that all commercial exploitation of innovations based on biological resources would only be allowed if the commercial benefits were shared with the country from which the biological resource came. The application process for an intellectual property right would also be required to indicate the biological source and country of origin for the underlying resource. This would constitute notification and provide an opportunity for interested persons to object to the granting of the right.

In an indication of European responsiveness to this issue, in early 2000, the European Patent Office withdrew a patent held by the US firm W R Grace, for a process to extract oil from the neem tree (for which the native habitat is India

---

[169] See TRIPS Art. 27(1); and the very few and narrow exceptions under Art. 27(3)(a) and (b).

Note that in April 2001, the secretariats of the World Health Organisation and the World Trade Organisation held a joint "workshop" on the issue of affordable drugs. With participation by a wide-ranging group of experts and representatives of organisations and NGOs, the fact of the meeting taking place is a clear reflection of the WTO's awareness that a public health crisis cannot be responded to in purely trade terms. It might also indicate a growing "inter-disciplinary" quality to global law.

[170] See Mark Kruger, "Harmonizing TRIPS and the CBD: A Proposal from India", (Winter 2001) 10 *Minnesota Journal of Global Trade* 169.

and Southeast Asia) for use as a plant pesticide. Responding to a complaint filed by developing world activists, a panel of the European Patent Office agreed with the group alleging that Grace had engaged in "bio-piracy", and decided that the patent granted in 1994 was characterised by a "lack of novelty". An Indian firm had long been using the oil for fungicidal purposes, and the tree had been traditionally used for a variety of purposes.[171] A number of US multinational companies have applied for patents based on plants found in the developing world, despite long-standing local reliance on such plants for their special qualities in medicine or agriculture.[172]

There is little question but that the inclusion of intellectual property standards at the WTO will encourage the ongoing development of a European Community-wide system of protection for intellectual property rights.[173] The larger question pertains to Europe's posture in the WTO's review of the functioning of the TRIPS Agreement to date. As has been well documented, the developed and developing worlds are far apart in their assessment of the fairness and validity of the Agreement.[174] While the developing countries are seeking to extend deadlines for full implementation, and to clarify and roll back requirements for essential pharmaceuticals and agricultural products, the position of the developed world thus far has been to advocate better and fuller implementation, without altering the original Agreement.

One extreme view is that TRIPS should be returned to the WIPO (its natural home) where countries can choose to participate in the major intellectual property conventions or not. Resistance by developing countries to full implementation of the existing rules cannot be dismissed as "compliance problems".[175] However, it is extremely unlikely that this first "minimum standards" agreement at the WTO would be relinquished so easily. Inclusion of full protection for copyright and trademark properties, despite having major financial implications for developing-world businesses, have not attracted a global outcry and are unlikely to be set aside, despite national failures to fully comply.

Speaking at a conference sponsored by Oxfam in March 2001, EU Trade Commissioner Pascal Lamy was quoted as saying that,

[171] See Kruger, *supra* n. 142, at 174–175; and "W.R. Grace's Neem-Related Patent Withdrawn", Europe Agri, 9 June 2000.

[172] At a WTO Council meeting in April 2001, the EC submitted a paper on the topic of the relationship between the Convention on Biological Diversity and the TRIPS Agreement, see WTO Doc. IP/C/W/254. While acknowledging the developing country point of view, Europe emphasises the need to seek solutions in the "appropriate international instruments", as opposed to the scope and nature of Art. 27.3(b) of TRIPS. See *Bridges Trade Weekly Digest*, Vol. 5, No. 13, 10 April 2001.

[173] For a discussion of the implications of the TRIPS Agreement for disparities between Member State intellectual property regimes; as well as for disparities between Community IP rules and TRIPS, see Talia Einhorn, "The Impact of the WTO Agreement on TRIPS on EC Law: A Challenge to Regionalism", (1998) 35:5 *Common Market Law Review*, 1069–1099.

[174] See Frederick Abbott, "TRIPS in Seattle: The Not-So-Surprising Failure and the Future of the TRIPS Agenda", (2000) 18 *Berkeley Journal of International Law* 165.

[175] For a discussion of compliance issues, see Adrian Otten, "Implementation of the TRIPS Agreement and Prospects for Its Further Development", (Dec 1998) 1:4 *Journal of International Economic Law* 523–536.

"[a]s I believe it is important to protect creativity and innovation, I support the TRIPS Agreement. I also support this Agreement as I believe it provides the requisite flexibility to allow developing countries to reconcile specific policy objectives in such areas as public health and biodiversity with IPR laws".

He continued,

"However, if it is felt that there are fundamental problems in implementing this flexibility, the EU is prepared to promote discussion, within the WTO and other relevant organizations, to address and resolve these difficulties".

This might be taken to mean that the EU's position will be to "promote" the concerns of the developing world in addressing the United States in particular, and co-operating with developing countries to remove some of the stringency from this most controversial of WTO agreements.

4

"Free Trade in Investments"

IN THE EARLY years of post-colonial freedom, it was considered by developing countries to be one of the principal attributes of sovereignty that a newly independent state could regulate conditions placed on inward direct investment from abroad. To a degree unknown in the post-debt crisis era,[1] developing countries in the 1970s insisted on restricting the "right" to make such investments, to ensure that they as host countries would also be genuine beneficiaries of the wealth they were helping to create for the developed world investors. To be sure, it was not only the developing countries that were interested in providing themselves with insurance that investments into their territory would prove an overall advantage; developed countries too maintained rules for investments, especially in key sectors. However, it was the newly independent states that most feared domination by the capital of the developed states.[2]

The topic of free trade in investments, which ultimately involves the legal rights of investors, must begin with the question of whether foreign direct investment is inherently positive in all its aspects.[3] For many years, developing countries pursued a policy of "import substitution", attempting to develop indigenous industries rather than becoming reliant on imports.[4] At the same time, there was a consciously pursued policy of the diverse economy, as opposed to the "export cash crop" model more common in the post-debt crisis world.[5]

The Uruguay Round Agreement on Trade Related Investment Measures (TRIMS) is the first global-level agreement to enhance the rights of investors,

---

[1] See Rajesh Swaminathan, "Regulating Development: Structural Adjustment and the Case for National Enforcement of Economic and Social Rights", (1998) 37 *Columbia Journal of Transnational Law* 161, describing the process by which developing countries fund themselves in the debt crisis, followed by demands for the implementation of "structural adjustment" programmes.

[2] It is common sense that inward investment involves both costs and benefits for the host country. See Eric M Burt, "Developing Countries and the Framework for Negotiations on Foreign Direct Investment in the World Trade Organization", (1997) 12 *American University Journal of International Law and Policy* 1015, 1022.

[3] See Kenneth J Vandevelde, "The Political Economy of a Bilateral Investment Treaty", 92 *American Journal of International Law* 621 (1998). Vandervelde writes at 623: ". . . economic nationalists do not in all cases favor or oppose foreign investment. Economic nationalists in developed and developing states may perceive international investment flows as beneficial in one case and detrimental in another".

[4] See John Rapley, *Understanding Development: Theory and Practice in the Third World* (Boulder, CO: Lynne Rienner Publishers, 1996).

[5] See Tim Lang and Colin Hines, *The New Protectionism* (New York: New Press, 1993), at 84–86, 135.

although its terms were not presented in this light.[6] As with the other Uruguay Round Agreements, its effectiveness is dependent upon its integration into the larger web of WTO obligations and dispute settlement mechanisms. Pre-1995 GATT contained no specific provision to deal with the question of freedom in investments, although the issue of how far a contracting party could go in placing restrictions by the host country on freedom to invest did arise in a dispute of the 1980s.[7]

THE FIRA CASE

This complaint was brought by the United States against Canada, at a time when Canada was fearful of losing control of its economic life to its much larger neighbour.[8] In December of 1973, Canada had enacted a Foreign Investment Review Act,[9] with the purpose of ensuring that acquisitions of control of large Canadian businesses, or the establishment of new businesses within Canada by non-Canadians should be reviewed, and only allowed to proceed if the government had determined that these businesses were likely to be of significant benefit to Canada.[10]

The Canadian authorities were to examine the consequences of the investment in Canada in the light of the following factors: effects on local employment, on resource processing, and on utilisation of parts, components and services produced in Canada and on the level of exports from Canada. In addition, there would be an examination of the degree of participation by Canadians in the proposed enterprise, as well as of the effects on productivity and technological development, and on product innovation in Canada. There would also be analysis of effects on competition within industries in Canada, and of the compatibility of the proposed project with national industrial and economic policies.[11] These national conditions are all, in fact, classic "trade related investment measures"—or "TRIMs".

Under FIRA, investors were encouraged, although not strictly required, to submit written undertakings on the conduct of the proposed business.[12] The undertakings themselves were generally the result of detailed negotiations

---

[6] For a complete discussion of the international law of foreign investments, see Thomas L Brewer and Stephen Young, *The Multilateral Investment System and Multinational Enterprises* (Oxford, OUP, 1998); see also Michael J Trebilcock and Robert Howse, *The Regulation of International Trade*, 2nd edn. (London: Routledge, 1999), 335–366.

[7] See Jackson, *The World Trading System*, 2nd edn. (Cambridge MA: MIT Press, 1997) 244.

[8] *Administration of the Foreign Investment Review Act (FIRA)*, (1984) BISD 30th Supp, 140 [hereinafter *FIRA* Panel Report].

[9] Can. Stat., ch. 46, 1973–1974 SC 619.

[10] See Robert E Hudec, *Enforcing International Trade Law: The Evolution of the Modern GATT Legal System* 170–72 (New Hampshire: Butterworth Legal Publishing, 1993).

[11] *FIRA* Panel Report, at 142–143.

[12] *FIRA* Panel Report, at 143–146.

between the Canadian government and the potential investor.[13] Investments that were approved continued to be monitored by the government, and the submission of progress reports based on these undertakings was often required. It was significant that the Canadian act, in theory, provided for the possibility of the government seeking a court order to require the investor to comply with the terms of the undertaking given. In fact, such an action had never been attempted by the authorities.[14]

The US argued that the administration of the Canadian law violated Article III: 4, Article III:5, and Article XI of the GATT Agreement.[15] In particular, the US focused on the fact that foreign investors were encouraged by the Canadian government to purchase goods of Canadian origin in preference to imported goods.[16] The Canadian rebuttal was a broad and theoretical one, with implications for the development of future GATT jurisprudence. The Canadians insisted that a nation's investment laws were outside the scope of the GATT, as such laws remained a matter for national sovereignty, not of free trade.[17] The US insisted that only the promise of a benefit—here, permission for the investment to proceed—could induce investors to commit to purchasing Canadian goods, even where these were less attractive from a commercial point of view.[18]

On the larger issue of whether or not the GATT could interfere with national regulation of foreign direct investment, the panel stated that the General Agreement did not prevent Canada from exercising its sovereign right to regulate such investment.[19] However, the panel decided to examine the legal implications of the *undertakings* accepted by the Canadian government under the Act.[20] At this stage in GATT history, it appears that this provided a means for the panel to avoid, on the one hand, making any startling statement about the relationship between the GATT Agreement and free trade in investments, while on the other hand placing national investment laws within the scope of a familiar GATT analysis.

The panel examined the US complaint concerning undertakings to purchase goods of Canadian origin in preference to imported goods, or in specified amounts or proportions, in the light of Article III:4.[21] It found that, since under the Canadian Act a court order could be sought directing the business to comply with its own undertaking, and because the undertaking became part of the

---

[13] During the relevant period, the vast majority of all applications for investment had in fact been approved by the Canadian authorities. Most but not all businesses provided undertakings as part of their application.

[14] *FIRA* Panel Report, at 145–146.

[15] *FIRA* Panel Report, at 146.

[16] *FIRA* Panel Report, at 147.

[17] *FIRA* Panel Report, at 148–150.

[18] *FIRA* Panel Report, at 148–149.

[19] *FIRA* Panel Report, at 157.

[20] *FIRA* Panel Report, at 158.

[21] *FIRA* Panel Report, at 158.

conditions under which the investment proposal had been accepted, these did constitute "requirements" as the term was used in Article III:4.[22]

The panel also found that undertakings to purchase goods of Canadian origin did exclude the possibility of purchasing other available products, such that imports were clearly treated less favourably than domestic products; and thus that such requirements were inconsistent with Article III:4.[23] So, while the panel rejected certain of the US arguments (relating to Article III:5 and Article XI), it did find a violation of Article III:4 due to the nature and effect of the undertakings. The panel did not accept the Canadian argument that the purchase undertakings fell within an Article XX(d) exception, for the "effective administration of the Foreign Investment Review Act".[24] The panel advised Canada to bring its administration of FIRA into line with its GATT obligations, and specifically to ensure that imported products were not being treated less favourably than domestic products.[25] The FIRA law was ultimately repealed.

Developing countries, traditionally sensitive about their national authority to set conditions for foreign investors to abide by, were unhappy that the case had been heard at the GATT at all, and considered the panel decision to represent a breach of important GATT subject matter limitations. In one sense, their unease was completely justified. By contrast, those who wished to push for an expansion of GATT law towards the liberalisation of investments were dissatisfied with the cautious approach taken by the panel.[26] Interestingly, while the original GATT granted no national rights with respect to establishment of investments, there had been an attempt to include investment concerns in the defunct International Trade Organisation (ITO) of the 1940s.[27] The ITO, of course, never came into being.

INTERNATIONAL INSTRUMENTS TO PROTECT INVESTMENTS BEFORE THE ADOPTION OF THE TRIMS AGREEMENT

Trade-related investment measures (TRIMS), as discussed above, are requirements imposed by host countries to influence the commercial decisions of foreign investors, in favour of certain socio-economic policies of the host country. TRIMS encompass a wide range of national measures, including local content requirements, to increase local procurement by investors, or export volume

---

[22] *FIRA* Panel Report, at 159–162.

[23] *FIRA* Panel Report, at 162.

[24] *FIRA* Panel Report, at 164–165.

[25] *FIRA* Panel Report, at 167–168.

[26] The panel itself very purposely stressed that its holding was not designed to protect the interests of foreign investors per se. In other words, although the ultimate decision was that the act was GATT-illegal, the panel in its reasoning attempted to keep the ruling from pushing the GATT beyond its familiar parameters of trade in *goods*.

[27] See Burt, *supra* n. 2, at 1028–1029.

requirements, designed to improve a country's balance of payments situation by bringing in foreign currency.[28]

TRIMS might take the form of establishment restrictions, operating requirements, personnel entry restrictions, or financial restrictions on the relationship between the investor and the investment (such as a cap on the amount of compensation to be paid in the event of a taking by the national government.) Where there have been establishment requirements, these have taken the form of absolute prohibitions on any foreign investment, prohibition on investment in certain sensitive sectors, or limits on the percentage of foreign ownership allowed. Financial restrictions are likely to include requirements concerning the ability of the investor to remit profits. The underlying TRIMs concept is that foreign investors will only be allowed to enter or remain, depending upon how well they help to fulfil the host country's national objectives.[29]

The rationale for bringing investments within the scope of the GATT/WTO is that local content and export requirements allegedly distort trade because they have the effect of injuring producers of goods either in the investor's home country or in a third country. TRIMs are said to weaken the GATT's central postulate of comparative advantage.[30] Until the Uruguay Round Agreement on Trade-Related Investment Measures (the TRIMS Agreement), to be explored below, there was no overarching international structure for regulating investment or the controls applied by individual nations to direct investment. The TRIMS Agreement is itself only considered to be a first step in the larger project of creating such a regime, as it is not overtly protective of *investors'* rights.[31] Before exploring the TRIMS Agreement, one should be aware of the complex web of bilateral investment agreements, and of the several investment instruments at OECD level.

BILATERAL INVESTMENT TREATIES (BITS) AND BILATERAL INVESTMENT PROTECTION AGREEMENTS (BIPAS)

Apart from economic pressure and exhortation, and compliance brought about by the workings of the debt crisis, the principal legal vehicle by which the developed world has sought to protect its investments in the developing world has been the bilateral investment treaty.[32] The precursor to these specialised

---

[28] See Trebilcock and Howse *supra* n. 6 (1999), 337–339.

[29] See Robert H Edwards, Jr. and Simon N Lester, "Towards a More Comprehensive World Trade Organization Agreement on Trade Related Investment Measures", (1997) 33 *Stanford Journal of International Law* 169, 172–74.

[30] See Todd S Shenkin, "Trade-Related Investment Measures in Bilateral Investment Treaties and the GATT: Moving Towards a Multilateral Investment Treaty", (1994) 55 *University of Pittsburgh Law Review* 541, 551.

[31] The TRIMS Agreement comes in for harsh criticism for its incompleteness, in Paul Civello, "The TRIMS Agreement: A Failed Attempt at Investment Liberalization", (1999) 8 *Minnesota Journal of Global Trade* 97.

[32] Brewer and Young, *supra* n. 5, at 74–78; Vandervelde, *supra* n. 2.

bilateral agreements was the "Treaty of Friendship, Commerce and Navigation", which originated in the late 18th century.[33] The underlying principle of these very early trade treaties was mutual non-discrimination with regard to trade in goods and the unhindered carrying out of business within each other's territories. In the realm of trade in goods, the original GATT Agreement superseded many aspects of these treaties through its principle of multilateralism.

With regard to rules for foreign direct investment, however, the FCN treaties of an earlier era were taken over by the so-called bilateral investment protection agreements (or BIPAs) between the European states and other countries, many in the developing world, and the bilateral investment treaties (BITs) between the United States and other countries.[34] As will be shown below, the TRIMS Agreement was the first multilateral agreement on this subject, transcending bilateralism and involving both the developed and developing world. OECD agreements on investment have been limited by the nature of OECD membership.[35]

In the late 1950s, individual European countries began negotiating a very successful series of treaties called Bilateral Investment Protection Agreements, the first treaties to be devoted exclusively to the problems inherent in direct investment abroad. They were, as indicated, most significant with respect to the investment relationship with developing countries, since investor problems are more likely to arise in a less certain political environment. As a general rule, these treaties guarantee reciprocal equality of treatment with regard to maintenance of investments by individuals or corporations. For the most part, BIPAs did not provide national treatment or MFN with regard to investment *establishment* conditions. Thus, under the BIPA regimes, host countries were still permitted to screen foreign investments and impose performance requirements as the price of establishing an operation within the national territory.[36]

BIPAs were notable for having placed a limit on the ability of the host country to nationalise the operation represented by the investment, in that under these agreements nationalisation must be for a public purpose, be non-discriminatory and provide for full compensation to the investor for the loss. Most BIPAs call for dispute resolution through arbitration at the International Centre for Settlement of Investment Disputes (ICSID), the principal forum for hearing investment issues arising between investors and the host countries.[37] As

---

[33] See Kenneth J Vandevelde, United States Investment Treaties: Policy and Practice (Deventer; Boston: Kluwer Law and Taxation, 1992 edn.), 19–22.

[34] See Shenkin, *supra* n. 30, at 545–550.

[35] For a discussion of OECD activity in the area of inward investment, see Thomas L Brewer and Stephen Young, *The Multilateral Investment System and Multinational Enterprises* (Oxford: OUP, 1998) at 92–96.

[36] Shenkin, *supra* n. 32, at 574–575.

[37] The ICSID was created in 1966 with a view to relieving the World Bank of its responsibility of acting as mediators in investment-related disputes. The Bank's idea was that a specialised institution to facilitate the settlement of investment disputes between host governments and foreign investors could help promote such investment around the world. The agreement establishing the ICSID has been ratified by approximately 130 countries. All ICSID member countries must recognise and

of 1992, European states had over 400 individual BIPA treaties with developed, developing and former non-market states around the world.

The US began a programme of bilateral investment treaties in the early 1980s, long after the development of the European version. The main objectives of the US "BITs" paralleled those of the European BIPAs, especially with regard to protecting existing investments. Full compensation for nationalisation or other expropriation was a prominent feature of most BITs.[38] Dispute resolution is also through the "depoliticised" forum of the ICSID.

The American BITs are considered to go somewhat further than the European BIPAs, in that they often require national treatment with respect to establishment. However, BITs will routinely have an annex listing areas excluded from such commitments; for instance, national security-related industries, utilities, communications and banking. There is substantial variety in the level of obligation called for in individual BITs and BIPAs.

Before these treaties came into general use, investment disputes had been settled at diplomatic level, which was considered to be too high profile and too fraught with political considerations. It is interesting to note that some commentators feel that the WTO will eventually have to allow the direct participation of individual economic players, rather than relying on a country-to-country approach, as is the case now. This is especially true as the line between large corporate interests and the interests of governments becomes increasingly unclear.

THE OECD AND INVESTMENTS

The Organisation for Economic Co-operation and Development (OECD) is based in Paris and has 30 members from among the industrialised nations, with the EU Member States individual members in their own right. Countries "qualify" for OECD membership depending upon their level of development and wealth, and the OECD now includes, in addition to all the Member States of the EU, the US, Canada, Switzerland, Japan, Turkey, Australia, Norway, Mexico, Korea and Iceland, among others. Established in 1961 as a successor to the postwar Organisation of European Economic Co-operation, its aims were and are to promote economic growth, trade, and financial stability. It guards the interests of its developed country membership on the world stage, and generates numerous legal instruments designed to enhance trade liberalisation, at least within the club of developed nations.

The OECD investment framework is built around two codes binding on its members, as well as a declaration, dating from the 1970s.[39] The two binding

enforce ICSID arbitral awards. Most investment contracts between host governments and foreign investors refer specifically to the centre, as do many bilateral investment treaties between governments. It is important to note that dispute settlement is not confined to nation states, and that the bulk of settlements would involve aggrieved investors and host country governments.

[38] Shenkin, *supra* n. 32, at 576–582.
[39] Brewer and Young, *supra* n. 5, at 73–74; Trebilcock and Howse, *supra* n. 6, 356–357

instruments are the Code of Liberalisation of Capital Movements and the Code of Liberalisation of Current Invisible Operations. The Declaration on International Investment and Multinational Enterprises calls for national treatment in laws and regulations pertaining to inward investment.[40] The ultimate aim of the codes is expressed as follows: "That residents of different member countries should be as free to transact business with each other as are residents of a single country". While the codes are "binding" on members, it is important to recognise that the OECD system as a whole lacks formal dispute resolution mechanisms.

Under the Capital Movements Code, members are required to "progressively abolish . . . restrictions on movements of capital to the extent necessary for effective economic co-operation".[41] Members are allowed to invoke specific exemptions, and may also require reciprocity in some areas. The general undertaking (Article 1) is to "treat all non-resident owned assets in the same way irrespective of the date of their formation", and "to permit the liquidation of all non-resident owned assets and the transfer of such assets or of their liquid proceeds". Members are to avoid introducing new restrictions on the movement of capital. There are opt-outs for public order and essential security interests,[42] as well as for times of national economic and financial disturbance.[43]

The Invisibles Code[44] is mainly concerned with service businesses and financial transactions. It requires members to eliminate all restrictions on specified "invisible operations" of other members.[45] Operations covered include business and industry, trade, transport, insurance, films, tourism, advertising, professional services and registration of patents and trademarks. All OECD states maintain exceptions, notably in the insurance and transport sectors. The Code also calls for freedom to transfer profits, and freedom for transactions underlying the transfer of funds.[46] Under this code, as well, there are broad derogations permitted for public order, morals and security interests.[47]

Because the OECD provides no clear enforcement mechanism, effective legal penalties for non-compliance are non-existent. The OECD system works rather on a system of notification, consultation and ultimately shared interests. There is an oversight committee established for trade in investments. It is ironic that the OECD is active in this area, to the extent that the OECD member countries

[40] The OECD attempted something far more ambitious in the infamous Multilateral Agreement on Investment negotiations which collapsed in 1998 when the French government stated that it would no longer participate. For more on the aims and intentions of the MAI, which drew an extraordinary level of fire from community groups around the world, see discussion *infra*.

[41] OECD, Code of Liberalisation of Capital Movements, at Art. 1(a) [hereinafter Capital Movements Code].

[42] Capital Movements Code, at Art. 3.

[43] Capital Movements Code, at Art. 7.

[44] OECD, Code of Liberalisation of Current Invisible Operations [hereinafter Current Invisible Operations Code].

[45] Current Invisible Operations Code, at Art. 1.

[46] Current Invisible Operations Code, at Art. 1.

[47] Current Invisible Operations Code, at Art. 3.

already have comparatively liberal investment regimes, whereas the OECD countries are continually looking to achieve greater liberalisation for investment in non-OECD countries. As will be explored with regard to the failed Multilateral Agreement on Investment (MAI), it may be that the OECD's main function is to set out the conceptual framework for later global initiatives, and to demonstrate broad prior consensus among the world's major trading powers.

MULTILATERAL LIBERALISATION OF INVESTMENT REGIMES: THE TRIMS AGREEMENT

While TRIMs are most prevalent in certain industrial sectors in the developing world—especially automobiles, mining, machinery and equipment—most developed countries also rely on at least some TRIMs. The most common TRIM in developed countries is the local content requirement. The computer, information and telecommunication sectors have all been characterised by the extensive use of TRIMs. TRIMs are obviously of greatest concern to multi-national corporations large enough to shop for hospitable countries in which to locate their investments.

With the Uruguay Round Agreement on Trade Related Investment Measures (TRIMs Agreement), one sees introduced into global trade jurisprudence a more overt concern with the interests of the international investor than had been possible at the time of the FIRA case.[48] However, the agreement is sometimes criticised as little more than a codification of the FIRA ruling, in that its ultimate intention of facilitating investors remains obscured behind a stated concern for the effect of TRIMs on the free flow of goods in international trade. While the agreement is undoubtedly a major departure in extending the scope of GATT/WTO law to enhance the freedom of investors, it is generally perceived as a mere opening salvo.

Of all the Uruguay Round Agreements, the TRIMs Agreement is one of the most readable and direct; this conceptual departure is only about four pages long. Stating that WTO members recognise "that certain investment measures can cause trade-restrictive and distorting effects", the agreement makes clear that its scope is investment measures related to trade in goods only.[49] The Agreement refers the TRIMs issue back to the basic provisions of the GATT Agreement, stating that "no member shall apply any TRIM that is inconsistent with the provisions of Article III (national treatment) or Article XI (quantitative restrictions) of GATT 1994".[50]

The next section of the same article explains how this connection is to be effected. An annex to the TRIMs Agreement provides an illustrative (thus, non-exhaustive) list of TRIMs, which are to be *deemed* inconsistent with these two

---

[48] Trebilcock and Howse *supra* n. 6, 349–353; Brewer and Young, *supra* n. 5, at 124–125.
[49] Agreement on Trade-Related Investment Measures, Preamble [hereinafter TRIMs].
[50] TRIMs, Art. 2.

GATT articles. The annex states that TRIMs considered inconsistent with Article III: 4 on national treatment are the required purchase or use of products of domestic origin (either particular products, or volume or value of products, or a proportion of the local production, or a limitation on use of imported products as related to the volume of local product being exported). This "illustrative list" of certain types of TRIMs has the effect of creating per se violations of Article III:4.[51]

The annex also sets out the sort of TRIMs to be deemed inconsistent with the Article XI obligation of general elimination of quantitative restrictions.[52] These are TRIMs which restrict to a certain set amount the importation of a product used in the investment operation; or which restrict the importation of products through restricting the access of an enterprise to foreign exchange; or restricting the export of products either by type or volume. (The latter technique would decrease the "space" on the domestic market for competing products.)

The agreement allows developing countries to deviate from these rules for purposes of balance of payments problems, at least to the extent that they are allowed to deviate from Article III and XI of the GATT under those circumstances.[53]

The agreement also requires members to inform the Council for Trade in Goods within 90 days of entry into force of the WTO Agreement of any TRIMs not in conformity with the TRIMs Agreement.[54] All such TRIMs are to be eliminated within two years of the WTO Agreement coming into force in the case of developed countries; and within five years for developing countries, with seven years phase-in to be given to the least developed members.[55] Where special difficulties are demonstrated by developing countries, the Council may extend the transition period.[56]

During the transition period, TRIMs are not to be made more inconsistent with the basic obligations of the agreement.[57] No TRIM introduced within 180 days of the coming into force of the agreement may benefit from the transitional arrangements.[58] As with most of the Uruguay Round agreements, the TRIMs Agreement establishes a specialised committee to be open to all members, to facilitate consultations and to monitor the implementation of the agreement. Disputes are, as would be expected, to be settled under the DSU.[59]

The final article of the agreement may not strike the reader as significant; however, it may have major implications for the future of international investments. It states that within five years of the coming into force of the WTO Agreement, the Council for Trade in Goods is to review the operation of the

---

[51]   TRIMs, Art. 2:1.
[52]   TRIMs, Art. 2:2.
[53]   TRIMs, Art. 4.
[54]   TRIMs, Art. 5.
[55]   TRIMs, Art. 5:2.
[56]   TRIMs, Art. 5:3.
[57]   TRIMs, Art. 5:4.
[58]   TRIMs, Art. 5:4.
[59]   TRIMs, Art. 7.

Agreement and to propose amendments to its text. "In the course of this review", the provision continues, "the Council for Trade in Goods shall consider whether the agreement should be complemented with provisions on investment policy and competition policy".[60] The question of which members and which forces are actively seeking to develop the WTO in the direction of these expanded subject areas (and by contrast, which are seeking to restrain such extensions) has everything to do with the future of the world trading system.

EXPORT SUBSIDIES LAW DOVETAILS WITH TRIMS

The subject of export subsidies may seem quite separate from that of TRIMs. However, it is no longer possible to assume that the problem of export subsidies is confined to subsidies offered to national companies on national soil, and certain subsidies may be made available by the host country to investors making specified business decisions—such as purchasing a particular amount of local product from the host country. Indeed, the Uruguay Round Agreement on Subsidies and Countervailing Measures (the SCM or Subsidies Agreement),[61] which continued the general trend in GATT law in making it more difficult for countries to subsidise exports, also contained crossover provisions on TRIM-like subsidies. The Agreement targets certain subsidies typically offered by host countries to companies controlled by *foreign* investors on the soil of the subsidy granting state, in legal terms treating some TRIMs as export subsidies, and thus extending the reach of anti-TRIMs law while at the same time enhancing subsidies law.[62]

GATT/WTO subsidies law will be dealt with in detail in a separate section of this study. However, before moving on to the first major dispute involving the TRIMs Agreement, it is necessary to understand how measures that fall most comfortably under the rubric of "TRIMs" were shared between the TRIMs and Subsidies Agreements.

---

[60] TRIMs, Art. 9. See WTO, Minutes of the Meeting of the Council for Trade in Goods held 24 January 2000, at http://www.wto.org, wherein it was noted that the Council for Trade in Goods had formally opened the Review of the Operation of the TRIMs Agreement on 15 October 1999. The US representative pointed out that the WTO was separately pursuing a work programme in trade and competition. Developed and developing countries were divided over the question of whether or not the TRIMs standards should be eased, with the US in particular insisting that the review should not lead to a lowering of standards established in the TRIMs Agreement.

It is significant that at the same Council meeting, a substantial number of developing countries made requests for extensions of time for phasing out TRIMs that had been notified to the WTO.

[61] See Agreement on Subsidies and Countervailing Measures [hereinafter Subsidies Agreement].

[62] Art. 3 of the Subsidies Agreement describes "prohibited subsidies" as follows: "Except as provided in the Agreement on Agriculture, the following subsidies, within the meaning of Art. 1, shall be prohibited: (a) subsidies contingent, in law or in fact, whether solely or as one of several other conditions, upon export performance, including those illustrated in Annex I; (b) subsidies contingent, whether solely or as one of several other conditions, upon the use of domestic over imported goods. A Member shall neither grant nor maintain subsidies referred to in paragraph 1".

From its inception, the GATT had difficulty in completely outlawing subsidies granted by contracting parties to exporting industries, in particular in the realm of primary products.[63] Participating countries have been extremely inventive in finding ways, through taxation and other programmes, to provide the most favourable possible conditions for their exporting companies. Under Article XVI, GATT law prohibited export subsidies on manufactured goods, and restricted their use for the promotion of exports of primary products. However, in subsidies as in dumping, the primary role of GATT seemed to be in preventing countries applying countervailing duties (and anti-dumping duties) from using these as protectionist devices.

The new Subsidies Agreement (SCM) deals with two essential areas of concern: categorising subsidies in light of their trade effects, and creating rules for the imposition of countervailing duties on unlawfully subsidised products.[64] Prohibition or restriction on certain kinds of subsidies had remained undeveloped within the GATT, with more detailed emphasis on the question of what constitutes a proportional response (in the form of a countervailing duty) to the subsidies of others. The new Subsidies Agreement clearly identified impermissible export subsidies, and consequently provides clear causes of action to challenge damaging subsidies. WTO members thus have available to them more direct and effective remedies than were available under the old GATT system.

The Subsidies Agreement creates three categories of subsidies (green light, yellow light and red light), green light subsidies being allowed as not damaging to trade; yellow light actionable in certain circumstances, and red light subsidies prohibited.[65] To be prohibited or actionable, or to invite a countervailing duty, a subsidy must be specific, which essentially means that access to the subsidy must be limited; it must not be generally available to all industries.[66]

It is significant that the "prohibited subsidies" are those which are "contingent upon export performance; or those contingent upon the use of domestic over imported goods". While this could refer to a situation where a national government was offering a subsidy to its own industry, it could just as likely refer to a situation where the subsidy involved a TRIM; that is, some form of preference to be given to an industry placed in the territory of the subsidy-giving state by a foreign investor, a subsidy contingent on that investor granting preferential treatment to domestic (host country) goods and services, or attaining a certain level of exports. It is again noteworthy that this type of subsidy alone is "prohibited", and that special expedited remedies are available to respond to it.[67]

Next in the hierarchy of subsidies are those, which are "actionable". These subsidies can be the target of a legal action at the WTO if they cause injury to

---

[63] See GATT, Art. XVI, Section B.

[64] Subsidies Agreement, Arts. 3–9, 10–23.

[65] Subsidy is defined as a financial contribution by a government or public body within the territory of the member, where there is a transfer of funds, or government revenue is foregone, or the government provides goods or services, or where there is income or price support.

[66] Subsidies Agreement, Art. 2.

[67] Subsidies Agreement, Arts. 3–4.

domestic industry, nullification or impairment of benefit, or serious prejudice to the interests of another member.[68] Serious prejudice is further defined, in a section enumerating circumstances in which this will be deemed to have occurred.[69]

The agreement next treats *non*-actionable subsidies, the green light type of subsidy. These exist where the subsidy was not specific, or where the subsidy was aimed at such objectives as research and development, regional aid, environmental adaptation, or similarly benign types of official assistance. There is a truncated form of dispute settlement available where a member feels that a subsidy meeting the "non-actionable" criteria is nevertheless causing "serious adverse effects to domestic industry".[70] The next section of the agreement contains the rules for determining the countervailing duties to be placed on unlawfully subsidised products, and will be treated in a later section of this study.

The Subsidies Agreement also contains an important section on special treatment to be granted to developing countries with regard to the new subsidy rules.[71] The agreement acknowledges that subsidies "may play an important role in economic development programmes".[72] Not surprisingly, the precise nature of the different and special treatment for developing countries is couched in imprecise terms. The "prohibition" in prohibited subsidies does not apply at all to the least developed countries; nor to other developing countries for a period of eight years, subject to compliance with provisions requiring them to phase out their export subsidies over the eight years.[73] Export subsidies are not to be increased during that period. Where countries have reached "export competitiveness" based on an analysis of their world market share in a product, the possibilities for continuing to apply export subsidies are much less generous.[74]

Article 27.7 is extremely important in the dispute context, in that it states that where these conditions are met, the provision on remedies against prohibited subsidies shall not apply; rather, the relevant remedies will be those attaching to "actionable subsidies". In other words, in the case of developing countries availing themselves of the transition, they will not be subject to the rigours of a complaint seeking remedies under the "prohibited subsidies" section; rather, what would otherwise be *prohibited* subsidies will be treated for the purposes of an action against a developing country as actionable subsidies. This means that harm or serious prejudice would have to be clearly shown by the complainant to be the result of the subsidy. Thus, the "automatic proscription" implications

---

[68] The agreement specifically removes agricultural subsidies from the scope of the agreement, referring us to Art. 13 of the specialized Agreement on Agriculture.

[69] Subsidies Agreement, Arts. 5–7.

[70] Subsidies Agreement, Arts. 8–9.

[71] See Part VIII, Art. 27.

[72] Subsidies Agreement, Art. 27.1.

[73] Subsidies Agreement, Art. 27.2, 3.

[74] Subsidies Agreement, Art. 27.5.

of the prohibited subsidies section would not apply to developing countries for the relevant transition period.[75]

In a further gesture of goodwill towards developing countries, but one which makes a complicated legal situation even more so, actionable subsidies other than those which cover operating losses or involve more than 5 per cent ad valorem of the industry, may not be responded to under the remedies section of the "actionable subsidies" unless nullification or impairment are found to exist so as to displace or impede imports into the market of the subsidising country, or unless there is injury to the domestic industry of an importing country.[76] In other words, the evidentiary burden for countries taking action against developing countries under the section on remedies for actionable subsidies is substantially higher. We will see in the Indonesian Automobile case what the exact nature of that evidentiary burden is.

INVESTING IN INDONESIA'S AUTOMOBILE INDUSTRY

The first major TRIMs dispute to be decided at the WTO[77] was indicative of the political issues underlying the adoption of the agreement. It also presented a stark example of the purposes behind those sections of the Subsidies Agreement, which can be applied to what would normally be thought of as TRIMs issues.

The action was brought against Indonesia by the US, EC and Japan.[78] All three complainants had grievances relating to Indonesia's development of a so-called "national car production program", which it had created through a combination of financial incentives, investment restrictions, and selective protectionism. Indonesia is the type of developing country of greatest interest to the developed world for inward investment purposes; with a huge pool of inexpensive labour, and at the same time a massive potential market for the products of the investment. Indonesia, in common with countries like Brazil, has also been extremely concerned with maintaining control over key industries such as automobile production, and determined to screen investments in key sectors for their conformity with national industrial policies.

The Indonesian measures challenged included a 1993 Incentive System, mainly duty relief on imports of auto parts and subparts based on the local content of the finished product; also, exemption from or reduction of luxury sales

---

[75] In a further softening of the rules towards developing countries, Art. 27.8 states that there will be no presumption of serious prejudice as described in Art. 6, para. 1 of the Agreement where the defendant country is a developing country; rather, such prejudice will be required to be proven by positive evidence.

[76] Subsidies Agreement, Art. 27.9.

[77] *US, EC and Japan v. Indonesia: Certain Measures Affecting the Automobile Industry*, Report of the Panel, 2 July 1998 (WT/DS54, 55, 59, 64/R) [hereinafter *Indonesian Automobile Industry Panel Report*].

[78] Japan was involved in fewer legal issues overall, but since all three complaints were heard by the same panel, this study will not attempt to separate out which parties emphasised which issues.

tax for certain categories of motor vehicles.[79] A 1996 National Car Program also gave a special status to car companies meeting criteria as to national ownership of facilities, with benefits including exemption from luxury taxes on sales and from import duties for parts.[80] Other elements of the National Car Program involved preferential loans.[81]

Indonesia's legal strategy in this case is noteworthy. As will be shown, Indonesia made a judgement that it would have an easier time defending its position under the Subsidies Agreement than under the TRIMs Agreement, because of the extra burden of proof on complainants challenging developing countries' "TRIM-like subsidies". This is a theme that pervades Indonesia's legal position in the case.[82]

The first major issue raised by the complainants was that of the car programme's "local content requirement". They alleged that linking sales tax benefits to cars incorporating a certain percentage (in value) of domestic product, and granting customs duty benefits for imported parts used in cars incorporating a certain percentage of domestic product violated Article III:4 of the GATT Agreement and Article 2 of the TRIMs Agreement (stating that no member shall apply any TRIM in a manner inconsistent with GATT Articles III and XI). There was a further argument that differential tax benefits violate Article III:2 of the GATT Agreement. Article I:1 of the GATT agreement was said to be violated by these tax and customs duty differentials, in that Korean companies willing to comply with the terms of Indonesia's national programme were gaining unfair advantages.

The complainants alleged "serious prejudice" as a result of the Indonesian subsidies; serious prejudice as described in Article 6 of the Subsidies Agreement.[83] In addition, the complainants stated that Indonesia had extended existing subsidies in violation of the Subsidies Agreement (Article 28). The US made several innovative arguments under the TRIPs Agreement (Article 65.5), regarding problems in acquiring and maintaining trademarks under the national car programme. As indicated, Indonesia attempted to convince the

---

[79] *Indonesian Automobile Industry* Panel Report, paras. 2.4–2.32.

[80] *Indonesian Automobile Industry* Panel Report, paras. 2.33–2.41.

[81] *Indonesian Automobile Industry* Panel Report, paras. 2.42–2.44.

[82] The case begins with a tussle over whether or not Indonesia should be allowed to be represented before the panel by private lawyers. In light of the fact that developing countries were allowed to rely on private counsel in the *EC Banana* case, Indonesia was allowed to choose whatever counsel it saw fit, including private lawyers. Indonesian Automobile Industry Panel Report, paras. 14.1–14.2.

[83] Art. 6(3) of the Subsidies Agreement reads as follows: "Serious prejudice in the sense of paragraph (C) of Art. 5 may arise in any case where one or several of the following apply: (a) the effect of the subsidy is to displace or impede the imports of a like product of another Member into the market of the subsidizing Member; (b) the effect of the subsidy is to displace or impede the exports of a like product of another member from a third country market; (c) the effect of the subsidy is a significant price undercutting by the subsidized product as compared with the price of a like product of another member in the same market or significant price suppression, price depression or lost sales in the same market; (d) the effect of the subsidy is an increase in the world market share of the subsidizing Member in a particular primary product or commodity as compared to the average share it had during the previous period of three years and this increase follows a consistent trend over a period when subsidies have been granted".

panel that the dispute was covered exclusively by the Subsidies Agreement, and thus that the other arguments relating to Article III of the GATT Agreement, and to the TRIMs Agreement should not be raised in this case.[84]

On this initial point, the panel pointed out that there is a presumption in WTO law against conflict within the various GATT/WTO instruments. The panel noted that both the GATT's Article III on national treatment and its Article XVI on subsidies and countervailing measures have been part of the GATT since its inception.[85] As to whether the dispute can be covered by both the Subsidies Agreement and the TRIMs Agreement, the panel stated "In the case of the TRIMs Agreement, what is prohibited are TRIMs in the form of local content requirements, not the grant of an advantage, such as a subsidy".[86] It went on to rule that the two agreements may have "overlapping coverage" in that they may simultaneously apply to a single legislative act, but as they have "different foci" they impose different types of obligation.[87] The panel described the obligations contained in the agreements as "cumulative", such that different aspects of the same national measure can be the objects of challenge under various WTO provisions.

Causes of action under the trims agreement: local content requirements linked to tax and customs duty breaks

The complainants pointed to the TRIMs annex list of measures that are to be considered inconsistent with Article III of the GATT. Indonesia made the interesting argument that, while its subsidies may at times indirectly affect the investment decisions of the recipient of a subsidy, these decisions "are not the object, but rather the unintended result of the subsidy".[88] Indonesia continued to insist that these subsidies had not been adopted as investment regulations.

However, the panel rejected this characterisation, saying that it was incorrect to limit the concept of TRIMs only to measures taken explicitly in regard to foreign investment. The TRIMs Agreement, the panel explained, is not concerned with subsidies as such, but with local content requirements, compliance with which may be encouraged through providing any type of advantage.[89] The panel noted that statements taken from official depictions of the national car programme indicated an intention to strengthen domestic industrial development through the contested measures.[90] Thus in the panel's view, the measures

---

[84] See *Indonesian Automobile Industry* Panel Report, paras. 14.26–14.27.

[85] *Indonesian Automobile Industry* Panel Report, paras. 14.28–14.36. The panel states, "This implies that the drafters of GATT 1947 intended these two sets of provisions to be complementary".

[86] *Indonesian Automobile Industry* Panel Report, para. 14.50.

[87] *Indonesian Automobile Industry* Panel Report, paras. 14.47–14.55.

[88] *Indonesian Automobile Industry* Panel Report, para. 14.70.

[89] *Indonesian Automobile Industry* Panel Report, para. 14.73.

[90] In the panel's interesting formulation: "On the basis of our reading of these measures applied by Indonesia under the 1993 and 1996 car programs, which have investment features and which refer

fell within "any reasonable interpretation of the term investment measures".[91] The panel insisted that with regard to the problem of whether to characterise a measure as an *investment* measure, the analysis must centre on the manner in which a measure relates to investment.

Crucially, it did not matter to the panel whether the host country considers the measures to be TRIMs or something else, such as subsidies. The TRIMs Agreement, the panel said, does not say that a measure is not an investment measure simply because the member in question does not classify it as such, or simply because it is not specifically adopted as an investment measure.[92] As to whether or not the measures are "trade related", local content requirements by definition favour the use of domestic over imported products, and thus, in the panel's view, affect trade.[93] The Indonesian insistence on investor compliance with provisions for the purchase of domestic origin products in order to obtain benefits was just the sort of measure referred to in Item 1(a) of the "Illustrative List of TRIMs", annexed to the TRIMs Agreement.[94] And on the question of whether the tax and duty benefits were "advantages" as required by the chapeau to the Illustrative List of TRIMs, the panel stated that of course they were, and that the Indonesian measures do violate Article 2.1 of the TRIMs Agreement.[95]

Sales tax discrimination as an Article III:2 (GATT) violation

Indonesia continued to try to maintain the focus on the "subsidies" aspect of its programme.[96] It argued that there was a conflict between Article III:2 of GATT and the Subsidies Agreement, and that to apply Article III:2 to what were really subsidies would reduce the Subsidies Agreement to an "inutility". Continuing this theme, Indonesia said that the Subsidies Agreement "explicitly authorises" WTO members to provide subsidies that would be prohibited if evaluated under Article III:2 of the GATT.[97] (In effect that the Subsidies Agreement allows measures in the form of subsidies that might otherwise be prohibited by the terms of Article III:2.)

---

to investment programs, we find that these measures are aimed at encouraging the development of a local manufacturing capacity for finished motor vehicle and parts . . . in Indonesia. [T] hese measures necessarily have a significant impact on investment in these sectors".

[91] *Indonesian Automobile Industry* Panel Report, para. 14.80.
[92] *Indonesian Automobile Industry* Panel Report, para. 14.81.
[93] *Indonesian Automobile Industry* Panel Report, para. 14.82.
[94] *Indonesian Automobile Industry* Panel Report, para. 14.88.
[95] *Indonesian Automobile Industry* Panel Report, para. 14.91. The panel pointed out that such violations may be justified under Art. 3,4, or 5 of TRIMs, including the possible 5-year phase-in period for developing countries. Indonesia had not attempted to mount any such defences.
  Also, because TRIMs violations are based by reference on violations of Art. III (or XI) of the GATT Agreement, the panel did not bother to proceed to carry out an Art. III analysis, citing judicial economy.
[96] *Indonesian Automobile Industry* Panel Report, para. 14.97.
[97] *Indonesian Automobile Industry* Panel Report, para. 14.98.

The panel remained adamantly opposed to this sort of logic, refusing to view the various GATT/WTO legal instruments as the sort of cross-referential legal melange advocated by Indonesia.[98] Article III:2 is concerned with discriminatory taxes; not with subsidies. So it was the panel's view that the Subsidies Agreement and Article III:2 may be concerned with different aspects of the same legislation; an identical position to the Panel's analysis of the relationship between subsidies and TRIMs.[99]

To establish an Article III:2, first sentence, violation, it must be shown that imported products are taxed in excess of domestic like products.[100] Indonesia did not dispute the fact that it taxed imported cars at higher rates than domestic cars. The panel found sufficient similarity between at least some of the imported and domestic cars to say that they were "like" products for purposes of Article III:2.[101] The higher tax resulted, according to the panel, only because of product origin or because of lack of sufficient local content. The panel stated that "In our view, such an origin-based distinction in respect of internal taxes suffices in itself to violate Article III:2".[102] The Panel further ruled that the Indonesian programmes violated Article III:2, second sentence, since any directly competitive car (as opposed to a "like" product) would be taxed differently as well, so as to afford protection to domestic production.[103]

---

[98] *Indonesian Automobile Industry* Panel Report, para. 14.98. The panel stated: ". . . Whether or not the Subsidies Agreement is considered generally to 'authorise' members to provide actionable subsidies so long as they do not cause adverse effects to the interests of another member, the Subsidies Agreement clearly does not authorise members to impose discriminatory product taxes".

[99] *Indonesian Automobile Industry* Panel Report, para. 14.99.

[100] *Indonesian Automobile Industry* Panel Report, para. 14.107.

[101] *Indonesian Automobile Industry* Panel Report, paras. 14.110–14.111.

[102] *Indonesian Automobile Industry* Panel Report, paras. 14.113–14114.

[103] *Indonesian Automobile Industry* Panel Report, paras. 14.115–14.117. Art. III:2 of the General Agreement states that "The products of the territory of any contracting party imported into the territory of any other contracting party shall not be subject, directly or indirectly, to internal taxes or other internal charges of any kind in excess of those applied, directly or indirectly, to like domestic products. Moreover, no contracting party shall otherwise apply internal taxes or other internal charges to imported or domestic products in a manner contrary to the principles set forth in paragraph 1". And *Art. III* explains that "A tax conforming to the requirements of the first sentence of paragraph 2 would be considered to be inconsistent with the provisions of the second sentence only in cases where competition was involved between, on the one hand, the taxed product and, on the other hand, a directly competitive or substitutable product which was not similarly taxed". See also the Report of the Appellate Body in *Canada, EC and US* v. *Japan: Taxes on Alcoholic Beverages*, issued 4 October 1996, adopted 1 November 1996 (WT/DS8/AB/R, WT/DS10/AB/R, WT/DS11/AB/R) From H (2)(a): "If imported and domestic products are not 'like products' for the narrow purposes of Art. III:2, first sentence, then they are not subject to the strictures of that sentence and there is no inconsistency with the requirements of that sentence. However, depending on their nature, and depending on the competitive conditions in the relevant market, those same products may well be among the broader category of 'directly competitive or substitutable products' that fall within the domain of Art. III:2, second sentence. How much broader that category of 'directly competitive or substitutable products' may be in any given case is a matter for the panel to determine based on all the relevant facts in that case."

CLAIMS OF MFN VIOLATIONS

It has been noted that certain Korean companies supplying cars and car parts were able to avail themselves of sales tax and customs duty exemptions where the parent companies complied with the terms of the Indonesian car programme. The panel took as its task under the MFN analysis to determine whether the advantages accorded to "national" cars and components from Korea were also unconditionally accorded to the products of other WTO members, as required by Article I.[104]

The panel said of the special arrangements entered into between Indonesia and the Korean manufacturers that the rights of WTO members could not be made dependent or conditional upon any private contractual obligations in place.[105] The existence of such conditions, the panel continued, was inconsistent with Article I:1 of the GATT Agreement, which requires that tax and customs duty benefits accorded to one member be accorded immediately and unconditionally to all other members.[106] Under the car programme, the discrimination is between what the panel called "complying" and "non-complying" imports.

CLAIMS OF SERIOUS PREJUDICE UNDER THE SUBSIDIES AGREEMENT

The complainants maintained that the tax and tariff exemptions of the car programme were specific subsidies that had caused serious prejudice to the complainants' interests under Article 5(c) of the Subsidies Agreement, one of the criteria for determining an "actionable subsidy".[107] Since the complainants were challenging a measure of a developing country, the evidentiary burden was, as indicated above, still higher, such that complainants were required to show that the effect of the alleged subsidies was (a) to displace or impede imports of like products (coming from complainants' countries), and (b) a significant price undercutting by the subsidised national car, as compared with cars from complainants' countries.[108]

---

[104] The differences in tax and duty rates were striking: no duty rates as compared with 200%; no sales tax as compared with 35% sales tax. Indonesian Automobile Industry Panel Report, para. 14.145.

[105] *Indonesian Automobile Industry* Panel Report, para. 14.145.

[106] *Indonesian Automobile Industry* Panel Report, para. 14.146.

[107] *Indonesian Automobile Industry* Panel Report, paras. 14.153–14.154.

[108] *Indonesian Automobile Industry* Panel Report, paras. 14.154. Art. 27.8 of the Subsidies Agreement states that "There shall be no presumption in terms of para. 1 of Art. 6 that a subsidy granted by a developing country Member results in serious prejudice, as defined in this Agreement. Such serious prejudice, where applicable under the terms of para. 8, shall be demonstrated by positive evidence, in accordance with the provisions of paras. 3 through 8 of Art. 6". And in Art. 27.9: "Regarding actionable subsidies granted or maintained by a developing country Member other than those referred to in para. 1 of Art. 6, action may not be authorized or taken under Art. 7 [on remedies for actionable subsidies] unless nullification or impairment of tariff concessions or other obligations under GATT 1994 is found to exist as a result of such a subsidy, in such a way as to displace

The panel noted that action may not be taken pursuant to Article 7 of the Subsidies Agreement against a developing country member "unless nullification or impairment of tariff concessions or other obligations under GATT 1994 is found to exist as a result of such subsidy".[109] The complainants argued that while there was no presumption of serious prejudice resulting from the subsidy, it could be demonstrated through positive evidence, as indicated in Article 27.8 of the Subsidies Agreement.[110] Following this logic, the panel allowed the complainants to proceed to "demonstrate" serious prejudice to their interests.

There was a relatively heavy burden of proof to demonstrate, as a threshold matter, that the products in question were "like" products for purposes of Article 6 of the Subsidies Agreement.[111] Indonesia understandably argued that the national car was a "low technology, no frills" budget car, filling a particular market niche at the bottom end.[112] So the panel compared the types of cars involved in the complaint, both in the national car programme and those of export interest to the complainants, in painstaking detail. Only certain of the European cars were determined to be "like" products when compared with the national car; the European and US upper-end cars did not succeed. In addition, while some lower end cars were planned by the US to enter the Indonesian market, none of the US cars that were at the time being directed at that market met the standard for "like" cars, as compared with the national cars.[113]

Moving on, the panel examined whether, under Article 6 (3) of the Subsidies Agreement, the complainants had shown that the effect of the subsidies had been to displace or impede exports of the relevant models to Indonesia.[114] The panel reviewed masses of market share data provided by complainants, and concluded as an initial matter that the data was not conclusive as to the effect on the complainants' market share of the introduction of the national subsidised car.[115]

However, the panel stated that market displacement may also exist where it is demonstrated that in the absence of a subsidy, sales *would have* increased—not only in the case where there has been a demonstrable decline. The complainants would be required to provide positive evidence for such a claim, however.[116]

---

or impede imports of a like product of another Member into the market of the subsidizing developing country Member or unless injury to a domestic industry in the market of an importing Member occurs".

[109] *Indonesian Automobile Industry* Panel Report, para. 14.156 (citing Art. 27.9 of the Subsidies Agreement).

[110] *Indonesian Automobile Industry* Panel Report, para. 14.158.

[111] *Indonesian Automobile Industry* Panel Report, para. 14.169. The panel adopted a moderate stance on the nature of the complainants' burden of demonstrating serious prejudice through positive evidence.

[112] *Indonesian Automobile Industry* Panel Report, para. 14.183.

[113] *Indonesian Automobile Industry* Panel Report, paras. 14.198–14.204. The panel made the interesting, and startlingly anachronistic, finding that "the US cannot seek to establish serious prejudice to US companies based outside the US when their products bound for Indonesia are not of actual US origin".

[114] *Indonesian Automobile Industry* Panel Report, paras. 14.208–14.222.

[115] *Indonesian Automobile Industry* Panel Report, para. 14.222.

[116] *Indonesian Automobile Industry* Panel Report, paras. 14.223–14.224.

Again, the panel reviewed masses of market data relating to plans by the complainants to expand within the Indonesian market, and found it inconclusive. The evidence might have been probative, the panel said, except that it remained general and relatively undocumented.[117]

However, apart from displacement, the complainants also had an opportunity to demonstrate that they had suffered serious prejudice because of price undercutting caused by the Indonesian car subsidies programme. Because of the likeness of some European cars to the Indonesian cars in question, the EC succeeded in establishing serious prejudice through price undercutting, albeit with respect to a narrow range of cars, whereas the US did not.[118] The EC provided actual detailed data on comparative features and prices of the cars, as a result of which the panel was convinced of serious prejudice to EC interests in the form of price undercutting.

TRIPS ARGUMENTS

The final arguments in the case were brought by the US, and concerned problems of access to the national car trademark in Indonesia.[119] The US claimed that Indonesia was violating Article 3 (national treatment) of the TRIPs Agreement, in that its car programme caused discrimination with respect to the acquisition and maintenance of trademarks.[120] The panel noted that developing countries do not have any special phase-in rights for the TRIPs provision on national treatment.[121] The main US contention was that any trademark that could apply to a "national" motor vehicle had to be acquired by an Indonesian company, whether a joint venture or a wholly owned Indonesian company.[122] The US, though, was not able to provide data to convince the panel that this had led to actual discrimination with regard to the use of trademarks.[123]

All the US had shown was that cars marketed under the national car programme were required to bear a trademark belonging to an Indonesian-owned company which had created that trademark; and that because of this, trademarks owned by non-Indonesian companies could not be used for inclusion in the national car programme. The panel continued:

---

[117] *Indonesian Automobile Industry* Panel Report, para. 14.226. "In the view of the panel, neither the EC nor the US has demonstrated by positive evidence that the effect of subsidies to the . . . National Car has been to displace or impede imports of like passenger cars from the Indonesian market within the meaning of Art. 6.3(a) of the Subsidies Agreement".

[118] *Indonesian Automobile Industry* Panel Report, paras. 14.237–14.255.

[119] *Indonesian Automobile Industry* Panel Report, paras. 14.263–14.282.

[120] *Indonesian Automobile Industry* Panel Report, para. 14.263.

[121] *Indonesian Automobile Industry* Panel Report, para. 14.266.

[122] *Indonesian Automobile Industry* Panel Report, para. 14.267.

[123] *Indonesian Automobile Industry* Panel Report, para. 14.268. The panel said that "the facts brought before us do not point to any difference in the applicable law for acquiring trademark rights between that applying to companies of other WTO members and that applying to the company operating under the national car program". *Indonesian Automobile Industry* Panel Report.

"While this may give rise to questions regarding the scope for the use of trademarks owned by US companies on cars under the national car program, it does not . . . pose a problem regarding the [non-discriminatory] acquisition of trademark rights".[124]

The US also failed in its arguments regarding the maintenance of trademark rights. The US had reasoned that if a foreign company became a partner in the national car programme, it would have to acquire a new, Indonesian owned trademark for the purpose. The panel dismissed that argument, on the grounds that the Indonesian requirement applies to pre-existing trademarks of both domestic and foreign companies.[125]

The Indonesian car dispute is a clear example of a carefully designed national subsidy and investment-measure programme to enhance industrial capability and competitiveness by selective protectionism in a key sector. While hardly a paragon of economic probity or transparency, the national car programme had a cogent economic purpose, and represented an attempt to maintain national control over a central sector of the economy.[126] As has been demonstrated, the scope of the new causes of action under the Uruguay Round Agreements have made it impossible to defend many of the familiar elements of the traditional "Asian tiger" economies. It is of the greatest interest that Indonesia never got around to appealing the panel's ruling to the Appellate Body. In the meantime, the Asian economic and monetary crisis hit, leaving Indonesia eager for economic assistance from the International Monetary Fund. Ironically, one of the promises made by the Indonesian government as a condition for the receipt of such aid was that it would eliminate its "national car" programme.[127]

THE CANADIAN AUTOMOTIVE INDUSTRY

A recent complaint brought by the EC and Japan against Canada's automotive regime bore some resemblance to the Indonesian case, and also touched tangentially on the TRIMs Agreement.[128] At issue was an exemption from customs duties accorded by Canada on the import of cars, subject to certain TRIM-like conditions. This system of exemptions arose from Canada's implementation of

---

[124] *Indonesian Automobile Industry* Panel Report, para. 14.268.

[125] *Indonesian Automobile Industry* Panel Report, paras. 14.270–14.273.

[126] The national car programme was notorious for the fact that it was controlled by then President Suharto's son. "PT Timor Putra Nasional (TPN), 99% owned by Suharto's youngest son Hutomo 'Tommy' Mandala Putra, was given special tax privileges under the veteran leader's national car program in 1996. It was once a 'spoiled child, but now it has to fend for itself,'" Indonesian automotive producers association chairman Herman Lateif said, following the WTO dispute and the Indonesian financial crisis of 1998. See Bhimanto Suwastoyo, "Suharto-linked firm shelves national car dream", Agence France Presse, 18 October 1998.

[127] See Indonesia Letter of Intent, 31 Oct 1997, at http://www.imf.org/external/np/loi/103197.htm. For background on this situation, see Bhimanto Suwastoyo, "Indonesian car program loses tax edge in IMF-supported reforms", Agence France Presse, 15 January 1998.

[128] See *EC and Japan* v. *Canada: Measures Affecting the Automotive Industry*, Report of the Panel, 11 February 2000 (WT/D139, 142/R) [hereinafter *Canadian Automotive Industry* Panel Report].

an Auto Pact with the United States in 1965, designed to settle a long-running dispute between Canada and the US over trade in cars, and to encourage US manufacturers to expand their production operations in Canada.[129]

Canada continued to apply an updated version of its original set of exemptions under the Motor Vehicle Tariff Order 1998, and other Special Remission Orders. The essential qualification for manufacturers, those who had been in operation in Canada during the "base year" commencing 1 July 1963, and those who had not, was that they maintain a certain ratio of the net sales value of their vehicles produced in Canada in relation to the net sales value of all vehicles sold for consumption in Canada; as well as a certain level of Canadian value added to their vehicles.

The EC and Japan raised a number of claims, relying on Articles I and III:4 of the GATT, the TRIMs Agreement, the GATS Agreement, and the Agreement on Subsidies and Countervailing Measures.[130] In fact, the TRIMs Agreement was not ultimately dealt with by the panel, since it decided not to follow the issue sequence of the *Indonesian Automobile* panel report. While recognising that from the point of view of the Indonesian panel, the TRIMs claims were "more specific" than the Article III claim, the Canadian Automotive Industry panel said that the TRIMs Agreement was *not* more specific for the claims that it was then addressing.[131] If these are TRIMs, the panel reasoned, their consistency with Article III:4 may not be able to be determined by reference to the illustrative list of TRIMs appended to the Agreement; but might instead require, in any event, an analysis under Article III:4.[132] So for this panel, the more efficient resolution involved proceeding to an Article III:4 analysis.

Having then found a violation of Article IIII:4 in the Canadian measures, the panel followed the *Banana* panel's reasoning, to the effect that no additional analysis of the TRIMs provisions was required.[133] The view of the *Banana* panel had been that "with the exception of its transition provisions, the TRIMs Agreement essentially interprets and clarifies the provisions of Article III (and Article XI) where trade-related investment measures are concerned". In that regard, the TRIMs Agreement was said not to "add to or subtract from those GATT obligations, although it clarifies that Article III:4 may cover investment-related matters".[134]

---

[129] See *Canadian Automotive Industry* Panel Report, para. 10.49.

[130] It is often stated that the GATS Agreement is the "real" WTO investment agreement, in that it deals with the right of establishment for businesses in the territory of other WTO members, where those members have decided to liberalise the relevant service markets. See discussion of GATS, *infra*.

[131] *Canadian Automotive Industry* Panel Report, para. 10.63.

[132] *Canadian Automotive Industry* Panel Report, para. 10.63.

[133] In the panel's view, the Canadian value added requirements affect the internal sale or use in Canada of imported parts, material and equipment for use in the production of motor vehicles. *Ibid.* at para. 10.85. The Art. III:4 claim is rejected with respect to the Canadian "ratio requirements". *Ibid.* at para. 10.150.

[134] See *Banana* Panel Report discussion *infra* p. 257 and following, para. 7.185. The *Banana* panel went on to state that: "A finding that the measure in question would not be considered a trade-related investment measure for the purposes of the TRIMs Agreement would not affect our findings

The *Canadian Automotive Industry* panel also found that certain aspects of the challenged Canadian measures violated Articles II and XVII (MFN and national treatment, respectively) of the General Agreement on Trade in Services (GATS), in that complaintants' services and service suppliers were being accorded less favourable treatment than Canadian services and service suppliers, or other members' services and suppliers.[135]

THE MULTILATERAL AGREEMENT ON INVESTMENTS (MAI)

Public reaction to the now infamous MAI must be seen as a precursor to the anti-WTO uprising in Seattle in 1999. The lesson of MAI was that a well-organised network of NGOs and citizens' groups could at least suspend negotiations aimed at expanding the scope of global economic governance in the interests of multinational enterprises.[136] The MAI, though created under the auspices of the OECD, was meant to act as a model for a *global* agreement on freedom of investment. It was strongly suspected that after its acceptance by the OECD countries, the Agreement would be introduced at the WTO, with the aim of including developing countries as well. By 1998, under pressure of intense public criticism, negotiations on MAI were shelved, with OECD governments stating that they needed to "consult public opinion" before finalising an acceptable investment agreement. It is assumed that the OECD will continue to seek consensus on a final text.[137]

A key objective of the MAI was to openly protect the rights of international investors, allowing them to bring actions against host country governments to challenge investment restrictions. The strongly negative reaction of NGOs and other interested parties was due to the fact that national regulations could be seen to constitute "expropriation" of investors' assets, leading to MAI legal actions through which multinational corporations would in effect gain control over key regulatory powers of national governments. Analogies were drawn between the MAI and North American Free Trade Agreement's (NAFTA's) chapter 11 on investments, under which investors have successfully challenged

in respect of Art. III:4, since the scope of that provision is not limited to TRIMS and, on the other hand, steps taken to bring the EC's licensing procedures into conformity with Art. III:4 would also eliminate the alleged non-conformity with obligations under the TRIMS Agreement". *Banana* Panel Report, para. 7.186.

[135] *Canadian Automotive Industry* Panel Report, para. 11.1. It should be noted that none of the issues on appeal dealt with the TRIMS Agreement. The Appellate Body upheld the panel's rulings on most, though not all, of the appeal questions.

[136] See discussion in Trebilcock and Howse *supra* n. 6, at 357–366. Also see Guy de Jonquieres, "Retreat over OECD pact on investment", *Financial Times* (London), 21 October 1998.

[137] For the most recent official negotiating text, consult the OECD website, http://www.oecd.org//daf/investment/fdi/mai/negtext.htm, The MAI Negotiating Text (as of 24 April 1998).

national environmental regulations of the NAFTA parties alleged to act as expropriations of their investments.[138]

The negotiating text of the MAI is striking in several respects. It naturally contains the predictable requirements of MFN and national treatment for investments and investors of other contracting parties.[139] Beyond that, however, the definition of "investment" is as broad as could possibly be; referring to "every kind of asset owned or controlled, directly or indirectly, by an investor", including enterprises, equity participation, bonds, rights under contracts, intellectual property claims, licenses and authorisations, and all sorts of tangible and intangible property.[140] The Agreement would prohibit a broad range of trade-related investment measures, including domestic content requirements, employment commitments, and requirements "to achieve a given level or value of research and development in [the host country's] territory".[141] There is a general exceptions clause, similar to Article XX of the GATT, allowing restrictions where "necessary" for the enforcement of laws and regulations not inconsistent with the Agreement, as well as for the protection of health and conservation of exhaustible natural resources.[142] The Agreement includes a non-discrimination provision for the granting of authorisations for exploring for and producing minerals, including hydrocarbons.[143]

The section of the Agreement on Not Lowering Standards (Labour and Environment) would utterly fail to meet the objections of MAI's critics.[144] (It is also unclear whether even this mild provision would find its way into a final version of the Agreement.) Three of the four "alternatives" provided recognise that it is "inappropriate" for parties to encourage investment by lowering regulatory standards. Each of the alternatives contains the conceptually naïve proposition that parties *should not* waive or lower standards for this purpose; and that standards should not be more favourable for investors from other parties than they would be for nationals of the host country. This is substantially different from establishing minimum regulatory standards for parties to adhere to; obviously, under the MAI, parties would still have the option of simply carrying out an across-the-board lowering of standards.[145]

Investors must be accorded "fair and equitable treatment and full and constant protection and security", and parties may not "impair by unreasonable or discriminatory (or unreasonable and discriminatory) measures the operation, management, maintenance, use, enjoyment or disposal of investments in its

---

[138] See William Crane, "Corporations Swallowing Nations: The OECD and the Multilateral Agreement on Investments", (Summer 1998) 9 *Colorado Journal of International Environmental Law and Policy* 429, 448–453.

[139] MAI, April 1998 text, at 13.

[140] MAI, April 1998 text, at 11.

[141] MAI, April 1998 text, at 18.

[142] MAI, April 1998 text, at 23.

[143] MAI, April 1998 text, at 43.

[144] MAI, April 1998 text, at 54–55.

[145] There is soft-law linkage of the MAI to the OECD's Guidelines for Multinational Enterprises. See MAI, April 1998 text, at 96–97.

territory of investors of another Contracting Party".[146] Full and prompt compensation must be paid for expropriation or nationalisation; we have already examined concern over the fact that "expropriation" could be defined to include regulatory measures that increase costs for investors.

The section on MAI dispute settlement deserves particular scrutiny.[147] In investor-state disputes, the investor has a substantial degree of control over the tribunal before which the matter will be heard. In the event that special arbitration is chosen, the tribunal "shall comprise three arbitrators, one appointed by each of the disputing parties, and the third, who shall be the presiding arbitrator, appointed by agreement of the disputing parties".[148] While this type of investor-state relationship is not unique to the MAI, it gave rise in this context to strong concerns that national regulation in a broad range of countries would be placed in a vulnerable position before NAFTA-like panels.[149]

Among free trade agreements, the EC has been distinguished by its commitment to the promotion of environmental, labour and social policy, in addition to "common market" principles. Through elaborate accession agreements and wealth transfers to aspiring entrants, the EC has protected itself with remarkable success, if not perfection, against a "race-to-the-bottom" syndrome more characteristic of NAFTA and the WTO. In this light, and given the fact that the French government in particular played an important role in the suspension of the MAI talks in 1998, EC attitudes towards their resumption, and towards the finalisation of an MAI text, will be crucial.

The European Commission has repeatedly stated that the proper forum for detailed negotiations on a global regime for investment protection should be the World Trade Organisation.[150] Citing the problems caused during the OECD negotiations on MAI due to lack of transparency, the Commission's public position is that future WTO negotiations on the subject should include "access to investment opportunities; protection of investment and right to regulate; sustainable development; and investors' responsibilities".[151] It remains to be seen whether the EC would accept a soft-law approach to these "non-trade" regulatory concerns. However, it stands to reason that acceptance of the MAI text in its most recent form would expose substantial areas of European regulation to adverse legal decisions before NAFTA-like tribunals; a result with grave and far-reaching consequences, and about which different sectors of influence in Europe continue to hold conflicting views.

---

[146] MAI, April 1998 text, at 57–58.

[147] MAI, April 1998 text, at 63–76.

[148] MAI, April 1998 text, at 72.

[149] See Peter T Muchlinski, "The Rise and Fall of the Multilateral : Where Now?" (Autumn 2000) 34 *International Lawyer* 1033.

[150] See Multilateral Issues: Trade and Investment, *at* http://europa.eu.int/comm/trade/miti/invest/index_en.htm, April 2000.

[151] See Muchlinski, *supra* n. 149.

5

"Trade and the Environment": International Trade Rules and National Regulation of the Environment

IN NO AREA has the WTO's "democratic deficit" been more striking, or more criticised, than in the trade and environment debate. Domestic environmental regulation enjoys a precarious existence at best, even in the wealthiest countries, and the revelation that existing environmental laws could be essentially overturned by the workings of the GATT/WTO came as a shock to a disparate set of constituents in a large number of countries. In trade disputes dealing with environmental or public health issues, the WTO's one-dimensional quality—in contrast to the EU's multi-dimensional approach—is painfully apparent. The WTO decision-making bodies take no genuine position on domestic environmental regulation, because they have no position to take. Yet they have a legal power and responsibility—at least in terms of the WTO's self-constructed authority—to reject or allow that regulation.

In this sense, while some of the best scholarship in WTO law is expended on trade and environment issues, there has been an academic tendency to focus on, even mystify, the evolution of the view taken by the panels, and Appellate Body, of the articles of GATT/WTO law relevant to an environmental dispute. This is at the expense of examining the larger effects of the operation of GATT/WTO law on the global environment. The challenge for a broader academic community will be to scrutinise the relationship of WTO law to domestic regulation from a wider perspective, a task scarcely yet begun.

The EU has groped its way towards an articulation of relationships among various sectors of law—economic, environmental, social—while this is a process that does not yet exist at global level. It is difficult to see how it could exist at "WTO" level specifically, in that WTO law assumes a hierarchy in which trade principles trump most other values, at least some of the time, and certainly whenever the WTO bodies are so inclined in their reasoning. It is particularly difficult in the trade and environment debate to discuss actual WTO disputes without becoming mired in the self-referential discourse characteristic of WTO studies. But a discussion that links the disputes to the world must be attempted. Especially with regard to "trade and environment", the academic task must be to

promote a wider study of GATT/WTO law by those with an interest in the interaction of economic law with non-economic law; and to move beyond analyses of
the WTO's relationship merely with its own history and values.

An important fact underlying the ubiquitous trade and the environment
debate is that the international trade regime, while capable of threatening
domestic environmental laws, itself does not contain or refer to any set of minimal environmental standards. The urgent question is whether or not the WTO
will assist in generating such a set of minimum standards, or lose legal credibility. There will be consequences as the realisation grows that trade rules and
principles have become linked with an enhanced legal and judicial system, and
that hard-won national (or supranational) environmental regulations may lose
out to trade rules, with the countries that adopted these regulations at considerable cost required to abandon them.

An often overlooked link between trade and the environment is the fact that
a globalising economic system increases general incentives for engaging in international exchange. With growth-oriented policies, and the demands of maintaining competitiveness, it is clear that there will be environmental impacts in
terms of conventional pollution, as well as in overbuilding, forest and species
depletion, and the proliferation of industrial farming methods. Modern trade
law, designed with the single purpose of increasing trade flows, is unlikely to
have a neutral effect on the world's environment.[1]

A second link involves a natural tendency for trading countries to try and bol-
ster the effectiveness of their own environmental regulation, as well as to influence the environmental behaviour of others, by resorting to trade measures.
This tendency in its most blatant form is an import ban on products obtained or
processed in what the importing nation considers to be an environmentally
destructive fashion. From the viewpoint of the newly enhanced WTO regime,
such bans become problematic when they are justified by reasons that lie in the
grey area between hard scientific evidence and national sensitivity to a particular environmental issue. Far from moving in the direction of allowing more discretion to nations in enacting environmental regulation, the Uruguay Round
made it substantially more difficult for any trading member to adopt "greener"
measures than any other member, insofar as such measures impinge upon the
WTO trading rules.[2]

Since the famous *Tuna-Dolphin* case of 1991,[3] the question has been asked
many times: Should the world trading body, the agenda of which is only to facilitate trade, be allowed to invalidate a member nation's regulatory choice as to

---

[1] See Steven Shryban, "The World Trade Organization: The New World Constitution Laid
Bare", (1999) 29:4 *Ecologist* 270–275; and reviewing arguments raised against free trade, see
Matthew A Cole, "Examining the Environmental Case Against Free Trade", (1999) 33:5 *Journal of
World Trade* 183–196.

[2] For a general discussion of contemporary issues in trade and the environment, see Michael
Ferrantino, "International Trade, Environmental and Public Policy", 20:1 *World Economy* 43–72.

[3] *US—Restrictions on Imports of Tuna*, (1991), BISD 39th Supp, 155; reprinted in 30 ILM 1594
(1991) [hereinafter *Tuna-Dolphin* Panel Report].

method of responding to another country's environmental practice, where that response is at variance with conventional trade rules? With the Uruguay Round and the creation of the Agreement on Sanitary and Phytosanitary Measures (the SPS Agreement) and the Agreement on Technical Barriers to Trade (TBT Agreement), the rules for the application of public health and environmental measures became clearer and stricter. Whether the general position adopted during the Uruguay Round, as reflected in these agreements, will hold up in the next round of WTO negotiations remains to be seen.

Certain mainstream theories advocate a true reconciliation of the apparently conflicting ethos of liberal trade and that of environmental protection. Some have called for a world environmental organisation to parallel the WTO, or indeed an environmental organisation within the WTO itself.[4] However, it may sometimes happen that environmental protection and trade rules find themselves in genuine opposition, incapable of being truly reconciled. It is also not clear how effective even a minimum environmental standards convention to run alongside the WTO would be; it is likely that trade rules would continue to trump measures in the public interest in certain circumstances.[5] Any environmental system brought within the WTO umbrella would inevitably continue to scrutinise environmental measures for their trade disrupting or trade restrictive properties.[6]

By contrast, the EU has managed to handle this matter because environmental protection and other public interest values have been explicitly articulated by the foundational treaties and by the European Court of Justice. This has provided a rationale for restraining the operation of trade ("internal market") principles in some contexts. The WTO contains no such alternative set of legal values, thus the sense of awkwardness in those disputes where the Appellate Body attempts to recognise the importance of national laws made in the public interest. Apart from Article XX of the GATT, and certain abstract statements made in the preamble to the WTO Agreement, on what basis is the Appellate Body supposed to have a "view" of the public interest?

Many commentators insist that only wealth can create the conditions for environmental protection, and that only free trade can continue to produce such wealth. If one accepts this thesis, then it becomes impossible to advocate a rollback in the level of trade liberalisation as a partial cure for the world's environmental woes. However, insofar as the striking increase in the movement of products around the world bears some responsibility for global environmental

---

[4] A classic in this regard is Daniel Esty's "Greening the GATT: Trade, Environment and the Future", *Institute of International Economics* (Washington, 1994).

[5] Esty, one of the leading advocates for a "greener" WTO, divides national environmental measures into what he calls swords and shields; swords referring to measures aimed outwardly, beyond the national territory, and often taking the form of import bans; the shields being defensive measures within the national territory such as requirements of meeting extremely high national product standards.

[6] For a general discussion of the options facing the WTO, see Dale Arthur Oesterle, "The WTO Reaches Out to the Environmentalists: Is It Too Little, Too Late?", (1999) *Colorado Journal of International Environmental Law Yearbook* 1.

problems, the "downstream" effects of international trade law must be faced as well. If, as is likely, there is an attempt in future WTO rounds to bring environmental considerations within the ambit of GATT/WTO principles, it is probable that environmental measures will continue to be scrutinised for their trade effects, and not the other way around.[7] Again, global governance on a more complex EU model may be the best, or the only, long-term solution.

PRE-URUGUAY ROUND

The GATT system did not require any minimum set of environmental standards from its participating countries, just as it did not insist upon minimum labour standards. As the GATT had no pretensions to developing a system of global governance, with concerns reaching beyond economic liberalisation, neither did it respond to the potential problem of a regulatory "race-to-the-bottom". The only GATT provision dealing explicitly with environmental matters was Article XX, an all-purpose defence clause, allowing countries to adopt otherwise GATT-illegal measures, if necessary to enforce national laws in the public interest, and as long as these measures did not constitute arbitrary discrimination, or a disguised restriction on trade. Especially relevant to environment disputes are Article XX(b), concerning measures "necessary to protect human, animal or plant life or health," and Article XX(g), concerning measures "relating to the conservation of exhaustible natural resources if such measures are made effective in conjunction with restrictions on domestic production or consumption".

The most famous pre-Uruguay Round environmental case, and the one that sent shock waves through the environmental community, was the so-called "*Tuna-Dolphin*" case of 1991.[8] It was this dispute that demonstrated the power of GATT law over national regulation, and generated an outpouring of academic interest in the "trade and environment" conflict. The idea that GATT law, little understood and highly technical, could undo years of legislative effort was devastating, and resulted in some of the most intensive scrutiny of GATT law by non-specialists in recent times.

TUNA-DOLPHIN

A panel was formed in 1991 to hear a challenge by Mexico against a US law called the Marine Mammal Protection Act of 1972, as amended in 1982 and

---

[7] Esty recommends first looking at environmental measures to try and unmask hidden trade barriers, with intention to discriminate triggering the strictest scrutiny. Then there would be an examination of the "environmental legitimacy" of the measure. To date, no mainstream commentators have called for a minimum standards convention, a set of environmental standards to which all WTO members should adhere. It is likely, though, that in order to retain its legitimacy, the WTO will need to incorporate more than simply methods for scrutinising national environmental laws.

[8] See *supra* n. 3.

1990. The Act prohibited the capture or killing and/or import into the US of marine mammals, except when explicitly authorised by the US government. Section 101(a)(2) of the Act also stated that the Secretary of the Treasury would ban the importation of fish caught with technology which resulted in the incidental killing or injury of mammals in excess of US standards.[9] Particular types of nets considered to lead to excess levels of accidental dolphin deaths were cited, as well as certain areas where dolphins were more likely to be located in large numbers.[10] The dispute began when the US ordered embargoes against tuna caught by certain foreign fleets, pending a demonstration by their home countries that the US MMPA standards were being complied with. The US was only willing to lift these embargoes where documentary evidence was provided that the necessary net technologies had been introduced.[11] At the same time as the MMPA was being challenged at the GATT, so was the US Dolphin Protection Consumer Information Act, under which the label "dolphin safe" was limited to products known to be obtained using the approved technology.

Mexico argued that the US action constituted a quantitative restriction (QR) in violation of Article XI of the General Agreement, and that the specific area designations were impermissible discriminatory measures and in violation of Article XIII.[12] Mexico also argued that the MMPA constituted a violation of Article III, since in Mexico's view a measure regulating a product "could not legally discriminate between domestic and imported products based solely on the production process".[13]

The US argued that the measures imposed under the MMPA were not covered by Article XI, but were rather internal regulations affecting "the sale, purchase, distribution or use" of tuna in a manner consistent with Article III of the GATT Agreement.[14] Under Article III, the US insisted, where it had requirements in place regarding the production method for a particular product, it "could then exclude imports of that product that did not meet the United States requirement".[15] Even if the US law was found not to be consistent with Article III, the US argued, its measures were justified by the exceptions available under Article XX(b) and XX(g). As indicated above, Article XX(b) allowed GATT-illegal measures which were necessary to protect human, animal or plant life or health. Article XX(g) created a similar exception for measures relating to the conservation of exhaustible

---

[9] For a full discussion of the factual aspects of the case, see *Tuna-Dolphin* Panel Report, paras. 2.1–2.12.

[10] The US fishing fleet was granted permits allowing for a certain number of incidentally taken dolphin. Where other nations were considered to be exceeding the level allowed to the US fleet, the products of those foreign fleets could not be imported into the US.

[11] *Tuna-Dolphin* Panel Report, paras. 2.7–2.8. Similar restrictions were introduced against fish products from countries acting as commercial intermediaries, having processed the fish caught by national fleets not considered to meet the US standards for dolphin protection.

[12] *Tuna-Dolphin* Panel Report, paras. 3.10–3.15.

[13] *Tuna-Dolphin* Panel Report, para. 3.16.

[14] *Tuna-Dolphin* Panel Report, para. 3.11.

[15] *Tuna-Dolphin* Panel Report, para. 3.19.

natural resources if such measures were taken in conjunction with restrictions on domestic production or consumption.[16]

One of the most interesting Article XX issues to arise in this case had to do with whether the US could lawfully attempt to impose extraterritorial restrictions on fishing methods of other contracting parties under the guise of protecting natural resources. The US countered—with a logic deriving from the world of environmental law, rather than trade law—that without such restrictions on imports, domestic regulations would be ineffective at conserving dolphin.[17]

The panel in its ruling gained instant notoriety for its alleged failure to consider the particular ethos of environmental law in analysing the matter of the US embargo. The panel first turned to the proper categorisation of the US measure: it rejected the US argument that the restriction was consistent with Article III; Article III:4, the panel pointed out, "refers solely to laws, regulations and requirement affecting the internal sale, etc. of products". "This suggests", the panel went on, "that Article III covers only measures affecting products as such".[18] Concluding that the US was attempting to regulate how the tuna was caught, the panel concluded that the contested law could not be seen as a mere "regulation affecting a product". The panel stated resoundingly that

> "Article III:4 . . . obliges the US to accord treatment to Mexican tuna no less favourable than that accorded to US tuna, whether or not the incidental taking of dolphins by Mexican vessels corresponds to US vessels".[19]

The underlying reason, the legal rationale, for the differential treatment—the linkage between the taking of dolphin and the importation of tuna— was not of legal interest to the panel. Under GATT law, the US could only maintain "internal regulations" consistent with the Note at Article III by confining itself to considerations relating to the product alone. In this case, according to the panel, the manner of harvesting by which the product was obtained was not relevant, since the regulations covering the taking of dolphin did not affect the tuna as a product.[20]

The panel went on to find that the direct import prohibition on certain tuna products from Mexico and the relevant provisions of the MMPA were inconsistent with Article XI:1, as they acted as impermissible QRs. No ruling on Article XIII, the non-discriminatory use of QRs, was considered necessary.[21]

---

[16] *Tuna-Dolphin* Panel Report, paras. 3.27–3.52.

[17] *Tuna-Dolphin* Panel Report, paras. 3.31–3.39. A number of third parties expressed dissatisfaction with the US position. While many had sympathy with the general goals of the US legislation, they questioned its extraterritorial methodology. These countries, many of which were affected as intermediary exporting countries, included Australia, Canada and the EC, as well as Indonesia, Japan, Korea, Norway, Thailand and Venezuela.

[18] *Tuna-Dolphin* Panel Report, para. 5.11.

[19] *Tuna-Dolphin* Panel Report, para. 5.15.

[20] *Tuna-Dolphin* Panel Report, paras. 5.14–5.16.

[21] *Tuna-Dolphin* Panel Report, paras. 5.17–5.19.

A widely discussed aspect of the dispute was that found in the panel's discussion of the Article XX defence raised by the US. With regard to Article XX(b), Mexico argued that this provision could not apply to a measure imposed to protect the life or health of animals outside the jurisdiction of the contracting party taking the measure. Any such measure could not be considered "necessary" as required by Article XX, Mexico maintained, since other kinds of international co-operation were available.[22] Examining the draft history of Article XX(b), the panel agreed with Mexico, concluding that it was in fact meant to refer to the life and health of humans, animals and plants within the national jurisdiction of the country adopting the measure.[23] The panel noted that Article XX(b) allows parties to "impose trade restrictive measures inconsistent with the General Agreement to pursue overriding public policy goals to the extent that such inconsistencies were unavoidable". As for this "unavoidable" quality, the panel wrote that

> "if the broad interpretation of Article XX(b) suggested by the US were accepted, each contracting party could unilaterally determine the life or health protection policies from which other contracting parties could not deviate without jeopardizing their rights under the General Agreement".[24]

Thus it was made clear that, in the panel's view, trade rights held by parties under the GATT agreement may trump rights of other parties to adopt legislation that would, in the name of environmental protection, affect trade freedom. Questions of effectiveness in environmental terms did not, of course, enter into the panel's legal reasoning.

In dealing with Article XX(g) on the conservation of natural resources, the panel followed analogous reasoning. It noted that Article XX(g) required that measures relating to the conservation of exhaustible natural resources be taken in conjunction with restrictions on domestic production or consumption, and thus be aimed at making domestic regulations effective.[25] Again, the panel left no room for doubt as to its vision of Article XX defences: "A country can effectively control the production or consumption of an exhaustible natural resource only to the extent that the production or consumption is under its jurisdiction".[26] The panel rejected an extrajurisdictional, or extraterritorial, approach to the application of Article XX(g), as it had with regard to Article XX(b). The panel also found the restrictions against intermediate trading nations to be inconsistent with Articles III and XI.[27] However, the tuna labelling scheme,

---

[22] *Tuna-Dolphin* Panel Report, para. 5.24.

[23] *Tuna-Dolphin* Panel Report, para. 5.26.

[24] *Tuna-Dolphin* Panel Report, para. 5.27. It was made clear that, in the panel's view, trade rights held by parties under the GATT agreement must trump rights of other parties to adopt legislation that would, in the name of environmental protection, affect trade freedom.

[25] *Tuna-Dolphin* Panel Report, paras. 5.30–5.34.

[26] Panel Report, 5.31. And further: "The panel considered that if the extrajurisdictional interpretation of Art. XX(g) suggested by the US were accepted, each contracting party could not deviate without jeopardizing their rights under the General Agreement". Panel Report, 5.32.

[27] *Tuna-Dolphin* Panel Report, paras. 5.35–5.40.

based as it was on consumer choice rather than on a trade measure, was found to be GATT-permissible.[28]

Not suprisingly, the panel report was blocked by the US. Nevertheless, environmentalists took the panel decision as a sign that the GATT could be employed by commercial interests to invalidate environmental regulations which tended to have a fragile status in any event. While the US had indicated a willingness to bring its legislation in line with the GATT ruling, it did not move quickly enough to satisfy its critics.[29] In 1993, the EC, being dissatisfied with the failure to adopt the panel report, and realising the public relations value of the issue, brought a second GATT challenge to the MMPA, focusing on the issue of intermediary exporting countries.[30] The panel again found the US law to be GATT-illegal because of its extrajurisdictional qualities.

In this second ruling, the panel emphasised the fact that the US was attempting to impose international standards unilaterally, with the danger that the multilateral nature of the GATT could be threatened.[31] The panel displayed scant interest in the fact that the philosophy underlying the US law was broadly similar to that underlying the Convention on International Trade in Endangered Species (CITES), which operates as a web of national refusals to trade in species considered to be made more vulnerable by such trade.[32]

The primary conflict in *Tuna-Dolphin* I and II—concerning national power to employ trade policy in the service of environmental goals—prefigures the difficulties raised by the SPS Agreement in the Uruguay Round, as well as later disputes such as the one involving endangered sea turtles. While the *Tuna-Dolphin* rulings were never officially adopted by the GATT parties, the US made certain efforts to eliminate the objectionable extraterritorial aspects of its law.

THE *THAI CIGARETTES* CASE[33]

Well before the adoption of the SPS Agreement in 1995, it was clear that GATT participating countries would face limitations in their ability to defend restrictions on imports damaging to the public health, unless those arguments were based on a combination of sound science and trade logic. As seen in this dispute, the foundational GATT concepts of non-discrimination in trade matters made it extremely difficult for countries to claim that trade competition itself could be indirectly damaging to the public interest.

---

[28] *Tuna-Dolphin* Panel Report, paras. 5.41–5.44.

[29] See MJ Trebilcock and R Howse *The Regulation of International Trade* (London: Routledge, 1999) at 410.

[30] GATT Doc. DS29/R (1994).

[31] *Tuna-Dolphin II* Panel Report, (1994) 33 ILM 839 para. 5.26.

[32] The US argument in this regard is outlined in the *Tuna-Dolphin II* Panel Report, paras. 3.14 and 3.23.

[33] *Thailand—Restrictions on importation of cigarettes*, (1990) BISD 37th Supp, 200 [hereinafter *Thai Cigarettes* Panel Report].

Under Thailand's Tobacco Act of 1966, import licenses were required for foreign cigarette imports. Yet for ten years prior to this dispute being brought, Thailand had granted almost no such licenses.[34] The US argued that Thailand's tobacco policy constituted a violation of Article XI of the General Agreement; Thailand's main defence was under Article XX (b), concerning measures necessary for the protection of human, animal or plant life.[35]

The panel conceded that smoking was dangerous and that national measures designed to reduce smoking do fall within the scope of Article XX(b). Demonstrating its early sense of the legal relationship existing between trade and environmental concerns, "the panel noted that this provision clearly allowed contracting parties to give priority to human health over trade liberalisation"; however, for a measure to be covered by Article XX(b) it had to be "necessary", as that term is used in Article XX.[36] And in this context, the measure can only be "necessary" when there are no GATT-consistent, or less GATT inconsistent measures reasonably available by which the same health policy may be achieved.[37]

Concerning the necessity of its restrictions, Thailand had argued that there were harmful effects in importing cigarettes per se, as opposed to producing the same product domestically, both in terms of harmful ingredients in cigarettes (the quality issue), and in terms of the level of consumption (the quantity issue).[38] Regarding the allegedly harmful ingredients, the panel ruled that a non-discriminatory content labelling system and a ban on the specific harmful substances would be an alternative consistent, or less inconsistent, with the General Agreement.[39]

More interestingly, Thailand had argued that competition between imported and domestic cigarettes would necessarily lead to an increase in the total sales of cigarettes and that Thailand therefore had no option but to prohibit cigarette imports.[40] Not surprisingly, the panel rejected this speculative approach. It suggested lowering national demand by a curb on cigarette advertising, in conjunction with existing "non-discriminatory" methods already in place, such as warnings on cigarette packs.[41] The panel noted that under GATT rules, government monopolies could regulate the overall supply of cigarettes, provided imported products did not receive less favourable treatment.[42] The panel thus concluded that there were available to Thailand various measures, based on

[34] For the facts underlying the dispute, see *Thai Cigarettes* Panel Report, paras. 6–11.

[35] *Thai Cigarettes* Panel Report, para. 21.

[36] *Thai Cigarettes* Panel Report, para. 73.

[37] *Thai Cigarettes* Panel Report, paras. 74–81. *Thai Cigarettes* Panel's interpretation of the meaning of "necessary" in Art. XX is based on the panel report in the *Aramid Fibres* case (section 337) of 1989.

[38] *Thai Cigarettes* Panel Report, para. 76.

[39] *Thai Cigarettes* Panel Report, para. 77.

[40] See *Thai Cigarettes* Panel Report, para. 27. In the Thai view, the benefits of international competition in products did not extend to cigarettes, since improved marketing techniques could only lead to greater consumption.

[41] *Thai Cigarettes* Panel Report, para. 78.

[42] *Thai Cigarettes* Panel Report, para. 79.

recommendations by the World Health Organization, which could control both quantity and quality without being discriminatory, as the existing measures were. The panel's emphasis on mainstream international standards as a proper set of guidelines for national policy anticipates the logic of the Uruguay Round SPS Agreement. Thailand accepted the panel's rulings, and the report was adopted.

TRADE AND THE ENVIRONMENT, POST-URUGUAY ROUND

It is of some interest that one of the first decisions handed down by the new and more legalistic WTO had the effect of invalidating a provision of the US Clean Air Act, in a dispute brought by a diverse range of countries including Venezuela, Brazil, the EU and Norway.[43] The dispute involved a decision by Congress to direct the US Environmental Protection Agency to promulgate new regulations on the composition and emissions effects of automotive fuel so as to improve air quality in the most polluted areas of the US. While the facts of the case are fairly narrow and technical, the ruling confirmed the fears of many after Tuna Dolphin that environmental laws would routinely fall to trade considerations where "unnecessary" discrimination was found by a panel.[44]

But without question, the most far-reaching addition to the "trade and the environment" debate by the Uruguay Round was the Agreement on Sanitary and Phytosanitary Measures (SPS Agreement). The essential focus of this agreement is the extent to which national governments may adopt trade-restrictive measures in light of national environmental and health policy, particularly with respect to food additives or other food production methods. The SPS Agreement purported to define the manner in which member governments should create measures which reflect national policy regarding plant and animal health, as well as human health which depends upon these standards.[45] The Agreement established standards for reviewing the legality of national health regulations;

---

[43] *Brazil and Venezuela v. United States: Standards for Reformulated and Conventional Gasoline*, Report of the Panel, 29 January 1996 (WT/DS2/R); Report of the Appellate Body, 29 April 1996 (WT/DS2/AB/R).

[44] The complainants argued, under Art. I and III of the General Agreement, and under the new Technical Barriers to Trade Agreement, that the US manner of evaluating the properties of gasoline discriminated against domestic and imported varieties and thus altered the conditions of competition between these products. The US failed in its attempt to defend under the Art. XX concept of "necessity", arguing that it was forced to create different methods for evaluating imported products, as quality verification would be far more difficult. The panel ruled that preventing imported gasoline from benefiting from sales conditions as favourable as that enjoyed by US producers was not necessary to any stated US legislative goal.

[45] Annex A of the Agreement defines sanitary or phytosanitary measure as "any measure applied (a) to protect animal or plant life or health in the territory of the member from risks arising from the entry, establishment or spread of pests, diseases, or disease-causing organisms; (b) to protect human or animal life or health within the territory of the member from risks arising from additives, contaminants, toxins or disease-causing organisms in food; (c) to protect life or health . . . from risks arising from diseases carried by animals, plants or products thereof; or (d) to prevent the entry, establishment or spread of pests.

and thus in effect established precisely how sensitive a member country of the WTO was "entitled" to be in this context.[46]

The Agreement's preamble

"reaffirms that no member should be prevented from adopting or enforcing measures necessary to protect human, animal or plant life or health, subject to the requirement that these measures are not applied in a manner which would constitute a means of unjustifiable discrimination between members where the same conditions prevail or a disguised restriction on international trade".

It states that harmonisation through a multilateral agreement on this subject should be based on international standards.[47] As will be shown below, this reference is in fact to selected mainstream, and not necessarily stringent, international standards.

Since the application of the Article XX defence in the environmental context has been characterised by a certain lack of clarity, the SPS Agreement took as its task to provide rules for the application of Article XX (b). Article 1, defining the scope of the SPS Agreement, states that it applies to "all sanitary and phytosanitary measures which may, directly or indirectly, affect international trade".[48] Article 2 makes clear that members shall ensure that protective measures will only be applied to the extent necessary to protect life or health—thus making clear that the scrutiny will be directed at the national measure, and how it relates to a demonstrable risk. It further states that national measures must be based upon "scientific principles and . . . not maintained without sufficient evidence", with a particular exception to be discussed at length below.

Harmonisation, a well-known concept in the European law context, has not been widely invoked in GATT/WTO law. However, Article 3 of the SPS Agreement encourages harmonisation based on international standards, which will be "deemed necessary to protect human, animal or plant life". The article

---

[46] The Agreement has received extensive academic attention, no doubt because it provides a dramatic instance of global rules capable of trumping sensitive national regulations. See Joost Pauwelyn, "The WTO Agreement on Sanitary and Phytosanitary (SPS) Measures as Applied in the First Three SPS Disputes", (1999) 2:4 *Journal of International Economic Law* 641; and Donna Roberts, "Preliminary Assessment of the Effects of the WTO Agreement on Sanitary and Phytosanitary Trade Regulations", (1998) 1:3 *Journal of International Economic Law* 377.

[47] It could be argued that the SPS Agreement still allows freedom to members in the setting of their standards of protection, as, in fact, the Appellate Body asserted in the Beef Hormones case, discussed below. Nevertheless, ordinary analysis of the subject indicates that the inevitable outcome of the application of the Agreement is the imposition of uniformity in the face of scientific uncertainty. See David G Victor, "The Sanitary and Phytosanitary Agreement of the World Trade Organization: An Assessment After Five Years", 32 *NYU Journal of International Law and Policy* 865. See also Fiona MacMillan and Michael Blakeney, "Regulating GMOs: Is the WTO Agreement on Sanitary and Phytosanitary Measures Hormonally Challenged?", (2000) 6:4 *International Law and Regulation* 131–40.

[48] The Uruguay Round did not create any set of minimum environmental standards to which WTO member countries would be obliged to adhere. The agreement is only concerned with defining the circumstances under which members have gone too far in adopting measures to respond to unsafe animal or plant products exported by another member.

says that members may in fact introduce a higher level of protection in this field than what is seen in the relevant international standard, if there is a scientific justification, or based upon the Article 5 "assessment of risk and determination of the appropriate level of . . . protection" standard.

Article 5 on the issue of risk assessment and "the determination of the appropriate level of sanitary or phytosanitary protection" is crucial to understanding the methodology of the SPS Agreement. It states that members shall ensure that the measures they adopt in this area are based on an assessment "taking into account risk assessment techniques developed by the relevant international organisations". Thus, the risk assessment method itself becomes a reviewable part of the member's protective measure. Members are further required to take into account the objective of minimising negative trade effects.

Paragraph 7 of Article 5 deals with the situation where the relevant scientific evidence is insufficient. In such a case, the member may provisionally adopt measures on the basis of available information, including that derived from international organisations and from other members. More objective information must then be sought and the measure "periodically reviewed". Under paragraph 8 of the article, where a member believes that a measure adopted by another member is constraining its exports, that member may seek and obtain an explanation of the reasons for the measure.

Predictably, disputes under the agreement will be heard under the Dispute Settlement Understanding. A specialised committee is set up to monitor the process of harmonisation in this area, and to maintain contact with the relevant international organisations. The phase-in times for members are two and five years, for developed and developing countries respectively, but only if the full application of the agreement "is prevented by a lack of technical expertise, technical infrastructure or resources". This exception does not extend to the requirement that national protective measures be explained and justified if requested, in the event that a clear basis for the measure does not exist in an international agreement on the subject.

THE AGREEMENT ON TECHNICAL BARRIERS TO TRADE (TBT AGREEMENT)

The conceptual basis of this agreement is roughly similar to that of the SPS Agreement, although to date it has not proven as significant in terms of generating WTO litigation. Expanding on the technical barriers code dating from the Tokyo Round, the avowed purpose of the TBT Agreement was to "ensure that technical regulations and standards, including packaging, marking and labelling requirements, and procedures for assessment of conformity with technical regulations and standards" "do not create unnecessary obstacles to trade". Here too, national powers to regulate and set standards are under scrutiny.

The Agreement is meant to cover all products—industrial and agricultural, with the exception of government purchases and matters already dealt with in the SPS Agreement. (Article 1) Under Article 2 .2, members of the WTO must ensure that technical regulations are not adopted with a view to creating, or with the effect of creating, unnecessary obstacles to trade. As with the SPS Agreement, international standards relating to legitimate national regulatory objectives are to be relied upon, unless the international standard "would be ineffective or inappropriate means for the fulfilment of the legitimate objectives pursued, for instance because of fundamental climatic or geographical factors or fundamental technological problems". (Article 2.4)

The Agreement sets out, in Annex 3, a "Code of Good Practice for the Preparation, Adoption and Application of Standards", to be adopted by "standardising bodies" in the various member countries. The main purpose of the code is to encourage national standardising authorities to follow procedures in the adoption of standards so as to accord national treatment to products of other WTO members, and avoid the creation of unnecessary obstacles to trade. Article 12 recognises the special difficulties developing countries may have in this area. Article 13 establishes a Committee on Technical Barriers to Trade to encourage consultation among members on the operation of the Agreement. Dispute settlement for matters relating to the TBT Agreement is under the Dispute Settlement Understanding (DSU) (Article 14).

THE *"BEEF HORMONES"* DISPUTE[49]

This case, brought by the US against the EC, explored the WTO-consistency of the EC's general ban on the importation of beef from cattle treated with hormones for growth promotion purposes. The dispute is unquestionably one of the most important to have been heard thus far at the WTO, in particular because of the stark opposition it demonstrated between a European regulatory impulse and the scientific rigour of post-Uruguay Round trade law.[50] Not surprisingly, the main causes of action derived from the SPS Agreement.[51]

By way of factual background, in 1981, the EC adopted Directive 81/602, requiring that EC Member States prohibit the administration to farm animals of certain chemical substances designed to promote growth, a list that was expanded upon

---

[49] *US v. EC: EC Measures Concerning Meat and Meat Products*, Report of the Panel, 18 August 1997 (WT/DS26/R) [hereinafter *Beef Hormones* Panel Report]; *US v. EC: EC Measures Concerning Meat and Meat Products*, Report of the Appellate Body, 16 January 1998 (WT/DS26,48/AB/R) [hereinafter *Beef Hormones* Appellate Body Report].

[50] See, for example, Michele D Carter, "Selling Science Under the SPS Agreement: Accommodating Consumer Preference in the Growth Hormones Controversy", (1997) 6 *Minnesota Journal of Global Trade* 625.

[51] In addition to its reliance on the SPS Agreement, the US also tried to raise arguments under the Agreement on Technical Barriers to Trade, on the theory that the EC ban included both sanitary and phytosanitary measures and technical regulations. However, the panel ruled that the TBT Agreement was not relevant to the dispute, insofar as the TBT Agreement itself explicitly excluded SPS measures from its ambit.

in 1988. The 1988 directive on the subject also required the prohibition of importation of animals or meat from animals to which these substances had been administered, with certain enumerated exceptions for therapeutic treatment purposes.[52]

The US claimed that the European measures violated the SPS Agreement, as well as Articles I and III of the General Agreement.[53] As the case necessarily revolved around scientific evidence, and theories of science itself, it is important to note that Article 11.2 of the SPS Agreement allows for the panel to seek expert advice on its own, as well as the studies it accepts from the parties to the dispute. Article 13 of the DSU also gives panels a general right to seek appropriate expert advice from any source thought relevant by the panel.[54] In its complaint, the US contested the EC ban on imports of meat and meat products from cattle treated with any of six specific hormones used for growth promotion purposes, three of them naturally occurring and three of them synthetic.[55]

The parties agreed that the EC measures in question fell under footnote 4 to Annex A of the SPS Agreement: concerning a "contaminant", including "pesticides and veterinary residues and extraneous matter".[56] Despite the fact that the EC measures were in force before the SPS Agreement itself, the panel stated that as they were of the sort that affect international trade, their being in force before the Agreement was not relevant.[57]

The EC presented a creative and far-reaching argument concerning the relationship between the SPS Agreement and Article XX of the GATT Agreement, to the effect that the substantive provisions of the SPS Agreement do not impose obligations additional to those of Article XX(b) of the General Agreement.[58] In essence, Europe was attempting to argue that there must be a violation of the GATT Agreement before the SPS Agreement is activated; further, that the SPS Agreement acts as an interpretive tool to assist in the application of Article XX. The EC motivation was undoubtedly to prevent the panel from engaging in a separate SPS Agreement analysis before turning to Europe's Article XX(b) defenses. But is it possible that Europe really imagined that the SPS Agreement did not impose its own separate and substantive obligations on members? In any event, the panel rejected this attempt to alter the course of the dispute.[59] There

---

[52] See the panel's factual description in the *Beef Hormones* Panel Report, paras. 2–4, 2.1–2.5,.

[53] *Beef Hormones* Panel Report, paras. 3.1–3.3.

[54] See *Beef Hormones* Panel Report, paras. 8.5–8.11. Canada, with similar interests to the US in this dispute, brought a nearly identical case that was heard by the same panel.

[55] *Beef Hormones* Panel Report, para. 8.2.

[56] *Beef Hormones* Panel Report, paras. 8.21–8.22.

[57] *Beef Hormones* Panel Report, paras. 8.22–8.28.

[58] *Beef Hormones* Panel Report, para. 8.33.

[59] "We note . . . that the general approach adopted in Art. XX(b) of the GATT is fundamentally different from the approach adopted in the SPS Agreement. Art. XX(b), which is not limited to sanitary or phytosanitary measures, provides for a general exception which can be invoked to justify any violations of another GATT provision. The SPS Agreement, on the other hand, provides for specific obligations to be met in order for a member to enact or maintain specific types of measures, namely sanitary and phytosanitary measures". *Beef Hormones* Panel Report, para. 8.39.

is no requirement, the panel said, that there be shown a prior violation of a GATT provision (for instance, of Article III or Article XI), before the SPS Agreement applies.[60] Given this underlying logic, it is not surprising that the panel decided that it would be more efficient to examine the SPS Agreement first; to be followed by an examination of any possible GATT violations.[61]

The panel identified its own task as being, first, to determine whether there were international standards relevant to the EC measures, and whether the measures were based on these standards. Secondly, if there were no such standards, to examine whether the EC could justify its measures under Article 3.3 of the SPS Agreement.[62]

Preliminary questions were raised concerning the burden of proof under the SPS Agreement: would the party imposing the protective measure bear the burden of justifying it, or would the complainant bear a burden of showing that there was insufficient risk to justify the measure? The panel reached the unsurprising conclusion that the initial burden of proof rests with the complaining party in establishing a prima facie case of inconsistency with the SPS Agreement. Thus, the US had first to present factual and legal arguments that, if unrebutted, would demonstrate a violation of the SPS Agreement. Once the prima facie case was made out, the burden of proof would shift to the responding party with respect to the obligations imposed by the SPS Agreement.[63]

The panel proceeded to the question of whether there were relevant international standards for the growth hormones in question. For matters relating to food safety, paragraph 3(a) of Annex A of the SPS Agreement refers to the standards established by the Codex Alimentarius Commission (a joint FAO/WHO advisory body) relating to food additives and drug pesticide residues.[64] The panel found that Codex standards existed for five of the six banned hormones.[65] As three of the hormones in question were naturally occurring, Codex said that it was "unnecessary" to set acceptable levels for daily intakes or residues for them. It was the Codex view that "residues resulting from the use of this substance as a growth promoter in accordance with good animal husbandry practice are unlikely to pose a hazard to human health".[66] Residues from meat were

[60] *Beef Hormones* Panel Report, paras. 8.36–8.41.

[61] *Beef Hormones* Panel Report, para. 8.42. The principal US arguments concern the following articles of the SPS Agreement: Art. 2 on basic rights and obligations of members; Art. 3 on the objective of harmonisation of sanitary measures based on international standards; and Art. 5 on the obligation of risk assessment and the determination by members of the appropriate level of sanitary protection.

[62] *Beef Hormones* Panel Report, paras. 8.43–8.47.

[63] *Beef Hormones* Panel Report, paras. 8.51–8.55.

[64] *Beef Hormones* Panel Report, para. 8.56.

[65] Codex establishes "Acceptable Daily Intakes" and "Maximum Residue Limits", among other recommended standards, for veterinary drugs. One important source of recommendations for the establishment of such standards is the joint FAO/WHO Expert Committee on Food Additives (JECFA), which is made up of individual scientists. Codex may or may not accept the recommendations of the committee. It is also worth noting that member countries of Codex are also not obliged to accept Codex's advice.

[66] *Beef Hormones* Panel Report, para. 8.62.

said by Codex to be far lower than what is produced by human beings naturally, or found in other foods.

With regard to two of the three synthetic hormones at issue, the panel cited the Codex standards for safe maximum residues. The principal European counter-argument was that the Codex standards were not relevant, insofar as Codex has only set maximum residue levels, rather than a standard for the ongoing use of these hormones as growth promoters.[67] But the panel found the language of the SPS Agreement to be unambiguous—either a relevant international standard existed, or it did not. So with regard to this initial question, the panel determined that standards did exist for five of the six hormones.[68]

The panel's next step was to analyse whether, under Article 3.1 of the SPS Agreement, the EC measures were "based on" the relevant international standards. The panel's point of reference was that, if the level of protection is different from the international standards in question, it could not be said to be *based on* the international standard.[69] Again, following in the logical sequence apparently demanded by the structure of the agreement itself, the panel found that the level of protection was not based on the international standard.[70] It then moved on to Article 3.3 of the Agreement, which governs the situation wherein sanitary measures are not based upon the international standard. This provision allows a separate and higher standard when there is a "scientific justification", or where a member determines the separate standard to be appropriate "in accordance with the relevant provisions of paragraphs 1–8 of Article 5"—in other words, the risk assessment provisions. The separate standard must also be consistent with other provisions of the agreement.[71]

The panel provided a doctrinaire interpretation of the meaning of "based on" a national risk assessment, which must itself be "a scientific examination of data and factual studies". What the risk assessment may not be seen as, the panel said, is "a policy exercise involving social value judgements made by political bodies". As the panel saw it, each member must decide "the extent to which it can accept the potential adverse effects related to a specific substance which have been identified in the risk assessment". In other words, in the panel's view, complete rejection of any and all risk is not within the power of the WTO member country.

The question then was whether the EC had demonstrated that its measures were *based on* a risk assessment.[72] It was pointed out that the EC had presented

---

[67]   *Beef Hormones* Panel Report, paras. 8.63–8.67. Ironically, the Codex standards for these hormones were completed six months after the SPS Agreement came into effect. Thus, the EC claimed to have been unaware of the fact that these particular standards would become binding on it by virtue of the SPS Agreement. *Beef Hormones* Panel Report, para. 8.68.

[68]   *Beef Hormones* Panel Report, para. 8.69.

[69]   *Beef Hormones* Panel Report, paras. 8.72–8.73.

[70]   *Beef Hormones* Panel Report, para. 8.77.

[71]   *Beef Hormones* Panel Report, para. 8.79.

[72]   *Beef Hormones* Panel Report, para. 8.90.

certain reports and studies in an attempt to justify its trade measures,[73] and thus the panel proceeded on the assumption that the EC had met its burden of demonstrating the existence of a risk assessment, carried out in accordance with the requirements of Article 5.[74] The more difficult issue, however, was whether the contested measure was based on the risk assessment that had been shown to have taken place.[75]

Displaying little interest in the complex nature of legislative drafting, the panel made a great deal of the fact that the preambles to the relevant directives do not refer to the scientific studies invoked by the EC, but rather to the "non-scientific" reports and opinions of the European Parliament and the EC Economic and Social Committee.[76] According to the panel, these inputs "cannot be part of a risk assessment".[77] The panel also accused the EC of considering certain reports by individual scientists only for purposes of this litigation; thus, such studies could not have formed the basis for the original trade ban.[78] For these reasons, the EC was not found to have met its burden of proving that it honoured the procedural requirement imposed by Article 5.1; that is, that the measure actually be based on the risk assessment.[79]

Turning to the substantive scientific issues, the panel stated that none of the evidence offered by Europe indicated that an identifiable risk arose from the hormones "if good practice is followed" in their administration for growth promotion purposes.[80] The panel further stated that individual studies showing carcinogenic effect of hormones did not investigate the effect of residues of the hormones in meat.[81] The panel's conclusion was thus that there was no scientific evidence available that concluded that an identifiable risk arises from the use of any of the hormones at issue, at least for "growth promotion purposes in accordance with good practice".[82]

The EC raised a number of other arguments that highlighted the line of demarcation between the bare, scientific concerns of the SPS Agreement and the broader considerations that led to the imposition by the EC of the ban. While scientifically unproveable to some degree, the very real concerns mentioned by the EC were risks arising from the nature and mode of action of the hormones;

---

[73] These included the EC Scientific Veterinary Committee Report and monographs of the International Agency for Research on Cancer, among others. Also included were JECFA Reports of 1988 and 1989 on the general relationship between hormones and cancer, and opinions by various academic specialists in the field. *Beef Hormones* Panel Report, paras. 8.108–8.111.

[74] *Beef Hormones* Panel Report, para. 8.112.

[75] The panel states, "In our view, the member imposing a sanitary measure needs to submit evidence that at least it actually took into account a risk assessment when it enacted or maintained its sanitary measure in order for that measure to be considered as based on a risk assessment".

[76] *Beef Hormones* Panel Report, para. 8.114.

[77] *Beef Hormones* Panel Report, para. 8.114.

[78] *Beef Hormones* Panel Report, para. 8.115.

[79] *Beef Hormones* Panel Report, para. 8.116.

[80] *Beef Hormones* Panel Report, para. 8.124.

[81] JECFA, for instance, did recognise the potential carcinogenic effect of these hormones, but not as residues in hormone-treated meat. Beef Hormones Panel Report, para. 8.128.

[82] *Beef Hormones* Panel Report, para. 8.134.

risks arising from combinations of hormones, and the special problem of multiple exposures; risks related to detection and control; and perhaps most importantly, the risks relating to the "inherent limits to science".[83] The panel's response to these arguments was withering.[84] The panel supported the US view that it was for the EC to prove that its ban was based on its risk assessment; not for the complainant to prove that there was no risk.[85]

The last significant issue in the dispute may appear to be legal overkill, but in fact proved very important in the context of appeal. The question concerned whether, even supposing the EC had established its scientific reasons for adopting the measures in question, their trade effects had been minimised, and whether they had led to arbitrary discrimination, in a manner forbidden by Article 5.5.[86] The panel ruled that there was no evidence to support the European argument that the effects of hormones exogenously produced were different from those endogenously produced.[87] But did this difference in levels of protection constitute arbitrary or unjustifiable discrimination? The panel was blunt in its determination that the EC had provided no justification for the different treatment, and that this treatment was in fact arbitrary.[88] As to whether this in turn indicated a disguised restriction on trade, within the meaning of Article 5.5 of the SPS Agreement, the panel found just such an impermissible restriction.[89]

The panel provided a separate analysis on the question of the European response to the administration of synthetic, as opposed to natural, hormones for growth promotion purposes.[90] The outcome was no different in this context. Experts advising the panel had stated that synthetic hormones could be better detected and controlled; also that synthetic and natural hormones were both treated under international standards according to a "no appreciable risk" level.[91] The ban on synthetic hormones was another arbitrary restriction on trade, according to the panel.[92]

---

[83] *Beef Hormones* Panel Report, para. 8.139.

[84] The panel stated that the EC "apparently considers that the residual risk, albeit minute and not appreciable, constitutes the risk (derived from a risk assessment) on which the EC ban is based in accordance with Art. 5.1, arguing that, according to EC risk management, risk other than zero is not acceptable". *Beef Hormones* Panel Report, para. 8.149.

[85] *Beef Hormones* Panel Report, paras. 8.150–8.156.

[86] *Beef Hormones* Panel Report, para. 8.163.

[87] In that regard, all the experts consulted by the panel indicated that even if the residues could be qualitatively distinguished, their potential adverse effects could not. *Beef Hormones* Panel Report, para. 8.187.

[88] *Beef Hormones* Panel Report, para. 8.197.

[89] The panel found further reasons for a determination of arbitrary discrimination. It stated that the EC had other motives than the protection of human health in its ban on the use of natural hormones. It mentioned such motives as the need to harmonise regulatory schemes across Europe, in order to remove competitive distortions and in turn to increase consumption and reduce European beef surpluses.

[90] *Beef Hormones* Panel Report, para. 8.207.

[91] *Beef Hormones* Panel Report, para. 8.213.

[92] *Beef Hormones* Panel Report, para. 8.214.

It is of legal interest that, having found these violations of the SPS Agreement, the panel considered it unnecessary to examine whether Articles I and III of the GATT Agreement had been violated. Had violations of the General Agreement been established, the panel explains, it would have been necessary to see whether the violations were justified under an Article XX defence. In such a case, the panel stated that it would have had to revert to an interpretation of the SPS Agreement anyway, under which inconsistencies had already been shown.[93] The panel's view appears to be that, in order to succeed under an Article XX (b) defence, one must show that there has been no violation of the SPS Agreement.[94]

The reasoning of the Appellate Body Report in *Beef Hormones* demonstrates a clear contrast in legal *approach*, if not ultimate substance, between the two judicial bodies.[95] Whereas panels are appointed for the matter at hand, the Appellate Body is a permanent institution, whose members sit for four year periods, and as such the Appellate Body appears to have a greater concern for remaining within the strict interpretative limits of the WTO agreements as actually written. In this dispute, while upholding the ultimate conclusion reached by the panel, the Appellate Body was both more cautious and more legally precise; its reasoning also left open the door for Europe to provide scientific evidence of a sort that would endow its beef ban with WTO-legality.

The Appellate Body agreed with the panel's general proposition that the complaining party must first set out a prima facie case; after which the burden of proof shifts to the defending party. However, the Appellate Body rejected a further view expressed by the panel view that , under the SPS Agreement, there is a special and distinct evidentiary burden placed on members imposing SPS measures not based on international standards. The Appellate Body stated that there is no generalised burden of proof particular to the SPS Agreement.[96]

With regard to the standard of review, the EC argued that the panel erred by not giving due deference to the EC decision to impose a higher level of protection than that recommended by Codex Alimentarius. The panel was also said to have

[93] *Beef Hormones* Panel Report, paras. 8.272–8.273.

[94] The panel made some interesting concluding remarks. It said that "in order to avoid any misunderstanding as to the scope and implications of the findings above", it would "like to stress that it was not our task to examine generally the desirability or necessity of the EC Council Directives in dispute. The ability of any member to take sanitary measures which do not affect international trade was not in issue in the present case . . . Likewise, the ability of any member to enact measures which are intended to protect not consumer health but other consumer concerns was not addressed. In this regard, we are aware that in some countries where the use of growth promoting hormones is permitted in beef production, voluntary labelling schemes operate whereby beef from animals which have not received such treatment may be so labelled". *Beef Hormones* Panel Report, para. 8.274.

[95] See Layla Hughes, "Limiting the Jurisdiction of Dispute Settlement Panels: The WTO Appellate Body Beef Hormone Decision", (1998) 10 *Georgetown International Environmental Law Review* 915.

[96] *Beef Hormones* Appellate Body Report, paras. 97–109. The Appellate Body says that the proper way for the panel to proceed is to ensure that the complaining party has presented legal arguments sufficient to demonstrate that the EC measures were inconsistent with the obligations assumed under each article of the SPS Agreement. Only after such a prima facie determination has been made out may the onus be shifted to the EC to bring forward evidence and arguments to disprove the complaining party's claim.

failed to accord deference to the EC's scientific assessment and its adherence to the precautionary principle.[97] The Appellate Body pointed out that the SPS Agreement itself is silent as to the issue of the appropriate standard of review.[98] Generally speaking, the Appellate Body continued, the panel's analysis must always be guided by Article 11 of the DSU, which refers to an "objective assessment of the facts". Thus, the Appellate Body said that it would determine whether or not this is what the panel carried out.[99]

As for the importance of the precautionary principle, the Appellate Body stated that this had not been written into the SPS Agreement as a ground for justifying SPS measures that are otherwise inconsistent with the obligations of members set out in particular provisions of the agreement. However, according to the Appellate Body, the principle is reflected in the agreement at several places, where it is recognised that members may establish their own high level of protection. (See Articles 3.3 and 5.7)[100] The Appellate Body confirmed that panels should recognise that members act from prudence and precaution where risks of irreversible damage to human health are concerned. However, the precautionary principle does not, by itself, and without a "clear textual directive to that effect", relieve a panel from applying the normal principles of treaty interpretation.[101] Thus, the panel's basic ruling that the precautionary principle does not override the provisions of Articles 5.1 and 5.2 of the SPS Agreement was upheld.[102]

With regard to the role of scientific evidence, and the panel's obligations under Article 11 of the DSU, the Appellate Body found no significant distortion of the evidence as presented by the EC.[103] Even though it was acknowledged that the panel made certain "errors" in its treatment of that evidence, none was sufficiently serious to impinge upon the panel's proper assessment of the evidence.[104] The Appellate Body upheld the panel's right under the SPS Agreement and the DSU to seek out whatever information, from whichever experts, the panel itself deems to be appropriate.[105]

The Appellate Body then took on the more difficult question of obligations under Article 3 of the Agreement, which calls on members to base their national measures on available international standards. The Appellate Body, displaying the legal restraint that has become its characteristic, rejected the panel's interpretation of "based on" as meaning " conforming to".[106] According to the

---

[97] *Beef Hormones* Appellate Body Report, para. 110.
[98] *Beef Hormones* Appellate Body Report, para. 114.
[99] *Beef Hormones* Appellate Body Report, paras. 116–119.
[100] *Beef Hormones* Appellate Body Report, para. 124.
[101] *Beef Hormones* Appellate Body Report, para. 124.
[102] *Beef Hormones* Appellate Body Report, para. 125.
[103] *Beef Hormones* Appellate Body Report, paras. 135–145.
[104] See, for example, *Beef Hormones* Appellate Body Report, para. 138.
[105] *Beef Hormones* Appellate Body Report, paras. 147–149.
[106] *Beef Hormones* Appellate Body Report, paras. 162–163. The Appellate Body stated that the language of Art. 3 indicates that "harmonisation of SPS measures of members on the basis of international standards is projected in the Agreement as a goal, yet to be realised, in the future". See *Beef Hormones* Appellate Body Report, para. 165.

Appellate Body, the international standards should not be read so as to have obligatory force and effect. In the Appellate Body's view, when a member adopts a set of international standards as its domestic standards, then this enjoys a presumption of consistency with GATT law. Under Article 3.3 of the SPS Agreement, a member may set its own different standard, which may be higher than the relevant international standard. Significantly, the Appellate Body stated that "the right of a member to determine its own appropriate level of sanitary protection is an important right".[107] But what is the scope of this "important right"?

The Appellate Body elaborated that this right was not an absolute or unqualified right. The higher national level of protection must, it said, be consistent with the SPS Agreement generally, including the Article 5 provisions on risk assessment. The Appellate Body agreed with the panel that the EC was required to comply with Article 5.1.[108]

The question then arose as to whether the EC, by maintaining SPS measures not based on a risk assessment, acted inconsistently with the requirements of Article 5.1. The Appellate Body ruled that the panel's finding that a minimum magnitude of risk had to be found had no basis in the SPS Agreement itself,[109] providing another instance of the Appellate Body pulling back from the over-zealous interpretative method of the panel. As the Appellate Body saw it, a panel is only authorised to determine whether or not an SPS measure is "sufficiently supported or reasonably warranted by" the risk assessment.[110] It seemed at this stage in its reasoning that the Appellate Body's analysis might take a broader, more generous view of the *nature* of a valid risk assessment. It stated that the panel was in error when it excluded "all matters not susceptible of quantitative analysis by the empirical or experimental laboratory methods commonly associated with the physical sciences".[111]

The Appellate Body then chided the panel for having looked to the preamble of the European legislation for clues as to its WTO legality.[112] It explained that the requirement that an SPS measure be "based on" a risk assessment is a substantive requirement that there be a "rational relationship" between the measure and the risk assessment.[113] Significantly, the Appellate Body recognised that

---

[107] *Beef Hormones* Appellate Body Report, paras. 170–172.

[108] *Beef Hormones* Appellate Body Report, Appellate Body Report, para. 176–177. The Appellate Body stated that "the requirements of a risk assessment under Art. 5.1, as well as of 'sufficient scientific evidence' under Art. 2.2, are essential for the maintenance of the delicate and carefully negotiated balance in the SPS Agreement between the shared, but sometimes competing, interests of promoting international trade and of protecting the life and health of human beings".

[109] *Beef Hormones* Appellate Body Report, para. 186.

[110] *Beef Hormones* Appellate Body Report, para. 186.

[111] *Beef Hormones* Appellate Body Report, para. 187. The Appellate Body went further and said that "It is essential to bear in mind that the risk that is to be evaluated . . . is not only risk ascertainable in a science laboratory operating under strictly controlled conditions, but also risk in human societies as they actually exist, in other words, the actual potential for adverse effects on human health in the real world where people live and work and die".

[112] *Beef Hormones* Appellate Body Report, para. 191.

[113] *Beef Hormones* Appellate Body Report, para. 193.

there is often divergence of view between representatives of the mainstream scientific community and "other responsible views". This in and of itself, the Appellate Body said, does not necessarily indicate the lack of such a relationship between the measure and the risk assessment, especially in cases where the risk involved is "life threatening in character".[114]

Despite the apparently greater generosity of the Appellate Body, however, its view of the EC measure and its relationship to a risk assessment is apparently not so different from that expressed by the panel. It concurred with the panel's conclusion that the scientific reports listed do not rationally support the EC import prohibition. The Appellate Body agreed that the studies cited by Europe only deal with the hormones in general, and not with the specific risk posed by hormones used for growth promotion.[115]

In the words of the Appellate Body:

> "We affirm, therefore, the ultimate conclusion of the panel that the EC import prohibition is not based on a risk assessment within the meaning of Articles 5.1 and 5.2 of the Agreement and is, therefore, inconsistent with the requirements of Article 5.1".

To be consistent with Article 3.3, the Appellate Body noted, a measure must also be consistent with Article 5.1, and the EC has failed on both these counts.[116]

It is on the final issue that the Appellate Body made a major conceptual break with the panel's approach; this was the question of whether the European measure was, in the language of Article 5.5, discrimination or a disguised restriction on international trade.[117] This matter was of real importance, since if the panel's view were to be upheld, the measure could not be saved by an adjustment of the risk assessment problem, since the measure would remain WTO-illegal. The Appellate Body took into account the fact that the primary motivation in enacting the legislation was the protection of human health. In its view, the fact that there is more hormone treated beef in the US and Canada merely reflects the reality that such treatment has been allowed in those countries.[118]

This position apparently left the door open to the EC to produce adequate scientific evidence of health risks from the use of hormones in growth promotion. It clearly begged the question, though, regarding the limits of science and the role of the precautionary principle. So, while the EC fared better with the Appellate Body than with the panel to this extent, the Appellate Body nonetheless finished with a recommendation that the DSB request the EC to bring its SPS measures which are inconsistent with the Agreement into conformity with its

---

[114] *Beef Hormones* Appellate Body Report, para. 194.
[115] *Beef Hormones* Appellate Body Report, paras. 196–209.
[116] *Beef Hormones* Appellate Body Report, paras. 208–209.
[117] *Beef Hormones* Appellate Body Report, paras. 210–246.
[118] See *Beef Hormones* Appellate Body Report, paras. 243–246. The Appellate Body stated at para. 245: "We are unable to share the inference that the panel apparently draws that the import ban on treated meat and the Community-wide prohibition on the use of the hormones here in dispute for growth promotion purposes in the beef sector were not really designed to protect its population from risk of cancer, but rather to keep out US and Canadian hormone-treated beef and thereby to protect the domestic beef producers in the EC".

obligations.[119] In the absence of timely EC compliance with the ruling, the US was authorised to apply tens of millions of dollars in retaliatory tariffs against various European products. Negotiations have continued to seek a satisfactory conclusion to the dispute, with a focus on increased access to the European market for hormone-free beef from the US.[120]

In one sense, this dispute was about the precautionary principle. In attempting to clarify the scientific basis of national protective measures, the SPS Agreement is plainly at conceptual loggerheads with the precautionary principle. To introduce the precautionary principle as an explicit feature of WTO law would require a major revision of the SPS Agreement, and a rethinking of the premises upon which it is based. It has been pointed out that the compatibility of the SPS Agreement and the precautionary principle is questionable at best.[121] On the other hand, to ignore the developments in international environmental law leading to the articulation of the precautionary principle, and to continue to apply the SPS Agreement with full rigour, risks further erosion of the WTO's legitimacy.[122]

THE *SEA TURTLE* CASE[123]

This dispute was in essence a replay of some of the issues from Tuna Dolphin, but in the far more high-stakes legal world of the WTO. In the view of some, it also represented the serious disproportion in the balance between trade and conservation concerns, since the devices being required by the US as the price of entry for shrimp products into the US market were relatively simple. By comparison, the consequence for sea turtles of failure to make the innovations would be dire.[124] In this case as well, although the panel and the Appellate Body ultimately arrive at the same place, the panel's decision is distinguished by its interpretative bravado, and the Appellate Body's by restraint and precision.

---

[119] *Beef Hormones* Appellate Body Report, para. 255.

[120] See "US Cattlemen call for EU compensation offer", *Agra Europe*, 13 October 2000; and "EU and US move towards resolving beef hormone trade dispute", European Information Service, *European Report*, 13 June 2001.

[121] Hans-Joachim Priess and Christian Pitschas, "Protection of Public Health and the Role of the Precautionary Principle Under WTO Law: A Trojan Horse Before Geneva's Walls?", (Dec 2000) 24 *Fordham International Law Journal* 519.

[122] One legal adviser in the European Commission's Legal Service raises the problem of lack of procedural regularity in the use of "science" and scientific experts by the WTO's decision-making bodies. See Theofanis Christoforou, "Settlement of Science-Based Trade Disputes in the WTO: A Critical Review of the Developing Case Law in the Face of Scientific Uncertainty", (2000) 8 *NYU Environmental Law Journal* 622.

[123] *Malaysia, Thailand, India and Pakistan v. US: Import Prohibition of Certain Shrimp and Shrimp Products*, Report of the Panel, 15 May 1998 (WT/DS58/R) [hereinafter *Sea Turtles* Panel Report]; *Malaysia, Thailand, India and Pakistan v. US: Import Prohibition of Certain Shrimp and Shrimp Products*, Report of the Appellate Body, 12 October 1998 (WT/DS58/AB/R) [hereinafter *Sea Turtles* Appellate Body Report].

[124] It is noteworthy that all seven species of sea turtle are included in an appendix to the 1973 Convention on International Trade in Endangered Species (CITES), forbidding trade in the listed animals.

The US had reached the conclusion that the principal reason for the high death rate of sea turtles was the activity of shrimp trawlers. Protected under domestic and international law, the sea turtle was disappearing due to the tendency of the turtles to become enmeshed in devices used to catch shrimp.[125] The US authorities developed simple machines called "turtle excluder devices", or TEDs, which acted as trapdoors to release the turtles and other large fish or animals. When voluntary use did not prove effective, the US made the use of TEDs mandatory for all its own fleet. In 1989, the US enacted a law that forbade imports of shrimp coming from countries whose fleets were not employing the turtle-saving technology. All supplying countries would have to provide documentation of TED use, to the extent that they were operating in areas known to host sea turtles.[126]

The complainants' main argument was built around Article XI: 1, to the effect that the US restrictions were virtually identical to those discussed in the *Tuna I* and *Tuna II* cases, where the selective US tuna ban was found to violate Article XI. As in *Tuna Dolphin*, the US defended itself under Article XX (b) and (g), acknowledging that its measures were restrictions on imports.[127]

The US took the opportunity to argue that Article XX (b) and (g) (despite the *Tuna Dolphin* rulings) have no

> "jurisdictional limits, nor limitations on the location of . . . natural resources to be . . . conserved and that, under general principles of international law relating to sovereignty, states have the right to regulate imports within their jurisdiction".[128]

The panel's methodology here was bold. It questioned whether Articles XX (b) and (g) even apply when a member has taken a measure "conditioning access to its market for a given product on the adoption of certain conservation policies by exporting members".[129] While acknowledging that Article XX accommodates a broad range of measures, the panel stated: "by accepting the WTO Agreement, members commit themselves to certain obligations which limit their right to adopt certain measures".[130] So, to decide the scope of Article XX, the panel looked first at the article's "chapeau", which states that the measure in

---

[125] For a discussion of the factual background to the case, see *Sea Turtles* Panel Report, paras. 11–15.

[126] *Sea Turtles* Panel Report, paras. 2.14–2.16. The panel made a controversial decision to refuse submissions made by NGOs on the subject of TEDs, on the grounds that it had not itself sought the submission. The US then used the NGO material as part of its own submission, Panel Report paras. 7.7–7.10.

[127] See *Sea Turtles* Panel Report, paras. 7–15. As the panel puts it: "Even if the . . . US declaration does not amount to an admission of a violation of Art. XI:1, we consider that the evidence made available to the panel is sufficient to determine that the US prohibition of imports of shrimp from non-certified members violates Art. XI:1". And: "In other words, the US bans imports of shrimp or shrimp products from any country not meeting certain policy conditions. We . . . note that previous panels have considered similar measures restricting imports to be 'prohibitions or restrictions' within the meaning of Art. XI". *Sea Turtles* Panel Report, para. 7.16.

[128] *Sea Turtles* Panel Report, para. 7.24.

[129] *Sea Turtles* Panel Report, para. 7.26.

[130] *Sea Turtles* Panel Report, para. 7.26.

question cannot be applied in a manner that constitutes arbitrary or unjustifiable discrimination.[131]

The complainants argued that the US measure adds costs and renders their operations less competitive; the US argued in turn that all exporting nations are treated alike in this matter. The panel found that the US was indeed discriminating between certified (i.e., technology-compliant) countries and non-certified countries, but asked whether this was occurring in an unjustified way, within the meaning of Article XX's "chapeau".[132] The panel stated that this could only be answered within the light of the overall purposes and meaning of the GATT and WTO Agreements.[133]

The panel examined past case law interpreting Article XX, and concluded that Article XX had been seen as a "limited exception;" not capable of being used so as to defeat the overall purposes of the General Agreement.[134] Taking up the preamble to the WTO Agreement, the panel reviewed the overall purposes of the WTO legal system; pointing out that while sustainable development is mentioned, mutually advantageous trade relations are featured. It concluded that "while environmental considerations are important for the interpretation of the WTO Agreement, the central focus of that agreement remains the promotion of economic development through trade", and "that the provisions of GATT are essentially turned toward liberalisation of access to markets on a non-discriminatory basis".[135] The panel stated that by its very nature, the WTO "favours a multilateral approach to these issues".[136]

The panel proceeded to theorise that

"a measure adopted by a member which, on its own, may appear to have a relatively minor impact on the multilateral trading system, may nonetheless raise a serious threat to that system if similar measures are adopted by the same or other members".[137]

The panel saw the US measure in this case as just such a threat to the multilateral trading system.[138] Based on this reasoning, the panel concluded that the US

---

[131] *Sea Turtles* Panel Report, paras. 7.28–7.29.

[132] *Sea Turtles* Panel Report, paras. 7.31–7.34.

[133] *Sea Turtles* Panel Report, para. 35. This was a peculiar approach, since Art. XX presupposes a GATT violation, and may allow it, if the challenged measure serves an enumerated national purpose, and as long as it is not a disguised restriction on trade, or arbitrarily discriminatory.

[134] *Sea Turtles* Panel Report, para. 7.40.

[135] *Sea Turtles* Panel Report, para. 7.42.

[136] The panel returned to its curious notion that "the chapeau of Art. XX . . . only allows members to derogate from GATT provisions so long as, in doing so, they do not undermine the WTO multilateral trading system, thus abusing the exceptions contained in Art. XX". This again failed to answer the question of what a member would need an Art. XX exception for, if not a unilateral measure at variance with the underlying presumptions of the GATT Agreement. See *Sea Turtles* Panel Report, para. 7.44.

[137] *Sea Turtles* Panel Report, para. 7.44.

[138] The panel stated: "In our view, if an interpretation of the chapeau of Art. XX were to be followed which would allow a member to adopt measures conditioning access to its market for a given product upon the adoption by the exporting members of certain policies, including conservation policies, GATT 1994 and the WTO Agreement could no longer serve as a multilateral framework

measure was "unjustifiable" within the meaning of the "chapeau" of Article XX. The US TEDs law was ruled to be "unjustifiable discrimination between countries where the same conditions prevail *and thus . . . not within the scope of measures permitted under Article XX*". (emphasis author's)

In another peculiar interpretative twist, the panel said that before making a definitive finding on this point, it would hear US arguments relating to Article XX. The US pointed out that there are numerous import bans under international agreements for the protection of animals, whether within or outside of the national jurisdiction. The panel rejected this, stating that no international agreement allows or requires the US "to impose an import ban on shrimp to protect sea turtles". The panel insisted that its finding was limited to measures conditioning access to the US market for a given product on the adoption by the exporting member of certain conservation policies.[139]

The panel failed to adequately address the argument that the US action is soundly based in the CITES Convention. The panel's contention that CITES is about banning trade in endangered species, whereas the shrimp is not endangered, clearly missed the larger context of the US measure.[140] The panel concluded that the US action violated Article XI:1 of GATT 1994, and that it could not be justified under Article XX of the GATT. Under the panel's reasoning in the Sea Turtles case, it is difficult to see how any GATT-illegal measure could be justified under Article XX, especially with regard to internationally mobile natural resources.[141]

The US appealed this decision on two main points: That the panel had erred in refusing to accept the NGO submissions; and that it had erred in finding that the US measure constituted unjustifiable discrimination and was therefore not within the scope of measures permitted by Article XX.[142]

---

for trade among members as security and predictability of trade relations under those agreements would be threatened."

[139] The US also raises the extraterritorial issue, but the panel denies that its finding is based on this question. The panel focuses firmly on its conclusions that WTO members cannot force other members to adopt certain conservation policies via import embargoes.

The US also argued that the sea turtle was a shared global resource, migrating thousands of miles in a lifetime, across jurisdictions. But the panel responds that this would imply a "common interest" in the resource concerned; and that if such a common interest existed, it would be better addressed through the negotiation of international agreements than by such unilateral measures conditioning market access on the adoption of certain policies. The panel called on the US to enter into negotiations to search for a commonly acceptable conservation method—but failed to explain what leverage a country would have over exporting countries unwilling to adopt the relevant technology!.

[140] *Sea Turtles* Panel Report, para. 58. The panel is careful to leave the impression that it is not interfering with environmental regulation. It states that "we do not suggest that import markets must exist as an incentive for the destruction of natural resources. Rather, we address a particular situation where a member has undertaken unilateral measures which, by their nature, could put the multilateral trading system at risk". *Sea Turtles* Panel Report, para. 7.60.

[141] For a critique of the panel's reasoning, see Geert Van Calster, "The WTO Shrimp/Turtle Report: Marine Conservation v. GATT Conservatism?", (1998) 7:11 *European Environmental Law Review* 307–314.

[142] *Sea Turtles* Appellate Body Report, paras. 9–28.

The Appellate Body made short work of the first point. It affirmed the fact that the WTO dispute settlement process is limited to members of the WTO; also, only WTO members having a "substantial interest" may be third parties to a dispute. No one outside these members has a legal right to participate. However, the Appellate Body disagreed with the panel that it was bound to refuse unsolicited NGO submissions, since under the DSU the panel may accept or decline information from any source it sees fit. According to the Appellate Body, "The panel erred in its legal interpretation that accepting non-requested information from non-governmental sources is incompatible with the provisions of the DSU".[143]

As for the more substantive issue concerning Article XX, the Appellate Body made clear that it did not approve of the manner in which the panel interpreted the structure of Article XX. In the Appellate Body's view, the panel followed the wrong sequence of reasoning; it should first have determined whether the challenged measure was one falling under one of the Article XX headings; then, the first section (chapeau) of Article XX can be examined.[144] The Appellate Body, with great understatement, pointed out that it is likely a "common aspect" of measures falling within the (a)–(j) exceptions of Article XX that a member would condition access to its market on whether an exporting member complied with or adopted a policy unilaterally prescribed by the importing member.[145] The Appellate Body also made the eminently sensible statement that the measures falling within Article XX's category headings are considered to be highly important—thus qualifying for an exception to the GATT rules.[146] Thus, the panel had made a significant error in its legal interpretation. The Appellate Body reversed the panel's ruling that the US measure did not fall not within the scope of measures permitted under the "chapeau" of Article XX.

The Appellate Body further ruled that sea turtles could be seen as falling under the heading "exhaustible natural resources" as that phrase is used in Article XX(g). Referring to the status of the sea turtle under the CITES Convention, the Appellate Body stated that the US measure "relates to" the conservation of those resources, as required by Article XX.[147] As far as the Article XX "chapeau" is concerned, the measure must not be arbitrary or discriminatory.[148] The Appellate Body noted that the US had argued that an alleged discrimination between countries where the same conditions prevail is not unjustifiable where the policy goal of the Article XX exception being applied

---

[143] *Sea Turtles* Appellate Body Report, paras. 99–110.

[144] *Sea Turtles* Appellate Body Report, paras. 114–120.

[145] *Sea Turtles* Appellate Body Report, para. 121.

[146] The Appellate Body states: "Paragraphs (a) to (j) comprise measures that are recognised as important and legitimate in character. It is not necessary to assume that requiring from exporting countries compliance with, or adoption of, certain policies . . . prescribed by the importing country, renders a measure a priori incapable of justification under Art. XX". *Sea Turtles* Appellate Body Report, para. 121.

[147] *Sea Turtles* Appellate Body Report, paras. 125–134; paras. 135–142.

[148] *Sea Turtles* Appellate Body Report, para. 150.

provides a rationale for the justification. The US maintained that the conservation goal could, in effect justify the discrimination.[149] But here the Appellate Body disagreed with the US position.[150]

"The policy goal of the measure at issue", the Appellate Body said, "cannot provide its rationale or justification under the standards of the chapeau of Article XX". Just because a measure falls within the scope of Article XX, the Appellate Body reasoned, does not then mean that the measure necessarily complies with the requirements of the "chapeau". "To accept the arguments of the US", the Appellate Body stated, "would be to disregard the standards established by the chapeau".[151]

The Appellate Body noted that the "chapeau" was designed to prevent abuse of the Article XX exception. In the environmental context, the Appellate Body saw a balance between the right of members to invoke an Article XX exception, and on the other hand, "the substantive rights of the other members under the GATT 1994".[152] The Appellate Body appeared closer in spirit here to the reasoning of the panel, as it emphasised the rights and expectations of WTO participant nations, and the power of such rights to trump other regulatory considerations.[153] Article XX exceptions are, in the Appellate Body's analysis, "limited and conditional".[154]

The next question had to be whether in fact the US restriction amounted to unjustifiable discrimination.[155] The Appellate Body was nearly as critical of the US programme as the panel had been. Calling the US TEDs requirement "a rigid and unbending standard", the Appellate Body concluded that

> "it is not acceptable, in international trade relations, for one WTO member to use an economic embargo to require other members to adopt essentially the same comprehensive regulatory programme, to achieve a certain policy goal, as that in force within that member's territory, without taking into consideration different conditions which may occur in the territories of those other members".[156]

The Appellate Body even upbraided the US for not having created bilateral agreements on this subject with the parties concerned.[157] It was highly critical of the

---

[149] *Sea Turtles* Appellate Body Report, para. 148.
[150] *Sea Turtles* Appellate Body Report, para. 149.
[151] *Sea Turtles* Appellate Body Report, para. 149.
[152] *Sea Turtles* Appellate Body Report, para. 156.
[153] The Appellate Body stated "To permit one member to abuse or misuse its right to invoke an exception would be effectively to allow that member to degrade its own treaty obligations as well as to devalue the treaty rights of other members". *Sea Turtles* Appellate Body Report, para. 156.
[154] *Sea Turtles* Appellate Body Report, para. 157.
[155] *Sea Turtles* Appellate Body Report, para. 161.
[156] *Sea Turtles* Appellate Body Report, para. 164.
[157] The Appellate Body also pointed to the existence of a convention signed in 1996, though not yet ratified, between the US and a number of countries. Called the Inter-America Convention on the protection and conservation of sea turtles, it would require each country to the convention to take appropriate measures within its own jurisdiction. *Sea Turtles* Appellate Body Report, para. 169.

unilateral character of the US measure, which, it said, "heightens the disruptive and discriminatory influence of the import prohibition and underscores its unjustifiability".[158]

The Appellate Body had equally harsh words regarding the manner of administration of the US programme. Non-certified exporting countries were being denied due process and basic fairness, the Appellate Body stated, and were discriminated against *vis-à-vis* those members granted certification. Thus, to the extent that the measure displays qualities of arbitrary discrimination, it could not, in the Appellate Body's view, meet the test of the "chapeau" of Article XX.[159]

Like the panel, the Appellate Body was eager to disclaim any intention to prevent members from protecting their environmental resources.[160] However, the Appellate Body's assumption that these various spheres of law can be separated and considered in isolation from one another gives rise to serious systemic issues; issues which must be addressed in the upcoming round of negotiations on further trade liberalisation, or in some other international forum.[161] As the Appellate Body saw the situation,

> "WTO members are free to adopt their own policies aimed at protecting the environment as long as, in so doing, they fulfil their obligations and respect the rights of other members under the WTO Agreement".[162]

This formulation raises at least as many questions as it answers, concerning the power of environmental consideration to trump trade rules, and trade principles to trump environmental regulations.

---

[158] *Sea Turtles* Appellate Body Report, para. 172.

[159] *Sea Turtles* Appellate Body Report, paras. 178–184.

[160] The Appellate Body wrote: "In reaching these conclusions, we wish to underscore what we have not decoded in this appeal. We have not decided that the protection and preservation of the environment is of no significance to the members of the WTO—clearly, it is. We have not decided that the sovereign nations that are members of the WTO cannot adopt effective measures to protect endangered species, such as sea turtles. Clearly, they can and should. And we have not decided that sovereign states should not act together bilaterally, plurilaterally, or multilaterally . . . to protect endangered species or to otherwise protect the environment. Clearly, they should and do". Describing its own decision, the Appellate Body explained that "What we have decided in this appeal is simply this: although the measure of the US in dispute in this appeal serves an environmental objective that is recognised as legitimate under paragraph (g) of Art. XX of the GATT 1994, this measure has been applied by the US in a manner which constitutes arbitrary and unjustifiable discrimination between members of the WTO, contrary to the requirements of the chapeau of Art. XX". *Sea Turtles* Appellate Body Report, paras. 185–186.

[161] The internally contradictory nature of the Appellate Body's reasoning has given rise to a variety of critical responses. See, for example, Omar Ranne, "More Leeway for Unilateral Measures?", (Mar–April 1999) 34:2 *Intereconomics* 72–83; and Geert Van Calster, "The WTO Appellate Body in Shrimp/Turtle: Picking Up the Pieces", (1999) 8:4 *European Environmental Law Review* 111–15.

[162] *Sea Turtles* Appellate Body Report, para. 186.

Changes made by the United States in its TED-related guidelines in order to comply with the rulings of the Appellate Body in the original Sea Turtles case did not satisfy Malaysia, which had recourse to Article 21.5 of the DSU.[163] Malaysia insisted that the United States was not in any event entitled to maintain an import ban outside the framework of an international agreement on the conservation of sea turtles; also, that the revised guidelines in use by the US were still not in compliance with the Appellate Body Report, since the US continued to impose its own conservation policies on other WTO members, as disallowed by the Appellate Body.[164]

This Article 21.5 proceeding has received a great deal of attention, since it marks the first time that a party has successfully relied on an Article XX defense to justify a unilateral environmental measure. However, it should be noted that the decisions taken in this Article 21.5 procedure, that of the panel and that of the Appellate Body, raise as many questions as they settle. The case does not clarify the relationship between international trade law and international environmental agreements; and it does offer the strange spectacle of the WTO judicial bodies overseeing national methods of implementation of an environmental policy embodied in an environmental statute. The source of this WTO authority *vis-à-vis* other areas of law remains extremely unclear.

The panel took up the question of the US failure to negotiate an international agreement for the conservation of sea turtles, an issue that had loomed large in the original panel and Appellate Body decisions.[165] It was primarily the absence of such negotiations that led to determinations of "unjustifiable discrimination" in the mode of application of the US measure. The panel in the Article 21.5 proceeding then went on to determine the scope of US obligations with respect to the negotiation of an international agreement.[166] As the US measure and its implementing regulations had been found to be "provisionally justified" by the Appellate Body, the panel proceeded to conduct an examination in the light of the chapeau of Article XX.[167]

---

[163] Art. 21.5 reads in part as follows: Where there is disagreement as to the existence or consistency with a covered agreement of measures taken to comply with the recommendations and rulings such dispute shall be decided by recourse to these disputes settlement procedures, including wherever possible resort to the original panel.

United States—Import Prohibition of Certain Shrimp and Shrimp Products; Recourse to Art. 21.5 by Malaysia, Report of the Panel, 15 June 2001 (WT/DS58/RW), (hereinafter *Sea Turtles Art. 21.5 Panel Report*).

[164] *Sea Turtles Art. 21.5* Panel Report, para. 5.1.

[165] *Sea Turtles Art. 21.5* Panel Report, para. 5.29.

[166] *Sea Turtles Art. 21.5* Panel Report, para. 5.3.

[167] *Sea Turtles Art. 21.5* Panel Report, para. 5.42.

Invoking the Appellate Body report, the panel noted that determination of an abuse of Article XX rights is dependent upon the "line of equilibrium" between the right of a member to invoke an exception under Article XX, and the rights of other members under the substantive provisions of GATT 1994. Where this line should be drawn is in turn dependent upon the factual context for any given case.[168]

Here, the factual context involved the biology of sea turtles, a subject requiring concerted action on the part of various countries.[169] The panel noted the WTO preamble and its mention of sustainable development as a value; as well as international instruments for the protection of sea turtles, to which the US and Malaysia were parties. It also noted that Article 31.3 of the Vienna Convention states that in interpreting a treaty, rules of international law applicable between the parties should be taken into account.[170] These factors, according to the panel, meant that the line of equilibrium should be seen as moving towards multilateral, and away from unilateral, solutions. US efforts, the panel explained, in the direction of good faith negotiations to protect the sea turtle, must involve a "continuity of efforts", with US endeavours to create such an agreement required to be "assessed over a period of time".[171]

The panel's view was that the earlier Appellate Body decision must lead to the conclusion that the requirement placed on the US was one of negotiation, not necessarily conclusion of an international agreement for the conservation of sea turtles, and that the US might be able to apply a unilateral measure in the interim.[172] However, "serious efforts" to "negotiate in good faith" were required to take place before the imposition of such a unilateral import prohibition.[173]

Looking at the evidence of US efforts to carry on such negotiations from the adoption of the Appellate Body Report up through the time of the Article 21.5 panel's establishment, the panel concluded that the US had in fact made substantial efforts.[174] It noted a "changed situation" and a sustained pace of negotiations, with a prospect for their completion in 2001.[175] The panel stated that the US measures would only be permitted under Article XX if they were also allowed under an international convention; or if taken further to the completion of serious good faith efforts to reach a multilateral agreement.[176]

It should be noted that the panel's reasoning does little to deal with the question of a nation's actual rights to impose trade restrictive measures in the name of conservation. In one sense, evidence of "multilateral interest" in conserving a natural resource in the form of a multilateral convention on the subject dodges

---

[168] *Sea Turtles Art. 21.5* Panel Report, para. 5.51.
[169] *Sea Turtles Art. 21.5* Panel Report, para. 5.52.
[170] *Sea Turtles Art. 21.5* Panel Report, paras. 5.53–5.57.
[171] *Sea Turtles Art. 21.5* Panel Report, para. 5.60.
[172] *Sea Turtles Art. 21.5* Panel Report, paras. 5.64–5.65.
[173] *Sea Turtles Art. 21.5* Panel Report, para. 5.65.
[174] *Sea Turtles Art. 21.5* Panel Report, para. 5.80.
[175] *Sea Turtles Art. 21.5* Panel Report, para. 5.87.
[176] *Sea Turtles Art. 21.5* Panel Report, para. 5.88.

the question of the rights of members where no such widely-held value can be demonstrated. The panel could not resist making the statement that "the possibility to impose a unilateral measure to protect sea turtles under Section 609 is more to be seen, for the purposes of Article XX, as the possibility to adopt a *provisional* measure allowed for emergency reasons than as a definitive 'right' to take a permanent measure. The extent to which serious good faith efforts continue to be made may be reassessed at any time".[177] It is extraordinary that so many commentators greeted this decision as a conceptual breakthrough in the interpretation of WTO law. More extraordinary is the degree of legal authority over national regulatory processes that the panel continues to attribute to itself.

The panel then turned to the question of the "insufficient flexibility" of the 1996 US guidelines, as criticised by the Appellate Body for the fact that the US approach had the effect of mandating the use of TEDs by shrimp-harvesting nations. The panel noted with approval that the revised US guidelines offer the possibility for countries to be certified, without necessarily using TEDs, so long as they can demonstrate a programme similar in effectiveness to that of the US.[178] (This difference is perhaps of questionable value, since the panel acknowledged that the US State Department knows of no other measures apart from TEDs that are comparable in effectiveness to the use of TEDs.)[179] The US managed to satisfy the panel that its revised guidelines were now sufficiently flexible.[180] The US also convinced the panel that it had corrected inconsistencies and due process problems in its guidelines, substituting a more transparent and predictable set of procedures for those previously in operation.[181]

The original Appellate Body Report had not examined whether the US measure was a "disguised restriction on trade", but the *Article 21.5* panel took up this point, making the interesting observation that "the fact that, on its face, a law has been narrowly tailored to achieve a bona fide conservation plan does not mean that, when applied, it does not constitute a disguised restriction on trade".[182] However, in this instance, by allowing exporting countries to apply programmes not based on mandatory use of TEDs, and by offering technical assistance to develop the use of TEDs in third countries, the US had demonstrated that its Section 609 was not being applied so as to constitute a disguised restriction on trade.[183] In a manner reminiscent of the "diplomatic" 1950s, the US and Malaysia were urged to "work together to conclude an agreement taking account of the principle that States have common but differentiated responsibilities to conserve and protect the environment".[184]

---

[177]   *Sea Turtles Art. 21.5* Panel Report, para. 5.88.
[178]   *Sea Turtles Art. 21.5* Panel Report, paras. 5.95–5.97.
[179]   *Sea Turtles Art. 21.5* Panel Report, para. 5.98.
[180]   *Sea Turtles Art. 21.5* Panel Report, para. 5.104.
[181]   *Sea Turtles Art. 21.5* Panel Report, paras. 5.121–5.136.
[182]   *Sea Turtles Art. 21.5* Panel Report, para. 5.140.
[183]   *Sea Turtles Art. 21.5* Panel Report, para. 5.143.
[184]   *Sea Turtles Art. 21.5* Panel Report, para. 7.2.

Again, it should be noted that the *Article 21.5* panel assumed for the WTO institutions a major oversight role in the exercise of national discretion with regard to laws based on public policy considerations, where those laws have trade restrictive effects. The upshot of the panel's decision might be seen as requiring the US to actually shoulder a good deal of the regulatory costs of those countries it hopes to influence in terms of a policy for the protection of sea turtles; in any event, the regulatory cost to the US clearly rises with the burden of demonstrating to the WTO complete good faith participation in a negotiating process on an ongoing basis.

On the other hand, in the wake of the *Article 21.5* decision, there have also been rumblings of discontent that the US is being allowed to engage in WTO-illegal behaviour, so long as its application of the law in question was of a certain nature. It is plain that the relationship between trade law and environmental law remains to be sorted out at a far more conceptual, and fundamental, level than has been the case to date.

The Appellate Body in *Sea Turtles, Article 21.5*

Malaysia raised several issues on appeal to the Appellate Body, but did not prevail on any. It first argued that the Article 21.5 panel improperly limited its analysis to the recommendations and ruling of the DSB, as opposed to examining the consistency of the US implementing measure with the provisions of the GATT 1994.[185] As a general matter, the Appellate Body considered that the panel had properly examined Section 609 as part of its examination of the totality of the new measure, had correctly found that Section 609 had not been changed since the original proceedings, and had "rightly concluded that our ruling in United States—Shrimp with respect to the consistency of Section 609, still stands".[186] The Appellate Body supported the panel's approach in examining only the *application* of the measure, as found in the revised US guidelines, to see whether this application constituted arbitrary or unjustifiable discrimination, in violation of the chapeau of Article XX.[187]

More substantively, Malaysia appealed the panel's conclusion that "Section 609 . . . is justified under Article XX of the GATT 1994 as long as the conditions stated in this report, in particular the ongoing serious, good faith efforts to reach a multilateral agreement, remain satisfied".[188] Malaysia first questioned the panel's finding with respect to the extent of the duty of the US to pursue international

---

[185] *United States—Import Prohibition of Certain Shrimp and Shrimp Products, Recourse to Article 21.5 of the DSU by Malaysia*, 22 October 2001 (WT/DS58/AB/RW) [hereinafter *Sea Turtles AA 21.5 Appellate Body Report*], para. 83.

[186] *Sea Turtles Art. 21.5 Appellate Body Report*, para. 96.

[187] *Sea Turtles Art. 21.5 Appellate Body Report*, para. 98.

[188] *Sea Turtles Art. 21.5 Appellate Body Report*, paras. 111–112.

cooperation in protecting sea turtles.[189] Its contention was that demonstrating good faith efforts to negotiate, as opposed to an obligation to conclude, an agreement was not sufficient to meet the requirements of the chapeau of Article XX.[190] In formulating its view, the Appellate Body took into account the language of the chapeau, the fact that the US had adopted a "cooperative approach" with some, but not all, shrimp harvesting countries, and the actual language of Section 609 requiring the US Secretary of State to initiate negotiations for the development of international agreements on this subject.[191]

The Appellate Body first made the common-sensical observation that acceptance of Malaysia's argument could lead to a situation where the negotiating partners of the US would essentially have veto power over whether the US could fulfill its WTO obligations; a clearly unreasonable position.[192] It pointed out that "it is one thing to prefer a multilateral approach in the application of a measure that is provisionally justified under one of the subparagraphs of Article XX of the GATT 1994; it is another to require the conclusion of a multilateral agreement as a condition of avoiding "arbitrary or unjustifiable discrimination" under the chapeau of Article XX". The Appellate Body continued, "We see, in this case, no such requirement".[193]

Malaysia further argued that the panel was incorrect in its determination that a measure can meet the requirements of Article XX if it is "flexible enough, both in design and application, to permit certification of an exporting country with a sea turtle protection and conservation programme 'comparable' to that of the United States".[194] Malaysia insisted that regardless of the manner of application, the US measure continued to constitute arbitrary and unjustifiable discrimination, because it still conditions access to the US market on compliance with standards "unilaterally prescribed by the United States".[195]

The Appellate Body noted that it had itself stated in its report in the original *United States—Sea Turtles* case that conditioning access to a member's market on whether the exporting member has complied with a unilaterally prescribed policy was to some degree a common aspect of measures falling within the scope of Article XX.[196] Malaysia, the Appellate Body stated, missed the significance of this statement as one of principle that was "central to the ruling" in the underlying dispute.[197] Beyond this, though, the Appellate Body noted that in *Sea Turtles, Article 21.5*, the panel had satisfied itself that the new US measure, "in design and application, does not condition access to the United States market on the adoption by an exporting Member of a regulatory programme aimed at the protection and the

---

189 *Sea Turtles Art. 21.5* Appellate Body Report, para. 114.
190 *Sea Turtles Art. 21.5* Appellate Body Report, para. 116.
191 *Sea Turtles Art. 21.5* Appellate Body Report, paras. 119–122.
192 *Sea Turtles Art. 21.5* Appellate Body Report, para. 123.
193 *Sea Turtles Art. 21.5* Appellate Body Report, para. 124.
194 *Sea Turtles Art. 21.5* Appellate Body Report, para. 136.
195 *Sea Turtles Art. 21.5* Appellate Body Report, para. 136.
196 *Sea Turtles Art. 21.5* Appellate Body Report, para. 137.
197 *Sea Turtles Art. 21.5* Appellate Body Report, para. 138.

conservation of sea turtles that is essentially the same as that of the United States".[198] As the Appellate Body saw the problem, Malaysia was questioning whether the panel had erred in inferring from the earlier Appellate Body report that the chapeau of Article XX permits a measure which requires only "comparable effectiveness"—rather than "essentially the same" practices.[199]

The Appellate Body supported the panel's position, stating that "there is an important difference between conditioning market access on the adoption of essentially the same programme, and conditioning market access on the adoption of a programme comparable in effectiveness".[200] It concluded that the revised US guidelines, on their face, "permit a degree of flexibility that . . . will enable the United States to consider the particular conditions prevailing in Malaysia if, and when, Malaysia applies for certification".[201]

Thus, the Appellate Body made Article XX history with its statement that "we uphold the finding of the panel . . ." that Section 609 of Public Law 101–162, as implemented by the revised guidelines . . . and as applied so far by the United States authorities, is justified under Article XX of the GATT 1994 as long as the conditions stated in the findings of this Report, in particular the ongoing serious, good faith efforts to reach a multilateral agreement, remain satisfied".[202] However, despite the nominally more environmentally-friendly panel and Appellate Body decisions set out above, it is unlikely that there will be any early conclusion to the long-running "trade and the environment" debate.

THE CANADIAN SALMON CASE[203]

This highly technical case, decided under the SPS Agreement and based strongly on the Beef Hormones ruling, is not as complex as it first appears. The case was brought by Canada, to protest measures by Australia restricting the import of fish, particularly salmon, that had not been subject to prescribed heat treatment prior to export. Australia had in recent years developed its own salmon industry with introduced species; its restrictive measures reflected concern with certain diseases that could be brought into Australia through uncooked Canadian salmon. There was no risk to human health, but rather to the animal health of Australia's own fish stocks.[204]

---

[198] *Sea Turtles Art. 21.5 Appellate Body Report*, para. 140.
[199] *Sea Turtles Art. 21.5 Appellate Body Report*, para. 143.
[200] *Sea Turtles Art. 21.5 Appellate Body Report*, para. 144.
[201] *Sea Turtles Art. 21.5 Appellate Body Report*, para. 148.
[202] *Sea Turtles Art. 21.5 Appellate Body Report*, para. 152.
[203] *Canada v. Australia: Measures Affecting Importation of Salmon*, Report of the Panel, 12 June 1998 (WT/DS18/R) [hereinafter *Canadian Salmon* Report of the Panel]; *Canada v. Australia: Measures Affecting Importation of Salmon*, Report of the Appellate Body, 20 October 1998 (WT/DS18/AB/R) [hereinafter *Canadian Salmon* Appellate Body Report].
[204] See *Canadian Salmon* Panel Report, discussion of the factual background to the case, paras. 2.1–2.30.

Beginning in the 1970s, Australia had adopted a number of measures requiring particular heat treatments as a condition of fish importation. In late 1996, the Director of Quarantine made a recommendation that uncooked, wild, ocean-caught salmon products not be permitted into Australia. Canada argued that these measures were inconsistent with Article XI of the GATT, as well as with Articles 2, 3 and 5 of the SPS Agreement.[205] Both sides agreed that the Australian restrictions were SPS measures within the agreement's definition. Following on from the *Beef Hormones* decision, the panel examined the SPS arguments first.

Australia argued that there were no relevant international guidelines for some of the animal diseases it was concerned with; where there were such guidelines, Australia claimed that it had quite validly chosen to adopt a higher level of protection, as permitted under the SPS Agreement.[206] As far as the latter diseases were concerned, Annex A of the SPS Agreement refers to the standards of the International Office of Epizootics as being the relevant international organisation. Because the IOE standards do not address all the diseases the Australians were concerned about, the panel decided to look at the basic obligations and risk assessment provisions of the SPS Agreement first.[207] The panel stated that if a violation of Article 5 is found, there will be a presumed violation of Article 2.2.[208]

Canada argued that the report presented by Australia to accompany its 1996 ban did not constitute an adequate risk assessment, especially since a full evaluation of each disease would be required. Canada asserted that the "heat treatment" requirement was not based on a risk assessment, as required by the Appellate Body in the *Beef Hormones* case—that is, a risk assessment of a kind to ensure a rational relationship between the restrictions and the scientific evidence.[209]

The panel responded to Australia's argument that members need not provide a quantitative risk assessment, but may also, especially where data is not complete, engage in a qualitative assessment, and need not separately evaluate the risk of occurrence for each disease and for each measure that might be applied.[210] As the panel framed the issue, members must first identify the relevant diseases; then evaluate the likelihood of the establishment of those diseases. Performing a nearly interminable technical evaluation of the contents of the 1996 Australian report, the panel concluded as an initial matter that it did meet

---

[205] *Canadian Salmon* Panel Report, paras. 3.1–3.3. The Canadian complaint in fact encompasses a series of measures, including earlier heat treatment standards, culminating in the 1996 ban.

[206] *Canadian Salmon* Panel Report, para. 8.45.

[207] *Canadian Salmon* Panel Report, paras. 8.46–8.47.

[208] *Canadian Salmon* Panel Report, para. 8.52.

[209] *Canadian Salmon* Panel Report, paras. 8.61–8.63.

[210] The panel stated that the relevant definition of risk assessment is that found in paragraph 4 of Annex A to the SPS Agreement; that is, "Evaluation of the likelihood of entry, establishment or spread of a pest or disease within the territory of an importing member according to the sanitary or phytosanitary measures which might be applied, and of the associated potential biological and economic consequences". *Canadian Salmon* Panel Report, para. 8.69.

this first test.[211] But as to whether or not the Australian measure was "based on" the risk assessment, the reader was told that even the 1996 report acknowledges that there is insufficient data on whether or not heat treatment inactivates the disease agents being considered.[212]

In fact, there appeared a distinct lack of certainty as to whether heat is effective for all the disease-causing pathogens included by Australia in its ban.[213] The panel stated that Canada had raised a presumption that there was no rational relationship between the measure and the risk assessment, whereas Australia had not in turn rebutted that presumption. Thus, according to the panel, the measure was not "based on" a risk assessment as required by Article 5.1.[214]

As in the *Beef Hormones* case, the panel went on to examine whether, had there been found a rational relationship between the risk assessment and the measure, the measure would nonetheless have been deemed a form of unjustifiable discrimination or a disguised restriction on trade.[215] It was noted that Australia tolerated other types of fish imports, in contrast to its blanket ban on wild salmon.[216] Following another dense and technical discussion of the salmon ban, the panel concluded that the measure was unjustly discriminatory towards the Canadian products, since different levels of risk should bring different levels of protection. Again, the panel concluded that Canada had raised a presumption that the distinctions in levels of protection imposed by Australia between salmon and other fish resulted in a disguised restriction on international trade. And Australia, according to the panel, had again failed to rebut that presumption.[217]

Finally, Canada alleged that the measures were more trade restrictive than they needed to be to achieve the appropriate level of protection, maintaining that there was no technical reason for the level of protection chosen by Australia.[218] The panel agreed that there were less trade restrictive options reasonably available to Australia, and that Australia had not demonstrated that heat treatment was even the most effective way of reducing the risk it invoked.[219]

The principal issue on appeal related to the validity of the Australian risk assessment.[220] As to whether the 1996 report constituted a proper risk assessment, the Appellate Body stated that "it is not sufficient that a risk assessment conclude

---

[211] *Canadian Salmon* Panel Report, para. 8.92.
[212] *Canadian Salmon* Panel Report, para. 8.98.
[213] *Canadian Salmon* Panel Report, para. 8.98.
[214] *Canadian Salmon* Panel Report, paras. 8.99–8.100.
[215] *Canadian Salmon* Panel Report, para. 8.102.
[216] *Canadian Salmon* Panel Report, para. 8.129.
[217] *Canadian Salmon* Panel Report, paras. 8.130–8.159.
[218] *Canadian Salmon* Panel Report, paras. 8.161–8.162.
[219] *Canadian Salmon* Panel Report, paras. 8.166–8.183.
[220] As a secondary issue, the Appellate Body found that the panel erred in looking at both the earlier heat treatment requirements, as well as the 1996 ban on wild salmon. Although the treatment conditions had made it nearly impossible to import fresh salmon, the Appellate Body insisted that "the SPS measure at issue in this dispute can only be the measure which is actually applied to the product at issue".

that there is a possibility of entry, establishment or spread of diseases . . ."[221] The Appellate Body ruled that the assessment must "evaluate the 'likelihood'—i.e., the probability, of entry . . .", and the relationship of this likelihood to the SPS measure under scrutiny. While the likelihood may be expressed either quantitatively or qualitatively, the Appellate Body was clear on the fact that risk assessment must be an "ascertainable risk"—not "theoretical uncertainty".[222] So, unlike the panel, the Appellate Body found that the 1996 Australian report failed to meet the standard for a proper risk assessment under the agreement.[223] But as to the ultimate question, the Appellate Body naturally agreed with the panel that the Australian measure is not "based on" a risk assessment, as required by Article 5.1 of the SPS Agreement.[224]

Following a highly detailed examination of the Australian measures, the Appellate Body upheld the panel's finding that there was unjust discrimination against Canadian salmon; also that the measure constituted a disguised restriction on international trade, therefore violating Article 5.5.[225] As to the matter of whether less trade restrictive measures were available to Australia (such as various forms of testing) the Appellate Body made some important conceptual statements about the nature of the obligations imposed by the SPS Agreement under Article 5.6.

Each member, the Appellate Body explained, must determine its appropriate level of protection. But this should not be taken to mean that an importing member is

> "free to determine its level of protection with such vagueness or equivocation that the application of the relevant provisions of the SPS Agreement, such as Article 5.6, becomes impossible".[226]

The Appellate Body continued, stating that

> "it would obviously be wrong to interpret the SPS Agreement in a way that would render nugatory entire articles or paragraphs of articles of this agreement and allow members to escape from their obligations . . ."[227]

The 1996 Australian report did not allow verification of whether alternatives to a ban were considered, the Appellate Body concluded. While there may have been a violation of Article 5.6, the Appellate Body stated that it had not been provided with the information to make such a determination.[228]

As in the Beef Hormones case, complaints were raised as to the panel's handling of evidence put forward by the defending party. And as in that case, the

---

[221] *Canadian Salmon* Appellate Body Report, Part V.B., para. 12.
[222] *Canadian Salmon* Appellate Body Report, Part V.B., paras. 13–14.
[223] *Canadian Salmon* Appellate Body Report, Part V.C. paras. 1–10.
[224] *Canadian Salmon* Appellate Body Report, Part V.C., para. 11.
[225] *Canadian Salmon* Appellate Body Report, Part V.C.3, paras. 1–20.
[226] *Canadian Salmon* Appellate Body Report, Part V.D., para. 12.
[227] *Canadian Salmon* Appellate Body Report, Part V.D., para. 12.
[228] *Canadian Salmon* Appellate Body Report, Part V.E., paras. 1–4.

Appellate Body found that there was no "egregious error to call into question the good faith of the panel", a standard of review quite generous towards the panel. Panels, the Appellate Body said, "are not required to accord to factual evidence of the parties the same meaning and weight as do the parties".[229]

THE *ASBESTOS* CASE: HOW REAL IS THE CHANGE OF EMPHASIS?

The outcome of this dispute was long awaited. In light of the earlier WTO "environmental" cases, there was a sense that the panel and Appellate Body might, by declaring a French asbestos ban to be GATT-illegal, cause more outrage than ever among the WTO's critics—especially since the ban involved extremely dangerous substances and well-established science.[230] As it turned out, the case represents the first time in GATT/WTO history that a panel recognised the necessity of a measure to protect public health, as per Article XX(b). It is hardly surprising that the decisions, especially that of the Appellate Body, managed to avoid such a crisis by bending GATT/WTO law somewhat more in the direction of the public interest, although not so strongly or unambiguously as to set the stage for a new relationship between international trade law and domestic regulation in the public interest. It could be said that the only basis for such an altered relationship would be in a more generous reasoning of the Appellate Body; as neither the letter nor the spirit of GATT/WTO law provide grounds for the articulation of a public interest ethos. The WTO can only *tolerate*—via Article XX, for instance—national regulation in the public interest; it is not logically capable of *embracing* it.

Because the Appellate Body decision especially was more accepting of the domestic regulation than was the case in previous challenges to environmental or public health laws, it generated a striking level of debate among academic commentators on either side of the trade and environment divide.[231] But in reality, the vexed relationship between domestic regulation and trade principle is essentially unaltered by this decision, which in effect only holds back the overreaching that had taken place in WTO disputes since 1995. The case does not clarify; it restrains the strongest form of free trade impulse, in favour of ambiguity and political peace.

---

[229] *Canadian Salmon* Appellate Body Report, Part VI.B., paras. 4–6.

[230] *Canada v. EC: Measures Affecting Asbestos and Asbestos-Containing Products*, Report of the Panel, 18 September 2000 (WT/DS135/R) [hereinafter *EC Asbestos* Panel Report]; *Canada v. EC: Measures Affecting Asbestos and Asbestos-Containing Products*, Report of the Appellate Body, 12 March 2001 (WT/DS135/AB/R) [hereinafter *EC Asbestos* Appellate Body Report].

[231] Professor Robert Howse, in particular, has lead an international discussion, centred around his view that the Appellate Body decision represents an important breakthrough in the development of WTO law and its relationship to environmental regulation. See, for example, Robert Howse and Elisabeth Tuerk, "The WTO Impact on Internal Regulations—A Case Study of the *Canada—EC Asbestos* Dispute", in *The EU and the WTO: Legal and Constitutional Aspects*, Grainne De Burca and Joanne Scott (eds.) (Hart Publishing: Oxford, 2001).

To state this more clearly, the problem of the vulnerability of domestic regulation in the face of WTO challenges remains unsolved, because the underlying legal relationship remains unsolved. Whereas some WTO law specialists have seen this case as a breakthrough in the Appellate Body's interpretation of Article III:4; it may be that the case merely presents a panel (in its treatment of Article XX(b)) and Appellate Body (in its treatment of Article III) less inquisitorial, and less dismissive of the public interest defences put forward by the regulating party.

In one sense, the dispute is less interesting than the *Beef Hormones* case, because the dangers posed by the asbestos products in question were so clearly established. The relationship of GATT/WTO law to domestic regulation is truly fraught when the motivations underlying the domestic legislation are complex; with the public interest motivation not obviously dominant, and not a subject of general scientific consensus.

The measure at issue in the *Asbestos* case is a French Decree, issued in 1996, essentially banning the import, use or sale of asbestos fibres, or asbestos-containing products.[232] The rationale for the ban was protection for both workers and consumers. A separate provision of the decree created temporary exceptions for the use of products containing chrysotile fibres where no substitute for that fibre is available, as long as certain safety criteria are adhered to.[233] Canada's chief complaints fell under the Agreement on Technical Barriers to Trade, and Articles III and XI of the GATT.[234] As a general matter, Canada argued that unlike other varieties of asbestos, chrysotile fibres are capable of being used without creating any appreciable risk to human beings or the environment, assuming "controlled use".[235] Canada termed this level of ban "irrational and disproportionate", a radical measure unjustified by expert scientific opinion. Canada further argued that in terms of international trade, the ban created a barrier to the importation of chrysotile fibres, as it "upsets the competitive relationship between chrysotile fibre and like (substitute) products of French or foreign origin, it is [also] a discriminatory measure".[236] The EC strongly denied that the methods of controlled use advocated by Canada reduce the risk of deadly diseases associated with chrysotile.[237]

The EC also refuted the argument that the risks associated with the substitute products are unknown, and possibly just as dangerous as chrysotile. Whereas the risks from chrysotile are well established, the EC insisted, the substitute products have long been in use, without any significant risks having been identified.[238] Most importantly, the EC argued that "substitute products are not like products because they are less dangerous and their chemical composition differs".[239]

---

[232] Decree No. 96–1133 of 24 December 1996. See *EC Asbestos* Panel Report, paras. 2.3–2.5.
[233] *EC Asbestos* Panel Report, paras. 2.5–2.6.
[234] *EC Asbestos* Panel Report, para. 3.1.
[235] *EC Asbestos* Panel Report, para. 3.9.
[236] *EC Asbestos* Panel Report, para. 3.12.
[237] *EC Asbestos* Panel Report, paras. 3.13–3.14.
[238] *EC Asbestos* Panel Report, paras. 3.17–3.19.
[239] *EC Asbestos* Panel Report, para. 3.19.

In the Canadian view, the French law represented "un phénomène de psy-chose collective", the result of widespread alarmism in the press, and the anxi-ety of politicians to appear to be responsive to public mistrust of the regulatory authorities.[240] Europe responded that a large number of countries have intro-duced blanket bans on asbestos, or planned to do so.[241] It also pointed out that "with a view to ensuring a high level of health protection in the European Community and preserving the unity of the single market", numerous pieces of Community legislation on the subject of asbestos had been adopted over the past twenty years. The culmination of this legislative effort was a total ban on the use of all asbestos fibres except chrysotile, the use of which was nonetheless prohibited for fourteen categories of product. A comprehensive ban inclusive of chrysotile was in the EC's legislative pipeline.[242] France's tradition of legislative protection for worker health and safety was noted.[243]

The panel's findings

The first substantive issue to be addressed by the panel was the applicability of the Agreement on Technical Barriers to Trade to the French decree.[244] The Canadian argument was that the Decree is a technical regulation because it lays down a characteristic of a product, a process and a production method, as well as admin-istrative regulations applicable to a product.[245] Naturally, the Canadian strategy was to force the EC to defend the measure under the rigours of the TBT Agreement. The product characteristic the Canadian argument referred to is the absence of asbestos fibres. The decree, according to this view, imposes restrictions on production methods by prohibiting the incorporation of asbestos.[246]

The European counter-argument was that the Decree cannot be seen as a technical regulation because the TBT agreement doers not cover "general pro-hibitions on the use of a product for reasons to do with the protection of public health", and that these fall instead under the GATT. The EC position was that a technical regulation lays down characteristics with which a specific product must comply, "in particular if it is to be released for free circulation on a given market".[247] It is a compelling argument, to the extent that this does seem to be

[240] *EC Asbestos* Panel Report, para. 3.26.
[241] *EC Asbestos* Panel Report, para. 3.31.
[242] *EC Asbestos* Panel Report, paras. 3.32–3.35.
[243] *EC Asbestos* Panel Report, paras. 3.36.
[244] *EC Asbestos* Panel Report, para. 8.18.
[245] *EC Asbestos* Panel Report, para. 8.20. The panel cited to the definition of technical regulation found in Annex 1.1 to the TBT Agreement: "Document which lays down product characteristics or the related processes and production methods, including the applicable administrative provisions, with which compliance is mandatory. It may also include or deal exclusively with terminology, symbols, packaging, marking or labeling requirements as they apply to a product, process or production method".
[246] *EC Asbestos* Panel Report, para. 8.21.
[247] *EC Asbestos* Panel Report, para. 8.22.

the underlying nature of the TBT Agreement; to accept the Canadian view would be to enlarge the scope of the definition of "technical regulation" significantly.

However, the EC also went on to argue that to adopt the Canadian position would "be equivalent to nullifying the effect of certain provisions of the GATT 1994, for example Articles I and III, which apply to general prohibitions".[248] Whatever the strength of this position, it does seem that there is sense to the EC position that "the object and purpose of the TBT Agreement is to deal with technical regulations and standards, not to resolve market access problems associated with general prohibitions".[249]

The panel took as its starting point the idea that for the TBT Agreement to apply to the Decree, the measures imposed under the decree must fall within the definition of "technical regulation" in Annex 1.1 to the TBT Agreement. The panel stated that it would examine the general prohibition contained in the Decree, and the exceptions to the prohibition, separately, to see whether they did in fact fall within this definition.[250] Taking up the prohibition first, the panel noted that the measure "is a general ban excluding a given product from the French market as such or when it is incorporated in other products not specified in the Decree". The panel stated that its findings did not extend to other factual situations.[251] Examining the language of Annex 1.1 of the TBT Agreement, the panel concluded that "a technical regulation is a regulation which sets out the specific characteristics of one or more identifiable products in comparison with general characteristics that may be shared by several unspecified products".[252]

By contrast, the panel pointed out that

> "the ban introduced by the decree is generally applicable both to asbestos and products containing it, in other words, a very large number of products which the Decree does not identify by name nor even by function or category".[253]

As the panel reasoned, the "characteristics" must be differentiated from the identification of the product itself. "The purpose of the measure, the panel explained, must be "to define the characteristics of products which can be introduced into the territory of the country applying the measure identified".[254] Seen in this light, the EC ban was not considered by the panel to meet the criteria of the definition of "technical regulation".

The panel pointed out that to ban the import of a product, it is not necessary to define its characteristics. "What is banned", the panel stated, "is not asbestos which possesses certain characteristics, but all types of asbestos". Indeed, products

---

248 *EC Asbestos* Panel Report, para. 8.23.
249 *EC Asbestos* Panel Report, para. 8.25.
250 *EC Asbestos* Panel Report, paras. 8.28–8.33.
251 *EC Asbestos* Panel Report, para. 8.35.
252 *EC Asbestos* Panel Report, para. 8.39.
253 *EC Asbestos* Panel Report, para. 8.40.
254 *EC Asbestos* Panel Report, para. 8.41.

whose characteristic would be that they contained asbestos, the panel noted, are not identified in the Decree.[255]

The panel then turned to the question of the general purposes of the TBT Agreement. The panel found upon examining the preamble that

> "The TBT Agreement . . . aims to improve market access by encouraging inter alia the use of international standards, while at the same time exercising control over the development and use of standards at the national level".[256]

The panel reasoned that had the Members intended the TBT Agreement to apply to general bans, the most extreme type of market access restriction, they would surely have mentioned this in the text of the Agreement. Rather, the panel stated,

> "it would appear that the purpose of the TBT Agreement is to prevent much more complex situations than a straightforward unconditional ban on a product, which is covered by the very strict provisions in Article XI:1 of the GATT 1994".

A general prohibition does not deal with the technical specifications and standards behind which protectionist intent may easily hide—and which was intended to be dealt with by the TBT Agreement.[257] Summing up its view, the panel stated that

> "the TBT Agreement appears to have been adopted in order to strengthen the disciplines applicable to the specific area of manufacturing standards, where they appeared to be insufficient to prevent certain forms of protectionism".[258]

The panel set out three elements that must be present in order for the measure to be considered a technical regulation: (1) the measure affects one or more given products; (2) it specifies the technical characteristics of the products which allow them to be marketed in the Member state that took the measure; and (3) compliance is mandatory.[259] Because the prohibition on asbestos and asbestos containing products did not meet all these criteria, the panel did not consider it to be a technical regulation under the definition offered in the TBT Agreement.[260] The panel reached a different conclusion, however, with respect to the part of the Decree dealing with the exceptions to the general ban on asbestos and products containing asbestos.

The EC argued that the exceptions should similarly not be seen as falling under the TBT Agreement, due to their ancillary nature. In the panel's view, however, there is no reason why two parts of the same text should not have a different legal characterisation.[261] The panel pointed out that the regulation

---

[255] *EC Asbestos* Panel Report, paras. 8.42–8.44.
[256] *EC Asbestos* Panel Report, para. 8.48.
[257] *EC Asbestos* Panel Report, para. 8.49.
[258] *EC Asbestos* Panel Report, para. 8.55.
[259] *EC Asbestos* Panel Report, para. 8.57.
[260] *EC Asbestos* Panel Report, para. 8.61.
[261] *EC Asbestos* Panel Report, para. 8.66.

created under the Decree does identify the products benefiting from an exception, in the form of an exhaustive list drawn up by the relevant Ministers.[262] In light of this, and the mandatory compliance, the panel concluded that the exceptions section of the Decree does come within the scope of the definition of technical regulation in Annex 1.1 of the TBT Agreement.[263]

The panel's application of Articles III and XI of the GATT to this complaint

While Canada raised arguments under both Articles III and XI of the GATT, the panel said that it is "difficult to see" whether Canada was claiming that even if the ban were covered under Article III:4, it was also covered by Article XI:1. The panel did not go on to consider this issue, on the grounds that this matter did not form part of the terms of reference given to the panel by the DSB.[264] (Because the panel decided that Article III:4 is relevant to the situation at hand, it did not go on to analyse the measure under Article XI:1.)

This dispute has generated enormous interest because of the conclusions reached by the panel and the Appellate Body with regard to the role of Article III in the trade-environment debate. In this case, the "like" products in question are the asbestos (specifically, chrysotile)-containing products and their substitutes legally in use in France. In order for Canada to be successful in its claims under Article III, it would have to show the requisite degree of similarity between the products banned by France, and the products used as substitutes by France. Otherwise, there could be no claim of "preference" being shown towards the substitute products.

As far as the panel's methodology is concerned, it first examined whether the substitute products in and of themselves are products "like" chrysotile fibre. Next, the panel examined certain products using asbestos on the one hand, and those using substitute fibres on the other. The panel set out the criteria for "likeness" in Article III:4, as articulated by the Working Party in the Border Tax Adjustments case of 1970. (Report of the Working Party, adopted 2 December 1970, BISD 18S/97). That decision called for a "case by case" approach to this question—including consideration of issues relating to the product's "end uses in a given market". Elements of that include consumers' tastes and habits, as well as the product's properties, nature and quality. The Appellate Body in the *Japan—Alcoholic Beverages* case added tariff classification to the list of elements to be considered.[265] The *Asbestos* panel also noted that the Appellate Body in the *Japan—Alcoholic Beverages* case affirmed the discretion of panels

---

[262]   *EC Asbestos* Panel Report, para. 8.67.
[263]   *EC Asbestos* Panel Report, para. 8.69–8.70. However, since Canada did not make any specific claims regarding the exceptions per se, and their relationship to the TBT Agreement, the panel did not reach any findings concerning the exceptions. EC Asbestos Panel Report, para. 8.72.
[264]   *EC Asbestos* Panel Report, para. 8.99.
[265]   *EC Asbestos* Panel Report, para. 8.113.

to decide the likeness question, in that "no single approach would be appropriate to every single case".[266]

Properties, nature and quality of the products

The Canadian argument was that chrysotile and substitute fibres were the same, because they were all fibres. "Products", Canada insisted, "may be considered like despite their differing impact on health".[267] The EC, on the other hand, made the important argument that, in that none of the substitute products is classified as a proven carcinogen for humans, these are "radically different" products. Summing up the European position, the panel noted:

> "In such a situation the health risk posed by the product must necessarily be taken into account. A dangerous product should be regarded as being different in nature and quality from a harmless or less dangerous product".[268]

In a manner very different from what the Appellate Body would decide, the panel drew back from accepting the EC view that the inherent risk associated with the product should become part of the Article III analysis. This is not, the panel contended, a "scientific classification exercise". "The objective of Article III", it reasons, "concerns market access for products". "It is with a view to market access", the panel stated, "that the properties, nature and quality of imported and domestic products have to be evaluated".[269]

The panel noted that asbestos is clearly unique in terms of its specific composition. On the other hand, many other industrial products have the same use as asbestos.[270] In this case, the panel believed that the "end use of the products should affect the way in which we examine the properties of the fibres compared". In this light, the panel considered that the chrysotile fibres, while having a separate chemical structure, nevertheless are "like" the substitute product with respect to their properties.[271]

The panel next dealt with the question of whether risk is relevant to the similarity of the products. It noted

> "the risk of a product for human or animal health has never been used as a factor of comparison by panels entrusted with applying the concept of 'likeness' within the meaning of Article III".

That no panel had ever been called on to treat this issue the panel attributed to the "economy" of GATT, the "primordial role" of which is to "ensure that a

---

[266] *EC Asbestos* Panel Report, para. 8.115.
[267] *EC Asbestos* Panel Report, para. 8.118.
[268] *EC Asbestos* Panel Report, para. 8.119.
[269] *EC Asbestos* Panel Report, para. 8.122.
[270] *EC Asbestos* Panel Report, para. 8.123.
[271] *EC Asbestos* Panel Report, paras. 8.124–8.126.

certain number of disciplines are applied to domestic trade regulations.[272] In the panel's view, Article XX(b) is designed to take care of issues related to health risks. According to the panel, introducing a risk analysis into the Article III likeness analysis would have the effect of distorting the rights and obligations negotiated under the GATT. Thus, in no sense did the panel find it "appropriate" to apply the risk criterion when examining the properties, nature or quality of the products concerned.[273]

For these and related reasons, the panel found that the products were "in certain circumstances, similar in properties, nature and quality, and have similar end-uses". In light of this, chrysotile fibres and the substitute products "are like products within the meaning of Article III:4 of the GATT".[274]

The question remaining for the panel was whether there had been less favourable treatment for "like" Canadian products, and, if so, whether this could be justified under Article XX.

Canada argued that the Decree altered the conditions of competition between substitute fibres and products containing them of French origin, and chrysotile fibres and related products from Canada. Canada also alleged de facto discrimination, citing the healthy state of the French PVA fibres industry.[275] The EC for its part emphasised the purposes underlying Article III, and the intention underlying the Decree. The French authorities, the EC argued, had no intention of protecting domestic products, but rather just to protect human health against the risks associated with asbestos.[276] The panel, however, once again appeared to have a "tin ear" for legal complexity.

The panel simply recited the logic of its Article III analysis—the products had been found to be like products, France did produce substitute fibres, and the Decree did establish less favourable treatment for asbestos and products containing asbestos. Thus, *de jure*, the Decree treated imported chrysotile fibres less favourably.[277] So the panel did not deviate from past practice in finding a violation of Article III:4. However, one could say that its Article XX analysis that follows was significantly different in tone and outcome from earlier panel reports.

In one sense, the panel's task with respect to Article XX was less problematic because of the established scientific view as to the dangers of asbestos use. Where this case differs rather starkly from the Beef Hormones case, for instance, is in the fact that the risk posed by asbestos has been so clearly demonstrated, and is so broadly accepted by a variety of interested parties. While Canada argued that contemporary methods of use of chrysotile fibres do not pose any health risk to humans, the EC was confident in its assertion that "scientists and international organizations" recognise the risks associated with asbestos use.[278]

[272] *EC Asbestos* Panel Report, para. 8.129.
[273] *EC Asbestos* Panel Report, paras. 8.129–8.131.
[274] *EC Asbestos* Panel Report, para. 8.144.
[275] *EC Asbestos* Panel Report, para. 8.151.
[276] *EC Asbestos* Panel Report, para. 8.153.
[277] *EC Asbestos* Panel Report, paras. 8.154–8.157.
[278] *EC Asbestos* Panel Report, paras. 8.160–8.165.

The panel said that it would "take into account the extent of the health problem in assessing the necessity of the measure" adopted by France. "Thus", said the panel, "if we were to conclude that the health hazard represented by chrysotile or chrysotile-cement was less than the EC allege, less vigorous measures might then be justified".[279]

The panel insisted that its role was not to settle a scientific debate—but rather

"to determine whether there is sufficient scientific evidence to conclude that there exists a risk for human life or health and that the measures taken by France are necessary in relation to the objectives pursued".[280]

The panel reviewed the scientific certainty attached to the cancer risks linked to asbestos use, and concluded that

"the doubts expressed by Canada with respect to the direct effects of chrysotile on mesotheliomas and lung cancers are not sufficient to conclude that an official responsible for public health policy would find that there was not enough evidence of the existence of a public health risk".[281]

It noted that the scientists it consulted considered that the existence of a threshold below which exposure does not present any risks "had not been established for any of the diseases attributable to chrysotile, except perhaps asbestosis". This statement undermined the Canadian view of the safety of controlled use.[282] In light of the evidence presented, the panel concluded that the EC had made out a prima facie case for the existence of a health risk in connection with the use of chrysotile, one that had not been rebutted by Canada. Thus, the panel accepted that the prohibition found in the Decree "falls within the range of policies designed to protect human life or health".[283]

The panel moved on to examine whether or not the measure as designed was "necessary"—and thus whether or not less restrictive measures might have been available to France. (Recall that Canada had argued that a total ban was not necessary within the meaning of Article XX, in that controlled use provided sufficient protection.)[284] The panel accepted the EC view, supported by various experts, that controlled use was not a reasonable alternative for all relevant sectors, and thus—in light of the French objectives—could not be considered to furnish a less trade restrictive alternative capable of accomplishing the same ends.

In terms of legal discourse, it could be said that the panel was laying new emphasis on the matter of France's public health objectives and goals. The panel was eager to make clear that it was not questioning French regulatory goals, and that the public health objectives could not in themselves be scrutinised by the

---

[279] *EC Asbestos* Panel Report, para. 8.176.
[280] *EC Asbestos* Panel Report, paras. 8.181–8.182.
[281] *EC Asbestos* Panel Report, para. 8.188.
[282] *EC Asbestos* Panel Report, para. 8.191.
[283] *EC Asbestos* Panel Report, paras. 8.193–8.194.
[284] *EC Asbestos* Panel Report, para. 8.196.

panel. There was a tone of caution and respect regarding the "public health" dimension that had arguably not been present in, for instance, the panel report in the Sea Turtles case as regards the protection of natural resources.

It is also interesting to read the panel's analysis of the Article XX "chapeau" issue in the light of its treatment of this matter in the Sea Turtles case. With regard to the issue of discrimination, the EC emphasised that the French measure applied equally to products from all countries, and contained nothing improper or abusive in its manner of application. For its part, Canada insisted that the measure was motivated by the desire "to reassure a panicked population".[285] The panel accepted the EC view, working from the text of the Decree, which mentions only product type and not origin. The panel concluded that the EC had made out a prima facie case that the Decree did not constitute arbitrary or unjustifiable discrimination in its application, one that Canada had not rebutted.[286]

As to whether or not the measure was a disguised restriction on trade, the panel stated that "a restriction which formally meets the requirements of Article XX(b) will constitute an abuse if such compliance is in fact only a disguise to conceal the pursuit of trade-restrictive objectives".[287] In this regard, the panel reiterated its position that the Decree was necessary to achieve a public health objective.[288] Nothing in the "design, architecture and revealing structure" of the measure led the panel to conclude that the French authorities had protectionist motives. The panel pointed out the contradiction in Canada's arguments that the measure was the result of both a deliberate attempt at protectionism, and a hurried response to public pressure.[289] In addition, the information available to the panel did not suggest that the import ban had benefited the French substitute fibre industry to the detriment of third country producers to a degree that would lead the panel to find a disguised restriction on international trade.[290] Thus, the panel found that the Decree satisfied the terms of the Article XX chapeau.[291]

THE APPELLATE BODY AND THE *ASBESTOS* DISPUTE

Whereas the panel went some distance towards softening the WTO's rhetorical posture on the subject of environmental and/or public health measures, the decision of the Appellate Body went significantly farther. The resultant academic debate centred on whether the appellate decision represented a genuine and permanent shift in the fortunes of domestic regulation in the public interest when challenged before the WTO. The principal innovation cited was the Appellate

---

[285]   *EC Asbestos* Panel Report, paras. 8.224–8.225.
[286]   *EC Asbestos* Panel Report, paras. 8.228–8.230.
[287]   *EC Asbestos* Panel Report, para. 8.236.
[288]   *EC Asbestos* Panel Report, para. 8.237.
[289]   *EC Asbestos* Panel Report, para. 8.238.
[290]   *EC Asbestos* Panel Report, para. 8.239.
[291]   *EC Asbestos* Panel Report, para. 8.240.

Body's interpretation of the meaning of Article III "likeness". For the skeptic, it is unclear how this decision represents change of a magnitude to allay objections to the relationship of the WTO to national law and/or to other sectors of law—as opposed to the lesser relationship between the WTO institutions and individual provisions of GATT/WTO law.[292]

The first issue raised on appeal was whether the panel was correct in finding that the ban on asbestos and asbestos-containing products was not a technical regulation under the TBT Agreement. What was at stake here, of course, was whether it was necessary to defend the ban under that Agreement—or whether the ban was fundamentally separate from measures the TBT Agreement sought to impose discipline on. (The panel, we recall, had accepted the latter position.) Canada argued that the panel should have seen the French measure as a single, unified measure—taking both the ban and its exceptions together. Canada also urged the Appellate Body to agree that a general prohibition could indeed constitute a technical barrier to trade.[293]

The Appellate Body stated that the "proper legal character of the measure at issue cannot be determined unless the measure is examined as a whole". It pointed out that the measure contained both a prohibition and temporary exceptions, and was composed of "both prohibitive and permissive elements".[294] The Appellate Body reviewed the main elements of the definition of "technical regulation" as found in the TBT Agreement—concluding that such a regulation must be a document which lays down product characteristics—compliance with which is mandatory.[295]

The Appellate Body confirmed that a technical regulation must be applicable to an identifiable group of products in order to be enforceable, but disagreed with the panel that such a regulation must apply to given products that are "actually named, identified or specified in the regulation". Indeed, in the Appellate Body's view, there might be sound reasons for devising a technical regulation in such a way that the products are not expressly identified, but rather made identifiable through the "characteristic" that is the subject of the regulation.[296] The Appellate Body agreed that if the measure contained only a prohibition on the use of asbestos fibres, it might not constitute a technical regulation.[297] However, it pointed out that the measure regulated asbestos by regulating products that use asbestos fibres—effectively imposing characteristics on all products. Thus the products in question were in that way identifiable—"all products must be asbestos free; any products containing asbestos are prohibited". Compliance with the prohibition was also mandatory.[298]

---

[292] *Canada v. EC: Measures Affecting Asbestos and Asbestos-Containing Products*, Report of the Appellate Body, 12 March 2001 (WT/DS135/AB/R).

[293] *EC Asbestos* Appellate Body Report, paras. 59–62.

[294] *EC Asbestos* Appellate Body Report, para. 64.

[295] *EC Asbestos* Appellate Body Report, paras. 67–68.

[296] *EC Asbestos* Appellate Body Report, para. 70.

[297] *EC Asbestos* Appellate Body Report, para. 71.

[298] *EC Asbestos* Appellate Body Report, para. 72.

The Appellate Body agreed with the panel that the exception to the prohibition set out product characteristics for a narrowly defined group of products.[299] Thus, while cautioning that not all internal measures covered by Article III:4 are technical regulations within the meaning of the TBT Agreement, the Appellate Body reversed the panel's conclusion that the TBT Agreement does not apply to the asbestos ban found in the Decree.[300] However, because the panel had made no findings regarding Canadian claims under the TBT Agreement, and since the TBT Agreement has not yet been interpreted in a WTO dispute, the Appellate Body concluded that there was insufficient legal basis for it to examine these Canadian claims.[301]

We recall that the Asbestos panel had declined to include the risk issue in its analysis of whether or not the products in question (chrysotile-containing fibres and substitute products) were actually like products for purposes of Article III:4. The panel decided to stay with the traditional market-based concept in deciding that these were in fact like products. The Appellate Body reviewed the Border Tax Adjustments criteria used by the panel: properties, nature and quality of the products; end-uses of the products; consumers' tastes and habits; and the tariff classification of the products. The EC asked the Appellate Body to consider that Article III:4 "calls for an analysis of the health objective of the regulatory distinction made in the measure between asbestos fibres and related products, and all other products". Under this view, products should not be regarded as like "unless the regulatory distinction drawn between them 'entails a shift in the competitive opportunities' in favor of domestic products".[302]

Reviewing various definitions of "likeness", the Appellate Body quoted an earlier decision of its own to the effect that "dictionary meanings may leave interpretive questions open". The definition of "like", for instance, does not indicate which characteristics are important in assessing likeness; it does not provide guidance on the question as to the degree to which products must share characteristics in order to be like; it also does not indicate "from whose perspective likeness should be judged".[303]

The Appellate Body pointed out that, unlike Article III:2, Article III:4 does not contain any reference to "directly competitive or substitutable products"—rather, only to "like products".[304] It also looked at the general principle invoked in Article III:1, again quoting its own earlier decision—to the effect that Article III is designed to ensure that internal measures not be applied to imported and domestic products so as to afford protection to domestic production. WTO members must provide "equality of competitive conditions for

---

[299] *EC Asbestos* Appellate Body Report, para. 74.
[300] *EC Asbestos* Appellate Body Report, paras. 75–77.
[301] *EC Asbestos* Appellate Body Report, paras. 81–83.
[302] *EC Asbestos* Appellate Body Report, para. 86.
[303] *EC Asbestos* Appellate Body Report, para. 92.
[304] *EC Asbestos* Appellate Body Report, paras. 94–96.

imported products in relation to domestic products".[305] The Appellate Body stated that this general principle informs Article III:4.

The Appellate Body reasoned that the word "like" in Article III:4 must be interpreted to apply to products that are in a competitive relationship; and thus "a determination of likeness is fundamentally a determination about the nature and extent of a competitive relationship between and among products".[306]

The Appellate Body returned to the basic interpretive model provided by the *Border Tax Adjustments* case and the four criteria derived from that—physical properties, end uses, consumer perceptions, and international tariff classification.[307] Interestingly, it stated that these criteria, while providing an analytical framework, "are neither treaty-mandated nor a closed list of criteria that will determine the legal characterization of the products". In assessing likeness, the duty remains, the Appellate Body stated, to examine all the pertinent evidence.[308] "The kind of evidence to be examined", the Appellate Body said, "will, necessarily, depend upon the particular products and the legal provision at issue".[309]

The main European argument on appeal was that the panel erred in adopting an "excessively commercial or market access approach" in comparing the products in question; that it placed excessive reliance on the single factor of end-use; and that it failed to include consideration of the health risk factors associated with asbestos.[310]

The Appellate Body was highly critical of the panel's method of analysing likeness. "Having adopted an approach based on the four criteria set forth in Border Tax Adjustments", the Appellate Body stated, "the panel should have examined the criteria relating to *each* of those four criteria and, then, weighed *all* of that evidence . . . in making an overall determination . . ." The panel instead decided that the products were "like" after examining only the first of the four criteria. It summarily decided that there was likeness under the second criteria, without analysis; and failed to consider the last two elements. The Appellate Body wrote that

". . . a determination on the 'likeness' of products cannot be made on the basis of a partial analysis of the evidence, after examination of just one of the criteria the panel said it would examine".[311]

The Appellate Body further objected to the manner in which the panel collapsed consideration of the physical properties of the products and their end-uses. While acknowledging that asbestos is a unique product, the panel then went on to say that while the products were not "like" in terms of their physical

---

[305] *EC Asbestos* Appellate Body Report, para. 97.
[306] *EC Asbestos* Appellate Body Report, para. 99.
[307] *EC Asbestos* Appellate Body Report, para. 101.
[308] *EC Asbestos* Appellate Body Report, para. 102.
[309] *EC Asbestos* Appellate Body Report, para. 103.
[310] *EC Asbestos* Appellate Body Report, para. 104.
[311] *EC Asbestos* Appellate Body Report, para. 109.

properties, in terms of "market access" issues, the products may replace each other, and thus are "like". This the Appellate Body saw as, in effect, a discussion of the end use issue.[312]

The Appellate Body stated that the physical properties of the products deserve separate and full treatment. Similar end-uses, the Appellate Body insisted, do not make products with different properties like in their properties.[313] Very significantly, the Appellate Body agreed with the EC that evidence relating to health risks might be pertinent to an examination of likeness; however, the Appellate Body found that this can be achieved under the existing criteria of physical properties and consumers' tastes and habits.[314] The Appellate Body went on to state that the very carcinogenity or toxicity of chrysotile asbestos fibres is "a defining aspect of [their] physical properties".[315] The Appellate Body rejected the panel's idea that including evidence relating to health risks in the likeness analysis nullifies the effect of Article XX(b). Just because such a view of Article III:4 might mean less frequent recourse to Article XX does not, in the Appellate Body's view, deprive Article XX (b) of its *effet utile*.[316] The Appellate Body found that the panel erred in excluding the health risks associated with chrysotile fibres from its examination of the physical properties of that product.[317]

Under the methodology proposed by the Appellate Body, where products have been found to be different on the basis of the first criterion, there is then a heavy burden placed on the complainant to establish that, despite this finding, "there is a competitive relationship between the products such that all the evidence, taken together, demonstrates that products are like under Article III:4 of the GATT 1994".[318]

The Appellate Body proceeded to criticise the panel for its failure to adequately deal with the issue of end-uses; it further said that a panel in such a case—where the fibres are physically very different—could not possibly conclude that these are like products without examining evidence relating to consumers' tastes and habits.[319] Taking this point further, the Appellate Body said that

"in this case especially, we are also persuaded that evidence relating to consumers' tastes and habits would establish that the health risks associated with chrysotile asbestos fibres influence consumers' behaviour with respect to the different fibres at issue".

With regard to the fibres, the consumer is the manufacturer incorporating the fibres into another product, according to the Appellate Body. In this respect, the

---

[312] *EC Asbestos* Appellate Body Report, para. 110.
[313] *EC Asbestos* Appellate Body Report, paras. 111–113.
[314] *EC Asbestos* Appellate Body Report, para. 113.
[315] *EC Asbestos* Appellate Body Report, para. 114.
[316] *EC Asbestos* Appellate Body Report, para. 115.
[317] *EC Asbestos* Appellate Body Report, para. 116.
[318] *EC Asbestos* Appellate Body Report, para. 118.
[319] *EC Asbestos* Appellate Body Report, paras. 119–121.

manufacturer cannot ignore the preferences of the ultimate consumer in the marketplace, the Appellate Body reasoned. Fear of liability would also influence manufacturers, it said. The Appellate Body rejected the Canadian argument that where a measure such as this has disturbed the normal conditions of competition between the products, then consumer tastes and habits become irrelevant.[320] For all the reasons set out above, the Appellate Body reversed the panel's conclusion that the products in question were "like" products for purposes of Article III:4.[321] Following this logic, the Appellate Body also reversed the panel's conclusion that chrysotile fibre products and fibro-cement (substitute) products are like products within the meaning of Article III:4.[322]

The Appellate Body went on to "complete the like product analysis" under Article III:4 of the GATT, in its words, basing its analysis on the facts in the record.[323] In light of the matter of carcinogenicity referred to above, the Appellate Body found that the products in question are very different.[324] With regard to end uses, the Appellate Body was dissatisfied that the panel had relied on evidence of "overlapping end uses"; there is an absence of evidence, the Appellate Body said, about the entire range of end uses, as opposed to a simple focus on overlapping end uses.[325] As to consumer tastes, no evidence was presented on this score; thus, "there is no basis for overcoming the inference, drawn from the different physical properties, that the products are not like".[326] And, "as far as tariff classification is concerned, the products have separate classifications". While this is not decisive, the Appellate Body stated that it also "tends to indicate" that the fibres in question are not like products.[327] The Appellate Body reached similar conclusions with regard to the products containing the fibres in question.[328]

In sum, Canada did not succeed in establishing to the Appellate Body's satisfaction that the measure at issue was inconsistent with Article III:4 of the GATT 1994.[329]

Canada appealed a number of the panel's conclusions relating to Article XX(b) of the GATT. The first Article XX issue was whether or not it was shown that the use of chrysotile-cement products posed sufficient risk to human health to allow the measure to fall within the scope of application of the phrase "to protect human . . . life or health" in Article XX(b.) The panel's conclusion had been that the EC had made out a prima facie case that this was so, and that this had remained unrebutted by Canada. The panel had determined that the measure fell

---

[320] *EC Asbestos* Appellate Body Report, para. 122.
[321] *EC Asbestos* Appellate Body Report, para. 126.
[322] *EC Asbestos* Appellate Body Report, paras. 127–132.
[323] *EC Asbestos* Appellate Body Report, para. 133.
[324] *EC Asbestos* Appellate Body Report, paras. 134–136.
[325] *EC Asbestos* Appellate Body Report, paras. 137–138.
[326] *EC Asbestos* Appellate Body Report, para. 139.
[327] *EC Asbestos* Appellate Body Report, paras. 140–141.
[328] *EC Asbestos* Appellate Body Report, paras. 142–147.
[329] *EC Asbestos* Appellate Body Report, para. 148.

within the category of measures "embraced by Article XX(b) of the GATT".[330] Canada's contention on appeal was that the panel had drawn erroneous conclusions from the evidence (contained in seven scientific sources) before it.[331]

Citing Article 11 of the DSU, the Appellate Body emphasised the traditional discretion accorded panels as triers of fact. In this regard, the Appellate Body stated,

> "the panel was entitled, in the exercise of its discretion, to determine that certain elements of evidence should be accorded more weight than other elements—that is the essence of the task of appreciating the evidence".[332]

The Appellate Body saw Canada's appeal on this point "as, in reality, a challenge to the panel's assessment of the credibility and weight to be ascribed to the scientific evidence before it". The Appellate Body stated that it would only interfere with the panel's conclusion where it believed that the panel had exceeded the bounds of its discretion. And in this case, according to the Appellate Body, "nothing suggests that the panel exceeded the bounds of its lawful discretion". The Appellate Body found in fact that the panel's conclusion that the fibres constituted a risk to human health was indeed borne out by the scientific evidence relied on.[333] Thus, the Appellate Body upheld the panel's conclusion that the measure "protects human life or health" within the meaning of Article XX(b) of the GATT 1994.[334]

Canada also appealed the panel's conclusion that the measure was "necessary" as that term is used in Article XX. The most important of Canada's arguments in this respect involved the "controlled use" option rejected by the panel. The Appellate Body took the occasion to discuss what constitutes a "reasonably available" alternative measure; in this case, an alternative to the prohibition on the use of asbestos fibres. Referring to its own reasoning in the Korean Beef case, the Appellate Body wrote that the more vital the interest being pursued, the easier it is to accept the necessity of the measures adopted. In this case, according to the Appellate Body, "the value pursued is both vital and important in the highest degree". In the Appellate Body's view, the remaining question was simply whether "there is an alternative measure that would achieve the same end and that is less restrictive of trade than a prohibition".[335]

The Appellate Body stated "France could not reasonably be expected to employ any alternative measure if that measure would involve a continuation of the very risk that the Decree seeks to 'halt'." That would in effect prevent France from "achieving its chosen level of health protection", the Appellate Body reasoned. Accepting the panel's findings with regard to the health risks still associated with controlled use in some circumstances, the Appellate Body

---

[330] *EC Asbestos* Appellate Body Report, para. 157.
[331] *EC Asbestos* Appellate Body Report, para. 158.
[332] *EC Asbestos* Appellate Body Report, para. 161.
[333] *EC Asbestos* Appellate Body Report, para. 162.
[334] *EC Asbestos* Appellate Body Report, para. 163.
[335] *EC Asbestos* Appellate Body Report, paras. 169–172.

upheld the panel's finding that controlled use would not allow France to achieve its chosen level of health protection by halting the spread of asbestos-related health risks. Thus, controlled use was not a viable alternative use, and the panel's conclusion that there was no reasonably available alternative to the measure adopted was upheld by the Appellate Body.[336]

Canada also appealed the panel's conclusions by invoking Article 11 of the DSU, which requires panels to make an objective assessment of the matter before them. This requirement, Canada argued, implies that "scientific data must be assessed in accordance with the principle of the balance of probabilities;" and that where the evidence is divergent or contradictory, the principle of the preponderance of the evidence implies that the panel "must take a position" as to the respective weight of the evidence.[337]

In essence, the Appellate Body stated, Canada was arguing that the panel did not take sufficient account of certain evidence, and at the same time placed too much weight on certain other evidence. "Thus", wrote the Appellate Body, "Canada is challenging the panel's exercise of discretion in assessing and weighing the evidence." The Appellate Body then reiterated that the panel had not exceeded its proper exercise of discretion as a trier of fact.[338]

Reverting to its reasoning in the *Beef Hormones* case, the Appellate Body made the point that a WTO member is not automatically obliged to follow majority scientific opinion in setting its health policy. There may well be divergent, but qualified and respected, opinion, according to the Appellate Body. "Therefore", it wrote, "a panel need not, necessarily, reach a decision under Article XX (b) of the GATT 1994 on the basis of the 'preponderant' weight of the evidence".[339]

It is hardly surprising that, in the face of so much international criticism surrounding the "trade and the environment" question, the panel and Appellate Body should tread lightly when it came to invalidating domestic regulation in the matter of a clear danger to public health. This dispute dealt with health matters that were in no way disputed or ambiguous—at least as to the main point: that asbestos causes terrible human diseases. What is truly extraordinary (although it appears that many have lost sight of this), is that the fate of such a regulation should be subject to a WTO decision at all!

CONCLUSION

"Trade and the environment" as a subject matter has become the focus of intense international attention in recent years, in part because it represents the clearest example of the clash between national regulatory objectives and the

---

[336] *EC Asbestos* Appellate Body Report, paras. 174–175.
[337] *EC Asbestos* Appellate Body Report, para. 176.
[338] *EC Asbestos* Appellate Body Report, para. 177.
[339] *EC Asbestos* Appellate Body Report, para. 178.

demands of global trade principles. For those involved in the implementation of environmental legislation, often after long and difficult political battles, it has been especially galling to see these victories eroded by a handful of comparatively unforgiving trade rules that make no concession to the ethos underlying environmental law. Whether the relationship between trade rules and environmental protection will be adjusted in the upcoming trade round is a major issue. Ironically, the developing world, which has perhaps the most to gain in the long-term from environmental protection, is apparently the most vocally opposed to an enhanced role for environmental principles within the WTO regime. (That is, if we understand the term "developing world" to mean the trade ministries of those countries.) It is clear, however, that a series of cases such as the Sea Turtles dispute (where relatively minor technical changes by the complainants could lead to dramatic conservation gains) has done much to discredit the legal and institutional validity of the WTO. The "trade and environment" debate has posed the most serious challenge to the WTO's continuing authority.

As a general matter, those involved in the trade and environment debate break down into two groups: those who believe that reform is needed to provide greater accommodation for national environmental measures within the world exchange system, and those who do not. The former group may be broken down again into smaller units, notably those who believe that the existing provisions of the GATT/WTO can be read and interpreted so as to provide that accommodation, and those who insist that only global institutional development will result in long-term environmental protection. (This discussion leaves aside the important, but rather separate, groups calling for a return to greater localism in economic organisation.) It would seem that, as NGOs and citizen groups become more informed in the technical aspects of international trade law, that a more generous reading of existing GATT/WTO law will simply not prove adequate to meet their concerns.[340]

It is likely that the next round of WTO negotiations will see some attempt to "reconcile" trade and environment concerns. If only for the sake of preserving the WTO's political legitimacy, some version of "global environmental law" may be created. This could take the form of an agreement allowing greater freedom for countries to implement national environmental law with trade restrictive properties, or a requirement that WTO member countries maintain a minimum standard of environmental protection, on the model of the TRIPs Agreement.[341] At this stage of legal development, the former possibility seems far likelier than the latter.

---

[340] Another possible approach to the conflict between trade and the environment is that taken by David Driesen in "What is Free Trade? The Real Issue Lurking Behind the Trade and Environment Debate", (2001) 41 *Virginia Journal of International Law* 279. Professor Driesen suggests that a failure to adequately define free trade and its goals has caused excessive intervention by the WTO bodies into national regulation.

[341] See Steve Charnovitz, "World Trade and the Environment: A Review of the New WTO Report", (2000) 12 *Georgetown International Environmental Law Review* 523; and Daniel C Esty, "Toward Optimal Environmental Governance", (1999) 74 *New York University Law Review* 1495.

6

The Trouble with Trade in Agriculture

AGRICULTURAL PRODUCTS HAVE always been treated differently from manufactured goods in the GATT system. This sense of difference, known as "agricultural exceptionalism", was taken for granted over many decades.[1] The fact that food security, rural life and culture were intimately tied to viable national agricultural structures meant that the key participants in the GATT system were not willing to open up trade in primary products to the same level of competition as other goods. It is for this reason that the Uruguay Round Agreement on Agriculture must be seen as a dramatic first step towards economic integration in food; as well as the first step towards dismantling the traditional protection of the rural sector, with all that this implies for national, and European, life.

In light of WTO developments since 1995, it is impossible to isolate "trade in agricultural products" from many other "trade and" issues, notably trade and environmental protection. Nevertheless, there is clear justification for focusing here on the social and cultural implications of further liberalisation of the global market in agricultural products. Without question, the Uruguay Round Agreement on Agriculture only hastened a process of agricultural rationalisation already well underway; nevertheless, the Agreement provided an international stamp of approval for the conceptual inclusion of agriculture within the developing system of global economic integration. It has been well stated that the Agriculture Agreement's importance "lies more in precedent and principle than in performance",[2] as actual implementation of the Agreement's obligations has been mixed at best.

The basic GATT Agreement allowed for wider subsidisation of agricultural products than for manufactured goods;[3] it also allowed for freer use of

---

[1] See Dimitris Moutsatsos, "The Uruguay Round Agreement on Agriculture: Issues and Perspective", in Sanoussi Bilal and Pavlos Pezaros (eds.) *Negotiating the Future of Agricultural Policies: Agricultural Trade and the Millennium WTO Round* (The Hague: Kluwer Law International, 2000) 29–50; 29–30; and Randy Green, "Part II: Review of Substantive Agreements: Panel IIC: Agreement on Agriculture: the Uruguay Round Agreement on Agriculture", (2000) 31 *Law and Policy in International Business* 819.

[2] See Green, *supra* n. 1, at 819.

[3] See GATT Art. XVI:B(3), which stated only that "contracting parties should seek to avoid the use of subsidies on the export of primary products". Para. 3 continues "If, however, a contracting party grants directly or indirectly any form of subsidy which operates to increase the export of any primary product from its territory, such subsidy shall not be applied in a manner which results in that contracting party having more than an equitable share of world export trade in that product, account being taken of the shares of the contracting parties in such trade in the product during a

quantitative restrictions against agricultural and fisheries imports, as long as the restrictions were applied as part of a general and non-discriminatory programme of surplus reduction.[4] While numerous disputes were brought before the GATT over the years regarding the most excessive forms of agricultural protectionism, it was generally accepted that primary products would continue to enjoy a special status in the GATT system. It was also accepted that the concepts of comparative advantage and wealth creation that drove an ever more ambitious world trade system could have only limited application to the sphere of rural life and farmers. That this paradigm changed radically in the latter stages of the Uruguay Round negotiations must be largely put down to a new EC willingness to contemplate the end of a protected and heavily subsidised farming sector in Europe.[5]

While it is often assumed in Europe that the EC finally had little choice but to succumb to US exhortations, this is far too simplistic a view. The most active GATT parties seeking agricultural liberalisation were the members of the so-called Cairns group, including New Zealand, Australia and Canada. These countries had the most to gain from a transformation of world agricultural markets so as to favour the advantages of large and efficient holders. They also had least to fear from a strict reduction in national subsidy programmes, since their farmers would likely survive in the most rigorous global conditions. Without the distortion caused by continued flooding of world markets with over-subsidised European and US products, moreover, their global position would be even stronger.

The US is not infrequently held up as a model of intensive, industrial, laissez-faire agriculture, whereas the US farming sector has in fact enjoyed enormous subsidy programmes, without which many US holdings would not survive. There has been traditional resistance within the US to free trade in agriculture, resistance of a scope and character not unlike that found in Europe.[6] However, perhaps no GATT contracting party had engaged in subsidies as elaborate or extensive as those created over the years by Europe's Common Agricultural Policy (CAP). Even from a practical point of view, it was clear that eastward expansion of the EC could hardly take place without substantial reform of the CAP, as this programme had been consuming a huge proportion of the overall EC budget. Faced with an untenable future, the EC took hold of the opportunity presented by the Uruguay Round talks; if the perception existed that this had

previous representative period, and any special factors which may have affected or may be affecting such trade in the product".

    [4] See GATT Art. XI:2(3).

    [5] The EC has traditionally promoted its internal agricultural market as motivated by concern for the family farm and preservation of the countryside, although its record in this regard is mixed. See Al J Daniel, Jr, "Agricultural Reform: The European Community, the Uruguay Round, and International Dispute Resolution", (1994) 46 *Arkansas Law Review* 874.

    [6] For a description of recent moves to deregulate the US farming sector, see Robert Scott, "Exported to death: The Failure of Agricultural Deregulation", (2000) 9 *Minnesota Journal of Global Trade* 87.

been "forced" by the US, that helped to defuse negative political pressures. With that decision, the European farming sector was to some extent subjected to principles of global free trade, in a manner that has not yet been fully acknowledged in the European agricultural sector itself.[7]

We have noted in the *Early GATT* section that trade battles involving the effect of subsidised agricultural products on national shares of the world market go back as far as the 1950s. Similar disputes, with complainants asking panels to restrain the European subsidy system to the extent allowable under existing GATT law, arose periodically throughout GATT's litigation history. Inside and outside the GATT system, trade wars, threats and counter-threats of punitive tariffs and other forms of retaliation, were a constant feature of agricultural trade up through the conclusion of the Uruguay Round negotiations. Each expansion of the EC led inevitably to intensive negotiations aimed at compensating Europe's trade partners for anticipated losses as yet more formerly "national" territory disappeared into the highly protected CAP zone.[8]

PRE-URUGUAY ROUND

The most famous battle from the long-running trade war between the US and EC over European agricultural subsidies is found in the famous Oilseeds case of the late 1980s.[9] As background, it should be noted that the US went into high gear during that period, bringing a large number of primary product related disputes before the GATT. This in turn must be seen in the context of the fact that the Uruguay Round negotiations, lasting from 1986 though 1994, were finding agriculture to be the most difficult and contentious of all the issues on the table. Indeed, it looked for most of this period as if there would be no ultimate agreement on agriculture. During the late 1980s, the US brought complaints against Norway, Sweden, Korea, Japan and Canada, in addition to the EC. Several of these cases were settled by agreement, while the US managed to win the others in panel rulings.[10]

The oilseed issue was a highly significant one from the point of view of US agricultural exporters. One of the "deals" struck between the US and the EC on the agricultural front in the 1960s, during the creation of the common agricultural policy, allowed individual European countries to end certain GATT tariff bindings on key products such as cereals, while the EC would, in return, give

---

[7] Pavlos Pezaros, "The Common Agricultural Policy in the Pliers of the Multilateral Trading System: Origins, Evolution and Future Challenges", in *Negotiating the Future of Agricultural Policies: Agricultural Trade and the Millennium WTO Round*, *supra* n. 1 at 51, 65–67.

[8] Robert E Hudec, *Enforcing International Trade Law: The Evolution of the Modern GATT Legal System* 328 (New Hampshire: Butterworth Legal Publishing, 1993).

[9] A panel report issued part way through this battle: *US v. EC: Payments and Subsidies Paid to Processors and Producers of Oilseeds and Related Animal-feed Proteins*, Report of the Panel, 25 January 1990 (L/6627–37S/86) [hereinafter *Oilseeds* Case].

[10] See Hudec, *supra* n. 8, at Appendix/Part I.

tariff-free access to US exports of oilseeds and non-grain animal feeds. Due to the livestock industry boom in Europe, the market represented by this concession had also grown enormously in value over the years.[11]

However, moving towards the mid-1980s, the US share of the European market in oilseeds was beginning to decline, with a number of new market entrants—notably Brazil—gaining export strength. The EC also began to increase its own production of subsidised oilseeds. In fact, apart from the unnaturally high price paid on the production side, Europe was also paying a subsidy to processors using European oilseeds to make up for the higher input prices they faced.

US producers of soya beans were incensed over EC intervention in this area, and filed a section 301 complaint with the US trade authorities,[12] which led to a complaint by the US being filed before the GATT.[13] The basis of the complaint was the agreement negotiated with Europe during the 1960s, allowing US oilseeds tariff-free access.[14] The effect of the new European subsidy, the US argued, was identical to the favourable tariff the US believed to have been eliminated. In other words, the US price advantage had been cancelled out by the EC subsidy. The US alleged that the EC had violated Article III:4 of the General Agreement on national treatment,[15] and made a second argument based on Article XXIII:1(b), non-violation nullification or impairment, concerning the loss of the value of the tariff concession.[16]

Although the complaint was filed in 1988, the EC managed to prevent the panel from sitting for an entire year. When the panel finally did sit to hear the case, Europe argued that its subsidies were not the cause of the reduction in US market share; rather, the US was simply losing out to other, more efficient, exporters. As the panel saw it, since payments to users of oilseed inputs often exceeded even the amount needed to offset the higher European prices, these payments unquestionably led to less favourable treatment of exports and violated Article III:4.

As far as the loss of expectation under the 1960s tariff concession was concerned, production subsidies introduced to growers after the granting of the tariff concession in question did constitute non-violation nullification or impairment.[17] The effect of the subsidies was to insulate domestic producers from price competition.

Rather than blocking the adoption of this report outright, the EC reserved its right to challenge the panel's findings on certain enumerated points. In 1991,

---

[11] See Hudec, *supra* n. 8, at 150.

[12] §301 of the 1974 Trade Act allowed US producer interests to petition the President to take action against unfair trading practices by other countries. See James R Arnold, "The Oilseeds Dispute and the Validity of Unilateralism in a Multilateral Context", (1994) 30 *Stanford Journal of International Law* 187, 189–90.

[13] See *ibid.*, at 187.

[14] See *ibid.*, at 189.

[15] *Oilseeds* Case, para. 36.

[16] *Oilseeds* Case, para. 53.

[17] *Oilseeds* Case, para. 152.

Europe altered its subsidy regime by shifting all payments to the production side, terminating payments to processors. The same GATT panel was then asked to meet again to examine the question of whether these changes sufficed to make the remaining subsidies GATT-legal.

The panel found at that point that the Article III:4 violation had ended, but that the "nullification or impairment" problem continued. The panel suggested a re-negotiation of the tariff binding under Article XXVIII of the General Agreement.[18] The EC blocked adoption of this second report; but then obtained authority to renegotiate the old tariff bindings. The diplomatic wrangling that followed is typical both of pre-1995 GATT, and of international agricultural disputes in general. Europe and the US were unable to agree on the amount of compensation to be offered by the EC; the US then attempted to submit the question to arbitration, a proposition refused by the EC. The US sought the authority to retaliate under Article XXIII:2, but this request was blocked by Europe. Towards the end of 1992, the US announced an intention to impose large retaliatory tariffs on hundreds of millions of dollars worth of European imports. However, at the brink, a mutually agreeable solution was announced, involving limitations on European soya bean production.[19] As often happened in disputes at the latter end of the Uruguay Round negotiations, reference was made to the agricultural agreement then being hammered out at the GATT. While the US adopted a less strident position on oilseeds, the EC implied that it would take a more conciliatory line on agricultural reform generally.

AGRICULTURE ENTERS THE GLOBAL FREE TRADE SYSTEM

The Uruguay Round Agreement on Agriculture is a framework document, setting out general intentions, whereas more detailed information on commitments is found in individual country schedules.[20] Of the WTO Agreements, it is particularly impenetrable in style, and for the uninitiated, very difficult to parse. Given the fact that it represents a revolutionary departure in the lives of millions of rural people, it seems odd that this, of all the agreements, should be presented in such unnecessarily turgid language. (By contrast, the TRIMs Agreement, or even the TRIPs Agreement, for instance, can be read by almost anyone with comparative ease.) There is a stark contrast between the rather simple concepts behind the agreement, its brevity, and its user-unfriendly diction.

The preamble to the Agreement sets out a commitment to a long-term objective of "progressive reductions in agricultural support and protection",

[18] *Oilseeds* Case, para. 151.

[19] Agreement was reached in the famous Blair House Accords of November 1992, to which some European Member States were strongly opposed. See Daniel, *supra* n. 5, at 876; Robert P Cooper, III, "The European Community's Prodigal Son—The Common Agricultural Policy—Undergoes Reform: Will Multilateral Trading Schemes Fostered by the GATT Blossom or Wither and Die?", (1995) 1 *Columbia Journal of European Law* 233, 273–74.

[20] See Moutsatsos, *supra* n. 1 (describing the Agreement on Agriculture's contents).

and the establishment of a "fair and market-oriented agricultural trading system". The first major commitments are found in Article 4 on market access. This article states that market access commitments by members, contained in their schedules, relate both to reductions in tariffs and other market access concessions. Measures "required to be turned into" customs duties (such as quantitative restrictions on imports) shall not be reverted to. Despite the use of the passive voice here, this provision is taken to mean that non-tariff restrictions will be turned into tariffs ("tariffication") by members. It has been agreed that all agricultural tariffs are to be reduced by 36 per cent for developed countries, and 24 per cent for developing countries, with a phase-in period of six and ten years, respectively. The least-developed countries are exempted from these tariff reduction rules. Article 5 contains a safeguard clause for special measures to be taken in the event of an import surge. The additional duty allowed is only to be maintained until the end of the year in which it is applied, and its size is restricted under an elaborate formula based on the concept of an import "trigger level". The question of whether or not to maintain these special trigger mechanisms in any revised agreement is highly controversial.

Article 6 is on the subject of "Domestic Support Commitments", referring to general supports for the agricultural sector. Domestic support measures which are considered to have a minimal effect on trade (the so-called "green box" supports) are to be excluded from reduction commitments; these include research, disease control and infrastructure developments.[21] Income supports not tied to production are also to be allowed. Similarly, structural adjustment assistance, payments under environmental programmes and under regional assistance programmes are exempted from reductions.

A related form of subsidy, the "blue box subsidy", acts as an exemption from the general rule that subsidies linked to production must be reduced or maintained within de minimus levels.[22] The "blue box" exemption applies to support payments connected with acreage or headage, as long as they accompany schemes to curb production or place agricultural land in set-aside programmes. The EU is the most notable, and one of the few, users of this exemption. While Europe is insisting on its continuance, there are strong arguments being put forward for phasing it out.[23]

All remaining non-exempted supports and payments (the "amber box" supports), product and non-product based, are to be put together in a member's assessment of "Total Aggregate Measurement of Support".[24] Included in this general support calculation are market price supports, direct payments and input

---

[21] These exceptions are described in detail in Annex 2 to the Agreement on Agriculture.

[22] See WTO, *Agriculture Negotiations: Backgrounder, "Domestic Support"*, at http://www.wto.org/english/tratop_e/agric_e/negs_bkgrnd07_domestic_e.htm.

[23] See Dimitris Moutsatsos, "The Uruguay Round on Agriculture: Issues and Perspective", in *Negotiating the Future of Agricultural Policies: Agricultural Trade and the Millennium Round*, *supra* n. 1 at 39.

[24] For details, refer to the Agreement on Agriculture, Annex 3.

subsidies. This aggregate support is to be reduced by 20 per cent over the implementation period mentioned above, with developing countries also having higher exemption levels.

Arguably the most significant aspect of the Agreement is found in Article 9 on export subsidies. This article contains a list of the sort of export-driven subsidies the Agreement is intended to reduce. Members are required to reduce the value of direct export subsidies to a level 36 per cent below their 1986–1990 level, over the course of the implementation period. In addition, the quantity of subsidised export products are to be reduced by 21 per cent. Developing countries are to meet a target approximately two-thirds that of the developed members, and over a 10 year, rather than a 6 year, period.Critics have noted that export subsidies are still a major factor in the "distortion" of trade in agricultural products.[25]

It is important to note the "peace provision" of Article 13, which is entitled "Due Restraint". This amounts to an understanding that WTO legal actions that could be taken in the subsidies area will not be taken with regard to agricultural policy, as long as there is conformity with the Agreement on Agriculture. There is also an understanding that "restraint" will be used in the application of countervailing duties under the General Agreement. The peace provisions are to be applicable during the implementation period. Interestingly, in the definitional section, we are informed that in this context "the implementation period means the six-year period commencing in the year 1995, except that, for the purposes of Article 13, it means the nine year period commencing in 1995".

Article 14 of the Agreement states that members agree to give effect to the Agreement on the Application of Sanitary and Phytosanitary Measures. A Committee on Agriculture is set up under Article 17 to monitor implementation of this agreement. The EC position is to integrate agricultural and environmental concerns more closely in the upcoming round, as part of Europe's commitment to multifunctionality.[26]

Article 20, on "Continuation of the reform process", makes clear that this agreement is merely the first phase of a long-term reduction of agricultural support and protection. It says:

> "Recognising that the long-term objective of substantial progressive reductions in support and protection resulting in fundamental reform is an ongoing process, members agree that negotiations for continuing the process will be initiated one year before the end of the implementation period".

This takes into account the experience gleaned over the implementation period, the effects on world trade in agriculture, and non-trade concerns. As described

[25] See Don Kenyon, "Position of the Cairns Group on the New Round", in *Negotiating the Future of Agricultural Policies: Agricultural Trade and the Millennium WTO Round, supra* n. 1 at 243, 246, suggesting that clear arrangements for phasing out export subsidies should be part of the new round.

[26] See ch. 5, *infra* (discussing the Agreement on Sanitary and Phytosanitary Measures).

below, the EC is the standard-bearer for "non-trade concerns" in the upcoming round of negotiations; namely, social, cultural and environmental values associated with the agricultural sector. Also mentioned as considerations are the needs of developing countries and the objective to establish a fair and market-oriented agricultural trading system. To be put on the agenda is the question, "What further commitments are necessary to achieve the above-mentioned long-term objectives?"[27]

CANADA'S "EXPORT SUBSIDIES"

The first case to have been decided under the Agriculture Agreement[28] provides important insight into how we can expect the Agreement (and its likely successors) to be interpreted. It is important to note that potential subsidies-based claims under WTO law have been put in abeyance by the operation of the Agriculture Agreement's "peace clause". There are also numerous agriculture-related disputes that appear in other guises; as conflicts under the environmental or safeguard provisions of the WTO. The Canadian milk case stands nearly alone as a dispute decided primarily under the specific terms of the Agriculture Agreement.

As background, it should be noted that Canadian milk production is highly regulated by a number of public entities; prices and production volumes are fixed by federal and provincial authorities to guarantee adequate returns for producers and adequate national supply for consumers.

Canadian milk production is divided into two categories: fluid milk (40 per cent of the total, destined for milk and cream); and industrial milk (60 per cent of the total, to be used in butter, cheese, milk powders and so forth). While fluid milk is generally consumed within Canada, industrial milk crosses provincial and national borders. At national level, regulation is undertaken by the Canadian Dairy Commission; at provincial level, the milk marketing boards co-ordinate quotas and set prices. These boards must be used as intermediaries in the selling of milk. The ultimate use and destination of milk is a highly planned matter, with a yearly scheme that divides milk into distinct categories according to projected requirements.

The main claim of both the US and New Zealand was that the level of Canadian exports achieved through the scheme entitled the "Special Milk Classes" resulted in Canada exceeding the export subsidy commitments it had

---

[27] The point has been made that many of the dramatic impacts that might have been expected from the Uruguay Round Agreement on Agriculture did not materialise. On the other hand, the Agreement provided for a substantial change in the rules of engagement for future negotiations on agricultural trade. See Green, *supra* n. 1.

[28] *US and New Zealand v. Canada: Measures Affecting the Importation of Milk and the Exportation of Dairy Products*, Report of the Panel, 17 May 1999, (WT/DS103,113/R) [hereinafter *Canadian Milk* Panel Report].

entered into under the Agriculture Agreement.[29] The Canadian plan called for milk to be divided into 5 classes, according to end use and destination; classes 1–4 being milk for use on the domestic market, and class 5 for export, or of a type facing competition domestically.[30] Classes 5(d) and (e), challenged here, indicated milk for use in exported products. An essential aspect of the scheme was the removal of milk surpluses. The complainants alleged violations of Articles 3.3,[31] 8,[32] and 10.1[33] of the Agriculture Agreement, which taken together require members to live up to the terms of their own commitments on export subsidies, while also prohibiting them from finding alternative means for circumventing those obligations.[34]

The complainants maintained that either the milk classes are export subsidies under Article 9.1, and thus should be counted against Canada's export subsidy reduction commitments,[35] or they were an export subsidy not listed in Article 9.1, applied in a manner that circumvented Canada's export subsidy commitments, in violation of Article 10.1 of the Agreement.[36] The US made the related argument that the Canadian classifications violated Article 3 of the Subsidies Agreement.[37] Canada for its part denied that its scheme was an export subsidy at all.[38]

A secondary claim made by the US was that access to the tariff rate quota granted by Canada for fluid milk in the Uruguay Round negotiations was being restricted, contrary to Canadian obligations under Article II of the General Agreement, and Article 3 of the Agreement on Import Licensing Procedures.[39] The Canadian restrictions in question required that entries with the quota must be for personal, consumer use, and were limited to entries valued at less than $20 each.[40]

As the complainants saw it, under milk classes 5(d) and 5(e), processors of dairy products for export were given access to milk at lower prices than those applying to milk for manufacture of the same products for domestic consumption. This

---

[29] *Canadian Milk* Panel Report, paras. 1.5–1.6.

[30] *Canadian Milk* Panel Report, paras. 2.38–2.40.

[31] Agreement on Agriculture, Art. 3.3: Subject to the provisions of paras. 2(b) and 4 of Art. 9, a Member shall not provide export subsidies listed in para. 1 of Art. 9 in respect of the agricultural products or groups of products specified in Section II of Part IV of its Schedule in excess of the budgetary outlay and quantity commitment levels specified therein and shall not provide such subsidies in respect of any agricultural product not specified in that Section of its Schedule.

[32] Agreement on Agriculture, Art. 8: Each member undertakes not to provide export subsidies otherwise than in conformity with this Agreement and with the commitments as specified in the Member's Schedule.

[33] Agreement on Agriculture, Art. 10.1: Export subsidies not listed in para. 1 of Art. 9 shall not be applied in such a manner which results in, or which threatens to lead to, circumvention of export subsidy commitments; nor shall non-commercial transactions be used to circumvent such commitments.

[34] *Canadian Milk* Panel Report, paras. 3.7, 3.9.

[35] *Canadian Milk* Panel Report, para. 3.6.

[36] *Canadian Milk* Panel Report, para. 3.9.

[37] *Canadian Milk* Panel Report, para. 3.13.

[38] *Canadian Milk* Panel Report, paras. 3.5, 3.8, 3.12.

[39] *Canadian Milk* Panel Report, para. 3.14.

[40] *Canadian Milk* Panel Report, para. 3.14.

was done to remove milk surpluses and allow Canadian processors/exporters to compete in world export markets. Only government intervention made this possible, even though the scheme was not directly paid for by government funds. As the system functioned, the government required a pooling of returns from these lower-cost exports with the higher returns obtained from more expensive milk sold on the domestic market. (The pooling occurred only with respect to in-quota milk, excluding out of quota milk.)

The Canadian view was that the programme was not directed by the government, but was producer-driven.[41] Canada saw its government role as a limited one of "oversight" only. Canada pointed out that under the Agriculture Agreement, members were required to replace earlier QRs with tariffs.[42] Under the earlier QR regime (based on GATT Article XI:2(c)(1)) Canada had imposed domestic restrictions on milk production.[43] Under the new regime, since that was not required, Canada was free to produce more milk for export. The tariffs, Canada explained, led to higher domestic prices, while for exports, the world market price demanded lower prices. Thus, "a system of sales at differing prices . . . is the consequence".[44] The Canadians insisted that the resultant two-tiered system was not a subsidy.[45] Otherwise, a member imposing tariffs on imports of a product could no longer export that same (domestically produced) product without it being considered an export subsidy.[46]

As a preliminary matter, the panel noted that Article 3 of the Subsidies Agreement contains a general prohibition on export subsidies. However, this prohibition is qualified by the phrase: "except as provided in the Agreement on Agriculture, the following subsidies shall be prohibited". Article 21 of the Agriculture Agreement also provides that "the provisions of GATT 1994 and of other Multilateral Agreements (including the Subsidies Agreement) shall apply subject to the provisions of this Agreement". It was clear to the panel that under the Agriculture Agreement, members may use export subsidies only to the limits of their commitments as specified in their own member's schedule. Anything beyond this is prohibited by Article 3.3, Article 8, and Article 10 of the agreement.[47] The panel saw the role of the Subsidies Agreement in this case as important to the contextual interpretation of the relevant provisions of the Agriculture Agreement on export subsidies.

---

[41] "Canada submits that milk producers producing for export follow commercial considerations and react to world market signals, not to government directions". *Canadian Milk* Panel Report, para. 7.12.

[42] *Canadian Milk* Panel Report, para. 7.14.

[43] *Canadian Milk* Panel Report, para. 7.14.

[44] *Canadian Milk* Panel Report, para. 7.14.

[45] *Canadian Milk* Panel Report, para. 7.14.

[46] *Canadian Milk* Panel Report, para. 7.14.

[47] The panel noted that the use of export subsidies beyond the scheduled limits is also, in principle, actionable under the prohibition in Art. 3 of the Subsidies Agreement. But by virtue of Art. 13(c)(I) of the Agreement on Agriculture, export subsidies that conform fully to Part V (export subsidy commitments) are exempt from actions based on Art. 3 of the Subsidies Agreement for the duration of the implementation period (through 2003).

The panel pointed out that this was the first case brought before a panel involving the substantive provisions of the Agreement on Agriculture.[48] The panel examined the position of the Agreement with regard to the question of export subsidies. It was noted that the Agreement seeks a fair and market-oriented trading system in agricultural products, and reductions in agricultural supports over an agreed period of time.[49] Other objectives cited are liberalisation in agricultural trade, and greater import access, especially through limitations on national subsidies. Each member has undertaken not to provide export subsidies otherwise than in conformity with the Agreement on Agriculture and the commitments specified in the national schedule.[50] Since under Article 3.3, members must not provide export subsidies as listed in Article 9.1 beyond the limits specified in the national commitments, the first question for the panel to consider was whether or not the Canadian Special Milk Class scheme did in fact involve an export subsidy as listed in Article 9.1.[51]

Article 10.3 of the Agreement indicates that in just such situations, where a member is denying that the product in question is subsidised, the burden of proof is on the defending party. The complainants focused on the export subsidy "types" set out in Articles 9.1 (a) and (c), which the panel took up in separate analyses. Going through the necessary element for each of the subsidy types, the panel found that the Canadian action met the conditions for both.[52] Thus, Canada did not prevail on its argument that its action did not constitute an export subsidy on the product in question.[53] As the panel's reasoning went, access by exporters to the less expensive milk was by government action, and conferred a special benefit that is to be considered an export subsidy. The panel's conclusion was that:

---

[48] *Canadian Milk* Panel Report, para. 7.24.

[49] *Canadian Milk* Panel Report, para. 7.25.

[50] The basic definition of export subsidies found in Art. 1(e) calls them "subsidies contingent upon export performance, including the export subsidies listed in Art. 9 of this Agreement. Art. 9 has a far more elaborate list.

[51] Art. 9.1: The following export subsidies are subject to reduction commitments under this Agreement:

(a) the provision by governments or their agencies of direct subsidies, including payments-in-kind, to a firm, to an industry, to producers of an agricultural product, to a cooperative or other association of such producers, or to a marketing board, contingent on export performance;

(b) the sale or disposal for export by government or their agencies of non-commercial stocks of agricultural products at a price lower than the comparable price charged for the like product to buyers in the domestic market;

(c) payments on the export of an agricultural product that are financed by virtue of governmental action, whether or not a charge on the public account is involved, including payments that are financed from the proceeds of a levy imposed on the agricultural product concerned or on an agricultural product from which the export product is derived;

(d) the provision of subsidies to reduce the costs of marketing exports of agricultural products (other than widely available export promotion and advisory services) including handling, upgrading and other processing costs, and the costs of international transport and freight;

(e) internal transport and freight charges on export shipments, provided or mandated by governments, on terms more favourable than for domestic shipments;

(f) subsidies on agricultural products contingent on their incorporation in exported products.

[52] *Canadian Milk* Panel Report, para. 7.114.

[53] *Canadian Milk* Panel Report, para. 7.114.

"according to figures submitted by Canada, the total amount of exports generated through classes 5(d) and (e) exceeds Canada's quantity reduction commitment levels, as set out in its schedule for all the dairy products in dispute . . .".[54]

This was contrary to Canadian obligations under Article 3.3 of the agreement.[55] Therefore, by extension, Canada had also violated Article 8 of the agreement.[56]

The final, and secondary, issue concerns the US allegation that by adding extra restrictions on access to Canada's tariff-rate quota (i.e., that the products be for personal consumption and that they be not more than $20 per entry), Canada had violated Article II: 1(b)[57] of the General Agreement. Canada argued that this limited access condition was provided for in its schedule, read in the light of its negotiating history. The two specific conditions at issue here were not, in fact, mentioned in Canada's schedule. The phrase actually used in the Canadian schedule is as follows: "This quantity represents the estimated annual cross-border purchases imported by Canadian consumers".[58] Not surprisingly, the panel found it difficult to read specific access restrictions into the phrase.

The panel referred to the purpose of Article II of GATT 1994: to "preserve the value of tariff concessions negotiated" between members.[59] Any later reductions in that value would upset the balance of concessions. Ostensibly relying on reasoning introduced by the Appellate Body in the *Indian Pharmaceuticals* case, the panel stated that it

"cannot read access restrictions imposed by Canada in its current schedule. The principles of security and predictability as well as those of treaty interpretation, do not 'condone the importation into a treaty of words that are not there or the importation into a treaty of concepts that are not intended' ".[60]

Thus, Canada was found to have acted inconsistently with its obligations under Article II:1(b) of the General Agreement.[61]

---

[54] *Canadian Milk* Panel Report, para. 7.115.

[55] In case the Appellate Body might not agree with its interpretation of whether the Canadian measures were export subsidies under Art. 9.1, the panel went on to analyse the case under Art. 10.1, for instances where commitment levels are exceeded, but where circumvention of the commitments occurs through subsidies not listed in Art. 9.1. Here, too, the panel found a violation by Canada, relying in part on the definition of export subsidy provided in Annex I of the Subsidies Agreement. This definition includes government-mandated schemes for the provision of goods on more favourable terms for use in exported goods. See *Canadian Milk* Panel Report, paras. 7.117–7.133

[56] See *Canadian Milk* Panel Report, para. 7.134. Having decided the case under the provisions of the Agriculture Agreement, the panel refrained, in the interests of judicial economy, from treating it under the prohibition against export subsidies found in Art. 3 of the Subsidies Agreement. See *Canadian Milk* Panel Report, para. 7.141.

[57] See *Canadian Milk* Panel Report, para. 7.142. Art. II:1(b) of the General Agreement states that imported products described in the schedule shall "subject to the terms, conditions, or qualifications set forth in the schedule, be exempt from ordinary customs duties in excess of those set forth and provided therein".

[58] *Canadian Milk* Panel Report, para. 7.148.

[59] *Canadian Milk* Panel Report, para. 7.154.

[60] *Canadian Milk* Panel Report, para. 7.154.

[61] *Canadian Milk* Panel Report, para. 7.154. Although the US had raised a possible violation under Art. 3 of the Licensing Agreement, the panel decided that it was not necessary to proceed to that issue.

On appeal, Canada argued that the Panel, in its decision, had erred in equating "payments in kind" (as found in the special milk classes) with "direct subsidies", for purposes of Article 9.1(a) of the Agriculture Agreement.[62] Canada's contention was that when goods are sold at less than normal price, the purchasers are not receiving payments in kind, but are simply paying less for the goods they receive.[63] It similarly maintained that the panel erred in finding under Article 9.1(c) that "payments" were "financed by virtue of governmental action" in the milk classification system. Canada further contended that the panel was wrong in its assessment of provincial milk marketing boards as governmental agencies, and that the panel failed to address their "high degree of independence" and their discretion.[64]

The reasoning of the Appellate Body is symptomatic of two aspects of its developing jurisprudence. First of all, there is the Appellate Body's resistance to the interpretative looseness that characterises certain panel reports. On the other hand, the decision is strikingly formalistic; built around a technical and linguistic analysis, removed from Canada's attempt to launch a more serious challenge to the conceptual limits to "export subsidy" as used in the Agriculture Agreement.

The Appellate Body reviewed the panel's analysis of Article 9.1(a): The panel equated a payment in kind with a direct subsidy, and then equated a payment in kind with a benefit. Then, if there was a benefit, there was also a direct subsidy; and if the benefit was provided by governments or their agencies, then there was an export subsidy as listed in Article 9.1(a) of the Agreement on Agriculture.[65] The Appellate Body found this to be a "flawed interpretive approach", since the one concept does not necessarily lead to the other.

While reversing the panel's conclusions on this point because of this flawed interpretative base, the Appellate Body did not find it necessary to examine whether export subsidies are conferred through the special milk classes. This is because the Appellate Body *was* able to accept the panel's logic and reasoning with regard to Article 9.1(c); that the term "payment" under that provision may include the provision of milk to processors for export under the special milk classes and, additionally, that these classes are payments made by virtue of governmental action.[66]

As set out above, the US had also claimed that Canada placed restrictions on access to its market for fluid milk, in a manner inconsistent with Canada's GATT Article II:1(b) obligations. The Appellate Body, responding to Canada's argument that it had indicated these restrictions in the language of its national schedule of commitments, disagreed with the panel that Canada had unlawfully

---

[62] *US and New Zealand* v. *Canada: Measures Affecting the Importation of Milk and the Exportation of Dairy Products*, Report of the Appellate Body, 13 October 1999 (WT/DS103/AB/R), [hereinafter *Canadian Milk* Appellate Body Report] para. 20 .

[63] *Canadian Milk* Appellate Body Report, para. 22.

[64] *Canadian Milk* Appellate Body Report, para. 26.

[65] *Canadian Milk* Appellate Body Report, para. 91.

[66] *Canadian Milk* Appellate Body Report, paras. 113–115.

restricted access for fluid milk to "consumer packaged milk for personal use". It did, however, agree with the panel that by restricting access to the tariff-rate quota for fluid milk to entries valued at less than $20 Canadian, Canada had acted inconsistently with its obligations under GATT Article II:1(b).

As with many other decisions of the Appellate Body, its elaborate divergence from the panel's reasoning is not reflected in a substantively different outcome from the point of view of the defendant member. The Appellate Body's disapproval is of the inexactitude in the reasoning of the panel; it does not display significantly greater liberality with respect to the right of a member to retain a national measure amounting to an export subsidy under the Agriculture Agreement.

THE MILLENNIUM ROUND ON AGRICULTURE

As was the case in the Uruguay Round, it is likely to prove profoundly difficult to attain global agreement on necessary changes to the system of trade in agricultural products in the upcoming round of negotiations. The EC faces, in this new round, the pressure of two imperatives: the need to respond to the demands of the United States and the Cairns group of countries; and the need to achieve enough reform of the common agricultural policy to allow for enlargement of the EU into Eastern Europe.[67] It is widely doubted that the European reforms to date, under the title of "Agenda 2000", are adequate with respect to current WTO commitments, let alone sufficient to future liberalisation.[68]

The main content of the Agenda 2000 package set out commitments to cut the intervention price for cereals by 20 per cent in one step, while increasing the arable area payment by approximately half the price cut. A three-stage support reduction of 30 per cent for beef will also replace intervention with private storage aid. Intervention prices for butter and skim milk powder will be reduced by 15 per cent over a four-year period, with the milk quota regime extended until 2006.[69] The EC has relied heavily on the Agriculture Agreement's Special Safeguard Provision, especially to maintain its market in sugar and butter.[70] It has been noted that Agenda 2000 contains no commitments to tariff cuts, placing the EU at odds with its own commitments under the Agreement on Agriculture.[71]

[67] See Ian Sturgess, "The Agenda 2000 CAP Reform and the 'Millennium' Round: Negotiations on Agriculture", in *Negotiating the Future of Agricultural Policies: Agricultural Trade and the Millennium WTO Round, supra* n. 1 at 97–111 (2000). "Agenda 2000 is fundamentally about the enlargement of the European Union (EU) to the east (and south). It concerns not only which countries shall join the EU and how they shall do so but also how to make their accession affordable for the EU budget in the next decade".

[68] See Alan Swinbank, "EU Agriculture, Agenda 2000 and the WTO Commitments", 22 *World Economy* 41–54 (1999).

[69] *Ibid.*, at 43.

[70] *Ibid.*, at 44–45.

[71] *Ibid.*, at 47.

The US and the Cairns group are vocally dissatisfied with the stated EU positions on the upcoming round, based mainly on the comparatively modest Agenda 2000 programme, as indicated above.[72] The most recently published proposals of the European Commission regarding the Community's negotiating position would indicate a continuation of themes from the Uruguay Round, and a rejection of any radical restructuring of its system of payments.[73]

The EC position reflects its Agenda 2000 programme, with emphasis on further tariff reductions according to set, minimum reductions; further reductions in export refunds; a continuation of the system of domestic supports established in the Uruguay Round; attention to "non-trade" concerns of the agricultural sector; and special and differential treatment for developing countries, designed to increase market access for these countries.

SUBMISSIONS OF WTO MEMBERS AT THE OUTSET OF THE NEW ROUND

A perusal of the submissions of WTO members on the subject of changes to the agricultural trading system reveals widespread dissatisfaction with the results of the Uruguay Round Agreement, and a general belief in its ineffectuality in bringing about fundamental change in trade of primary products. As in the last round, it can be expected that the European position will ultimately prove decisive in determining the degree to which there will be deviation from existing rules and patterns.

In its comprehensive negotiating proposal of December 2000, the EC "underlines its full commitment to the continuation of the reform process" begun in the Uruguay Round; while insisting that this reform process aimed at a balance "between trade concerns—market access, export competition, domestic support—and non-trade concerns, which reflect important societal goals".[74] At the outset, it is emphasised that to attain the goal of further liberalisation, "it is vital to muster public support, which can only be achieved if other concerns are met, in particular the multifunctional role of agriculture". This the submission says covers "the protection of the environment and the sustained vitality of rural communities, food safety and other consumer concerns including animal welfare".[75]

Reference is made to the particular needs of developing countries, as well as to Europe's own immediate problem, how to reconcile the demands of the common agricultural policy with the expansion of the Community eastwards.[76] With regard to market access, the EC supports "a commitment as to the overall

---

[72] See Sturgess, *supra* n. 60, at 101.

[73] MEMO/01/28, EU makes proposal for "win-win" solution to WTO agricultural negotiations.

[74] EC Comprehensive Negotiating Proposal, 14 December 2000, WTO Document G/AG/NG/W/90, 1, available at http:\\www.wto.org [hereinafter EC Submission].

[75] EC Submission, at 1.

[76] EC Submission, at 1.

average reduction of bound tariffs and a minimum reduction per tariff line, as was the case in the Uruguay Round".[77] It states that the Special Safeguard Clause had proven

> "a very useful adjunct to the process of tariffication as it provides a limited degree of reassurance that this will not lead to sudden or unpredictable surges in imports or sharp reductions in import prices".

Without this special provision, the EC argues, "the only remaining form of recourse in such situations would be the relevant safeguard provisions in the WTO, under which much more trade-disruptive measures are permitted".[78] The submission adopts a skeptical attitude towards any moves to remove remaining export subsidies; Europe will negotiate further reductions, it says; however, this will occur only "on the condition that all forms of export subsidisation are treated on an equal footing".[79] The submission refers in particular to failures to include reductions in export credits in agriculture.[80]

With respect to domestic supports, the EC proposes that "the concept of 'blue' and 'green' boxes should be maintained, as well as the general rules and disciplines applying to them", but expresses willingness "to discuss the detailed rules on domestic support".[81] The final substantive sections of the European submission cover non-trade concerns and the needs of developing countries. The EC seems determined to preclude the elimination of European measures

---

[77] EC Submission, at 2.

[78] EC Submission, at 2.

[79] Contrast this statement by the Cairns group: "There is no justification for export subsidies to continue in agriculture. Export subsidies for industrial products were eliminated by the GATT more than 40 years ago . . . Consistent with the WTO commitments to fundamental reform, resulting in correcting and preventing restrictions and distortions in world agricultural markets, the Cairns Group seeks the complete elimination of all forms of agricultural export subsidies". WTO Negotiations on Agriculture, Cairns Group Negotiating Proposal: Export Competition, WTO Document G/AG/NG/W/11, at 1, available at http:\\www.wto.org. In its proposal on market access, the Cairns Group calls for "vastly improved market access opportunities for all agricultural and agrifood products", involving "deep cuts to all tariffs using a formula approach which delivers greater reductions on higher level tariffs, including peak tariffs, and eliminates tariff escalation, and establishes maximum levels for all tariffs". WTO Document G/AG/NG/W/54, at 2.

[80] EC Submission, at 3. On the problem of export credits, see Ian Sturgess, "The Liberalisation Process in International Agricultural Trade: Market Access and Export Subsidies", in *Negotiating the Future of Agricultural Policies: Agricultural Trade and the Millennium WTO Round*, *supra* n. 1 at 135, 152.

[81] EC Submission, at 4. It should be noted that many developing countries have a strongly negative position towards the maintenance of "green" and "blue box" supports. See Agreement on Agriculture: Green Box/Annex 2 Subsidies, Proposal to the June 2000 Special Session of the Committee on Agriculture by Cuba, Dominican Republic, Honduras, Pakistan, Haiti, Nicaragua, Kenya, Uganda, Zimbabwe, Sri Lanka and El Salvador, 23 June 2000, WTO Document G/AG/NG/W/14, available at http:\\www.wto.org [hereinafter Cuba et al Submission]: "While the Agreement on Agriculture assumes that the domestic support, decoupled from production, will have no or minimal impact on production levels, studies have shown that it is virtually impossible to break links between income support and marginal costs and returns, particularly when the support runs into billions of dollars". And, "The Green Box . . . masks huge supports that continue to be provided by OECD countries". And further, "Subsidies previously classified as trade distorting were obviously shifted to the non-trade distorting category. The problem is that the Green Box criteria have not been vigorously defined". Cuba et al Submission, at 3.

aimed at protecting the rural environment and the "sustainable vitality" of rural areas as a result of future WTO litigation. Such multifunctional measures should be "accommodated" by the Agreement on Agriculture, the EC argues. It also calls for a clarification of the precautionary principle and how it can be implemented in the food safety context.[82]

The EC pledges to include agricultural products in its newly announced programme to accept virtually all products from the developing world on a duty-free basis, the "all-but-arms" programme. It calls for international food aid programmes to be restricted to forms that do not damage local food production and the marketing capacities of the recipient countries.[83]

Finally, as if recalling the turbulent GATT relationships of the late 1980s, the EC submission states that, "The need for a continuation of a 'peace clause' is the logical corollary of the specific nature of the Agreement on Agriculture". It maintains that the peace clause "defines the conditions under which specific support measures may be granted, and therefore contributes to the enforcement of the reduction commitments which were agreed".[84] The EC document contains no hint of a wish or intention to move beyond the conceptual framework provided by the Uruguay Round Agreement, except to ensure that the non-trade values of agriculture are preserved. It would seem, in fact, that the EC is making the preservation of these values a necessary precondition to further liberalisation. This position is not without its paradoxes.

In one sense, what one finds in the European submission is a repeat of the paradox underlying the CAP itself. It is a fact that the CAP was "the first and only subordination of agriculture and agricultural trade to the discipline of an international organisation like the EU".[85] It has been pointed out that the CAP "is one of the very few policy areas (another being trade policy) where national decision-making competences have been completely surrendered to the EU institutions".[86] It is ironic that while the CAP is considered to be intensely protectionist, it was itself an early and utterly innovative move towards Europe-wide liberalisation of trade in agricultural products.[87]

The EC Treaty provisions on the CAP reflect the same ambivalence as that seen in the EC's submission on the upcoming agriculture talks at the WTO, discussed above. It is not self-evident that any system of agricultural integration can in fact increase productivity and contribute to optimum utilisation of the

---

[82] EC Submission, at 4.

[83] EC Submission, at 5.

[84] EC Submission, at 6.

[85] See Pezaros, *supra* n. 7. See also Jim Dixon, "Nature Conservation and Trade Distortion: Green Box and Blue Box Farming Subsidies in Europe", (Spring 1999) 29 *Golden Gate University Law Review* 415. Dixon states that "European agriculture can be characterised as polarised between, on the one hand, cultural landscapes where farming is extensive . . . and production is often on a sub-optimal scale and undertaken on family farms" and "on the other hand . . . modern technologies, increased efficiency in production and . . . ambitious to meet global market demands". Dixon, at 417.

[86] Pezaros, *supra* n. 7, at 52.

[87] Pezaros, *supra* n. 7, at 52.

factors of production, while at the same time ensuring a fair standard of living for the agricultural community, and stabilising markets.[88] With enormous surpluses, under fire for the extensive subsidisation of goods for export, and undergoing a livestock disease crisis, it may be that the EC is asserting its intention to continue to maintain this contradictory situation as is; that to accelerate the demise of its farming sector through the operation of the WTO is not something Europe is politically prepared to grapple with. This, however, does not foreclose the possibility of a last-minute revision of this position, as happened in late 1993 at the conclusion of the contentious Uruguay Round negotiations on agriculture.[89]

It is ironic that while engaging in agricultural trading behaviours heavily criticised by the developing country bloc, Europe has nonetheless strongly embraced the concept of special and differential treatment for developing countries in this area. In its customary role as the voice of developing country concerns, India in its submission to the latest WTO negotiations has pointed out that for these countries, supply gaps are developmental problems; that many farm holdings are small and productivity low.[90] Thus, India states, developing country policies for agriculture "aim at harnessing the potential for increasing . . . production". In addition, agriculture in the developing world has "meagre domestic support" and there is a "virtual absence of export subsidies", so that "it is obvious that developing countries are not in any way responsible for the current distortions in international trade in agriculture".

India argues in favour of conceptualising developing country agriculture in terms of food security and poverty alleviation. This would require such differential treatment as retention of appropriate levels of tariffs, the creation of a special safeguard measure for developing countries, and exemption from the requirement to provide minimum market access.[91] India points to the fact that access by developing countries to developed world markets has, if anything, worsened in the period since the adoption of the Agreement on Agriculture.[92] In common with much of the developing world, India argues that the wealthy countries have continued to provide so-called "green" and "blue" box payments to farmers in a manner that has maintained distortions in agricultural trade. India accuses the developed countries of shifting their subsidies from one category to

---

[88]   Treaty of Rome, Art. 33 (ex Art. 39).

[89]   The French Agriculture Minister, Jean Glavany, was quoted as saying that the common agricultural policy is "outdated" and should be "reoriented" away from a policy of maximum output through guaranteed prices and export subsidies, and brought in the direction of greater food quality. See "France Ready for EU Agricultural Reform", by Michael Mann, *Financial Times*, 10 April 2001

[90]   Negotiations on WTO Agreement on Agriculture: Proposals by India in the areas of: (i) Food Security, (ii) Market Access, (iii) Domestic Support, and (iv) Export Competition, 15 January 2001, WTO Document G/AG/NG/W/102, available at http:\\www.wto.org [hereinafter India Submission].

[91]   India Submission, at 4–5.

[92]   India Submission, at 6.

another in such a way as to continue to deny market access to developing countries in precisely those areas where they have the greatest comparative advantage.[93]

India terms agriculture "the only sector of the world economy still marked by the existence of export subsidies".[94] The Uruguay Round disciplines have proven "grossly inadequate" to correct the distortions caused by export subsidies, India argues. India complains that certain developed countries complied with commitments in the aggregate, while increasing subsidies for certain products; and further that export credits, guarantees and insurance programmes have not been included in the export subsidy reduction commitments under the Agreement on Agriculture.[95]

It has been said that the Uruguay Round Agreement on Agriculture was in essence "an agreement between the EC and the United States", despite the many other countries with vital interests in this area.[96] If this is so, and if it has implications for the upcoming agricultural negotiations, it is difficult to see how the "European model" of agriculture will be reconciled with the far more "matter of fact" version proposed by the Americans. For the US, the challenge is to

> "build upon that foundation [of the Uruguay Round Agreement on Agriculture] by accelerating the process of reducing trade distortions while preserving the appropriate role for governments to address agricultural concerns in a on-trade-distorting fashion".[97]

The US-declared position is one of support for "policies that address non-trade concerns, including food security, resource conservation, rural development, and environmental protection", but these are not presented as central concerns with the potential to influence the shape of future agricultural trade.[98]

The basic US position includes proposals

> "to reduce substantially or eliminate disparities in tariff levels among countries, to reduce substantially or eliminate tariff escalation, and ensure effective market access opportunities for all products in all markets",

and

> "to reduce to zero the levels of scheduled budgetary outlays and quantity commitments through progressive implementation of annual reduction commitments over a fixed period".[99]

Calling the present use of domestic supports for agriculture "disproportionate", the US calls for substantial reductions, as well as simplification in the

---

[93] India Submission, at 10–14.
[94] India Submission, at 15.
[95] India Submission, at 15.
[96] See Dixon, *supra* n. 84.
[97] Proposal for Comprehensive Long-Term Agricultural Trade Reform, Submission from the United States, WTO Document G/AG/NG/W/15, 23 June 2000, available at http:\\www.wto.org [hereinafter US Submission].
[98] US Submission, at 2.
[99] US Submission, at 3.

method by which these are determined.[100] With regard to the needs of developing countries, the US emphasises "capacity building" with the assistance of the developed countries, along with continuation of the "special consideration" given to developing countries in the implementation of tariff reduction commitments.[101] The US also supports the creation of

> "additional criteria for exempt support measures deemed essential to the development and food security objectives of developing countries to facilitate the development of targeted programs to increase investment and improve infrastructure".[102]

It is likely that the upcoming round of agriculture negotiations will also depend upon the *ultimate* intentions of the United States and the EC. The other main blocs are the developing countries (seeking greater market access in developed countries, and also greater possibilities for the creation of a special "development box" to allow for the fostering of their own agricultural sector); and the Cairns Group and their supporters, countries with an interest in seeing a far more radical dismantling of agricultural subsidisation in the US and the EC.

Europe is unique in that no other country or group of countries has ever maintained a system as elaborate as the CAP; likewise, no other developed country grouping is seeking the protection of the "life of the countryside" and non-trade values as overtly as is the EC. The US reshaped its own system of agricultural supports in 1996 with the passage of the Federal Agricultural Improvement and Reform Act (FAIR), which abolished production-related deficiency payments to farmers, while maintaining production-neutral subsidy payments.[103] The European concern about the FAIR act was that the US would be able to argue that its subsidy system had been entirely de-coupled from production, and could thus be classified under the permissible "green box" subsidies. By contrast, much of the European subsidy system remains tied to production, and thus has a less certain status under the WTO rules.[104] For farmers who enter the new US "flexibility contracts", payments will be made regardless of the current commodity prices. However, the weakness in the new US system is in the tendency of Congress to supplement the existing prices when commodity prices are low, thus gravitating back towards a more traditional deficiency payment.[105]

---

[100]   US Submission, at 4.

[101]   US Submission, at 5.

[102]   US Submission, at 5.

[103]   Federal Agricultural Improvement and Reform Act of 1996, Pub. L. No.104–127. 110 Stat. 888. See "US Farm Act threatens EU subsidies", *Agra Europe* (London), 20 September 1996.

[104]   See Christopher R Kelley, "Recent Federal Farm Program Developments", (Spring 1999) 4 *Drake Journal of Agricultural Law* 93. Professor Kelley writes: "[The FAIR Act] suspended or repealed the authority for the making of direct income transfers known as 'deficiency payments' to producers of feed grains, wheat, upland cotton, and rice under the respective acreage reduction programs for each of these commodities . . . [D]eficiency payments had been the primary and most visible instrument of the domestic commodity programs. They were the so-called 'safety net' that provided income to farmers when prices were low". Kelley at 96.

[105]   See Kelley, *supra* n. 102, at 100.

European commentators have pointed out the lack of clarity of the current US position, leaving the US "ambivalent between supply controls, protection and support versus liberalisation", and also "arguably in no more liberally defensible a position than is the European Union".[106] It has been argued that the principal effects of the Uruguay Round Agreement on Agriculture were the lowering of farm prices, the encouragement of global monopolies in the production and marketing of food, and export dumping on a grand scale.[107]

At the outset of the new round of agriculture negotiations, the impenetrability of the language of the initial agreement, and the failure of the WTO to provide a neutral analysis of the agreement's principal results on the ground to date, are serious disadvantages. Without political consensus on such issues as the most desirable size of farming units, the role of food security and environmental protection, the influence of multinational agribusiness, and the principal intended outcomes of any further reform, the next agreement on agriculture is likely to remain as obscure in its general aims and effects as the first one.

Thus far, WTO members have managed to pursue slow-motion reform under the auspices of the Agreement on Agriculture. There is little doubt but that the greatest challenge to European agriculture lies just ahead, as far more concrete adjustment is sought by the United States and the Cairns Group, and by certain developing countries.[108] Europe will be bound to resist serious attack on remaining tariff rate quotas, export subsidies, and "blue box" subsidies exemptions.[109] Lingering concerns from the *Beef Hormones* case will likely prompt the EC to insist on a review of the functioning of the SPS Agreement with respect to food safety.[110] Particularly in the wake of a colossal farming crisis brought on by BSE and the resurgence of hoof and mouth disease, it remains to be seen to what degree Europe will hold out for its "European model" of farming; or respond instead to the combined influence of global competition and the economic imperatives of eastward enlargement.

---

[106] See "FAIR not a permanent change in US farm policy", *Agra Europe* (UK), 29 November 1996, (referring to the views of Professor David Harvey of Newcastle University).

[107] See Mark Ritchie and Kristin Dawkins, "WTO Food and Agricultural Rules,: Sustainable Agriculture and the Right to Food", (Winter 2000) 9 *Minnesota Journal of Global Trade* 20–23.

[108] See William A Kerr, "The Next Step Will be Harder: Issues for the New Round of Agricultural Negotiations at the World Trade Organization", (2000) 34 *Journal of World Trade* 123–140.

[109] *Ibid.*, at 126. Kerr also points out that Japan will resist any further liberalisation, in order to preserve its agricultural sector employment. However, as in the last round, Japan will no doubt be forced to make concessions as the EC significantly relaxes its resistance to sweeping changes. *Ibid.*, at 128.

[110] *Ibid.*, at 136–37.

7

Safeguards: Escape Clauses and the Power of Self-Protection

IT WAS MENTIONED in the chapter on early GATT that the late 1970s and the 1980s saw a sharp rise in reliance on Voluntary Export Restraints (VERs), supposedly voluntary agreements between importing and exporting countries. Under a VER, an importing country would threaten retaliatory action unless the exporting country agreed to ease up on its level of exports. On the surface, this was undertaken with bilateral co-operation; in terms of GATT principle, this sort of arrangement was felt to be unlawful, but it remained unclear who the natural plaintiff would be for any GATT litigation. It was long recognised that such arrangements were antithetical to the essential concept espoused in Article XIX of the General Agreement; that safeguard actions—national self-protection measures—should be completely transparent.

As will be demonstrated, one very important change brought about by the Uruguay Round was that VERs have become per se unlawful; these agreements can no longer be entered into without violating the new Safeguards Agreement. Interestingly, it was the unpopularity of GATT's Article XIX as a remedy that contributed to the broad use of secretive VERs. One panel decision in particular, arising from a complaint brought by Hong Kong against Norway and adopted in 1980, had turned countries away from reliance on Article XIX safeguard measures.[1] As it happens, this case arose in the context of a highly managed sector of international trade, textiles. The more specialised considerations now governing safeguard restrictions in the textile trade are dealt with in chapter 8.

As factual background to the *Hong Kong* v. *Norway* textiles case, up until the end of 1977, at which point the MultiFibre Arrangement (MFA)[2] was being re-negotiated, Hong King and Norway conducted their trade relations in textiles under an MFA-based agreement. This agreement determined the level of textiles Norway would accept from Hong Kong. At the time this dispute arose, the two countries were seeking, unsuccessfully, to agree on a mutually acceptable level for the future.

---

[1] See *Hong Kong* v. *Norway: Restrictions on imports of certain textile products* (1980), BISD 27th Supp, 119.

[2] As with certain other commodities and product types, textiles have not traditionally been freely traded. Rather, they have been managed under a massive web of bilateral agreements called the MultiFibre Arrangement, through which developed countries would control the amount of low-cost textile they would allow into their territories, and developing countries would be guaranteed a certain level of market access at an acceptable price.

In 1978, Norway introduced temporary import control measures on textile products from certain countries, including Hong Kong. In the expectation of acceding to a renewed MFA in the near future, Norway also managed to enter into market access agreements on textile imports with six developing countries (not including Hong Kong) on terms relatively favourable to these countries. Not long after, Norway invoked Article XIX[3] of the General Agreement and said that it was preparing new global quotas on certain textile items. Hong Kong called for a fair share of Norway's global quota in these products, on terms similar to those granted to the other six developing countries. When it failed in this, Hong Kong proceeded to bring an action before the GATT, under Article XIII:2[4] of the General Agreement.

This case posed a major question with regard to the use of Article XIX safeguard restrictions by contracting parties to the GATT: namely, whether non-discrimination principles apply when quantitative restrictions are imposed on grounds of Article XIX, or whether governments may use Article XIX restrictions "selectively", when the imports actually causing the injury are limited to one or two countries?

Hong Kong argued that Norway's six bilateral agreements with other textile-exporting countries had not been concluded or justified under either the MFA or under any provision of GATT, and that as a general matter Article XI prohibits such import restrictions. Thus, in Hong Kong's view, Norway's bilateral agreements with the other parties had no GATT standing. The result of those agreements, according to Hong Kong, was that Norway's global quota had been reduced and with it, of course, Hong Kong's share of the overall global quota. At the very least, Hong Kong argued, Norway should make its action consistent with Article XIII:2(b), a provision which requires fair allocation of a global QR to all interested supplying countries. Such an approach, it was argued, would at least allow Hong Kong a fair share of trade with Norway.

---

[3] Art. XIX:1(a): If, as a result of unforeseen developments and of the effect of the obligations incurred by a contracting party under this Agreement, including tariff concessions, any product is being imported into the territory of that contracting party in such increased quantities and under such conditions as to cause or threaten serious injury to domestic producers in that territory of like or directly competitive products, the contracting party shall be free, in respect of such product, and to the extent and for such time as may be necessary to prevent or remedy such injury, to suspend the obligation in whole or in part or to withdraw or modify the concession.

[4] Art. XIII:2: "In applying import restrictions to any product, contracting parties shall aim at a distribution of trade in such product approaching as closely as possible the shares which the various contracting parties might be expected to obtain in the absence of such restrictions . . .

(d) In cases in which a quota is allocated among supplying countries, the contracting party applying the restrictions may seek agreement with respect to the allocation of shares in the quota with all other contracting parties having a substantial interest in supplying the product concerned. In cases in which this method is not reasonably practicable, the contracting party concerned shall allow to contracting parties having a substantial interest in supplying the product shares based upon the proportions, supplied by such contracting parties during a previous representative period, of the total quantity or value of imports of the product, due account being taken of any special factors which may have affected or may be affecting the trade in the product . . ."

Norway's own argument was that recent imports of low-cost textiles, including those from Hong Kong, had risen dramatically. Whatever unilateral measures it had taken, it was within its rights to do so under the MFA, since the MFA made provision for the possibility of jointly agreed, reasonable departures from particular elements of the umbrella agreement. Norway further argued that its Article XIX action was in full conformity with the General Agreement. The six agreements, it said, had been entered into before its decision to invoke Article XIX.

The panel was of the view that the type of action chosen by Norway—that is, quantitative restrictions (QRs) limiting the importation of the textile categories in question, as a form of emergency action under Article XIX—was subject to the requirements of Article XIII, providing for non-discriminatory administration of quantitative restrictions. The panel focused on the language of Article XIII, to the effect that distribution of trade "should approximate as closely as possible the shares which the various contracting parties might have expected to obtain in the absence of such restrictions". Norway, having given a partial allocation of its quota to the six countries, should be considered to have acted under Article XIII:2(d).

The panel further found that Hong Kong had a substantial interest in exporting these products, and thus a right to expect the allocation of a share of the quota in accordance with Article XIII:2(d), based on the trade volumes of a previous representative period of time. The panel found that Norway had not acted under Article XIX consistently with Article XIII:2(d), and called upon it to terminate its action, or make it consistent with Article XIII. While Norway accepted the ruling, the EC for its part "reserved its position" with regard to the implications of the panel report.[5] Of greatest significance after this case was the fact that when a contracting party invokes Article XIX and on that basis imposes a quantitative restriction on imports, Article XIII principles on non-discrimination apply. This meant that Article XIX action would be more costly, because the interests of all significant trading partners would have to be taken into account when designing QR allocations. Thus, the ruling contributed directly to the proliferation of unilateralist actions during the 1980s, since countries found unattractive this requirement to treat all suppliers even-handedly when invoking the escape clause.

The original GATT Agreement included a safeguard provision, as do other free trade agreements, as an inducement to participation. That is, it offered the prospect that, if concessions made within the context of GATT proved too politically costly, participating countries could take emergency action to protect the endangered economic interest within their own territory. When the use of Article XIX safeguard measures proved too costly, then contracting parties reverted to VERs.[6] The Uruguay Round Agreement on Safeguards, described

---

[5] Over the next few years, Norway terminated the objectionable favouritism shown to selected trading partners.

[6] See Ernesto M Hizon, "The Safeguard Measure/VER Dilemma: The Jekyll and Hyde of Trade Protection", (Fall 1994) 15 *Journal of International Law and Business* 105.

below, by both proscribing VERs, and making the use of Article XIX safeguards far more costly than before, significantly limited the freedom of WTO members to engage in protectionism, and thus significantly eroded the concept of a "safety valve" within the GATT/WTO system.

THE URUGUAY ROUND AGREEMENT ON SAFEGUARDS:
NEW RULES FOR INVOKING ARTICLE XIX

The Agreement on Safeguards is one of the most important in the entire body of Uruguay Round Agreements. Since safeguards are the route by which countries can undo, however temporarily, the unintended consequences and effects of trade liberalisation, these measures act as political insurance against the resistance of internal political constituencies. In the event that a GATT/WTO party grants a trade concession, then finds itself inundated in an unforeseen way with foreign products, such that a domestic industry is threatened with injury (and clearly the subtextual issue here is job maintenance), there must be an escape clause available to soften the blow. Indeed, without some form of escape clause, it is doubtful that trade agreements would get off the ground at all, as the risks would be too great.

The basic safeguard provision of the General Agreement, found in Article XIX, was fairly open-ended. Even though the *Hong Kong* v. *Norway* panel decision made it necessary for Article XIX to be invoked according to principles of non-discrimination, the time frame and scope of safeguard actions were nonetheless left for the most part up to the importing country. In light of the fact that the Uruguay Round Agreements in the aggregate brought about greater legalism and a stricter form of trade liberalisation, it should come as no surprise that safeguard measures also became more difficult and costly to invoke, and far less of an open-ended invitation to protect vulnerable national economic sectors. No longer an opt-out for the adversely affected, the new agreement ensured that GATT/WTO safeguards would be no more than an "opportunity to adjust", in the parlance of the post-1995 trade ethos.

The Safeguard Agreement's preamble states its purpose: to "re-establish multilateral control over safeguards and eliminate measures that escape such control". Article 1 on the scope of the Agreement asserts that it will "establish rules for the application of safeguard measures" under Article XIX. Article 2 first reiterates the conditions for applying Article XIX measures (only where there have been determinations of serious injury or threat of serious injury to a domestic industry),[7] then goes on to state that "safeguard measures shall be applied to a product being imported, irrespective of its source". Article 3 requires an investigation of the

---

[7] Art. 4 provides a clearer definition of "serious injury", including the following elements: a significant overall impairment in the position of a domestic industry. "Domestic industry" should be taken to mean at least a "major proportion of the total domestic production of those products". A causal link must be shown, on the basis of objective evidence, between increased imports and the serious injury or threat of serious injury.

"injury" to domestic industry, including public notification of the initiation of the investigation, as well as hearings, with findings to be published.

Article 5 deals with the application of safeguard measures—the new rules for invoking Article XIX. Article 5(1) says that members shall only apply safeguard measures to the extent necessary. If a QR is used, it cannot lower the quantity of imports below the average of the last three representative (recent) years, unless there is some clear indication that some other level is necessary to prevent serious injury. Article 5(2) appears to codify the Hong Kong-Norway case, stating that where a quota is allocated among supplying countries, the allocation must occur proportionately, based on trade shares in a previous representative period. The conditions for departure from this non-discrimination principle (valid only where there is actual injury) are set out in Article 5(2)(b); this must be under the auspices of the Committee on Safeguards, and be the result of a disproportionate recent increase from certain exporting members.

Article 7, on the duration and review of safeguard measures, is extremely important, in that it places a clear time line on the adoption of safeguard measures. Article 7(1) states that safeguards may only be applied for as long as necessary; the relevant period shall not exceed four years, unless it is extended under Article 7(2). Under Article 7(2), the member's authorities must determine (using criteria outlined earlier) that (i) the safeguard measure continues to be necessary, and (ii) there is evidence that the industry is adjusting, and that the conditions of Articles 8–10 are observed. Article 7(3) creates a firm rule that the total period of application should not exceed four years, and must not in any event exceed eight years. This temporal limitation on the use of safeguards alters the expectations and incentives of WTO members, in that it ensures that protection for a particular industry, at least through the use of safeguards, cannot continue indefinitely.

Under Article 7(4), all measures applied for more than one year must be "progressively liberalised" at regular intervals; this on the theory that industries will better "adjust". Renewed safeguards cannot be more restrictive than the situation at the end of the first phase.[8] Looked at in its entirety, the effect of Article 7 is unmistakable. The objective is to make it far more burdensome for members to invoke Article XIX in order to protect vulnerable industries.

Article 8 requires that members applying such measures compensate adversely affected members by granting other trade concessions. If no such accord is reached, the adversely affected member may apply to the Council for Trade in Goods to suspend concessions against the member applying the safeguard measure.

Article 9 is on the treatment of developing countries in the application of safeguards. Such measures are not to be applied against products from developing countries where the developing country's share of exports in that product to the

---

[8] Under Art. 7(5), where an imported product has once had a safeguard measure applied to it, and where there has then been a period of non-application of two years, no second application can be allowed for as long a period of time, with some highly technical exceptions.

importing member is not over 3 per cent, and if developing countries with less than 3 per cent import share do not collectively account for more than 9 per cent of the total of such exports to the affected member. Developing countries may apply a safeguard for two years beyond the maximum length of time allowed other member countries; re-application restrictions are also eased somewhat for developing countries.

Article 10, on pre-existing Article XIX measures, states that all safeguard measures in being when the WTO Agreement came into force must be terminated not later than eight years after they were applied, or five years after the date of entry into force of the WTO Agreement.

Article 11, hidden away in the body of the overall agreement, is of striking importance for contemporary economic relations; it states that no emergency action on imports by a member under Article XIX can be applied except in conformity with Article XIX and the Safeguards Agreement. In other words, there can be no more unilateral safeguard actions, outside the scope of GATT/WTO law. Article 11(1)(b) says clearly that no VER, Orderly Marketing Agreement (OMA) or similar measure, whether on the import or export side, can be sought or taken, either by one or more members. Any such arrangements are to be ended, either by being brought into conformity with the Agreement, or phased out altogether.[9]

Under Article 11(2), all VERs are to be phased out within four years at the most, with each member entitled to keep one VER until the end of 1999.[10] Interestingly, 11(3) states that "members shall not encourage or support the adoption or maintenance by public and private enterprises of non-governmental measures equivalent to those referred to in paragraph 1". This provision takes account of the fact that VERs could be carried out unofficially, and achieve the same protective effect.

Article 12 creates an obligation to notify when a country is engaging in an investigation or extending a safeguard measure, to the extent that all relevant evidence must be provided to the Committee on Safeguards. The Committee has the power to demand additional information from the member. Adequate consultations with affected parties must also be a feature of plans to apply a safeguard measure. The Committee on Safeguards, established under Article 13, is to monitor implementation of the Safeguards Agreement, and, if requested, make a finding as to whether the procedural requirements of the agreement have been complied with as to a particular national measure. The Committee must also monitor the phasing out of national safeguard measures, as described above.

---

[9] It should be noted that under Art. 11(1)(c), there is a specific statement that the Safeguards Agreement does not apply to measures taken under a GATT article other than Art. XIX, or other multilateral agreements, or other agreements entered into within the framework of the GATT. This is important in the textiles context, since the new textiles trading scheme, to be discussed below, has an entirely separate safeguard regime.

[10] The only registered exception of this kind is the large OMA agreed between Europe and Japan, which limits the number of imported passenger cars, and light commercial vehicles and light trucks to be exported to Europe. As required, this is in effect only until the end of 1999.

On request, the Committee is required to review whether a given proposal to suspend concessions (i.e., in response to another member's safeguard restriction) is "substantially equivalent", that is, equivalent to the value of what was believed to be lost. Disputes arising under the agreement are of course conducted under the terms of the Dispute Settlement Understanding.

DISPUTES UNDER THE SAFEGUARDS AGREEMENT

It was to be expected that the Safeguards Agreement would generate significant litigation over the question of whether a member imposing an emergency safeguard measure had honoured the new and more stringent requirements. It is starkly evident that with each new dispute, the cost of national protection through the use of traditional safeguards is rising. Not only are the front-end costs of deciding to apply a safeguard far greater (in anticipation of possible review by a WTO panel and the Appellate Body), but the additional cost of defending that decision before a panel in the event of a challenge is also significant.

KOREAN SKIMMED MILK POWDER

When the EC brought a challenge in 1998 to a Korean safeguard measure pertaining to skimmed milk powder preparations,[11] it is hardly surprising that Korea's first line of defence was that the EC had no real commercial interest in the matter; and that the complainants were simply looking to establish some nice precedents on the use and abuse of safeguards, and had happened upon the Korean attempt to protect Korean farmers.[12]

The panel pointed out that there is no requirement in the WTO that the parties have a demonstrable economic interest in the issues to be resolved; at least since the *Banana* decision, there was no need to show a genuine commercial motive in order to obtain locus standi before a WTO panel.[13] In the panel's view,

> "even assuming that there is some requirement for economic interest, we consider that the EC, as an exporter of milk products to Korea, had sufficient interest to initiate and proceed with these dispute settlement proceedings".[14]

Since a determination by the Korean trade authorities to apply a safeguard measure was under challenge, and by extension the quality of official data upon which this decision was based, it is hardly surprising that the proper standard of

---

[11] *EC v. Korea: Definitive Safeguard Measure on Imports of Certain Dairy Products*, Report of the Panel, 21 June 1999 (WT/DS98/R) [hereinafter *Korean Dairy Safeguards* Panel Report].

[12] See description of factual aspects, *Korean Dairy Safeguards* Panel Report, paras. 2.1–2.8. Regarding the alleged EC lack of an economic interest in the matter, see paras. 7.8–7.15.

[13] *Korean Dairy Safeguards* Panel Report, para. 7.13.

[14] *Korean Dairy Safeguards* Panel Report, para. 7.14.

review by the panel should loom large as an issue. The panel relied on its mandate under Article 11 of the DSU. It explained,

> "We consider that for the panel to adopt a policy of total deference to the findings of the national authorities could not ensure an 'objective assessment' as set out in Article 11 of the DSU".

Neither does the panel see its own review as a "substitute for the proceedings conducted by national investigating authorities".[15] The panel conceived of its task as an objective assessment of the review conducted by the national investigating authorities, in this case the Korean Trade Commission.[16] The panel said that it would examine the entire underlying report prepared by the Korean authorities, not just the notifications made to the Committee on Safeguards. While no particular method is prescribed to the member country, the panel would ensure that the member can "demonstrate that it did address the relevant issues".[17]

The EC claims were under both GATT Article XIX and the Safeguards Agreement.[18] As for the first European argument, that Korea should have, in line with the language of Article XIX, shown that the import situation was the result of "unforeseen developments", the panel agreed that the obligations of Article XIX and the Safeguards Agreement were generally cumulative, and did not conflict with one another.[19]

However, it rejected the European argument that this imposed a separate obligation on the defendant country to demonstrate the unforeseen circumstances. Reviewing the historical context under which the provision was written into Article XIX, the panel reasoned that it would have been unthinkable that a trade minister would negotiate a tariff concession in the knowledge and expectation that there would be increased imports leading to serious injury to a domestic industry.[20] In the panel's view, this interpretation of the opening

---

[15] *Korean Dairy Safeguards* Panel Report, para. 7.30.

[16] The panel elaborated on this: "For us, an objective assessment entails an examination of whether the KTC had examined all facts in its possession or which it should have obtained in accordance with Art. 4.2 of the Agreement on Safeguards . . . whether adequate explanation had been provided of how the facts as a whole supported the determination made and, consequently, whether the determination made was consistent with the international obligations of Korea". Para. 7.30.

[17] *Korean Dairy Safeguards* Panel Report, para. 7.31.

[18] *Korean Dairy Safeguards* Panel Report, para. 7.33. Noting that Art. XIX :1(a) had mentioned "unforeseen developments" leading to the need to protect one's domestic industries, while the Safeguards Agreement did not repeat that phrase, the EC made the argument that Korea ought to have shown that the import trends under investigation were in fact the result of "unforeseen developments". As far as the Safeguards Agreement is concerned, Europe argued that Korea had failed to address whether the conditions under which the products being investigated were imported were of such a nature as to cause serious injury to the domestic industry producing like or directly competitive products.

[19] *Korean Dairy Safeguards* Panel Report, paras. 7.37–7.39.

[20] In the panel's words, ". . . the proposition 'as a result of unforeseen developments and of the effect of the obligations incurred by a contracting party under this agreement' does not address the conditions for Art. XIX measures to be applied but rather explains why a provision such as Art. XIX may be needed". *Korean Dairy Safeguards* Panel Report, paras. 7.41–7.45.

language of Article XIX "is compatible with the object and purpose of GATT which was to ensure some certainty and predictability in tariff bindings and other GATT obligations".[21] As to why the phrase was not repeated in the Safeguards Agreement, by the time of the Uruguay Round negotiations, it was no longer necessary to make this point. Thus, according to the panel, there was no legal violation in the fact that Korea did not conduct an examination as to whether the import surge and negative effect on domestic industry were the result of "unforeseen developments".[22]

The more substantive arguments centred on Korea's alleged deficiencies with respect to the obligations imposed by Articles 2.1, 4.2, and 5.1 of the Safeguards Agreement.[23] Referring to Article 2.1, the EC argued that the phrase "under such conditions" imposed a separate obligation on the country applying the measure to actually consider such "conditions", including price, which was allegedly not considered by Korea.[24] While price would nearly always be relevant in the determination of injury, the panel said, it rejected the idea that Article 2.1 imposes any such explicit and separate obligation. Rather, it imposes a general requirement on the importing country to "perform an adequate assessment of the impact of the increased imports at issue and the specific market under investigation".[25]

---

[21] *Korean Dairy Safeguards* Panel Report, para. 7.46.

[22] *Korean Dairy Safeguards* Panel Report, paras. 7.47–7.48.

[23] The relevant provisions read as follows:

"Art. 2.1: 'A member may apply a safeguard measure to a product only if that member has determined, pursuant to the provisions set out below, that such product is being imported into its territory in such increased quantities, absolute or relative to domestic production, and under such conditions as to cause or threaten to cause serious injury to the domestic industry that produces like or directly competitive products'."

Art. 4.2(a): In the investigation to determine whether the increased imports have caused or are threatening to cause serious injury to a domestic industry under the terms of this Agreement, the competent authorities shall evaluate all relevant factors of an objective and quantifiable nature having a bearing on the situation of that industry, in particular, the rate and amount of the increase in imports of the product concerned in absolute and relative terms, the share of the domestic market taken by increased imports, changes in the level of sales, production, productivity, capacity, utilization, profits and losses, and employment.

(b) The determination referred to in subparagraph (a) shall not be made unless this investigation demonstrates, on the basis of objective evidence, the existence of the causal link between increased imports of the product concerned and serious injury or threat thereof. When factors other than increased imports are causing injury to the domestic industry at the same time, such injury shall not be attributed to increased imports.

(c) The competent authorities shall publish promptly, in accordance with the provisions of Art. 3, a detailed analysis of the case under investigation as well as a demonstration of the relevance of the factors examined.

Art. 5.1: "A member shall apply safeguard measures only to the extent necessary to prevent or remedy serious injury and to facilitate adjustment. If a quantitative restriction is used, such a measure shall not reduce the quantity of imports below the level of a recent period which shall be the average of imports in the last three representative years for which statistics are available, unless clear justification is given that a different level is necessary to prevent or remedy serious injury. Members should choose measures most suitable for the achievement of these objectives".

[24] *Korean Dairy Safeguards* Panel Report, para. 7.49.

[25] *Korean Dairy Safeguards* Panel Report, paras. 7.51–7.52.

The EC further claimed that, in its evaluation of serious injury to its domestic industry, Korea failed to correctly examine all relevant factors of an objective and quantifiable nature having a bearing on the situation of the domestic industry, as required by Article 4.2 of the Safeguards Agreement.[26] The panel proceeded to analyse whether Korea examined all relevant facts in its possession, or which should have been obtained under Article 4.2, and whether it provided an adequate explanation of how those facts as a whole supported the determination made.[27] In this assessment of Korea's analysis, the panel found several troubling gaps: A lack of consideration of certain of the factors listed in Article 4.2—for instance capacity utilisation and productivity; failure to examine all relevant market sectors, as opposed to a select sampling; and failure to provide sufficient reasoning on choices which affected Korea's consideration of factors, and how these factors support a finding of serious injury.[28]

The panel went through the individual elements of the Korean Trade Commission's report; some of the enumerated factors were shown to have been adequately considered, while others were not. Because of the existence of these gaps, the panel found that Korea did not meet the requirement to consider each of the factors set out in Article 4.2.[29] The panel noted that Article 2.1 permits the application of a safeguard only if there has been a determination of serious injury pursuant to Article 4.2—that is, in accordance and conformity with the terms of Article 4.2.[30]

The second arm of the panel's Article 4.2 analysis concerned the EC claim that Korea had not demonstrated a causal link between increased imports and serious injury to the domestic industry producing like or directly competitive products. In the panel's view, it was not strictly speaking necessary to treat this issue, since it had already been shown that Korea did not address all of the injury factors listed in Article 4.2, and thus had acted in contravention of that article. However, the panel decided to offer some general comments relevant to the matter of sufficient demonstration of a causal link between imports and injury.[31]

Under Article 4.2, a causal link must be shown for the safeguard measure to be valid; it must be demonstrated that the injury is not due to something other than the increased imports. The panel noted that Korea had an obligation not to attribute to increased imports any injury caused by other factors.[32] However, the Korean report suggested that a number of complex issues relating to supply and demand, quite apart from the issue of imports, were also at work.[33]

[26] *Korean Dairy Safeguards* Panel Report, paras. 7.54–7.55.
[27] *Korean Dairy Safeguards* Panel Report, para. 7.55.
[28] *Korean Dairy Safeguards* Panel Report, para. 7.58.
[29] *Korean Dairy Safeguards* Panel Report, paras. 7.60–7.85.
[30] *Korean Dairy Safeguards* Panel Report, paras. 7.60–7.85.
[31] *Korean Dairy Safeguards* Panel Report, para. 7.87.
[32] *Korean Dairy Safeguards* Panel Report, paras. 7.89–7.90.
[33] *Korean Dairy Safeguards* Panel Report, paras. 7.92–7.95.

The EC made claims under Article 5.1 of the Safeguards Agreement, to the effect that when a WTO member takes a safeguard measure, it needs to prove that the measure is necessary and should justify its "adequacy" in remedying injury and facilitating adjustment. The EC alleged that Korea did not give consideration to adjustment plans, or consider other types of measures than a quota. Korea was also alleged to have failed to show that the level of the quota was necessary to remedy serious injury or facilitate adjustment.[34] While all of these claims, if approached technically, might appear absurdly narrow to the general reader, in fact, Europe's insistence signals the end of the era of casual, unilateral safeguard actions by GATT/WTO countries. The point of these claims was to establish *that each and every factor* mentioned in the Safeguards Agreement must be taken seriously.

For its part, Korea argued that it was free to decide that the four- year quota was the most appropriate remedy for its problem, and that there is no obligation to demonstrate that this is the most suitable measure to achieve these objectives.[35]

The panel interpreted Article 5 as establishing certain rules that come into play only after a decision has been taken to adopt a safeguard measure. Once the conditions have been complied with, the decision itself cannot be further challenged; however, the panel cautions, Article 5.1 does in fact contain a very specific obligation. This is

> "to apply a measure that is commensurate with the goals of preventing or remedying the serious injury suffered by the domestic industry and of facilitating the adjustment of the domestic industry".[36]

The elements of any measure—product coverage, form, duration, and level—must be no more restrictive than necessary. And this in turn, the panel stated, must be reviewable by a panel. For this reason, members must provide a reasoned explanation as to how the particular measure decided upon complies with Article 5.1.[37]

And the panel agreed with the EC to the extent that Korea had apparently not explained how it had concluded that the measure adopted was necessary.[38] The panel stated that "mere description" of alternative measures is insufficient; rather, there must be

> "some discernible reasoning as to why the measure recommended or adopted is preferable to the others, specifically with respect to achieving the objectives of remedying the serious injury and facilitating adjustment".[39]

---

[34] *Korean Dairy Safeguards* Panel Report, para. 7.97.
[35] *Korean Dairy Safeguards* Panel Report, para. 7.98.
[36] *Korean Dairy Safeguards* Panel Report, paras. 7.98–7.99.
[37] *Korean Dairy Safeguards* Panel Report, para. 7.101.
[38] The panel wrote: "We note the absence of any discussion or analysis indicating the considerations underlying the choice of the measure adopted and any explanation as to why the Korean authorities concluded that the measure was necessary to remedy the serious injury and facilitate adjustment." *Korean Dairy Safeguards* Panel Report, para. 7.104.
[39] *Korean Dairy Safeguards* Panel Report, para. 7.105.

The EC succeeded on a further claim under Articles 12.1 and 12.2 that the Korean notifications of injury and the decision to apply a safeguard were not sufficiently timely. While Korea met the test for sufficiency of information notified, that was not the case for the speed with which it made its intentions known to those trading partners with an interest in the matter.[40] The EC's claim that Korea provided insufficient information to form the basis for meaningful consultations was rejected by the panel.[41]

THE APPELLATE BODY ON KOREAN DAIRY SAFEGUARDS

The EC appealed the panel's rejection of its argument that Korea had violated Article XIX:1 of the GATT due to the failure of the Korean authorities to examine whether the increase in imports was "as a result of unforeseen developments".[42] The Appellate Body recalled that the panel had stated that the clause relating to unforeseen developments in Article XIX did not add conditions for any measure to be applied pursuant to Article XIX, but rather served as an explanation as to why an Article XIX measure may be needed.[43] The panel nonetheless asserted that the obligations found in Article XIX and those found in the Safeguards Agreement were cumulative, a proposition with which the Appellate Body agreed.[44] The Appellate Body pointed out the links between Article XIX and the Agreement, in particular the fact that the Agreement establishes rules for the application of Article XIX safeguard measures.[45]

Based on the principle that all of the provisions of a treaty must be given meaning and legal effect, the Appellate Body stated its belief that the clause found in Article XIX:1, "as a result of unforeseen developments", must have meaning. In this light, it explicitly rejected the panel's view that this phrase does not add conditions for measures to be applied pursuant to Article XIX.[46] As to the actual meaning that must therefore be granted to the clause, the Appellate Body interpreted unforeseen to indicate "unexpected", pointing to independent circumstances which must be demonstrated as a matter of fact before a safeguard measure can be applied consistently with Article XIX of the GATT.[47]

The Appellate Body also emphasised the fact that Article XIX actions are in essence "emergency actions",

---

[40]   *Korean Dairy Safeguards* Panel Report, paras. 7.112–7.145.
[41]   *Korean Dairy Safeguards* Panel Report, paras. 7.146–7.153.
[42]   *EC v. Korea: Definitive Safeguard Measure on Imports of Certain Dairy Products*, Appellate Body Report, 14 December 1999 (WT/DS98AB/R) [hereinafter *Korean Dairy Safeguards* Appellate Report] at para. 68.
[43]   *Korean Dairy Safeguards* Appellate Body Report, para. 70.
[44]   *Korean Dairy Safeguards* Appellate Body Report, paras. 74–76.
[45]   *Korean Dairy Safeguards* Appellate Body Report, para. 77.
[46]   *Korean Dairy Safeguards* Appellate Body Report, para. 82.
[47]   *Korean Dairy Safeguards* Appellate Body Report, paras. 84–85.

"to be invoked only in situations when, as a result of obligations incurred under the GATT 1994, an importing Member finds itself confronted with developments it had not 'foreseen' or 'expected' when it incurred that obligation".[48]

Article XIX provides an extraordinary remedy which allows members to provide a temporary re-adjustment of the balance in the level of concessions, giving the domestic industry time to adjust to new competitive conditions.[49] While reversing the panel's conclusion with respect to the obligations imposed by the clause in Article XIX pertaining to "unforeseen" developments, the Appellate Body noted that the panel did not make any factual findings as to whether the increase in imports was the result of unforeseen developments. To this extent, the Appellate Body stated that it was "not in a position to complete the analysis and make a determination as to whether Korea acted inconsistently with its obligations under Article XIX:1(a)".[50]

With respect to Article 5.1 of the Safeguards Agreement, the Appellate Body found a relatively minor error in part of the panel's reasoning, while agreeing with most of it.[51] Korea had argued that by finding that Members must impose measures no more restrictive than necessary, and that they must provide a reasoned explanation as to how the authorities reached a conclusion that the measure in question satisfied all the requirements set out in Article 5.1, the panel had in effect imposed on members a new obligation not actually found in that provision.[52] The Appellate Body agreed with the panel that the first sentence of Article 5.1 imposes an obligation on members applying a safeguard measure "to ensure that the measure applied is commensurate with the goals of preventing or remedying serious injury and of facilitating adjustment". Whatever form the safeguard takes, the Appellate Body agreed that it must be applied "only to the extent necessary" to achieve the goals set out in the first sentence of Article 5.1.[53]

The Appellate Body also affirmed that the second sentence of Article 5.1 requires a clear justification from the member if the measure takes the form of a quantitative restriction which reduces the quantity of imports below the average of imports in the last three representative years. But the Appellate Body stated that nothing in Article 5.1 establishes such an obligation for a safeguard measure other than a QR which reduces the quantity of imports below that level. The panel had not made any factual determinations as to whether the

---

[48] *Korean Dairy Safeguards* Appellate Body Report, para. 86.
[49] *Korean Dairy Safeguards* Appellate Body Report, para. 87.
[50] *Korean Dairy Safeguards* Appellate Body Report, para. 92.
[51] Art. 5.1 of the Agreement reads as follows: "A Member shall apply safeguard measures only to the extent necessary to prevent or remedy serious injury and to facilitate adjustment. If a quantitative restriction is used, such a measure shall not reduce the quantity of imports below the level of a recent period which shall be the average of imports in the last three representative years for which statistics are available, unless clear justification is given that a different level is necessary to prevent or remedy serious injury. Members should choose measures most suitable for the achievement of these objectives."
[52] *Korean Dairy Safeguards* Appellate Body Report, paras. 94–95.
[53] *Korean Dairy Safeguards* Appellate Body Report, para. 96.

Korean safeguard was of such a type; and so the Appellate Body simply said that it was not in a position to make a determination as to the consistency of Korea's safeguard measure with the second sentence of Article 5.1 Again, whatever the differences in interpretation of the Safeguards Agreement as between the panels and Appellate Body, the totality of the logic of the agreement is clear: the burden of justification on WTO members imposing safeguard measures is heavy, and freedom to rely on safeguards to respond to pressure from endangered economic constituencies, severely limited.

ARGENTINE FOOTWEAR SAFEGUARDS

The case against Korea offered a useful exploration of the rules relating to the application of safeguard measures in a post-Uruguay Round world. The EC took a similar case against Argentina,[54] which also led to interesting formulations by the panel and Appellate Body concerning the freedom of a member country to impose safeguards. The dispute involved European dissatisfaction with the manner in which Argentina had applied safeguards to protect its footwear industry, and raised a number of issues concerning the obligations of WTO members who are also parties to regional free trade agreements, in the context of determining the proper scope of safeguard measures.

The EC argued that Argentina had imposed Article XIX safeguard measures as a substitute for other protective duties that had been found GATT-illegal in an earlier WTO action.[55] Argentina had embarked upon a major programme of trade liberalisation at the beginning of the 1990s, especially as part of its participation in South American regional trade agreements (MERCOSUR), but then began to introduce counter-measures to protect its threatened industries. For this reason, Argentina had imposed so-called "minimum specific duties" on footwear and other items of apparel, although these had been found to be inconsistent with GATT obligations, in that they caused Argentina to charge a customs duty higher than the one it had committed itself to in its GATT schedule.[56] While the GATT-illegal duties on footwear were abolished in 1997, it was alleged by the EC that the safeguard measures complained of in this dispute were designed to replace them.[57] Argentina's definitive safeguard measure on footwear was imposed in September of 1997, valid for three years.[58]

---

[54] *EC v. Argentina: Safeguard Measures on Imports of Footwear*, Report of the Panel, 25 June 1999 (WT/DS121/R) [hereinafter *Argentine Footwear Safeguards* Panel Report].

[55] *Argentine Footwear Safeguards* Panel Report, para. 4.8.

[56] In fact, Argentina abolished its special duties on footwear in advance of the first panel ruling; then turned to the safeguard measure. In the meantime, the panel found the same type of special duties on apparel and textiles to be GATT-illegal. All of the specific duties were then abolished, but the footwear safeguard that Argentina had imposed remained. Europe then brought this WTO challenge to the safeguard measure.

[57] *Argentine Footwear Safeguards* Panel Report, paras. 4.9–4.10.

[58] *Argentine Footwear Safeguards* Panel Report, paras. 8.1–8.11.

The EC complained that Argentina had failed to examine whether or not the increased imports were a result of "unforeseen developments", relying on arguments similar to those raised in the *Korean Dairy Safeguards* dispute.[59] The panel in this case summed up its view of the relationship between the obligations imposed by the Safeguards Agreement and by GATT Article XIX in this way:

"It appears that the negotiators intended the new Safeguard Agreement to comprehensively cover the field of the application of safeguard measures and deliberately chose not to include the unforeseen developments criterion in the new comprehensive agreement. As a result, since we must give meaning to the fact that the new Safeguards Agreement does not in so many words make a single reference to the unforeseen developments condition, conformity with the explicit requirements and conditions embodied in the Safeguards Agreement must be sufficient for the application of safeguard measures within the meaning of Article XIX of GATT".[60]

Thus, as in the *Korean Dairy Safeguards* case, the panel declined to accept the EC's view that, with the coming into effect of the Safeguards Agreement, Article XIX continues to impose a separate obligation based on the language of "unforeseen developments". For this reason, the panel saw no basis to address the EC's claims under Article XIX "separately and in isolation from those under the Safeguards Agreement".[61]

One of the EC's "core allegations" against Argentina's safeguard investigation was that Argentine authorities had conducted an analysis of imports, injury and causation on the basis of statistics for all imports (including imports from MERCOSUR countries as well as from third countries), and then impermissibly applied the safeguard measure only against imports from non-MERCOSUR countries.[62] The EC argued that it would only have been acceptable to exclude the MERCOSUR countries from the safeguard measure in the event that they had been excluded from the investigation as well; that is, from the injury and causation analyses. For its part, Argentina accused the EC of adding obligations to the Safeguards Agreement that are simply not there, in that Articles 2 and 4 refer only to imports, without any further limitation.[63] (The issue of exclusion of trading partners in regional trade arrangements from the scope of safeguard measures receives more complete treatment in the discussion of the *US Wheat Gluten Safeguards* dispute, below.)

The panel dealt at length with the footnote to Article 2 on the role of customs unions in the adoption of safeguard measures, especially this sentence:

"When a safeguard measure is applied on behalf of a member state [that is, of the free trade area], all the requirements for the determination of serious injury or threat thereof shall be based on the conditions existing in that member state and the measure shall be limited to that member state".

---

[59] *Argentine Footwear Safeguards* Panel Report, para. 8.47.
[60] *Argentine Footwear Safeguards* Panel Report, para. 8.67.
[61] *Argentine Footwear Safeguards* Panel Report, para. 8.69.
[62] *Argentine Footwear Safeguards* Panel Report, para. 8.72.
[63] *Argentine Footwear Safeguards* Panel Report, para. 8.74.

(Under the footnote, it would also be possible for a safeguard measure to be taken on behalf of the whole customs union, in which case the conditions prevailing within the bloc as a whole would be relevant.)

The panel agreed with Argentina that the footnote does not prevent the inclusion of imports from other states of the customs union in the injury and causation analysis.[64] But it also agreed with the EC that there must be *parallelism*—that the imports from one's regional trade partners cannot be included in the analysis, if the safeguard measure then excludes those regional partners from its scope.[65] This interpretation is supported, the panel stated, by the overall purpose of the agreement, which was "to re-establish multilateral control over safeguards and to eliminate measures that escape such control". Thus, strict interpretation and implementation of the agreement was called for.[66] The panel's conclusion is that

> "in the case of a customs union the imposition of a safeguard measure only on third-country sources cannot be justified on the basis of a member-state-specific investigation that finds serious injury or threat thereof caused by imports from all sources of supply from within and outside a customs union".[67]

The panel then turned to Argentina's investigation, to see whether it had established the "essential conditions" under the Safeguards Agreement for imposing a safeguard measure. In a manner similar to that followed in the *Korean Dairy Products* case, the panel assessed whether the Argentine investigation was flawed, and by extension whether it failed to provide sufficient justification for the safeguard measure adopted. Responding to the relentless set of EC arguments, the panel provided an exhaustive evaluation of the quality of the Argentine evidence which, in nearly all respects, proved wanting.[68]

Argentina failed both to demonstrate significant increases in imports, or to explain the injurious effects on its domestic industry. It failed to show rises in imports over the relevant period, failed to look at all factors necessary for a serious injury determination, and failed to show, through adequate explanation, a causal link between increased imports and injury to domestic industry. "Therefore", the panel stated, "we find that Argentina's investigation and determinations of increased imports, serious injury and causation are inconsistent with Articles 2 and 4 of the Safeguards Agreement". (8.280) The factual

---

[64] *Argentine Footwear Safeguards* Panel Report, para. 8.79.

[65] *Argentine Footwear Safeguards* Panel Report, para. 8.87.

[66] *Argentine Footwear Safeguards* Panel Report, para. 8.88. The panel went on to examine Art. XXIV of the General Agreement, to determine whether it in any way prohibits a member of a free trade bloc from imposing safeguard measures against the products of other members of the same bloc. Despite Argentina's arguments to that effect, the panel found nothing in the language of Art. XXIV that would in itself act as such a prohibition. Paras. 8.93–8.101.

[67] *Argentine Footwear Safeguards* Panel Report, para. 8.102.

[68] *Argentine Footwear Safeguards* Panel Report, paras. 8.129–8.274.

determination that would provide the only sound legal basis for the safeguard measure was lacking; the Argentinian measure was found unlawful.[69]

ARGENTINE FOOTWEAR AND THE APPELLATE BODY

The Appellate Body reversed the panel on several issues.[70] Following similar reasoning to its holding in the *Korean Dairy Safeguards* case, the Appellate Body overruled the panel with respect to the relationship between Article XIX of the GATT and the Safeguards Agreement.[71] As Article XIX "continues to have full force and effect", the obligation of demonstrating unforeseen developments continues to fall on WTO members. The panel's interpretation would fail to give "meaning and legal effect" to Article XIX, and thus to "all relevant terms of the WTO Agreement".[72]

The Appellate Body also disagreed with the panel's view that the footnote to Article 2.1 of the Safeguards Agreement applies in this case. The Appellate Body pointed out that "MERCOSUR did not apply these safeguard measures, either as a single unit or on behalf of Argentina".[73] The measures were applied by Argentina as Argentina, a member of the WTO.[74] However, with regard to the issue of a necessary parallelism between the scope of the investigation and the scope of application of the safeguard measure, the Appellate Body agreed that these must correlate. On the ultimate point, the Appellate Body concurred with the panel's view that Argentina's investigation, evaluating injury caused by imports from all sources, could not serve as the basis of a restrictive measure that excludes imports from other MERCOSUR countries from the application of the safeguard measures.[75] The Appellate Body upheld the panel's conclusions with respect to the quality of the evidence relied on by Argentina in making its determinations. "We uphold the panel's conclusions", the Appellate Body wrote, "that Argentina's findings and conclusions regarding causation were not adequately explained and supported by the evidence".[76]

US SAFEGUARDS ON WHEAT GLUTEN

The scope of the evidentiary burden placed on parties applying safeguard measures continues to be refined by decisions of the panels and Appellate Body. In a

[69] *Argentine Footwear Safeguards* Panel Report, paras. 8.275–8.285; 8.286. The panel wrote, ". . . we find that Argentina's investigation provides *no* legal basis for the application of the definitive safeguard measure at issue, or any safeguard measure".

[70] *EC* v. *Argentina: Safeguard Measures on Imports of Footwear*, 14 December 1999 (WT/DS121/AB/R) [*Argentine Footwear Safeguards* Appellate Body Report].

[71] *Argentine Footwear Safeguards* Appellate Body Report, paras. 76–98.

[72] *Argentine Footwear Safeguards* Appellate Body Report, para. 88.

[73] *Argentine Footwear Safeguards* Appellate Body Report, paras. 106–107.

[74] *Argentine Footwear Safeguards* Appellate Body Report, para. 108.

[75] *Argentine Footwear Safeguards* Appellate Body Report, paras. 111–114.

[76] *Argentine Footwear Safeguards* Appellate Body Report, para. 146.

manner familiar from other topics in WTO law, the Appellate Body in interpreting the Safeguards Agreement tends to be critical of impressionistic reasoning on the part of the panels, while affirming the ultimate determinations of those panels. This is plainly the case in a complaint brought by the EC against the US in 1999, with regard to a definitive safeguard measure applied by the US against imported wheat gluten.[77]

As factual background, in January of 1998, the United States International Trade Commission (USITC) determined that wheat gluten was being imported into the US in such increased quantities as to be a substantial cause of serious injury to the domestic wheat gluten industry, and in May of 1998 a definitive safeguard was imposed "to facilitate positive adjustment to competition from imports of wheat gluten".[78] The measure chosen was a QR on certain imports of wheat gluten to the US for a period of three years, with annual increases of 6 per cent in the second and third years of the restriction. Wheat gluten originating in NAFTA countries was excluded from the scope of the QR. The quota was allocated among supplying countries on the basis of average shares in the period covered by the crop years ending 30 June 1993 through 30 June 1995.[79] (Wheat gluten, for which there are four principal US suppliers, is a product made from wheat flour, of which 80 per cent is consumed in the US as input for the baking industry, for use in high fibre breads. The remainder is used by the pet food industry.[80]) The EC contention was that the US had not adequately demonstrated a link between increased imports of wheat gluten and injury to the US domestic industry.

The panel made some interesting comments about the appropriate standard of review by the panel of the factual data relied upon by the US authorities. It stated that Article 11 of the DSU provides the appropriate standard for determining the consistency of a safeguard measure with the Safeguards Agreement: objective assessment of the facts of the case.[81] Taking into account the findings of earlier panels on this score, the panel stated that neither *de novo* review nor "total deference to the findings of the national authorities" would be proper, as neither would provide for an objective assessment of the facts as called for in Article 11 of the DSU.[82]

The panel affirmed that it would examine whether the USITC considered all the relevant facts, as required by Article 4.2 of the Safeguards Agreement; whether the USITC demonstrated a causal link between the increased imports and serious injury, without attributing to the imports injury caused by other factors; and whether the published report of the investigation contained an

[77] *EC v. US: Definitive Safeguard Measures on Imports of Wheat Gluten from the European Communities*, Report of the Panel, 31 July 2000 (WT/DS166/R), [hereinafter *US Wheat Gluten* Panel Report].

[78] *US Wheat Gluten* Panel Report, paras. 2.1–2.7.

[79] *US Wheat Gluten* Panel Report, para. 2.8.

[80] *US Wheat Gluten* Panel Report, para. 2.9.

[81] *US Wheat Gluten* Panel Report, para. 8.2

[82] *US Wheat Gluten* Panel Report, para. 8.5.

adequate and reasonable explanation of how the facts in the record supported the determination made.[83] Its review, according to the panel, was not to be "a substitute for the investigation conducted by the USITC". "Our role", noted the panel, "is limited to a review of the consistency of the US measure with the Agreement on Safeguards and Articles I and XIX of the GATT 1994".[84]

As to the threshold matter of whether or not there had been an "increase in imports", as required by both Article XIX of the GATT and Article 2.1 of the Safeguards Agreement, the panel referred to the finding of the Appellate Body in the Argentina—Footwear Safeguards case, that the increase must be "sufficiently recent, sudden, sharp and significant, both quantitatively and qualitatively, to cause or threaten to cause serious injury".[85] Taking note of the data relied on by the US authorities, the panel determined that the USITC Report did provide an "adequate, reasoned and reasonable explanation of how the facts support the determination made".[86]

The EC alleged that the USITC had failed to evaluate all relevant factors having a bearing on the situation of the US industry as required by Article 4.2(a) of the Safeguards Agreement; and also that the findings of the USITC with regard to the factors it did investigate were not supported by the evidence.[87] The US, emphasising its national discretion in the matter, argued that the USITC determination was based on the whole record, including an examination of all factors mentioned in Article 4.2(a). In this regard, the US insisted, the relative weight accorded to each factor was within the discretion of the competent national authorities, as long as they reached a reasoned conclusion.[88]

The panel, reviewing the language of Article 4.2(a), determined that the competent authorities were obliged to evaluate all relevant factors of objective and quantifiable nature having a bearing on the industry in question.[89] As to whether the USITC examined all relevant factors, its report made clear that in any case all factors *listed* in Article 4.2(a) were examined, although this was not determinative with regard to the total obligation imposed on the US authorities.[90] The panel dismissed EC arguments that the US had not properly treated data concerning two of the listed factors, productivity and profits, finding that the US had properly gathered and treated the available data, and thus did not violate Article 4.2(a) of the Safeguards Agreement.[91]

The EC further argued that the US had failed to consider certain other relevant factors not listed in Article 4.2(a). The panel agreed with the proposition that an investigating authority must evaluate all relevant factors, whether or not

---

[83] *US Wheat Gluten* Panel Report, para. 8.5.
[84] *US Wheat Gluten* Panel Report, para. 8.6.
[85] *US Wheat Gluten* Panel Report, para. 8.31.
[86] *US Wheat Gluten* Panel Report, paras. 8.32–8.34.
[87] *US Wheat Gluten* Panel Report, para. 8.36.
[88] *US Wheat Gluten* Panel Report, para. 8.37.
[89] *US Wheat Gluten* Panel Report, paras. 8.38–8.39.
[90] *US Wheat Gluten* Panel Report, paras. 8.40–8.41.
[91] *US Wheat Gluten* Panel Report, paras. 8.42–8.56.

listed, but rejected the idea that the USITC had failed to consider the issues raised by the EC.[92]

The EC also made the more fundamental challenge that the serious injury determination of the USITC was not consistent with the Safeguards Agreement. The panel accepted the US view that the determination can only be made on the basis of an evaluation of the overall position of the domestic industry, in light of all relevant factors having a bearing on the situation of that industry. But it also stated that the serious injury found must be current, including the time up to the end of the investigation period.[93] The EC argued that there was an upturn at the end of the investigation period and that the US industry was not in a state of serious injury at that time.[94]

While agreeing that the USITC could have included a more thorough explanation of why the decrease in inventories and upturn in sales, production and capacity towards the end of the investigation period did not detract from the USITC's determination of serious injury, in its totality, the panel found, the determination provided an "adequate, reasoned and reasonable" explanation. Thus, the overall US determination of serious injury was not inconsistent with Article 4.2(a) of the Safeguards Agreement, as the USITC "did not fail to evaluate all relevant factors having a bearing on the state of the industry in determining serious injury".[95]

However, the panel went on to say, Article 4.2(b) of the Agreement requires that a determination under Article 4.2(a) shall not be made unless the investigation demonstrates a causal link between increased imports and serious injury.[96] This issue of the proper demonstration of a casual link became the most important of the case.

The panel pointed out that the demonstration of a causal link between increased imports and serious injury is a fundamental requirement for the imposition of a safeguard measure, as required by both Article XIX of the GATT and Article 2.1 of the Agreement on Safeguards. The panel in this case affirmed the three-part approach to causation relied upon in the Argentina Footwear Safeguard dispute, as follows: (i) Did the upward trend in imports coincide with the downward trends in injury? (ii) Did the conditions of competition between the imported and domestic product demonstrate the existence of the casual link between imports and any injury? And (iii) Whether other factors were analysed, and whether it was established that injury caused by other factors were in fact attributed to imports.[97]

As for the first factor, the panel stated that the USITC Report "indicates a general coincidence of [these] trends", and thus that it "contains an adequate, reasoned and reasonable explanation of how the facts support its findings with

[92]   *US Wheat Gluten* Panel Report, paras. 8.67–8.77.
[93]   *US Wheat Gluten* Panel Report, paras. 8.79–8.81.
[94]   *US Wheat Gluten* Panel Report, para. 8.78.
[95]   *US Wheat Gluten* Panel Report, paras. 8.84–8.89.
[96]   *US Wheat Gluten* Panel Report, para. 8.89.
[97]   *US Wheat Gluten* Panel Report, para. 8.91.

respect to this aspect of the causation analysis".[98] With regard to the second arm of the causation analysis, concerning conditions of competition, the panel noted that the EC maintained that the USITC did not conduct a separate price analysis, and that there was no evidence of consistent underselling.[99]

The panel agreed that the USITC might have provided a "more robust explanation" as to how pricing data interrelated with the movement of trends in imports. However, since the annual average trends in price as identified by the USITC supported the statement of the USITC, according to the panel, it also found that the report contained an "adequate, reasoned and reasonable explanation of how the facts supported the determination made on this point". The report, the panel stated, likewise contained a demonstration of the relevance of this factor.[100] To this extent, the panel found that the USITC did not act inconsistently with the obligations imposed by the phrase "under such conditions" in Article XIX:1(a) of the GATT and Article 2.1 of the Safeguards Agreement.[101] The EC had argued that the USITC did not, in the context of determining causation, deal with certain relevant factors, notably the relationship between wheat protein premiums and price. However, the panel found that the US authorities did adequately address this issue.[102]

The US analysis foundered, however, on the EC argument that the USITC attributed to imports injury caused by other factors. The EC alleged that the US had used a preponderance test, based on whether or not imports were a "substantial cause" of the injury, which in the European view was an unknown standard in WTO law. The EC argument was that members must determine whether the imports taken alone had caused serious injury; not whether certain other causes are a more important cause of serious injury than increased imports, as relied on in US law.[103]

The panel then considered the nature of the obligations imposed by Article 4.2(b) with respect to the causation analysis that investigating authorities in general must conduct. In this regard, the panel stated that

> "where a number of factors, one of which is increased imports, are sufficient collectively to cause a 'significant overall impairment of the position of the domestic industry,' but increased imports alone are not causing injury that achieves the threshold of 'serious' within the meaning of Article 4.1(a) of the Agreement, the conditions for imposing a safeguard measure are not satisfied".

The panel continued by stating that in such a situation the imports may be causing injury, and there may be a causal link—but if this injury is not serious, the circumstances permitting the imposition of a safeguard measure are not present.[104]

---

[98] *US Wheat Gluten* Panel Report, paras. 8.92–8.101.
[99] *US Wheat Gluten* Panel Report, paras. 8.103–8.109.
[100] *US Wheat Gluten* Panel Report, paras. 8.110–8.117.
[101] *US Wheat Gluten* Panel Report, para. 8.118.
[102] *US Wheat Gluten* Panel Report, paras. 8.119–8.127.
[103] *US Wheat Gluten* Panel Report, paras. 8.128–8.130.
[104] *US Wheat Gluten* Panel Report, paras. 8.136–8.139.

The panel stated that while the Safeguards Agreement does not impose any particular method for assessing whether other factors are also causing injury, the method chosen by the US must demonstrate that imports are causing injury.[105] As the panel put it, Articles 4.2(a) and (b) of the Agreement "require that increased imports per se are causing serious injury". "Furthermore" the panel wrote", the investigating authority must conduct an investigation that ensures that any injury caused by other factors is not attributed to increased imports".[106]

The flaw found by the panel in the USITC Report was that the US authorities failed to separate out the injury caused by imports on their own—the panel saw no evidence, in other words, that the US had not attributed injury caused by other factors to imports. As for the methodology used by the US (the US determination that "increased imports are both an important cause of serious injury and a cause that is greater than any other cause"), the panel stated that "A demonstration that a given causal factor did not make an equal or greater contribution to serious injury than imports does not demonstrate that such factor made no contribution at all to serious injury".[107] The panel found that the US ought to have ensured that serious injury would still exist if the other factors causing injury were removed.[108] Thus, the examination of the US ITC was determined by the panel to be not consistent with the requirements of Article 4.2(b) of the Agreement on Safeguards.[109]

The final issue of importance involved the question of the USITC's exclusion of imports of Canadian wheat gluten from its causation analysis, on the basis that Canada is part of NAFTA, and that Article XXIV allowed this exclusion.[110] The EC argument was that this exclusion was not permissible under the logic of Article 4.2 of the Agreement. The panel noted that the US applied the safeguard measures after conducting a global investigation of the product being imported into the US from all sources, and after examining the effects of those imports on US industry. It was on that basis, the panel explained, that the US determination of serious injury was made.[111]

The panel found that

> "the text of Articles 2.1 and 4.2 contains a requirement of symmetry between the scope of the imported products subject to the investigation and the scope of the imported products subject to the application of the measure".

The phrase "a product" in Article 2.1, according to the panel, must correspond to the phrase "such product" in the same article.[112] The panel made a similar

---

[105] *US Wheat Gluten* Panel Report, para. 8.140.
[106] *US Wheat Gluten* Panel Report, para. 8.143.
[107] *US Wheat Gluten* Panel Report, paras. 8.145–8.151.
[108] *US Wheat Gluten* Panel Report, para. 8.152.
[109] *US Wheat Gluten* Panel Report, para. 8.153.
[110] *US Wheat Gluten* Panel Report, para. 8.155.
[111] *US Wheat Gluten* Panel Report, paras. 8.160–8.164.
[112] *US Wheat Gluten* Panel Report, para. 8.167.

determination with respect to Article 4.2(a): that the "products concerned" must also form the basis for the determination of serious injury and causal link.[113]

The panel said that it had found "further confirmation" of its view in the text of Article 2.2, which states that "safeguard measures shall be applied to a product being imported irrespective of source".[114] In the case before it, the panel found that this necessary symmetry had not been achieved.[115] Taken to its logical conclusion, the panel explained, the US approach could exclude a number of country sources where the source of the product was a number of relatively small contributors to the whole.[116] Thus, the US was required under Articles 2.1 and 4.2 to apply the measures to imports from all sources, including Canada, a NAFTA country.[117]

As to the US argument that Article XXIV allowed it to exclude Canadian products from its analysis, the panel was unpersuaded. While Article XXIV of the GATT may provide a defence to a claim of violation under another covered agreement, the panel found the obligations at issue here under Articles XXIV and XIX to be cumulative.[118] Since the US was not making the larger argument that Article XXIV of the GATT provides a defence to a violation of the Safeguards Agreement, the panel insisted that it was not required to rule on that general question here.[119] It returned to the principle that the scope of the imported products subject to investigation must parallel the scope of the products subject to the application of the measure. The panel's view was not altered by the fact that footnote 1 to the Safeguards Agreement stated that the non-discriminatory requirement of Article 2.2 of the Agreement is not pertinent in assessing the safeguards treatment accorded by a customs union or an FTA member to goods originating in other participating countries.[120] By failing to achieve this symmetry, the panel reasoned, the US has acted inconsistently with Articles 2.1 and 4.2 of the Safeguards Agreement.[121] The US also lost on some essentially technical issues having to do with notification.

---

[113] *US Wheat Gluten* Panel Report, para. 8.168. The panel stated: "In our view, there is no basis in Art. 4.2 SA for a distinction to be drawn on the basis of the origin of a product when examining the element of causation in safeguards investigation."

[114] *US Wheat Gluten* Panel Report, para. 8.170. The panel cited the Argentina Footwear Safeguards case, where the panel had determined that there should be parallelism between the scope of the investigation and the application of the safeguard measures.

[115] *US Wheat Gluten* Panel Report, paras. 8.171–8.173.

[116] *US Wheat Gluten* Panel Report, para. 8.176.

[117] *US Wheat Gluten* panel Report, para. 8.177.

[118] *US Wheat Gluten* Panel Report, paras. 8.178–181.

[119] *US Wheat Gluten* Panel Report, para. 8.183.

[120] *US Wheat Gluten* Panel Report, paras. 8.178–8.181.

[121] *US Wheat Gluten* Panel Report, para. 8.182.

THE APPELLATE BODY AND CAUSALITY

The principal issues on appeal had to do with the methodology relied on by the US in its Article 4.2(b) causality analysis. The US urged the Appellate Body to find that to cause means in this context to bring about a result—whether alone or in combination with other factors; not as the Panel held regarding increased imports, "to cause on its own".[122] The US further argued that the panel did not adequately examine the meaning of the expression "under such conditions" in Article XIX:1(a) of the GATT. That term, according to the US, should have been taken to indicate increased imports within the "totality of attendant circumstances and existing state of affairs that lead imports to cause injury". This should include "factors that may have rendered a domestic industry more (or less) susceptible to injury".[123]

The US also asked the Appellate Body to reverse the panel's finding that the exclusion of Canadian products from the safeguard measure was inconsistent with Article 2.1 and 4.2 of the Safeguards Agreement.[124] Among other arguments, the US insisted that there is no implied symmetry, as found by the panel, between the scope of a safeguard investigation and the scope of the application of the safeguard measure.[125]

For its part, the EC challenged the panel's interpretation of Articles 4.2(a) and (b) of the Agreement, to the effect that the competent authorities are only required to evaluate factors actually raised as relevant by the interested parties. The EC contended that the USITC Report should have contained analysis of the protein content of wheat; which, according to the EC, is the single most important factor determining the price of wheat gluten.[126] The EC further maintained that in the light of Article 11 of the DSU, the panel applied an inappropriate standard of deference towards the US authorities, and failed to provide an adequate and reasonable explanation for its findings.[127]

The Appellate Body first took up the matter of whether the USITC had evaluated all relevant factors as required by Article 4.2(a) of the Agreement. In the Appellate Body's view, the obligation to evaluate relevant factors must be seen in the light of the duty of the competent authorities to conduct an investigation. Whether or not a factor is relevant should be based on evidence that is objective and quantifiable.[128] It turned to the requirements for carrying out an investigation,

---

[122] See *EC v. US: Definitive Safeguard Measures on Imports of Wheat Gluten from the European Communities*, Report of the Appellate Body, 22 December 2000 (WT/DS166/AB/R) [hereinafter US *Wheat Gluten* Appellate Body Report], para. 9.

[123] *US Wheat Gluten* Appellate Body Report, para. 10.

[124] *US Wheat Gluten* Appellate Body Report, para. 12.

[125] *US Wheat Gluten* Appellate Body Report, para. 13.

[126] *US Wheat Gluten* Appellate Body Report, para. 22.

[127] *US Wheat Gluten* Appellate Body Report, para. 24. The EC further argued that the panel erred in its position on judicial economy, in that it ought to have heard the EC claim under Art. XIX:1(a) of the GATT. Para. 29–30.

[128] US *Wheat Gluten* Appellate Body Report, para. 52.

as described in Article 3.1 of the Safeguards Agreement, including the steps that must be included as part of the investigation and the fact that interested parties are clearly meant to be a primary source of information.[129] The Appellate Body agreed with the EC that the authorities may not limit their consideration to issues raised by these parties, where other factors might also be relevant; however, the Appellate Body did not accept the EC position that the competent authorities have an "open-ended and unlimited duty to investigate all available facts that might possibly be relevant".[130]

As for the specific question of whether an evaluation of the protein content of wheat should have been carried out, the Appellate Body noted that the Report did mention a weather-related deficiency in wheat protein content during 1993, leading to price effects in 1994. Since the surge in imports occurred in 1996 and 1997, the Appellate Body was of the opinion that there was no reason to conclude that the USITC was required to evaluate the protein content of wheat as a relevant factor under Article 4.2(a) of the Agreement.[131]

"Accordingly", the Appellate Body concluded, "albeit for different reasons, we uphold the panel's finding that the US has not acted inconsistently with Articles 4.2(a) and 4.2(b) of the SA" with respect to this issue.[132]

The Appellate Body then treated the fundamental matter of causality and the Safeguards Agreement. The Appellate Body noted that, in essence, the panel had found that the increased imports must in and of themselves be capable of causing injury that is serious.[133] Looking at the text of Article 4.2(b), the Appellate Body stated that in its view, the language of the first sentence does not suggest that the imports must be the sole cause of serious injury, or that the other factors causing serious injury must be excluded from the determination of serious injury. "To the contrary", it wrote, "the language of Article 4.2 (b), as a whole, suggests that 'the causal link between increased imports and serious injury may exist, even though other factors are also contributing 'at the same time,' to the situation of the domestic industry".[134]

Indeed, the Appellate Body continued, it is just because there can be several factors, besides the imports, contributing simultaneously to the situation that the last sentence of Article 4.2(b) states that the competent authorities shall not attribute to increased imports injury that is being caused by other factors. What is important, the Appellate Body stated, is to separate out the effects caused by the different factors in bringing about the injury.[135] In terms of the methodology to be pursued by the national authorities, the Appellate Body stated that the first step under Article 4.2(b) must be to distinguish between the injurious effects caused to the domestic industry by increased imports and that caused by other

[129] *US Wheat Gluten* Appellate Body Report, paras. 53–54.
[130] *US Wheat Gluten* Appellate Body Report, paras. 55–56.
[131] *US Wheat Gluten* Appellate Body Report, paras. 57–58.
[132] *US Wheat Gluten* Appellate Body Report, para. 59.
[133] *US Wheat Gluten* Appellate Body Report, para. 66.
[134] *US Wheat Gluten* Appellate Body Report, para. 67.
[135] *US Wheat Gluten* Appellate Body Report, para. 69.

factors. The final step is to determine whether a causal link exists between increased imports and serious injury.[136]

In a more serious divergence from the panel, the Appellate Body went on to state that this need to distinguish between the effects of the several factors does not necessarily imply that increased imports on their own must be capable of causing serious injury; nor that injury caused by other factors must be excluded from the determination of serious injury.[137]

The Appellate Body declared itself "fortified in its interpretation" by the language of Article 2.1 of the Agreement, since, under Article 2.1, "the causation analysis embraces two elements: the first relating to increased imports specifically, and the second to the 'conditions' under which imports are occurring".[138] For these reasons, the Appellate Body reversed the panel's interpretation of Article 4.2(b) to the effect that increased imports alone, and in and of themselves must be capable of causing injury that is serious.[139]

But the Appellate Body went on to provide its own causation analysis as a substitute for the flawed one it had just reversed.[140] It identified four factors indicated by the USITC which, besides the increased imports, had a bearing on the situation of the domestic industry. Of these, the Appellate Body noted, the panel made most mention of capacity utilisation.[141] The facts showed that there was an increase in average capacity and a decrease in production, such that capacity utilisation fell dramatically during the investigation period, while the market share of imports was rising.[142] The USITC Report noted that had it not been for the increase in imports, the industry would have operated at a higher level of capacity and would have been profitable.[143]

The Appellate Body rejected the US position that the data in the USITC Report on increases in capacity and on capacity utilisation are not relevant under Article 4.2(b) of the Agreement.[144] "The data before the USITC", stated the Appellate Body, "therefore suggest that the increases in average available capacity in the domestic industry may have been very important to the overall situation of the domestic industry in 1997". The Appellate Body went on to say that it was not suggesting that capacity utilisation was the sole cause of serious injury in the domestic industry; nor that increased imports had no relevance. "Rather", the Appellate Body reasoned,

---

[136] *US Wheat Gluten* Appellate Body Report, para. 69.

[137] *US Wheat Gluten* Appellate Body Report, para. 70.

[138] *US Wheat Gluten* Appellate Body Report, paras. 75–76.

[139] *US Wheat Gluten* Appellate Body Report, para. 79. The Appellate Body also wrote that it was reversing the panel's conclusions on the issue of causation as found in para. 8.154 of the panel report, "as these are based on an erroneous interpretation of Art. 4.2(b)".

[140] *US Wheat Gluten* Appellate Body Report, para. 80. The Appellate Body wrote that it would "complete the legal analysis on this issue on the basis of the factual findings of the panel and the undisputed facts in the panel record".

[141] *US Wheat Gluten* Appellate Body Report, para. 80.

[142] *US Wheat Gluten* Appellate Body Report, para. 81.

[143] *US Wheat Gluten* Appellate Body Report, para. 82.

[144] *US Wheat Gluten* Appellate Body Report, para. 88.

". . . the data relied upon by the USITC indicate that the relationship between the increases in average capacity, the increases in imports and the overall situation of the domestic industry was far more complex than suggested by the test of the USITC Report".[145]

The Appellate Body found itself not satisfied that the USITC "adequately evaluated the complexities" of whether the increase in average capacity during the relevant period was causing injury to the domestic industry at the same time as increased imports. An essential requirement of Article 4.2(b), the Appellate Body reasoned, was for the competent authorities to examine whether factors other than increased imports are simultaneously causing injury. Where this does not occur, it continued, the authorities cannot ensure that injury caused by other factors is not attributed to increased imports.[146]

Thus, the fatal flaw in the methodology of the USITC was that it did not demonstrate that any injury caused to the domestic US industry by increases in average capacity was not being attributed to increased imports; in consequence, according to the Appellate Body, the USITC could not establish the existence of the causal link required by Article 4.2(b) between increased imports and serious injury.[147] The Appellate Body agreed with the panel on the ultimate point, that the US had acted inconsistently with its obligations under Article 4.2(b) of the Agreement on Safeguards.

As tends to happen when the Appellate Body overturns the reasoning of a panel, we are left with a decision—here with respect to causation—that appears to some extent to provide more freedom to WTO members to regulate their own economies. In this dispute, the legal rule set down by the panel had the virtue of clarity, and seemed to be in accord with the spirit of the Safeguards Agreement, which is undoubtedly to make it more difficult to apply safeguard measures. However, the Appellate Body objected to the narrowness of the panel's approach, while at the same time proceeding to invalidate the US measure based on its own more complex, if somewhat less precise, reasoning.

The US appealed the panel's finding concerning the lawfulness of the US exclusion of Canadian products from its safeguard measure, having included these products in its initial investigation. The US argued that the panel failed to take sufficient account of the fact that, following its determination that imports from all sources were causing serious injury, the US authorities had then conducted a separate examination of the effects of Canadian imports alone. On the basis of that examination, the US maintained, the USITC found that Canadian imports were not contributing importantly to the serious injury caused by

---

[144] *US Wheat Gluten* Appellate Body Report, para. 88.

[145] *US Wheat Gluten* Appellate Body Report, para. 90. The Appellate Body continued, "On this issue, the USITC simply observed that 'but for the increase in imports, the [domestic] industry would have operated at 61% of capacity in 1997, which is much closer to the level at which the industry operated early in the investigative period when it operated reasonably profitably'."

[146] *US Wheat Gluten* Appellate Body Report, para. 91.

[147] *US Wheat Gluten* Appellate Body Report, para. 91.

imports.[148] The US also argued that the panel had failed to take into account the legal relevance of footnote 1 to the Agreement on Safeguards, as well as that of Article XXIV of the GATT.[149]

The Appellate Body turned to Articles 2.1 and 2.2 of the Safeguards Agreement. Article 2.1, it noted, sets forth the conditions for imposing a safeguard measure; Article 2.2 of the agreement provides that a safeguard measure "shall be applied to a product being imported irrespective of its source", and "sets forth the rules for the imposition of a safeguard measure".[150] The Appellate Body noted that the phrase "product . . . being imported" appears in both Articles 2.1 and 2.2—and that it would be unwarranted to treat these as having different meanings. Since Article 2.1 embraces imports coming from all sources, these must correspond to the imports mentioned in Article 2.2.[151] To accept the US view, then, would necessitate an "incongruous" interpretation of the relation between these two provisions.

As for the US' assertion that it had examined the importance of the Canadian imports separately, the Appellate Body stated that in fact the US did not make any explicit determination relating to increased imports, excluding imports from Canada. In the Appellate Body's view, the US did not establish explicitly that imports from sources excluding Canada satisfied the conditions for the application of a safeguard measure, as required by Articles 2.1 and 4.2 of the agreement.[152]

With regard to the panel's finding that it could rule on the EC claim without having recourse to Article XXIV or to footnote 1 of the Safeguards Agreement, the Appellate Body stated that it found no error in the panel's approach, and had no finding to make on these issues.[153] Concerning the US obligation to notify of its investigation and its decision to apply a safeguard measure under Article 12 of the Safeguards Agreement, the Appellate Body upheld the panel on certain points, and reversed it on others.[154]

US MEASURES ON IMPORTS OF LAMB MEAT

The relentlessness of the challenge to national safeguard measures is clearly seen in the complaint brought by Australia and New Zealand, against a decision of the United States to impose a definitive safeguard measure against lamb meat from those countries, based on a finding of threat of serious injury to the domes-

---

[148] *US Wheat Gluten* Appellate Body Report, para. 94.
[149] *US Wheat Gluten* Appellate Body Report, para. 94.
[150] *US Wheat Gluten* Appellate Body Report, para. 95.
[151] *US Wheat Gluten* Appellate Body Report, para. 96.
[152] *US Wheat Gluten* Appellate Body Report, para. 98.
[153] *US Wheat Gluten* Appellate Body Report, para. 99
[154] See generally, *US Wheat Gluten* Appellate Body Report, paras. 101–146.

tic industry.[155] This case and others make it obvious that the political nature of a safeguard measure sits uneasily alongside the legalism of the WTO Safeguards Agreement, making it extremely difficult for any national safeguard measure to stand up to a legal challenge.

Australia and New Zealand claimed that the US had violated GATT Article XIX, by imposing its safeguard measures despite the fact that the increased imports were not a result of unforeseen developments. On the contrary, the increase in imports was a result of a decrease in US production due to the removal of subsidies under the Wool Act, and thus "could and should have been foreseen by the United States".[156] As to the relationship between obligations under Article XIX of the GATT and the Agreement on Safeguards, the panel noted that earlier case law had contained rulings that these applied on a cumulative basis. Thus, there was no basis for arguing that obligations explicitly referred to in Article XIX but not in the agreement had been superseded by the agreement. Rather, "all of the relevant provisions of the Safeguards Agreement and GATT Article XIX must be given meaning and effect".[157]

The panel does not accept the complainants' view that this necessitates a "two part causation approach"—with establishment of the existence of unforeseen development to be separated from the phrases "in such quantities" and "under such conditions".[158] The complainants emphasised the fact that the US failed to comply with its obligations in this regard, since the report published by the US ITC contained no explicit consideration of the question.[159] The panel noted that the structure of Article XIX suggests that a demonstration of the existence of the circumstance of "unforeseen developments" must be based on factual evidence which was before the competent authority at the time the investigation was carried out. Despite the fact that the agreement does not contain a specific publication requirement for these unforeseen developments, the panel found that:

> "no matter how such a conclusion is presented in an authority's determination, there needs to be a conclusion that makes clear that changes that had not been anticipated had taken place in the market, and that these changes had resulted in a situation in which increased imports were causing or threatening to cause serious injury".[160]

The principal US defence in this regard had to do with the fact that a shift of the product mix from frozen to chilled/fresh lamb meat toward the end of the investigation period brought about increased competition between domestic and imported lamb, constituting an "unforeseen development". In

---

[155] *New Zealand and Australia v. US: Safeguard Measures on Imports of Fresh, Chilled or Frozen Lamb Meat from New Zealand and Australia*, Report of the Panel, 21 December 2000, (WT/DS177/R; WT/DS178R) [hereinafter *US Lamb Meat Safeguards* Panel Report].

[156] *US Lamb Meat Safeguards* Panel Report, para. 7.4.

[157] *US Lamb Meat Safeguards* Panel Report, paras. 7.10–7.11.

[158] *US Lamb Meat Safeguards* Panel Report, paras. 7.13–7.16.

[159] *US Lamb Meat Safeguards* Panel Report, para. 7.25.

[160] *US Lamb Meat Safeguards* Panel Report, paras. 7.25–7.31.

the US view, this allowed it to impose its safeguard consistently with the requirements of Article XIX concerning "unforeseen developments".[161] The panel in turn examined whether this had been demonstrated as a matter of fact by the USITC.[162] Looking in detail at the language used by the USITC to describe this market phenomenon, the panel found nothing to suggest the conclusion that the shift in product mix had a "profound effect on the US market for lamb meat and was unforeseen".[163] The panel found only "descriptive statements" in the USITC Report—not the separate legal requirement of a conclusion regarding unforeseen developments, as required by GATT Article XIX.[164]

The complainants alleged that the US wrongly defined the domestically-produced product that was "like" the imports at issue such as lamb meat. They complained that the USITC should not have included growers and feeders of live lambs in the relevant "industry" under Article 4.1(c) of the Agreement on Safeguards.[165] (Obviously, the freedom with which a defending party is allowed to define the relevant domestic industry affects the ease, or difficulty, with which safeguard measures may be imposed.) The panel found that the phrase "producers as a whole", as found in Article 4.1(c) "is not related to the process of manufacturing or transforming raw materials and inputs into a final product", so that there is "no contextual support for including producers of raw materials or inputs as part of the industry producing a like product".[166]

The panel stated that the WTO offered a "safety valve" in the form of safeguard measures as a response to increased imports causing serious injury to domestic industry. At the same time, the panel was clear that these national measures are characterised by their emergency and extraordinary nature.

> "A conceptual approach to defining the relevant domestic industry which would leave it to the discretion of competent national authorities how far upstream and/or downstream the production chain of a given 'like' end product to look in defining the scope of the domestic industry could easily defeat the Safeguards Agreement's purpose of reinforcing disciplines in the field of safeguards and enhancing rather than limiting competition".[167]

Following on a survey of the relevant GATT case law, the panel stated that the reasoning of those earlier panels "supports the interpretation that the domestic industry should be defined as the producers as a whole of the like end-product,

---

[161] *US Lamb Meat Safeguards* Panel Report, paras. 7.32–7.34.
[162] *US Lamb Meat Safeguards* Panel Report, para. 7.37.
[163] *US Lamb Meat Safeguards* Panel Report, paras. 7.38–7.39.
[164] *US Lamb Meat Safeguards* Panel Report, paras. 7.42–7.45.
[165] *US Lamb Meat Safeguards* Panel Report, paras. 7.46–7.47. Art. 4.1(c) states that a domestic industry "shall be understood to mean the producers as a whole of the like or directly competitive products operating within the territory of a Member, or those whose collective output of the like or directly competitive products constitutes a major proportion of the total domestic production of those products".
[166] *US Lamb Meat Safeguards* Panel Report, para. 7.74.
[167] *US Lamb Meat Safeguards* Panel Report, para. 7.77.

i.e., lamb meat in this case". The panel also agreed with the conclusion of those panels that separability of operations and data between different stages of production, rather than vertical integration, common ownership or economic interdependence "are relevant for determining the scope of the industry" in a manner consistent with Article 4.2(c) of the Safeguards Agreement.[168] In the panel's view, the USITC incorrectly included producers of live lambs in its investigation.[169]

Complainants also claimed that the USITC examination of whether threat of serious injury exists did not meet the standard required by Article 4.1(b) of the Agreement, which must include a prospective analysis of the industry's condition. Complainants argued that, based on past trends in supply and demand, there should be an analysis of how prices were likely to develop in the future. They insisted that the US ought to have provided more "prospective facts" of this kind.[170] The panel rejected the contention that the time period relied on by the US authorities was too short; and more generally that there was any "conceptual fault" with the USITC's approach in its "threat of serious injury" determination.[171]

However, the panel went on to carry out a separate analysis of whether the US determination of "threat of serious injury" is "sufficiently fact-based and sufficiently forward-looking to meet the demands of the requirements of Articles 4.1(a) and (b) and 4.2(a)".[172] On the one hand, the panel found that the data relied on by the USITC confirmed the determination that a significant overall impairment in the position of the domestic industry was clearly imminent.[173] But in looking at the representativeness of the data collected, the panel found a problem.

While agreeing that the agreement does not specify any particular methodology for ensuring representativeness of data in an investigation, the panel nonetheless stated that—as conceded by the USITC itself—the questionnaire responses relied on did not constitute a "statistically valid sample of the producers" forming an essential part of the domestic industry. The panel concluded, in agreement with the complainants, that the data used by the USITC was not sufficiently representative of "those producers whose collective output . . . constitutes a major proportion of the total domestic production of those products" within the meaning of Article 4.1(c) of the Safeguards Agreement.[174]

In a re-run of the causation issues raised in the *US Wheat Gluten* case, complainants argued that the US was not employing the correct standard for attributing injury to increased imports. As the *Wheat Gluten* appeal was

---

[168] *US Lamb Meat Safeguards* Panel Report, para. 7.109.
[169] *US Lamb Meat Safeguards* Panels Report, para. 7.118.
[170] *US Lamb Meat Safeguards* Panel Report, paras. 7.179–7.182.
[171] *US Lamb Meat Safeguards* Panel Report, paras. 7.189–7.195.
[172] *US Lamb Meat Safeguards* Panel Report, para. 7.196.
[173] *US Lamb Meat Safeguards* Panel Report, para. 7.204.
[174] *US Lamb Meat Safeguards* Panel Report, paras. 7.208–7.221.

pending at the time of this panel report, the panel repeated its view that increased imports must by themselves be necessary and sufficient to threaten injury.[175] In a manner parallel to the panel's finding in the *Wheat Gluten* case, the *Lamb Meat* panel found that with regard to causation the US had violated Article 4.2(b) of the Agreement on Safeguards. And although the Appellate Body upheld the panel on other issues, it reversed the panel (but on other grounds found against the United States), on the causation issue—in a manner similar to its reasoning in *Wheat Gluten*.[176]

SAFEGUARDS DISPUTES SEEN IN THE AGGREGATE

With each issue raised in each instance of litigation under the Safeguards Agreement, the cost of protection for vulnerable sectors of the national economy necessarily increases. The cases discussed above demonstrate clearly how far we have come from the time during which Article XIX could be invoked without any great concern about the quality of one's evidence being put to the test, or in the alternative, when VERs could be entered into even more easily and painlessly than Article XIX protective measures. From a comparatively open-ended opt-out, a freely invoked power to protect at-risk economic sectors, WTO countries are now faced with the prospect of the most intense scrutiny of their attempts to invoke emergency measures.

Not only are there the costs of carrying out the exhaustive studies that would allow for the proper application of the measures; there is also the prospect of defending the evidence relied on and conclusions based on that evidence at the WTO. It could well be that, in the end, WTO member countries will find it easier to cut loose the political constituencies that have traditionally demanded temporary, emergency protection in the first place. And there is little doubt that the terms of the Agreement on Safeguards contain an ultimate disincentive to reliance on safeguard measures. With the agreement, safeguards as a tool of national protectionism have been demoted; they are truly temporary, for emergency use, and indicative only of an "opportunity to adjust".

---

[175] *US Lamb Meat Safeguards* Panel Report, paras. 7.227–7.258.

[176] *New Zealand and Australia v. US: Safeguard Measures in Imports of Fresh,Chilled or Frozen Lamb Meat from New Zealand or Australia*, Report of the Appellate Body, 1 May 2001, (WT/DS177/AB/R). See the Appellate Body's discussion of causation issues, paras. 162–188. At para. 188, the Appellate Body wrote that "the USITC, in its Report, did not adequately explain how it ensured that injury caused to domestic industry by factors other than increased imports was not attributed to increased imports. In the absence of such an explanation, we uphold, albeit for different reasons, the Panel's conclusion that the United States acted inconsistently with Art. 4.2(b) of the Agreement on Safeguards, and, hence, with Art. 2.1 of that Agreement".

8

Liberalising the Textile Trade: The only Uruguay Round Agreement of Clear Benefit to the Developing World?

W E HAVE ALREADY encountered the unique characteristics of the global textile trade.[1] That the textile trade has traditionally been highly controlled can be explained by the simple fact that, had it been liberalised, most textile-related employment in the developed world would have been lost, as production shifted to a more natural base in the developing world. Since the 1960s, developing country producers/exporters and developed country importers have been essentially divided into two blocs, which took the legal form of the MultiFibre Arrangement (MFA).

John Jackson has written that one of the most "pronounced anomalies of our liberal trade period since World War II has been an elaborate system of voluntary agreements which perpetuates a quota system for international trade in textiles and clothing".[2] While there are other highly regulated areas of international trade—principally commodities such as steel, tin, some types of tropical timber, sugar, coffee and rubber—the textile system has been one of the most far-reaching, and also one of the most politically contentious.

Briefly stated, the MFA worked in the following way: a framework was established for textile-importing countries to negotiate with the textile-exporting countries in the developing world, with a resultant formation of a vast web of bilateral export restraint agreements.[3] These agreements were arrived at in the context of a world-wide "target agreement"—a projected percentage (typically 6 per cent) for growth in overall exports from the developing world to the developed world.[4] It is crucial to understand that the MFA system did not rely on a multilateralising concept; rather, it remained bilateral in its orientation.

While a general target would be set for global expansion in the level of exports, and though individual bilateral agreements also contained quantitative

---

[1] See ch. 7 on safeguards and *Hong Kong v. Norway: Restrictions on inports of certain textile products* (1980), BISD 27th Supp, 119.

[2] John H Jackson, *The World Trading System: Law and Policy of International Economic Relations*, 2nd edn. (Cambridge, MA: MIT Press, 1991) 181.

[3] *Ibid.* at 182.

[4] *Ibid.*

targets, there was flexibility for responding to economic conditions built into the system. Individual countries could negotiate to accept a far lower rate of import increase in a given year.[5] The MFA itself allowed for both emergency restraining agreements and also called for an equitable distribution of market share among supplying countries, although this was not as strict as in the case of GATT Article XIX safeguards in the wake of the *Hong Kong* v. *Norway* panel decision.[6]

The textile industry has always occupied a sensitive position in national economies. It was, after all, the bedrock of the industrial revolution in most countries, and has traditionally been strongly protected. While extremely labour-intensive, textile production is not particularly capital-intensive, and is often regarded as the first stepping stone out of an agrarian society. In recent times, most countries find themselves attempting to produce textiles for the same over-supplied world market. In developing countries in particular, the textile industry is heavily export-driven, and there is substantial over-capacity. With this in mind, it could be said that the Uruguay Round Agreement on Textiles and Clothing (ATC) provided a greater benefit to the developing world than any other innovation in GATT/WTO law, and certainly the least ambiguous one. On the other hand, to the extent that multinational corporations are seizing the opportunity to shift textile and clothing production to lower-cost locations, it must be remembered that the textile industry has been characterised by egregious labour abuses as well.[7] It is likely that future debate on the linkage between trade and labour standards will centre on examples from the clothing industry.

It is also important to keep in mind that the early GATT recognised that textile products would be treated as separate from other types of manufactured goods. All efforts over the years to liberalise the sector failed, until of course the Uruguay Round negotiations. Starting around 1960, a distinct textile trading regime developed under the auspices of GATT. Conferences were held to gain agreement from the major players on both sides as to what level of change they could accept in the trade over a future period. The principal objection was said to be the avoidance of "market disruption".[8] It is of significance that under the MFA, textile trading was not subject to the non-discrimination rules of GATT, nor to the general prohibition against quantitative restrictions.[9] The MFA was generally renegotiated and applied in four-year blocs, starting in the early 1970s,

[5] John H Jackson, *The World Trading System: Law and Policy of International Economic Relations*, *supra* n. 2, at 182.

[6] For a discussion of the legal implications of individual country textile quotas within Europe, see the discussion below.

[7] See, for example, Claudia R Brewster, "Restoring Childhood: Saving the World's Children from Toiling in Textile Sweatshops", (Spring 1997) 16 *Journal of Law and Commerce* 191.

[8] Jackson, *supra* n. 2, at 294.

[9] While the agreements of the 1960s restricted themselves to cotton, as of 1970 an increasing array of products were made from other, "manufactured" fibres. Then a new global regime, to include many new fibres and wool, while incorporating the old agreements, came under discussion. The first officially named MultiFibre Arrangement, or MFA, came into force in 1974.

the operative concept being "controlled expansion" in trade between the developing and developed world.[10]

Under the MFA, a multilateral institution called the Textiles Surveillance Body was established with the task of supervising the implementation of the MFA. As a legal entity, the MFA has been called a "multilateral contract, freely entered into by those wishing to participate". Extensions of the agreement have added to the fibre types covered.

It would have been difficult for the developed world, in light of the numerous demands it was making on the developing world during the Uruguay Round negotiations, to refuse to liberalise the textile sector. A major criticism of the MFA was that it not only allowed quotas, but was actually based on them; while it was supposed to provide temporary protection for jobs in the textile sector in the developed world, in fact the MFA looked set to become a way of life. The Uruguay Round ATC was so contentious that it took seven years to negotiate; its aim is in fact to phase out all special protections in the sector, and to integrate textiles into the larger GATT/WTO system for freely traded goods. Assuming that the ATC proceeds according to plan, special protection measures for textiles and clothing will no longer exist by the year 2005.

STRUCTURE AND CONTENT OF THE AGREEMENT ON TEXTILES AND CLOTHING

Article 1 of the ATC says that it will set out provisions to be applied by Members during a transition period while textiles and clothing are integrated into the GATT system. To facilitate this, it says, members should allow for "continuous autonomous industrial adjustment" and increased competition in their markets. The concept of an opportunity to adjust is familiar from other sectors of WTO law; indeed, it is the theme that runs consistently through virtually all of the instruments created by the Uruguay Round.

The products to be covered under the ATC are set out in an annex to the agreement, but include virtually all traded textiles. Article 2 requires that all quantitative restrictions in existence through bilateral agreements on the effective date of the WTO Agreements are to be notified in detail within 60 days to the new Textiles Monitoring Body. All these pre-existing restrictions will then be governed by the terms of this new agreement.[11] Pre-existing restrictions not so notified must be terminated within 60 days.[12]

---

[10] See Jackson, *supra* n. 2, at 181–83.

[11] Art. 2(4) states that the restrictions so notified "shall be deemed to constitute the totality of such restrictions applied by the respective members on the day before entry into force of the WTO Agreement. No new restrictions (in terms of products or members) shall be introduced except under the provisions of this Agreement or relevant GATT 1994 provisions".

[12] Any unilateral action under Art. 3 of the MFA and in prior existence may remain in effect for a period not exceeding 12 months, but it must be reviewed by the Textiles Surveillance Body, set up under the old MFA.

Under Article 2(8), there is a schedule for the full integration of all products into the GATT system, in a number of stages, with all national restrictions being eliminated within 121 months. There is also a schedule (see Articles 2(13) and 2 (14)) for mandatory minimum increases in the level of restrictions on imports relative to MFA bilateral agreements in effect prior to the entry into force of the WTO Agreement. The clear intention of these provisions is to eliminate restrictive bilateral agreements altogether by the end of the transition period.

Article 2(20), while unpleasantly technical, amounts to a statement that, with respect to the use of Article XIX non-tariff safeguards, within a year of a textile being brought within GATT discipline (i.e., being eliminated from MFA protection), the party invoking Article XIX will be quite constrained in how it can use the GATT safeguard. As well as quantitative limits on the level of restriction allowed, it is also the case that after one year of invoking the Article XIX safeguard measure, mandatory progressive liberalisation in market access for that product also applies.

Article 3 requires notification of all unilateral, non-MFA measures in force, whether or not they are consistent with the provisions of the GATT. Article 3(2) states that members maintaining such restrictions, unless justified under the GATT (i.e., Article XIX), have the choice of either bringing these measures into conformity with the GATT within one year, or phasing them out progressively according to a set programme. The phase out cannot be longer than this agreement; in other words, ten years. Article 5 contains provisions against circumvention of the ATC's purposes through such means as re-routing or falsifying place of origin.

Article 6 of the ATC describes the specialised textile safeguards that are to apply during the transition period, the so-called "transitional safeguards". This provision is likely to be a focus of textile-related trade friction in the years leading up to the end of managed trade in textiles.

Article 6(1) states that "the transitional safeguard should be applied as sparingly as possible, consistently with the provisions of this article and the effective implementation of the integration process under this agreement". As to when such a safeguard can be applied, the conditions are not unlike those under Article XIX:

> "when it is demonstrated that a particular product is being imported into its territory in such increased quantities as to cause serious damage, or actual threat thereof, to the domestic industry producing like and/or directly competitive products".

The damage must be "demonstrably" caused by such increased quantities in total imports of that product, and not by other factors such as technological changes, or changes in consumer preference. One notes again the high evidentiary burden and associated costs attached to a safeguard action.[13]

---

[13] The third paragraph of this article provides a list of elements to which the safeguard-adopting country must look to determine these effects—productivity, wages, inventories, investments, etc. Paragraph 4 says that the threat must be from a sharp increase in imports.

One of the key elements of the Article 6 transitional safeguard for textiles is that this is applied on a member-to-member basis; members are not bound by considerations of non-discrimination in invoking the transitional safeguard, and indeed must identify a particular country as a source of the problem. In an important sense, this adds a different evidentiary burden, in that it may not be a simple matter to prove that one particular country is causing damage to one's national industry.

Article 6(6) requires that more favourable treatment is to be accorded to "re-imports" by a member of products that same member has exported to another member for purposes of processing and subsequent re-importation. Article 6 (7) says that where there is mutual agreement on the need for export restraint, the level decided upon must be fixed at a level not lower than the actual level of exports or imports from the member concerned during the 12 month period terminating two months preceding the month in which the request for consultations was made. The Textile Monitoring Body (TMB) (see discussion below) has the interesting role of determining whether the agreement is "justified". Under Article 6(10), where agreement has not been reached, the party proposing the safeguard action may go ahead and place the restraint on the products concerned, with either party then able to refer the issue to the TMB. The TMB will then, within 30 days, examine the situation and make appropriate recommendations.

Article 6(12) says that a member may maintain measures applied under Article 6 for either up to 3 years without extension, or until the product is integrated into the GATT, whichever comes first. Paragraph 13 of Article 6 says that if the restraint remains in force for more than one year, the level of growth in the amount imported must be not less than 6 per cent per year, unless otherwise justified to the TMB.

Article 7 is a type of "fairness provision" for the agreement. It commits members to improved market access for textile products, fairness in the areas of anti-dumping, subsidies and intellectual property rights as these relate to textile trade. It also contains a general commitment to avoiding discrimination against the textile sector in national import policy. Article 7(3) grants members the right to bring problems with other members' measures before the DSB.

Article 8 establishes the Textiles Monitoring Body (TMB). The TMB is to have a chair and ten members, a membership meant to be of "broad representation", and rotating participation. Members of the TMB are to be appointed by the Council for Trade in Goods, and they are required to act in their own personal capacity, rather than as representatives of any government interest. The TMB has many functions, among them an arbitration-like role, and a pre-litigation advisory role. It is also empowered to make recommendations to members. A matter should only go to the DSB if a member considers itself unable to conform to a recommendation of the TMB.

Article 9 concludes the ATC by reiterating the fact that it is to be terminated in the 121st month of the WTO Agreement, "on which date the textiles and clothing sector shall be fully integrated into GATT 1994". It also makes clear that "there shall be no extension of this agreement". What is certain, then, is that at the end of the transition period, member countries wishing to protect textile sector employment will have little choice but to invoke Article XIX safeguard measures. And we have already examined in detail why that has also become a far more costly and difficult proposition.

LITIGATION UNDER THE ATC

It is hardly surprising that developing countries should have seized upon the opportunity to bring disputes before the WTO under the ATC. After all, those countries in the developed world that were to lose employment as textile trade became deregulated were very likely to try and avoid the full force of these changes through manipulation of the complex safeguards regime for textiles.

Two such cases were brought by Costa Rica and India respectively against the United States, and clearly demonstrated that the US was likely to employ the remaining safeguard options to the maximum extent possible. These cases demonstrate the importance of this sector of trade to the developing world, and the value to them of the causes of action found in the ATC.

Costa Rica and others v. US: Restrictions on imports of cotton and man-made fibre underwear[14]

The background to this case reflects a difference in approach to the "re-importation" of cotton goods from the Caribbean area before and after the US elections of 1992. The panel noted that, starting in 1990, the US underwear manufacturing industry had undergone a major change in industrial arrangements. Instead of producing and assembling domestically, companies had taken to producing component parts in the US, cutting them, and then assembling them into the garments abroad. Then, the finished good would be returned to the US for marketing.[15]

This device represented the US policy of encouraging "co-production" as it was called, as part of its "Caribbean Basin Initiative". The objective was closer trade links with Mexico, the Caribbean, and the so-called Andean countries in a broad grouping including Costa Rica.[16] The general idea, simply put, was that while "making use of the labour force available outside the country", US companies could still keep their market share, as well as control over the levels of production, as well as over marketing.[17]

[14] *Costa Rica and others v. US: Restrictions on imports of cotton and man-made fibre underwear*, Panel Report, 8 November 1996, (WT/DS24/R) [hereinafter *US Underwear Imports* Panel Report].
[15] *US Underwear Imports* Panel Report, para. 2.1.
[16] *US Underwear Imports* Panel Report, paras. 2.1–2.6.
[17] *US Underwear Imports* Panel Report, para. 2.1.

A provision in the US tariff schedule allowed the re-importation of goods assembled abroad from US components of this kind, at extremely low or tariff free rates, as long as only assembly had occurred abroad, with no other changes having been made to the product.[18] Despite this, such goods were still classified as foreign goods and as imports into the United States.[19] The relevant re-importation programmes, which served both development and industrial objectives from the US' point of view, included a Guaranteed Access Level for such products up to a very high quota level.[20]

It should be recalled that Article 2 of the Textile Agreement required that all members should make notification of existing bilateral restrictions on textiles, and agree not to make new ones. Article 4 also stated that changes in the practices and procedures in these restrictions should not upset the access balance available to members and should not "disrupt trade".

However, in early 1995, the US authorities identified a "situation of serious damage or actual threat thereof" with respect to its underwear industry because of imports from seven geographically dispersed countries, including Costa Rica. In March of 1995, the US initiated a safeguard procedure under Article 6 of the ATC, with a view to establishing a quantitative restriction. (As noted above, there is a three-year maximum on such actions under Article 6(12).) It also gave a "statement of serious damage" as the factual basis for its action.[21]

The US could not reach agreement with Costa Rica, among others, on an acceptable level of restriction, and imposed a 12-month restraint, referring the matter to the Textiles Monitoring Body, as per Article 6.10 of the ATC.[22] The TMB, in carrying out its review, could find no evidence of serious damage, although it failed to reach a consensus as to whether or not there was an actual threat of serious damage.[23] The TMB encouraged the countries involved to reach a mutually satisfactory solution, although this did not prove possible.[24]

What Costa Rica was seeking through the dispute settlement system was the withdrawal of the unilateral US restriction on the products in question. Costa Rica alleged that in fact no damage was being done to US manufacturing industry. Rather, the US was simply trying to cut down on its re-import trade. Since the focus of the ATC is on damage to the industry rather than only to employment per se, the US was in somewhat of a conceptual bind. Also, the increase in this sort of trade could not, according to Costa Rica, be considered increased "imports" within the meaning of Article 6.2 of the ATC.[25]

---

[18] *US Underwear Imports* Panel Report, paras. 2.2–2.3.

[19] *US Underwear Imports* Panel Report, paras. 2.4–2.5. The dutiable value of the final product was reduced by deducting the cost of the (US-derived) components from the final product, so that in essence a duty was generally only payable on the assembly cost.

[20] *US Underwear Imports* Panel Report, para. 2.6.

[21] *US Underwear Imports* Panel Report, para. 2.9.

[22] *US Underwear Imports* Panel Report, paras. 2.10–2.12.

[23] *US Underwear Imports* Panel Report, para. 2.16.

[24] *US Underwear Imports* Panel Report, para. 2.16.

[25] *US Underwear Imports* Panel Report, para. 3.1 (summarising the Costa Rican position).

India, with its keen interest in the workings of the new ATC, fully supported Costa Rica and argued that the Costa Rican imports were almost entirely made from US components, as well as being manufactured in Costa Rica by US manufacturers. As India saw it, if US industry participates voluntarily in such a programme, how could it be said to be contributing to "actual damage" to US industry? Costa Rica had questioned the quality of the US evidence purporting to show a causal link between imports from other countries and the drop in US employment in that sector.[26]

For its part, the US argued that the new regime brought into being under the Agreement on Textiles and Clothing is in essence a safeguards regime, just as are Article XIX and the WTO's Agreement on Safeguards. In other words, both these "permit a member to restrict trade in fairly traded goods on the basis of a determination made by that member, subject to certain limits".[27] What both sides agreed on was the fact that as a so-called "transitional safeguard", this measure must be applied in accordance with Article 6 of the ATC.

The main charges to be explored are that the US did not show serious damage as required by Articles 6.2 and 6.4; and also that the US should have granted more favourable treatment to re-imports from Costa Rica, as required by Article 6.6(d) of the ATC, when the restriction was applied. This leads in turn to the charge that the US violated Article 2.4, which says that "no new restrictions in terms of products or members shall be introduced except under the provisions of this agreement or relevant GATT 1994 provisions".[28]

In its findings, the panel turned first to the requirements of Article 6.2, which makes the application of a transitional safeguard conditional on a finding by the member concerned that a product is being imported in such increased quantity as to cause serious damage or actual threat thereof to the domestic industry producing like and/or directly competitive products. In contrast to Article XIX safeguard measures, Article 6.4 requires that damage be assessed on a member by member basis; that is, the complainant country must show exactly how

---

[26] *US Underwear Imports* Panel Report, para. 4.1.

[27] *US Underwear Imports* Panel Report, para. 5.44.

[28] Art. 6(2) states that "Safeguard actions may be taken under this Article when, on the basis of a determination by a Member, it is demonstrated that a particular product is being imported into its territory in such increased quantities as to cause serious damage, or actual threat thereof, to the domestic industry producing like and/or directly competitive products. Serious damage or actual threat thereof must demonstrably be caused by such increased quantities in total imports of that product and not by such other factors as technological changes or changes in consumer preference."

Art. 6(4) states that "Any measure invoked pursuant to the provisions of this Article shall be applied on a Member by Member basis. The Member or Members to whom serious damage, or actual threat thereof, referred to in paras. 2 and 3, is attributed, shall be determined on the basis of a sharp and substantial increase in imports, actual or imminent, from such a Member or Members individually, and on the basis of the level of imports as compared with imports from other sources, market share, and import and domestic prices at a comparable stage of commercial transaction; none of these factors, either alone or combined with other factors, can necessarily give decisive guidance. Such safeguard measures shall not be applied to the exports of any Member whose exports of the particular product are already under restraint under this Agreement."

another member's exports are causing the damage.[29] There is no requirement of non-discriminatory self-protection until the MFA is phased out, and textile trade returned to general GATT/WTO rules. One might say that there is a requirement of differentiation, according to the national source of the damage-causing imports.

The panel pointed out that Article 6 does allow members to adopt new restrictions after the coming into being of the WTO, but this requires that serious damage or a threat of serious damage be proven. Also, the damage must be plainly attributable to a particular member through demonstrable evidence.[30] The panel looked at whether the US evidence supported either of these propositions. The US lost both with regard to underlying causality and to attribution of damage to an individual member's exports. The panel concluded that the US had failed to comply with its obligations under Articles 6.2 and 6.4.[31]

As to the more specialised point under Article 6.6(d)—that where a transitional safeguard measure is to be applied, members must grant more favourable treatment to re-imports—the panel agreed with Costa Rica on this issue as well.[32]

The fact that the Article 6 provisions had been violated in this way also meant that Article 2.4 had been likewise violated, since Article 2.4 says that any new restrictions must be seen as exceptions to the terms of Article 2 (i.e., no new restrictions after those in place in January 1995), and must meet the conditions imposed by Article 6.[33] The panel recommended that the US be required by the DSB to bring its challenged measures into line with its obligations under the ATC, and to immediately withdraw its restriction against Costa Rican imports.[34]

Interestingly, only Costa Rica lodged an appeal, on the few narrow points upon which it did not prevail with the panel. It succeeded in obtaining a ruling from the Appellate Body that the US could not impose a restraint between the time of publication of the notice of consultations and the date of formal application of the measure.[35] The US had argued that it needed to protect itself against a speculative flood of imports before the restraint went into effect, but the Appellate Body did not find this sufficient justification for extending the scope of the permissible restriction.[36]

---

[29] *US Underwear Imports* Panel Report, para. 7.22.

[30] *US Underwear Imports* Panel Report, paras. 7.23–7.24.

[31] See *US Underwear Imports* Panel Report, paras 7.25–7.52; and 7.53–7.55 (discussing actual threat of serious damage).

[32] *US Underwear Imports* Panel Report, paras. 7.45–7.59.

[33] *US Underwear Imports* Panel Report, paras. 7.70–7.71.

[34] *US Underwear Imports* Panel Report, para. 8.3.

[35] *Costa Rica and others* v. US: *Restrictions on imports of cotton and man-made fibre underwear* 10 February 1997 (WT/DS24/AB/R) [hereinafter *US Underwear Imports* Appellate Body Report] pp. 11–17.

[36] *US Underwear Imports* Appellate Body Report, pp. 17–20.

India v. US: Measures Affecting Imports of Woven Wool Shirts and Blouses from India[37]

This case is another example of a developing country seizing upon the ATC to challenge developed-world protectionism in the textile sector. As factual background, the last of the US-India bilateral agreements entered into under the MFA expired at the end of 1994. From the beginning of 1995, such trade was governed entirely under the terms of the ATC.[38] Simultaneously, the US sought to place temporary safeguard measures on woven woollen shorts and blouses originating in India.[39]

Unable to reach agreement with India on this, the US proceeded to apply a one-year restraint on the relevant products.[40] In its review, the TMB concluded that the US has demonstrated an "actual threat of serious damage".[41] India charged that the US had violated Article 2, 6, and 8 of the ATC, on notification of pre-existing bilateral agreements restraining textile exports, transitional safeguard measures, and on the role of the TMB, respectively.[42]

A main element of contention was the adequacy of a document issued by the US in the context of its April 1995 request for consultations with India, and entitled "Statement of Serious Damage". In it, the US said that sharp and substantial increases in imports from India of these products were causing serious damage or actual threat of serious damage to US industry. In July of that year, the US implemented a restraint on imports of the goods in question. As mentioned, the TMB found that the US had demonstrated an actual threat of serious damage, attributable to a sharp rise in the level of imports from India.

According to the Indian claim, the US failed to demonstrate the threat of serious damage because the data it provided was flawed. India also alleged procedural violations regarding the quality and extent of the consultations—specifically, that the US failed to consult on the value of the proposed safeguard action.[43] In particular, the US was alleged to have failed to obtain the endorsement of the TMB before imposing its safeguard action.[44] The US rejoined that the TMB did in fact confirm its conclusions on the question of actual threat of damage.[45]

---

[37] *India v. US: Measures Affecting Imports of Woven Wool Shirts and Blouses*, Panel Report, 6 January 1997 (WT/DS33/R) [hereinafter *Indian Wool Shirts* Panel Report]; *India: Measures Affecting Imports of Woven Wool Shirts and Blouses from India* Appellate Body Report, 25 April 1997 (WT/DS33/AB/R) [hereinafter *Indian Wool Shirts* Appellate Report].

[38] *Indian Wool Shirts* Panel Report, para. 2.1.

[39] *Indian Wool Shirts* Panel Report, para. 2.3.

[40] *Indian Wool Shirts* Panel Report, paras. 2.5–2.8.

[41] *Indian Wool Shirts* Panel Report, para. 2.9.

[42] *Indian Wool Shirts* Panel Report, para. 3.1.

[43] *Indian Wool Shirts* Panel Report, para. 7.6.

[44] *Indian Wool Shirts* Panel Report, para. 7.6.

[45] *Indian Wool Shirts* Panel Report, para. 7.8.

There is an important initial issue raised as to what the standard of review ought to be in a dispute like this, where the validity of a restrictive measure really depends upon the quality of the factual evidence.[46] The panel noted that the ATC does not establish a standard of review for panels.[47] In light of this, it considered that Article 11 of the DSU, which "describes the parameters of the function of panels", was relevant.[48]

Under Article 11 of the Dispute Settlement Understanding, the panel said that it was limited to "making an objective assessment of the facts surrounding the application of the specific restraint (here, by the US), and of the conformity of such restraint with the relevant WTO agreements".[49] The panel pointed out that as far as the textile trade was concerned, DSU panels and the TMB have separate functions.[50] The TMB has broad powers of investigation and no clear terms of reference to restrict their inquiry. The TMB may engage in its own evidence-gathering procedures.[51]

A DSU panel, by contrast, "is not called upon to reinvestigate the market situation". A panel, in reviewing the "WTO-compatibility" of a decision to impose a national measure, must limit itself to the evidence used by the importing member in making its determination to impose the measure. So this panel saw its task as that of making "an objective assessment as to whether the US respected the requirements of Articles 6.2 and 6.3 of the ATC at the time of the determination".[52]

The panel's substantive findings were simple, but significant. First of all, it stated that the wording of Article 6.2 confirms that WTO members have a right to take safeguard actions; and that the decision to impose a safeguard measure must be based upon a demonstration, before the action is taken, that the increased quantities of imports are causing serious damage or actual threat of damage.[53] The panel then carried out a detailed analysis of the quality of evidence presented by the US as justification for its protective measure. Examining this evidence in the light of the requirements of Article 6.3 of the ATC (that such economic factors as productivity, wages, inventories, investments, etc., be looked at), the panel found that the US had failed to consider all the relevant elements, and that it had not proved damage causation to a sufficient degree.[54] However, India's further contention that a member's safeguard action was required to be specifically endorsed by the TMB was rejected by the panel in light of the fact that Article 8.9 of the ATC "confirms that the recommendations of the TMB are not binding". Therefore, in this case, too, a developing country

---

[46] See the arguments of the parties in *Indian Wool Shirts* Panel Report, paras. 7.10–7.11.
[47] *Indian Wool Shirts* Panel Report, para. 7.16.
[48] *Indian Wool Shirts* Panel Report, para. 7.16.
[49] *Indian Wool Shirts* Panel Report, para. 7.17.
[50] *Indian Wool Shirts* Panel Report, para. 7.18.
[51] *Indian Wool Shirts* Panel Report, paras. 7.19–7.20.
[52] *Indian Wool Shirts* Panel Report, para. 7.21.
[53] *Indian Wool Shirts* Panel Report, para. 7.24.
[54] *Indian Wool Shirts* Panel Report, paras. 7.51–7.52.

prevailed in its attempt to show that the US was misusing the safeguard rights available under the ATC.[55/56]

THE REQUIREMENTS OF JOINING AN ADVANCED CUSTOMS UNION:
INDIA V. TURKEY[57]

Perhaps the most interesting of the textile cases to date involves the peculiar role of Turkey, as both a major exporter and importer of textiles, poised to enter a customs union with the EC, and thereby required to bring its regime of textile imports in line with that of Europe. The significant question was whether the internal requirements of the customs union itself, a regional arrangement countenanced by Article XXIV of the General Agreement, could justify new restrictions by Turkey which ostensibly violated both Article XI of the General Agreement and the provisions of the Uruguay Round's Agreement on Textiles.

In March of 1996, India requested consultations with Turkey on the question of Turkey's unilateral imposition of quantitative restrictions on a broad range of textile and clothing products from India as from January 1996.[58] When talks did not proceed because of a disagreement on the appropriateness of EC participation, India proceeded to request the formation of a panel to hear its complaints under the GATT and the ATC.[59] The panel was established in March of 1998.[60]

The case raises intriguing questions as to the relationship between Article XXIV of the GATT and the possibility of violation of substantive GATT law in the name of Article XXIV obligations. The panel discussed the GATT history of Article XXIV, and pointed out that friction resulting from potential clashes between regional trade agreements and the GATT have traditionally been dealt with pragmatically, rather than comprehensively, with no clear statement of policy ever having been clearly worked out.[61] Especially in recent years, a number of new regional trade agreements had been notified to the WTO, and a new WTO committee on RTAs had been established.[62]

---

[55] Here, too, only the complainant party, India, appealed the case, and on comparatively narrow grounds. The Appellate Body upheld the panel's views on burden of proof, the role of the TMB, and on the concept of judicial economy.

[56] *Indian Wool Shirts* Panel Report, para. 7.57. Art. 8.9 of the ATC states that members shall endeavour to accept in full the recommendations of the TMB, which shall exercise proper surveillance of the implementation of such recommendations.

[57] *India* v. *Turkey: Restrictions on Imports of Textile and Clothing Products*, Report of the Panel, 31 May 1999 (WT/DS34/R) [hereinafter *Turkish Textile Restrictions* Panel Report].

[58] *Turkish Textile Restrictions* Panel Report, para. 1.1.

[59] " . . . India claimed that the restrictions imposed by Turkey were inconsistent with Turkey's obligations under Arts. XI and XIII of the GATT, and were not justified by Art. XXIV of GATT, which did not authorise the imposition of discriminatory quantitative restrictions and that the restrictions were inconsistent with Turkey's obligations under Art. 2 of the ATC".

[60] *Turkish Textile Restrictions* Panel Report, paras. 1.1–1.4.

[61] *Turkish Textile Restrictions* Panel Report, paras. 2.2–2.4.

[62] *Turkish Textile Restrictions* Panel Report, paras. 2.8–2.9.

As for the agreement between the EC and Turkey, the parties signed the "Ankara Agreement" on association in 1963, which envisaged the creation of a customs union by stages, leaving open the eventual possibility of Turkey's accession to the EC. Beginning in 1973, Turkey had begun to align its customs duties with those of the EC. The final phase of alignment was to occur between 1996 and 2001.[63]

As far as the trade context is concerned, the EC constitutes a full 50 per cent of Turkey's imports and exports. A striking 37 per cent of Turkey's exports are in the textile and clothing sector (10 per cent and 27 per cent respectively); and 7 per cent of imports are in that sector.[64] As explained above, after January 2005, no WTO country will be able to continue to apply discriminatory safeguard measures under the ATC.[65] At the time the ATC came into force, Turkey did not in fact maintain QRs on textile and clothing imports. Its own exports of textiles and clothing products were under restraint in the EC and other countries' markets under the terms of the MFA.[66]

In 1996, Turkey harmonised its customs duties in line with Europe's with respect to industrial goods generally.[67] Turkey accepted a number of European trade rules, including the regulations on imports of textiles and clothing—especially those contained in Council Regulation 3030/93.[68] During 1995, Turkey sent proposals to the countries whose imports of textiles were under restraint in the EC market, including to India, "to reach agreements for the management and distribution of quotas under a double checking system".[69] While asked to enter into negotiations with Turkey to that end, India protested that the intended restrictions "were in contravention of Turkey's multilateral obligations and declined to enter into discussions on the conditions proposed by Turkey".[70]

Turkey did manage to enter into restraint agreements with 24 other countries, and from January 1996, imposed unilateral restrictions on imports originating in 28 countries, including India.[71] Turkey's actions were in line with similar import restrictions in place for the EC.[72] The main issue in the dispute was whether Article XXIV of the GATT, the only legal justification offered by

---

[63] Entry into force of this "final phase of the customs union" between Turkey and the EC was notified to the WTO in December of 1995. *Turkish Textile Restrictions* Panel Report, paras. 2.10–2.17.

[64] *Turkish Textile Restrictions* Panel Report, paras. 2.21–2.22.

[65] *Turkish Textile Restrictions* Panel Report, para. 2.28.

[66] *Turkish Textile Restrictions* Panel Report, para. 2.30.

[67] *Turkish Textile Restrictions* Panel Report, para. 2.31.

[68] *Turkish Textile Restrictions* Panel Report, para. 2.34. This regulation "provided for the bilateral agreements with supplier countries to be implemented by a set of EC quantitative limits on certain imports and for a system of import surveillance".

[69] *Turkish Textile Restrictions* Panel Report, para. 2.34.

[70] *Turkish Textile Restrictions* Panel Report, para. 2.35.

[71] *Turkish Textile Restrictions* Panel Report, para. 2.36. Turkey imposed QRs on 19 categories of Indian textile and clothing products. Para. 2.38.

[72] *Turkish Textile Restrictions* Panel Report, para. 2.36.

Turkey for the contested measures, permitted the imposition of these restrictions on imports of textile and clothing products from India; restrictions that otherwise were inconsistent with Turkish obligations under Article XI:1 of GATT and Article 2.4 of the ATC.[73]

The panel considered Turkey's argument that Article XXIV, the right of WTO members to join in customs unions, also provided a "shield" from other WTO obligations that might be violated in the process.[74] A more subtle argument was that since the customs union is with the EC, which is in turn entitled under the ATC to maintain import restrictions on the same categories of products, then Turkey's conforming import restrictions are not in fact "new restrictions" in the sense that term is used in Article 2.4 of the ATC, as they are fully justified under Article XXIV.[75] India, in Turkey's view, "directed its complaint against Turkey concerning a measure taken by another entity"—either the customs union itself or the EC. These were "collective" measures for which Turkey was not individually responsible.[76]

But is it true that when WTO members enter into a customs union that there is of necessity fundamental change, as insisted upon by Turkey, both in their relationship with one another and in their relationship with other WTO members? The panel first turned to the question of whose (that is, which member's) measures were actually being challenged.

The panel noted that the measures were taken in a formal action by Turkey; the joint notification of the measures to the TMB by Turkey and the EC refer to the QRs being imposed by Turkey.[77] Since the customs union has no separate legislative body, the panel's view was that it had no authority to enact laws applicable to the territory of the customs union.[78] Apart from this, the customs union was also not a member of the WTO in its own right.[79] For these and other reasons, the panel determined that the measures were in fact Turkish measures.[80]

The panel discussed the nature of the traditional GATT prohibition against QRs; and the fact that this is the "cornerstone" of GATT law.[81] The panel repeated the GATT belief that while QRs impose absolute limits, MFN tariffs "permit the most efficient competitor to supply imports", and do not have the same distorting effect as QRs.[82] It is noted that from the earliest days of GATT,

---

[73] *Turkish Textile Restrictions* Panel Report, paras. 9.25–9.26. Turkey argued that the drafters of the original GATT had referred to the creation of customs unions as "desirable" in Art. XXIV:4, since these would lead to increased economic integration between the parties to the customs union. Para. 3.26. India argued that while Turkey may face conflicting obligations, the panel must address itself only to Turkey's WTO obligations. Para. 3.31.

[74] *Turkish Textile Restrictions* Panel Report, paras. 9.27–9.28.

[75] *Turkish Textile Restrictions* Panel Report, para. 9.29.

[76] *Turkish Textile Restrictions* Panel Report, para. 9.33.

[77] *Turkish Textile Restrictions* Panel Report, para. 9.36.

[78] *Turkish Textile Restrictions* Panel Report, para. 9.40.

[79] *Turkish Textile Restrictions* Panel Report, para. 9.41.

[80] *Turkish Textile Restrictions* Panel Report, para. 9.44.

[81] *Turkish Textile Restrictions* Panel Report, para. 9.63.

[82] *Turkish Textile Restrictions* Panel Report, para. 9.63.

agricultural and textile products have enjoyed exceptions to the general prohibition against QRs.[83] The need to eliminate these exceptions is reflected in the new Uruguay Round Agreements, notably in the ATC.[84] In these circumstances, India had made out a prima facie case of the imposition of QRs by Turkey.[85]

As for the ATC, Article 2 allows some exceptions to the Article XI and XIII prohibition for members who had MFA restrictions in place and notified these to the WTO within 60 days.[86] Four WTO members notified such pre-existing restraints to the WTO: Canada, the EC, Norway and the US.[87] Apart from these, no new QRs introduced by a member can benefit from the exceptions provided after the 60-day period.[88] The panel also noted that there is no relationship between the Article 6 transitional safeguard provisions of the ATC and the issue of new QRs under that agreement.[89] Turkey's measures must be seen as "new" measures, as discussed in Articles 2.4 and 3.3 of the agreement, the only justification for which would have to stem from Article XXIV.[90] The panel concluded that unless justified by Article XXIV the measures are inconsistent with Articles XI and XIII of the GATT "and they would necessarily violate also Article 2.4 of the ATC".[91]

Turkey made persuasive, if profoundly flawed, arguments about the nature of Article XXIV of the General Agreement. In its view, Article XXIV has the power to wash away the WTO-inconsistency of almost any new measures pursued in the course of adopting the requirements of the customs union.[92] The panel in turn provided an important analysis of the workings of Article XXIV within the entire WTO system.

The panel pointed out that, given the desirability of customs unions in increasing freedom of trade, members forming a customs union may depart from the MFN principle as to the trade between themselves, in conformity with the conditions of Article XXIV.[93] However, this is not without qualification, the panel continued, and Article XXIV:4 makes clear that such agreements must not

---

[83] *Turkish Textile Restrictions* Panel Report, paras. 9.64–9.65.
[84] *Turkish Textile Restrictions* Panel Report, para. 9.65.
[85] *Turkish Textile Restrictions* Panel Report, para. 9.66.
[86] *Turkish Textile Restrictions* Panel Report, para. 9.68.
[87] *Turkish Textile Restrictions* Panel Report, para. 9.69.
[88] *Turkish Textile Restrictions* Panel Report, para. 9.69.
[89] *Turkish Textile Restrictions* Panel Report, para. 2.74.
[90] *Turkish Textile Restrictions* Panel Report, paras. 2.78–2.80.
[91] *Turkish Textile Restrictions* Panel Report, para. 9.86.
[92] The panel writes that "For Turkey, Art. XXIV (paras. 5–9) is to be viewed as *lex specialis* for the rights and obligations of WTO members at the time of the formation of a regional trade agreement. . . . In Turkey's view, the WTO consistency of the measures challenged by India depends on the WTO consistency of the Turkey—EC customs union (of which they are an integral part) and the WTO consistency of both the customs unon and its measures is to be determined with reference to the provisions of paras. 5 to 9 of Art. XXIV only and no other GATT provisions". Para. 9.88.
   India's response to this is that "Members forming a customs union could legally circumvent the WTO procedural and substantive requirements with respect to QRs, which the signatories of the WTO agreements could no longer operate as a legal framework providing effective assurances of market access and the WTO dispute settlement procedures would be rendered ineffective." Para. 9.89.
[93] *Turkish Textile Restrictions* Panel Report, para. 9.98.

be formed for the purpose of raising barriers to the trade of other members with such territories.[94] Scrutiny of such arrangements by GATT committees had thus far proved unsuccessful, and no customs union has received a definite finding of GATT/WTO consistent by an examining body.[95]

Turkey maintained that it had met the relevant conditions; that Article XXIV:5(e) only required that the overall incidence of duties and other regulations of commerce not be higher or more restrictive than before.[96] It pointed to the last sentence of paragraph 2 of the GATT 1994 Understanding on Article XXIV, which stated that

> "for the purpose of overall assessment of the incidence of other regulations of commerce for which quantification and aggregation are difficult, the examination of individual measures, regulations, products covered and trade flows affected may be required"

as confirmation of its position.[97] Under this view, had it been the intention of members to ban the imposition of new QRs whenever a customs union was being instituted, the reference to "other regulations of commerce" in Article XXIV:5 would be redundant.[98] Turkey insisted that the derogation envisaged by Article XXIV:5 encompasses all those rules from which derogation is necessary to permit the formation of customs unions.[99]

India's view was that Article XXIV:5 does not provide a legal basis for measures that are otherwise incompatible with GATT/WTO rules.[100] As it said, the terms of Article XXIV:5 "exempt from the other obligations under the GATT only measures inherent in the formation of a customs union or an FTA". And, it was pointed out, customs unions can be formed without the introduction of new QRs.[101] It argued that Article XXIV:6 recognises that on the occasion of a customs union being formed, tariff bindings may be increased.[102] Yet, India said, there is no corresponding mechanism for renegotiation and compensation for members affected by the introduction or increase of QRs that are otherwise WTO incompatible. Whereas QRs are in general prohibited, tariffs may be renegotiated. Had the Uruguay Round negotiators meant to extend Article XXIV:6 to QRs, this argument went, they would have formulated this provision accordingly.[103]

In a complex analysis of the meaning of Article XXIV:5(a), the panel stated that, along with paragraph 2 of the Understanding on Article XXIV, this provision provides for an economic test for assessing whether a customs unison is

---

[94] *Turkish Textile Restrictions* Panel Report, para. 9.103. The panel wrote: "The terms of Art. XXIV thus confirm that WTO members have a right, albeit conditional, to conclude trade agreements." Para. 9.103.

[95] *Turkish Textile Restrictions* Panel Report, para. 9.107.

[96] *Turkish Textile Restrictions* Panel Report, para. 9.109.

[97] *Turkish Textile Restrictions* Panel Report, para. 9.110.

[98] *Turkish Textile Restrictions* Panel Report, para. 9.111.

[99] *Turkish Textile Restrictions* Panel Report, para. 9.112.

[100] *Turkish Textile Restrictions* Panel Report, para. 9.113.

[101] *Turkish Textile Restrictions* Panel Report, para. 9.113.

[102] *Turkish Textile Restrictions* Panel Report, para. 9.114.

[103] *Turkish Textile Restrictions* Panel Report, para. 9.114.

compatible with Article XXIV.[104] (This is a different assessment from that called for in Article XXIV: 6, which deals with bound tariffs, which are regulated by the WTO, rather than applied duties generally.)[105] The panel explained that

> "in the context of the overall assessment of the potential trade impact of any such customs union . . . duties and all regulations which existed in one or more of the constituent members and/or form part of the customs union treaty must be taken into account".[106]

The panel stated clearly that in its view, the concept "other regulations of commerce" includes QRs, as well as other types of regulation—technical, environmental, and so forth.[107]

But while the language of Article XXIV:5(a) authorises the formation of customs unions, the panel said,

> "it does not contain any provision that either authorises or prohibits, on the occasion of the formation of a customs union, the adoption of import restrictions otherwise GATT/WTO incompatible, by any of the parties forming this customs union".[108]

The panel continued by noting that while Article XXIV:5(a) assumes that, as a result of a customs union, some applied duties may be higher, and other regulations of commerce may be more restrictive than before, "it does not specify whether such a situation may occur only through GATT/WTO consistent actions or may occur through GATT/WTO inconsistent actions".[109] In other words, Article XXIV itself is silent on this central question, and it is for the panel to decide what Article XXIV actually allows.[110] The general purpose of Article XXIV:5(a), then is to make sure that a new customs union is not used to increase trade barriers overall.

Continuing in this analysis, the panel noted that under Article XXIV:6 compensation is due if a pre-existing tariff binding is exceeded; there is, however, no parallel provision to compensate members for the introduction of QRs.[111] The panel concluded that this was the case because QRs are generally prohibited by GATT/WTO, while tariff increases above agreed upon bindings can be, as long as they are re-negotiated, WTO compatible.[112]

As the panel saw it, the provisions of Article XXIV:5(a) are informed by the language of Article XXIV:4, which states that there must not be a raising of trade barriers overall. The panel said that it consequently found that there is no

---

[104] *Turkish Textile Restrictions* Panel Report, para. 9.120.

[105] *Turkish Textile Restrictions* Panel Report, para. 9.118.

[106] *Turkish Textile Restrictions* Panel Report, para. 9.120.

[107] *Turkish Textile Restrictions* Panel Report, para. 9.120.

[108] *Turkish Textile Restrictions* Panel Report, para. 9.121.

[109] *Turkish Textile Restrictions* Panel Report, para. 9.121.

[110] According to the panel, what Art. XXIV:5(a) provides is "that the effects of the resulting trade measures and policies of the new regional agreement shall not be more trade restrictive, overall, than were the constituent countries' previous trade policies". Para. 9.121.

[111] *Turkish Textile Restrictions* Panel Report, para. 9.127.

[112] *Turkish Textile Restrictions* Panel Report, paras. 9.127–9.128.

legal basis in Article XXIV:5(a) for the introduction of QRs otherwise incompatible with GATT/WTO. The panel stated that

> "the wording of sub-paragraph 5(a) does not authorise members forming a customs union to deviate from the prohibitions contained in Articles XI and XIII of GATT or Article 2.4 of the ATC".[113]

Indeed, Article XXIV:5(a), the panel said,

> "provides for a prohibition against the formation of a customs union that would be more restrictive, on the whole, than was the trade of its constituent members, even in situations where there are no WTO-incompatible measures".

Turkey presented the alternative argument that it was obliged by the terms of Article XXIV:8 to adopt common QRs with Europe on textile imports.[114] The panel then considered whether Turkey was "required" to do this. The panel said that Article XXIV must be interpreted in a manner that avoids conflicts with other WTO provisions. With that in mind, can Articles XI and XIII, and Article XXIV:8(a) be interpreted so as to avoid a conflict requiring that one provision yields to another? Not surprisingly, the panel expressed a belief that there could be "harmonious interpretation".[115] Though a customs union may require that there be convergence across a wide range of policy areas, there can also be distinct exceptions in limited areas.[116] The panel interpreted Article XXIV:8(ii) to mean that members are allowed to form a customs union where one constituent member is entitled to impose QRs under a special transitional regime, and the other constituent member is not.[117] But the panel was again clear in its view that Article XXIV:8(a)(ii) does not provide authorisation for members forming a customs union to violate the prescriptions of Articles XI and XIII of GATT or Article 2.4 of the ATC.[118]

The overall purpose of the GATT, the panel reminded its readers, is to make trade less restrictive.[119] In this sense, according to the panel, the objectives of regional trading agreements and the GATT/WTO "have always been complementary".[120] The panel emphasised that the ATC itself has

> "put in place new disciplines regarding the introduction of QRs in the sector of textiles and clothing whereby, as of January 1, 1995, the global level of QRs in that sector could only decrease (setting aside the possibility for ATC compatible safeguard measures)".[121]

A bilateral agreement like that between the EC and Turkey does not, the panel said, "alter the legal nature of the measures at issue or the applicability of the relevant GATT/WTO provisions".[122]

---

[113] *Turkish Textile Restrictions* Panel Report, para. 9.134.
[114] *Turkish Textile Restrictions* Panel Report, para. 9.135.
[115] *Turkish Textile Restrictions* Panel Report, para. 9.147.
[116] *Turkish Textile Restrictions* Panel Report, para. 9.151.
[117] *Turkish Textile Restrictions* Panel Report, para. 9.151.
[118] *Turkish Textile Restrictions* Panel Report, para. 9.154.
[119] *Turkish Textile Restrictions* Panel Report, paras. 9.159–9.162.
[120] *Turkish Textile Restrictions* Panel Report, para. 9.163.
[121] *Turkish Textile Restrictions* Panel Report, para. 9.169.
[122] *Turkish Textile Restrictions* Panel Report, para. 9.178.

In fact, the actual agreement only required that Turkey apply "substantially the same commercial policy" as the European Community in the textile sector. This led the panel to find that Turkey has "some flexibility" under its agreement with Europe.[123] But even were this not the case, the panel said "such requirement would not be sufficient to exempt Turkey from its obligations under the WTO Agreement".[124]

A related and imaginative argument raised by Turkey had to do with whether a constituent member of a customs union could "pass on" a WTO right to other members of the customs union.[125] The panel rejected this proposition, noting that there is no such concept mentioned in Article XXIV, in the WTO Agreement, or even in international law generally.[126] In the panel's view, the "specific circumstances which serve as the legal basis for one member's exercise of such a specific right cannot suddenly be considered to exist for the other constituent members".[127] On a more philosophical note, the panel concluded that the right of WTO members to form a customs union must be exercised so as to ensure the WTO rights of third country members are also respected.[128] So the conclusion must be that Article XXIV is not, as Turkey argued, *lex specialis*, and does not create a self-contained legal regime insulated from the other provisions of GATT and the WTO Agreement.[129] Article XI being clear and unambiguous, and Article XXIV providing a conditional right, the wording of Article XXIV does not authorise a departure from the obligations contained in Articles XI or XIII, nor those contained in Article 2.4 of the ATC, according to the panel.[130] Any other conclusion, the panel said, would lead to "politically and economically absurd results".[131] In this particular case, the panel found, Turkey was in a position to avoid violations of Articles XI and XIII of the GATT, and of Article 2.4 of the ATC.[132]

Turkey's arguments before the Appellate Body[133]

Turkey appealed the panel's finding that Article XXIV of the GATT 1994 does not allow it to introduce, upon the formation of its customs union with the European Communities, quantitative restrictions on textile and clothing products

[123] *Turkish Textile Restrictions* Panel Report, para. 9.179.
[124] *Turkish Textile Restrictions* Panel Report, para. 9.182.
[125] *Turkish Textile Restrictions* Panel Report, para. 9.183.
[126] *Turkish Textile Restrictions* Panel Report, para. 9.184.
[127] *Turkish Textile Restrictions* Panel Report, para. 9.184.
[128] *Turkish Textile Restrictions* Panel Report, para. 9.184.
[129] *Turkish Textile Restrictions* Panel Report, paras. 9.186–9.187.
[130] *Turkish Textile Restrictions* Panel Report, para. 9.188.
[131] *Turkish Textile Restrictions* Panel Report, para. 9.188.
[132] *Turkish Textile Restrictions* Panel Report, para. 9.191.
[133] *India v. Turkey: Restrictions on Imports of Textile and Clothing Products*, Report of the Appellate Body, 22 October 1999 (WT/DS34/AB/R) [hereinafter *Turkish Textile Restrictions Appellate Body Report*].

which are inconsistent with Article XI and XIII of the GATT 1994 and Article 2.4 of the ATC.[134] In Turkey's view, Article XXIV does permit the

> "common regulation of commerce or a customs union in a particular sector to be determined by one of the constituent member's lawful QRs in that sector, provided that unified regulations are not on the whole more restrictive than the previous regulations of the constituent members".[135]

Turkey maintained, in particular, that the panel did not properly interpret the meaning of the "chapeau" of Article XXIV:5, in that the "chapeau" shows that Article XXIV allows WTO members to derogate under certain conditions from their WTO obligations.[136] Turkey made a number of other arguments, all connected with the panel's failure to appreciate the autonomous right granted to WTO members under Article XXIV.

The Appellate Body noted that the panel had referred only "in a passing and perfunctory way" to the "chapeau" of Article XXIV:5; focusing instead on paragraphs 5(a) and 8(a) of Article XXIV. The Appellate Body, however, stated that "the chapeau of paragraph 5 of Article XXIV is the key provision for resolving the issue before us in this appeal".[137]

The Appellate Body agreed with the panel that the terms of Article XXIV: 8(a)(ii), requiring that members of the customs union apply substantially the same duties and other regulation of commerce to external trade with third countries, offers a certain degree of flexibility to members of the customs union in the creation of their common commercial policy.[138] But given the language of the "chapeau", the Appellate Body reasoned that Article XXIV can in fact be invoked as a defence to a finding that a measure is inconsistent with certain GATT provisions, where the requirements of Article 5(a) are met.[139] The Appellate Body stated that it agreed with the panel that the terms of Article XXIV:5(a) provide that "the effects of the resulting trade measures and policies of the new regional arrangement shall not be more trade restrictive, overall, than were the constituent countries' previous trade policies".[140] In this regard,

---

[134] *Turkish Textile Restrictions* Appellate Body Report, para. 6.

[135] *Turkish Textile Restrictions* Appellate Body Report, para. 8.

[136] *Turkish Textile Restrictions* Appellate Body Report, para. 10; also give text of "chapeau".

[137] *Turkish Textile Restrictions* Appellate Body Report, para. 43. The section of the "chapeau" quoted by the Appellate Body reads: "Accordingly, the provisions of this Agreement shall not prevent, as between the territories of contracting parties, the formation of a customs union . . . provided that. . . ."

[138] *Turkish Textile Restrictions* Appellate Body Report, para. 50.

[139] *Turkish Textile Restrictions* Appellate Body Report, para. 52. As for the specific conditions, with respect to duties, Art. XXIV:5(a) requires that the duties applied by the constituent members of the customs union after the formation of the customs union shall not on the whole be higher . . . than the general incidence of the duties that were applied by each of the constituent members before the formation of the customs union. Para 53. And regarding "other regulations of commerce", Art. XXIV:5(a) requires that those applied by the members after the formation of the customs union shall not on the whole be . . . more restrictive than the general incidence of the regulation of commerce that were applied by each of the constituent members before the formation of the customs union. Para. 54.

[140] *Turkish Textile Restrictions* Appellate Body Report, para. 55.

Article XXIV:4 sets out the overriding purpose of the creation of customs unions, which must be to facilitate trade without creating adverse effects on the trade of other members. This overall purpose must inform our interpretation of the "chapeau" of paragraph 5.[141]

The Appellate Body therefore reasoned that Article XXIV might justify a measure that is inconsistent with certain other GATT provisions. But the defending party has a heavy burden to meet; it must show that the conditions set out in sub-paragraphs 8(a) and 5(a) are fulfilled; it must also show that the formation of the customs union would be prevented if it were not allowed to introduce the measure at issue.[142] The Appellate Body strongly implied that the panel ought to have addressed the threshold question of whether the arrangement between Turkey and the EC was in fact a customs union which met the requirements of Article XXIV:8(a) and 5(a).[143] The Appellate Body agreed with the panel that had Turkey not adopted the same QRs that are applied by the EC, that would not have prevented the formation of the customs union. In light of the "flexibility" enjoyed by the constituent members of the customs union, an arrangement could have been made whereby textiles and clothing originating in Turkey could have been distinguished from that originating in third countries and coming into Turkey, as one example of an alternative approach offered by the Appellate Body.[144]

Since Turkey was not required to apply the QRs in question in order to form its customs union, the Appellate Body concluded that the Article XXIV defence was not available to Turkey in this case. The Appellate Body made clear that it had made no finding on the issue of whether QRs found to be inconsistent with Articles XI and XIII of the GATT will ever be justified by Article XXIV.

These cases are of transitional interest, since textiles will lose their separate trade identity with the end of the ATC in 2005. There is no question but that this transition has major implications for employment in developed countries, although textile manufacturing had been gravitating towards the developing world well before the coming into force of the ATC. As this process continues, international labour standards in this sector are likely to become a greater focus of attention. During the latter stages of the transition, the question of whether developed countries are willing to carry out full implementation of the Agreement may also generate controversy. However, if the doctrine of comparative advantage has any validity, the MultiFibre Arrangement was surely one of the "most pronounced anomalies" of the postwar trading system.[145]

---

[141] *Turkish Textile Restrictions* Appellate Body Report, paras. 56–57.
[142] *Turkish Textile Restrictions* Appellate Body Report, para. 58.
[143] *Turkish Textile Restrictions* Appellate Body Report, paras. 59–60.
[144] *Turkish Textile Restrictions* Appellate Body Report, paras 61–62.
[145] Jackson, *supra* n. 2, at 181.

9

The Power of the General Agreement on Trade in Services (GATS)

W̲E̲ ̲H̲A̲V̲E̲ ̲S̲E̲E̲N̲ how a newly legalistic WTO dispute settlement system has combined with a plethora of new causes of action to form a potent regime for the application of trade principles. One of the new Uruguay Round Agreements in particular created rules for another sector of trade altogether; a sector of increasing interest to the developed countries in recent times, trade in services. It may seem merely logical, and rather unexciting, that trade in services should be added to the WTO's competence. After all, free trade in goods is a well-established notion, and services might at first glance appear simply to be one more area of tradable products. However, it could also be said that subjecting trade in services to free trade principles hitherto confined to goods brings the GATT/WTO system far more deeply into the actual structure of the national economy; its foundational apparatus, and its underlying vehicles of exchange.[1]

The Services Agreement is remarkable for the fact that it marks the first step in making it difficult (perhaps impossible) for WTO members to refuse rights of participation in their domestic economies, in almost any capacity, to non-nationals. Some have speculated that perhaps the Services Agreement, rather than TRIMs, is the real investment agreement, because of its profound implications for the organisation of the national financial sector and for rights of establishment. Along with the GATS Agreement itself, the separate protocols on such heavily regulated sub-sectors as financial services, telecoms and transport indicate that for the first time in economic history, not only the nationality of goods, but also the nationality of economic structures, may be about to crumble.

The wealthier developed countries were not willing to provide greater market access during the Uruguay Round negotiations unless the matters of intellectual property protection and freer trade in services were also included in the final trade package. Since the products of greatest export interest to the developed world were likely to require intellectual property protection and were increasingly likely

---

[1] For a discussion of the negotiations leading to the conclusion of the GATS Agreement, see Michael Trebilcock and Robert Howse, *The Regulation of International Trade*, 2nd edn. (Routledge, London, 1999) 278–320 . The authors also provide a detailed look at the individual provisions of the GATS. *Ibid*. at 280–291. See also J Steven Jarreau, "Interpreting the General Agreement on Trade in Services and the WTO Instruments Relevant to the International Trade of Financial Services: The Lawyer's Perspective", (Fall 1999) 25 *North Carolina Journal of International Law and Commercial Regulation* 1, 11–27 (describing how services entered the GATT/WTO agenda).

to involve the provision of services, it is not surprising that the first step was taken in the liberalisation of services trading. However, it is important to realise that the GATS is in fact a first step, and operates on the sort of incremental basis that characterised the early GATT.[2] As will be shown, member countries may make both negative and positive commitments. The agreement does not require liberalisation in any particular type of service, but it does create a framework for voluntary commitments, upon which members are expected to build over time.[3] This incrementalism is part of the fundamental GATT genius—the insight that members would not accept, and in political terms could not absorb, a sudden entry of basic services from abroad. Instead, by the time members have become accustomed to the idea of internationally traded services, a second stage agreement will have been largely negotiated.

A second factor to be borne in mind while examining the Services Agreement is that it appears to have vast, and thus largely untested, power to invalidate national laws. It will take some years of litigation before there is clear idea of what the true scope of the term "services" is. Even at this early stage, though, it is safe to say that services can refer even to the "service" of providing a tradable good. Whether or not the drafters of the Agreement intended the term to be interpreted so broadly is unclear. But this is an issue of particular importance in the context of the EC Banana Regime case, discussed below.

THE GENERAL AGREEMENT ON TRADE IN SERVICES (GATS)

The GATS enjoys a separate legal status within the GATT/WTO legal corpus.[4] Its preamble recognises the growing importance of trade in services and expresses an intention of liberalisation in this sector, as well as a corresponding commitment to "successive rounds of multilateral negotiations" on the subject.[5]

Article 1 discusses the scope and definition of the GATS Agreement, and sets out a kind of chart of possible service transaction configurations. These include: the supply of a service (i) from the territory of one member into the territory of any other member (as in the case of holiday tours); or (ii) in the territory of one member to the service consumer of any other member (providing advice to a consumer in another country); or (iii) by a service supplier of one member, through commercial presence in the territory of any other member (requiring

---

[2] See Trebilcock and Howse, *supra* n. 1, at 280–281.

[3] For insight into the emphasis on reciprocity found in the GATS, see Anders Ahnlid, "Comparing GATT and GATS: Regime Creation Under and After Hegemony", (1996) 3:1 *Review of International Political Economy* 65–94.

[4] See André Sapir, "The General Agreement on Trade in Services", (Feb 1999) 33:1 *Journal of World Trade* 51–66; and Friedl Weiss, "The General Agreement of Trade in Services 1994", (Oct 1995) 32:5 *Common Market Law Review* 1177–1225.

[5] For analysis of issues relevant to the upcoming round of negotiations in services, see Rudolf Adlung, "Liberalizing Trade in Services: from Marrakech to Seattle", (Sept–Oct 1999) 34:5 *Intereconomics* 211–22.

movement to set up the commercial entity); or (iv) by a service supplier of one member, through presence of natural persons of a member in the territory of any other member (requiring movement of the natural person). These distinctions may seem either trivial or obvious, but in fact, they are highly significant when one considers the elaborate regulation governing each category of activity within the national territories, and how such regulations may be affected by liberalisation.[6]

Article II of the Agreement sets out a general MFN obligation, with respect to the treatment that must be given to service suppliers of other WTO members. Article II, paragraph 2 states that "[a] member may maintain a measure inconsistent with paragraph 1 provided that such a measure is listed in, and meets the conditions of, the Annex on Article II exemptions". The interesting feature here is that the individual member can opt out of applying MFN to particular areas of the services trade.[7]

Article III is a transparency requirement, under which all national measures relating to the Services Agreement must be notified to the Council for Trade in Services.

Article V, on the subject of "economic integration", warns that the Services Agreement is not to prevent any WTO member from being a party to or entering into an agreement liberalising trade in services among parties to that (other) agreement. As long as the agreement provides for the elimination of virtually all discrimination in a substantial number of sectors, and as long as new discriminatory measures towards the outside world are prohibited, such an agreement will not be contrary to the GATS. (The echo of Article XXIV of the GATT, on regional trade agreements, is unmistakable.) Paragraph 4 of Article V says that such agreements shall be designed to facilitate trade between the parties to the agreement and not to raise the overall level of external barriers.

Article VI, on the subject of domestic regulation, states that in those sectors where commitments are undertaken, members shall ensure that all measures

---

[6] Excluded from the scope of the basic agreement are services supplied "in the exercise of governmental authority", echoing a similar exclusion of government purchased goods from national treatment rules under the original GATT, Art. III:8.

[7] Annex II specifies the conditions under which a member may be exempted from the MFN obligation. New exemptions (post-1995) are to be dealt with under para. 3 of Art. IX of the WTO Agreement, which requires a waiver of WTO obligations, approved of by a ¾ majority of members.

Under para. 3 of the Annex, the Council for Trade in Services will review exemptions within 5 years. The Council will examine whether the conditions still exist that gave rise to the exemption, and will also set the date for a further review. Under paras. 5 and 6, exemptions must terminate when they say they will. In any event, they are not to last for longer than 10 years, and they are to be subject to negotiation in subsequent trade rounds.

Under para. 7, members must notify the Council when the exemption has been "brought into conformity" with Art. II of the Agreement.

As Trebilcock and Howse explain, Art. II of the GATS is "a compromise between American insistence that . . . the USA should not be required to open up its markets to countries not prepared to provide an adequate equivalent degree of market access, and the concerns of many other Members that the GATS not evolve into a tangled web of bilateral sectoral deals, i.e. into a regime of sectoral managed trade at odds with basic GATT principles of rules- based multilateral liberalization". *Ibid.* at 283.

affecting trade in services are administered fairly and impartially. There is a requirement that judicial, arbitral or administrative tribunals review decisions affecting trade in services. Paragraph 4 of Article VI cites the objective of ensuring that measures relating to professional qualification and licensing requirements do not constitute unnecessary barriers to trade in services. Thus the Council for Trade in Services "shall, through the appropriate bodies it may establish, develop any necessary disciplines". The "disciplines" will ensure that the requirements are based on objective and transparent criteria, "such as competence and the ability to supply the service". Under paragraph 5, where the member has undertaken a commitment in a particular sector, licensing and other requirements shall not be applied so as to nullify or impair these commitments.

Article VII encourages agreements between members facilitating mutual recognition of qualifications to provide a service. Paragraph 5 says, however, that "wherever appropriate, recognition should be based on multilaterally agreed criteria".

Article VIII on monopolies and exclusive service suppliers does not disallow such arrangements, but establishes a requirement that Article II on MFN be adhered to in this context, and that activities in these sectors honour other commitments entered into by members under the GATS.

Article IX is striking in that it clearly anticipates the eventual inclusion in the WTO of competition rules. It states that certain business practices other than monopolies "may restrain competition and thereby restrict trade in services". Thus, in paragraph 2, members must enter into consultations with other members with a view to eliminating such practices. This is an inconclusive provision, but the setting out of an informational and reformist burden on members engaging in such practices is significant.

Article X put off the question of emergency safeguard measures with regard to services. It calls for multilateral negotiations on this subject to be completed within 3 years. However, paragraph 2 allows members to withdraw specific commitments for emergency safeguard purposes after a period of one year from the date of the commitment coming into force, if the member can show cause that it cannot wait for the result of the negotiations on services safeguards.

Freedom of international financial transfers relating to specific commitments is required under Article XI. Article XIII contains an exception to this, which allows restrictions in the service area and its underlying financing so long as there is a serious balance of payments difficulty. However, such a restrictive measure must be temporary. Article XIII calls for multilateral negotiations on the eventual inclusion of government procurement in services within the Agreement.

The GATS has a general exceptions provision in Article XIV, of a type quite similar to Article XX of the GATT Agreement. Non-discriminatory measures may be applied in the services context in order to, among other objectives, protect public morals; human, animal and plant life or health; or, if necessary, secure compliance with laws relating to the prevention of fraudulent practices and the protection of the privacy of individuals, among other objectives. Article XV calls for negotiations to eliminate trade-distorting subsidies in the services area.

Part III of the GATS, commencing with Article XVI, describes the actual procedures by which members are to make individual service-liberalising commitments. Part 2 of Article XVI on market access lists the types of measures members may not maintain or adopt in sectors where market access commitments have been undertaken towards service providers from other WTO members, unless otherwise indicated in the member's schedule. The list includes the following: limitations on the number of service suppliers, or on the total value or number of service transactions; limits on the number of persons a supplier may employ; restrictions on the type of legal entity through which a service may be provided; and limitations on the participation of foreign capital in the service operation.

Article XVII requires national treatment for other members' service suppliers. Under paragraph 3, treatment shall be considered "less favourable" if it modifies the conditions of competition in favour of services or suppliers of the member, in comparison with like services or suppliers of any other member. This provision is obviously analogous to Article III of the original GATT Agreement.

Part IV, on the subject of "Progressive Liberalisation", displays the gradualism so characteristic of GATT/WTO legal development. Paragraph 1 of Article XIX, on negotiation of specific commitments, requires that members shall enter into successive rounds of negotiations not later than five years from the date of entry into force of the WTO Agreement and periodically thereafter, with a view to achieving a "progressively higher level of liberalisation".[8]

Article XX outlines the nature of national schedules of specific commitments, with Article XXI providing the procedures for modifying these scheduled commitments. The core concept here is that measures inconsistent with Article XVI on market access and Article XVII on national treatment must be set out in a national list. Terms and limitations on market access, as well as qualifications on national treatment, must be described by the member imposing the restriction. These "negative commitments" must be annexed to the Agreement and form an integral part of it. Under Article XXI, modification of schedules may take place at any time after three years have elapsed since the commitment was entered into. Paragraph 2 provides a requirement that members modifying a schedule enter negotiations for compensating any adversely affected member. Under paragraph 4, modification may not take place until compensation is set in conformity with the findings of an arbitration carried out for that purpose.

---

[8] Not surprisingly, this is followed by a limitation. Para. 2 of Art. XIX says that this liberalisation shall take place with due respect for national policy objectives and the level of development of individual members. The situation of developing countries will be taken into account and lower levels of market access expected from these members. The Council for Trade in Services is to carry out an assessment of trade in services and establish guidelines for the ongoing negotiations.

Disputes under the GATS Agreement are, as would be expected, handled within the structures of the DSU.

Annexes to the Services Agreement represent areas where trade liberalisation is both politically sensitive and contentious, as well as being very high on the trade agenda, including financial services, telecommunications, and air and maritime transport services.

The protocol on financial services encompasses insurance, banking, and general financial management services; with a substantial list of related activities appended.[9] Members are encouraged to regularise their approach to those measures taken to protect the interests of investors, depositors, and policy-holders, and to ensure the stability of the financial system.[10] Such measures are not to be used as a means of avoiding members' commitments under the Services Agreement. Members have somewhat greater freedom of exemption from the MFN commitment in the financial services sector,[11] and are given an option of earlier modification of commitments made in their individual schedules regarding financial services.[12]

The annex on telecommunications says that each member must ensure that any service supplier of any other member is to be accorded access to and use of telecommunications networks and services on a non-discriminatory basis for the supply of a service included in an individual country's schedule.[13] Members are to ensure that no condition is imposed on access to telecommunications networks other than what is necessary to safeguard public sector responsibilities, or to protect technical integrity. Developing countries may apply access conditions in order to strengthen their own domestic telecommunications infrastructure. Technology transfer to developing countries in this sector is encouraged. The application of Article II of the Services Agreement (the MFN principle) was postponed with regard to telecommunications.[14]

---

[9] See Wendy Dobson and Pierre Jacquet, *Financial Services Liberalization in the WTO*, (Institute for International Economics, Washington, 1998); see also Peter Morrison, "WTO Agreement Liberalizes Financial Services Market", 17:8 *International Financial Law Review* 53–56; and Dilip K Das, "Trade in Financial Services and the Role of the GATS Against the Backdrop of the Asian Financial Crises", (Dec 1998) 32:6 *Journal of World Trade* 79–114.

[10] On this point, see Sydney J Key, "Trade Liberalization and Prudential Regulation: the International Framework for Financial Services", (Jan 1999) 75:1 *International Affairs* 61–75.

[11] See Yi Wang, "Most Favored Nation Treatment Under the General Agreement on Trade in Services—And its Application in Financial Services", (Feb 1996) 30:1 *Journal of World Trade* 91–124.

[12] On the European dimension, see Philippe Metzger, "GATS and the European Union: Free Trade in Banking? I & II", *College of European Working Papers* No. 14 (1995), 13–76; 77–149.

[13] See Miriam Gonzalez-Durante, "Telecommunications and GATS 2000", (Dec 1999) 5:6 *International Trade Law and Regulation* 155–57; and Rachel Frid, "The Telecommunications Pact under the GATS: Another Step Towards the Rule of Law", (1997) 24:2 *Legal Issues of European Integration* 67–96.

[14] For an interesting case study on the specific effects of global telecommunications liberalisation, see Jennifer Laura Feltham, "Polish Communications Law: Telecommunications Takes Off in Transition Countries But at What Price Are They Becoming Wired?" (2000) 33 *Vanderbilt Journal of Transnational Law* 147.

GATS AT WORK: THE *BANANA* DISPUTE[15]

The issues raised in the famous *Banana Regime* case of 1997 were both great in number and of a striking complexity.[16] However, it was the powerful combination of GATT and GATS arguments put forward by the complainant parties that made the case so significant in the developing history of WTO case law.[17] In a manner that is sure to have profound implications in future WTO disputes, the Banana panel agreed with the US that the concept of "services" underlying the Services Agreement could be extended to include the "service" of providing or supplying a tradable good. Thus, many cases involving trade in goods are also likely to have a GATS component.

Bananas as a product were among the last holdouts in the creation of a Single European Market. It proved extremely difficult to devise a Europe-wide system for banana imports: a common regime that would satisfy numerous conflicting interests. When the EC did finally manage to affect a very complex and cumbersome compromise in 1993, it was negated at the WTO in a stunning and wide-ranging panel report handed down in May of 1997. The decision of the Appellate Body, essentially supportive of the panel report, followed in September 1997.[18]

The banana dispute is a clear instance of a WTO member's non-trade values coming into conflict with rules designed solely to promote liberalised trade. (It should go without saying that non-trade values only co-exist with protectionist motives, or regulatory values with a possibly protectionist effect.) As a starting point, it is necessary to realise that the various European Member States had very different interests when it came to the banana trade, because of the particular historical relationships maintained by those Member States with certain banana-exporting countries—mainly the so-called "ACP" countries—African, Caribbean and Pacific. Prior to the 1993 regime coming into force, the European dilemma was that some Member States imported their bananas from former colonies (each tending to prefer countries from their own historical sphere of influence), whereas others—notably Germany—relied upon the cheaper and more efficiently produced Latin American bananas, which were grown for the most part within the zone of US economic control.[19]

---

[15] *Ecuador, US and others v. EC: Regime for the Importation, Sale and Distribution of Bananas, Report of the Panel*, 22 May 1997 (WT/DS27/R) [hereinafter *Banana* Panel Report]; *Ecuador, US and others v. EC: Regime for the Importation, Sale and Distribution of Bananas, Report of the Appellate Body*, 25 September 1997 (WT/DS27/AB/R) [hereinafter Banana Appellate Body Report].

[16] The panel itself stated at the outset of its "findings" that, "this case is an exceedingly complex one". *Banana* Panel Report, para. 7.1.

[17] For an entertaining and complete discussion of the unique complexities of this case, see Raj Bhala, "The Bananas War", (2000) 31 *McGeorge Law Review* 839.

[18] In analysing the WTO dispute, it is worth anticipating our discussion of *Germany v. Council*, case C–280/93, ECR I–4973, wherein Germany attempted to challenge the banana regime on a number of grounds, including that it failed to comply with GATT law.

[19] See Bhala, *supra* n. 17, at 848–849.

In fact, the EC found itself, with regard to bananas, caught in a web of conflicting legal obligations. Under a "banana protocol" of 1956 (annexed to the Convention on Association of Overseas Countries and Territories with the Community, and as allowed for under Article 136 of the Treaty), Germany enjoyed a special arrangement that allowed it to import an annual quota of bananas free of customs duty. The abolition of Germany's special quota was made explicitly dependent upon the future realisation of the Common Market.[20] However, as has been noted, conflicting interests within the Community prevented the establishment of a single market in bananas until 1993. Other countries, which had come to rely mainly, if not entirely, on Latin American sources, were the Benelux countries, Denmark and Ireland. However, there was a 20 per cent tariff rate on bananas imported into these countries, in contrast to Germany's tariff-free quota.[21]

Then there were those countries—notably France, Italy and the UK—which imported bananas from their former colonies in Africa, the Caribbean and the Pacific region. These countries enjoyed significantly preferential trade terms with Europe under the Lomé Conventions (as of 1991, Lomé IV was in force).[22] To further complicate matters, special banana trade terms existed for territories of Spain and Portugal (Madeira and the Canary Islands) under their Treaties of Accession to the EC.[23]

Before the WTO banana dispute under examination here, there were in fact two earlier GATT panel decisions relating to European banana import practices. The earliest case, decided just before the inception of the new Europe-wide banana regime, declared the restrictions imposed by the ACP-sourcing EC member States to be GATT-illegal, and injurious to the Latin American producing states which brought the case. Soon after the creation of the new EC banana regime in 1993, Latin American producers brought another case against the EC, and won again.[24]

Those earlier panels had twice rejected the argument that GATT Article XXIV on the subject of free trade agreements (in this case, the Lomé Convention) justified the clear violation of Article I of the General Agreement, especially since the Lomé Conventions were trade and aid agreements, and not based on genuine reciprocity. The panels further refused to recognise an Article XX(h) exception (on commodity agreements), since the Lomé Convention was not in any sense a commodity agreement open to all. The panels rejected what was actually the most important, if least "legal" of the arguments: that the ACP countries would be economically devastated by a more drastic change in the

---

[20] See *Germany* v. *Council, supra* n. 18.

[21] See Bhala, *supra* n. 17, at 849.

[22] The Lomé Convention has been superceded by the new ACP-EC Agreement, the Cotonou Agreement of 2000.

[23] See Bhala, *supra* n. 17, at 848–850.

[24] See *ibid*. at 849–851.

European banana import regime. Under the pre-1995 GATT regime, these panel reports remained unadopted, having been blocked by the EC.[25]

Because of the changes brought about by the Uruguay Round, potential complainants against the European banana regime were guaranteed that a new panel report could not be blocked. Also, the Uruguay Round Agreements created important new causes of action that could assist in the construction of a successful case against Europe.

OUTLINE OF THE 1993 EUROPEAN BANANA REGIME

The EC is the world's largest importer of bananas, closely followed by the US. Within Europe, Germany has the highest rate of national consumption of bananas. The preamble to Regulation 404/93 on the common organisation of the market in bananas states that the new regime should permit Community-produced bananas and ACP bananas to be sold at satisfactory prices within the Community, without undermining imports of bananas from other third country suppliers. The regulation set out common quality and marketing standards across the Community. Title IV of the regulation, dealing with rules for trade with third country suppliers, was intended to protect ACP suppliers against a total loss of market share by regulating the proportion of share available to the various supplying regions. It is quite clear that full liberalisation of the banana trade would lead to such a collapse of the market for ACP bananas. The Community might have opted to source largely from ACP countries alone, had Germany not had such a strong vested interest in maintaining its supply of Latin American bananas.

The system of licenses was the most vexed, and legally complex, aspect of the regime. It was through an elaborate licensing regime that the EC sought to control not only the volume of bananas from each source, but also to protect the *traders* dealing in bananas. It was to be expected that there would be strong competition to obtain licenses for the importation of the cheaper Latin American bananas. With each source of bananas controlled for amount by a system of tariff quotas (the tariff would rise exorbitantly if the quota for each type was exceeded), the licensing system controlled *access* to trade in the various banana categories. This occurred against a background of established trade relationships between European traders, and the respective exporting source countries. However, the licenses were themselves tradable, and pre-existing trade relationships were not set in stone. Of enormous irritation to the Germans in particular was the fact that in order to expand one's current trade in Latin American bananas, it was necessary to buy a certain level of ACP bananas. Thus, no one could choose to develop a large-scale trade in Latin American

[25] See *EEC: Import Regime for Bananas*, DS38/R (not adopted); and *EEC: Member States' Import Regime for Bananas*, DS32/R (not adopted).

bananas without dealing to some degree in ACP bananas. On top of this, the system ensured that a certain significant percentage of licenses to deal in Latin American bananas were granted in the first instance to companies that had traditionally dealt in ACP bananas. In an elaborate scheme designed to maintain this delicate balance, the licenses were allocated so as to prevent a rush in the direction of Latin American bananas, by slowing down the ability of the larger companies to deal exclusively in those products. The idea was that trade in ACP bananas would be "subsidised" by the profits to be made in Latin American bananas.

Under the new regime, Latin American bananas were to come into the EC at a 20 per cent ad valorem duty, with 30 per cent of the total licenses to deal in these bananas allocated to dealers who had traditionally dealt in ACP and Community bananas. 65.5 per cent of the licenses went to traditional dealers in Latin American bananas, and 3.5 per cent to market newcomers. ACP bananas were to receive tariff free access to the European market, and could be imported under far simpler procedures than the third country bananas.

The dispute under discussion was brought before the WTO by Ecuador, Guatemala, Honduras, Mexico and the United States. Prior to the action being brought, certain other Latin American producing countries had entered into an arrangement with the EC in 1994, called the Banana Framework Agreement (BFA). The purpose of this agreement was obviously to ensure that there would be no further GATT/WTO challenges to the European banana trading system; in this, however, since not all the Latin American producer countries could be induced to participate, the agreement failed to achieve its purpose. In return for their co-operation, the BFA countries were granted better rates of tariff and guaranteed individual quotas. Designed to last until 2002, the agreement included Colombia, Costa Rica, Venezuela and Nicaragua.

Even the panel itself began its analysis by stating that "[t]his case is an exceedingly complex one".[26] There were six principal parties to the case, including the EC, and a full 20 third-party observers. This means that nearly one third of all WTO members at the time were one way or another involved in this case.[27]

---

[26] *Banana* Panel Report, para. 7.1.

[27] The panel granted more generous terms of third party participation to various countries than was strictly required under the wording of the DSU. This was because of the scale of the economic effect on those parties wishing to be heard and to remain as observers to the dispute. *Banana* Panel Report, para. 7.8.

The complainants objected to the presence of private lawyers in the proceedings. The panel's decision in this instance was that only government representatives could actually attend panel meetings. A number of reasons were given for this, including the fact that according to past practice, private lawyers were excluded when there was an objection from a party to the proceedings. The panel also said that there were concerns about the implications for costs on smaller members, and whether the presence of private lawyers would change the "intergovernmental character of WTO dispute settlement proceedings". As the panel saw it, no party would be adversely affected by this decision because each could still consult with their private lawyers in the course of the panel proceedings, and receive whatever advice they needed in the course of preparing their written submissions from non-governmental experts. *Banana* Panel Report, paras. 7.10–7.12.

A procedural point of some significance was the argument made by the EC that the US had no real legal interest in the outcome of the case. Banana exports from the US were minimal at best; virtually non-existent. The EC insisted that the US had not suffered any nullification or impairment of WTO benefits as required by Article 3.3 or 3.7 of the DSU.[28] Since there were no "advisory" opinions in the WTO system, the EC argued, the US could not bring this complaint from whose resolution it could not receive any effective remedy.[29]

The EC went so far as to say that this kind of dispute would undermine the DSU by leading to a situation of litigation "by all against all".[30] But the panel took a literal view of the matter. It stated that "no provision of the DSU contains any explicit requirement that a member must have a 'legal interest' as a prerequisite for requesting a panel . . ." and further that "we fail to see that there is, or should be, a legal interest test under the DSU".[31] The panel also said that

> "this view is corroborated by past GATT practice, which suggests that if a complainant claims that a measure is inconsistent with the requirements of GATT rules, there is not a requirement to show actual trade effects".[32]

In this regard, the panel scarcely took into account the changes brought about by the introduction of a binding dispute resolution system, and the implications for a new form of locus standi appropriate to the developing WTO system. Interestingly, the panel insisted that the GATT had been interpreted so as to protect "competitive opportunities" and not "actual trade flows".[33] It revisited a number of old GATT cases to demonstrate the traditional GATT emphasis on the "potentialities of exporters".[34] Clearly, this point of view provided an extremely broad mandate for the panel's own involvement in the trade behaviour of member countries.

The panel concluded,

> "even if the US did not have even a potential export interest, its internal market for bananas could be affected by the EC regime and that regime's effect on world supplies and prices".[35]

In the panel's opinion, the cost of bringing cases is sufficient deterrent to a situation of "all litigating against all".[36] This is surely as generous an approach to locus standi as one could imagine.

---

[28] *Banana* Panel Report, para. 7.48.
[29] *Banana* Panel Report, para. 7.48.
[30] *Banana* Panel Report, para. 7.47.
[31] *Banana* Panel Report, paras.7.49–7.50.
[32] *Banana* Panel Report, para. 7.50.
[33] *Banana* Panel Report, para. 7.50.
[34] *Banana* Panel Report, para. 7.50.
[35] *Banana* Panel Report, para. 7.50.
[36] *Banana* Panel Report, para. 7.51.

THE *BANANA* PANEL ON THE SUBSTANTIVE ISSUES ARISING IN THE CASE

The first substantive issue to be dealt with by the panel was the question of the EC's allocation, through tariff quotas, of market share for bananas among the various producing countries. The complainants argued that there was no country-specific part of the overall tariff quota for them, in contrast to the quota granted to the ACP and BFA countries, and that this violated Article XIII of the GATT.[37] The European defence was that preferences for the ACP countries were part of the obligations imposed by the Lomé Convention, whereas the quota arrangements with the Latin American countries part of the BFA, as well as the quota granted to non-traditional ACP bananas, were part of the EC's GATT schedule relating to the Agreement on Agriculture.[38] Thus, the argument went, there could be nothing discriminatory about these arrangements, as they were in effect devised with the approval of the GATT/WTO.

The panel pointed out that

> "the wording of Article XIII is clear. If QRs are used (as an exception to the general ban on their use in Article XI), they are to be used in the least trade-distorting manner possible".[39]

Article XIII:5 plainly states that Article XIII applies to the administration of tariff quotas as well as QRs. Under Article XIII:2, the objective is to ensure that, under the regime imposed, there is a correspondence between the share granted to parties with an export interest in the product, and the shares that would have existed in the absence of the restriction. The panel emphasised that Article XIII allows for "exceptions to one of the most basic GATT provisions—the general ban on quotas and other non-tariff restrictions contained in Article XI".[40]

The panel then embarked on a complicated analysis of the role of Article XIII in a case such as this: Article XIII(2)(d) speaks of reaching agreement with all members having a substantial interest in supplying the product, as to the fair distribution of the quota, based upon a previous representative period. But the panel refused to see "substantial interest" as being entirely dependent upon shares from a previous period, and stated that a determination of substantial interest "might well vary somewhat based on the structure of the market".[41]

As it happened, some of the BFA parties did have a substantial market share in Europe, and some did not. Those taking this action, left out of the BFA, did not. Was the European action permissible, then, in light of the fact that all those with a substantial interest in the most literal sense did get some agreed share? The panel pointed out that among those without a literal substantial interest

---

[37] *Banana* Panel Report, para. 7.65.
[38] *Banana* Panel Report, para. 7.66.
[39] *Banana* Panel Report, para. 7.68.
[40] *Banana* Panel Report, para. 7.68.
[41] *Banana* Panel Report, paras. 7.83–7.84.

based on share, some were treated better than others. Some without a substantial interest were given an assignment by agreement.[42] The panel found this to be a violation of Article XIII, because it entails a discriminatory allocation of tariff quota share.[43]

THE LOMÉ WAIVER

Separate arguments were made with regard to the effect of Europe's "Lomé waiver" on the allocation of tariff quota shares to the ACP countries. In 1994, Europe sought from the GATT and received the so-called Lomé waiver for its special treatment of banana imports from ACP countries. This was extended by the WTO General Council in October 1996.[44] Under the terms of the extension, Europe's Article I obligations for products originating in the Lome countries were waived until the year 2000.[45] The precise language used was: "to the extent necessary to permit the EC to provide preferential treatment for products originating in ACP states as required by the . . . Fourth Lomé Convention".[46]

The panel asked whether the preferential treatment being shown to bananas was in fact "required" by the Lomé Convention; and also whether an Article I waiver extends as far as to cover a waiver of Article XIII obligations.[47]

For its part, the EC argued that a WTO panel was not authorised to interpret the meaning of the Lomé Convention. The panel replied that since the GATT contracting parties incorporated a reference to the Convention into the Lomé waiver, the meaning of the Convention became a GATT issue, at least to that extent.[48] In this light, the panel proceeded to examine the relevant provisions of the Convention.

Protocol 5 of the Convention states that

"In respect of banana exports to the Community markets, no ACP State shall be placed, as regards access to its traditional markets, in a less favourable situation than in the past or at present".[49]

The panel said that the complainants correctly pointed out that Protocol 5 does not guarantee that a certain level of banana exports will be achieved.[50] The panel reasoned that, since the ACP countries used to have heavily protected market access in a few Member States of the EC, "the issue is how the EC could fulfil its obligations under Protocol 5 on an EC-wide market".[51] The panel's

[42] *Banana* Panel Report, para. 7.89.
[43] *Banana* Panel Report, para. 7.90.
[44] *Banana* Panel Report, para. 7.96.
[45] *Banana* Panel Report, para. 7.96.
[46] *Banana* Panel Report, para. 7.96.
[47] *Banana* Panel Report, para. 7.96.
[48] *Banana* Panel Report, paras. 7.97–7.98.
[49] *Banana* Panel Report, para. 7.99.
[50] *Banana* Panel Report, para. 7.100.
[51] *Banana* Panel Report, para. 7.100.

view was that the EC was entitled to conclude that the Convention "required" the allocation to ACP countries in an amount equal to their pre-1991 best-ever exports to the EC—but not in amounts in excess of that.[52]

The panel's first inclination was to say that the Lomé waiver only covered GATT Article I violations. However, it looked at the question of whether the EC could honour its Lomé commitment only by a violation of Article XIII. In order to give what the panel calls "real effect" to the Lomé waiver, it needed to cover Article XIII to the extent necessary to allow Europe to allocate country-specific tariff quota shares through the method of calculation chosen.[53] Thus, logically, the waiver had to be interpreted by the panel to allow this.[54]

AGRICULTURE AGREEMENT ISSUES

The EC argued that the provisions of the Agriculture Agreement prevail over GATT rules such as Article XIII, and that the tariff commitments for BFA countries were included in the EC schedules to the Agriculture Agreement.[55] The panel accepted the general proposition, but said that there must also "be a provision of the Agreement on Agriculture that is relevant to the dispute, in order for this to apply".[56] Indeed, the panel continued, the whole purpose of the Agreement on Agriculture is to bring trade in agricultural products within the GATT discipline.[57] Further, the Agreement, while containing provisions on market access, does not allow for country-specific allocations of tariff quotas.[58] Article 4.2 of the Agreement actually prohibits the use of certain non-tariff barriers.[59] Therefore, the panel found no permission in the Agriculture Agreement for Article XIII-inconsistent allocations of market share and while the allocation to the ACP countries was saved, in the panel's view, by the Article I (and thus Article XIII) waiver, the BFA arrangements were not saved by any such "permission".

LICENSING PROCEDURES CHALLENGED UNDER GATT

The banana import licensing procedures, immensely complicated and clearly discriminatory, were challenged in over 40 claims made under the Uruguay Round Licensing Agreement, the TRIMS Agreement, and Articles I and III of the GATT Agreement.[60] As a general matter, insofar as the very complex

---

[52] *Banana* Panel Report, paras. 7.101–7.103.
[53] *Banana* Panel Report, para. 7.106.
[54] *Banana* Panel Report, para. 7.110.
[55] *Banana* Panel Report, paras. 7.112, 7.120.
[56] *Banana* Panel Report, para. 7.122.
[57] *Banana* Panel Report, para. 7.122.
[58] *Banana* Panel Report, para. 7.124.
[59] *Banana* Panel Report, para. 7.124.
[60] *Banana* Panel Report, para. 7.143.

scheme of allocating import licenses for Latin American bananas tended to encourage certain marketing practices, the system was found to infringe GATT/WTO rules with respect to nearly all of the grounds raised.[61] As noted above, the licensing scheme required that a trader purchase a certain quantity of Community or ACP bananas in order to increase market share of imports from Latin American countries. The panel found violations under all the instruments mentioned above except the TRIMS Agreement, which it found unnecessary to decide upon, having already established an Article III violation.[62] Interestingly, the Lomé waiver did not let Europe off the hook with regard to its Article I obligations for licensing procedures. The waiver, the panel said, must be interpreted narrowly.[63]

THE GATS ISSUES

The US put the GATS Agreement to brilliant and extremely effective use in this dispute. While the complainants enjoyed substantial success in their GATT-based arguments (relating to trade in goods), the GATS issues were by far the more interesting and innovative. The US and its co-complainants in the case argued that the European banana licensing procedures were inconsistent with Article II (MFN) and Article XVII (national treatment) of the GATS, insofar as they discriminated in favour of EC and ACP banana *distributors*. This logic represented a new concept at work in the GATT/WTO system. Not only could a domestic regime harm the interests of the producers of goods; it could simultaneously harm the interests of the distributors of those goods.

Interestingly, the EC had undertaken a full commitment to the liberalisation of its wholesale services sector, and included that in its GATS schedule. It was on this basis that the US argued that the EC was no longer free to restrict access to its services market in the manner apparent in its banana licensing scheme. The EC replied that the measures implementing the Community's banana regime were aimed at trade in goods, and did not affect trade in services in the true sense. Moreover, the EC insisted, the complainants' own service *suppliers* were not being discriminated against in any event.

The panel first asked whether the EC measures were measures affecting trade in services. The Europeans insisted that the GATS Agreement was "to regulate trade in services as such, and that it covers the supply of services as products in their own right".[64] Further, the EC argued that the GATS was not concerned with the indirect effects of measures relating to trade in goods on the supply of services. Europe pointed out, and with good reason, that if a national measure relating to trade in goods were covered by a GATT waiver, then the waiver

[61] See discussion in *Banana* Panel Report, paras. 7.168–7.273.
[62] *Banana* Panel Report, paras. 7.183–7.187.
[63] *Banana* Panel Report, paras. 7.196–7.204 (see especially para. 7.203).
[64] *Banana* Panel Report, para. 7.277.

could be voided by a finding of a GATS violation, which would be illogical.[65] This EC objection made a good deal of sense, and the distinction is an important one. Is the supply of goods (especially goods the subject of GATT-based arguments in the same dispute) a "service" in its own right, as that term is used in the agreement? Did the GATS Agreement intend that it should be so treated?

In an enormously important decision, the panel rejected the EC's view, and said that there can be overlap between the GATT and GATS Agreements. As the panel put it,

> "The scope of the GATS encompasses any measure of a member to the extent it affects the supply of a service regardless of whether such measure directly governs the supply of a service or whether it regulates other matters but nevertheless affects trade in services".[66]

There is a most significant discussion by the panel of the scope of the GATS Article II obligation.[67] The scope of GATS having been defined in Article I to include "measures by members affecting trade in services", any exception to the general obligation, the panel explained, must be explicitly provided for.[68] Article II:2 states that "A member may maintain a measure inconsistent with paragraph 1 provided that such a measure is listed in, and meets the conditions of, the Annex on Article II exemptions."

As the panel saw it, the EC had not listed any Article II-inconsistent measures relating to "wholesale trade services".[69] Thus, "[t]he EC is fully bound by its obligations under Article II:1 in relation to 'wholesale trade services' ".[70] The panel pointed out that Article XVII of the GATS, on national treatment, has a paragraph which says,

> "[f]ormally identical or formally different treatment shall be considered to be less favourable if it modifies the conditions of competition in favour of services or . . . suppliers of the Member compared to like services of any other member".

The panel also stated that this was the proper interpretation to put on the language of Article II. "Treatment no less favourable" should be interpreted as meaning that there should be no modification in the conditions of competition.[71]

From here it is only a short step to the panel finding that the licensing system constitutes discrimination against service suppliers of the complainants' origin,

---

[65] *Banana* Panel Report, para. 7.278.

[66] *Banana* Panel Report, paras. 7.282–7.286.

[67] *Banana* Panel Report, para. 7.298 and following.

   Art. II of the GATS Agreement states that "With respect to any measure covered by this Agreement, each member shall accord immediately and unconditionally to services and service suppliers of any other member treatment no less favorable than that it accords to like services and service suppliers of any other country."

[68] *Banana* Panel Report, para. 7.298.

[69] *Banana* Panel Report, para. 7.298.

[70] *Banana* Panel Report, para. 7.298.

[71] See *Banana* Panel Report, paras. 7.299–7.305.

in a manner inconsistent with the requirements of Articles II and XVII of the GATS Agreement.

THE EC BANANA REGIME AND THE APPELLATE BODY

Contrary to its usual stance, the Appellate Body took a stricter line than the panel against the challenged measures. As a preliminary matter, the Appellate Body decided that member countries should be allowed to have private counsel present during Appellate Body hearings.[72] The Appellate Body stated that

> "representation by counsel of a government's own choice may well be a matter of particular significance, especially for developing country members, to enable them to participate fully in dispute settlement proceedings".[73]

Because the Appellate Body's mandate is to review only issues of law or legal interpretations of the panel, the Body continued, "it is particularly important that governments be represented by qualified counsel in Appellate Body proceedings".[74]

As for the legal interest of the US in pursuing the complaint, the Appellate Body agreed with the panel that the US was fully justified, in that it had a "potential export interest" in bananas, and its own internal market would experience the effects of the EC regime on world supplies and prices of bananas.[75] The Appellate Body also agreed that nothing in the Agreement on Agriculture indicates that market access concessions made as a result of the agriculture negotiations could be inconsistent with the provisions of Article XIII of the GATT, thus disallowing this avenue of escape for the EC regarding the BFA arrangements.[76] Following upon this determination, the Appellate Body upheld the panel's strict view of Article XIII with respect to the non-discriminatory administration of tariff quotas. The Appellate Body resoundingly agreed that it was discriminatory for some but not all WTO members having a substantial interest in supplying bananas to the European market to be allocated specific shares.[77]

With regard to the Lomé waiver question, the Appellate Body adopted a stricter approach than the panel, as indicated above. The Appellate Body stated "[i]t is clear that the use of the term 'required' [in the waiver] is not accidental", and agreed with the panel that duty free market access and the allocation of tariff quota shares to traditional ACP suppliers (to the level of pre-1991 best ever export volumes) was "required".[78] However, as to whether the Article I waiver extends to Article XIII, the Appellate Body was firm. It

---

[72] *Banana* Appellate Body Report, paras. 4–12.
[73] *Banana* Appellate Body Report, para. 12.
[74] *Banana* Appellate Body Report, para. 12.
[75] *Banana* Appellate Body Report, paras. 132–138.
[76] *Banana* Appellate Body Report, paras. 153–158.
[77] *Banana* Appellate Body Report, paras. 159–163.
[78] *Banana* Appellate Body Report, paras. 168, 172–174, 178.

stated that "[t]he wording of the Lomé waiver is clear and unambiguous" and does not mention any other GATT provision.[79] The Appellate Body made the further interesting point that "although Articles I and XIII of the GATT are both non-discriminatory provisions, their relationship is not such that a waiver from the obligations under Article I implies a waiver from the obligations under Article XIII".[80] It commented that the GATT system had always been very limited and narrow in its approach to waivers, and that waivers are very rare.[81] As for certain of the differential procedures and administrative requirements attaching to the two licensing systems, depending on the source of the bananas involved, the Appellate Body upheld the panel's finding of Article I and Article III:4 violations.[82]

The Appellate Body added strength to the panel's findings on the relationship of the GATS Agreement to this case. The EC once again raised the fundamental argument that its licensing measures were not measures "affecting trade in services" within the meaning of Article I:1 of the GATS Agreement.[83] The complainants, for their part, argued that the GATT and GATS Agreements are not mutually exclusive, and may well overlap in this way.[84] The Appellate Body determined that there was "no legal basis for an a priori exclusion of measures within the EC banana import licensing regime from the scope of the GATS",[85] making the following important statement on the matter:

> "Whether a certain measure affecting the supply of a service related to a particular good is scrutinised under the GATT 1994 or the GATS, or both, is a matter that can only be determined on a case-by-case basis. For these reasons, we agree with the panel that the EC banana import licensing procedures are subject to both the GATT 1994 and the GATS, and that the GATT 1994 and the GATS may overlap in application to a particular measure".[86]

Thus, the potential scope of application of the GATS Agreement expanded enormously.

The EC, recognising the importance of the issues at stake, appealed the panel's finding that Article II of the GATS on MFN should be extended to interpret "treatment no less favourable" to mean "providing no less favourable conditions of competition".[87] The Appellate Body was less than satisfied that the panel relied on analogies to national treatment provisions in the GATT Article III and GATS Article XVII, when in fact the interpretation of MFN was at stake, and not national treatment. However, it stated that "[i]f Article II of the GATS (MFN) was not applicable to *de facto* discrimination, it would not be difficult—

---

[79] *Banana* Appellate Body Report, paras. 182–183.
[80] *Banana* Appellate Body Report, para. 183.
[81] *Banana* Appellate Body Report, para. 187.
[82] *Banana* Appellate Body Report, paras. 205–207; 208–216.
[83] *Banana* Appellate Body Report, para. 218.
[84] *Banana* Appellate Body Report, para. 219.
[85] *Banana* Appellate Body Report, para. 220.
[86] *Banana* Appellate Body Report, para. 221.
[87] *Banana* Appellate Body Report, paras. 228–230.

and indeed it would be a good deal easier in the case of trade in goods—to devise discriminatory measures aimed at circumventing the basic purpose of that Article".[88] Thus the Appellate Body upheld the panel on this point, at least with regard to the essentials, as well. It also upheld the panel on a number of specific points regarding violation of Articles II and XVII of the GATS Agreement by the banana regime licensing system.[89] The EC also failed in its attempt to revisit whether the US had experienced nullification or impairment, or had suffered no trade damage whatsoever.[90] On the substance, the banana regime case was a clean sweep for US-based transnational fruit traders, for an expansively minded WTO jurisprudence, and for the latent capabilities of the GATS Agreement.

After years of contention over the nature and scope of reform necessary for the EC to comply with the panel and Appellate Body reports, in April of 2001, the two principal parties finally reached agreement.[91] The agreement will require the EC to move in two stages to a tariff-only system by the year 2006, abandoning the licensing scheme that was so effectively targeted under the GATS Agreement. Until that time, a transitional "historical reference" licensing scheme will be introduced. The US agreed to suspend, also from July 1, the $200 million in sanctions that had been approved by the WTO, in the form of tariffs against various EC-produced goods. The US also agreed not to oppose a GATT Article I waiver that would allow the EC to continue preferential treatment for ACP countries under the Cotonou Agreement, the successor agreement to the Lomé Conventions.

FUJI-KODAK:[92] A SPECIAL ROLE FOR THE SERVICES AGREEMENT?

To understand this case fully in its contemporary context, it is first necessary to realise that Japan has occupied a peculiar place in the GATT system since its entry in 1955.[93] As might be expected, Japan has been an extraordinarily reluctant plaintiff at the GATT, although it has been a target of US and European complaints on a relatively frequent basis. Japan has also been a regular target of anti-dumping actions by a number of countries. Added to this is the fact that Japan, Europe and the US have found themselves in a unique trade triangle, with

---

[88] *Banana* Appellate Body Report, paras. 231–233.
[89] *Banana* Appellate Body Report, paras. 240–248.
[90] *Banana* Appellate Body Report, paras. 249–254.
[91] See Eliza Patterson, "US–EC Banana Dispute Agreement", *ASIL Insight*, available at http:www.asil.org/insights.htm.
[92] *US v. Japan: Measures Affecting Consumer Photographic Film and Paper*, report of the Panel, 31 March 1998 (WT/DS44/R) [hereinafter *Japan Film* Panel Report].
[93] Japan's entry into the GATT on 10 September 1955 was vehemently opposed by thirteen GATT members, including Australia, Austria, Belgium, Brazil, Cuba, France, Haiti, India, Luxembourg, the Netherlands, Rhodesia-Nyasalund, South Africa and the UK. Accordingly, under Art. 35 of GATT 1947, these countries were not obliged to accord Japan most-favoured-nation status. For an interesting analysis of Japanese trade issues, see David Flath, A Perspective on Japanese Trade Policy and Japan–US Trade Friction, at http://www.gsb.columbia.edu/japan/pdf/wp151.pdf.

the EC and US traditionally eager to establish favourable terms of trade with Japan.[94] Both the US and EC have found themselves at times in a state of trade conflict, and at others in a state of trade co-operation, with Japan. The prolonged Japanese recession of recent years, and the new legalism of the WTO, will clearly contribute to a change in these established trade configurations.

The Fuji-Kodak case has often been dismissed as a mere curiosity in the history of trade relations between the US and Japan, its importance not fully understood. Since the dispute represents one of the few occasions on which the US has failed at the GATT/WTO as plaintiff, it is worth examining US motives in shaping this unusual complaint.

The dispute began as a complaint made by the Kodak film company to the United States Trade Representative (USTR), to the effect that it was being excluded from the Japanese market by a supposedly "closed" distribution system. Kodak's argument was that Japan had allowed relationships between manufacturer, wholesalers, and retailers to form a sort of cartel, which had the effect of excluding Kodak from the Japanese film market. Fuji, in turn, maintained that Kodak had failed to reach Japanese consumers with product innovation.

Although no argument under the Services Agreement came to fruition in this case, the role of the Services Agreement in the background is worth noting. It could be said that the most powerful US arguments in the case were those brought under GATS. However, these were dropped before the case formally began—after the US apparently received from Japan an enormously significant concession concerning the liberalisation of its retail sector in general. The GATS issue was also unrelated to the main questions initially raised by Kodak. Kodak itself certainly did not include demands for liberalisation of the retail sector in its complaint to the USTR.

The initial WTO case was divided into three parts.[95] The first of these involved a competition law argument, in which the US argued that Japan was not enforcing its own competition laws, and was allowing the operation of the exclusionary cartels referred to above.[96] Although TRIMS states that competition rules might factor in future WTO provisions, there is at present no competition law aspect to WTO law. The US based this part of the case on an obscure 1960 GATT decision expressing a collective commitment to enforcing domestic competition laws, although the legal significance of this decision was unclear.[97] This arm of the case was ultimately suspended, but we will revisit the question of competition rules and the WTO in the section dealing with the WTO's Millennium Round.

---

[94] For a dramatic instance of this problematic triangular relationship, see *EC v. Japan: Trade in Semi-Conductors* Report of the Panel adopted on 4 May 1988 (L/6309–35S/116).

[95] *Japan Film* Panel Report, para. 1.2.

[96] *Japan Film* Panel Report, para. 4.18.

[97] Cabinet Decision Concerning Liberalization of Inward Direct Investment of 6 June 1967 ("1967 Cabinet Decision").

The second argument was based on GATS, and in light of the banana case, it is not unreasonable to think that the US could have won on this point. The gist of the US argument was that Japan's law protecting small and medium retailers[98] served to discriminate against the distribution of foreign products—specifically against film—on the theory that larger stores were more likely to carry foreign products.[99]

The US had, for years—notably under the Structural Impediments Initiative talks of the early 1990s—sought the abolition of this law, since it was seen as hindering the spread of US and other foreign mega-retailers in Japan, particularly in Japanese provincial areas.[100] In short, when Japan promised to abolish the Large Scale Retail Stores Law (LSRSL) and replace it with a far less obstructionist retail placement law, the US agreed to drop the GATS arm of this case. Thus, the US had achieved, through the power of GATS, something it had sought, quite apart from the Kodak complaint, for a number of years. Rather than economic protectionism, which was the overt rationale for the old LSRSL, the new laws had an environmental focus, and were based on a European model in order to secure them against future WTO challenge. While the old LSRSL had not been rigorously enforced in recent years either, it had nevertheless slowed the pace of mega-retailing in suburban Japan. The new law was unlikely to maintain this protection.

It is interesting to note that not one politician in Japan was reported to support this change in law. Through pressure exerted by MITI, in which the modernising and liberalising faction managed to prevail, politicians were convinced that this was a concession worth making, and that it would enhance Japan's reputation as an open economy.

The principal argument in the remaining case was that a group of Japanese government "counter measures" relating to the distribution sector, competition law and the retail sector, had constituted a non-violation nullification and impairment of US benefits under the WTO—benefits obtained through tariff concessions made by Japan over the decades in the film area.[101] There were also arguments made that these same measures had violated Article III:4 and Article X of the GATT Agreement.[102]

Without examining the panel's reaction to these arguments in detail, the Japanese side argued back strongly that the US was attempting to substitute prejudice and innuendo for genuine proof.[103] The panel was persuaded, and the US lost on all counts in the formal dispute.[104] It is of significance that, in fact, the US film market is a virtual mirror image of the Japanese film market—the same arrangements between and among manufacturer, wholesaler and retailer

---

[98] Called the Daitenho, it is generally referred to, in English, as the Large Scale Retail Stores Law (LSRSL).

[99] *Japan Film* Panel Report, para. 2.26.

[100] *Japan Film* Panel Report, paras. 5.127, 5.160.

[101] *Japan Film* Panel Report, at n. 220.

[102] *Japan Film* Panel Report, paras. 1.2, 3.7.

[103] *Japan Film* Panel Report, paras. 3.19, 3.21, 3.24, 3.33, 3.37.

[104] *Japan Film* Panel Report, paras. 10.402–10.404.

exist to a large degree. Additionally, Japanese film products manage to gain about the same level of market share in the US as US film manufacturers gain in Japan. The panel was unconvinced that the US had suffered loss of benefit, or that the Japanese had violated any GATT provision, based purely on a series of so-called government directives to the distribution sector.[105] The US did not appeal any aspect of the case, and the panel report was adopted.

The strategic use by the US of the GAT S Agreement in the context of the Fuji-Kodak case clearly demonstrates the Agreement's chameleon-like power. It seems capable of attaching itself to a wide variety of disputes, changing its character in order to challenge an equally broad array of national arrangements not contemplated as falling within the scope of the Services Agreement as originally conceived.

CANADIAN AUTOMOTIVE INDUSTRY CASE[106]

The EC and Japan raised arguments under Articles II and XVII (MFN and national treatment) of the GATS Agreement in their challenge to Canada's preferential treatment of certain auto companies, based on historical relationships and the maintenance of certain levels of domestic product input and Canadian value added. In a similar fashion to the web of challenges brought in the Banana dispute, in the Canadian Automotive Industry case the complainants also linked discrimination against certain foreign products to discrimination against foreign services and service suppliers—services closely related to the actual sale of the products in question, including their distribution. The expansive nature of the Services Agreement, first demonstrated in the *Banana* dispute, was strongly confirmed by the panel in the *Canadian Automotive Industry* case.

However, the Appellate Body demonstrated a certain degree of discomfort with the panel's expansive reading of the provisions of GATS Article II into this set of facts. While not overturning the panel's conclusion on the merits, the Appellate Body refused to uphold the panel's conclusions regarding GATS Article II on the basis that the panel did not sufficiently justify those conclusions. The Appellate Body made clear that the use of GATS for purposes such as the ones advanced by European and Japan in this case must be approached with the greatest caution, as explained below.

The complainants in this case argued that the import duty exemptions offered by Canada to certain manufacturers were inconsistent with GATS Article II (MFN), because US suppliers were granted more favourable status than those of either the EC or Japan.[107] They also complained that the Canadian value added requirements were inconsistent with Article XVII of the GATS (national

[105] *Japan Film* Panel Report, para. 10.401.
[106] See discussion of the *Canadian Automotive Industry* case as it relates to investment measures in ch. 4.
[107] *Canadian Automotive Industry* Panel Report, para. 10.223.

treatment), because in requiring manufacturers to achieve a minimum of Canadian value added in order to benefit from the import duty exemption, they gave more favourable treatment to services supplied in Canada than to services of other members supplied through modes 1 (cross border supply) and 2 (consumption abroad).[108]

Canada countered with the argument that the import duty exemption is not in fact a measure affecting trade in services, within the meaning of Article I of the Services Agreement. As far as Article II is concerned, Canada argued that the exemption does not modify the conditions of competition in favour of services and service suppliers of the US, largely because vertical integration in the industry makes competition at the wholesale level non-existent.[109]

As to whether the Canadian value added requirement violates Article XVII of the Services Agreement, Canada argued that it had inserted the relevant limitations on its commitments in these sectors. It further maintained that the supply of the relevant services through modes 1 and 2 would not be technically feasible from abroad in any event; and that, if feasible, there would be an inherent competitive disadvantage due to the foreign character of the service, not the Canadian value added requirement.[110]

The panel proceeded to an important discussion of the meaning of "measure affecting trade in services", as that language is used in Article I of the Services Agreement, and whether it is applicable to the import duty exemption in particular. The panel referred to the Banana decision, and noted that both the panel and Appellate Body in that case found that the term "affecting" in Article I of the GATS Agreement had a broad scope of application.[111] But rather than determine this issue in the abstract, the panel decided to address the larger question in the course of determining whether or not there had been unequal treatment for service suppliers from certain WTO members.[112]

With respect to a possible violation of Article II of the Services Agreement because of the import duty exemption, the complainants raised a convoluted argument. They maintained that the import duty exemption affects the supply of wholesale trade services, as it modifies the conditions of competition between the beneficiaries of the duty-free treatment and other wholesale trade service suppliers of imported motor vehicles that do not benefit from the same treatment. Since the exemption would affect the cost of the goods being distributed, it would indirectly affect the profitability of the related wholesale trade services.[113]

Eager to proceed to the broadest reading of the Services Agreement, the panel noted that it cannot be maintained that the exemption does not indirectly affect

---

[108] *Canadian Automotive Industry* Panel Report, para. 10.224.
[109] *Canadian Automotive Industry* Panel Report, para. 10.225.
[110] *Canadian Automotive Industry* Panel Report, para. 10.226.
[111] *Canadian Automotive Industry* Panel Report, para. 10.231.
[112] *Canadian Automotive Industry* Panel Report, para. 10.234.
[113] *Canadian Automotive Industry* Panel Report, paras. 10.237–10.238.

the supply of distribution services. As with the services at issue in the Banana case, the panel said,

> "the import duty exemption granted only to manufacturer beneficiaries bears upon conditions of competition in the supply of distribution services, regardless of whether it directly governs or indirectly affects the supply of such services".[114]

The panel treated the import duty exemption as falling in a category of measures, as identified by the Appellate Body in the Banana case, as involving a "service relating to a particular good or a service supplied in conjunction with a particular good", which "could be scrutinized under both the GATT 1994 and the GATS".[115]

Canada raised the powerful counter-argument that then all tariffs could be found to affect trade in services, especially distribution services. If that were the case, Canada continued, wouldn't certain GATT-legal measures in the form of tariffs become illegal when seen in the light of GATS?[116] The logic is impressive, and the panel declined to deal with the issue head on. Instead, the panel said that it need not determine that question, since it did not arise here. Rather, the panel stated, the issue was "the effect of measures which reserve access to duty-free goods to a closed category of service suppliers, while excluding others".[117]

The panel accepted the Banana analogy presented by the complainants, to the effect that there was no difference between the measures at issue in the two disputes. The panel stated,

> "We note that both sets of measures allow some wholesale trade service suppliers to import and resell under more favourable conditions, while putting at a competitive disadvantage other suppliers, who have to pay the tariff or buy the licenses out of the tariff quota".[118]

The panel further said that

> "In both cases there is an economic disadvantage. . . . [I]t is not relevant to distinguish between the measures at issue in EC—Bananas III and the measures at issue in this case on the basis of the extent of their effect on trade in services".[119]

The panel was unpersuaded by the arguments put forward regarding the effects of vertical integration in eliminating meaningful competition from the industry in any event. Rather, in the panel's view, because the benefit is granted to a limited and identifiable group of manufacturers and wholesalers of motor vehicles of some WTO members, the import duty exemption clearly does result in less favourable treatment accorded to services and service suppliers of other members within the meaning of Article II:1 of the Services Agreement.[120]

---

[114] *Canadian Automotive Industry* Panel Report, para. 10.239.
[115] *Canadian Automotive Industry* Panel Report, para. 10.239.
[116] *Canadian Automotive Industry* Panel Report, para. 10.240.
[117] *Canadian Automotive Industry* Panel Report, para. 10.242.
[118] *Canadian Automotive Industry* Panel Report, para. 10.246.
[119] *Canadian Automotive Industry* Panel Report, para. 10 246.
[120] *Canadian Automotive Industry* Panel Report, paras. 10.253–10.264.

The United States made submissions to the effect that Article V of the Services Agreement, which allows preferences within regional trade agreements (in a manner analogous to Article XXIV of the GATT Agreement), provides an exemption for Canada with regard to the violation of GATS Article II. The panel, however, accepted the view of complainants that these unilateral measures are not part of the NAFTA Agreement, and only benefit a small group of US service suppliers.[121]

The issue of Canadian value added and Article XVII (national treatment) of the Services Agreement were less controversial. It was noted that manufacturers receiving benefits under the Canadian regime were required to achieve a certain level of Canadian value added, with the purchase of various services also counting towards this aggregate level of CVA.[122] The complainants argued that this creates an incentive for beneficiaries to use services supplied within the Canadian territory, rather than like services from the territory of other WTO members, thus modifying the conditions of competition among service suppliers. Canada did not contest the effect on the supply of services of its CVA requirement.[123]

The panel accepted the principal arguments of the complainants, saying of the CVA requirement that it is "bound to have discriminatory effect against services supplied through modes 1 and 2, which are services of other members".[124] Canada did not appeal the panel's conclusion that the CVA requirements are inconsistent with Canada's obligations under Article XVII of the GATS.

GATS, THE IMPORT DUTY EXEMPTION, AND THE APPELLATE BODY

The Appellate Body, as indicated above, took a strikingly cautious line with regard to the application of Articles I and II of the Services Agreement to Canada's contested import duty exemption. While upholding the panel on a number of key issues, the Appellate Body backed away from endorsing the panel's enthusiastic extrapolation of the Banana panel and Appellate Body reasoning to the Canadian automotive dispute. In doing so, the Appellate Body expressed no real disapproval of the panel's approach; it merely implied that it wished to consider the scope of GATS in greater depth and in some other context.

Canada argued on appeal that the panel "mistakenly concluded that whether a measure is within the scope of GATS is determined by whether the measure is consistent with certain substantive obligations, such as Article II, and not by

---

[121] *Canadian Automotive Industry* Panel Report, paras. 10.269–10.272.

[122] *Canadian Automotive Industry* Panel Report, para. 10.291.

[123] *Canadian Automotive Industry* Panel Report, para. 10.292.

[124] *Canadian Automotive Industry* Panel Report, para. 10.307. Canada had attempted to argue that it had set out limitations in its schedule of GATS commitments, and thus was not bound to act in a non-discriminatory fashion regarding the services in question. However, the panel rejected this, stating that Canada had undertaken specific commitments in those sectors that the complainants claim to be affected by the CVA requirements, whereas the limitations that were listed do not cover the CVA requirements. See *ibid.*, para. 10.297.

whether the measure falls within Article I of the GATS".[125] The Appellate Body agreed that the panel skipped over a GATS Article I analysis, and stated that the logic of Article I:1 of GATS demanded that determination of whether a measure is covered by GATS must be made before the consistency of the measure in question with substantive provisions can be assessed.[126] Article II of GATS, the Appellate Body noted, states that it applies only to measures covered by the Agreement.[127]

What is required, the Appellate Body continued, to determine whether a measure is one affecting trade in services, is first an analysis of whether there is trade in services involved; and second, whether the measure affects trade in services within the meaning of Article I:1.[128] Having concluded that wholesale trade services of motor vehicles were at issue, and thus that there is trade in services, the Appellate Body proceeded to consider the fundamental issue of whether the measure affects trade in the service identified.[129]

The Appellate Body took note of Canada's contention, described above, that its import duty exemption, as tariff measure, is not a measure affecting trade in services, and that it should be seen as falling exclusively within the scope of GATT 1994.[130] It also noted that, relying on the Appellate Body in the Banana case, the panel identified the "service" at issue here as one "relating to a particular good", or "supplied in conjunction with the particular good", and one which could be scrutinised under both the GATT 1994 and GATS.[131] But the Appellate Body found that, unlike the situation in the Banana case, the panel in the Canadian Automotive case failed to examine any evidence relating to the provision of wholesale trade services of motor vehicles within the Canadian market, and thus

> "did not make any factual findings as to the structure of the market for motor vehicles in Canada, nor as to which companies actually provide wholesale trade services of motor vehicles".[132]

In this light, the Appellate Body further found that the panel had never examined "whether or how the import duty exemption affects wholesale trade service suppliers in their capacity as service suppliers". Rather, the panel simply applied the Banana case reasoning, without evidence of an actual similarity.[133] For this reason, the Appellate Body concluded that the panel did not provide a sufficient legal basis for its conclusion that the import duty exemption affects wholesale trade services of motor vehicles as services, or wholesale service sup-

---

[125] *Canadian Automotive Industry* Appellate Body Report, para. 148.
[126] *Canadian Automotive Industry* Appellate Body Panels Report, para. 151.
[127] *Canadian Automotive Industry* Appellate Body Panels Report, para. 152.
[128] *Canadian Automotive Industry* Appellate Body Panels Report, para. 155.
[129] *Canadian Automotive Industry* Appellate Body Report, paras. 156–158.
[130] *Canadian Automotive Industry* Appellate Body Report, para. 161.
[131] *Canadian Automotive Industry* Appellate Body Report, para. 162.
[132] *Canadian Automotive Industry* Appellate Body Report, paras. 163–164.
[133] *Canadian Automotive Industry* Appellate Body Report, para. 164.

pliers in their capacity as service suppliers. The panel was also faulted for its failure to articulate what it understood Article I:1 to require by the use of the term "affecting".[134] Very significantly, the Appellate Body stated that the panel ought to have then examined the facts surrounding the question of who supplies these services in Canada, and how such services are supplied. "It is not enough", the Appellate Body scolded, "to make assumptions". The panel should have "applied its interpretation of 'affecting trade in services' to the facts it should have found", the Appellate Body concluded.[135]

The Appellate Body conceded that the EC and Japan might well have been correct in their contention that the exemption has an effect on the operations in Canada of wholesale trade service suppliers in their capacity as service suppliers. But the panel merely made a conclusory statement, and according to the Appellate Body, that was "not good enough".[136]

Canada also argued that even if the GATS was held applicable to its measure, the panel erred in finding that the measure accorded less favourable treatment to services and service suppliers of any other WTO member under Article II:1 of the Services Agreement. The Appellate Body took up this question, examining whether the panel had set out the basis on which the measure accords less favourable treatment, either in fact or in law, to the services or service suppliers of certain Members.[137]

The Appellate Body was clearly concerned to set out interpretative guidelines for panels applying the *Banana* case reasoning to a wide variety of factual situations. The potential for the application of GATS to spin out of control is obvious, since virtually all disputes over trade in goods could be seen to have a services component of some kind. The question is whether the "services" are of a type and are "affected" in a manner contemplated by the Services Agreement itself.

The Appellate Body went on to state that if the determination is made that the measure is covered by GATS, then there must be an evaluation of whether the measure is consistent with the requirements of Article II:1 (MFN) of the Agreement. Article II:1 requires, the Appellate Body reminded us, that treatment by one member of services and service suppliers of any other member be compared with treatment of like services and suppliers of any other country. Taking these "core elements" into account, the Appellate Body reasoned, the panel should have interpreted Article II:1, made factual findings as to treatment of wholesale trade services and service suppliers of motor vehicles of different members present in Canada, and then applied its interpretation of Article II:1 to the facts as it found them.[138] Again, the Appellate Body was less than satisfied with the panel's approach; the panel "did none of this".[139] It did not inquire into the

---

134 *Canadian Automotive Industry* Appellate Body Report, para. 165.
135 *Canadian Automotive Industry* Appellate Body Report, para. 165.
136 *Canadian Automotive Industry* Appellate Body Report, para. 166.
137 *Canadian Automotive Industry* Appellate Body Report, para. 168.
138 *Canadian Automotive Industry* Appellate Body Report, para. 171.
139 *Canadian Automotive Industry* Appellate Body Report, para. 172.

structure of the wholesale trade services market in Canada; it did not explain how less favourable treatment resulted from the measure at issue. "Instead", the Appellate Body wrote, "it engaged in speculation about the 'possibility' of certain relationships".[140] When confronted with Canada's argument that the vertical integration in the industry actually eliminated competition between service suppliers at wholesale level, the panel, according to the Appellate Body, responded with findings that were in essence "pure speculation".[141] The Appellate Body found that the panel

> "failed to conduct an analysis of whether and how the import duty exemption affects wholesalers related to manufacturers which benefit from the import duty exemption, as compared with wholesalers related to manufacturers which do not benefit from the import duty exemption".[142]

The Appellate Body faulted the panel for finding a violation of Article II:1 of GATS on the basis that the import duty exemption was granted to a limited and identifiable group of manufacturers/wholesalers of motor vehicles. "The panel", wrote the Appellate Body, "appears to be saying here that the import duty exemption is granted to certain wholesalers of a limited number of members, and not to wholesalers of other members".[143] Therefore, the Appellate Body reasoned, the panel was "confusing the application of the import duty exemption to manufacturers with its possible effect on wholesalers".[144]

Most interesting of all, the Appellate Body objected to the fact that the panel conducted a goods analysis of the measure, and then "simply extrapolated its analysis of how the import duty exemption affects manufacturers to wholesale trade service suppliers of motor vehicles". The panel surmised that the import duty exemption "*ipso facto* affects conditions of competition among wholesalers *in their capacity as service suppliers*".[145] (Italics of the Appellate Body) As implied by the Appellate Body itself, these issues will require working out in the course of future complaints relying on the provisions of the Services Agreement. However, it is worth asking whether the Appellate Body did not protest too much at the panel's extrapolation, especially in the light of the expansionary legal overtones of the Banana case reasoning.

The Appellate Body made clear that it was not suggesting that the import duty exemption does not affect wholesale trade services of motor vehicles in Canada, nor that Canada is acting consistently with Article II:1 of the GATS. Rather, the Appellate Body stated, "We mean only to say that the panel, in this case, failed to substantiate its conclusion." As such, the Appellate Body had "no choice but to

---

[140] *Canadian Automotive Industry* Appellate Body Report, para. 172.
[141] *Canadian Automotive Industry* Appellate Body Report, paras. 172–174.
[142] *Canadian Automotive Industry* Appellate Body Report, para. 174.
[143] *Canadian Automotive Industry* Appellate Body Report, para. 180.
[144] *Canadian Automotive Industry* Appellate Body Report, para. 181.
[145] *Canadian Automotive Industry* Appellate Body Report, para. 181.

reverse the findings and conclusions of the panel relating to Article II:1 of the GATS".[146]

It is heartening that the Appellate Body has displayed an appropriate degree of caution, given the extraordinary legal potential of the Services Agreement, as shown in the *Banana* dispute, and as outlined in this chapter. It is worth quoting the final paragraph of the appeal decision in the *Canadian Automotive Industry* case in full:

> "In reaching our conclusion, we are mindful of the importance of the GATS as a new multilateral trade agreement covered by the WTO Agreement. This appeal is only the second case in which we have been asked to review a panel's findings on provisions of the GATS. Given the complexity of the subject matter of trade in services, as well as the newness of the obligations under the GATS, we believe that claims made under the GATS deserve close attention and serious analysis. We leave interpretation of Article II of the GATS to another case and another day".[147]

THE FUTURE OF GATS

The legal capabilities of the Services Agreement has everything to do with the wide range of meanings that adhere to the concept of "services" itself. To some extent, services indicate economic activity itself, and it is not surprising that the Appellate Body should engage in stock-taking before allowing panels to expand the scope of the agreement to an endless variety of factual situations. At the same time, strengthening the existing agreement will be at the top of the agenda for developed countries. In March 2001, service negotiating guidelines were agreed, which has been taken as "an important signal that WTO Members are ready and willing to move ahead in the mandated negotiations even in the absence of a new round [of negotiations]".[148] The WTO Services Council has presented these guidelines as "relatively development-friendly", in that they contain language addressing the concerns of developing countries over the liberalisation of their service sectors.[149]

The upcoming services negotiations have been targeted by NGOs on the basis that they represent a threat to basic services in the developing world, and will lead inevitably in the direction of privatisation and domination by multinational corporations of deregulated service sectors across the globe.[150] The WTO for its part has recently published a brochure entitled "GATS—Fact and Fiction", intended to counteract a growing movement against the further liberalisation of

---

[146] *Canadian Automotive Industry* Appellate Body Report, para. 183.
[147] *Canadian Automotive Industry* Appellate Body Report, para. 184.
[148] See *Bridges Trade Weekly News Digest*—Vol. 5, Number 12 (3 April 2001).
[149] *Ibid*.
[150] See Frances Williams, "WTO foresees tough talks on opening up of services provision; pressure group aims to highlight 'threat' to basic services", *Financial Times*, 16 March 2001, p. 12.

services.[151] This brief publication charges that "the negotiations and the GATS itself have become the subject of ill-informed and hostile criticism". "Scare stories", it says, "are invented and unquestionably repeated." The pamphlet derides the notion that "the right to maintain public services and the power to enforce health and safety standards are under threat", and argues that both are safeguarded under the Services Agreement. Readers are told, "Decision-making in open societies presupposes informed public discussion. It must be based on fact rather than fiction."

Each of the "charges" made by critics of the expansion of GATS are stamped with the word "FALSE", notably the accusation that the services negotiations will lead to loss of control by national governments over the provision of basic services, and the conditions for their regulation. The pamphlet also stamps as "FALSE" the charge that "GATS negotiations are secretive and anti-democratic". The pamphlet responds:

> "It is true that the GATS 2000 negotiations, like other negotiations in the WTO, are taking place between Governments and that meetings are not open to the press, the public or industry. But Governments are the representatives of their countries' interests as a whole, and have a legitimacy that the self-appointed spokespersons of special interests can never have".

It is unclear on what basis these remarks are made.

A major outstanding issue relating to the existing GATS Agreement is the proper interpretation of the concept of "necessity" as found in Article VI: 4 of the agreement, on Domestic Regulation. Paragraph 1 of Article VI says,

> "In sectors where specific commitments are undertaken, each member shall ensure that all measures of general application and affecting trade in services are administered in a reasonable, objective, and impartial manner".

Article VI: 4 was drafted to prevent measures relating to "qualification requirements and procedures, technical standards and licensing requirements" from becoming "unnecessary barriers to trade in services". It calls for the Council for Trade in Services to "establish any necessary disciplines" to that end, with the following goals in mind: that the national requirements be (a) based on objective and transparent criteria, such as competence and the ability to supply the service; (b) not more burdensome than necessary to ensure the quality of the service; and (c) in the case of licensing procedures, not in themselves a restriction on the supply of the service. A working party on domestic regulation was established for the purpose of developing the "disciplines" indicated.[152]

The EC released a communication to the working party on 1 May 2001, urging clarification of WTO members' obligations with regard to the Article VI:4

---

[151] See GATS—Fact and Fiction, at http://www.wto.org/english/tratop_e/serv_e/gats_factfiction_e.htm.

[152] See *Bridges Trade Weekly News Digest*—Vol. 5, Number 17 (8 May 2001). See also WTO Secretariat and Budget, at http://www.wto.org/test/english/thewto_e/secre_e/div_e.htm.

necessity concept. If this clarification does not occur, the European communication stated, there will be an "unpredictable mandate for dispute settlement
procedures to do so".[153] The EC urged that the WTO adopt an interpretation
similar to its own proportionality principle, under which a measure should not
be considered more trade-restrictive than necessary if it is proportionate to the
objective pursued. Based on its own legal regime, the EC explained that under a
proportionality analysis, the degree of permissible trade restrictiveness would
depend on the specific objective sought, and the validity of the policy objective
itself would not be assessed. Alternative approaches, such as the "least trade
restrictive" standard, would in the European view "unduly restrict the choice of
the regulatory tools available".

The WTO system could gain much from adopting balancing tests developed
by the European Court of Justice. However, these tests emanate from a system
with an avowed and traditional commitment to non-trade values, a position
that facilitates a more complex interpretive methodology for dealing with
clashes between trade and non-trade values. The paradox of the WTO is that,
while attempting to balance values, as a regime it has substantive allegiance only
to the values of trade liberalisation. It is the very open-endedness and unpre-
dictability of the Services Agreement that has called forth such an extreme reaction from the WTO's critics, and such a spirited defence by the WTO itself.

---

[153] See Bridges, *supra* n. 153.

10

National Measures Against Dumping and Subsidies

ANTI-DUMPING ACTIONS: THE LAST OF THE (SOMEWHAT) LOW-COST PROTECTIONIST DEVICES?

ANTI-DUMPING ACTIONS HAVE long been a favourite self-protective measure of GATT/WTO member countries, especially in the developed world. The original GATT did not take a clear legal position on the necessity of national anti-dumping laws; to the extent that many countries had laws setting out conditions for the application of anti-dumping duties and other self-help remedies, the GATT drafters recognised this as a common reality. Dumping itself was not legally restricted at GATT level, since dumping is inherently private behaviour—by firms engaged in price competition of a certain kind in foreign markets. However, the language of Article VI:1 of the GATT speaks of a recognition by the contracting parties that dumping

> "is to be condemned if it causes or threatens material injury to an established industry in the territory of a contracting party or materially retards the establishment of a domestic industry".

This condemnation leads to acceptance of national anti-dumping laws, but only within the limits set out in GATT/WTO anti-dumping rules.

GATT's primary concern in the anti-dumping context was that national anti-dumping measures should not function as protectionist devices in response to legitimate low-cost competition from abroad. Thus, GATT/WTO law on this subject has been characterised by the imposition of discipline with regard to the manner of application of anti-dumping measures. As GATT/WTO anti-dumping law has evolved over time, one has seen a lessening of the freedom with which members may act when imposing duties; national anti-dumping law, substantive and procedural, has come under increasing scrutiny as the conditions for the imposition of anti-dumping measures have become stricter.

We have explored the legal processes through which WTO members have become increasingly constricted in their freedom to indulge in protectionism. The multi-faceted Uruguay Round Agreements in particular have cut members off from a number of familiar safety valves; the aggregate effect of the agreements has been to subject national economies to the cold wind of GATT/WTO discipline on a far wider variety of fronts than heretofore. VERs are apparently unavailable; safeguards can only be used under strictly defined conditions; non-tariff barriers of all kinds must be justified or abandoned, to a degree unimaginable prior to 1995. The anti-dumping measure, while subject to a more restrictive set of conditions than in the past, is, however, still the easiest and simplest protectionist device available to member countries. The most basic reason for this is that if the GATT/WTO system were to set out an even greater number of restrictions in this area, with a view to eliminating anti-dumping actions or severely curtailing their use (as advocated by some), then this would have the effect of essentially affirming the propriety of "dumping". And this the WTO has not attempted to do; thus, the degree to which the form and nature of national anti-dumping actions may be curtailed is itself necessarily limited.

The anti-dumping measure is attractive to members in a number of ways: it can be imposed without regard for anti-discrimination principles, and thus has far lower negotiation costs attached than measures requiring agreement with all countries whose exports are being restricted. And, although the Uruguay Round Agreement on the Implementation of Article VI (Anti-Dumping) does increase the evidentiary burden on countries applying anti-dumping measures, it does not substantially restrict the right of WTO members to respond to perceived dumping activity by their trading partners.[1]

As with other topics within GATT/WTO law, anti-dumping law must be looked at in its totality, so that its true significance will not be lost. The typical users of the anti-dumping measure have historically been the developed countries, under threat from low-cost competition from Asia or the newly industrialised and developing worlds more generally. Thus, it is to be expected that aspects of the anti-dumping laws of the developed world would be subject to WTO challenge by aggrieved exporting countries, and to a large extent, this has been the case. However, an interesting phenomenon of recent times has been the use made by developing countries of GATT/WTO anti-dumping law to challenge the anti-dumping laws of other developing countries. Due to the enhanced procedural and evidentiary requirements imposed by the Uruguay Round Anti-Dumping Agreement, countries with a history of imposing anti-dumping duties have found their national laws challenged by would-be exporters frustrated by a continued "impressionistic" reliance on the spectre of dumping to justify what could be seen as pure self-protection, encouraged by national producer and labour interests. An examination of the anti-dumping-related disputes from 1995 until the present shows an eagerness to hold members to the letter of GATT/WTO anti-dumping law, perhaps with a view to cooling the enthusiasm of importing countries for this last "simple solution" to the problem of low-cost competitors.

---

[1] The Tokyo Round negotiations also introduced an Anti-Dumping Code, with the intention of making it more difficult for countries to apply anti-dumping duties.

PRE-1995 ACTIONS: JAPAN'S ANTI-DUMPING COMPLAINT[1a]

Japan had been a reluctant plaintiff at the GATT, apparently preferring to keep a low profile, while hoping for the best in terms of its international trade position. While the new WTO rules seem to have given Japan a new self-confidence, and removed some of its traditional defensiveness, Japan still has less frequent recourse to the complaint procedure than other major trading countries.

One of the most conceptually important cases brought by Japan before the GATT was on the issue of the excessively restrictive nature of European anti-dumping laws. The specific cause of Japan's grievance was the notorious EC "screwdriver operations" legislation of 1988.[2] There had in fact been EC-wide anti-dumping rules going back to the introduction of the common customs tariff in 1968.[3] This original anti-dumping regulation reflected the contents of the first (and ultimately unsuccessful) GATT Anti-Dumping Code, from the Kennedy Round, completed in 1967.

The first legislation naturally called for the imposition of duties by the Community authorities on dumped goods being sent into the Community for Community consumption. The 1988 revisions, the target of Japan's complaint, included rules on so-called "screwdriver operations", operations which allegedly represented an attempt by foreign producers to evade the stringency of the Community's anti-dumping rules. This evasion, or "circumvention", occurred when producers set up assembly operations within European territory to finish the manufacture of products that would otherwise (that is, if they were coming from the country of first origin) be subject to anti-dumping duties. The Community amendments in essence treated these products assembled in the Community as if they were coming from the third country in question.

Under the 1988 European regulation, anti-dumping duties could be imposed on such products where more than 50 per cent of parts derived from the country of exportation of the product subject to the original anti-dumping duty. However, these anti-dumping proceedings could be suspended where undertakings were

---

[1a] *Japan v. EEC: Regulation on Imports of Parts and Components*, Report of the Panel, adopted 16 May 1990 (L/6657–37S/132).

[2] See Council Regulation (EEC) No. 2423/88 of 11 July 1988 on protection against dumped or subsidised imports from countries not members of the European Economic Community. Art. 13.10 states that "definitive anti-dumping duties may be imposed . . . on products that are introduced into the commerce of the Community after having been assembled or produced in the Community, provided that: assembly or production is carried out by a party which is related or associated to any of the manufacturers whose exports of the like product are subject to a definitive anti-dumping duty; the assembly or production operation was started or substantially increased after the opening of the anti-dumping investigation; the value of parts or materials used in the assembly or production operation and originating in the country of exportation of the product subject to the anti-dumping duty exceeds the value of all other parts or materials used by at least 50%. . . ."

[3] See Council Regulation (EEC) 459/68 of the Council of 5 April 1968 on protection against dumping or the granting of bounties or subsidies by countries which are not members of the European Economic Community.

made by the manufacturer to source a certain percentage, generally 40 per cent, of parts and products from within the EC itself. Thus, in effect, a specialised rule of origin existed in the anti-circumvention context. Under ordinary rule of origin analysis, a number of factors, including the complexity of the last operation performed, and the alteration of the product in that process, are taken into account. Under the anti-dumping rules Japan complained of, however, the investigation turned on the percentage of local content in the creation of the final product.[4]

Japan complained of the fact that products locally assembled within the EC by Japanese manufacturers were being subject to anti-dumping duties, in violation of Article III:2. As for the requirement that imported parts should not represent more than a certain percentage of total parts in the finished products, Japan claimed that this constituted an internal requirement involving less favorable treatment of imports in violation of Article III:4. (Japan had also argued that the Tokyo Round Anti-Dumping Code, Article I, was violated, as duties placed on locally assembled products lacked the necessary findings of dumping and injury.[5] Although this was a compelling argument, it was ultimately not pursued by Japan.)

Especially by Japanese standards, this was a courageous complaint to have been brought, raising as it did challenging structural issues. The target of European concern was the expansion or setting up of assembly operations that tended to occur after anti-dumping investigations had been initiated. In fact, Europe was involved at the time in many "voluntary undertakings" regarding local content with manufacturers who hoped thereby to avoid anti-dumping duties on their assembled products.

Europe defended its measures under Article XX(d), concerning measures necessary to secure compliance with law or regulations not inconsistent with the provisions of the General Agreement. The panel found that the European duty was an "internal tax" of the sort prohibited by Article III:2; and that Europe's Article XX defence was invalid on the basis that Article XX does not allow the imposition of anti-dumping duties that are themselves outside the scope of the GATT's anti-dumping rules. The panel also held that the 40% local content undertakings required to avoid anti-dumping duties were in fact "internal requirements" as per Article III:4, concerning less favourable treatment of imported goods.

The EC objected very publicly to the panel's legal conclusions. The panel then set out a rebuttal of the EC's objections in an equally public manner.[6] Following

---

[4] Note that the EC did not place the anti-dumping duties on the actual imported parts, which would have been a more common method of responding to this kind of dumping.

[5] One of the important stand-alone codes brought into being by the Tokyo Round of negotiations was the Anti-Dumping Code. While this has been superceded by the Uruguay Round Anti-Dumping Agreement, it managed to substantially increase the evidentiary burden on countries imposing anti-dumping duties on exporting countries. It became clearly necessary to determine injury to domestic industry before imposing a duty. The code made plain that duties could only be maintained for as long as strictly necessary. A specialised dispute settlement procedure was created for the anti-dumping context.

[6] Hudec believes this to be a unique series of events in GATT history.

a course of action similar to that of the US in the *Aramid Fibres* case, the EC did not block adoption of the panel's report, but said that it would await the outcome of the Uruguay Round negotiations to see in what manner its anti-dumping regulations would have to be changed. The panel report was in this manner adopted in 1990. As it happened, the Uruguay Round negotiations, which were intended to deal with the problem of circumvention of anti-dumping laws, did not arrive at an agreement on the issue.

THE DEVELOPMENT OF EUROPEAN ANTI-DUMPING LEGISLATION

Of all the remedies available to European trade authorities to respond to undesirable behaviour on the part of trading partners, anti-dumping procedures are by far the most frequently relied upon. This is true in other major trading powers as well, and looks set to become even more the case in the wake of the Uruguay Round Agreements' restrictions on other types of protectionist measures.

As mentioned above, since there is no requirement in GATT law that anti-dumping measures must be applied in a non-discriminatory manner, far less is required by way of official negotiation costs. European industrial organisations are very familiar with the anti-dumping system, and employ specialised legal counsel to pressure the Commission into taking action against countries whose exporters are engaged in dumping.

The competence of the Community institutions to take action in the dumping area is exclusive, since dumping is plainly a part of the Common Commercial Policy, as described in Article 133 (ex Article 113) of the EC Treaty. After the end of the so-called transition period in 1968, no Member State has been able on its own to initiate anti-dumping action against third countries.

The European Commission takes a predominant role in the anti-dumping scheme.[7] It is the Commission that conducts the investigation to determine whether dumping has occurred, and then decides whether the evidence warrants a formal proceeding. The Commission may impose provisional duties, accept price undertakings from offending exporters, and terminate proceedings when appropriate. The Directorate handling anti-dumping actions within the Commission is a specialised section (C) of DGI, External Relations, having a staff of about 100 people.

It is the Council that has the power to order definitive anti-dumping duties; however, because the Council does not get involved in the factual investigation, its decision on duties tends to be no more than a legislative rubber stamp for the recommendations made by the Commission. There is also an Advisory

---

[7] The first legislation was Council Regulation 459/68; followed by Council Regulation 2423/88, both already discussed above; in turn superceded by Council Regulation (EC) No. 3283/94 of 22 December 1994 on protection against dumped imports from countries not members of the European Community, and further amended by Council Regulation (EC) No. 2331/96 of 2 December 1996; these were updated by Council Regulation (EC) No. 384/96 of 22 December 1995 on protection against dumped imports from countries not members of the European Community.

Committee on Anti-Dumping, composed of Member State officials, and chaired by a Commission representative. Although this committee has the formal power to veto relief sought by the Commission, this is a highly unlikely scenario. Member States do not even have access to confidential anti-dumping information gathered by the Commission.

In practice, no proceeding will be initiated unless a complaint is lodged with the Commission on behalf of a Community industry. As indicated above, this will normally be by the trade association representing the industry concerned. Under the 1994 regulation, the producers represented in this initial petition must produce at least 25 per cent of total production of the like product in the EU. The Commission spends about a month gathering answers to questionnaires from both exporters and importers relating to a potential anti-dumping action. Hearings held by the Commission are not accessible to the public.

Since 1968, Community anti-dumping legislation has required that three conditions be met before anti-dumping duties could be imposed; (i) that it be first established that dumping was taking place; (ii) that there was a material injury to a Community industry; and (iii) that there was a Community interest in the imposition of such duties. The term "Community interest", an interesting concept, was not plainly defined within the regulation itself, but normally involves a complex analysis and a balancing of factors: the interests of the domestic industry raising the complaint, the interests of consumers, and the interests of other industries (those relying on the lower-cost inputs, for instance).[8] Consumer groups had often complained that the Commission pays too much attention to the interests of the relevant domestic industry during such investigations. Where preliminary findings warrant the imposition of temporary anti-dumping duties, these can stay on a maximum of nine months, whereas six months would be the normal length.

COMMUNITY ANTI-DUMPING LAW AND THE PROBLEM OF CIRCUMVENTION[9]

Under the provisions of Regulation 2423/88 (the provisions challenged by Japan in the GATT "screwdriver" case), anti-dumping duties were extended to products assembled within the Community, assuming several conditions were met.[10] These were that the assembly or production had to be carried out by a party which was related to or associated with any of the manufacturers whose exports of the like product were subject to a definitive anti-dumping duty; and that the assembly operation in question had to have been started or substantially

---

[8] See Marc Wellhausen, "The Community Interest Test in Antidumping Proceedings of the European Union", (2001) 16 *American University International Law Review* 1027.

[9] See Simon Holmes, "Anti-circumvention Under the EU's New Anti-dumping Rules", (June 1995) 29:3 *Journal of World Trade* 161.

[10] As indicated in n. 2 above, the anti-circumvention section of the 1988 anti-dumping regulation was found in Art. 13, para. 10.

increased after the opening of the anti-dumping investigation. Further, it was necessary that the value of parts and materials used in the assembly or production, and originating in the country of export of the product subject to the anti-dumping duty, represents more than 50 per cent of the total value of parts and materials, with the remainder being EC-derived parts and materials.

In the many proceedings brought by the Commission under this Article 13(10) of the 1988 Regulation, the main question tended to boil down to a formulaic investigation into the percentage of parts value deriving from the relevant exporting country. In response, exporting countries began to shift their production to third countries—neither the home country of the exporter, nor European territory, since the 1988 legislation targeted screwdriver operations that were set up within the EC. However, this newer form of circumvention, shifting assembly to third countries not covered in the European legislation, elicited yet another legislative response.

We have mentioned that the Uruguay Round negotiations failed to produce a set of rules to deal with the circumvention problem generally for WTO members. Thus, Europe moved to further amend its dumping law to deal with the situation of circumvention through third-country assembly.[11] The principal change in this regard was that the Community could now impose anti-dumping duties on products or parts imported into the EC, regardless of where these had been assembled, whenever these were found to be circumventing anti-dumping duties already imposed by Europe on like products.[12] The ironic justification for this addition to the law was that limiting anti-circumvention measures to duties placed on EC-assembled products actually provided an incentive for Japanese companies to invest in third countries, rather than within the EC.

The 1996 regulation established a presumption of circumvention if the operation either started, or substantially increased, since or just prior to the initiation of an anti-dumping investigation; and if parts originating in the dumping country represented 60 per cent or more of total value of the parts for the final assembled product. However, where the product's value added (as distinct from the value of parts) deriving from the assembly procedure was more than 25 per cent of the total value, circumvention would not be considered to be taking place. A further requirement for a finding of circumvention was that the remedial effects of the duty were being undermined by the assembled product.[13]

---

[11] The preamble of Council Regulation (EC) No 384/96 states that "Whereas the 1994 Anti-Dumping Agreement does not contain provisions regarding the circumvention of anti-dumping measures, though a separate GATT Ministerial Decision recognizes circumvention as a problem and has referred it to the GATT Anti-Dumping Committee for resolution; whereas given the failure of the multilateral negotiations so far and pending the outcome of the referral to the GATT Anti-dumping Committee, it is necessary to introduce new provisions into Community legislation to deal with practices, including mere assembly of goods in the Community or a third country, which have as their main aim the circumvention of anti-dumping measures."

[12] See Art. 13 of Council Regulation 384/96.

[13] Circumvention is defined as "a change in the pattern of trade between third countries and the EU, stemming from a practice for which there is insufficient economic justification other than the imposition of an anti-dumping duty".

THE URUGUAY ROUND AGREEMENT ON THE IMPLEMENTATION OF ARTICLE VI
(ANTI-DUMPING)

This agreement is noteworthy mainly for the fact that it added more detailed rules to be followed in determining that products have in fact been dumped, and clearer criteria for determinations of injury to domestic industry. In reading the agreement, a question that arises is whether it made anti-dumping actions significantly more difficult to impose. That is, since the other Uruguay Round Agreements in the aggregate have made other national protective measures far more difficult to apply, to the extent that anti-dumping actions are still characterised by a substantial degree of national discretion, it is likely that anti-dumping actions will remain a preferred means of national self-protection for the foreseeable future. It is important to consider the extent to which the Uruguay Round altered the margin of discretion for national authorities engaging in anti-dumping actions. It is interesting to speculate as to how and why the WTO might attempt to restrict national access to this particular means of self-protection in the future.

Article 1 of the Agreement states that anti-dumping actions shall only be applied "pursuant to investigations initiated and conducted in accordance with the provisions of this agreement". Article 2 takes up the topic of "determination of dumping", providing rules for the national authorities in this regard. This section reiterates the three possible ways to identify that dumping is taking place: sale in one's market at a price lower than the price in the exporting market; or lower by comparison with a third country market supplied by the exporter; or if no such data is available, by reference to the basic costs of production plus a reasonable amount for profit. Paragraph 2.2.1.1 states that costs shall be calculated on the basis of records kept by the exporter or producer under investigation, as long as these meet normal accounting standards, and reasonably reflect the underlying costs.

What follows are highly technical rules to ensure that the calculation of costs be based on actual data, rather than speculation. While exacting, the rules could not be said to be excessively burdensome. Article 2.6 sets out a standard for "like product" appropriate to the anti-dumping context—that "like product" should be interpreted to mean "a product which is identical, i.e., alike in all respects to the product under consideration, or in the absence of such a product, another product which, although not alike in all respects, has characteristics closely resembling those of the product under consideration."

Article 3, on rules for the determination of injury, is similarly technical and does not really break new ground relative to existing GATT law. This article says that a determination of injury for purposes of Article VI must be based on positive evidence, and involve an objective examination of both the volume of dumped imports and the effect of these on prices in the domestic market for like products; and the consequent impact of these imports on domestic producers of such products. Investigating authorities must look at whether there has been a significant increase in dumped imports, and whether there has been significant price undercutting by the dumped import. This provision reminds us that the GATT never attempted to forbid dumping, but rather allowed a proportional response by participating countries to the import of dumped goods.

Article 3.4 requires that

> "the examination of the impact of the dumped imports on the domestic industry concerned shall include an evaluation of all relevant economic factors . . . having a bearing on the state of the industry".

These include decline in sales, profit, output, market share and productivity, as well as inventories, employment, wages, growth and any other relevant factors. The list is not exhaustive, and it aims to ensure that the anti-dumping measure is not used to shield the industry from other difficulties that may have entirely separate causes. Article 3.5 requires a demonstration that "the dumped imports are, through the effects of dumping . . . causing injury within the meaning of this Agreement". This causal relationship must be established by "an examination of all relevant evidence before the authorities". These authorities are further required to investigate other factors that may be responsible for the injury to the industry in question; including other types of competition not related to dumping.

Article VI of the GATT also allows anti-dumping actions when there is a threat of material injury to a domestic industry. In such a case, under Article 3.7, this "shall be based on facts and not merely on allegation, conjecture or remote possibility". A number of specific evidential factors, including the likelihood of substantially increased importation, must be taken into account.

Article 4 defines "domestic industry" as

> "the domestic producers as a whole of the like products or . . . those of them whose collective output of the product constitutes a major proportion of the total domestic production of those products".

Under certain circumstances, it may be appropriate to divide one's domestic market for purposes of the analysis. But when the national economies of two or more members have reached the level of integration indicated under the terms of Article XXIV, and the market is a single, unified market, then "the industry in the entire area of integration shall be taken to be the domestic industry referred to . . ." (Article 4.4)

Article 5 provides rules for the initiation and conduct of an investigation into alleged dumping. There must be a written application by the domestic industry claiming injury. This must include evidence of dumping and injury, as well as of a causal link between the dumped imports and alleged injury. "Simple assertion" is unacceptable. There follow unequivocal requirements as to the type of evidence to be included, particularly with regard to the volume of dumped imports, and the volume of production of the complainant, and the effects of the alleged dumping on the business.

Article 5.7 states that the evidence of both the dumping and the injury must be considered simultaneously in the decision on whether or not to initiate an investigation, and also in the course of the investigation. Where the authorities concerned are satisfied that there is insufficient evidence of either dumping or injury, the investigation must be terminated promptly. This is also true where the authorities determine that the margin of dumping is de minimis (less than 2 per cent, expressed as a percentage of the export price). Investigations must be concluded within one year, except in special circumstances, and in no case may they go on longer than 18 months.

Article 6 deals with evidence. The basic principle is that "all interested parties in an anti-dumping investigation shall be given notice of the information which the authorities require and ample opportunity to present in writing all evidence which they consider relevant in respect of the investigation in question". (Article 6.1) Rules follow on such issues as the time provided to exporters to answer questionnaires; protection of confidential information; notice of the allegations in the application, etc. Article 6.2 places an obligation on the national authorities for those with adverse views to present their side of the issues in person. Article 6.6 states that

> "Except in circumstances provided for in paragraph 8, the authorities shall during the course of an investigation, satisfy themselves as to the accuracy of the information supplied by interested parties upon which their findings are based".

The paragraph 8 exception involves a situation where information is refused by one of the parties, and the authorities must make a determination based on the available evidence.

Under Article 6.10, the national authorities must determine an individual margin of dumping for each known exporter of the product under investigation. Article 6.1. defines "interested parties" as including the exporter or foreign producer or the importer of the product, the government of the exporting member and producers of like product in the importing country. The authorities must also provide opportunities for industrial users of the product and consumer groups to be allowed to provide information regarding dumping, injury and causality. Authorities must be prepared to assist interested parties who might have difficulty providing this type of information, particularly small companies.

Article 7 on provisional measures sets out rules for responses that may occur during the investigation period, where a preliminary affirmative determination has been made of dumping and injury, and where the authorities "judge such measures necessary to prevent injury from being caused during the investigation". These provisional measures may take the form of a provisional duty, or a security by cash deposit or bond, equal to the amount of provisional duty estimated. Such measures may not be applied sooner than 60 days after the date of the initiation of the investigation.

Article 7.4 ensures that provisional measures shall be "limited to as short a period as possible, not exceeding four months", or under specially defined circumstances, not to exceed six months. Article 8 covers the question of price undertakings offered by the exporter. This provision says that the proceedings may be terminated without the imposition of any duties where there are satisfactory undertakings from the exporter to revise its prices or cease its exports at dumped prices such that the authorities are satisfied that the injury will be eliminated.[14]

Price undertakings may only be sought after a preliminary determination of dumping has taken place. Even where an undertaking is accepted, the authorities may decide (under Article 8.4) to continue with the investigation. Where the determination under such circumstances is ultimately negative, the undertaking will automatically lapse. Under Article 8.5, exporters may not be compelled to offer undertakings; also, the fact that such undertakings have not been offered cannot prejudice the determination of dumping or injury.

Article 9 gives rules for the imposition and collection of anti-dumping duties. Predictably, the amount of the duty may not exceed the margin of dumping as established under Article 2. (See Article 9.3) Article 9.3.2 allows for the prospective assessment of duties, but on condition of prompt refunds of any duty paid in excess of the margin of dumping. This would seem to leave in place a relatively high degree of freedom for national governments to use anti-dumping measures protectively. Article 10 sets out rules for the imposition of retroactive duties, in situations where provisional duties would have been appropriate, but were not applied.

Article 11 is of fundamental importance in the WTO anti-dumping scheme. The basic obligation on member countries is that "an anti-dumping duty shall remain in force only as long as and to the extent necessary to counteract dumping which is causing injury". (Article 11.1) Article 11.2 states that authorities shall review the need for the continued imposition of the duty, either on their own initiative or upon request of an interested party. If the review determines that the anti-dumping duty is no longer warranted, then the duty shall be terminated immediately.

Article 11.3 places a sunset clause on anti-dumping actions, saying that definitive duties shall be terminated not later than five years from imposition, or from the date of the most recent review (including dumping and injury), "unless the authorities determine, in a review initiated before that date . . . that the expiry of the duty would be likely to lead to continuation or recurrence of dumping and injury". A period of twelve months is allowed for such a review to take place in. This provision clearly grants a significant amount of freedom to members to maintain anti-dumping duties, particularly under the guise of preventing the "recurrence" of dumping.

---

[14] Interestingly, the provision also says "Price increases under such undertakings shall not be higher than necessary to eliminate the margin of dumping." And that, "It is desirable that the price increases be less than the margin of dumping if such increases would be adequate to remove the injury to the domestic industry."

Article 12 provides elaborate rules for public notice of investigations and decisions to impose duties; it also requires clear explanations to be given as to why a particular determination has been made. Article 13 states that where members have anti-dumping laws, they shall

"maintain judicial, arbitral, or administrative tribunals or procedures for the purpose, *inter alia*, of the prompt review of administrative actions relating to final determinations and reviews of determinations within the meaning of Article 11".

Article 24 allows anti-dumping actions to be taken on behalf of third countries, a traditional feature of GATT law. Article 15 asks that the special situation of developing countries be taken into account when imposing anti-dumping duties, but this is largely aspirational. Article 15 states "Possibilities of constructive remedies provided for by this agreement shall be explored before applying anti-dumping duties where they would affect the essential interests of developing country members".

Article 16 establishes a committee on anti-dumping practices, composed of representatives from all the members. The Committee is to function as a consultative body for members dealing with the Anti-Dumping Agreement; it is empowered to seek information from whatever source it deems appropriate. Members taking anti-dumping actions must report to this committee. Dispute settlement under the agreement is naturally to be conducted within the Dispute Settlement Understanding. (See Article 17)

WTO ANTI-DUMPING DISPUTES

If current trends continue, a high volume of complaints will be brought before the WTO under the provisions of the Uruguay Round Anti-Dumping Agreement. As all of these disputes follow a pattern of challenge to a use of national anti-dumping law allegedly not based on the standards established under GATT/WTO law, these disputes in particular are more engaging when conceived of in the aggregate than when examined individually.

What follows is a discussion of one "garden variety" dispute brought by Korea against the United States, and one more unusual dispute, involving the EC and Japan against the provisions of the US Anti-Dumping Act of 1916.

KOREA V. US: ANTI-DUMPING DUTY ON DYNAMIC RANDOM ACCESS MEMORY SEMICONDUCTORS (DRAMS)[15]

It was only to be expected that countries that were targets of frequent anti-dumping actions by the EC and the US would race to WTO panels to challenge

---

[15] *Korea v. US: Anti-Dumping Duty on Dynamic Random Access Memory Semiconductors (DRAMs)*, Report of the Panel, 29 January 1999 (WT/DS79/R) [hereinafter *Korean DRAMS* Panel Report].

some of the more obviously protectionist uses of anti-dumping law by these trading powers. While the Uruguay Round Anti-Dumping Agreement did not restrict the use of anti-dumping actions as dramatically as it might have, the evidentiary, technical and procedural burdens on those countries imposing anti-dumping duties were nevertheless increased. While the DRAMS case is quite dry and technical, the underlying theme is Korea's attempt to test the WTO as to how strict it will be with major importing countries regarding their reliance on anti-dumping actions. The result in this dispute was a mixed one for Korea.

Prompted by a complaint from the Micron Technologies Company, filed with the US International Trade Commission and the Department of Commerce, the US authorities found that dumping of dynamic random access memory semi-conductors (DRAMs) from Korea was occurring, and imposed an anti-dumping order. Subsequent reviews, requested by Korea, found that the dumping had ceased. The US nonetheless refused to revoke the anti-dumping order, even though it was not imposing an anti-dumping duty. The US rationale was that revocation of the order could lead to a recurrence of the dumping.[16] (Under the US anti-dumping regime, there may be an imposition of an anti-dumping order, without any actual anti-dumping duties being levied.)

As the US saw the issue, Korean producers had a history of dumping DRAMs in the US; a history that had to be taken into account. The question was whether the US Department of Commerce was required to revoke the anti-dumping order maintained by the US, when Korea had ceased its dumping of these products for three consecutive years, as revealed in the review.[17]

The 1997 US determination not to revoke the anti-dumping order was based on the relevant DOC regulations for making such determinations.[18] Korea based its complaint on Article 11.2 of the Uruguay Round Anti-Dumping Agreement, which states that "authorities shall review the need for the continued imposition of a duty . . . upon request of any interested party which submits information substantiating the need for a review". And further that "If, as a result of the review . . . the authorities determine that the anti-dumping duty is no longer warranted, it shall be terminated immediately".

At issue was whether Article 11.2 of the Anti-Dumping Agreement precluded an anti-dumping duty being deemed "necessary to offset dumping" where there

---

[16] See footnote 485 to para. 6.24 of the *Korean DRAMS* Panel Report: "In the US, an anti-dumping order does not of itself result in the levying of duties, but sets a rate of deposit for estimated duties to be paid on future imports. In the anniversary month of every order, interested parties may request an 'administrative review' of the anti-dumping order. . . . [T]he Department of Commerce calculates the anti-dumping duties actually owed on imports during the previous 12 months; and sets a new deposit rate on future imports. If the actual duties levied fall short of the deposit rate in the order, the excess is repaid."

[17] *Korean DRAMS* Panel Report, para. 4.103.

[18] Department of Commerce regulations, Section 353.25 (a)(2), which say in part that the Secretary may revoke an order in part if the Secretary concludes that, "[P]roducers or resellers covered by the order have sold the merchandise at not less than foreign market value for a period of at least three consecutive years; and that it is not likely that those persons will in the future sell the merchandise at less than market value . . ."

was no present dumping to offset. In other words, Korea would have the panel find that its three-year record of no dumping made it impossible for the US to continue to impose its order, even where there is no duty actually assessed, and even where the US believed that there was a threat of recurrence. Korea maintained that Article 11.2 of the agreement required duties to be revoked as soon as there was a finding of no dumping.[19]

This first pillar of the Korean argument fell quickly. The panel pointed out that Article 11.2 provides for a review of "whether the injury would be likely to continue or recur if the duty were removed or varied". This it saw as a necessarily prospective examination, and disagreed that Article 11. 2 precluded the continued imposition of a duty where there is no present dumping.[20]

Korea further argued that the US standard of review (with a finding of "not likely to recur" required, rather than a finding that the dumping is "likely" to recur) was contrary to Article 11.2 of the agreement.[21] The panel recounted that

> "if the Department of Commerce fails to satisfy itself that recurrence of dumping is 'not likely', it will find that there is a need for the continued imposition of the anti-dumping duty".[22]

The panel looked to the relationship between Article 11.1 and 11.2, 11.1 creating an "unambiguous requirement" that the duty shall remain in force "only as long as and to the extent necessary to counteract dumping which is causing injury".[23] The panel stated that the requirement imposed by Article 11.2 is not to be construed in any absolute or abstract sense, but rather as appropriate to the "practical reasoning" of a review. This, in the panel's view, was as applicable to recurrence of dumping as to cases of present dumping.[24]

The panel then looked at whether "a failure to find that the recurrence of dumping is 'not likely' meets the standards demanded by the agreement". Here the panel was in agreement with Korea, that "a failure to find that an event is 'not likely' is not equivalent to a finding that the event is 'likely' ".[25] Failure to find that something is unlikely does not mean that one has found that it is likely, the panel stated. "A finding that an event is 'likely' implies a greater degree of certainty", it found. Since the US standard gives no "predictive assurance", it is contrary to Article 11.2 of the agreement.[26] And since the US standard of review

---

[19] *Korean DRAMS* Panel Report, para. 6.24.

[20] *Korean DRAMS* Panel Report, at 137.

[21] Recall that the relevant section of the US regulations states that the Secretary may revoke an order in part if the Secretary concludes that "it is not likely that those persons will in the future sell the merchandise at less than foreign market value".

[22] *Korean DRAMS* Panel Report, para. 6.38.

[23] *Korean DRAMS* Panel Report, para. 6.41.

[24] *Korean DRAMS* Panel Report, para. 6.43.

[25] *Korean DRAMS* Panel Report, para. 6.45.

[26] "[W]e are unable to find that the s. 353.25(a)(2)(ii) 'not likely' criterion provides any demonstrable basis on which to reliably conclude that the continued imposition of the duty is necessary to offset dumping." *Korean DRAMS* Panel Report, para. 6.45.

was contrary to the agreement, it followed that the specific review results being challenged were also contrary to Article 11.2.[27]

Korea did not succeed with its next argument, to the effect that failure by the US to self-initiate an injury review violated Article 11.2 of the agreement. Specifically, Korea maintained:

> "after concluding for three years that no injury was occurring as a result of dumping, the authorities had an obligation on their own initiative to investigate whether injury as well as dumping would be likely to resume if the order were revoked".

The panel noted that this injury review is dependent upon a determination of whether dumping will recur, and that a finding of no dumping does not imply the necessity to initiate an injury review.[28] The Korean arguments would seem to an objective reader to be sound, and the panel's reaction quite cautious.

Korea also failed to convince the panel that the US had violated Article 2.2.1.1 of the agreement by rejecting an economic study regarding cost trends and cost data submitted by Korea for 1996. The panel wrote that the DOC was an "unbiased investigative authority" and also that Korea had made only "conclusory arguments in support of its claim that the DOC should not have rejected" a particular study.[29]

A further argument raised by Korea was that the Department of Commerce failed to satisfy itself as to the accuracy of data supplied by the petitioner, uncritically accepting and relying upon the petitioner's data without taking any steps to confirm that it was accurate. This was a clear attempt to test the nature of the evidentiary burden placed on the country imposing the anti-dumping measure—in this case, the US. The panel, though, pointed out that Article 6.6. of the agreement does not explicitly require members to verify the accuracy of such data; only that they "satisfy themselves as to the accuracy of the information".[30] This, according to the panel, could happen in any number of ways, including by reliance upon the reputation of the original source of the information supplied—consultancy firms, newspaper articles, etc. The panel then stated, "anti-dumping investigations would become totally unmanageable if investigating authorities were required to actually verify the accuracy of all information being relied on".[31] As the US insisted on the high reputations of these original sources of information, stating that Korea had failed to indicate anything in the record that the US should not have relied upon, the panel agreed with the US that Korea has not made out a prima facie case.[32]

Thus, the principal issue upon which Korea succeeded was the inconsistency of the US "not likely" standard with the requirements of Article 2.1 of the Anti-Dumping Agreement. This narrow victory, however, should be seen in its

---

[27] *Korean DRAMS* Panel Report, para. 6.51.
[28] *Korean DRAMS* Panel Report, para. 6.59.
[29] *Korean DRAMS* Panel Report, para. 6.69.
[30] *Korean DRAMS* Panel Report, paras. 6.75–6.76.
[31] *Korean DRAMS* Panel Report, para. 6.78.
[32] *Korean DRAMS* Panel Report, para. 6.80.

ambiguous context: While the margin of discretion left to national authorities in making anti-dumping orders and imposing anti-dumping duties is less than it was, there is still more discretion available for the application of these measures than in virtually any other sector of GATT/WTO law. It has been suggested that the US did not appeal this decision because the difference between the "not likely" standard and the "likely to recur" standard was small, and would be unlikely to have an impact on revocation decisions.[33] The parties notified the DSB in October of 2000 of a mutually agreeable solution, involving revocation by the United States of the anti-dumping order in question, following a sunset review by the Department of Commerce.

CHALLENGING US ANTI-DUMPING LEGISLATION

A panel was established in early 1999 to hear a complaint brought by the EC against an old and established (if infrequently invoked) statute, the Anti-Dumping Act of 1916.[34] The case was striking for the fact that a WTO panel, supported by the Appellate Body—as opposed to a US domestic court—actually struck down this venerable statute, rather than a measure applied under the statute.[35] Japan brought a similar complaint, with similar results, soon after.[36]

As background to the WTO case, in September 1997 a US District Court had ruled that Geneva Steel Company (a US steel producer) could proceed to the trial phase of a civil suit against Ranger Steel Supply and Thyssen Stahl AG, the latter being distributors of foreign steel in the US. Geneva Steel had filed suit against Ranger and Thyssen under the 1916 Act. Of great interest is the fact that the 1916 Act has always occupied a middle ground between anti-dumping and antitrust law, whereas the Geneva Steel court treated the action as a clear anti-dumping matter.[37] The Geneva Steel plaintiffs had argued that the defendants violated the 1916 Act through "systematically selling steel purchased abroad to customers in the United States, at prices substantially below the actual market value of the steel in the countries where the steel was made".[38] The defendants argued that the 1916 Act was an antitrust law, thus requiring proof of the

[33] Rosenthal and Vermylen, "The WTO Antidumping and Subsidies Agreements: Did the United States Achieve its Objectives During the Uruguay Round?", (2000) 31 *Law and Policy in International Business* 871.

[34] *EC v. US: Anti-Dumping Act of 1916*, Report of the Panel, 31 March 2000 (WT/DS136/R), [hereinafter *US Anti-dumping Act* Panel Report].

[35] On this point, see Jeffrey S Beckington, "The World Trade Organization's Dispute Settlement Resolution in the United States—Anti-Dumping Act of 1916", (Jan 2001) 34 *Vanderbilt Journal of Transnational Law* 199.

[36] See *US Anti-Dumping* Act Panel Report.

[37] See Dianne M Keppler, "The Geneva Steel Co Decision Raises Concerns in Geneva: Why the 1916 Antidumping Act Violates the WTO Antidumping Agreement", (1999) 32 *George Washington Journal of International Law and Economics* 293.

[38] As quoted in Keppler, *supra* n. 37, *Geneva Steel* v. *Ranger Steel*, 980 F Supp 1209 (D.Utah 1997).

defendants' "predatory intent".[39] However, the court ruled that if Geneva could prove merely that the defendants had acted "with the intent of injuring, by any means", the US steel industry, then Geneva would be entitled to damages under the 1916 Act.[40] It did not take Europe long to put the issue before the WTO: Could the US maintain anti-dumping legislation that set out separate and conflicting standards as compared with the GATT Article VI, and the WTO's Anti-Dumping Agreement?

The panel related that the US Congress had enacted the legislation under the heading of "Unfair Competition" in Title VII of the Revenue Act of 1916. Called the Anti-Dumping Act of 1916, it provided that it would be unlawful for any person importing articles into the US to systematically sell them at less than the actual market value or wholesale market price, as compared with the principal markets in the country of production or other foreign countries to which the products were commonly exported, provided that such acts were done "with the intent of destroying or injuring an industry in the US", or of preventing the establishment of an industry in the US, or restraining or monopolising any part of trade or commerce in such articles in the US. Any person found to have violated the Act would be guilty of a misdemeanour, punishable by a fine of not more than $5,000, or imprisonment not exceeding one year, or both. Any person injured by reason of a violation of the act could sue in US District Court, and receive threefold damages.[41]

The US also passed an Anti-Dumping Act in 1921, which allowed the Secretary of the Treasury to impose duties on dumped goods, regardless of the intent of the dumping party. This was repealed, but provided the model for the sections of the Tariff Act of 1930 dealing with dumping.[42] The panel outlined US laws applying to price discrimination within the US, where the effect is to substantially lessen competition or to tend to create a monopoly.[43]

The panel noted that the 1916 Act had been invoked very infrequently, and had never been reviewed by the US Supreme Court. Also, while the Justice Department had responsibility for prosecuting criminal violations of the 1916 Act, it had never successfully done so.[44]

The EC requested the panel to hold that the 1916 Act was in fact an anti-dumping measure, since it was targeted at imports, and price discrimination between the exporters' market, or a third country market, and the importing

---

[39] *Geneva Steel*, 980 F Supp at 1217.

[40] *Geneva Steel*, 980 F Supp at 1215.

[41] *US Anti-Dumping Act* Panel Report, para. 2.1. The panel explained that the business activity prohibited by the act was a form of international price discrimination, with two basic components: (1) The importer must have sold a foreign-produced product in the US at a price substantially less than the price for which the product was sold in the country of the foreign producer; (2) The importer must have undertaken the price discrimination "commonly and systematically". For criminal or civil liability to apply, there must have been intent to destroy or injure US industry. US Anti-dumping Act Panel Report, paras. 2.2–2.3.

[42] *US Anti-Dumping Act* Panel Report, paras. 2.7–2.8.

[43] *US Anti-Dumping Act* Panel Report, paras. 2.9–2.11.

[44] *US Anti-Dumping Act* Panel Report, paras. 2.13–2.16.

country's market—in terms which were "in substance identical" to Article VI:1 of the GATT. Europe argued that the US Act allowed action to be taken which would not be allowed under Article VI of the GATT, in particular because the remedies under the Act were not allowed under Article VI:2 of GATT. The EC maintained that the 1916 Act violated Articles VI:1 and VI:2 of the GATT, and also the WTO Anti-Dumping Agreement.[45]

The US defended that there was nothing in Article VI:2 of GATT that provided that anti-dumping duties were the exclusive remedy for dumping; and further that the 1916 Act was not even an anti-dumping statute governed by Article VI or the Anti-Dumping Agreement. Rather, the US submitted that the 1916 Act was "specifically targeted at a very narrow type of objectionable business activity involving antitrust-like predatory intent".[46]

The EC raised claims to the effect that the 1916 Act failed to respect procedural requirements as to the determination of material injury and the initiation and conduct of the investigation leading to the imposition of measures.[47] The US countered that a member is only bound to respect the provisions of the Anti-Dumping Agreement to the extent that it intends to impose anti-dumping duties; and that in this regard, the remedies under its 1916 Act fell outside the scope of that Agreement.[48]

Examining its plain text, the panel concluded that

> "the 1916 Act, based on an analysis of its terms, objectively addresses a type of transnational price discrimination that meets the definition of 'dumping' contained in Article VI:1 of the GATT . . ."[49]

As for the historical context in which the Act must be seen, the panel stated that

> "the historical context and legislative history do not confirm that the 1916 Act had a purely 'anti-trust' purpose, within the meaning of that concept today. Rather, it appears that anti-dumping as it is known today in international trade law, and anti-trust laws dealing with predatory pricing were part of the same notion of 'unfair competition' ".[50]

And, further, that

> "We note that evidence from the historical context of the 1916 Act supports our finding that the 1916 Act transnational price discrimination test corresponds to 'dumping' within the meaning of article VI".[51]

---

[45] *US Anti-Dumping Act* Panel Report, para. 3.17.
[46] *US Anti-Dumping Act* Panel Report, paras. 3.21–3.25.
[47] *US Anti-Dumping Act* Panel Report, para. 6.7. The US also attempted to argue that the 1916 Act was "non-mandatory law", since the Justice Department enjoyed discretion as to whether or not to file a suit. This would mean that the statute itself could not be examined for its WTO-compatibility, but rather only specific instances of its application. This argument was rejected by the panel, which disagreed with the US assessment of the character of its 1916 Act. See *US Anti-Dumping Act* Panel Report, paras. 6.12, 6.170.
[48] *US Anti-Dumping Act* Panel Report, para. 6.11.
[49] *US Anti-Dumping Act* Panel Report, para. 6.118.
[50] *US Anti-Dumping Act* Panel Report, para. 6.131.
[51] *US Anti-Dumping Act* Panel Report, para. 6.132.

The panel found no indication in its examination of the relevant case law that the statute was considered to be part of US anti-trust law, as distinct from anti-dumping law addressing topics falling within the scope of Article VI of the GATT.[52] Thus, having found that the 1916 statute addresses "dumping" within the meaning of Article VI, and the Anti-Dumping Agreement, the panel went on to examine the substance of the EC claim that the Act violated those laws.[53]

The panel noted the EC view that the 1916 Act violates Article VI:1, because that article "provides that dumping is to be condemned if it causes or threatens to cause injury to a domestic industry". The EC also argued that Article 3 of the Anti-Dumping Agreement lays down a detailed definition of "injury", and the manner in which injury must be established, whereas the 1916 Act contains nothing to ensure that the injury shown corresponds to the material injury standard of Article VI:1 of GATT and Article 3 of the Anti-Dumping Agreement. A further argument was that since other and separate intents were relevant under the 1916 Act, it could happen that measures would be authorised under the Act without an inquiry being carried out into the effects on domestic industry—thus setting up an anti-dumping regime separate and distinct from the one established in GATT/WTO law.[54]

The panel accepted the EC view of a clash between the Article VI:1 requirement of material injury or threat thereof, and the absence of this in the 1916 Act; as well as the fact that the 1916 Act required instead a showing of intent to injure or destroy a US domestic industry. It noted that intent might in fact be more difficult to establish than injury. However, the panel stated, identifying intent might not always require a finding of actual injury or threat thereof.[55] On this basis, the panel found incompatibility between the US Act and Article VI:1 of the GATT.[56]

The last major issue raised was whether Article VI of the GATT clearly required members to limit their anti-dumping remedies to the imposition of anti-dumping duties, as opposed to other types of remedy (fines or imprisonment) available under the 1916 Act, however infrequently these might be sought. The panel agreed that the ordinary meaning of Article VI:2 of the GATT would "support the view that anti-dumping duties are the only type of remedies allowed under Article VI:2".[57] In that the 1916 Act "failed to respect" procedural and due process requirements set out in the WTO Anti-Dumping Agreement, the panel also found a violation of Article 4 of that Agreement. Specifically, since Article 4 requires that a complaint be made on behalf of the domestic industry and be supported by a minimum proportion of the domestic industry, the fact that any person injured in business or property could bring an

[52] *US Anti-Dumping Act* Panel Report, para. 6.162.
[53] *US Anti-Dumping Act* Panel Report, para. 6.178 and following.
[54] *US Anti-Dumping Act* Panel Report, para. 6.178.
[55] *US Anti-Dumping Act* Panel Report, para. 6.180.
[56] *US Anti-Dumping Act* Panel Report, para. 6.181.
[57] *US Anti-Dumping Act* Panel Report, para. 6.190.

action under the 1916 Act was incompatible with Article 4. The panel noted that there was no evidence that a minimum representation level for a given industry must be established by the complainant before filing a case before a federal court.[58]

Finally, the EC argued that because Article 5.5 of the Anti-Dumping Agreement requires that notice be given to the government of the exporting country before an anti-dumping case is begun, the fact that the 1916 Act does not contain any similar requirement constitutes a violation of the Anti-Dumping Agreement.[59] The panel noted that the 1916 Act did not provide for any such notification, either under the civil or criminal tracks. The panel agreed that in this regard the 1916 Act violated Article 5.5 of the Anti-Dumping Agreement.[60]

On appeal, the Appellate Body upheld virtually all the panel's findings.[61] The two "philosophical" points raised by the US were that: (1) the panel did not have jurisdiction to examine the 1916 Act, since the complainants had not challenged a definitive anti-dumping duty, a price taking or a provisional measure—but rather the US legislation *as* legislation;[62] and (2) that Article VI of GATT did not apply to the 1916 Act, since the Act dealt with actions based on anti-competitive intent.[63]

As for the former point, the Appellate Body wrote that

"prior to the entry into force of the WTO Agreement, it was firmly established that Article XXIII:1(a) of the GATT 1947 allowed a CP to challenge legislation as such, independently from the application of that legislation in specific instances".[64]

As for the WTO Anti-Dumping Agreement, Article 17.4 does "set out certain conditions that must exist before a member can challenge action taken by a national investigating authority in the context of an anti-dumping investigation". However, the Appellate Body continued, "Article 17.4 does not address or affect a member's right to bring a claim of inconsistency with the Anti-Dumping Agreement against anti-dumping legislation as such".[65] The Appellate Body thus confirmed the panel's finding with respect to its own jurisdiction in this matter.[66]

As to the latter point, the Appellate Body stated that

"Even if the 1916 Act allowed the imposition of penalties only if the intent proven were an intent to monopolise or an intent to restrain trade (i.e., an 'anti-trust'-type intent),

---

[58] *US Anti-Dumping Act* Panel Report, para. 6.213.
[59] *US Anti-Dumping Act* Panel Report, para. 6.216.
[60] *US Anti-Dumping Act* Panel Report, para. 6.216.
[61] *EC v. US: Anti-Dumping Act of 1916*, Report of the Appellate Body, 28 August 2000 (WT/DS136/AB/R, WT/DS162/AB/R) [hereinafter *US Anti-Dumping Act* Appellate Body Report].
[62] *US Anti-Dumping Act* Appellate Body Report, paras. 52–56.
[63] *US Anti-Dumping Act* Appellate Body Report, para. 132.
[64] *US Anti-Dumping Act* Appellate Body Report, para. 60.
[65] *US Anti-Dumping Act* Appellate Body Report, para. 74.
[66] *US Anti-Dumping Act* Appellate Body Report, para. 83.

this would not transform the 1916 Act into a statute which does not provide for 'specific action against dumping', and thus would not remove the 1916 Act from the scope of application of Article VI".[67]

FUTURE DEVELOPMENT OF WTO ANTI-DUMPING LAW

It has been pointed out that the European Commission is prepared to engage in negotiations on possible reform of the WTO's Anti-Dumping Agreement, with a view towards easing the anti-dumping burden currently experienced by developing countries.[68] To date, the United States has apparently not displayed the same willingness. Among suggestions for reform is a pre-consultation process, whereby developing countries could demonstrate that the initiation of an anti-dumping investigation would affect one of its essential interests; in which case, the investigation would proceed only if the petition contained "serious evidence of injury", and only if the protection of domestic industry in the developed country (importing) member from imports from developing countries (considered in isolation from imports from developed countries) also represented an essential interest for that importing developed country member.[69] There is some indication that rules will be established for the application of national anti-circumvention measures as well.[70]

National anti-dumping measures are likely to remain a refuge for self-protection, in the larger context of an increasingly rules-bound international trade regime. As indicated above, a comparatively high volume of cases are being brought, seeking to challenge national anti-dumping provisions and practices that abuse the relatively open-ended anti-dumping disciplines of the GATT/WTO. To the extent that national anti-dumping laws are used as tools for resisting lower-cost competition from the developing world, they are anomalous and anachronistic; to the extent that they provide a protectionist safety valve for national labour and producer interests, they represent entrenched constituent interests unlikely to be dislodged by any internal WTO reform movement currently on the horizon.

THE SCOPE OF WTO SUBSIDIES LAW: RECENT DISPUTES UNDER THE SCM AGREEMENT

Article VI of the GATT established rules for the imposition of anti-dumping and countervailing duties. Countervailing duties are those imposed to counteract the

---

[67] *US Anti-Dumping Act* Appellate Body Report, para. 132.
[68] See Konstantinos Adamantopoulos and Diego DeNotaris, "The Future of the WTO and the Reform of the Anti-Dumping Agreement: A Legal Perspective", (Dec. 2000) 24 *Fordham International Law Journal* 30.
[69] *Ibid*. at 46–47.
[70] *Ibid*. at 56–57.

effect of unlawful subsidies placed on a particular product to encourage its export. As discussed in the context of the Indonesian Automobile case, the Uruguay Round Agreement on Subsidies and Countervailing Measures (the SCM Agreement) developed existing GATT law on the subject into a conceptually more elaborate system, with subsidies characterised as prohibited, actionable, or non-actionable, depending on their effects, presumed or proven, on trade. Part V, Articles 10 to 23 of the SCM Agreement, covers the "application of Article VI of GATT 1994". The procedures and conditions for the application of countervailing duties set out in that section parallel those set out for the imposition of anti-dumping duties in the Anti-Dumping Agreement.

Unlike the case with dumping (private behaviour, about which the GATT system could only be officially "disapproving"), export subsidies with trade distorting effects were outlawed under GATT's Article XVI from an early stage. Under Article XVI:3, the rules for the use of export subsidies on primary products were more flexible than those applicable to manufactured goods. Creative use of the GATT's anti-subsidies law to challenge trade practices of other countries is not new. However, with the advent of the SCM Agreement, a number of interesting and important disputes have arisen, two of which are described below.

NATIONAL TAX LAW AS AN EXPORT SUBSIDY: THE DISC CASE REVISITED

Following on from the famous DISC case of the 1970s and early 1980s, the United States reformed its tax law to take into account the requirements of GATT law. The result was a change from the "domestic international sales corporation" to the "foreign sales corporation". Perhaps in part because of the high profile complaints being brought by the US (*Beef Hormones* and *Bananas*), the EC in 1998 commenced an action at the WTO against the very FSCs that had resulted from the DISC case.[71] So while the dispute is noteworthy for an expansive interpretation of the Subsidies Agreement (SCM), the argument that GATT/WTO should not deal with national tax rules— or that export subsidies should not be conceived of so broadly— is hardly novel.

The principal EC claim was that the US FSC scheme confers subsidies within the meaning of Article 1 of the SCM Agreement, which are contingent on export performance within the meaning of Article 3.1(a) of the SCM Agreement, and thus prohibited.[72] The EC alleged that there were two subsidies involved in the US scheme: first, certain exemptions from income taxes for FSCs and their

---

[71] *EC v. US: Tax Treatment for "Foreign Sales Corporations"* Report of the Panel, 8 October 1999 (WT/DS108/R), [hereinafter US Foreign Sales Corporations Panel Report].

[72] US Foreign Sales Corporations Panel Report, para. 7.35. Art. 3.1(a) of the SCM Agreement reads as follows: "Except as provided in the Agreement on Agriculture, the following subsidies, within the meaning of Art. 1, shall be prohibited: (a) subsidies contingent, in law or in fact, whether solely or as one of several other conditions, upon export performance, including those illustrated in Annex 1 . . ." Art. 1 sets out the definition of a subsidy.

parent companies; and second, administrative pricing rules which derogate from normal transfer pricing rules and increase the amount of income shielded from taxation by the FSC exemptions.

In the EC view, these represented a financial contribution within the meaning of Article 1.1(a)(ii) of the SCM Agreement, since a government revenue that is otherwise due is foregone or not collected—and a benefit is conferred because the revenue foregone is equal to the amount of money which does not have to be paid in taxes by the FSCs and their parents.[73] The EC also argued that these subsidies were contingent on export performance, within the meaning of Article 3.1(a) because they depend on the amount of exempt foreign trade income that can only be produced by the export of US goods.

The FSC itself was a corporation maintained in a foreign country outside the US customs territory, under the requirements of Sections 921–927 of the US Internal Revenue Code. In contrast to the former DISCs, FSCs were required to be foreign corporations. The FSC was allowed to obtain a tax exemption on its foreign trade income, in particular "the gross receipts of any FSC which are generated by qualifying transactions, which generally involve the sale or lease of 'export property' ".[74] A portion of the company's foreign trade income is deemed to be not effectively connected with a trade or business in the US, and is not taxed in the US (exempt foreign trade income). The remainder is taxable to the FSC.[75] Several pricing rules are available to FSCs, depending on which allocation of income between the FSCs and their parent companies is most advantageous.[76]

The US position was that the FSC scheme did not confer any export subsidy at all; and that footnote 59 to item (e) of the Illustrative List of Export Subsidies (Annex I to the SCM Agreement) contained the "controlling legal standard" applicable to the EC's export subsidy claims. The US argued that this footnote indicated that income generated from foreign economic processes does not need to be taxed, and that the exemption of such income from tax in any form is not a prohibited subsidy.[77] The US also relied on a 1981 decision and understanding

---

[73] Art. 1.1(a)(ii) states that a subsidy shall be deemed to exist if "government revenue that is otherwise due is foregone or not collected (e.g. fiscal incentives such as tax credits); and (b) a benefit is conferred)".

[74] *US Foreign Sales Corporations* Panel Report, para. 2.1.

[75] *US Foreign Sales Corporations* Panel Report, para. 2.3.

[76] *US Foreign Sales Corporations* Panel Report, paras. 2.5–2.8.

[77] Footnote 59 reads: "The Members recognize that deferral need not amount to an export subsidy where, for example, appropriate interest charges are collected. The Members reaffirm the principle that prices for goods in transactions between exporting enterprises and foreign buyers under their or under the same control should for tax purposes be the prices which would be charges between independent enterprises acting at arm's length. Any Member may draw the attention of another Member to administrative or other practices which may contravene this principle and which result in a significant saving of direct taxes in export transactions. In such circumstances, Members shall normally attempt to resolve their differences using the facilities of existing bilateral tax treaties or other specific international mechanisms, without prejudice to the rights and obligations of Members under GATT 1994, including the right of consultations created in the preceding sentence.

Para. (e) is not intended to limit a Member from taking measures to avoid the double taxation of foreign-source income earned by its enterprises or the enterprises of another Member."

of the GATT Council, to the effect that the exemption from tax of income attributable to foreign economic processes does not constitute the foregoing of revenue that is "otherwise due" as in Article 1.1(a)(1)(ii) of the SCM Agreement. In that regard, the US argued that exempting foreign economic processes should not be considered "contingent on export performance".

Finally, the US maintained that footnote 59 allowed members to adopt practices that would distinguish between income derived from processes outside their territory and that derived from processes inside the territory—on condition that the overall allocation of income approximated arm's length results and did not result in a significant savings of direct taxes in export transactions. The US urged the panel to find that there was in its FSC scheme no export subsidy within the meaning of Article 3.1(a) of the SCM Agreement.[78]

The panel began by examining whether or not the FSC exemptions constituted a subsidy. Examining the language of Article 1 of the SCM Agreement, the panel noted that for there to be a benefit, there must be a financial contribution by a government (including revenue foregone); and that a benefit must be conferred thereby.[79] The US had argued that since under WTO rules members were not obliged to tax certain categories of income, their exemption could not constitute a subsidy, and certainly not an export subsidy. But the panel explained that the determination of whether or not revenue is "otherwise due" must involve a comparison between the "fiscal treatment being provided by a Member in a particular situation and the tax regime otherwise applied by that Member".[80]

The panel engaged in a lengthy analysis as to whether or not the 1981 understanding represented a binding part of GATT law;[81] its conclusion was that this understanding was not in fact part of GATT 1994, and did not represent subsequent practice in the application of GATT 1947.[82] The panel concluded that the understanding was in fact a "decision" within the meaning of Article XVI:1 of the WTO Agreement, and that it should be seen as guiding the WTO "to the extent relevant". "However", the panel wrote, "we consider that the 1981 understanding cannot provide guidance in understanding detailed provisions of the SCM Agreement which did not exist at the time the understanding was adopted".[83]

---

[78]   *US Foreign Sales Corporations* Panel Report, para. 7.36.

[79]   *US Foreign Sales Corporations* Panel Report, para. 7.40. In para 7.45, the panel wrote: "In accordance with its ordinary meaning, we took the term 'otherwise due' to refer to the situation that would prevail but for the measure in question. It is thus a matter of determining whether, absent such measures, there would be a higher tax liability."

[80]   *US Foreign Sales Corporations* Panel Report, para. 7.43.

[81]   See *US Foreign Sales Corporations* Panel Report, paras. 7.55–7.85.

[82]   The Understanding, adopted at the time of the adoption of the Tax Legislation (*DISC* case) panel reports, stated that: "The Council adopts these reports on the understanding that with respect to these cases, and, in general, economic processes (including transactions involving exported goods) located outside the territorial limits of the exporting country need not be subject to taxation by the exporting country and should not be regarded as export activities in terms of Art. XVI:4 of the General Agreement." The statement went on to say that arm's length pricing should be observed and that Art. XVI:4 does not prohibit the adoption of measures to avoid double taxation.

[83]   *US Foreign Sales Corporations* Panel Report, para. 7.85.

The panel noted that

"the United States' reference to the 1981 understanding is part of a broader argument that any revenue foregone as a result of FSC exemptions is not 'otherwise due' because it arises from income which is attributable to 'foreign economic processes' ".[84]

With regard to footnote 59, which receives the bulk of the panel's attention, the US had argued that

"the necessary predicate of footnote 59 is that income from foreign economic processes may be exempted from direct taxes. Were that not the case, the arm's length principle would be irrelevant. The arm's length principle prevents income from being inappropriately shifted between parties or functions".[85]

The panel conceded that the US argument on this score "is not without some persuasive force", and agreed that footnote 59 indicates that income from foreign sources may be exempted from direct taxes.[86] However, the panel said that there is also nothing in footnote 59 leading to the conclusion that

"a member that decides that it will tax income arising from foreign economic processes does not forego revenue 'otherwise due' if it decides in a selective manner to exclude certain limited categories of such income from taxation".[87]

The panel stated that it would determine whether revenue foregone was "otherwise due" on the basis of an examination of the fiscal treatment that would be applicable "but for" the measures in question.[88]

The panel reviewed the three forms of exemption the EC alleged deviated from the standard US tax regime. The first related to the rules for determining whether income of an FSC is domestic or foreign source income;[89] the second to the non-application to the foreign trade income of an FSC of the anti-deferral rules for foreign controlled corporations under the Internal Revenue Code.[90] The third concerned the tax treatment of dividends paid by FSCs to their parent corporations.[91] The panel concluded that applying a "but for" test to the FSC scheme, there could be no doubt that, in the absence of the FSC scheme, income which is shielded from taxation by that scheme would be subject to taxation, since it shields from taxation income that would be taxed in its absence.[92]

---

[84] *US Foreign Sales Corporations* Panel Report, para. 7.86.
[85] *US Foreign Sales Corporations* Panel Report, para. 7.89.
[86] *US Foreign Sales Corporations* Panel Report, para. 7.91.
[87] *US Foreign Sales Corporations* Panel Report, para. 7.92.
[88] *US Foreign Sales Corporations* Panel Report, para. 7.93.
[89] *US Foreign Sales Corporations* Panel Report, para. 7.95. The panel wrote: "[T]he European Communities is alleging that the rules provided for determining whether the income of a FSC is 'effectively connected with the conduct of a trade or business within the United States' exempt from taxation certain income of a FSC which in the case of a non-FSC would be treated as taxable by the United States."
[90] *US Foreign Sales Corporations* Panel Report, para. 7.96.
[91] *US Foreign Sales Corporations* Panel Report, para. 7.97.
[92] *US Foreign Sales Corporations* Panel Report, para. 7.98.

Looking at the FSC scheme as a totality, with the individual exemptions taken as one subsidy programme, the panel concluded that the scheme did "involve the foregoing of revenue which is otherwise due". The panel termed the exemptions "a systematic effort by the United States to exempt certain types of income which would be taxable in the absence of the FSC scheme".[93] For these reasons, the panel concluded that the various exemptions do give rise to a "financial contribution" within the meaning of Article 1.1(a)(1)(ii) of the SCM Agreement.[94] In light of the fact that the FSC scheme could provide a tax exemption as large as 15 to 30 per cent of gross income from exporting, the panel concluded, "the financial contribution clearly confers a benefit".[95]

Having found that the FSC scheme gives rise to a financial contribution that confers a benefit, constituting a subsidy within the meaning of Article 1 of the SCM Agreement, the panel's next task was to consider whether the subsidy was "contingent on export performance" within the meaning of Article 3.1(a) of the SCM Agreement.[96] We recall that under Article 3.1(a) of the SCM Agreement, those subsidies shall be prohibited which are "contingent, in law or in fact, whether solely or as one of several other conditions, upon export performance, including those illustrated in Annex I . . .". Since the subsidy in question is only available for "foreign trading income", which arises from the sale or lease of "export property", (property produced in the US for consumption outside the US), the panel concluded that it was indeed "contingent upon export performance".[97] The panel considered its conclusion confirmed by item (e) in the Illustrative List of Export Subsidies in Annex I to the SCM Agreement.[98]

The US maintained that while item (e) stated a general rule that exemption of taxes specifically related to exports was an export subsidy, footnote 59 "qualified the scope" of item (e), making it clear that "exempting income attributable for foreign economic processes from direct taxation is not a prohibited export subsidy" covered by item (e).[99] The hair-splitting carried on by the US in this instance is doubtless attributable to the ambiguity contained in the SCM Agreement, and indeed in GATT/WTO law since the conclusion of the DISC case.

---

[93]   *US Foreign Sales Corporations* Panel Report, paras. 7.99–7.100. The panel wrote that "application of special source rules for FSCs serves to protect a certain proportion of the foreign trade income of a FSC from direct taxation, whether or not that income would be taxable under the source rules provided for in Section 864 of the US Internal Revenue Code. The exemption from the anti-deferral rules of Subpart F of the US Internal Revenue Code ensures that the undistributed foreign trade income of a FSC is not immediately taxable to the US parent of a FSC, even though such income might otherwise be subject to the anti-deferral rules. Finally, the 100% dividends-received deduction ensures that, even when the FSC distributes earnings attributable to foreign trade income to the US parent company, the US patent will not be subject to US income taxes on that income. Taken together, it is clear that the various exemptions under the FSC scheme result in a situation where certain types of income are shielded from taxes that would be due in the absence of the FSC scheme".

[94]   *US Foreign Sales Corporations* Panel Report, para. 7.102.

[95]   *US Foreign Sales Corporations* Panel Report, para. 7.103.

[96]   *US Foreign Sales Corporations* Panel Report, para. 7.104.

[97]   *US Foreign Sales Corporations* Panel Report, para. 7.108.

[98]   *US Foreign Sales Corporations* Panel Report, paras. 7.109–7.112.

[99]   *US Foreign Sales Corporations* Panel Report, para. 7.113.

The panel could hardly resolve this dispute without an analysis of the relationship between item (e) of the Illustrative list, and the famous footnote 59—did the footnote "take the FSC exemptions outside the scope of item (e)"?

The panel rejected the US proposition that a qualification on the scope of item (e) could be implied from the language of footnote 59. In the panel's view, a broad exemption of income deriving from foreign economic activities from taxation might not be an exemption specifically related to exports, since the exemption would relate to income derived from any foreign economic activity, export or otherwise. The panel saw no contradiction between the principle that income arising from foreign economic activity may be exempted from direct taxes, and "the conclusion that the FSC exemptions are within the scope of item (e) because those exemptions are "specifically related to exports".[100]

The US, in a manner reminiscent of the DISC case, argued that its system of worldwide taxation, as opposed to a territorial system, places its exporting companies at a disadvantage, one that the FSC scheme was itself intended to redress.[101] The panel agreed that the WTO may not "dictate the type of tax system that should be maintained by a Member". The US, the panel affirmed, is free to retain its worldwide tax system, or any other tax system it sees fit. "What it is not free to do", the panel stated,

> "is to establish a regime of direct taxation, provide an exemption from direct taxes specifically related to exports, and then claim that it is entitled to provide such an export subsidy because it is necessary to eliminate a disadvantage to exporters created by the US tax system itself".[102]

The parallels with the *DISC* case are obvious here as well.

The US made the argument, highly reminiscent of that earlier case, that if the panel were to

> "rule in favour of the European Communities and reject the principle that foreign-source income need not be taxed, the result would be to condemn not only the FSC, but also territorial tax systems, including the tax systems of the EC Member States".

It was pointed out that the EC had advanced a theory that WTO Members were not prevented by the SCM Agreement from not taxing foreign source income, as long as this was done on a general basis. The panel insisted that there were no implications in its conclusions for the legality or otherwise of the tax systems of other members. "It will be up to any future panels that might be established," the panel wrote, "to examine the consistency of the tax regime before it in accordance with WTO requirements".[103] The panel's conclusion was that the US FSC scheme was indeed a subsidy contingent upon export performance

---

[100] *US Foreign Sales Corporations* Panel Report, para. 7.119.
[101] *US Foreign Sales Corporations* Panel Report, para. 7.121.
[102] *US Foreign Sales Corporations* Panel Report, para. 7.122.
[103] *US Foreign Sales Corporations* Panel Report, para. 7.123.

within the meaning of Article 3.1(a) of the SCM Agreement. The subsidies provided were accordingly prohibited.[104]

The EC also successfully argued that the FSC scheme represented an export
subsidy under the Agreement on Agriculture, and that the US had under its
scheme provided FSC subsidies on a quantity of exports in excess of its commitments under the Agreement on Agriculture, thus acting inconsistently with
Articles 3.3 and 8 of the Agriculture Agreement.[105]

The US did not succeed in its appeal of the panel's conclusions regarding the
status and meaning of the FSC scheme *vis-à-vis* the SCM Agreement. In particular, the Appellate Body rejected the US view of footnote 59, the most potent of
the US arguments.[106] The Appellate Body confirmed the panel's reasoning that
the issue was not whether a member was obliged to tax a particular category of
foreign-source income; rather, the true issue was indeed whether, having decided
to tax a particular category of foreign-source income, the US could be permitted
to carve out an export–contingent exemption from the category of foreign-
source income that is taxed under its other rules of taxation. The Appellate Body
rejected the US' notion that footnote 59 addresses this problem.[107]

In addition, while overturning some of the panel's conclusions with respect to
US commitments under the Agreement on Agriculture, the Appellate Body nevertheless found that the US had, through its FSC measure, applied export subsidies in a manner resulting in or threatening to lead to circumvention of its
export subsidy commitments under the Agriculture Agreements.[108]

SUBSIDIES TO THE AIRCRAFT INDUSTRY

The US and EC closely watched a dispute between Brazil and Canada relating
to national subsidies for the civilian aircraft industry.[109] The case was significant for the fact that it helped clarify the meaning of the term "benefit" in
Article 1.1(b) of the SCM Agreement. Brazil as complainant alleged that certain
Canadian measures constituted subsidies contingent on export performance,

---

[104] *US Foreign Sales Corporations* Panel Report, para. 7.130.

[105] See *US Foreign Sales Corporations* Panel Report, paras. 7.133–7.177.

[106] *EC v. US: Tax Treatment for "Foreign Sales Corporations"*, Report of the Appellate Body,
24 February 2000 (WT/DS108/AB/R), [hereinafter *US Foreign Sales Corporations* Appellate Body
Report].

[107] *US Foreign Sales Corporations* Appellate Body Report, para. 99.

[108] *US Foreign Sales Corporations* Appellate Body Report, paras. 122–154.

[109] *Brazil v. Canada: Measures Affecting the Export of Civilian Aircraft*, Report of the Panel,
14 April 1999 (WT/DS70/R), [hereinafter *Canadian Civil Aircraft* Panel Report]; and Report of the
Appellate Body, 2 August 1999 (WT/DS70/AB/R), [*Canadian Civil Aircraft* Appellate Body Report].
See also discussion by Paul C Rosenthal and Robert T C Vermylen (Spring 2000), "The WTO
Antidumping and Subsidies Agreements: Did the United States Achieve Its Objectives During the
Uruguay Round", 31 *Law and Policy in International Business* 871.

and thus violations of Article 3.1(a) of the SCM Agreement.[110] The particular measures complained of by Brazil were financing and loan guarantees provided by the Export Development Corporation, which included equity infusions for corporations specially established to assist the export of civil aircraft; funds provided by Technology Partnerships Canada (TPC); and various benefits provided by provincial governments.[111] A panel was established to hear the dispute on 23 July 1998.[112]

In defence of its measures, Canada argued that "a 'benefit' is conferred when a financial contribution by a public body (i) imposes a cost on the government, and (ii) results in an advantage above and beyond what the market could provide".[113] It maintained that the ordinary meaning of benefit is overly broad in the context of the SCM Agreement, in that that definition could include ordinary commercial activity, such as a commercial contract entered into by a government that accords an advantage to a firm, as compared with its competitors.[114]

Canada pointed to a number of elements of the SCM Agreement as "context" for its interpretation of the term "benefit". With regard to government credit, Canada stated that item (k) of the Illustrative List in Annex I gives guidance as to what constitutes a subsidy within the meaning of Article 1 of the SCM Agreement. In that regard, Canada submitted that there were two factors relevant to the question of whether credit terms constitute subsidies: (1) whether the government provide credit at rates below those which it has to pay for the funds; and (2) whether the credit secures a material advantage in the field of export credit terms.[115] Canada insisted that the particular mischief the SCM Agreement sought to avoid was national measures distorting the market by imposing a cost on the treasury of the member applying the measure, and conferring an advantage to the recipient "above and beyond the market".[116] Brazil raised strong objections to this "net cost to government" test, finding nothing in the SCM Agreement to suggest that this was necessary to a finding of an unlawful subsidy.[117]

The panel stated that the ordinary meaning of benefit clearly encompassed "some form of advantage", but this ordinary meaning did not include any notion of net cost to government. A financial contribution, the panel went on,

---

[110] Note that Canada also brought a complaint against Brazil with respect to its alleged subsidisation of its civilian aircraft industry. See *Canada v. Brazil: Export Financing Programme for Aircraft* Report of the Panel, 9 May 2000 (WT/DS46/RW). While the panel, upheld by the Appellate Body, found that Brazil had violated Art. 3.1 of the SCM Agreement, the Appellate Body also held that where a developing country member is accused of violating Art. 3.1, the complainant bears the burden of proving that the developing country member did not comply with Art. 27.4 of the SCM Agreement. (Art. 27.4 allows developing country members an eight year phase-out on condition that the level of subsidies is not increased.) Brazil was found not to have complied with Art. 27.4, however.

[111] See *Canadian Civil Aircraft* Panel Report, paras. 2.2 and 3.1 (for full details on the benefits).

[112] *Canadian Civil Aircraft* Panel Report, para. 9.3.

[113] *Canadian Civil Aircraft* Panel Report, para. 9.98.

[114] *Canadian Civil Aircraft* Panel Report, para. 9.99.

[115] *Canadian Civil Aircraft* Panel Report, paras. 9.100–9.101.

[116] *Canadian Civil Aircraft* Panel Report, para. 9.102.

[117] *Canadian Civil Aircraft* Panel Report, paras. 9.103–9.110.

only confers a benefit if it is provided on terms that are more advantageous than those that would have been available on the market.[118] The panel rejected all of Canada's "contextual" arguments in favour of a narrower reading of "benefit"—stating that the ordinary reading would not include ordinary commercial activity, since that kind of activity would not be seen to confer a benefit unless the terms of the contract were more advantageous than those that would have been negotiated on the open market.[119] The panel resoundingly dismissed Canada's interpretation of benefit as necessarily concluding a "net cost to government", finding that a financial contribution by a government confers a benefit, and thus constitutes a subsidy within the meaning of Article 1 of the SCM Agreement,

> "when it confers an advantage on the recipient relative to applicable commercial benchmarks, i.e., when it is provided on terms that are more advantageous than those that would be available to the recipient on the market".[120]

The panel's next task was to review each of the programmes alleged by Brazil to constitute impermissible subsidies.

Brazil attempted to challenge the Canadian Export Development Corporation programme *per se*—in that it is an agency of the government, with an express mandate of assisting Canadian corporations to compete in the global marketplace. Specific aspects of the programme include risk absorption services, export insurance, loan guarantees and equity investments.[121] The panel concluded that Brazil had not shown that the EDC programme actually mandates the granting of subsidies; thus, in accordance with established practice at the WTO, the panel could only evaluate instances of the application of the programme, rather than the programme *per se*.[122]

Following an exhaustive and highly fact-based analysis of the EDC debt financing programme, the panel remained unconvinced that this aspect of the programme constituted an unlawful export subsidy.[123] Brazil failed to establish a prima facie case with respect to every other aspect of the EDC programme—including loan guarantees, residual value guarantees and equity financing.[124]

The panel then turned to Brazil's arguments with respect to the "Canada Account", the funds of which were described by the EDC itself as funds

> "used to support export transactions which the federal government deems to be in the national interest but which, for reasons of size or risk, the EDC cannot support through regular export credits. Transactions are negotiated, executed and administered by the EDC on behalf of the government, and are accounted for separately on

---

[118] *Canadian Civil Aircraft* Panel Report, para. 9.112.
[119] *Canadian Civil Aircraft* Panel Report, paras. 9.113–9.119; 9.114.
[120] *Canadian Civil Aircraft* Panel Report, para. 9.120.
[121] *Canadian Civil Aircraft* Panel Report, paras. 9.121–9.122.
[122] *Canadian Civil Aircraft* Panel Report, paras. 9.124–9.129.
[123] *Canadian Civil Aircraft* Panel Report, paras. 9.131–9.184.
[124] *Canadian Civil Aircraft* Panel Report, paras. 9.183–9.191; 9.192–9.196; and 9.197–9.203.

the books of the Department of Foreign Affairs and International Trade (DFAIT). These activities are known collectively as the Canada Account".[125]

As Brazil again failed to establish that the Canada Account programme actually mandates the grant of subsidies contingent on export performance, the panel looked only at "the actual application of the Canada Account programme".[126]

The panel found first that the Canada Account debt-financing programme constitutes a financial contribution by a public body, and operates at less than commercial rates. Canada had failed, the panel said, to rebut this prima facie showing of the existence of a subsidy within the meaning of Article 1 of the SCM Agreement.[127] As to whether the Canada Account debt financing was contingent on export performance, within the meaning of Article 3.1(a) of the SCM Agreement, the panel noted that all EDC debt financing takes the form of export credits. The panel concluded that the debt financing was in fact "for export of goods", thus clearly contingent in law upon export performance, and thus that Canada had acted in violation of Article 3.2 of the SCM Agreement as well.[128]

While Brazil failed to convince the panel regarding several other of its allegations, it did succeed in establishing its case in the matter of certain repayable investments in projects that result in a high technology product for sale in export markets. Brazil challenges the "actual application" of the Technology Partnerships Canada, a programme created in 1996

> "to address the need by established companies in specific industrial segments to ensure that near-market products—those with a high potential to stimulate economic growth and job creation—actually reach the marketplace".[129]

Brazil maintained that the loans provided in these high-potential areas are not repayable if the project is unsuccessful; on the other hand, if the project achieves profitability, the loans do become repayable, but the government recovers its investment at a rate of return well below what would be expected in the market.[130] The panel then examined specific instances of investments through TPC.[131]

In light of the evidence, the panel stated that it was "in no doubt that TPC contributions constitute 'financial contributions' by a public body within the meaning of Article 1.1 of the SCM Agreement, as they are direct transfers of funds by the government of Canada, in the sense of Article 1.1(a)(1)(i)". And also that "Canada has not disputed this fact".[132] Stating that Brazil had shown

[125] *Canadian Civil Aircraft* Panel Report, paras. 9.204–9.205.
[126] *Canadian Civil Aircraft* Panel Report, paras. 9.208–9.213.
[127] *Canadian Civil Aircraft* Panel Report, paras. 9.220–9.226.
[128] *Canadian Civil Aircraft* Panel Report, paras. 9.227–9.231.
[129] *Canadian Civil Aircraft* Panel Report, para. 9.283.
[130] *Canadian Civil Aircraft* Panel Report, para. 9.284.
[131] *Canadian Civil Aircraft* Panel Report, paras. 9.285–9.304.
[132] *Canadian Civil Aircraft* Panel Report, para. 9.306.

that at least in these instances specific TPC contributions to the aircraft sector were negotiated on terms that do not provide for a commercial rate of return, the panel found that Brazil had established a prima facie case that TPC assistance to the Canadian regional aircraft industry confers benefits within the meaning of Article 1.1(b) of the SCM Agreement.[133] Despite Canada's objections to Brazil's methodology, the panel concluded that Canada had failed to rebut this prima facie case, and thus that TPC assistance constituted subsidies within the meaning of Article 1.1 of the SCM Agreement.[134]

The final element in the panel's investigation is the question of whether or not TPC assistance to the aircraft industry is contingent on export performance. Brazil argued that

> "the export orientation of the Canadian regional aircraft industry is the condition for the grant of the subsidies, in the sense that the subsidies 'would not have been granted were it not for the virtually total export orientation of the Canadian regional aircraft industry".[135]

Canada's counter-argument was that TPC provided support to a wide range of sectors and technologies, including nearly all industrial sectors in Canada; and that TPC does not have any export performance requirements as a condition of project support.[136] Canada further argued that while Brazil appeared to say that TPC was inconsistent with Article 3 of the SCM Agreement because "some of its contributions have been made in a sector that is export-oriented and to companies that export", that in fact is not the test in Article 3. Rather, Canada insisted that the aircraft industry generally, and everywhere it exists, has an export propensity due to market factors, and that it happens to be one of the most globalised industries. The panel noted that

> "Canada understand Brazil to argue that the mere fact that companies in the civil aviation sector engage in exports turns a programme that is also available for domestic markets into an export contingent subsidy".[137]

The panel engaged in an analysis of the phrases "contingent . . . in fact . . . upon export performance" and "in fact tied to . . . anticipated exportation or export earnings". It noted that the ordinary meaning of contingent is "dependent on;" whereas the ordinary meaning of tied to, as used in footnote 4,

> "requires a specific connection between the grant of the subsidy and 'actual or anticipated exportation or export earnings' in order for a subsidy to be 'contingent . . . in fact . . . upon export performance".

---

[133] *Canadian Civil Aircraft* Panel Report, para. 9.307.
[134] *Canadian Civil Aircraft* Panel Report, paras. 9.309–9.315.
[135] *Canadian Civil Aircraft* Panel Report, paras. 9.316–9.317.
[136] *Canadian Civil Aircraft* Panel Report, paras. 9.321–9.322.
[137] *Canadian Civil Aircraft* Panel Report, para. 9.325.

The panel stated that

"When read in the context of the 'contingency referred to in Article 3.1(a), we consider that the connection between the grant of the subsidy and the anticipated exportation or export earnings required by 'tied to' is conditionality".

The panel also noted that the parties agreed to this interpretation.[138]

In the panel's view, whether the "requisite conditionality" exists between the grant of TPC assistance and "anticipated exportation or export earnings" should be in light of whether the facts demonstrate that such assistance would not have been granted but for anticipated exportation or export earnings.[139] Naturally, the parties disagreed on which factors were relevant in determining whether the aircraft industry would not have received these grants were it not for the anticipated exports. Canada rejected Brazil's position that the test is fulfilled when a subsidy is granted because the recipient is anticipated to remain export-oriented; counter-arguing that Brazil's position was over-broad, in that if that view were accepted, then any subsidy that would assist in making national industries more efficient globally would be prohibited as an export subsidy.[140]

The panel stated that in its view Canada's arguments were based on a misunderstanding of Brazil's approach to *de facto* export contingency. The panel did not "understand Brazil to argue that any subsidy that could lead to increased exports is *de facto* export contingent". Rather, as the panel saw it, the panel is referring to subsidies that are granted precisely *because* they are expected to lead to increased exports.[141] It could be said, though, that Canada had presented a compelling argument that was not fully or satisfactorily dealt with by the panel.

The standard relied on by the panel was that "the factual evidence adduced must demonstrate that had there been no expectation of export sales . . . ensuing from the subsidy, the subsidy would not have been granted". The panel stated that this implied a "strong and direct link between the grant of the subsidy and the creation or generation of export sales". In that sense, in the panel's view, the closer the subsidy brings a product to sale on the export market, the greater the possibility that the facts might demonstrate that the subsidy would not have been granted but for the anticipated exports.[142] To this end, the panel reviewed all facts relevant to a determination of the existence of this link.[143]

Reviewing a number of elements in the descriptions and criteria of the relevant programmes, the panel concluded that

"these facts demonstrate that TPC funding in the regional aircraft sector is expressly designed and structured to generate sales of particular products, and that the Canadian government expressly takes into account, and attaches considerable importance to, the

---

[138] *Canadian Civil Aircraft* Panel Report, para. 9.331.
[139] *Canadian Civil Aircraft* Panel Report, para. 9.332.
[140] *Canadian Civil Aircraft* Panel Report, para. 9.333.
[141] *Canadian Civil Aircraft* Panel Report, para. 9.334.
[142] *Canadian Civil Aircraft* Panel Report, para. 9.339.
[143] *Canadian Civil Aircraft* Panel Report, para. 9.340.

proportion of those sales that will be for export, when making TPC contributions in the regional aircraft sector".

These facts, in the panel's view, met the "but for test" discussed above; and provided a sufficient basis for a prima facie case that they also

> "demonstrate that TPC assistance to the . . . industry is 'in fact tied to . . . anticipated exportation . . .' and are therefore 'contingent . . . in fact . . . upon export perform-ance" within the meaning of Article 3.1(a) of the SCM Agreement".[144]

Thus, Canada had not managed to rebut the prima facie case made out by Brazil on this score.[145] Concluding that the Canadian TPC programmes pro-vided "subsidies contingent upon export performance", the panel stated these were contrary to Articles 3.1(a) and 3.2 of the Subsidies Agreement.[146]

DISCIPLINING ANTI-DUMPING, ANTI-SUBSIDIES AND SUBSIDIES

Anti-dumping and anti-subsidies law have been traditionally linked because Article VI of the GATT concerned rules for the imposition of anti-dumping and countervailing duties. Contracting parties were to exercise caution, and meet certain standards, before engaging in self-protective measures designed to elim-inate the unfair competitive advantage represented by dumping or subsidisation by trading partners, in the event that injury was being caused by such practices. The Tokyo Round codes on these subjects raised the evidentiary and procedural burden for countries imposing such measures.

The Uruguay Round's Anti-Dumping Agreement further clarified the require-ments for the imposition of anti-dumping duties. As explained above, because GATT/WTO law can really do no more than "condemn" the private behaviour of dumping, and create rules for the application of national anti-dumping law, this agreement does not interfere with the activity of dumping—but only with the response of members to it. This is central to the logic of GATT/WTO's rela-tionship with the issue of dumping itself.

The Uruguay Round's Agreement on Subsidies and Countervailing Measures also contains more elaborate rules for the imposition of countervailing duties, in a manner analogous to the Anti-Dumping Agreement's rules. However, the SCM Agreement has also created a new system of evaluating the WTO-lawfulness of *subsidies*, establishing clear grounds for challenging a trading partner's subsidisation of its domestic industry. The WTO system is able to cre-ate such rules because subsidisation is, of course, inherently part of the behav-iour of governments and official bodies, and susceptible to regulation by the

---

[144] *Canadian Civil Aircraft* Panel Report, para. 9.341.
[145] *Canadian Civil Aircraft* Panel Report, para. 9.342.
[146] *Canadian Civil Aircraft* Panel Report, para. 9.348. Note that the Appellate Body upheld the panel on all points raised before it. See Canadian Civil Aircraft Appellate Body Report. See *supra* n. 109.

GATT/WTO system. Thus, the "discipline" with respect to subsidies is in two directions—against the subsidiser and against those members responding to subsidies. Dumping itself, as private behaviour, will remain a phenomenon concerning which GATT/WTO will not be able to take a legal position, except to the extent that it seeks to restrain members' responses to the dumping of their trading partners.

Part III
External Trade Relations of the European Union

11

European External Trade Relations: Uniformity Without

BUILDING BLOCKS OF THE COMMON COMMERCIAL POLICY

ARTICLE 14 (FORMERLY 7A), added to the European Treaty by the Single European Act, states that

> "the Community shall adopt measures with the aim of progressively establishing the internal market over a period expiring on the 31st December 1992 . . . The internal market shall comprise an area without internal frontiers in which the free movement of goods, persons, services and capital is ensured in accordance with the provisions of the Treaty".

If we see the economic agenda of the European trading bloc developing over time, it is clear that while the barriers are progressively dismantled internally, there must be a corresponding uniformity of approach by the constituent member states in their trade dealings with non-Member States. It is impossible to imagine intense internal integration without an equal measure of external uniformity.

From the earliest days of the Community, the most basic objectives of the EC have included these two inseparable aspects of economic integration. Article 3 of the Treaty, with its list of core Community activities, prominently includes first "the elimination, as between Member States, of customs duties and of quantitative restrictions on the import and export of goods, and of all other measures having equivalent effect"; and second, "the establishment of a common customs tariff and of a common commercial policy towards third countries".[1] It has been said that under the EC Treaty, "the Common Commercial Policy is the external side of the establishment of the internal market. If the latter were a building, the CCP would be its façade".[2]

The significance of a customs union, of course, is that third countries sending goods into the EC are to receive identical treatment, regardless of where the point of entry to the Community is. Once inside the customs union, imported and European goods ought to circulate freely among Member States, without

---

[1] Piet Eeckhout, *The European Internal Market and International Trade: A Legal Analysis* (Oxford: Oxford University Press, 1994). Eeckhout argues that it was not until 1988 that legal and political attention to the external dimension intensified, partly as a result of the Uruguay Round negotiations and their implications for a greater dose of international competition than ever before.

[2] *Ibid.* at p. 344.

being subjected to any customs charges and without encountering other discriminatory treatment. A common customs tariff has been in place for the
Community since July of 1968.[3] Across the EU, there is a common nomenclature
(system of products classification) for tariff-assessment purposes, a common
method of assigning value to products and a common method for determining
origin.

Both customs duties and quotas had been abolished among the member states
by the time the common external tariff was introduced in 1968. It is significant
that the EC Treaty did not contain any express prohibition against individual
Member States imposing charges equivalent to customs duties on products from
outside the Community. This problem, as will be discussed below, was dealt
with by the Court of Justice.

It is important to note that the Single European Act of 1987 had as one of its
objectives to replace national rules still seen as legally legitimate under former
Community decisions, but restrictive of trade between the Member States. As
far as methodology was concerned, Article 100a (now Article 95) brought in by
the Single European Act stated that the Council, in co-operation with the
Parliament, was allowed to act by qualified majority (rather than unanimity)
when harmonisation of national legislation was required in order to achieve the
internal market by the end of 1992.

The Common Commercial Policy derived from the original Articles 110–116
of the Treaty (now Articles 131–134), a section that has undergone significant
revision over the years. Article 110 stated that it was the aim of the Member
States in creating a customs union to "contribute to the harmonious development of world trade, the progressive abolition of restrictions on international
trade and the lowering of customs barriers", with an aspiration included for
increasing the "competitive strength of undertakings in the Member States as a
result of the abolition of customs duties between them". This article is reminiscent of the GATT Article XXIV idea that the creation of free trade areas and
customs unions ultimately contributed to the growth of global trade.

Article 133 (ex Article 113) is at the core of the CCP. It is fairly self-explanatory,
declaring that the CCP shall be based on uniform principles with regard to tariff
rates, the conclusion of trade agreements, the achievement of uniformity in liberalisation, in export policy and in protective trade measures, such as those imposed
in response to dumping and subsidies. Article 133, paragraph 3 states that in negotiations with other states or with international organisations, the Commission is
to make recommendations to the Council, and the Council is to authorise the
Commission to open the necessary negotiations. Thus, under the Treaty, it is the
Commission which has the actual task of conducting trade negotiations, for
instance at the GATT. This paragraph also makes reference to Article 300 (ex
Article 228), a provision that establishes the Commission's power to negotiate

---

[3] It is of some significance that duties paid under the common customs tariff are taken in as part
of the Community's own budget, with a 10% refund being returned to Member States to cover the
costs of administering their own systems.

and the Council's power to conclude (by qualified majority, on a proposal from the Commission) an international trade agreement. The Commission jealously guards this aspect of the Community's external personality.

Article 115 (now Article 134) virtually phased out by the Single Market programme, was in effect the only escape clause for Member States with respect to uniformity of approach in external trade matters, at least concerning the importation of third country goods. The case law, and the Community's Single Market legislative programme, have both acted to progressively restrict the ability of the Member States to invoke Article 115. It did, however, offer individual Member States a limited opportunity to take national protective measures against certain products where recommendations by the Commission had failed to prevent Member State differences in treatment of certain third party goods. Article 115 was, unsurprisingly, far more limited in scope than, for instance, Article XIX of the GATT (the safeguard clause), since under Article 115 the Commission could determine the national measure to be taken, and indeed had to specifically authorise it. The Commission could also demand the termination of such measures.

While apparently generous towards the economic sensitivities of the member states, and their particular trade needs *vis-à-vis* products entering from outside the EC, Article 115 in fact highlights how narrow the scope was for Member State discretion in the external trade field. Article 115 commonly arose in the context of the problem of overall Community quotas for the import of certain products, when that general quota was further subdivided into Member State quotas, leading to a failure to treat imports from the third party countries as being in "free circulation".

RULES OF ORIGIN

In the European context, the issue of product origin is especially important, since a determination of EC origin confers all the rights and privileges of the European market. Rules of origin represent a key element in the EC's customs legislation, which is in turn a central aspect of the basic customs union itself. When Community-wide legislation was first created on this subject,[4] there was no formal international agreement on methods for conferring origin. Since then, in 1977, the Community has accepted, in addition to its basic regulation, the principles of the Kyoto Convention on the simplification and harmonisation of customs procedures.

The basic Community rules on origin are found in Article 5 and 6 of the original regulation, or Articles 22–27 of the new regulation.[5] The Article 5 definition did not have a quantitative component; there was no set percentage of parts or

---

[4] Council Regulation 802/68. Now see Council Regulation 2913/92, establishing the Community Customs Code. Arts. 22–27 contain the same contents as the earlier regulation with regard to determining origin of goods.

[5] Art. 5 reads: "A product in the production of which two or more countries were concerned shall be regarded as originating in the country in which the last substantial process or operation that is economically justified was performed, and resulting in the manufacture of a new product or representing

value added, nor any other numerical formula leading to the conferral of Community origin on a product. Obviously, the Article 5 term "substantial process" needed judicial clarification. There were several early cases in which the Court of Justice did offer an interpretation of Article 5.

In an early case,[6] the Court of Justice found that origin must be based on "real and objective distinction between raw material and processed product", and that the last process referred to in Article 5 of the regulation is only substantial if the product that results has its own properties, properties it did not possess before that process of operation. The Court stated:

> "activities affecting the presentation of the product for the purposes of its use, but which do not bring about a significant qualitative change in its properties, are not of such a nature as to determine the origin of the product".

In the Yoshida cases,[7] the Court repudiated a Commission regulation that had in effect denied Community origin to slide fasteners made by Japanese companies within European territory. This specialised Commission regulation sought to make it more difficult for certain Japanese companies to claim EC origin, by specifying that origin of these products would depend upon where certain identified operations had taken place. The Court stated that the Commission had gone "back beyond the last process of the manufacture" of the product, thereby introducing criteria extraneous to those set out in the basic Community regulation on rules of origin.

The most important case on this subject was *Brother International*, decided by the Court of Justice in 1989.[8] In this case, the German customs authorities decided that certain typewriters being assembled by Japanese companies in Taiwan should properly be said to have Japanese origin. Had they been coming from Japan, they would have been subject to an anti-dumping order; a classic "circumvention" problem. In light of this, the German authorities proceeded to assess an equivalent anti-dumping duty on the typewriters coming into Germany from Taiwan, as if they had in fact been coming from Japan, an anti-circumvention remedy at the Member State level. The Japanese manufacturer objected on the basis that the parts manufactured in Japan were being assembled in a specially equipped factory located in Taiwan.[9]

---

an important stage of manufacture." Art. 6 says that "Any process or work in respect of which it is established, or in respect of which the facts ascertained justify the presumption that its sole object was to circumvent the provisions applicable in the Community or the member states to goods from specific countries shall in no case be considered, under Art. 5, as conferring on the goods thus produced the origin of the country where it is carried out."

    [6] See *Gesellschaft fur Überseehandel* v. *Handelskammer Hamburg*, Case 49/76 of 26 January 1977 [1977] ECR 41.

    [7] *Yoshida Nederland* v. *Kamer van Koophandel en Fabrieken voor Friesland*, Case 34/78 of 31 January 1979 [1979] ECR 115; and *Yoshida GmbH* v. *Industrie-und Handelskammer Kassel*, Case 114/78 of 31 January 1979 (1979) ECR 151.

    [8] *Brother International GmbH* v. *Hauptzollamt Giessen*, Case 26/88 [1989] ECR 4253, [1990] 3 CMLR 658 of 13 December 1989.

    [9] The German authorities in *Brother International* insisted that the plants in Taiwan were simply "screwdriver plants", and that, beyond mere assembly, some extra element of "intellectual

The question of origin in this context was referred to the Court of Justice under Article 234 (ex Article 177). The Court here clarified under what conditions the mere assembly of previously manufactured parts originating in some country other than the one where assembly occurs, is sufficient to confer the origin of the country where the assembly takes place.

As the Court saw it, Rule 6 of the Kyoto Convention shed some light on the enigmatic language of Article 5 of the origins regulation. Rule 6 says that operations that only contribute a small extent to the essential characteristics of the goods shall not be regarded as "substantial manufacturing or processing". On the list of operations that cannot be seen as substantial is "simple assembly operations", in turn defined as those which do not require specialised staff or special factories with particular equipment for the purpose of that assembly.

The Court said that, since the Kyoto Convention does not specify conditions under which other types of assembly may constitute a substantial process or operation, these must be reviewed on a case-by-case basis.[10] Where technical criteria are not decisive, the proper route, the Court said, is to take value added into account as an ancillary criterion.[11] The Court concluded that the assembly operation as a whole should involve an appreciable increase in the commercial value of the finished product.[12]

The Court rejected the German argument that it is necessary to determine whether the assembly involves any intellectual contribution, since, the Court said, that was not a criterion envisaged in Article 5 of the product origin regulation. Finally, with regard to the question as to whether transfer to another country in this way justifies an Article 6 presumption that the sole object of the transfer was to circumvent the applicable provisions,[13] the Court said plainly that a transfer of this kind is in itself not a ground for such a presumption, since a number of reasons could govern such a decision. However, the company concerned must show that there are other reasonable grounds than circumvention for carrying out assembly in the country from which goods were ultimately exported.

---

input" should be necessary to confer origin. They further argued that the Japanese practice of assembling in Taiwan could justify a presumption under Art. 6 of the origin regulation that the object of the Japanese manufacturers was to circumvent the applicable anti-dumping provisions.

[10] *Yoshida* is cited to the effect that an assembly operation can be seen to confer origin where it represents, from a technical point of view, the decisive production stage, during which the product becomes definite and the goods are given their specific qualities.

[11] This approach, the Court says, is validated by the Kyoto Convention, which allows for "substantial transformation" to be expressed in value added terms.

[12] In para. 23 of the decision, the Court states that where two countries are involved and technical criteria are not sufficient for a determination of origin, assembly of previously manufactured parts is not enough to confer origin on the country of assembly if the value added in the assembly country is appreciably less than the value which was imparted in the other country. In this case, the Commission estimated that less than 10% of the value was added in the country of assembly. In such an instance, the Court says, the amount of value added "cannot in any event be regarded as sufficient to confer on the finished product the origin of the country of assembly".

[13] Under Art. 6, the presumption depends on the sole objective of the transfer being to circumvent European anti-dumping law.

It is clear that the relative vagueness of the origin standard led to the European rules on circumvention in the 1988 and 1994 legislation. The 1994 amendments would have been directly relevant to the *Brother International* facts. The 1994 anti-dumping legislation undoubtedly reflected frustration on the part of the authorities at not being able to "transfer" origin back to the offending country more easily (as seen in *Brother International*) and also at not being able to settle the circumvention issue during the Uruguay Round negotiations.

EXTERNAL CHARGES EQUIVALENT TO CUSTOMS DUTIES

The European Treaty did not explicitly deal with the problem of Member States imposing external charges that might have effects equivalent to those of customs duties. Not surprisingly, it was left to the Court of Justice to sort this matter out, in a case involving a Belgian law setting up a social fund for diamond workers.[14] The fund was generated by making importers of rough diamonds subject to an importation charge. While Belgium had exempted diamonds coming from its European partners from such a charge, it remained in effect with regard to diamonds centering from third countries. Two representatives of the diamond industry submitted statements to the effect that since the coming into force of the common customs tariff in 1968, any separate contribution should be considered incompatible with the EC Treaty. The Belgian authorities countered with the argument that incompatibility with the Treaty could only be established where the Commission, acting under Articles 155 (now Article 211) and 169 (now Article 226), found a serious obstacle to the working of the customs union and the common customs tariff and had actually intervened to stop it. The case is interesting in part because the reason for the charge had nothing to do with customs duties *per se*; and in fact had a separate justification with a social dimension.

The Court invoked Article 3(b) (now Article 5) of the Treaty and the principles governing the creation of a customs union as found in Article 9. It describes the customs union as "one of the foundations of the Community", involving the elimination of customs duties between the Member States and of all charges having equivalent effect. As for the common customs tariff, this was designed to achieve equalisation of customs charges levied at the frontiers "in order to avoid deflection of trade in relations with third countries, and any distortion of free internal circulation or of competitive conditions".

The Court recognised that the Treaty says nothing about "charges having equivalent effect of customs duties" towards third countries. But, the Court said tellingly, "this does not mean that such charges may be maintained, still less introduced". What must be taken into account here, the Court said, are requirements resulting from the establishment of the common customs tariff and those resulting from the CCP, within the meaning of Articles 110–116 of

---

[14] *Sociaal Fonds voor de Diamantarbeiders* v. *NV Indiamex* [1973] cases 37 and 38/73 ECR 1609; [1976] 2 CMLR 222.

the Treaty (now Articles 131–134) which together regulate trade with third countries. The Court thus posited an interesting conceptual combination of the CCP and the CCT. It is clear, the Court continued, that Member States are prohibited from amending, by means of charges supplementing such duties, the level of protection defined by the CCT. Even where such (national) charges are not protective in character, the Court stated, they may still be irreconcilable with the requirements of a CCP and with Article 113 (now Article 133), which calls for "uniform" principles. The Court's theory here is dominated by the fact that Article 133 (ex Article 113) requires the general elimination of national disparities in the field of commerce affecting trade with third countries. The Court stated clearly that subsequent to the introduction of the CCT, all Member States are prohibited from introducing, on a unilateral basis, any new charges or from raising those already in force.

The outstanding question, then, involves the legal status of pre-CCT charges of this type. The Court said that it is for the Community to evaluate, and if need be to obligate Member States to eliminate, such charges. This depends upon some intervention, some action, by the Community authorities, but the Court did not agree that the Commission would have to identify some economic disruption before requiring the elimination of a national charge. No burden was placed on the Community authorities to justify their actions based upon a finding of disturbance. By implication, lack of uniformity in external tariffs would appear to be justification enough for disallowing a national charge with equivalent effect to an external tariff.

COMMUNITY COMPETENCE TO CONCLUDE AND PARTICIPATE IN INTERNATIONAL AGREEMENTS

Some international agreements involve the European Community institutions acting alone (without the participation of the Member States), as long as the subject matter of the agreement falls wholly within the external competence of the Community. By contrast, there are also "mixed agreements", involving the active participation of both the Community and the Member States, when competence belongs partly to the one, and partly to the other. There are also in some areas international agreements made by the Member States on their own behalf directly with third countries.

The European Treaty grants explicit treaty-making power to the Community in two areas: under Article 133 (ex Article 113) in the area of international commercial agreements, and in Article 238 (ex Article 181), dealing with association agreements.[15] Under Article 228 (ex Article 171), the Council is to conclude agreements after consultation with the European Parliament, but that is not the

---

[15] Association agreements with particular third countries often precede the membership of those countries in the EC; they generally involve a range of mutual rights and obligations, particularly with respect to trade matters.

case with agreements referred to in Article 133(3)—that is, agreements related to the CCP and trade/tariff agreements, including of course the GATT. However, Article 300(3) also states that: ". . . agreements establishing a specific institutional framework by organising cooperation procedures, [and] agreements having important budgetary implications for the community . . . shall be concluded after the assent of the European Parliament has been obtained." This was the case with the adoption of the Uruguay Round Agreements.

The power to make agreements with third countries of course goes to the heart of national sovereignty; consequently, there has been a long-running legal battle as to the scope of the Community's competence to conclude and participate in such agreements in the place of and acting for the EC Member States. The language of Article 300 (ex Article 228) would seem to imply that the Commission is to negotiate and the Council to conclude international agreements only where the Treaty specifically provides for this. As in so many other contexts, the Court of Justice has, through its decisions, greatly increased the Community's ability to expand its external competence, as will be shown below.

Since tariffs and trade (and commercial policy generally) were specifically mentioned in the Treaty as subject matter over which the Community had competence, it has generally not been problematic for the Community to enter into and conclude such agreements. However, where the areas covered in the third party agreement were partly in and partly outside the traditional subject matter of the CCP, the Community came to rely on a device called the "mixed agreement", although such an entity was nowhere mentioned in the EC Treaty itself. Most association agreements, in fact, involve co-operation in a number of fields, both trade and non-trade related. Thus, many of the trade and aid agreements, including the Lomé Convention (now succeeded by the Cotonou Agreement) entered into between the EC and countries representing former colonial possessions, were concluded under the mixed agreement formula. Ratification in such instances would be first by the individual Member States, then by the Community institutions. The issue of external competence takes on great significance in the controversial Opinion 1/94 of the Court of Justice, concerning the competence of the Community to conclude the Uruguay Round Agreements.

EXCLUSIVE COMPETENCE IN MATTERS FALLING UNDER THE CCP:
THE NATURE OF EXCLUSIVITY

Opinion 1/75 (OECD *Understanding on a local cost standard*):[16] the what and why of exclusive external competence

The Court of Justice was asked by the Commission under Article 300(6) (ex Article 228(6)) of the Treaty to examine the legality of the conclusion by the

---

[16] [1975] ECR 1355.

Community of an OECD agreement on the subject of credit cover for exporting firms for costs incurred in the importing countries. The Commission wished to have the Court's analysis as to whether the Community is competent to conclude the agreement, and, more importantly, whether this power to conclude is exclusive—that is, whether the Member States can be excluded altogether from participation.[17] The Commission had been responsible for presenting a common Community position on the matter at the OECD negotiations.

The Court stated that it would keep in mind Articles 112 and 113 of the EC Treaty (now Articles 132 and 133) in making its assessment of the agreement. Article 112 indicates that Member States are to harmonise the systems whereby they grant aid to exporters "to the extent necessary to ensure that competition between undertakings of the Community is not distorted". Article 113 is of course the key provision on the CCP, and commences with the statement that "The common commercial policy shall be based on uniform principles".

The Court said that it was clear that the subject matter of the understanding relates to a field in which the provisions of the Treaty recognise an external Community power. Export aid policy, the Court continued, is an important part of the CCP.[18] And there is no doubt about the fact that the Community has the power to adopt both internal rules and to conclude agreements with third countries to implement principles contained in Articles 112 and 113. However, the more significant question is whether and in what manner that power is exclusive.

The answer to this, said the Court, depends upon how the CCP is perceived within the Treaty. In the Court's view, the CCP exists for the defence of the common interest of the Community, and Member States must adapt to this. The Court was adamant that under this scenario, there is no role for the concurrent participation of the Member States.[19] The Court here assumed a "common interest" without explaining what precisely this interest consists of.

The Court saw concurrent participation in apocalyptic terms: it said that any individual action by the Member States in this regard would lead to "disparities . . . calculated to distort competition" between the undertakings of the various Member States in external markets. The only correct approach, the Court said, is "strict uniformity".

Were the Member States to act independently in these matters, the Court said that the "institutional framework" of the Community itself would be called into

---

[17] The subject matter of the agreement has to do with harmonisation of the level of financing offered to national exporters for their "local costs"—i.e., expenses incurred in the countries of destination for the exported goods. An excessive level of aid to one's exporters, above that offered by one's trade rivals, would represent a competitive advantage.

[18] There is Community legislation on the subject of export credit insurance, dating back to 1970 and 1971.

[19] A proper conception of the CCP, the Court said, "is incompatible with the freedom to which the Member States could lay claim by invoking a concurrent power, so as to ensure that their own interests were separately satisfied in external relations, at the risk of compromising the effective defense of the common interests of the Community".

question, along with "mutual trust", preventing the Community from "fulfilling its task in the defense of the common interest".

So in the Community's exclusive competence, based on a principle of "strict uniformity", participation by the Member States is ruled out completely as a threat to unity. The Court might have interpreted the principle as requiring a negotiated common position representing a balance between general and particular interests. Instead, without feeling the need to demonstrate empirically that such an interest exists, or in what form its exists, the Court asserted the primacy of the Community interest, and the fundamental need for the Community to be in an international position to defend it.

OPINION 1/78 (*THE NATURAL RUBBER AGREEMENT*)[20]

In this opinion, the Court sanctioned the use of mixed agreements, to allow the Community and the Member States to jointly participate in an international agreement where the subject matter made this necessary. It is also important for the expansionary approach taken by the Court in defining the scope of the CCP. Here the Commission asked the Court to analyse the Community's competence with regard to a worldwide commodity agreement, negotiated under the auspices of the UN, concerning the supply of natural rubber. The objectives of the agreement were to guarantee stable prices and supply in a manner beneficial to both the developed and developing worlds. Although the subject matter of the agreement was broad, the Commission argued that because its essentials fell within the exclusive competence of the Community, the entire agreement should be seen in this way.

For its part, the Council argued in favour of a mixed agreement format for negotiation and conclusion, since some of the subject matter was not covered by the traditional CCP; for example, issues of North-South co-operation, foreign aid, as well as the military and strategic aspects of natural rubber. A related issue was the proper financing of a "buffer stock" to be used to regulate the world price of natural rubber. The Commission argued in favour of Community financing, whereas the Council's view was that any Member State financing would require the adoption of a mixed agreement format.

The Court conceded that this agreement differed from "ordinary commercial and tariff agreements", since it was about structured trade and the organisation of a market in the product on a worldwide scale. As far as whether or not the agreement falls within the scope of Article 113, the Court took a simultaneously practical and daring point of view. Rather than measuring the commodity agreement against a pre-existing definition of the CCP, it measured the available definition of the CCP against the rise in global commodity agreements. The Court said, "it is clear that a coherent commercial policy would no longer be

---

[20] [1979] ECR 2871.

practicable if the Community were not also in a position to exercise its powers in connection with a category of agreement which is becoming one of the major factors in the regulation of international trade".

To opt for a narrower interpretation of the CCP, the Court explained, would be "to restrict the CCP to the use of instruments intended to have an effect only in the trading aspects of external trade", thus excluding "more highly developed mechanisms such as appear in the agreement envisaged". This type of restrictive view would, the Court said, risk causing disturbance in intra-Community trade by reason of the disparities that would then exist in certain sectors of economic relations with non-Member States.

The Court concluded that although there were effects brought about by the agreement on the economic policies of the Member States, such as the supply of raw materials or price policy, this "does not constitute a reason for excluding such objectives from the field of application of the rules relating to the CCP". This is also true of the question of the strategic importance of the product.

But this expansive definition of the CCP was not the end of the story. Although the Commission had argued that Community competence could not be made to depend upon financial arrangements, the Court nevertheless found that mixed competence would in fact be necessary if the Member States participated in the financing of the buffer stock. As the Court saw it, either solution was legally possible.

EXTERNAL AGREEMENTS ON NON-CCP SUBJECT MATTER:
HOW DOES THE COMMUNITY GAIN COMPETENCE?

Far more complicated is the situation where the subject matter of the third party agreement clearly does not fall under the CCP. While many non-CCP agreements may have an indirect relationship to trade matters, the route by which competence to conclude and participate in such agreements has been spelled out over time by the Court of Justice, since the Treaty itself was silent on the question of Community competence apart from in the enumerated areas described above. Had the Court decided in the early days that the Community's external competence was limited to those areas clearly enumerated in the Treaty, the Community would have been a much-reduced legal entity on the international stage.

THE *ERTA* CASE: PARALLELISM AND EXTERNAL COMPETENCE

One of the first cases to take on this issue was the *European Road Transport Agreement (ERTA)* case of 1971,[20a] a classic battle between the Commission

---

[20a] *Commission* v. *Council*, Case 22/70, [1971] ECR 263.

and the Council over the role of Member States in participating in a third party agreement on road transport in Europe. The Commission here asked the Court to annul a Council resolution allowing Member States involvement in the negotiations. The Commission's argument was that since a Council regulation had been created in 1969 on the same subject matter, though only applicable within EC territory, the Community alone had the power to conclude third party agreements on related topics.

The Commission also argued that since Article 75 (now Article 71) of the Treaty conferred broad powers on the Community to create a common transport policy within the Community, then these powers must be taken to include external relations as well.[21] The Council in turn argued that the Community institutions only have such third party powers as are specifically conferred on them, and that authority to supercede the Member States in making third party agreements of this kind cannot just be assumed.

The judgment made a great leap forward, asserting that since Article 210 of the Treaty states that the Community has a legal personality, this means that the Community can establish contractual links with third countries. In an extraordinary section, the Court stated that:

> "each time the Community, with a view to implementing a common policy envisaged by the Treaty, adopts provisions laying down common rules, the Member States no longer have the right, acting individually or even collectively, to undertake obligations with third countries which affect those rules".

Applying that principle to these facts, the Court found the internal and external rules to be inseparable.

The Court set out a scheme wherein Member States lose their power to act externally after the Community has acted internally—and acted on the basis of a Treaty mandate to create a common internal policy. At that point, the Community has vested in it the powers to act with respect to that subject matter as it appears in third party agreements with the Community.[22] With regard to the agreement in question, most of the negotiations had already been concluded before the transfer of power took place in 1969, at the time when Community legislation was created on the same subject matter. For this reason, the Court did not wish to precipitate a situation in which the negotiating entity was changed at that late date in the creation of the agreement. Under the circumstances, the Court found that the Council had not failed in its obligations under Article 71 (ex Article 75) and Article 300 (ex Article 228) of the Treaty. So, while the Commission had technically lost the case, in legal terms it had won an

---

[21] This is the doctrine Trevor Hartley refers to as "strong parallelism". See *The Foundation of European Community Law*, 3rd edn. (Oxford: Clarendon Press, 1994) at 172.

[22] This process, the Court says, excludes the possibility of concurrent powers for the Member States, since "any steps taken outside the framework of the Community institutions would be incompatible with the unity of the Common Market and the uniform application of Community law".

enormous conceptual victory.[23] The ability of the Community to expand its own external powers by taking action internally was now assured, at least in subject matter areas appropriate for the creation of a common policy, as specifically mentioned in the Treaty.[24]

INLAND WATERWAYS OPINION:[24a] A STRONGER PARALLELISM

In this case, too, the Commission asked the Court of Justice to evaluate the legality of an international agreement, here one negotiated among the Commission, Switzerland, and the EC Member States which had been members of a previous agreement on the same subject—reducing the surplus carrying capacity for goods on the European inland waterway system, so as to maintain prices for the freight industry. The Court identified the source of the Community's authority to legislate in this field in Articles 3 and 75—Article 75 being the provision calling for a common transport policy. The Court expanded on the ERTA doctrine by saying that external powers arise from internal powers, particularly in cases where the internal power has already been used to adopt measures for the attainment of common policies. The Court said that the exercise of the external powers "is, however, not limited to that eventuality".

The agreement in question set up a number of unique institutions, including a tribunal that envisaged a sharing of judicial personnel and resources with the Court of Justice itself, as well as a Supervising Board and a Board of Management. The Commission would be represented on the Supervisory Board, but would not have voting rights. The Board of Management would have weighted representation according to the size of the participating community. The Commission's original position was that the agreement would be administered by the Community presenting a common response to all points of principle raised within the working of the agreement. The Court here took a hard line on both Member State participation in the conclusion of the agreement and on the structure of the agreement itself. Member State participation in the creation of the new agreement would be tolerable only to the extent that this was necessary to revise the earlier treaties on the subject. Apart from that, the Court said, "the legal effects of the agreement with regard to the Member States result . . . exclusively from the conclusion of the latter by the Community".

---

[23]   See Hartley n. 21 *supra*, at 172. What the Court had left unsaid at this stage was that the very existence of an internal power of the Community's in a particular subject matter would, even if still unexercised, imply a corresponding external power, if only in certain circumstances.

[24a]   *Opinion given pursuant to Art. 228(1) of the EEC Treaty* (Opinion 1/76) [1977] ECR 741.

[24]   *Cornelius Kramer and Others* (Joined cases 3, 4 and 6/76) [1976] ECR 1279. In the Kramer case, concerning Member State powers to participate in an agreement on national quotas for fishing in the Northeast Atlantic, the Court stated that the authority of Member States is "transitional", and ends when the Community has taken legislative action. As soon as the Community institutions have implemented measures in an area, it is for the Community to participate in any related international agreements. The Community's duty consists in taking action where it is called upon to do so, and in assuming international obligations in the relevant subject matter area.

Beyond this, the Court found serious legal flaws in the outcome of the negotiations as well, since participation of the Member States had "produced results
. . . incompatible with the requirements implied by the very concepts of the
Community and its common policy". The Court found the role to be played by
the Community institutions in the agreement's scheme to be too limited, with
determinative functions being performed by the participating states. The Court
was characteristically apocalyptic about the consequences of allowing such an
arrangement to go forward. The agreement's provisions, the Court said,

"Call in question the power of the institutions of the Community and, moreover, alter
in a manner inconsistent with the Treaty the relationship between Member States
within the context of the Community as it was in the beginning and when the
Community was enlarged".

As the Court found the structure of the Agreement to be "incompatible with
the requirements of unity and solidarity", one sees the extent to which the Court
values external uniformity as a key ingredient in maintaining coherent
Community powers. In other words, there must not be an external configuration in the allocation of powers between Community and Member States that
does not mirror the existing internal configuration of those powers.[25]

AN EXPANDING DEFINITION OF THE COMMON COMMERCIAL POLICY

The CCP appears to be a concept capable of an ever-expanding interpretation, and
capable of absorbing many of the foreign policy issues that cling to foreign trade
matters. A case referred to the Court of Justice from the English Court of Appeal
raised important questions as to the relationship between foreign commerce and a
Member State's continuing power to decide its own foreign policy positions.[26]

The case arose from a decision by the Bank of England to refuse authorisation
for Barclay's Bank to transfer funds from a bank in Yugoslavia to an account
held by an Italian company, for the purpose of paying for medical products
approved for export from Italy to Montenegro.

As background, in 1992, a UN Security Council resolution imposed sanctions
against Yugoslavia (Serbia and Montenegro). All states were to prevent the supply from their territories of any commodities to any person in Yugoslavia,
although the prohibition excluded medical supplies and food. All states were

---

[25] The Court, in its Opinion 2/91 on *Community competence in the context of an ILO convention No. 170 on chemicals at work*, [1993] 3 CMLR 800, went beyond ERTA to say that sometimes
external competence could be gained through Community legislation, even where the internal legislation did not derive from a specific mention of Community powers in the Treaty. The Court
stated: ". . . The authority of the decision in that case [ERTA] cannot be restricted to instances where
the Community has adopted common rules within the framework of a common policy. In all areas
corresponding to the objectives of the Treaty, Art. 5 EEC requires Member States to facilitate the
achievement of the Community's tasks and to abstain from any measure which could jeopardize the
attainment of the objectives of the Treaty".

[26] *R v. HM Treasury and Bank of England* case C-124/95 [1997] ECR I-81.

also to prevent their nationals from making available any funds to that county, except payments for medical, food and humanitarian purposes.

The European Community then adopted a "Sanctions Regulation" to give effect to the UN resolution. It stated that exports to Serbia and Montenegro of medical or food products shall be subject to a prior authorisation to be issued by the competent authorities of the Member States. The UK adopted its own order prohibiting any person from supplying any goods to those countries except with a license granted by the Secretary of State. The order further said that no person could make any payment where this would make resources available to Serbia and Montenegro, except with the permission of the Treasury.

The Bank of England began to authorise transactions for the payment of humanitarian exports to Serbia and Montenegro. Barclay's, holder of an account of the National Bank of Yugoslavia, applied to the Bank of England to debit its account, most of which requests were accepted. Then came public reports to the effect that the system was being abused in favour of other parties, and the Treasury became stricter. It announced that such payments would only be authorised where the exported product had been from the UK. The Court of Appeal was unsure as to whether this decision was contrary to Article 113 (now Article 133) of the Treaty, in light of the EC's Sanctions Regulation.

The Court identified the first problem as involving the relationship between measures of foreign and security policy and the CCP. The UK argued that the validity of its measures cannot be affected by the exclusive competence of the Community in CCP matters, or by the Sanctions Regulation which merely implements at Community level the exercise of a Member State's competence in the field of foreign and security policy. While the Court agreed that Member States had retained their competence in the field of foreign and security policy, nonetheless they could not treat national measures whose effect is to restrict the export of certain products as falling outside the scope of the CCP on the ground that they have foreign and security objectives.

As to the scope of the CCP, the Court said that

> ". . . even if such measures do not constitute measures of commercial policy, they may nevertheless be contrary to the CCP . . . insofar as they contravene Community legislation adopted in pursuance of that policy".

Since the derogation from the general system of Community exports does not extend to exports of medical products, the Court said, "[i]t follows that those exports remain subject to the common system provided for by the export regulation". The Court found that the UK measure was a restriction on the payment of goods legally exported, and as an essential element in the export transaction, it was the equivalent of a quantitative restriction.

The UK insisted that its measure was based on the Article 11 exception for measures adopted on grounds of public policy or security. The Court responded that while measures imposed to apply UN sanctions fall within the Article 11 exception, Member State recourse to Article 11 ceases to be justified "if

Community rules provide for the necessary measures to ensure protection of the interests enumerated in that article."

It might be suggested that the Court wilfully ignored the fact that the whole point of the security exception is that Member States are likely to have different interpretations of the security issues involved. According to the Court, the Sanctions Regulation is designed to implement the UN Sanctions uniformly throughout the Community. "In that respect", the Court said, "Member States must place trust in each other". Other Member's authorisation procedures, in other words, must be accepted throughout the Community.

THE NEW COMMERCIAL POLICY INSTRUMENT AND THE TRADE BARRIERS INSTRUMENT[27]

This special European legislation was created as a response to the US Section 301 of the 1974 Trade Act.[28] Both instruments were designed to allow industry representatives to put public political pressure on the relevant trade authorities to take action against trading partners engaged in unfair trading practices. The New Commercial Policy Instrument, first created in 1984, has undergone changes in recognition of the outcome of the Uruguay Round negotiations and of the fact that Voluntary Export Restraints (VERs) have been made WTO-illegal in the WTO context. Whereas the earlier instrument could lead to actions either unilateral or as part of a GATT complaint, the new instrument is more limited in the action it indicates the authorities can take in response to unfair trading behaviour by others.

THE ORIGINAL REGULATION

Its preamble speaks of "strengthening the CCP" with regard to protection against illicit commercial practices of other states.[29] Under this instrument, the

---

[27] Council Regulation No 2641/84 on the strengthening of the common commercial policy with regard in particular to protection against illicit commercial practices; replaced by Council Regulation No 3286/94. For a broad discussion of the new instrument, see Candido Garcia Molyneaux, "The Trade Barriers Regulation: the European Union as a Player in the Gloablisation Game", 5:4 *European Law Journal*, 375–418

[28] "Section 301 of the Trade Act of 1974 is one of the most politically motivated provisions of United States trade laws . . . [It] authorizes and in some cases mandates unilateral United States retaliation if another nation is in breach of a trade agreement or engaging in unjustifiable, unreasonable or discriminatory conduct." Ralph H Folsom, Michael Wallace Gordon, John A Spanogle, *International and Investment Trade in a Nutshell*, 2nd edn. (St. Paul, Minn.: West Publishing, 2000), at 168.

[29] "Whereas in the light of experience and of the conclusions of the European Council of June 1982, which considered that it was of the highest importance to defend vigorously the legitimate interest of the Community in the appropriate bodies, in particular GATT, and to make sure the Community, in managing trade policy, acts with as much speed and efficiency as its trading partners, it has become apparent that the CCP needs to be strengthened."

Community was provided with procedures that would enable it to respond to illicit commercial practices, so as to ameliorate their injurious effects within the Community, and to ensure the full exercise of the Community's rights with regard to the commercial practices of third countries. The "illicit nature" of third country practices is said to be "evident from their incompatibility regarding international trade practices either with international law or with the generally accepted rules".[30]

Article 1 points out that procedures are being established to respond to illicit commercial practices, and to ensure the full exercise of the Community's rights with regard to the commercial practices of third countries. Article 2, on definitions, states that an illicit practice is one "either incompatible with international law or with the generally accepted rules". The "Community's rights" are defined as "international trade rights of which it may avail itself either under international law or under generally accepted rules". Community industry refers to producers "whose combined output constitutes a major proportion of total Community production of the products in question".

The procedures for lodging a complaint are described in Article 3. First, a representative of the industry files a complaint when the industry has suffered injury as a result of an illicit trade practice. The industry must provide sufficient evidence of the injury claimed. When consultations make it apparent to the Commission that there is sufficient evidence to justify an examination, and that it is in the interests of the Community, the Commission makes a formal announcement to that effect.

The Commission is given broad powers of investigation; it also receives submissions from interested parties. The Commission must present a report within five months of the initiation of procedures, but at the latest within seven months. There is a list of various economic and industrial factors to be taken into account during the Commission's examinations of injury (Article 8), no doubt on the theory that this instrument cannot be used for the purpose of general protection of flagging European industries.

A number of outcomes are possible (Article 9 and 10). The proceedings may of course be terminated; or, undertakings from third countries may be accepted. Article 10, on the adoption of commercial policy measures, states that where the examination leads to a conclusion that there must be a response to the illicit commercial practice, either with the aim of removing its injury or in order to ensure full exercise of the Community's rights, then the appropriate measures shall be determined in accordance with procedures set out in Article 11. As with the US section 301, this provision ensures that some steps will be taken by the authorities in the event that it is determined that Community rights have been violated by trading partners.

---

[30] It also mentions, as part of the regulation's purpose, that "the Community must act in compliance with its international obligations and, where such obligations result from agreement, maintain the balance of rights and obligation which it is the purpose of those agreements to establish."

The next paragraph states that where the Community's international obligations require consultation or dispute settlement, commercial policy measures shall only be decided upon after that procedure has been terminated, and "taking account of the procedure". While this did not give absolute precedence to a GATT outcome, it did imply that the Community would restrain its use of unilateral measures.

The article proceeds: "Any commercial policy measures may be taken which are compatible with existing international obligations and procedures", notably a withdrawal of negotiated concessions, the raising of existing customs duties, or the introduction of any other charge on imports; or the introduction of QRs or other measures. Clear reasons must be given for whatever response is chosen by the authorities.

The instrument that replaced the New Commercial Policy Instrument, popularly known as the Trade Barriers Instrument, reflected the results of the Uruguay Round negotiations.[31] Reference to the WTO is more prominent than was the case with GATT rules within the earlier instrument. The preamble mentions that the purpose is to lay down Community procedures

"in the field of common commercial policy in order to ensure the exercise of the Community's rights under international trade rules, in particular those established under the auspices of the World Trade Organisation".

It goes on to say that international trade rules are primarily those of the WTO, but that they can also be found in other trade agreements between the Community and third countries. The preamble also calls for transparency and a clear factual basis when the Community invokes its rights under international trade rules. The Community institutions are to react to trade obstacles "provided that a right of action exists, in respect of such obstacles, under applicable international trade rules". By comparison with the earlier trade instrument, it must be said that this one lays substantial emphasis on the need to resolve disputes with trading partners on the basis of agreements and also by acting in compliance with international obligations of the Community. The post–1995 trading world is far less tolerant of unilateral solutions.

Article 1 reiterates this deference towards the recognised legal rules.[32] The objective will be to remove adverse trade effects and injury. The procedures "shall be applied in particular to the initiation and subsequent conduct and termination of international dispute settlement procedures in the area of the common commercial policy".

The new instrument's definition of obstacles to trade is of importance. (Article 2) These shall be

---

[31] See Michael Sanchez Rydelski and G A V R Zonnekeyn, "The EC Trade Barriers Regulation: The EC's Move Towards a More Aggressive Market Access Strategy", 31: 5 *Journal of World Trade* 147–166; and Natalie McNelis, "The European Union Trade Barriers Regulation: A more effective instrument", 1:1 *Journal of International Economic law*, 149–155

[32] The regulation is to establish procedures governing "the exercise of the Community's rights under international trade rules, in particular those established under the auspices of the WTO".

"any trade practice adopted or maintained by a third country in respect of which international trade rules establish a right of action. Such a right of action exists when international trade rules either prohibit a practice outright, or give another party affected by the practice a right to seek elimination of the effect of the practice in question".

Thus the right to respond has been limited by a prior determination that there exists a cause of action under international trade rules.

These trade rules are further defined by specific reference to the WTO and other free trade agreements. As with the earlier instrument, injury could refer either to injury within the European market, or in some third country market.[33] The new instrument emphasises that its response will be guided by the outcome of WTO panel proceedings. "In particular", it says,

"where the Community has requested an international dispute settlement body to indicate and authorise the measures which are appropriate for the implementation of the results of an international dispute settlement procedure, the Community commercial policy measures which may be needed in consequence of such authorisation shall be in accordance with the recommendation of such international dispute settlement body".

The list of "possible outcomes"—withdrawal of concessions, raising duties, or introducing QRs—is not terribly different from those listed in the earlier instrument.

Where ultimately it is clear that all the international procedures have been gone through and it is decided to do "something" out of the list of possible responses, "the Council shall act in accordance with Article 113 of the Treaty, by a qualified majority, not later than 30 working days after receiving the proposal [by the Commission]".

THE COMMUNITY'S MONOPOLY TO INTERPRET GATT COMMITMENTS

In *Nederlandse Spoorwegen*,[34] importers were again attempting to challenge a Community move to reclassify a product, thus placing it in a higher tariff category than it had been under the former Dutch national classification rules. The importer argued that, since items in the former category had had their tariff level cut in half during a GATT negotiating round, the EC action was in contravention of Article II, as an invalid transfer of goods from one category to another.

The Court's response in an Article 177 reference (now Article 234) was that from July 1968, when the EC replaced the national customs tariff systems, the Community authorities alone have jurisdiction to interpret and determine the legal effect of the product heading concerned. Whatever mandatory force attached to the tariff under the national legal system from the point of view of

---

[33] As in the earlier instrument, this one makes clear that where the Community's international obligations require the prior discharge of an international procedure for dispute settlement, Community measures shall only be decided upon after that international procedure has been terminated, and taking account of the results.

[34] *Douaneagent der NV Nederlandse Spoorwegen v. Inspecteur der invoerrechten en accijnzen*, case 38/75 [1975] ECR 1439.

the national authorities, the Court said, "the interpretation of the national authorities cannot hold good under the Community legal system, this being applicable throughout the Member States".[35]

TRADE SAFEGUARDS FOR THE EC MEMBER STATES:
A RARE AND NARROW OPT OUT

Every free trade agreement must begin life with a safeguard provision attached. As free trade agreements also work according to a principle of gradual and imperceptible transition in economic loyalties, it makes good sense to allow participating states to avail themselves of opt outs where the political cost of accepting international competition is beyond what was expected. And the opt out clause provides a psychological safety valve for the drafters of the original agreement, giving them in turn a means of allaying public fears concerning the loss of domestic industries and familiar modes of employment.

Article 115 of the EC Treaty[36] (now Article 134) was just such a safeguard provision, although it is one of the narrowest of its kind imaginable. Article 115 provided a mechanism for pursuing acts of heresy within the European common market: where a product simply could not yet be brought within the ambit of common rules for import into EC territory, Member States could, with the permission of the Commission, for the time being treat such products differently from the other Member States. They could create separate national import regimes until such time as the common rules for import had been instituted. This would of course necessitate a partitioning of the internal market in such products, since it would make little sense to draw an external distinction (different tariffs, separate numerical quotas) if the products were then to be placed in free circulation within the EC. So the Article 115 exception, while ungenerous and narrow, nevertheless was the most fundamental exception to the most basic principles of the unified internal market of Europe.

---

[35] The Court's basic formulation is that "So far as the fulfillment of the commitments provided for by GATT is concerned, the Community has replaced the Member States, [so] the mandatory effect, in law, of these commitments must be determined by reference to the relevant provisions in the Community legal system and not to those which gave them their previous force under the national legal systems."

[36] Art. 115 reads: "In order to ensure that the execution of measures of commercial policy taken in accordance with this Treaty by any Member State is not obstructed by deflection of trade, or where differences between such measures lead to economic difficulties in one or more Member States, the Commission shall recommend the methods for the requisite co-operation between Member States. Failing this, the Commission may authorise Member States to take the necessary protective measures, the conditions and details of which it shall determine.

In case of urgency, Member States shall request authorisation to take the necessary measures themselves from the Commission, which shall take a decision as soon as possible; the Member States concerned shall then notify the measures to the other Member States. The Commission may decide at any time that the Member States concerned shall amend or abolish the measures in question.

In the selection of such measures, priority shall be given to those that cause the least disturbance to the functioning of the common market."

The seminal case on Article 115 is *Donckerwolcke*,[37] both rhetorically interesting and an unmistakable indication of the Court's view of national deviations from common market rules. Referred under Article 177 from a French court, the case raised fundamental questions concerning restrictions placed by the French authorities on goods that had ostensibly achieved free circulation status by virtue of having passed customs in another Member State.[38] While the Community free movement certificates did not indicate origin, the French national document did demand a statement of origin. In this instance, the Belgian companies declared the origin as Belgian, and were charged with contravention of French customs laws.[39] The French justified their policy by saying that they were following import trends with a view to obtaining authorisation from the Commission for protective measures under Article 115.

The Court of Justice saw the main issue in terms of the compatibility with the Treaty of monitoring measures introduced unilaterally by a Member State before it had obtained a derogation under Article 115 from the rules of free circulation. Not surprisingly, the Court said that the legal answers are to be found in the provisions on the customs union in Article 9, (now Article 23) covering all trade in goods between Member States, and the provisions of Article 113 (now Article 133), read together. The Court pointed out that under Article 9(2) (now Article 23(2)) of the Treaty, the provisions on intra-Community trade are identical with respect to products originating in the Community and in third countries, where the latter have attained free circulation. Since these third countries' products had become "wholly assimilated" to Community products, Article 30's (now Article 28) removing of quantitative restriction and measures having equivalent effect applies without distinction as to ultimate source. Thus, the Court found, even as a pure formality, national import licenses cannot be applied in intra-Community trade. Also, there can be no administrative procedure with different rules depending on first origin. Indeed, this is why the EC "movement certificate" introduced in 1960 purposely had no indication of ultimate origin. It was intended to guarantee free circulation regardless of first origin.

But the Court went on to draw a further link between this principle and the "progress" of the CCP in Europe. The application of the principles of free circulation, the Court said, is conditional upon the establishment of the CCP with respect to a particular product. While all goods were intended to be subject to identical conditions of importation throughout the Community by the end of the transition period, the CCP was not in fact achieved for all products by that deadline. This meant that differences between the Member States remained in

---

[37] *Suzanne Criel, née Donckerwolcke and Henri Schou v. Procureur de la Republique au Tribunal de Grande Instance, Lille and Director General of Customs*, Case 41/76 [1976] ECR 1921.

[38] The goods in question were textile products originating in the Middle East, then arriving in Belgium, from where they were sent on to France accompanied by "movement certificates" to show that the Belgian authorities attested to their free movement status.

[39] The penalties involved were severe—with suspended prison terms and fines far exceeding the value of the goods themselves. The French policy for certain sensitive goods such as textiles called for monitoring which included a statement of the original source of the goods.

place, and these differences were "capable of bringing about deflections of trade or of causing economic difficulties in certain Member States". These were the conditions that led to the operation of Article 115.

The Court explained that Article 115 allows for such difficulties to be avoided by giving the Commission the power to authorise Member States to take protective action via derogation from the principle of free circulation within the Community of products originating in third countries. But, the Court cautioned,

> "because [these derogations] constitute not only an exception to the provisions of Article 9 and 30 of the Treaty which are fundamental to the operation of the Common Market, but also an obstacle to the implementation of the CCP provided for by Article 113, *the derogations allowed under Article 115 must be strictly interpreted and applied*". (emphasis added)[39a]

Turning to the question of the French monitoring procedures, the Court said that as full responsibility for commercial policy was transferred to the Community under Article 113, national commercial policy measures after the end of the transition period are only permissible by virtue of "specific authorisation by the Community".[40]

If the incomplete state of the CCP gave rise to the application of Article 115,[41] it must be asked why it took so long for the CCP to encompass certain products. Where Member States exhibited extreme reactions to the prospect of competing with foreign products on terms dictated by Brussels—in other words, where products were notoriously "sensitive"—then an Article 115 derogation would come into play. Conventional wisdom has it that Article 115 measures hinder the completion of the Single Market in two ways.[42] First, there can be no genuine internal market for goods subject to different conditions of importation; and second, these differences distort competition, in that companies in the "protected" Member States are not operating under the same conditions as those established in less protected Member States, where there is full exposure to foreign competition. One of the principal objectives of the Single Market programme was to eliminate virtually all remaining uses of the Article 115 procedure.

It is natural for importers to attempt to challenge the use of national restrictions under Article 115. Because reliance on Article 115 depends upon a demonstration of particular national difficulties, restrictive measures are likely to be

---

[39a] *Suzanne Criel, nee Donckerwolcke and Henri Shou* v. *Procureur de la Republique au Tribunal de Grande Instance, Lille au Director General of Customs,* [1976] Case 41/76, ECR 1921, [1977] 2 CMLR 535.

[40] The Court found that while the French authorities could ask for the ultimate origin for purposes of gathering information relevant to an Art. 115 restriction, where there was non-compliance, the national authorities could not respond with disproportionate penalties, *"taking account of the purely administrative nature of the contravention"*. Any severe penalty, such as seizure of goods or costly fines would be seen as equivalent to a quantitative restriction, the Court said. An import license would have to be specifically authorised under Art. 115 in order to be compatible with the Treaty.

[41] See Eeckhout, *supra* n. 1.

[42] *Ibid.*

questioned on the basis that Community-wide action with regard to a particular product has made the use of the Article 115 process impossible. In other words, where the Community has already created some version of a Community-wide regime for the product, invoking Article 115 may be said to be no longer a legal option.

This was the argument raised in *Cayrol v. Rivoira & Figli*,[43] where the clash came between a Community-wide regulation that governed fruit imports from Spain for certain periods of the year, but appeared to leave other parts of the year unregulated. During these "open" periods, France instituted a set of Article 115 restrictions—in this case against grapes. In the Court's view, during the periods of the year uncovered by the Community-wide regulation, the differences that provided grounds for the operation of Article 115 restrictions reappeared. Thus, when the Community legislation does not apply in time, Article 115 cannot be said to be inapplicable. Clearly, it was not the case that just any Community-wide regime for the import of a product will wipe out the option of relying on Article 115.[44]

NATIONAL FREEDOM TO RESTRICT EXPORTS?

Similar issues arise where Member States attempt to create particular national restrictions on exports, generally because of the sensitive nature of the export in question. In *Bulk Oil v. Sun International*,[45] matters relating to a British ban on oil sales except to enumerated countries were referred to the Court of Justice. In *Bulk Oil*, British Petroleum had refused to supply oil it discovered was intended to be shipped to Israel, a country not approved for sales of British oil. The argument was raised that a 1975 free trade agreement with Israel precluded the imposition of such a restriction on exports to that country; and second, that Britain should have had specific authorisation from the Community before imposing such a restriction, in light of a 1969 regulation creating a uniform approach to Community exports generally.

In the Court's view, the agreement with Israel lays no obligation on either the Community or the Member States with regard to the introduction or abolition of quantitative restrictions on exports.[46] As for the regulation establishing common rules for exports,[47] its annex clearly states that the principle of freedom of

---

[43] *Leonce Cayrol v. Giovanni Rivoira & Figli*, Case 52/77 [1977] ECR 2261.

[44] The Court states "Member States cannot ignore the origin of goods in free circulation originating in third countries and presented for importation precisely in cases where, because the CCP has not been fully achieved, differences remain between the measures of commercial policy applied by the Member States and where deflections of trade or economic difficulties may be feared."

[45] *Bulk Oil v. Sun International Ltd and Sun Oil Trading Co*, Case 174/84 [1986] ECR 559.

[46] The Court writes that "[s]ince QRs on exports do not fall within the scope of the Agreement between the Community and the State of Israel the argument that the agreement deprived the Member States of their power to introduce such restrictions must be rejected".

[47] Council Regulation 2603/69.

exports will not apply to crude oil and petroleum. But does this then allow Member States to remove oil from its own list of freely exported goods without Community authorisation, despite the demands of Article 113 of the Treaty? While affirming the exclusivity of Community competence in this area, the Court found that the regulation provides specific authorisation for the imposition of QRs in the export of the enumerated products, such as oil. In a decision characterised by unusual generosity towards national difference, the Court found that the Council had properly decided to exclude, on a transitional basis, certain products from the common rules on exports.[48]

TWO VIEWS OF A SEGMENTED MARKET

The sensitivity of the textile sector that led to the MultiFibre Arrangement at global level also led to the internal partitioning of the European market. In the textile sector, one sees the clear interplay between managed international trade based on quotas and Article 115 safeguards within the EC. The famous *Tezi Textiel*[49] case arose from a refusal by the Dutch Minister for Economic Affairs to grant Tezi textile licenses to import into the Netherlands certain clothing that had originated in Macao, but that had attained free circulation in other Member States. Tezi took a direct action before the Court of Justice, seeking an annulment of the Commission's decision authorising the Benelux countries not to apply Community treatment to these articles of clothing.

The Community regulation governing the import of textiles from Macao reflected the agreements entered into under the MFA. Acting under Article 115, the Commission then gave its permission to the Benelux countries to subject these products to the grant of a license. The argument made was that when the Community has exercised its exclusive powers under Article 113 of the Treaty in a specific sector of the CCP, recourse to Article 115 derogations became impossible, and individual Member States could no longer seek permission for protective measures. Here, the exercise of Community power is said to be the negotiation of the MFA by the Commission, the quota levels of which were determined based upon an assessment of the interests of the Community's textile industry considered as a whole. The compelling argument was made that national measures taken in order to implement national sub-quotas fixed by the Community do not exhibit any disparity likely to lead to economic difficulties warranting a decision under Article 115.

The Commission denied that the regulation governing textile imports had rendered Article 115 inapplicable. Citing *Donckerwolcke*, the Commission maintained that the regulation still leaves disparities in the commercial policies

---

[48] "The Council can exclude a product like oil from the common rules on exports without contravening Art. 113, especially when that product is of vital importance for the economy of a state and for the functioning of its institutions and public services."

[49] *Tezi Textiel* v. *Commission*, Case 59/84 [1986] ECR 887.

of Member States, as it provides for national sub-quotas. Thus, goods from third countries are not being subject to the same conditions of import throughout the Community. Contrary to Tezi, the Commission insisted that these subdivisions are not just administrative, not merely for the convenient parcelling out of a global quota.

Basing its decision heavily on *Donckerwolcke*, the Court adopted a surprisingly tolerant view of the national sub-quotas. Repeating that the full application of the principle of free movement is conditional upon the establishment of the CCP, the Court identified the central question here as that of whether the regulation in question did in fact establish a CCP for these textile products. Did the regulation lead to uniform conditions for the importation of these textiles? The Court rather saw the regulation as a "step towards the establishment of a CCP based on Article 113". But it has not created uniform conditions of the sort required; indeed, the recital to the regulation, the Court indicated, states that the conditions of import for textiles "can be standardized only gradually". The Court made clear that in its view the disparities remaining are not merely attributable to sub-quotas allowed by the regulation.

The alternative argument put forward by Tezi was that the Commission should have satisfied itself that there was a real danger that increased competition would aggravate economic difficulties such that national protective measures were necessary. The Court agreed that the Commission is under an obligation to show great prudence and moderation in the exercise of its powers under Article 115. The limits of what the Commission may do—and the Court believed that these conditions had been satisfied in this case—is to authorise:

> "solely for serious reasons and for a limited period, after a full examination of the situation in the Member States seeking a decision under Article 115 and having regard to the general interests of the Community . . . the protective measures which cause the least disruption of intra-Community trade".

The post-Tezi world, though, is characterised by the phasing-out of reliance on Article 115; political difficulties in the creation of the Single Market were set aside in the name of the progress of economic integration. The need for national differences became less important, and less tolerated. The Court, too, was less willing to countenance internal sub-divisions of the market.

While not a case involving Article 115 *per se*, an action by the Commission against the Council on the issue of the Community's generalised system of preferences is taken as an indication of the Court's new firmer position *vis-à-vis* national quotas.[50] The European Community, in common with the US and other developed countries, and under the auspices of the GATT, created a generalised system of preferences for the importation of manufactured goods from developing countries. Based on regulations periodically adopted, the Community would suspend the official customs duty towards such products on

---

[50] *Commission* v. *Council*, Case 51/87 [1988] ECR 5459.

a unilateral basis; that is, without any requirement of reciprocity. For certain products, when reference bases were reached, the Commission was empowered to re-impose customs duties, if there were economic difficulties arising within the Community. While the product ceilings were administered by the Community, tariff quotas for the products were divided up among the Member States on the basis of national economic criteria.

The Commission contended that the administration of the GSP in Europe contravenes the principles of the customs union and the CCP.[51] *Diamantarbeiders*, and the equalisation of customs duties levied at the frontier, resurface in the Court's reasoning. The Court declared that it is hard to see how the national quota system devised to implement the GSP can be compatible with the uniform application of the CCT "and hence with the customs union itself". The Court was clearly troubled by the fact that a product may be subject to different customs requirements, depending on its point of entry into the Community, even where the Community quota has not been exhausted.

The obvious objection to this, however, was that the Court seemed to have approved of such sub-division in *Tezi*. The Court distinguished sharply between these two situations. In *Tezi*, the Court said, the issue was whether the Commission was entitled to authorise protective measures under Article 115 of the Treaty, where the CCP had not been fully achieved. Here, though, the question is whether "in view of the incomplete implementation of the CCP, the [Council] may also depart from the principles of the customs union". And the Court's conclusion was that "It should be self-evident that this is not the case".

OPINION 1/94: A RETREAT FROM ABSOLUTE UNIFORMITY?

The new subject matter introduced into GATT/WTO law through the conclusion of the Uruguay Round Agreements presented a major challenge to the Community institutions. We have seen that the Court had previously been all too willing to expand the definition of "common commercial policy" in order to affirm the competence of the Community to conclude the particular third party agreement in question. However, faced with the new substantive areas of WTO law, the Court took a different approach, much to the chagrin of those who wished to see both a stronger and more unified EU on the world stage, as well as a stronger embrace by Europe of GATT/WTO law.[52]

---

[51] The Commission's main contention is that when a particular Member State's share of the quota is used up, this may necessitate the reintroduction of the ordinary rate of duty under the CCT, even though it is possible that at the same time goods are being imported under the preference scheme into other Member States, since they have received less of their quota share.

[52] *Re: The Uruguay Round Treaties* (Opinion 1/94 of 15 November 1994), [1995] 1 CMLR 205. For a discussion of the larger implications of the opinion, see Nicholas Emilious, "The Death of Exclusive Competence?" 21:4 *European Law Review*, 294–311; and J H J Bourgeois, "The EC in the WTO and Advisory Opinion 1/94: an Echternach procession", (1995) 32 *Common Market Law Review*, 763.

It was pointed out in the introductory section that under Article IX of the Agreement Establishing the WTO, the EC was to have a number of votes equal to the number of the Member States that are members of the WTO. In addition, it was pointed out that the European Communities became an original member of the WTO, along with the states that had been parties to GATT 1947. The Uruguay Round negotiations were conducted on behalf of the Community and the Member States "by the Commission alone". However, this was explicitly not taken to mean that the question of competence with regard to particular issues within the new WTO agreements was decided in advance.

The Commission requested the Court of Justice to sort out these unresolved questions of competence, asking whether the EC had competence to conclude all parts of the WTO Agreement concerning the General Agreement on Trade in Services (GATS), and the Agreement on Trade-Related Aspects of Intellectual Property (TRIPs), either on the basis of Article 113 (now Article 133) of the Treaty alone, or in combination with Article 100a (now Article 95) or Article 235 (now Article 308). It was common ground that the conclusion of the WTO Agreement requires the assent of the European Parliament, in light of Article 228(3) (now Article 300(3)), since it provides for the establishment of a specific institutional framework.

It was acknowledged by the Council that "the exclusive competence of the Community covers almost all the provisions of GATT and its annexes and this competence derives from Article 113". However, the Council urged that Article 43 should be relied upon in relation to the agreements on agriculture and SPS measures, because these "concern not only the commercial measures applicable to international trade in agricultural products but . . . above all the internal system for the organisation of agricultural markets".

A contextual discussion of the nature of the GATS Agreement is provided. The Commission unsurprisingly emphasised the fact that the service sector is becomingly increasingly central to the export interests of the developed countries. It is pointed out that schedules of commitments under GATS have been submitted by both the European Community and by the Member States, with somewhat different conditions and restrictions applying to the different Member States.

The Commission's principal argument regarding GATS is that

"any agreement which is liable to have a direct or indirect effect on the volume or structure of commercial trade is a commercial policy agreement and must be concluded on the basis of Article 113".

It points to "links and similarities noted by economists between goods and services, both sectors forming part of the balance of trade".

The Council argued in return that "the interpretation of the common commercial policy advocated by the Commission leads to the transformation of that policy into a common policy on external economic relations". The Council noted that just such a proposition had been rejected at the Intergovernmental Conference on Political Union. The Council emphasised that an integral part of the provision of services involved the establishment of commercial presence for third country companies, an area governed by national law and not covered by the Common commercial policy. According to the Council,

> "international trade in services falls within Article 113 only in so far as the services in question are directly linked to the supply of goods (for example, the assembly of a machine)".

With regard to the TRIPS Agreement, the Commission stated that trade in counterfeit products causes harm to Community industry; and that

> "the lack of effective protection of intellectual property rights in certain non-member countries is regarded as having the same effect on 'goods subject to intellectual property rights' as any other restriction on imports".

Its arguments regarding TRIPS and Article 113 closely parallel those concerning GATS and Article 113: that "the rules relating to intellectual property rights are closely linked to trade in the products and services to which they apply". The Commission also advocated reliance on either Article 235 or 100a of the Treaty as alternative bases for a finding of exclusive Community competence to conclude GATS and TRIPS. The Commission argued strongly that to have the Community be a party to the new WTO law alongside the Member States, "the coherence of the internal market would be prejudiced".

The Court turned to the question of whether the WTO Agreement on Agriculture should fall under Article 113, or rather under the Treaty provisions dealing with the common agricultural policy. The Court found here that while even Community directives dealing with agricultural trade with non-member countries were intended to achieve one or more of the objectives of the CAP, that was not the case with respect to the WTO's Agreement on Agriculture. Rather, the Agreement was "to establish a fair and market-oriented agricultural trading system". The fact that the Agreement requires internal measures to be adopted on the basis of Article 43 of the EC Treaty does not prevent the international commitments from being entered into on the basis of Article 113 alone.[53] Concerning the SPS Agreement, since its objective is "the establishment of a multilateral framework of rules and disciplines to guide the development, adoption and enforcement of sanitary and phytosanitary measures in order to minimise their negative effects on trade", this too can be adopted on the basis of Article 113 alone.[54]

The Court then went on to examine the relationship between Article 113 and the GATS and TRIPS agreements, respectively. The Court pointed out that the Commission argued that GATS should be seen to fall within the common commercial policy, "without any need to distinguish between the different modes of supply of services"—in particular, between the cross-frontier supply of services and the supply of services through a commercial presence in the country of the

---

[53] Para. 29.
[54] Para. 31.

person to whom they are supplied. The Commission had also argued that international commercial agreements on transport fall within the CCP and not within the Treaty title on the common transport policy.[55]

The Court first considered services other than transport, and then the particular services comprised in transport. It first revisited Opinion 1/75 (*OECD—Local cost standard*), noting "the Court recognised the exclusive competence of the Community, without drawing a distinction between goods and services".[56] In Opinion 1/78 (*Natural Rubber Agreement*), the Court rejected an interpretation of Article 113 "the effect of which would be to restrict the common commercial policy to the use of instruments intended to have an effect only on the traditional aspects of external trade". That opinion also pointed out that the enumeration of subjects covered in Article 113 was meant to be a non-exhaustive enumeration.[57]

The Court acknowledged the importance of the Commission's argument to the effect that the definition of the CCP must remain open to world trade trends, and that in light of this, "trade in services cannot immediately, and as a matter of principle, be excluded from the scope of Article 113".[58] But the Court stated that the definition of trade in services in the GATS Agreement itself would have to be taken into account, "in order to see whether the overall scheme of the Treaty is not such as to limit the extent to which trade in services can be included in Article 113".[59] The Court divided the concept of services according to the modes identified in the GATS Agreement, Article I(2)—whether cross-frontier supply (no one moves), consumption abroad (consumer moves); commercial presence (supplier creates a branch); or the presence of natural persons (supplier moves as a natural person).[60]

The Court determined that in the "cross-frontier supply" situation, where the supplier remains in one country and the consumer of the service in another, the situation is "not unlike trade in goods, which is unquestionably covered by the common commercial policy within the meaning of the Treaty". The Court saw no difficulty with such a service falling within the CCP.[61] However, the Court stated that the same could not be said of the three other modes of supply.[62] The Court pointed out that the Treaty distinguished in Article 3 between the common commercial policy and "measures concerning the entry and movement of persons", such that "the treatment of nationals of non-member countries on crossing the external frontiers of Member States cannot be regarded as falling within the common commercial policy". The Court further pointed out that the Treaty had separate chapters on the free movement of natural and legal

[55] Para. 36.
[56] Para. 38.
[57] Para. 39.
[58] Para. 41.
[59] Para. 42.
[60] Para. 43.
[61] Para. 44.
[62] Para. 45.

persons, thus demonstrating that these matters did not fall within the common commercial policy.[63]

The Court then turned to the question of the provision of services in the transport sector. It noted that transport was also the subject of a specific title in the Treaty, and that

> "it was precisely in relation to transport policy that the Court held for the first time that the competence of the Community to conclude international agreements 'arises not only from an express conferment by the Treaty—as is the case with Article 113 and 114 for tariff and trade agreements and Article 238 for association agreements—but may equally flow from other provisions of the Treaty and from measures adopted, within the framework of those provisions, by the Community institutions' ".

The Court's view was that the idea underlying the ERTA case was that "international agreements in transport matters are not covered by Article 113.[64]

The Court turned to the Commission argument that the Community had exclusive competence in the TRIPs subject matter in that "the rules concerning intellectual property rights are closely linked to trade in the products and services to which they apply". As with the provisions of the GATS Agreement, the Court here distinguished between those provisions of TRIPs dealing with "specific rules as to measures to be applied at border crossing points" and all other provisions of the TRIPs Agreement. The Court declared that inasmuch as an existing Community regulation concerned a prohibition on the release into free circulation of counterfeit goods, it was "rightly based on Article 113 of the Treaty". Certain provisions of TRIPs Agreement involve measures to be taken by customs authorities at the external frontiers of the Community, and thus these sections of TRIPs may be "adopted autonomously by the Community institutions on the basis of Article 113". Likewise, it is "for the Community institutions alone to conclude international agreements on such matters".[65] But the Court rejected the Commission's arguments with respect to all other sections of the TRIPs Agreement.[66]

The Court conceded the relationship between intellectual property and trade in goods, noting, "intellectual property rights enable those holding them to prevent third parties from carrying out certain acts". But this alone, the Court stated, "is not enough to bring [these rights] within the scope of Article 113". Intellectual property rights, in the Court's view, "do not relate specifically to international trade", insofar as they "affect internal trade just as much as, if not more than, international trade".[67]

The Court pointed out that since TRIPs establishes rules in areas for which there are no Community-level harmonisation measures, to accept the

[63] Para. 46.
[64] Para. 48.
[65] Para. 55. However the Court rejected the Commission's arguments with respect to all other sections of the TRIPS Agreement.
[66] Para. 56.
[67] Para. 57.

Commission's position "would make it possible at the same time to achieve harmonisation within the Community and thereby to contribute to the establishment and functioning of the Common Market".[68] The Community is competent under Articles 100 and 100a of the Treaty, as well as Article 235, to harmonise Community rules on intellectual property, but

> "those measures are subject to voting rules (unanimity in the case of Articles 100 and 235) or rules of procedure (consultation of the Parliament in the case of Articles 100 and 235, the joint decision-making procedure in the case of Article 100a) which are different from those applicable under Article 113".[69]

In what hardly represented as surprising a departure as sometimes alleged, the Court wrote that

> "If the Community were to be recognised as having exclusive competence to enter into agreements with non-member countries to harmonise the protection of intellectual property and, at the same time, to achieve harmonisation at Community level, the Community institutions would be able to escape the internal constraints to which they are subject in relation to procedures and to rules as to voting".[70]

To some extent at least, this is simply fact.

The Court was unmoved by references to other third party agreements based on Article 113 of the Treaty, which contained provisions relating to the protection of intellectual property. The Court stated that where these were limited and ancillary provisions, there was no implication that the Community had exclusive competence to conclude an international agreement "of the type and scope of TRIPS".[71]

The Court next took up the Commission's alternative arguments, based on the Community's implied powers. As far as GATS is concerned,

> "the Commission cites three possible sources for exclusive external competence on the part of the Community: the powers conferred on the Community institutions by the Treaty at internal level, the need to conclude the agreement in order to achieve a Community objective, and, lastly, Articles 100a and 235".[72]

The first argument was that for each provision of GATS, the Community had a corresponding internal power, set out specifically in the chapters on the right of establishment, freedom to provide services and transport. The Commission maintained "exclusive external competence flows from those internal powers".[73] This was firmly rejected by the Court.

Even in the field of transport, the Court stated, the Community's exclusive external competence does not flow *automatically* from its power to lay down

[68] Para. 58.
[69] Para. 59.
[70] Para. 60.
[71] Para. 68.
[72] Para. 73.
[73] Para. 74.

rules at internal level.[74] Drawing on the ERTA judgment, the Court pointed out that Member States "only lose their right to assume obligation with non-member countries as and when common rules which could be affected by those obligations come into being". "Only in so far as common rules have been established at internal level does the exclusive competence of the Community become exclusive", the Court concluded.[75] This does not make the establishment of exclusive competence in these areas impossible; it merely makes them subject to the internal legislative activity the Court emphasised in this opinion.

The Commission had argued that the Member States'

> "continuing freedom to conduct an external policy based on bilateral agreements with non-member countries will inevitably lead to distortions in the flow of services and will progressively undermine the internal market".[76]

While not rejecting the possibility of such distortion, the Court replied that there is

> "nothing in the Treaty which prevents the institutions from arranging, in the common rules laid down by them, concerted action in relation to non-member countries or from prescribing the approach to be taken by the Member States in their external dealings".

The Court pointed to various pieces of Community legislation in the transport sector that called for just such concerted action.[77]

The Court further noted that, in contrast to the chapter on transport, the treaty chapters on the right of establishment and on freedom to provide services do not explicitly extend Community competence to "relationships arising from international law". Rather, the sole objective of those chapters "is to secure the right of establishment and freedom to provide services for nationals of Member States". Those sections of the Treaty, the Court continued, contain no provisions on the first establishment of nationals of non-member countries and the rules "governing their access to self-employed activities". Thus, there can be no inference drawn from these provisions that the Community

> "has exclusive competence to conclude an agreement with non-member countries to liberalise first establishment and access to service markets, other than those which are the subject of cross-border supplies within the meaning of GATS, which are covered by Article 113 . . ."[78]

The Commission also submitted that, based on Opinion 1/76 (*Inland Waterways*), exclusive external competence is not limited to cases in which use has already been made of internal powers to adopt measures for the attainment of common policies. It should be recalled that in that case, the Court of Justice

---

[74] Para. 77.
[75] Para. 77.
[76] Para. 78.
[77] Paras. 79–80.
[78] Para. 81.

moved beyond the parallelism of ERTA, and especially in light of the special circumstances of the Inland Waterways legal structure that had been set up under
the agreement, stated that it was not necessarily the case that external competence should in all cases be paralleled by already-exercised internal powers. As
the Commission relied on the Inland Waterways holding, "it is enough that the
Community's participation in the international agreement is necessary for the
attainment of one of the objectives of the Community".[79]

The Court summed up the Commission's position with respect to both internal and external factors: on the one hand, without exclusive Community participation in the GATS and TRIPS agreements, "the coherence of the internal
market would be impaired". And as for external issues, "the European
Community cannot allow itself to remain inactive on the international stage".[80]
But the Court rejected this interpretation of Opinion 1/76.[81]

Opinion 1/76, explained the Court, related to separate issues entirely: the
rationalisation of the economic situation in the inland waterways sector in several Member States. Since vessels from Switzerland were involved by virtue of
their navigation on the waterways in question, it was not possible to achieve the
objective of the agreement through "autonomous common rules". In such a
case, or in other similar situations, it may be that external powers "may be exercised, and thus become exclusive, without any internal legislation having first
been adopted".[82]

That is not the case with regard to services, the Court pointed out. "Attainment
of freedom to provide services for nationals of the Member States", the Court
stated,

> "is not inextricably linked to the treatment to be afforded in the Community to nation-
> als of non-member countries or in non-member countries to nationals of Member
> States of the Community".[83]

The Court then dealt with the Commission's arguments concerning Articles
100a and 235, as applied to the GATS agreement. As for 100a, where the internal power to harmonise has not yet been exercised, this power "cannot confer
exclusive external competence in that field on the Community". As for Article
235, which enables the Community to "cope with any insufficiency in the powers conferred on it, for the achievement of its objective, it "cannot in itself vest
exclusive competence in the Community at international level".[84] The Court
noted that while the only explicitly mentioned objective in the chapters on the
right of establishment and on freedom to provide services is the attainment of
those freedoms for Member State nationals,

---

[79] Para. 82.
[80] Para. 83.
[81] Para. 84.
[82] Para. 85.
[83] Para. 86.
[84] Paras. 88–89.

"it does not follow that the Community institutions are prohibited from using the powers conferred on them in that field in order to specify the treatment which is to be accorded to nationals of non-member countries".

In other words, it is open to the Community to take those legislative steps if it so chooses. The Court reviewed various existing legislation that already contain just such "external provisions".[85]

The Court's conclusion was that where the Community has included within internal legislation "provisions relating to the treatment of nationals of non-member countries, or expressly conferred on its institutions powers to negotiate with non-member countries", the Community then "acquires exclusive external competence in the spheres covered by those acts".[86] In this sense, exclusive competence with respect to a particular subject matter could be "created" through a particular piece of legislation.

In addition, the Court stated that the same applies where the Community

"has achieved complete harmonisation of the rules governing access to a self-employed activity, because the common rules thus adopted could be affected within the meaning of the ERTA judgement if the Member States retained freedom to negotiate with non-member countries".[87]

However, this is not the case, the Court pointed out, in all service sectors—as the Commission itself accepted.[88] The Court's conclusion was thus that competence to conclude GATS is to be shared between the Community and the Member States.

The Court presented similar reasoning with regard to the application of Opinion 1/76 to the TRIPS context. The Court stated "unification or harmonisation of intellectual property rights in the Community context does not necessarily have to be accompanied by agreements with non-member countries in order to be effective".[89]

The Court examined whether legislative acts already adopted by the Community "could be affected within the meaning of the ERTA judgment in the conclusion of TRIPs", as argued by the Commission. The Court pointed out that the degree of harmonisation achieved to date within the Community with regard to certain areas covered by TRIPs "is only partial", and with regard to other areas "no harmonisation has been envisaged".[90] The Court did affirm that the Community is competent to harmonise matters "directly affecting the establishment or functioning of the common market" under Article 100. "But the fact remains", the Court stated, "that the Community institutions have not hitherto

---

[85] Paras. 90–94.
[86] Para. 95.
[87] Para. 96.
[88] Para. 97.
[89] Para. 100.
[90] Para. 103.

exercised their powers in the field of the 'enforcement of intellectual property rights,' except in Regulation 3842/86 laying down measures to prohibit the release for free circulation of counterfeit goods".[91] Thus, the Community and the Member States are jointly competent to conclude the TRIPs Agreement.[92]

The Court accepted as "quite legitimate" the Commission's concerns that there would be problems with administration of the agreements in the event of joint competence having been established. The Court stated in this regard that

"any problems which may arise . . . as regards the co-ordination necessary to ensure unity of action where the Community and the Member States participate jointly cannot modify the answer to the question of competence".[93]

By way of comfort, the Court continued that in such a case

"it is essential to ensure close co-operation between the Member States and the Community institutions, both in the process of negotiation and conclusion and in the fulfilment of the commitments entered into".

The source of the obligation to co-operate, as the Court termed it, is in the "requirement of unity in the international representation of the Community". The Court also noted the fact that it would be especially imperative to co-operate in the case of the WTO Agreements, where the agreements were "inextricably interlinked", particularly with regard to the cross-retaliation possible under the Dispute Settlement Understanding.[94]

The uproar that greeted this opinion is based on some questionable assumptions. It was assumed by many that this decision of the Court represented a major departure from its earlier approach to questions of the external presence of the Community on the world stage, and demonstrated a political retrenchment in favour of the power of the Member States. However, the implications here for a restoration of power to the Member States is small indeed. More importantly, the opinion could actually be seen as pro-Community *vis-à-vis* the WTO, rather than as a departure in the long-running battle between the Community and the Member States over issues of external competence.[95] The Court did not indicate in the least that there was a problem with continuing the expansion of the Community's external competence. However, it did not choose to allow internal harmonisation of Community law through the

---

[91] Para. 104.
[92] Para. 105.
[93] Para. 107.
[94] Para. 109.
[95] For an analysis of the reaction to the opinion, see Pierre Pescatore, "Opinion 1/94 on 'Conclusion' of the WTO Agreement: is there an escape from a programmed disaster?", (1999) 36:2 *Common Market Law Review* 387–405. For a discussion of implications for the future participation in the WTO of the Community, see Meinhard Hilf, "The ECJ's Opinion 1/94 on the WTO. No Surprise, but Wise?" (1995) 6:2 *European Journal of International Law* 245–259.

substantive provisions of GATT/WTO law—a fairly sensible position, in light of the implications for future effects on the international Community legal regime.[96]

---

[96] The Court's conclusions were confirmed in Opinion 2/92 of 24 March 1995, *Re: The OECD Third Revised Decision on National Treatment*.

The Amsterdam Treaty added the following provision to Art. 133 (ex Art. 113): "The Council, acting unanimously on a proposal from the Commission and after consulting the European Parliament, may extend the application of paras. 1 to 4 to international negotiations and agreements on services and intellectual property insofar as they are not covered by these paragraphs". The continuing requirement of unanimity should be noted.

12

The European Court of Justice Meets GATT Law: The Power of First Impressions

THE EUROPEAN COURT of Justice first characterised "GATT law" as an international agreement lacking clarity, definition and firm enforcement procedures.[1] While a part of Community law by virtue of international obligations falling on the Community, GATT law was treated as a set of rules that the Community must adhere to; yet, where the Community did not follow these rules, no person had the right or the power to compel it to from within. While the Community regime itself was so obviously "legal" from the perspective of the Court of Justice, and even though other international agreements between the Community and third parties did have effects within the Community legal order, the GATT was of a significantly different nature.[2] At least ostensibly, it was principally because of the GATT's negotiation-based, diplomatic methodology that it could not grant rights to individuals, and could not in turn lead to the invalidation of a Community measure.[3]

But did the Court of Justice fully acknowledge the power, or properly characterise the methodology of the GATT? In its reasoning, it is unlikely the Court provided the true reason why it concluded that GATT law was not capable of conferring rights upon individuals within the Community. If the Court of Justice did underestimate the power of the GATT, it did so wilfully. It was surely not simply misled by the ambiguous form in which the original GATT was, of necessity, drafted. It could be argued that the Court of Justice could not give direct effect to GATT/WTO law on substantive grounds—at least not without rendering numerous Community laws vulnerable to GATT challenges from within. The fact of the General Agreement's unique multilateral status no doubt made "direct effect" impossible from the start, quite apart from questions

---

[1] See *International Fruit Company NV and Others* v. *Produktschap voor Groenten en Fruit*, Cases 21–24/72, [1972] ECR 1219.

[2] For an early and quite complete discussion of the Court's approach to direct applicability and direct effect of international agreements within the Community legal order, see J H J Bourgeois, "Effects of International Agreements in European Community Law: Are the Dice Cast?" (1984) 82 *Michigan Law Review* 1250.

[3] For a full treatment of direct applicability and direct effect of international agreements within the Community legal system , see Ilona Cheyne, "International Agreements and the European Community Legal System", (1994) 19:6 *European Law Review* 581–598.

of clarity and enforceability of individual GATT provisions.[4] It is obvious that the entire context of adoption of the General Agreement, both as to scope, purpose and membership, was very different from any other agreement to which the Community was a party, with far broader tracts of law marked "unknown", at least with respect to the implications of allowing the full application of GATT law.

It is true that Europe's largest trade rival, the United States, also refuses to give "direct effect" to GATT law provisions. On the other hand, allowing individuals to rely on provisions of agreements entered into by the Community and another party in order to challenge a Community measure is not unusual in the European scheme; the Court of Justice is not notoriously unwilling to allow such effects to provisions of agreements entered into by the Community with third parties. From the *Haegeman* judgment,[5] the Court of Justice made clear that it would interpret international agreements entered into between the Community and non-member countries as if these agreements were "acts of the Community" for purposes of Article 177 references.[6] It has been pointed out that the principal concern of the Court of Justice in this regard is to ensure that there be "uniform application of the law deriving from international agreements concluded by the Community throughout the whole Community", in that the international agreements reflect a common policy of the Community itself.[7] In the view of the Court of Justice, only the EC Treaty—and not secondary legislation of the Community—is superior to the Community's international commitments.[8]

The US, by contrast, is primarily "dualist" in its approach to international agreements, and would be less likely in any event to allow challenges to domestic law by persons standing on international law commitments of the United States.[9] Perhaps predictably, so entrenched, or so purposeful, were the Court of

---

[4] See Judson Osterhoudt Berkey, "The European Court of Justice and Direct Effect for the GATT: A Question Worth Revisiting", (1998) 9:4 *European Journal of International Law* 626–657. Berkey makes the interesting point that "the practical position of the Community in the GATT 47 was different than its position in the other international agreements. [Those others] . . . involved countries which were in a much weaker bargaining position than the Community. Because these agreements allowed the parties to withdraw from the agreement if they so desired, the EC could use threats to do so, and the resulting loss of treaty benefits for the other party, as a means of forcing compliance with the agreement's obligations . . . In the GATT 47, however, the Community was not in as strong a position to influence the policies of the contracting parties".

[5] *Haegeman* v. *Belgium*, Case 181/73, [1974] ECR 449.

[6] See Kuilwijk's discussion of this point, *The European Court of Justice and the GATT Dilemma*, (Beuningen: Center for Critical European Legal Studies Series, 1996). "The Haegman judgment", writes Kuilwijk, "may serve to illustrate that the Court of Justice also regards the relationship between international law and Community law as monist". At 82.

[7] Kuilwijk, *supra* n. 6, at 89.

[8] See the *Radio Tubes* case, *Commission* v. *Government of the Italian Republic*, Case 10/61 [1962] ECR 1.

[9] See Ronald A Brand, "Direct Effect of International Economic Law in the United States and the European Union", (1996/7) 17 *Journal of international Law and Business* 556. Brand writes that "In the Trade Agreements Act of 1979, Congress made clear that the implementation of the Tokyo Round Agreements, negotiated under the GATT framework, would not allow any provi-

Justice's views on the GATT, that even a Member State in a direct action before the Court itself was not allowed to invoke the GATT.[10]

For those who saw GATT law as the ultimate guarantor of commercial freedom in a centralising Europe, the enduring perspective first articulated in *International Fruit* has been an intellectual and economic tragedy. For them, the GATT was the repository of economic rights, rights to free trade, ideally possessed by European citizens doing business in a Europe that had embraced the GATT, and had replaced the Member States before it, in order to look after the "common interest". But seen from the opposite point of view, the Community had an internal mandate to enact laws that might well not be in accordance with free trade principles, since the Community, unlike the GATT system, very explicitly embedded commercial considerations within a variety of non-economic policies. It remained for the Community institutions to maintain this balance; and for the Court of Justice to decide, on the basis of Community law as a totality, when the Community institutions had got the balance wrong.

Whatever the true reasons for its reluctance to give GATT law a more central place in the EC regime, the Court of Justice adopted a fundamental rationale in *International Fruit* that was not completely convincing or logical. This rationale has been re-packaged in the post-1995 GATT/WTO, in ways to be explored below. Whereas the old GATT was deceptively haphazard in tone, no one could make that mistake with regard to the WTO Agreements. However, the Court has not moved to alter the effect of GATT/WTO law within the Community legal order.

THE COURT AND THE GATT AGREEMENT

Commission v. Italy[11]

In this early case, Italy attempted to rely upon its GATT obligations to defend itself against a legal challenge brought by the European Commission to certain of Italy's customs duties. While Italy's position seems naïve in retrospect, the Court's decision does draw a clear distinction between intra-Community and international trade. Whereas Italy had decided upon its level of duties for radio parts during GATT negotiations of the 1950s, it balked at lowering these towards its European partners under the first wave of EC-wide liberalisation under Article 14 of the Treaty.[12] Italy said that, under its GATT-based commitments (it became

---

sion of those agreements to prevail over a US statute, regardless of when the statute was enacted"; and further that "The Urgugay Round Agreements Act of 1994 continued this progression toward full prohibition of direct effect of international trade agreements in challenges to either federal or state law." At 569 and 571.

[10] *Germany* v. *Council*, Case C–280/93, [1994] ECR I–4973.

[11] Case 10/61 [1962] ECR 1.

[12] The Italian government is arguing that Art. 234 of the Treaty, which states that "the rights and obligations arising from agreements concluded before the entry into force of this Treaty between

a GATT member in 1950), it had "not only obligations, but also rights which must be maintained in accordance with Article 234 of the EC Treaty".

The Court accepted the Commission's argument that by assuming a new obligation which is incompatible with rights held under a prior treaty a State gives up the exercise of these rights to the extent necessary for the performance of its new obligations. "In matters governed by the EC Treaty", the Court stated, "that Treaty takes precedence over agreements concluded between Member States before its entry into force, including agreements made within the framework of GATT". It is clearly the Court, and not the Member State, which enjoys the power to interpret obligations arising from agreements into which the Member State had previously entered. "The manner in which Member States proceed to reduce customs duties amongst themselves", the Court concludes,

> "cannot be criticised by third countries, since the abolition of customs duties is accomplished according to the provisions of the Treaty and does not interfere with the rights held by third countries under agreements still in force".

International Fruit[13]

The seminal decision of the Court of Justice with regard to the nature and character of the GATT, and its role in the Community legal regime, is *International Fruit* of 1972. The Court's rhetorical presentation of the GATT Agreement displayed no consciousness of the GATT's history or its power; to the degree that the Court's description of the GATT is accurate, it is also startlingly incomplete. However, as indicated above, this must be seen as intentional and purposeful.

The background to the case is the adoption by the Council of a regulation in 1969[14] on the common organisation of the market in fruit and vegetables, with the objective of introducing standardisation by the Member States in their treatment of third country exports into the Community. Under the regulation, Member States were not to apply quantitative restrictions or measures having equivalent effect on imports, including apples. The regulation also said that if such imports threatened the objectives of Article 33 (ex Article 39) of the Treaty on the common agricultural policy, then "appropriate measures" may be taken with respect to trade until the disturbance had disappeared. In such a situation, the Commission was to take action, either on its own or at the request of a Member State. Predictably, in 1970, the Commission adopted a regulation[15] laying down

---

one or more Member States on the one hand, and one or more third countries on the other hand, shall not be affected by provisions of this Treaty", allows it to maintain its GATT obligations as they are.

[13] *International Fruit Company NV and others* v. *Produktschap voor Groenten supra* n. 1.
[14] Regulation No 2513/69.
[15] Regulation No 459/70.

protective measures for the importation of apples. Imported apples would be required to have import licenses, applications for which would be reported to the Commission by Member States, with the objective that the Commission could thereby assesss the market situation. Amending legislation set an upper limit for the issuing of import licenses for apples.[16]

The original plaintiffs in the Dutch court were importers of fruit who in 1970 applied to the Dutch agency with responsibility for import certificates for foreign apples. Based on the Community regulations, the Dutch agency rejected the application, since the relevant numbers had been exceeded. The most interesting argument raised by the plaintiffs was that the Community regulations on which the Dutch action was based were inconsistent with the General Agreement, to which the Community was a party. The Court had first to answer whether in this instance international law could be relied upon to evaluate the validity of a Community measure. If it could, the Court would have to determine whether the regulations being challenged were contrary to Article XI of the GATT Agreement, as alleged.

As an initial matter, the Court held that its jurisdiction extended to all grounds capable of invalidating Community measures, such that it could examine the validity of such a measure in the light of international law. However, there were two fundamental conditions to be met before the relevant provisions of international law could be found capable of invalidating a Community measure. In other words, the Court set out preconditions for the international law in question to qualify as capable for this purpose.

The first condition was that the validity of the Community measure could only be affected if the Community was in fact bound by the provision. The second condition had the circularity of direct effect analyses in other contexts: before a citizen could go before a national court relying on a provision of international law, that provision would have to be capable of conferring rights on citizens of the Community which they could invoke before national courts.

The Court first discussed whether the Community was bound by the GATT, a proposition with two slightly related meanings, depending upon whether one emphasises the word "Community" or the word "bound". The Court looked at the history of the GATT in Europe at the time the EC Treaty was promulgated. The original Member States of the EC were bound as contracting parties to the GATT, and the aims of the EC Treaty were in many ways similar to the GATT objectives, the Court explained. Noting that although the Community had never formally acceded to the GATT as a separate entity, the Court stated that the Community had assumed the functions of tariff and trade policy under Article 113 (now Article 133) of the Treaty.

Following this logic, the Court said that "by conferring those powers on the Community, the member States showed their wish to bind it by the obligations

---

[16] Regulation 565/70.

entered into under the General Agreement. Also, the other GATT contracting parties have recognised the transfer of CCP powers to the Community institutions.[17]

The second point to be addressed was whether the provisions of the General Agreement confer rights on citizens of the Community, on which in turn they can rely before their national courts in contesting the validity of a Community measure. For this purpose, the Court stated that it would look at the "spirit, the general scheme and the terms of the General Agreement". In its consideration of the nature of the GATT, the Court launched into a kind of parody of the language of the General Agreement. As has been discussed at length above, there were important political and legal reasons why the GATT was originally drafted in uncertain and even ambiguous language. However, citing this language as indicative of its non-legal nature, the Court of Justice found the GATT generally inappropriate for purposes of direct effect.

What, in the Court's view, was defective in the GATT for this purpose? First, that the GATT was founded on the principle of negotiations undertaken on the basis of "reciprocal and mutually advantageous arrangements". As the Court saw the GATT, it was characterised by great flexibility, especially with regard to the possibility of derogation, to the measures which can be taken by the contracting parties when they are confronted with exceptional difficulties, and to the methods of conflict resolution between the parties.

With ill-disguised scepticism, the Court raised a number of specific GATT articles by way of example. The Court expressed difficulty with the language of Article XXII, which requires that parties grant each other "sympathetic consideration" when consultation by another party is requested; it cited Article XXV, which requires that contracting parties "act jointly". As far as Article XXIII nullification or impairment of benefit was concerned, the Court's objection was that the contracting parties themselves carry out the investigations and that they also authorise the suspension of concessions by the aggrieved party. As for the Article XIX safeguard provision, the Court stated that the contracting party adversely affected by its own concessions within the GATT retains the power of unilaterally suspending concessions—hardly the formula of a precise, legally binding system, as the Court interpreted the process.

While the Court might have severed individual GATT provisions for analysis, it did not. The Dutch plaintiffs had based their argument on Article XI of the GATT, the provision making quantitative restrictions generally unlawful. This provision was of course roughly analogous to common market rules disallowing quantitative restrictions in intra-Community trade. But without considering Article XI in the specific, the Court rejected the GATT Agreement itself as inherently incapable of containing a provision, any provision, that could provide clear

---

[17] The Court stated that ". . . insofar as under the EC treaty the Community has assumed the powers previously exercised by Member States in the area governed by the General Agreement, the provisions of the Agreement have the effect of binding the Community".

rights to individuals. The cumulative effect of the Court's assessment of various GATT articles was that

> "Those factors are sufficient to show that, when examined in such a context, Article XI of the General Agreement is not capable of conferring on citizens of the Community rights which they can invoke before the courts."

Therefore, the Court concluded, the EC regulations in question "cannot be affected by Article XI of the General Agreement".

To some the Court of Justice created an artificial focus on the amorphous nature of the GATT Agreement in order to justify its conclusion that GATT's individual provisions could in no way have direct effect within the Community legal order. It has been noted in chapter 2 how coercive even the early GATT was, and in what idiosyncratic manner it was coercive. Thus, it might be concluded that the Court's line of reasoning in *International Fruit* is at best incomplete. There might have been other, more satisfying reasons to deny such effect to the General Agreement, but the Court preferred to characterise the GATT as more voluntary, and less legally binding, in nature than it actually was.

THE COURT OF JUSTICE AND OTHER FREE TRADE AGREEMENTS

Bresciani[18] and the Yaounde Convention

The Court of Justice had far less trouble with granting effect to the provisions of other free trade agreements within the Community legal order. Even where particular provisions of the free trade agreement were indistinguishable from provisions of the General Agreement, the *International Fruit* decision meant that the GATT itself, in the most general sense, was incapable of allowing any of its own provisions to be invoked by individuals. It must be noted that in *Bresciani*, the implications were less dramatic, in that the importer was invoking an EC-based convention, in order to challenge a national—rather than a Community—law.

In the late 1960s, an Italian importer was bringing cowhides from France and from Senegal into Italy, Senegal being a party to the Yaounde Convention, precursor to the Lomé Conventions. Under Italian law, all products of animal origin were required to be inspected at the frontier for public health reasons, with a collection taken to cover the costs of the inspection.

Bresciani objected before the national court to the charge on inspections for the French imports under ex-Article 13(2) of the EC Treaty, disallowing customs duties on imports among the Member States. For the products from Senegal, he objected under Article 2(1) of the Yaounde Convention of 1963,

---

[18] *Conceria Daniele Bresciani v. Amministrazione Italiana delle Finanze (preliminary ruling requested by the Tribunale of Genoa)* Case 87/75, [1976] ECR 129 [1976] 2 CMLR 62.

which stated that goods originating in associated states under the convention would benefit, on import into a Member State of the EC, from the progressive abolition of customs duties and charges having equivalent effect between the Member States. Furthermore, Article 2(1) of the 1969 convention stated that products originating in the associated states would be admitted into the EC free of duties and charges having equivalent effect.

As far as the intra-Community charge is concerned, the Court was not impressed by arguments that the cost is proportional to the inspection. If it is an inspection in the public interest, it is not a service to the importer; it is a charge having equivalent effect to a customs duty. Such costs, the Court held, must be met from public funds in the importing state.

To analyse the effect of the provisions of the Yaounde Convention, the Court stated that the "spirit, general scheme and wording" of the agreement must be looked at. The Yaounde Convention, entered into with countries the Community wished to assist in their development, was concluded on the European side by both the Member States and the Community. While the Community had a far more clear-cut obligation to abolish customs duties and charges having equivalent effect than did the developing countries parties to the convention, the Court found that certain of its provisions were capable of direct effect. Article 2(1) of the convention refers to ex-Article 13 of the Treaty, the Court points out, such that "the Community undertook precisely the same obligation towards the associated states to abolish charges having equivalent effect as, in the Treaty, the Member States assumed towards each other".

As to the nature of the obligation, the Court found it to be "specific and not subject to any implied or express reservation on the part of the Community". It was thus "capable of conferring on those subject to Community law the right to rely on [the convention's provision on charges] before the courts".

LIMITS TO THE SIMILARITY BETWEEN CONCEPTS COMMON TO THE EC TREATY AND FREE TRADE AGREEMENTS: *POLYDOR*

This case, referred to the Court of Justice from the UK courts,[19] raised the question of whether case law interpreting a provision of the EC Treaty could be assumed to apply to a nearly identical provision when located in a free trade agreement. RSO, holder of a number of copyrights, licensed separate distributors in the UK and Portugal, prior to Portugal's accession to the EC. Certain traders attempted to import recordings from Portugal deriving from the licensee in Portugal, without first receiving the permission of Polydor or RSO. The record shop owners argued that Polydor could not enforce its rights under the national copyright act, because of the terms of the free trade agreement created between

---

[19] *Polydor Ltd & RSO Records Inc* v. *Harlequin Record Shops Ltd*, Case 270/80 [1982] ECR 329.

the EC and Portugal in 1972.[20] The claim was that, under *Bresciani*, provisions of the free trade agreement had direct effect; and further, that the European case law on Articles 30 and 36, (now Articles 28 and 30) to which Articles 14(2) and 23 of the free trade agreement closely paralleled, prevented the restraint of importation of these products without the intellectual property right holder's consent.

The Court pointed out that it was well-established in Community law that the exercise of a commercial property right , including the exploitation of a copyright, could not prevent the importation of a product from one Member State into another, where that product had been lawfully placed on the market by the proprietor or with his consent. As to whether the same doctrine applied to provisions similar to Articles 30 and 36, as found in the FTA between the EC and Portugal, the Court stated that it would look at the "object and purpose of the free trade agreement", and its wording. The Court identified the purposes of the free trade agreement as the extension of economic relations between the parties, as part of the "construction of Europe". To that end, the parties had decided to "eliminate progressively the obstacles to substantially all their trade", as that term is found in Article XXIV of the GATT Agreement.

The Court found that while certain provisions of the free trade agreement were in some ways similar to those of the Treaty,

> "such similarity of terms is not a sufficient reason for the transposing to the provisions of the agreement the [Community] case law, which determines in the context of the Community the relationship between the protection of industrial and commercial property rights and the rules on the free movement of goods".

The objectives of the EC Treaty include the principle that national laws on commercial property may not have the effect of leading to an artificial partitioning of the common market. But in the context of the FTA with Portugal, those considerations did not obtain. Thus, the case law must be limited to the interpretative context which is specific to the EC Treaty itself. As the Court concluded, restrictions on trade in goods in the context of the free trade agreement might be justified on grounds of commercial property protection, whereas such justification would not be recognised within the Community.

KUPFERBERG: WHY SO DIFFERENT FROM *INTERNATIONAL FRUIT*?

The reasoning of the Court of Justice in *Kupferberg*[21] contrasts sharply with that of *International Fruit*, and the discrepancy is left unexplained by the Court

---

[20] Specifically, Art. 14(2) of the FTA states that "quantitative restrictions on imports are to be abolished from January 1973 and all measures having equivalent effect to QRs on imports must be abolished not later than January 1975". Art. 23 of the same agreement states that "the agreement shall not preclude restrictions on imports or exports justified on grounds of public morality, law and order or public security, . . . protection of individual or commercial property", etc. But also that "such restrictions must not . . . constitute a means of arbitrary discrimination or a disguised restriction on trade between the contracting parties".

[21] *Hauptzollamt Mainz v. C.A. Kupferberg & Cie.*, Case 104/81 [1982] ECR 3641.

itself. It was apparent after *Kupferberg* that the Court had more complex reasons than those stated in *International Fruit* for resisting the notion of direct effect or direct applicability for GATT law within the EC legal regime. In *Kupferberg*, the Court was also interpreting a free trade agreement with elements of ambiguity and non-legal features of the kind the Court had emphasised in denying effect to the GATT Agreement. However, these elements were not a bar to direct effect in *Kupferberg*.

The case, referred to the Court of Justice by a German court, was brought by an importer attempting to rely on a provision of the free trade agreement with Portugal in order to obtain a lower rate of equalisation duty for certain kinds of Portuguese spirits. His argument was that, had the same product been of German origin, it would have enjoyed a lower rate of internal duty. The importer cited Article 21 of the free trade agreement, which he argued to be "essentially the same" as Article 95 (now Article 90) of the EC Treaty. The Court was called upon to answer the question whether the free trade agreement's provision contained a similar prohibition against discrimination as that found in the Treaty.[22]

The Court affirmed the role of Member States in ensuring compliance with the obligations arising from those agreements which are entirely within the competence of the Community institutions to deal with under Article 228.[23] Several Member States had submitted observations denying the direct effect of free trade agreements between the EC and the Community, basing their arguments in particular on the distribution of powers in regard to external relations of the Community. Interestingly, especially in the light of *International Fruit*, these Member States had also argued against direct effect by pointing out that the free trade agreement relied upon reciprocity, had special arrangements for the settlement of disputes, and safeguard clauses allowing parties to derogate from the agreement. In other words, these Member States were encouraging the Court to apply the reasoning of *International Fruit* to its interpretation of this free trade agreement, which shared elements of structural ambiguity with the General Agreement.

The Court discussed the procedures for consultation within the FTA, but found that these special structures did not exclude *all judicial application* of the agreement. The court displayed a willingness to treat the provisions of free trade agreements as severable—although this had not been true of its approach to the

---

[22] Art. 21 of the agreement stated that "the contracting parties shall refrain from any measure or practice of an internal fiscal nature establishing, whether directly or indirectly, discrimination between the products of one contracting party and like products originating in the territory of the other contracting party".

Art. 95 of the EC Treaty rules out discriminatory internal taxation on similar products of the Member States.

[23] The Court says that "in ensuring respect for commitments arising from an agreement concluded by the Community institutions the Member States fulfill an obligation not only to the non-member country but also and above all in relation to the Community which has assumed the responsibility for the due performance of the Agreement".

GATT agreement. In *Kupferberg*, it isolated the relevant provisions, and then declared these to be capable of direct effect. The Court's conviction was not weakened by the fact that the agreement was, in the overall sense, less than structurally solid in every way. In the Court's view, a free trade agreement between the Community and a third country can easily contain precise provisions capable of direct effect, as well as special diplomatic procedures that are in no sense strictly "legal".[24]

And what of the safeguard clauses, the opt outs, that loomed so large in the Court's reasoning in *International Fruit*? The Court's answer was that these apply only in specific circumstances and after consideration by the joint committee. The safeguard provisions, the Court stated emphatically, "do not affect the provisions prohibiting tax discrimination", and are not sufficient in themselves to affect "the direct applicability which may attach to certain stipulations in the agreement". The Court finds that

"neither the nature nor the structure of the agreement concluded with Portugal may prevent a trader from relying on the provisions of the said agreement before a court in the Community".

Having established this as a general matter, the Court looked at the specific provisions being invoked. Article 21 of the agreement sought to prevent the trade liberalisation envisaged in the agreement from being "rendered nugatory by the fiscal practices of the contracting parties". The Court did not add here that this was also the purpose of the related GATT provisions—to prevent tariff reductions from being substituted for by other forms of protection. "If the products of one party were taxed more heavily than similar products which it encounters on the market of the other party", the Court explained, "then the liberalisation which is the underlying objective of the agreement would be nullified". Article 21 of the FTA imposed what the Court called "an unconditional rule against discrimination in matters of taxation", dependent only on a finding that the products affected are of like nature.[25]

DIRECT EFFECT FOR ASSOCIATION AGREEMENTS: *SEVINCE*[26]

This case came before the Court of Justice on reference from the Dutch court of last instance in administrative matters, arising from a complaint by Mr Sevince, a Turkish national, concerning the refusal of the Dutch authorities to grant him

---

[24] The Court wrote: "The fact that a court of one of the parties applies to a special case before it a provision of the Agreement involving an unconditional and precise obligation and therefore not requiring any prior intervention of the joint committee does not adversely affect the powers that the agreement confers on that committee."

[25] The Court made clear, however, that it does not consider the two provisions to be identical, and insists that they must always be interpreted in their own contexts.

[26] *S.Z. Sevince v. Staatssecretaris Van Justitie*, Case C–192/89, [1990] ECR I–346.

a permit to reside in the Netherlands. The refusal was on the grounds that the family circumstances which had justified the grant of the permit no longer existed. The Court of Justice was asked to interpret provisions of decisions of the Council of Association, which had been created under the Agreement establishing an Association between the European Economic Community and Turkey, signed in 1963, and concluded on behalf of the Community by a Council decision.[27]

The content of the decisions on which Mr Sevince had relied was that a Turkish worker who had been in legal employment for a set number of years in a Member State had free access in that Member State to any paid employment.[28] The first question the Court answered had to do with whether an interpretation of the relevant decisions could be given under an Article 177 (now Article 234) reference. The Court first noted that it had consistently held that "the provisions of an agreement concluded by the Council under Articles 228 and 238 EEC form an integral part of the Community legal system as from the entry into force of that agreement". The Court had also held that decisions such as the decisions of the Council of Association in question, in the same way as the Agreement itself, form an integral part of the Community legal system.[29] Thus, the Court did have jurisdiction to give preliminary rulings on decisions adopted under the Agreement.[30]

As to whether the relevant provisions of the decisions have direct effect within the Member States, the Court cited the *Demirel* case,[31] in which it had stated that for a provision in an agreement concluded by the Community with non-member countries, such a provision:

> "must be regarded as being directly applicable when, regard being had to its wording and the purpose and nature of the agreement itself, the provision contains a clear and precise obligation which is not subject, in its implementation or effects, to the adoption of any subsequent measure".[32]

The Court then examined the provisions in question to determine whether or not they satisfied these criteria, and set out a number of reasons for finding them capable of direct effect.

The Court found that both provisions contain clear, precise and unequivocal terms; and that this capacity for direct applicability was confirmed by the overall purpose and nature of the decisions and of the agreement. The Court further identified these purposes, one of which was " to promote the continuous and balanced strengthening of trade and economic relations between the parties", with a view to helping Turkey strengthen its economy and prepare for the creation of a customs union with the EC.[33]

---

[27] Sevince Judgment, para. 1.
[28] *Ibid*. Para. 4.
[29] *Ibid*. Paras. 8 and 9.
[30] *Ibid*. Para. 10.
[31] Case 12/86 [1987] ECR 1573.
[32] *Ibid*. Para. 15.
[33] *Ibid*. Paras. 17–20.

No other features of the decisions—the fact that procedures for applying the rights granted were to be established under national rules—altered the Court's determination of capability of direct effect. The fact that the agreement contained safeguard clauses, allowing the parties to derogate in certain circumstances, was likewise not a matter to alter the Court's view. Citing *Kupferberg*, the Court stated that it must be observed that the safeguard clauses "apply only to specific situations". The Court continued that "Otherwise than in the specific situations which may give rise to their application, the existence of such clauses is not in itself liable to affect the direct applicability inherent in the provisions from which they allow derogations. . . ."[34]

The contrast between the Court's approach in *International Fruit* on the one hand, and *Kupferberg* and *Sevince* on the other, could hardly be plainer, and the reasons should be sought elsewhere than in the "clarity" of an agreement's provisions, or indeed in the agreement's overall purposes, despite the Court's own emphases. There is in fact a contextual logic to the Court's position that is simply not fully reflected in the rather narrow and stylised reasoning offered. This is the fact that bringing GATT law fully into the Community legal system by granting its provisions, or even certain of them, direct applicability and/or direct effect would have larger and ongoing effects on the Community's own freedom to legislate. This is not the case with regard to any of the other agreements examined by the Court in cases that are often raised by way of contrast to *International Fruit*. The overriding contextual reality is that the Community itself would not be compromised by having its acts challenged in light of the provisions of the far more limited agreements over which it exerts far greater control; the subject matter of these agreements is generally speaking a creature of the Community's own needs and intentions, in a manner far different from the subject matter of GATT/WTO law.

WHEN IS GATT LAW COMMUNITY LAW?

Two cases from the 1970s illustrate the point that an identical obligation may be seen as part of Community law even where it began as a GATT obligation, as long as it has been recast in the form of a Community legislative instrument.

The *Schluter* case[35] dealt with issues arising from exchange rate fluctuations, with the result that several Member States were put at a disadvantage regarding payments made to them under the common agricultural policy. Acting on a system enacted by the Council to alleviate the effects of the monetary emergency, these Member States began to charge a special levy on selected third country agricultural products at the border. The objective was of course to neutralise a temporary competitive disadvantage of their own products.

[34] *Ibid*. Paras. 23–25.
[35] *Carl Schlüter v. Hauptzollamt Lörrach* case 9/73 [1973[ECR 1135.

Predictably, these measures were challenged by importers of the third country products. The central question was whether the measures allowing the special levies could be challenged on the grounds that a special levy of this sort exceeded the bound tariff rate agreed to in the GATT. The Court pointed out that the tariff can be "located" as it were in both the GATT schedule of commitments and in the annex to the EC's own common customs tariff. The importer/plaintiff, in fact, had based his action on both sources of law.

Regarding the possibility of relying on GATT to invalidate a Community regulation, the Court followed *International Fruit* exactly. In its excessive "flexibility", the GATT was simply inappropriate for the purpose. However, the identical commitment entered into by the EC could be successfully invoked by a plaintiff, if reference was made to the bound duty as included under the heading of "agreed duties" in the common customs tariff. The Court concluded that "this provision, having been incorporated into a Community regulation, is capable of giving rise to rights of which parties may avail themselves in a court of law".

This was so, in the Court's view, because the obligation in that form was clear and precise, and left no margin of discretion to the authorities by whom it was applied. In this instance, however, the Court found that the "compensatory amounts" being charged were corrective in nature and designed to allow a normal flow of trade, not to hamper it. As exceptional measures, the levies were found not to contravene the provisions of the common customs tariff.

CONTINUING EFFORTS TO INVOKE GATT LAW: *SIOT*[36] AND *SPI & SAMI*[37]

Despite the Court's firm holding in *International Fruit* that GATT law could not be invoked within the European legal system, at least not before the national courts, business persons seeking to assert "economic rights" or "rights to free trade" continued to make the attempt.

In *SIOT*, a case referred to the Court of Justice by the Italian Corte Suprema di Cassazione, the company responsible for the oil pipeline running through Italy brought a challenge to charges assessed under an Italian law for all goods loaded and unloaded at port, regardless of their source. The oil in question originated in non-GATT countries and was transferred through Italy to both EC and non-EC GATT countries. The company raised the argument that the Italian law was incompatible with the GATT's Article V on freedom of transit.[38]

The Court pointed out that the EC Treaty does not expressly lay down rules on goods in transit; it is only in the GATT that one finds explicit provisions on

---

[36] *Societa Italiana per l'Oleodotto Transalpino (SIOT)* v. *Ministero delle Finanze* Case 26/81 [1983] ECR 731.

[37] *Amministrazione delle Finanze dello Stato* v. *Societa Petrolifera Italiana SpA (SPI), & SpA Michelin Italiana (SAMI)*, Cases 267–269/81 [1983] ECR 801.

[38] The company also argued that the charge is inconsistent with Community law; specifically, with Art. 113, and certain Community regulations on transit.

this issue. Nevertheless, the Court set out first principles with regard to the matter of transit within the Community. From the basic provisions on free movement of goods, the Court said, it was clear that Member States must not impede the movement of goods within the Community. The Court noted that the preamble to the regulation on this subject linked measures to facilitate transit with the functioning of the customs union.[39]

The Court stated that the questions put by the Italian court relating to transit to third countries involved an interpretation of the legal significance of the charges as seen in the light of Article 113 of the EC Treaty and Article V of the GATT. As there was no specific commitment between the EC and Austria (the third country in question here), the Court acknowledged that only Article V of the GATT offered any relevant law on the subject, as it plainly prohibited "transit duties". However, as was established in *International Fruit*, the Court repeated that the GATT has no direct effect in Community law, and individuals could not rely on a GATT provision to challenge the imposition of a charge for the loading and unloading of goods in transit.

Interestingly, however, the court said that this in no way affected the Community's obligation to ensure that the provisions of GATT were observed in its relations with non-Member States. But since Article 113 did not in itself contain any legal criterion sufficiently precise to enable an assessment of the contested transit charge, there was no rule which might be relied upon to challenge it.

There is a lack of precision in the Court's statement that the Community is "under an obligation to ensure that the provisions of GATT are observed", since the Court is equally clear that this obligation is unenforceable, in any event by individuals through national courts of the Member States. The declaration of obligation might be seen as an invitation to Community action in the relevant subject area, but outside the realm of direct enforcement without the intervention of a Community act.

A sister case, *SPI and SAMI*, decided at the same time, involved a challenge to Italian charges for administrative services for imported goods. First applied in the 1950s, the charge was not abolished until 1971. While abolished restrospectively for Community goods back to the end of the transition period in 1968, the principal question turned on the status of the charges on third country goods during the entire period. The claim made by companies seeking a refund for charges was based on Article II and III of the GATT. The Court noted that the duty was introduced by Italy at a point in time when Italy had acceded to the GATT but before Member State commitments had been replaced by a Community-wide tariff schedule. There were Community-wide tariff protocols created, however, during the 1960s, before the Community had formally taken over the role of the Member States at the GATT.

---

[39] Drawing on the holding in the *Diamentarbeiders* case, the Court said that just because the Treaty does not prohibit a certain charge, does not mean such a charge "may be introduced or maintained".

The Court repeated its view that the GATT must be applied uniformly throughout the Community. Under *International Fruit*, the official point in time at which to identify the substitution of the Community institutions for the Member States as a negotiating presence at the GATT is the creation of a common customs tariff in 1968. Thus, it is from that point that the Court of Justice must interpret all GATT provisions as part of a Community commitment. But as the GATT tariff protocols of 1962 and 1967 were Community acts, they also fall within the jurisdiction of the Court to give preliminary rulings on the significance of their content.

As for the period after 1968, since the GATT tariff protocols did not have direct effect, the legality of the imposition of the administrative duty had to be considered in the light of *Diamentarbeiders*, from which it followed that, under the common customs tariff and the CCP, Member States could not unilaterally raise the level of the external tariff by the imposition of such a charge. But since the charge was in effect before 1968, it could only become inapplicable in the event of special provisions having been adopted by the Community to that effect. Since this did not happen, the charges were lawfully applied until their repeal in 1971.

As for the period of time before the creation of the common customs tariff, the Court looked at the nature and effect of the first EC-wide tariff protocols of 1962 and 1967. During that period, the Member States were in the process of bringing their national tariffs into line with a common external tariff. Thus, in the Court's view, the early EC protocols "did not constitute a definite obligation for the Member States, but represented rather an objective by reference to which [the Member States] were to direct their measures of alignment". So those protocols did not protect individuals against the imposition by a Member State of a charge on products imported from non-member countries.

THE GROWING GATT/WTO–EC LAW STRUGGLE

The position taken by the Court of Justice towards GATT law within the European legal regime is of great political and practical significance. For those who believe that the construction of Europe is a step on the road towards a freely trading globalised world, resistance by the Court to the direct application of international trade principles is taken as a sign of a negative and inefficient "fortress Europe". Interestingly, the principles applied so eagerly, and often so radically, by the Court in the internal construction of the fledgling Community order do not translate into global level. Free trade principles are tools to serve certain purposes, and must be understood in their context; they serve needs in particular contexts of political economy. They are functional, and do not translate precisely from one regime to another.

There is no absolute reason why the Court of Justice should find it right and proper that the Member States should cede large areas of economic sovereignty—

internal and external—to the Community, while failing to grant the same status to the same principles when they appear at global level, despite the legal relationship between the Community and GATT/WTO law. It is true that important values of the individual Member States, and/or their protectionist impulses, have fallen to the demands of the Community's internal integration. This was justified by a complex political project. The limits to the reach of the Treaty and the Court of Justice are found in the jurisprudence of Articles 30 and 36 (now Articles 28 and 30). But more importantly, many of the values of the Member States have been collectivised in Community law itself. The basis for the imposition of common legislation, along with the striking down of restrictive Member State laws, is the effort to provide convergence and ensure integration that goes beyond the purely economic.

In the 1980s, the Court of Justice appeared to move closer towards granting greater effect to GATT law within the European legal system, as will be discussed in the context of the *Fediol* case, below. In an action brought by Germany challenging the validity of the EC's 1993 banana regime[40] the Court drew back from allowing a Member State to rely on GATT law to challenge anti-free trade Community legislation. While this was disappointing to some, the trend has continued, and the Court is unlikely to alter its view of the proper relationship between Community law and multilateral trade law.

The GATT/WTO system holds up a mirror to the techniques of economic integration within Europe, and the image sent back is a contradictory one. It is clear that as the WTO expands its field of concerns, so too will the *external* power of the EC tend to expand along with it. (This is true despite the moderate approach taken by the Court in Opinion 1/94, discussed in the previous chapter.) In this sense, increased GATT/WTO power is paralleled by increased European external powers, and enhanced global competence for the Community institutions. Nevertheless, where individual constituents within Europe (such as the German banana traders) attempt to rely upon GATT law to resist the encroachments of a centralising and/or protectionist Europe, the Court must take the side of the Community institutions against the Member State (in the case of *Germany* v. *Council*, the Member State as proxy for its transnational economic operators) within the EC. So far, under the approach taken by the Court, the GATT has given external power to the Community by virtue of Article 133 (ex Article 113), but has not been allowed to take it away from within—at least where the Community institutions are concerned.

After *International Fruit*, it was quite clear that the Court would not permit individuals to proceed to national courts relying on GATT law in attempts to invalidate either Community or national actions. But there were other possible configurations that had not been clarified. Could affected persons take *direct* actions before the Court of Justice to challenge Community acts that were contrary to GATT principles? Or more compelling yet, what about Member States

[40] *Germany* v. *Council, supra* n. 10.

which considered that they were being forced by Community acts to adopt measures contrary to their economic interests—and incidentally contrary to GATT law? Would they have a greater right to rely on GATT law to request the Court to invalidate such a Community measure?

HIGH WATER MARK OF GATT LAW IN THE COMMUNITY LEGAL ORDER: *FEDIOL*[41]

After the Court of Justice's decision in this case, one began to hear of the "promise of *Fediol*". Had this promise borne fruit, many actions of the Community institutions would have been subject to a GATT analysis as a condition of their lawfulness; if not for citizens before national courts, then at least for those who could gain access to the Court of Justice directly.

The Fediol group[42] had brought a complaint to the Commission under the New Commercial Policy Instrument, alleging "illicit" trading practices by Argentina, the substance of which was that the Argentine authorities were charging for the export of soya beans at a higher rate than processed soya products, with the aim of limiting the export of the raw product. The objective of this policy, Fediol argued, was to restrict the supply of the beans on the Argentine market, and lower the input price for Argentine processors, in turn helping Argentine processors to sell more of the finished product on the international market.

Fediol went before the Court of Justice seeking an annulment of the Commission's decision to reject their complaint, and the Court's refusal to initiate an investigation. In attempting to convince the Commission of the illicit nature of the Argentine behaviour, Fediol had cited various provisions of GATT law—Articles III, XI, and XXIII, as well as Article XX, of the General Agreement. The Commission had responded that Argentina's system of differential charges on exports did not run counter to the rules of international law cited by Fediol. The substance of Fediol's challenge to the Commission's decision was solely that the Commission's conclusion with respect to the GATT lawfulness of Argentina's behaviour was erroneous.

For obvious reasons, the admissibility issue is the central one in this case. The Commission's natural argument is that the submissions made by Fediol are based on GATT law and thus inadmissible; that with regard to the protections afforded by the new Commercial Policy Instrument, complaints relating to the Commission's actions must be limited to those based on disregard of procedural guarantees, infringement of Community law, or a serious mistake in the exercise of Commission powers. The Commission argued that the New Commercial Policy Instrument conferred on it broad discretion to make decisions, taking into account political considerations unreviewable by the Court. In this view,

---

[41] *Fediol v. EC Commission*, Case 70/87 [1989] ECR 1781.
[42] EEC Oil Crushers and Oil Processors' Federation.

the Commission's task under the instrument was to determine what the "Community interest" was, and how best to defend it.

The Court might easily have deflected the GATT issue by deferring to the Commission's discretion and the delicate politico-economic calculation it is bound to make. Instead, it looked squarely at the decision the Commission had in fact made in this instance, and saw no issue to be dealt with but that relating to the GATT.[43] This was because the Commission had apparently rejected the federation's petition on the sole basis of the Commission's interpretation of GATT law. In rejecting the Commission's arguments on admissibility, the Court seemed to move its jurisprudence a step closer to accepting GATT law as a core element in the European legal regime.

The Commission had understandably maintained that the Court could only review the Commission's interpretation of GATT rules insofar as the misapplication of these rules amounted to an infringement of Community law which vests rights in individuals, since GATT rules were not in themselves sufficiently precise to give rise to such rights. The Court conceded that it had held, on a number of occasions, that GATT provisions were not capable of conferring rights on citizens which they could invoke before national courts. But then the Court made the statement which led to speculation that its former GATT-related jurisprudence might be coming to an end. The Court explained that it could not be inferred from those earlier judgments that citizens could not,

> "in proceedings before the Court, rely on the provisions of GATT in order to obtain a ruling on whether conduct criticised in a complaint lodged under Article 3 of Regulation No 2641/84 constitutes an illicit commercial practice within the meaning of the regulation".

The Court further stated that

> "The GATT provisions form part of the rules of international law to which Article 2(1) of that regulation refers, as is borne out by the second and fourth recitals of its preamble, read together".

Referring to the Court's earlier decision to the effect that the GATT was exceptionally broad and flexible, the Court stated that this

> "does not, however, prevent the Court from interpreting and applying the rules of GATT with reference to a given case, in order to establish whether certain specific commercial practices should be considered incompatible with those rules".

As for the GATT provisions, in the Court's words they "have an independent meaning which, for the purposes of their application in specific cases, is to be determined by way of interpretation".

---

[43] The Court stated: "It should be pointed out that the decision at issue contains no assessment regarding the Community's interest in the initiation of an examination procedure or even regarding the injury or threat to the Community industry concerned arising from the practice in question. The contested decision confines itself to the finding that the charging of differential rates of duty is not contrary to the GATT provisions. And because that assessment was made prior to the assessment of the Community's interest, it requires separate consideration . . ."

Apparently unfazed by its own *International Fruit* analysis of the special procedures for the settlement of disputes found in the GATT system, and turning *Kupferberg* on its head, the Court stated that in *Kupferberg* "the mere fact that contracting parties have established a special framework for implementing the agreement is not sufficient to exclude all judicial application of that agreement". Thus, the presence of these characteristics in the GATT is no longer the decisive issue. As the Court interprets its own role here, since economic agents are entitled to make complaints to the Commission under the New Commercial Policy Instrument, those same agents are then entitled to request the Court to exercise its powers of review over the legality of the Commission's decision applying those provisions.

The rest of the judgment is taken up with the Court conducting just such an analysis. The Court considered the substantive provisions of the GATT raised by *Fediol*, and evaluated the quality of the Commission's decision. The federation failed on each substantive point. The Court saw no merit in *Fediol*'s GATT arguments, which were, it should be noted, clumsily crafted.[44] Nevertheless, the Court came closer in *Fediol* than it ever has to granting GATT law a powerful place within the European legal regime. It could be said that the Court did no more than second guess the Commission's interpretation of GATT law, for purposes of ensuring that the Commission was acting properly under the New Commercial Policy Instrument. But it is not surprising that after *Fediol*, it was assumed that in certain circumstances at least, persons coming directly before the Court of Justice could invoke GATT provisions in order to challenge Community acts.

A similar conclusion can be drawn from the *Nakajima* case,[45] in which a company against which an anti-dumping order was made by the European authorities went before the Court of Justice, arguing that the Community authorities had not assessed the anti-dumping duties in a manner that conformed with the GATT Anti-Dumping Code of 1979, based on Article VI of the GATT. The Court's view was that Nakajima was not attempting to rely on the direct effect of the GATT provisions. Rather, its invocation of GATT law was found to be "incidental" to its questioning of the legality of the Community regulation imposing the anti-dumping duty. The Court stated that *International Fruit* established that the provisions of the General Agreement had the effect of binding the Community. Similarly, the GATT Anti-Dumping Code had been brought into Community law through implementing legislation specifying that the GATT Anti-Dumping Code elaborates rules for the application of Article VI

---

[44] The Court took a particularly restrictive view of Art. III of the GATT, stating that it does not apply here because the duties are placed on exported goods. As for Art. XI, the Court stated that it does not include restrictions arising from taxes or other charges, whereas here the measures being complained of are export duties. Fediol made an argument under Art. XX, using this as the basis of a complaint; the Court rightly pointed out that Art. XX is about derogations, and does not provide a prohibition in itself on certain trade behaviour. Similar arguments are made by the complainants under Art. XXIII, and these meet with a similarly skeptical response by the Court.

[45] *Nakajima All Precision Co v. Council*, Case 69/89 [1991] ECR I–2069.

of the General Agreement.[46] The Court saw its role as ensuring compliance with the international obligations the Community legislation was designed to achieve. In this light, it examined whether the Council went beyond the legal framework laid down, and thus whether the Council was in breach of the GATT Anti-Dumping Code. Apart from the rather dry subject matter (the permissible methods of calculating normal value for domestic and export price), the Court engaged in an important analysis of whether the Council had complied with what were in essence its GATT obligations. In the end, as with *Fediol*, the Court disagreed that there was any discrepancy between the Community law on anti-dumping and the GATT Anti-Dumping Code upon which it was based.

WHEN A MEMBER STATE'S INTERESTS LIE WITH GATT LAW:
GERMANY V. COUNCIL[47]

After the *Fediol* and *Nakajima* cases, it remained to be seen how the Court of Justice would react to a Member State bringing a challenge to a Community act on the basis of GATT law. In retrospect, it was perhaps naïve to have thought that the Court would look favourably on such a challenge, given the explosive political implications. If a Member State could assert on behalf of its own traders that a Community action had endangered their economic rights, the Community's power to enshrine the "Community interest" generally into law would be seriously weakened. For although the German case was carefully crafted, and careful to avoid such statements, it was clear that the foundation of Community competence was at stake, particularly where conflicting needs across Europe made clumsy compromise a necessity.

In May of 1993, Germany brought an action directly before the Court seeking a declaration that parts of the Council regulation creating a common organisation of the market in bananas[48] were void. Germany had since the 1950s enjoyed the privileges of a special "banana protocol" to the EC Treaty, allowing its traders to import a large annual quota of duty free bananas from Latin America. The abolition of that quota had been made explicitly dependent upon the realisation of the common market.[49]

The preamble to the 1993 Community legislation stated that the common organisation of the market for bananas should permit Community produced and ACP bananas to be sold at satisfactory prices within the Community without

---

[46] The Court also points out that the preamble to the 1988 anti-dumping regulation says that it was adopted in accordance with existing international obligations, in particular those arising from Art. VI of the General Agreement and the Anti-Dumping Code.

[47] *Germany v. Council, supra* n. 10.

[48] Council Regulation 404/93 of 13 February 1993 on the common organisation of the market in bananas (OJ 1993 L 47).

[49] The banana protocol stated that "Any decision to abolish or amend this quota shall be taken by the Council, acting by a qualified majority on a proposal from the Commission."

undermining imports of bananas from other third country suppliers. As has been discussed in the context of the WTO Banana dispute above, prior to the adoption of this regulation, the various Member States of the Community had pursued their own interests in conducting banana trade, based largely on historical associations. Of the Member States, Germany was the largest consumer and the strongest advocate of an open approach that would allow it to continue sourcing Latin American bananas on low-tariff terms.

It has already been pointed out that in creating the 1993 regulation, the Community institutions had to consider multiple and conflicting interests within the Community regarding the banana trade, interests both economic and political. The result was a clumsy if ingenious compromise, that left German fruit traders with a serious sense of grievance. The most important of the German arguments pitted GATT law against a Community regulation created by reference to the "Community interest"—here an internally contradictory one—with earlier GATT decisions clearly stating that the European banana regime (before and after the 1993 regulation) was GATT-unlawful. There could hardly be a more appropriate scene for challenge by a Member State to interference by the Community institutions with "free trade rights".

The Court stated that "The Federal Republic of Germany submits that compliance with GATT rules is a condition of the lawfulness of Community acts, regardless of any question as to the direct effect of GATT, and that the Regulation infringes certain basic provisions of GATT".[50] The Court noted that it had already been held that the provisions of GATT "have the effect of binding the Community". "However", the Court added, reverting entirely to the spirit of *International Fruit*", [the Court] has also held that in assessing the scope of GATT in the Community legal system, the spirit, the general scheme and the terms of GATT must be considered".[51]

Perhaps most disappointing, or unsatisfying, about this judgment is the fact that the very difference that led so many to await the Court's decision—the fact that the challenge was being brought by a Member State—is left largely unaddressed by the Court. The *International Fruit* doctrine is merely transposed onto this new situation, with little justification for making so total a transfer. The Court stated that it was "settled law" that the GATT is based on the principle of negotiations which are undertaken on the basis of "reciprocal and mutually advantageous arrangements". Its provisions are flexible, some allowing for derogations, especially as regards safeguards and dispute settlement. The Court essentially quoted from its own set of characterisations from *International Fruit*, with no concession to difference of situation, and no more nuanced assessment of the operation of GATT law.[52]

---

[50] *Germany* v. *Council*, para. 103.
[51] *Ibid*. Para. 106.
[52] *Ibid*. Paras. 106–108.

At paragraph 109, the Court stated that

"Those features of GATT, from which the Court concluded that an individual within the Community cannot invoke it in a court to challenge the lawfulness of a Community act, also preclude the Court from taking provisions of GATT into consideration to assess the lawfulness of a regulation in an action brought by a Member State under the first paragraph of Article 173 of the Treaty."

The Court repeated that the "special features" indicated above showed that GATT rules "are not unconditional", and that

"an obligation to recognize them as rules of international law which are directly applicable in the domestic legal systems of the contracting parties cannot be based on the spirit, general scheme or terms of GATT".[53]

The Court then repeated the *Fediol* doctrine to the effect that only where the Community itself intended to implement a particular obligation entered into within the framework of GATT, or where the Community act expressly referred to provisions of GATT, would the Court review the lawfulness of a Community act from the point of view of the GATT rules.[54] Thus, it was not open to Germany to "invoke provisions of GATT to challenge the lawfulness of certain provisions of the Regulation".[55]

Germany had made other important arguments relating to breaches of Community law, notably that the banana regulation constituted a breach of fundamental rights of its traders, and had led to unjustifiable discrimination.

"The loss of market share suffered by those [German] operators constitutes an infringement of their right to property, their freedom to pursue their trade or business and their acquired rights".[56]

Keeping Kuilwijk's theory in mind, it is apparent that for Germany, GATT law is a source of such rights, rights already recognised in other ways within the Community legal order itself.

But the Court approached this problem from the larger point of view required to synthesize conflicting interests. It recognised that the regulation had caused disparate changes in the situations of the various categories of economic operators among whom the tariff quota was divided. Operators who had dealt with third country bananas "now find their import possibilities restricted". "However", the Court said,

"such a difference in treatment appears to be inherent in the objective of integrating previously compartmentalised markets, bearing in mind the different situations of the various categories of economic operators before the establishment of the common organization of the market".

---

[53] *Ibid*. Para. 110.
[54] *Ibid*. Para. 111.
[55] *Ibid*. Para. 112.
[56] *Ibid*. Para 64.

The regulation has a larger purpose, which the Court found justified the differences in treatment identified. "The Regulation", the Court continued, "is intended to ensure the disposal of Community production and traditional ACP production, which entails the striking of a balance between the two categories of economic operators in question".[57]

Germany was unable to rely on GATT law to protect the trading rights and interests of its national traders, even though they were clearly disadvantaged by the operation of the 1993 banana regulation. GATT law will not be allowed to trump the Community interest. Rights and obligations will be balanced according to Community concerns, which are more complex than those enshrined in the GATT. The Member States may not use the text of the General Agreement as a kind of economic constitution, though Germany made an extremely compelling attempt to do just that.

PORTUGUESE REPUBLIC V. COUNCIL OF THE EUROPEAN UNION[58]

There was a sense, after the changes that occurred at WTO level after the conclusion of the Uruguay Round, that the reasoning of *International Fruit*, which had served as a precarious basis for the Court of Justice to refuse GATT law direct effect within the Community legal order, would not endure. After all, the Court had long relied on the dubious but ostensibly appropriate conclusion that GATT law lacked clear and binding requirements and dispute settlement procedures; it was, in the Court's long-held view, incapable of conferring rights upon individuals, nor even upon Member States, within the Community, on the basis of which they could challenge inconsistent Community law provisions. The Court's true reasons for denying direct effect were doubtless more complex than those stated; the subtext for *International Fruit* and cases following has been outlined in the introductory chapter to this work. However, with the ease and convenience of the facially irrefutable, the Court continued, even in *Germany* v. *Council*, to rely upon the well-worn phrases of *International Fruit* in order to fend off attacks by GATT principle on Community laws that could be seen as conflicting with the international trade rules. Until the creation of the WTO in 1995, and the coming into effect of the Uruguay Round Agreements, there was no mechanism by which to test the limits of the *International Fruit* "reasoning", or to push the Court into either allowing direct effect to GATT/WTO law—highly unlikely as has been suggested—or at last providing a more satisfying set of reasons. Not surprisingly, just such a case arose not long after the coming into force of WTO law.

In May of 1996, Portugal brought an action under Article 230 (ex Article 173) of the Treaty, seeking the annulment of a Council decision concerning the conclusion

---

[57] Paras. 73–74.
[58] *Portuguese Republic* v. *Council*, Case C–149/96, [1999] ECR I–8395.

of Memoranda of Understanding between the European Community and the Islamic Republic of Pakistan and between the European Community and the Republic of India on arrangements in the area of market access for textile products.[59] As factual background, the Uruguay Round negotiations came to an end in December 1993, after which the Director General of GATT invited some of the participants to "pursue their negotiations on access to the market, with a view to reaching a more complete and better balanced market access package".[60] Negotiations on market access for textile products between the Community and India and Pakistan were pursued by the Commission, with the assistance of a "textile committee" designated by the Council. In April of 1994, despite the fact that the negotiations on market access in textiles were not yet completed with Pakistan and India, the President of the Council and the Commission member with responsibility for external relations signed the Final Act concluding the multilateral trade agreements of the Uruguay Round, the WTO Agreement and all its annexed agreements on behalf of the EU. These included the Agreement on Textiles and Clothing (ATC) and the Agreement on Import Licensing Procedures.[61]

In late 1994, the Commission, and Pakistan and India, signed two Memoranda of Understanding between the European Community and India and Pakistan on arrangements in the area of market access for textile products.[62] Under the Memorandum of Understanding with Pakistan, Pakistan agreed to eliminate all QRs applicable to textile products listed in Annex II to the Memorandum. The Commission undertook to

> "give favourable consideration to requests which the government of Pakistan might introduce in respect of the management of existing [tariff] restrictions for exceptional flexibility . . . and to initiate immediately the necessary internal procedures in order to ensure 'that all restrictions currently affecting the importation of products off the handloom and cottage industries of Pakistan are removed before entry into force of the WTO' ".[63]

The Memorandum between India and the Community stated that the Indian government was to bind the tariff it applied to textile and clothing items listed in an attachment, and that these would be notified to the WTO secretariat within 60 days of the date of entry into force of the WTO. It also provided that India could introduce alternative specific duties for particular products. For its part, the EC agreed to "remove with effect from 1 January 1995 all restrictions currently applicable to India's exports of handloom products and cottage industry products; and also to give favourable consideration to "exceptional flexibilities" for any and all categories under restraint, up to amounts indicated in the memorandum for 1995 through 2004.[64]

---

[59] See Council Decision 96/386/EC of 26 February 1996, OJ 1996 L 153, p. 47.
[60] Judgment Para. 3.
[61] Judgment Paras. 5–6.
[62] *Ibid.* Para. 10.
[63] *Ibid.* Para. 10.
[64] *Ibid.* Para. 11.

The content of the memoranda was approved in the contested Council decision of February 1996. Approval was by qualified majority, with Spain, Greece and Portugal voting against it. Community legislation lays down rules for imports into the Community of textile products originating in third countries which are linked to the Community by agreements, protocols or arrangements, or which are members of the WTO.[65] Article 2(1) of the Community regulation stated that the importation of textile products listed in Annex V originating in enumerated countries were to be subject to annual quantitative limits set down in the annex. The release for free circulation into the Community of imports subject to the Annex V limits was to be subject to the presentation of an import authorisation issued by the Member States' authorities.[66] Article 3(1) of the regulation specified that the limits referred to in Annex V did not apply to specified cottage industry and folklore products, which had to be accompanied by a certificate meeting separate conditions.[67]

In April of 1995, a Council Regulation granted financial assistance to Portugal for the purpose of modernising its textile and clothing industries. In December 1995, a Commission Regulation amended the annexes of the principal regulation on textile trade, to reflect the arrangement with India concerning the abolition of restrictions on market access for certain folklore and cottage industry products originating in India.[68] While the original Commission regulation reflecting the agreements was made invalid because of a procedural defect, a later regulation was created to fulfil the same purpose.

Portugal's challenge to the decision concluding the memoranda of understanding was based first on the argument that it had breached rules and fundamental principals of WTO law; and second that it had breached rules and fundamental principles of the Community legal order.[69] With regard to WTO law, Portugal relied on GATT 1994, the ATC and the Agreement on Import Licensing Procedures.[70] Portugal attempted to distinguish the situation at hand from that of *Germany* v. *Council*, in that while GATT was confirmed not to have direct effect in that case, the Court of Justice also held that "that does not apply where the adoption of the measures implementing obligations assumed within the context of the GATT is in issue or where a Community measure refers expressly to specific provisions of the General Agreement". Portugal argued that the Court had stated in paragraph 111 of the *Germany* v. *Council* judgment that in such a case, the Court must review the legality of the Community measure in the light of the relevant GATT rules. Here, Portugal maintained, that is in fact the case, since the decision in question reflected an

---

[65] Para. 15. See Council Regulation (EEC) No 3030/93 of 12 October 1993 on common rules for imports of certain textile products from third countries, as amended by Council Regulation (EC) No 3289/94 of 22 December 1994.

[66] Para. 17.

[67] Para. 18.

[68] Paras. 19–20.

[69] Para. 24.

[70] Para. 25.

understanding negotiated "for the specific purpose of applying the rules in GATT 1994 and the ATC".[71] The counter-argument proposed by the Council, the Commission and the French government was that the decision was not a "Community measure" intended "to transpose certain provisions of the ATC into Community law".

The Portuguese government made the important argument, the argument "waiting to happen", that GATT 1947 was not at issue in this case; rather, that GATT 1994 and WTO agreements were the focus, these being significantly different from GATT 1947, "in particular in so far as they radically alter the dispute settlement procedure".[72] As Germany had also argued in the earlier case, Portugal insisted that the issue was not direct effect; rather, it concerned "the circumstances in which a Member State may rely on the WTO agreements before the Court for the purpose of reviewing the legality of a Council measure".[73]

As to the WTO question, the Court stated that while it is true that the WTO agreements differ significantly from the provisions of GATT 1947, "the system resulting from those agreements nevertheless accords considerable importance to negotiation between the parties".[74] Examining the structure of the DSU, the Court wrote that although the main purpose is to secure the withdrawal of measures found to be inconsistent with WTO rules, the DSU also provides that "where immediate withdrawal of the measures is impracticable, compensation may be granted on an interim basis pending the withdrawal of the inconsistent measure".[75] The Court noted that where compliance is not forthcoming within a reasonable period of time, the DSU allows for negotiations between the parties with a view to finding mutually acceptable compensation.[76]

The Court concluded from this that

> "to require the judicial organs to refrain from applying the rules of domestic law which are inconsistent with the WTO agreements would have the consequence of depriving the legislative or executive organs of the contracting parties of the possibility afforded by Article 22 of that memorandum of entering into negotiated arrangements even on a temporary basis".[77]

While not stated in the clearest possible manner, the Court here has decided to emphasise the freedom of WTO members to negotiate alternative modes of dispute settlement; and not the fact that there is now the possibility of a binding decision regarding the WTO-illegality of the domestic law. Offering compensation,

---

[71] Para. 28.

[72] Para., 31.

[73] Para. 32. The Court wrote that "The Portuguese Government maintains that such a review is justified in the case of measures such as the contested decision which approve bilateral agreements governing, in relations between the Community and non-member countries, matters to which the WTO rules apply." Para. 33.

[74] Para. 36.

[75] Para. 37.

[76] Paras. 38–39.

[77] Para 40.

which is essentially compliance with a penalty, does not thereby make the GATT/WTO-illegal measure GATT-legal.

The Court pointed out that some of the Community's principal trading partners have concluded that the WTO agreements are not "among the rules applicable by their judicial organs when reviewing the legality of their rules in domestic law". The Court is of course well aware that the United States implementing legislation explicitly rejected the idea of direct effect within the US legal order for the Uruguay Round Agreements.[78] While this does not in itself constitute a "lack of reciprocity" in the implementation of the agreements, the Court noted that the WTO agreements are based on "reciprocal and mutually advantageous arrangements", and must be distinguished from agreements concluded between the Community and third parties, such as the Court had interpreted in the *Kupferberg* case.[79] In the WTO context, such lack of reciprocity could lead to "disuniform application of the WTO rules", according to the Court.[80]

While overtly political, the Court at least provides a more honest appraisal of why it cannot grant such effect to WTO law within the Community legal order when it writes that

"To accept that the role of ensuring that those rules comply with Community law devolves directly on the Community judicature would deprive the legislature or executive organs of the Community of the scope for manoeuvre enjoyed by their counterparts in the Community's trading partners".[81]

More generally, the Court displayed its traditional disinclination to allow the Community legislature's freedom to be restricted by reference to GATT law. The Court concluded that

"having regard to their nature and structure, the WTO agreements are not in principle among the rules in the light of which the Court is to review the legality of measures adopted by the Community institutions".[82]

Reverting to the *Fediol* and *Nakajima* holdings, the Court stated that

"it is only where the Community intended to implement a particular obligation assumed in the context of the WTO, or where the Community measure refers expressly to the precise provisions of the WTO agreements, that it is for the Court to review the legality of the Community measure in question in the light of the WTO rules".[83]

---

[78] Para. 43.

[79] Para. 45.

[80] Para. 45.

[81] Para. 46.

[82] Para. 47. The Court further noted at para. 48 that Decision 94/800, on the adoption of the WTO agreements, stated that "by its nature, the Agreement establishing the World Trade Organization, including the Annexes thereto, is not susceptible to being directly invoked in Community or Member State courts". (It should, however, be pointed out that this statement found in such a decision rather begs the question.) The Court here differed from the position of the Advocate General in this case, who concluded that Portugal should be able to rely on WTO law, since unlike GATT 1947, the WTO agreements contained a binding, rule-based system. See Opinion of Advocate General Antonio Saggio, 25 February 1999.

[83] Para 49.

And the Court held that this was not the situation in this case, since

> "the contested decision is not designed to ensure the implementation in the Community legal order of a particular obligation assumed in the context of the WTO, nor does it make express reference to any specific provisions of the WTO agreements".

Rather, "its purpose is merely to approve the Memoranda of Understanding negotiated by the Community with Pakistan and India".[84]

Portugal made a number of interesting, though unsuccessful, arguments to the effect that rules and fundamental principles of the Community legal order had also been breached. The most relevant of these was the allegation of a breach of the principle of legitimate expectations, as regarded "economic operators in the Portuguese textile industry".[85] In particular, Portugal argued that its textile industry was

> "entitled to expect that the Council would not substantially alter the timetable and rate of the opening of the Community market in textile products to international competition, as fixed in the WTO Agreements, particularly in the ATC, and in the applicable Community legislation . . . [transposing] the rules set out in the ATC into Community law".[86]

The Court noted Portugal's view that the adoption of the decision in question did create significant acceleration of the process of liberalising the Community market, and thus altered the framework set up under the ATC. That alteration did cause harm to the Portuguese textile operators.[87]

The Court dismissed Portugal's arguments since it was

> "settled law that the principle of respect for legitimate expectations cannot be used to make a regulation unalterable, in particular in sectors—such as that of textile imports—where continuous adjustment of the rules to changes in the economic situation is necessary and therefore reasonably foreseeable".[88]

As with *International Fruit*, there are logical inconsistencies in the Court's position on the effect in the Community legal order of WTO law.[89] The Court did not really examine the specific nature and provisions of WTO law, and did not fully analyse how it differed from the earlier GATT system it replaced. As it did in *International Fruit*, the Court in *Portugal* v. *Council* focused on only one aspect of the WTO regime, taking it out of context, and thus reducing the scope of WTO law with which it would have to contend for purposes of deflecting yet another attempt to submit Community law to GATT legality.[90] But

---

[84] Para. 51.
[85] Para. 69.
[86] Para. 70.
[87] Para. 71.
[88] Para. 75.
[89] See Patricia Egli and Juliane Kokott, "International Decision: *Portuguese Republic* v. *Council of the European Union*", 94 *American Journal of International Law* 740 (2000).
[90] For an analysis of the similarity of approach taken by the Court in these cases, see Geert Zonnekeyn, "The Status of the WTO Agreements in the EC Legal Order After the Portuguese Textiles Case", (May 2000) 6:2 *International Trade Law and Regulation* (London), 42–47.

while commentators have waited for the outcome of this case, believing that the Court would be unable to continue the line of reasoning commenced in *International Fruit*, in one sense the Court had even less reason after 1995 to subject Community acts to the discipline of GATT/WTO legality. As has been pointed out many times, the difference between the GATT and other international agreements entered into by the Community was not so much in structure or even content; hence the accusations of inconsistency in the Court's approach to GATT law. Rather, the GATT was unique in its broad multilateralism, its unpredictable outcomes, and its potential to invalidate domestic law. While the Court was satisfied to dismiss the GATT for purposes of direct effect in that it was structurally incapable of providing direct effect, due to its negotiation-based character, in fact it was the Community's lack of control over GATT outcomes that was undoubtedly at the root of the Court's reluctance. It is impossible to imagine another international trade agreement that could so threaten the regulatory discretion of the Community legislative mechanism; and also impossible to conceive of another international agreement that could provide so many causes of action within which to challenge Community legislation in unexpected and creative ways.

Yet because the Court chose the particular emphasis it did in *International Fruit*, it was expected that this rationale would have to give way in light of the developments of the Uruguay Round and the creation of the WTO. However, a Court reluctant to grant such effect to GATT law could hardly be expected to "invite in" a creature as extensive as the WTO, with its numerous attendant agreements, capable of presenting challenges to countless Community legislative programmes.

In this light, the Court's unwillingness to allow international harmonisation through the adoption of the Uruguay Round Agreements in *Opinion 1/94*, and its unwillingness to grant GATT/WTO law full effect in the Community legal order, starting with *International Fruit* and continuing through *Portugal v. Council*, have much in common. GATT/WTO law is not merely a set of international obligations, freely undertaken, falling only on the regulatory efficiency of the Community. Rather, as has been discussed throughout this book, and demonstrated in the narrative discussion of numerous disputes, it is a unique kind of law, having open-ended implications, capable of interfering with legislative and regulatory programmes of the widest variety.

If the EU itself suffers from accusations of a democratic deficit, and a failure to honour many legitimate purposes of Member State law, for the EU to cede further control to GATT/WTO law by granting it the same status as other international commitments of the EU could lead to startling outcomes. To allow direct effect of WTO law would, in effect, shift the WTO's dispute resolution system to the EU itself, with the Court of Justice in effect taking the role of a panel. It should also be noted that the issues raised in *International Fruit* were far simpler than those that would be bound to arise today, given the proliferation of causes of action under WTO law.

Osterhoudt Berkey has made the important point that GATT law is probably not an appropriate source of "individual rights" in any event, in that the GATT is "ultimately an agreement regulating the rights and obligations of its members [and] not individuals".[91] It may be that advocating the direct application of GATT/WTO law within the Community legal order may simply be a way of expressing dissatisfaction with the EU's own legislative ethos, a wish for the EU itself to orient itself as a political matter more in the direction of a globally-focused efficiency. There are economic rights within the European legal order, but they are circumscribed by other values that enjoy equal legal status within that order. Granting direct effect to GATT/WTO law would privilege one set of Community concerns over another, and threaten the subject matter complexity discussed in chapter 1.

Kuilwijk has argued that

"Certainly, granting direct effect to GATT would mean a shift of power within the Community from the executive to the judiciary branch. However, such a shift of power would enhance both procedural and substantive rights of individuals in the Community and would help the political institutions to overcome the lobby pressures which lead them to violate the law to the detriment of the Community's public interest".

He continues:

"Direct effect also would impede the Community's ability to violate the law in a reaction to violations by other WTO Members. It would force the Community to use the proper procedures under the GATT treaty. In the view of the Council, this is too much to ask. It therefore explicitly has excluded the direct effect of the WTO agreements. It still is the Court of Justice, however, which has the final word on this matter".[92]

While this is a compelling argument in favour of direct effect for GATT/WTO in the Community legal order, it also sets out precisely why direct effect is not possible. Along with all other WTO members, the EU now has a clear penalty to pay in the event of non-compliance with an adverse WTO ruling. However, the cumulative effect of these rulings will influence the EU in its approach to the future development of GATT/WTO law. It is plain that the crisis of legitimacy so often discussed since the events of Seattle in late 1999 will not be easily answered. The EU, as an alternative model of international economic, political and social integration, is in a unique position to assist in complexifying the future WTO, or in bringing other international agreements on other subjects up to the legal status currently enjoyed by the WTO alone.

---

[91] See above n. 4.
[92] Kuilwijk, above n. 6 at 345.

Index